M000313953

CDX Learning Systems™

FUNDAMENTALS OF
Mobile Heavy Equipment
SECOND EDITION

TASKSHEET MANUAL

JONES & BARTLETT
LEARNING

World Headquarters
Jones & Bartlett Learning
5 Wall Street
Burlington, MA 01803
978-443-5000
info@jblearning.com
www.jblearning.com

Jones & Bartlett Learning books and products are available through most bookstores and online booksellers. To contact Jones & Bartlett Learning directly, call 800-832-0034, fax 978-443-8000, or visit our website, www.jblearning.com.

978-1-284-19649-8

Production Credits
Director of Product Management: Laura Pagluica
Product Manager: Kevin Murphy
Content Strategist: Christine Scheid
Project Manager: Jessica deMartin
Project Specialist: Allie Koo
Director of Marketing Operations: Brian Rooney
Marketing Specialist: Emma Limperis
Product Fulfillment Manager: Shawn Marquis
Composition: S4Carlisle Publishing Services
Project Management: S4Carlisle Publishing Services
Cover Design: Scott Moden
Text Design: Scott Moden
Media Development Editor: Faith Brosnan
Rights Specialist: Maria Leon Maimone
Cover Image (Title Page, Part Opener, Chapter Opener): © Chris Henderson/Corbis/Getty Images
Printing and Binding: LSC Communications

6048

Printed in the United States of America
25 24 23 22 21   10 9 8 7 6 5 4 3 2 1

Contents

Section 1: Safety/Administrative

Chapter 1: Identification and Use of Basic Hand Tools

Learning Objective/Task	CDX Tasksheet Number	AED Reference Number
• Identify basic hand tools by their proper name.	1a1001	AED 1a.1
• Demonstrate the proper use of basic hand tools.	1a1002a	AED 1a.1
• Demonstrate the proper use of drill bits.	1a1002b	AED 1a.1
• Demonstrate the proper use of taps, dies, and thread chasers.	1a1002c	AED 1a.1
• Perform broken bolt removal and thread repair.	1a1002d	AED 1a.1
• Identify grade, pitch, and size of standard and metric fasteners.	1a1002e	AED 1a.1
• Utilize mechanical and hydraulic pullers.	1a1003	AED 1a.1
• Test operation and calibration of precision hand tools.	1a1004	AED 1a.1

Learning Objective/Task	CDX Tasksheet Number	AED Reference Number
• Torque and de-torque fasteners to specification.	1a1006	AED 1a.1
• Measure parts using precision measuring tools and gauges.	1a1007	AED 1a.1
• Measure engine speed and pulses per revolution.	1a1009	AED 1a.1
• Measure pressure, flows, and temperature.	1a1010	AED 1a.1
• Measure specific gravity of fuel, coolant, and electrolyte.	1a1011	AED 1a.1

Materials Required

- Standard toolkit and other tools as required
- 30 basic hand tools chosen by the supervisor/instructor to complete the task
- Tags numbered 1–30 for labeling tools/parts across tasks
- $5/16''$ drill bit
- Drill bit sharpening equipment
- $3/14'' \times 2'' \times 2''$ flat bar stock (for continued use in Tasks 1a1002b–1a1002d)
- Steel rule standard and metric
- Letter punch
- Prick punch
- Pin punch
- Bench vise
- $3/8''$ electric drill
- Layout fluid (if desired)
- Standard tap and die set
- Standard thread chaser set
- $3/8''$-16 × 2 grade 5 bolts
- Clamp or hammer
- Extractor set with manufacturer's directions
- $3/8''$-16 grade 5 nuts
- $3/4'' \times 2'' \times 2''$ flat bar stock from lab task (from completed Task 1a1002c)
- $1/2''$ breaker bar
- Thread locking compound
- Thread insert kit with manufacturer's directions
- Welding equipment
- 10 common fasteners chosen by the supervisor/instructor to complete the task
- Steel rule (metric and standard)
- Thread pitch gauge (metric and standard)
- Bolt diameter gauge (metric and standard)
- Fastener grade marking chart (metric and standard)
- Gears pressed to shafts
- Bearings pressed to hollow shafts
- Bushing pressed in bore
- Bearing cup pressed in bore

- Lip-type seal pressed in bore
- Bearing pressed in bore
- Mechanical two-jaw puller
- Mechanical three-jaw puller
- Step plate
- Mechanical slide hammer
- Bearing cup puller
- Lip-type seal puller
- Push puller
- Centering plate
- Bearing pulling attachment
- Hydraulic puller
- Inside micrometer and master gauge
- Outside micrometer and master gauge
- Depth micrometer and master gauge
- Split ball gauge and master gauge
- Dial bore gauge and master gauge
- Pressure gauge and master gauge tool
- Hydrometer
- Refractometer
- Torque wrench
- Six standard or metric fasteners chosen by the supervisor/instructor to complete the task
- Torque wrench ft-lb, N·m clicker-style
- Torque wrench ft-lb, N·m dial-style
- Torque wrench in-lb, N·m clicker-style
- Torque wrench in-lb, N·m dial-style
- Angle gauge
- Metric torque chart
- Standard torque chart
- Step method torque procedure
- Engine assembly
- One standard fastener
- One metric fastener
- One standard washer
- One metric washer
- Six additional parts chosen by the supervisor/instructor to complete the task
- Tags numbered 5–9 for labeling parts
- Straight edge (standard and metric)
- Micrometer (standard and metric)
- Caliper (standard and metric)
- Bore gauge (standard and metric)
- Dial indicator (standard and metric)
- Feeler gauge set (standard and metric)
- Various machines
- Speed/rpm indicators

- Magnetic/optical tachometers and pulse generators
- Various machines or hydraulic tables
- Pressure/flow gauges and meters, manometers, and vacuum gauges
- Temperature gauges, pyrometers, thermocouples, and infrared thermometers
- Personal protective equipment (PPE)
- Various fuel samples
- Various coolant samples
- Various electrolyte samples
- Various batteries for testing electrolyte
- Various hydrometers/refractometers

Safety Considerations
- Comply with personal and environmental safety practices associated with clothing; eye protection; hand tools; power equipment; proper ventilation; and the handling, storage, and disposal of chemicals/materials in accordance with local, state, and federal safety and environmental regulations.
- Tools allow us to increase our productivity and effectiveness. However, they can also cause severe injury or death if used improperly. Make sure you follow the manufacturer's operation procedures.

CDX Tasksheet Number: 1a1001

Student/Intern Information

Name _____ Date _____ Class _____

Machine, Customer, and Service Information

Machine used for this activity:

Make _____ Model _____

Hours _____ Serial Number _____

Materials Required
- Standard toolkit and other tools as required
- 30 basic hand tools chosen by the supervisor/instructor to complete the task
- Tags numbered 1-30 for labeling tools

Task-Specific Safety Considerations
- Comply with personal and environmental safety practices associated with clothing; eye protection; hand tools; power equipment; proper ventilation; and the handling, storage, and disposal of chemicals/materials in accordance with local, state, and federal safety and environmental regulations.
- Tools allow us to increase our productivity and effectiveness. However, they can also cause severe injury or death if used improperly. Make sure you follow the manufacturer's operation procedures.

▶ **TASK** Identify basic hand tools by their proper name.　　　**AED** *1a.1*

Student Instructions: Read through the entire procedure prior to starting. Prepare your workspace and any tools or parts that may be needed to complete the task. When directed by your supervisor/instructor, begin the procedure to complete the task, and comment or check the box as each step is finished. Track your time on this procedure for later comparison to the standard completion time (i.e., "flat rate" or customer pay time).

Time off_____

Time on_____

Total time_____

Procedure	Step Completed
1. Select Tool #1 and write its correct name below:	☐
2. Select Tool #2 and write its correct name below:	☐
3. Select Tool #3 and write its correct name below:	☐

4. Select Tool #4 and write its correct name below:	☐
5. Select Tool #5 and write its correct name below:	☐
6. Select Tool #6 and write its correct name below:	☐
7. Select Tool #7 and write its correct name below:	☐
8. Select Tool #8 and write its correct name below:	☐
9. Select Tool #9 and write its correct name below:	☐
10. Select Tool #10 and write its correct name below:	☐
11. Select Tool #11 and write its correct name below:	☐
12. Select Tool #12 and write its correct name below:	☐
13. Select Tool #13 and write its correct name below:	☐
14. Select Tool #14 and write its correct name below:	☐
15. Select Tool #15 and write its correct name below:	☐
16. Select Tool #16 and write its correct name below:	☐
17. Select Tool #17 and write its correct name below:	☐

18. Select Tool #18 and write its correct name below:	☐
19. Select Tool #19 and write its correct name below:	☐
20. Select Tool #20 and write its correct name below:	☐
21. Select Tool #21 and write its correct name below:	☐
22. Select Tool #22 and write its correct name below:	☐
23. Select Tool #23 and write its correct name below:	☐
24. Select Tool #24 and write its correct name below:	☐
25. Select Tool #25 and write its correct name below:	☐
26. Select Tool #26 and write its correct name below:	☐
27. Select Tool #27 and write its correct name below:	☐
28. Select Tool #28 and write its correct name below:	☐
29. Select Tool #29 and write its correct name below:	☐
30. Select Tool #30 and write its correct name below:	☐

Non-Task-Specific Evaluation	Step Completed
1. Tools and equipment were used as directed and returned in good working order.	☐
2. Complied with all general and task-specific safety standards, including proper use of any personal protective equipment (PPE).	☐
3. Completed the task in an appropriate time frame (recommendation: 1.5 or 2 times the flat rate).	☐
4. Left the workspace clean and orderly.	☐
5. Cared for customer property and returned it undamaged.	☐

Student signature _____ Date _____

Comments:

Have your supervisor/instructor verify satisfactory completion of this procedure, any observations made, and any necessary action(s) recommended.

Evaluation Instructions: The scoring box below is intended to act as a guide for both student and supervisor/instructor. Each criterion listed will help students to understand what is expected of them and help supervisors/instructors to articulate the level of success at a particular task. The scoring is set up to allow a second attempt at each task (see the Test and Retest columns). Scoring is designed only to award students points for task criteria that were completed correctly. Points are lost for failure to complete the employability requirements (see Non-Task-Specific criteria). When all criteria are evaluated, tally the points for a total at the bottom of each column.

Tasksheet Scoring

Evaluation Items	Test		Retest	
	Pass	Fail	Pass	Fail
Task-Specific Evaluation	**(1 pt)**	**(0 pts)**	**(1 pt)**	**(0 pts)**
1. Student correctly identified at least seven tools.				
2. Student correctly identified at least 14 tools.				
3. Student correctly identified at least 21 tools.				
4. Student correctly identified all 30 tools.				
Non-Task-Specific Evaluation	**(0 pts)**	**(−1 pt)**	**(0 pts)**	**(−1 pt)**
Student successfully completed at least three of the non-task-specific steps.				
Student successfully completed all five of the non-task-specific steps.				
Total Score: <total # of points / 4 = %>				

Supervisor/Instructor:

Supervisor/instructor signature _____ Date _____

Comments:

```
[                                                    ]
[                                                    ]
[                                                    ]
```

Retest supervisor/instructor signature _____ Date _____

Comments:

```
[                                                    ]
[                                                    ]
[                                                    ]
```

CDX Tasksheet Number: 1a1002a

Student/Intern Information

Name _____ Date _____ Class _____

Machine, Customer, and Service Information

Machine used for this activity:

Make _____ Model _____

Hours _____ Serial Number _____

Materials Required

- Standard toolkit and other tools as required
- 30 basic hand tools chosen by the supervisor/instructor to complete the task
- Tags numbered 1–30 for labeling tools

Task-Specific Safety Considerations

- Comply with personal and environmental safety practices associated with clothing; eye protection; hand tools; power equipment; proper ventilation; and the handling, storage, and disposal of chemicals/materials in accordance with local, state, and federal safety and environmental regulations.
- Tools allow us to increase our productivity and effectiveness. However, they can also cause severe injury or death if used improperly. Make sure you follow the manufacturer's operation procedures.

▶ **TASK** Demonstrate the proper use of basic hand tools. **AED 1a.1**

Time off _____

Time on _____

Total time _____

Student Instructions: Read through the entire procedure prior to starting. Prepare your workspace and any tools or parts that may be needed to complete the task. When directed by your supervisor/instructor, begin the procedure to complete the task, and comment or check the box as each step is finished. Track your time on this procedure for later comparison to the standard completion time (i.e., "flat rate" or customer pay time).

Procedure	Step Completed
1. Select Tool #1 and demonstrate its proper use, care and maintenance, and safe operating procedure. Have your supervisor/instructor verify satisfactory completion of these procedures. Supervisor's/instructor's initials: _____	☐

2. Select Tool #2 and demonstrate its proper use, care and maintenance, and safe operating procedure. Have your supervisor/instructor verify satisfactory completion of these procedures. Supervisor's/instructor's initials: _____	☐
3. Select Tool #3 and demonstrate its proper use, care and maintenance, and safe operating procedure. Have your supervisor/instructor verify satisfactory completion of these procedures. Supervisor's/instructor's initials: _____	☐
4. Select Tool #4 and demonstrate its proper use, care and maintenance, and safe operating procedure. Have your supervisor/instructor verify satisfactory completion of these procedures. Supervisor's/instructor's initials: _____	☐
5. Select Tool #5 and demonstrate its proper use, care and maintenance, and safe operating procedure. Have your supervisor/instructor verify satisfactory completion of these procedures. Supervisor's/instructor's initials: _____	☐
6. Select Tool #6 and demonstrate its proper use, care and maintenance, and safe operating procedure. Have your supervisor/instructor verify satisfactory completion of these procedures. Supervisor's/instructor's initials: _____	☐
7. Select Tool #7 and demonstrate its proper use, care and maintenance, and safe operating procedure. Have your supervisor/instructor verify satisfactory completion of these procedures. Supervisor's/instructor's initials: _____	☐
8. Select Tool #8 and demonstrate its proper use, care and maintenance, and safe operating procedure. Have your supervisor/instructor verify satisfactory completion of these procedures. Supervisor's/instructor's initials: _____	☐
9. Select Tool #9 and demonstrate its proper use, care and maintenance, and safe operating procedure. Have your supervisor/instructor verify satisfactory completion of these procedures. Supervisor's/instructor's initials: _____	☐

10. Select Tool #10 and demonstrate its proper use, care and maintenance, and safe operating procedure. Have your supervisor/instructor verify satisfactory completion of these procedures. Supervisor's/instructor's initials: _____	☐
11. Select Tool #11 and demonstrate its proper use, care and maintenance, and safe operating procedure. Have your supervisor/instructor verify satisfactory completion of these procedures. Supervisor's/instructor's initials: _____	☐
12. Select Tool #12 and demonstrate its proper use, care and maintenance, and safe operating procedure. Have your supervisor/instructor verify satisfactory completion of these procedures. Supervisor's/instructor's initials: _____	☐
13. Select Tool #13 and demonstrate its proper use, care and maintenance, and safe operating procedure. Have your supervisor/instructor verify satisfactory completion of these procedures. Supervisor's/instructor's initials: _____	☐
14. Select Tool #14 and demonstrate its proper use, care and maintenance, and safe operating procedure. Have your supervisor/instructor verify satisfactory completion of these procedures. Supervisor's/instructor's initials: _____	☐
15. Select Tool #15 and demonstrate its proper use, care and maintenance, and safe operating procedure. Have your supervisor/instructor verify satisfactory completion of these procedures. Supervisor's/instructor's initials: _____	☐
16. Select Tool #16 and demonstrate its proper use, care and maintenance, and safe operating procedure. Have your supervisor/instructor verify satisfactory completion of these procedures. Supervisor's/instructor's initials: _____	☐
17. Select Tool #17 and demonstrate its proper use, care and maintenance, and safe operating procedure. Have your supervisor/instructor verify satisfactory completion of these procedures. Supervisor's/instructor's initials: _____	☐

18. Select Tool #18 and demonstrate its proper use, care and maintenance, and safe operating procedure. Have your supervisor/instructor verify satisfactory completion of these procedures. Supervisor's/instructor's initials: _____	☐
19. Select Tool #19 and demonstrate its proper use, care and maintenance, and safe operating procedure. Have your supervisor/instructor verify satisfactory completion of these procedures. Supervisor's/instructor's initials: _____	☐
20. Select Tool #20 and demonstrate its proper use, care and maintenance, and safe operating procedure. Have your supervisor/instructor verify satisfactory completion of these procedures. Supervisor's/instructor's initials: _____	☐
21. Select Tool #21 and demonstrate its proper use, care and maintenance, and safe operating procedure. Have your supervisor/instructor verify satisfactory completion of these procedures. Supervisor's/instructor's initials: _____	☐
22. Select Tool #22 and demonstrate its proper use, care and maintenance, and safe operating procedure. Have your supervisor/instructor verify satisfactory completion of these procedures. Supervisor's/instructor's initials: _____	☐
23. Select Tool #23 and demonstrate its proper use, care and maintenance, and safe operating procedure. Have your supervisor/instructor verify satisfactory completion of these procedures. Supervisor's/instructor's initials: _____	☐
24. Select Tool #24 and demonstrate its proper use, care and maintenance, and safe operating procedure. Have your supervisor/instructor verify satisfactory completion of these procedures. Supervisor's/instructor's initials: _____	☐
25. Select Tool #25 and demonstrate its proper use, care and maintenance, and safe operating procedure. Have your supervisor/instructor verify satisfactory completion of these procedures. Supervisor's/instructor's initials: _____	☐

26. Select Tool #26 and demonstrate its proper use, care and maintenance, and safe operating procedure. Have your supervisor/instructor verify satisfactory completion of these procedures. Supervisor's/instructor's initials: _____	☐
27. Select Tool #27 and demonstrate its proper use, care and maintenance, and safe operating procedure. Have your supervisor/instructor verify satisfactory completion of these procedures. Supervisor's/instructor's initials: _____	☐
28. Select Tool #28 and demonstrate its proper use, care and maintenance, and safe operating procedure. Have your supervisor/instructor verify satisfactory completion of these procedures. Supervisor's/instructor's initials: _____	☐
29. Select Tool #29 and demonstrate its proper use, care and maintenance, and safe operating procedure. Have your supervisor/instructor verify satisfactory completion of these procedures. Supervisor's/instructor's initials: _____	☐
30. Select Tool #30 and demonstrate its proper use, care and maintenance, and safe operating procedure. Have your supervisor/instructor verify satisfactory completion of these procedures. Supervisor's/instructor's initials: _____	☐

Non-Task-Specific Evaluation	Step Completed
1. Tools and equipment were used as directed and returned in good working order.	☐
2. Complied with all general and task-specific safety standards, including proper use of any personal protective equipment (PPE).	☐
3. Completed the task in an appropriate time frame (recommendation: 1.5 or 2 times the flat rate).	☐
4. Left the workspace clean and orderly.	☐
5. Cared for customer property and returned it undamaged.	☐

Student signature _____ Date _____

Comments:

Have your supervisor/instructor verify satisfactory completion of this procedure, any observations made, and any necessary action(s) recommended.

Evaluation Instructions: The scoring box below is intended to act as a guide for both student and supervisor/instructor. Each criterion listed will help students to understand what is expected of them and help supervisors/instructors to articulate the level of success at a particular task. The scoring is set up to allow a second attempt at each task (see the Test and Retest columns). Scoring is designed only to award students points for task criteria that were completed correctly. Points are lost for failure to complete the employability requirements (see Non-Task-Specific criteria). When all criteria are evaluated, tally the points for a total at the bottom of each column.

Tasksheet Scoring

Evaluation Items	Test		Retest	
	Pass	Fail	Pass	Fail
Task-Specific Evaluation	**(1 pt)**	**(0 pts)**	**(1 pt)**	**(0 pts)**
1. Student correctly demonstrated the proper use, care and maintenance, and safe operating procedure for at least seven tools.				
2. Student correctly demonstrated the proper use, care and maintenance, and safe operating procedure for at least 14 tools.				
3. Student correctly demonstrated the proper use, care and maintenance, and safe operating procedure for at least 21 tools.				
4. Student correctly demonstrated the proper use, care and maintenance, and safe operating procedure for all 30 tools.				
Non-Task-Specific Evaluation	**(0 pts)**	**(−1 pt)**	**(0 pts)**	**(−1 pt)**
Student successfully completed at least three of the non-task-specific steps.				
Student successfully completed all five of the non-task-specific steps.				
Total Score: <total # of points / 4 = %>				

Supervisor/Instructor:

Supervisor/instructor signature _____ Date _____

Comments:

Retest supervisor/instructor signature _____ Date _____

Comments:

CDX Tasksheet Number: 1a1002b

Student/Intern Information

Name _____ Date _____ Class _____

Machine, Customer, and Service Information

Machine used for this activity:

Make _____ Model _____

Hours _____ Serial Number _____

Materials Required

- Standard toolkit and other tools as required
- $5/16''$ drill bit
- Drill bit sharpening equipment
- $3/14'' \times 2'' \times 2''$ flat bar stock
- Steel rule standard and metric
- Letter punch
- Prick punch
- Pin punch
- Bench vise
- $3/8''$ electric drill
- Layout fluid (if desired)

Task-Specific Safety Considerations

- Comply with personal and environmental safety practices associated with clothing; eye protection; hand tools; power equipment; proper ventilation; and the handling, storage, and disposal of chemicals/materials in accordance with local, state, and federal safety and environmental regulations.
- Tools allow us to increase our productivity and effectiveness. However, they can also cause severe injury or death if used improperly. Make sure you follow the manufacturer's operation procedures.

▶ **TASK** Demonstrate the proper use of drill bits.

AED
1a.1

Time off_____

Time on_____

Total time_____

Student Instructions: Read through the entire procedure prior to starting. Prepare your workspace and any tools or parts that may be needed to complete the task. When directed by your supervisor/instructor, begin the procedure to complete the task, and comment or check the box as each step is finished. Track your time on this procedure for later comparison to the standard completion time (i.e., "flat rate" or customer pay time).

Procedure	Step Completed
1. Select a ⁵⁄₁₆″ drill bit.	☐
a. Inspect the drill bit condition. Is it safe to use? Yes ☐ No ☐	☐
b. Sharpen the ⁵⁄₁₆″ drill bit following your shop's procedures.	☐
2. Select a ³⁄₄″ × 2″ × 2″ piece of flat bar stock provided by your supervisor/instructor.	☐
a. Measure and mark (using a prick) the locations in Figures 1-1 and 1-2: 18/32" 25 mm 18/32" 11 mm Figure 1-1 Figure 1-2	☐
3. Stamp your initials into the flat bar stock using a letter punch.	☐
4. Center punch the marks you measured above.	☐
5. Secure your flat bar stock into a bench vise.	☐
6. Chuck the ⁵⁄₁₆″ drill bit into an electric drill provided by your supervisor/ instructor.	☐
7. Drill a ⁵⁄₁₆″ hole through the bar stock at your measured/marked location in Figure 1-1.	☐
8. Drill a ⁵⁄₁₆″ blind hole 1¼″ deep into the bar stock at your measured/ marked location in Figure 1-2.	☐
9. Store your drilled flat bar stock for future lab tasks.	☐
10. Return any tools you used to their proper location.	☐

Non-Task-Specific Evaluation	Step Completed
1. Tools and equipment were used as directed and returned in good working order.	☐
2. Complied with all general and task-specific safety standards, including proper use of any personal protective equipment (PPE).	☐
3. Completed the task in an appropriate time frame (recommendation: 1.5 or 2 times the flat rate).	☐
4. Left the workspace clean and orderly.	☐
5. Cared for customer property and returned it undamaged.	☐

Student signature _____ Date _____

Comments:

Have your supervisor/instructor verify satisfactory completion of this procedure, any observations made, and any necessary action(s) recommended.

Evaluation Instructions: The scoring box below is intended to act as a guide for both student and supervisor/instructor. Each criterion listed will help students to understand what is expected of them and help supervisors/instructors to articulate the level of success at a particular task. The scoring is set up to allow a second attempt at each task (see the Test and Retest columns). Scoring is designed only to award students points for task criteria that were completed correctly. Points are lost for failure to complete the employability requirements (see Non-Task-Specific criteria). When all criteria are evaluated, tally the points for a total at the bottom of each column.

Tasksheet Scoring

Evaluation Items	Test		Retest	
	Pass	Fail	Pass	Fail
Task-Specific Evaluation	**(1 pt)**	**(0 pts)**	**(1 pt)**	**(0 pts)**
1. Student correctly determined the safety of the drill bit and sharpened it according to their shop's procedures.				
2. Student accurately measured and marked the specified locations on their flat bar stock.				
3. Student stamped their initials properly and correctly center punched their measured marks.				
4. Student drilled holes correctly and in the proper locations.				
Non-Task-Specific Evaluation	**(0 pts)**	**(−1 pt)**	**(0 pts)**	**(−1 pt)**
Student successfully completed at least three of the non-task-specific steps.				
Student successfully completed all five of the non-task-specific steps.				
Total Score: <total # of points / 4 = %>				

Supervisor/Instructor:

Supervisor/instructor signature _____ Date _____

Comments:

Retest supervisor/instructor signature _____ Date _____

Comments:

CDX Tasksheet Number: 1a1002c

Student/Intern Information

Name _____ Date _____ Class _____

Machine, Customer, and Service Information

Machine used for this activity:

Make _____ Model _____

Hours _____ Serial Number _____

Materials Required

- Standard toolkit and other tools as required
- Bench vise
- Standard tap and die set
- Standard thread chaser set
- $^3/_8$"-16 × 2 grade 5 bolts
- $^3/_4$" × 2" × 2" flat bar stock (from completed Task 1a1002b)
- Clamp or hammer

Task-Specific Safety Considerations

- Comply with personal and environmental safety practices associated with clothing; eye protection; hand tools; power equipment; proper ventilation; and the handling, storage, and disposal of chemicals/materials in accordance with local, state, and federal safety and environmental regulations.
- Tools allow us to increase our productivity and effectiveness. However, they can also cause severe injury or death if used improperly. Make sure you follow the manufacturer's operation procedures.

▶ **TASK** Demonstrate the proper use of taps, dies, and thread chasers.

Student Instructions: Read through the entire procedure prior to starting. Prepare your workspace and any tools or parts that may be needed to complete the task. When directed by your supervisor/instructor, begin the procedure to complete the task, and comment or check the box as each step is finished. Track your time on this procedure for later comparison to the standard completion time (i.e., "flat rate" or customer pay time).

Time off_____

Time on_____

Total time_____

Procedure	Step Completed
1. Select a $^3/_8$"-16 taper tap and inspect its condition. Is it safe to use? Yes ☐ No ☐	☐
2. Select a $^3/_8$"-16 bottoming tap and inspect its condition. Is it safe to use? Yes ☐ No ☐	☐
3. Select a tap handle and inspect its condition. Is it safe to use? Yes ☐ No ☐	☐
4. Select your $^3/_4$" × 2" × 2" piece of flat bar stock used in Task 1a1002b and reference Figures 1-1 and 1-2. Figure 1-1 Figure 1-2	☐
5. Secure your flat bar stock into a bench vise.	☐
6. Using the $^3/_8$"-16 taper tap, cut threads in the predrilled hole from Figure 1-1.	☐
7. Using the $^3/_8$"-16 bottoming tap, cut threads in the predrilled hole from Figure 1-2.	☐
8. Install a $^3/_8$"-16 × 2" bolt in each of the threaded holes.	☐
a. Do the bolts thread in by hand easily? Yes ☐ No ☐	☐
9. Remove bolts from the block.	☐
a. Clamp the bolts in the vise at threads to cause distortion or hit threads with hammer to distort them.	☐
10. Secure a bolt into a bench vise with threads facing up.	☐
11. Select a $^3/_8$"-16 die and cut the damaged threads to straighten them out.	☐
a. Install the bolt back into the block bolt hole. It should thread in easily.	☐
12. Select a $^3/_8$"-16 thread chaser and straighten the damaged threads.	☐
a. Install the bolt back into the block bolt hole. It should thread in easily.	☐
13. Store your drilled flat bar stock for future lab tasks.	☐
14. Return any tools you used to their proper location.	☐

Non-Task-Specific Evaluation	Step Completed
1. Tools and equipment were used as directed and returned in good working order.	☐
2. Complied with all general and task-specific safety standards, including proper use of any personal protective equipment (PPE).	☐
3. Completed the task in an appropriate time frame (recommendation: 1.5 or 2 times the flat rate).	☐
4. Left the workspace clean and orderly.	☐
5. Cared for customer property and returned it undamaged.	☐

Student signature _____ Date _____

Comments:

Have your supervisor/instructor verify satisfactory completion of this procedure, any observations made, and any necessary action(s) recommended.

Evaluation Instructions: The scoring box below is intended to act as a guide for both student and supervisor/instructor. Each criterion listed will help students to understand what is expected of them and help supervisors/instructors to articulate the level of success at a particular task. The scoring is set up to allow a second attempt at each task (see the Test and Retest columns). Scoring is designed only to award students points for task criteria that were completed correctly. Points are lost for failure to complete the employability requirements (see Non-Task-Specific criteria). When all criteria are evaluated, tally the points for a total at the bottom of each column.

Tasksheet Scoring

Evaluation Items	Test		Retest	
	Pass	**Fail**	**Pass**	**Fail**
Task-Specific Evaluation	**(1 pt)**	**(0 pts)**	**(1 pt)**	**(0 pts)**
1. Student properly cut threads into the two predrilled holes.				
2. Student distorted the bolt threads as directed.				
3. Student correctly cut and straightened the damaged threads.				
4. Student easily installed the bolts back into the block bolt holes.				
Non-Task-Specific Evaluation	**(0 pts)**	**(−1 pt)**	**(0 pts)**	**(−1 pt)**
Student successfully completed at least three of the non-task-specific steps.				
Student successfully completed all five of the non-task-specific steps.				
Total Score: <total # of points / 4 = %>				

Supervisor/Instructor:

Supervisor/instructor signature _____ Date _____

Comments:

Retest supervisor/instructor signature _____ Date _____

Comments:

CDX Tasksheet Number: 1a1002d

Student/Intern Information

Name _____ Date _____ Class _____

Machine, Customer, and Service Information

Machine used for this activity:

Make _____ Model _____

Hours _____ Serial Number _____

Materials Required

- Standard toolkit and other tools as required
- Bench vise
- Extractor set with manufacturer's directions
- Standard thread chaser set
- $^3/_8$"-16 × 2 grade 5 bolts
- $^3/_8$"-16 grade 5 nuts
- $^3/_4$" × 2" × 2" flat bar stock from lab task (from completed Task 1a1002c)
- $^1/_2$" breaker bar
- Thread locking compound
- Thread insert kit with manufacturer's directions
- Welding equipment

Task-Specific Safety Considerations

- Comply with personal and environmental safety practices associated with clothing; eye protection; hand tools; power equipment; proper ventilation; and the handling, storage, and disposal of chemicals/materials in accordance with local, state, and federal safety and environmental regulations.
- Tools allow us to increase our productivity and effectiveness. However, they can also cause severe injury or death if used improperly. Make sure you follow the manufacturer's operation procedures.

▶ **TASK** Perform broken bolt removal and thread repair. _____ **AED** 1a.1

Time off_____

Time on_____

Student Instructions: Read through the entire procedure prior to starting. Prepare your workspace and any tools or parts that may be needed to complete the task. When directed by your supervisor/instructor, begin the procedure to complete the task, and comment or check the box as each step is finished. Track your time on this procedure for later comparison to the standard completion time (i.e., "flat rate" or customer pay time).

Total time_____

Procedure	Step Completed
1. Select your ³⁄₄″× 2″× 2″ piece of flat bar stock used in Tasks 1a1002b and 1a1002c.	☐
2. Secure your flat bar stock into a bench vise.	☐
3. Apply thread locking compound to the threads and install a ³⁄₈″-16 × 2″ bolt in each of the threaded holes.	☐
a. Write the torque specification below: _____ lbs	☐
b. Torque to specification.	☐
4. Using a ¹⁄₂″ breaker bar, tighten each bolt beyond its yield point until its head breaks off.	☐
5. Remove the broken bolt using the extractor set, following the manufacturer's directions. Have your supervisor/instructor verify satisfactory completion of these procedures. Supervisor's/instructor's initials: _____	☐
6. Secure your flat bar stock into a bench vise.	☐
7. Apply thread locking compound to the threads and install a ³⁄₈″-16 × 2″ bolt in each of the threaded holes.	☐
a. Write the torque specification below: _____ lbs	☐
b. Torque to specification.	☐
8. Using a ¹⁄₂″ breaker bar, tighten each bolt beyond its yield point until its head breaks off.	☐
9. Weld a nut to the top of the broken bolt and let it cool to the touch. (**Note:** If you have not taken a welding class, see your supervisor/instructor.)	☐
10. Remove the broken fastener using a wrench that fits the welded nut. Have your supervisor/instructor verify satisfactory completion of these procedures. Supervisor's/instructor's initials: _____	☐
11. Ask your supervisor/instructor to damage the threads in your flat bar stock.	☐
12. Secure your flat bar stock into a bench vise.	☐
13. Replace the damaged threads with a thread insert, following the manufacturer's directions.	☐
14. Show the thread insert repair in the flat bar stock to your supervisor/instructor for inspection. Have your supervisor/instructor verify satisfactory completion of these procedures. Supervisor's/instructor's initials: _____	☐
15. Return any tools you used to their proper location.	☐

Non-Task-Specific Evaluation	Step Completed
1. Tools and equipment were used as directed and returned in good working order.	☐
2. Complied with all general and task-specific safety standards, including proper use of any personal protective equipment (PPE).	☐
3. Completed the task in an appropriate time frame (recommendation: 1.5 or 2 times the flat rate).	☐
4. Left the workspace clean and orderly.	☐
5. Cared for customer property and returned it undamaged.	☐

Student signature _____ Date _____

Comments:

Have your supervisor/instructor verify satisfactory completion of this procedure, any observations made, and any necessary action(s) recommended.

Evaluation Instructions: The scoring box below is intended to act as a guide for both student and supervisor/instructor. Each criterion listed will help students to understand what is expected of them and help supervisors/instructors to articulate the level of success at a particular task. The scoring is set up to allow a second attempt at each task (see the Test and Retest columns). Scoring is designed only to award students points for task criteria that were completed correctly. Points are lost for failure to complete the employability requirements (see Non-Task-Specific criteria). When all criteria are evaluated, tally the points for a total at the bottom of each column.

Tasksheet Scoring

	Test		Retest	
Evaluation Items	**Pass**	**Fail**	**Pass**	**Fail**
Task-Specific Evaluation	**(1 pt)**	**(0 pts)**	**(1 pt)**	**(0 pts)**
1. Student installed bolts into the threaded holes using the correct torque specification each time.				
2. Student properly removed the broken bolt with an extractor set, following the manufacturer's directions.				
3. Student properly welded a nut to the broken bolt and removed the broken fastener.				
4. Student properly replaced the damaged threads with a thread insert, following the manufacturer's directions.				
Non-Task-Specific Evaluation	**(0 pts)**	**(−1 pt)**	**(0 pts)**	**(−1 pt)**
Student successfully completed at least three of the non-task-specific steps.				
Student successfully completed all five of the non-task-specific steps.				
Total Score: <total # of points / 4 = %>				

CDX Tasksheet Number: 1a1002e

Student/Intern Information

Name _____ Date _____ Class _____

Machine, Customer, and Service Information

Machine used for this activity:

Make _____ Model _____

Hours _____ Serial Number _____

Materials Required

- Standard toolkit and other tools as required
- 10 common fasteners chosen by the supervisor/instructor to complete the task
- Tags numbered 1–10 for labeling fasteners
- Steel rule (metric and standard)
- Thread pitch gauge (metric and standard)
- Bolt diameter gauge (metric and standard)
- Fastener grade marking chart (metric and standard)

Task-Specific Safety Considerations

- Comply with personal and environmental safety practices associated with clothing; eye protection; hand tools; power equipment; proper ventilation; and the handling, storage, and disposal of chemicals/materials in accordance with local, state, and federal safety and environmental regulations.
- Tools allow us to increase our productivity and effectiveness. However, they can also cause severe injury or death if used improperly. Make sure you follow the manufacturer's operation procedures.

▶ TASK Identify grade, pitch, and size of standard and metric fasteners.　　**AED 1a.1**

Time off_____

Time on_____

Total time_____

Student Instructions: Read through the entire procedure prior to starting. Prepare your workspace and any tools or parts that may be needed to complete the task. When directed by your supervisor/instructor, begin the procedure to complete the task, and comment or check the box as each step is finished. Track your time on this procedure for later comparison to the standard completion time (i.e., "flat rate" or customer pay time).

Procedure	Step Completed
1. For this task, you will identify the grade, pitch, and size of various fasteners using identification markings, pitch/thread gauges, bolt gauges, and steel rule. If the fastener is metric, then measurements must be taken and documented in metric measures. If the fastener is standard, then measurements must be taken and documented in standard measures.	

2. Select Fastener #1. Identify its grade, pitch, diameter, and length and write the values below. Be sure to include millimeters or inches: ☐

Grade _____

Pitch _____

Diameter _____

Length _____

3. Select Fastener #2. Identify its grade, pitch, diameter, and length and write the values below. Be sure to include millimeters or inches: ☐

Grade _____

Pitch _____

Diameter _____

Length _____

4. Select Fastener #3. Identify its grade, pitch, diameter, and length and write the values below. Be sure to include millimeters or inches: ☐

Grade _____

Pitch _____

Diameter _____

Length _____

5. Select Fastener #4. Identify its grade, pitch, diameter, and length and write the values below. Be sure to include millimeters or inches: ☐

Grade _____

Pitch _____

Diameter _____

Length _____

6. Select Fastener #5. Identify its grade, pitch, diameter, and length and write the values below. Be sure to include millimeters or inches: ☐

Grade _____

Pitch _____

Diameter _____

Length _____

7. Select Fastener #6. Identify its grade, pitch, diameter, and length and write the values below. Be sure to include millimeters or inches: ☐

Grade _____

Pitch _____

Diameter _____

Length _____

8. Select Fastener #7. Identify its grade, pitch, diameter, and length and write the values below. Be sure to include millimeters or inches: Grade _____ Pitch _____ Diameter _____ Length _____	☐
9. Select Fastener #8. Identify its grade, pitch, diameter, and length and write the values below. Be sure to include millimeters or inches: Grade _____ Pitch _____ Diameter _____ Length _____	☐
10. Select Fastener #9. Identify its grade, pitch, diameter, and length and write the values below. Be sure to include millimeters or inches: Grade _____ Pitch _____ Diameter _____ Length _____	☐
11. Select Fastener #10. Identify its grade, pitch, diameter, and length and write the values below. Be sure to include millimeters or inches: Grade _____ Pitch _____ Diameter _____ Length _____	☐
12. Return any tools you used to their proper location.	☐

Non-Task-Specific Evaluation	Step Completed
1. Tools and equipment were used as directed and returned in good working order.	☐
2. Complied with all general and task-specific safety standards, including proper use of any personal protective equipment (PPE).	☐
3. Completed the task in an appropriate time frame (recommendation: 1.5 or 2 times the flat rate).	☐
4. Left the workspace clean and orderly.	☐
5. Cared for customer property and returned it undamaged.	☐

Student signature _____ Date _____

Comments:

Have your supervisor/instructor verify satisfactory completion of this procedure, any observations made, and any necessary action(s) recommended.

Evaluation Instructions: The scoring box below is intended to act as a guide for both student and supervisor/instructor. Each criterion listed will help students to understand what is expected of them and help supervisors/instructors to articulate the level of success at a particular task. The scoring is set up to allow a second attempt at each task (see the Test and Retest columns). Scoring is designed only to award students points for task criteria that were completed correctly. Points are lost for failure to complete the employability requirements (see Non-Task-Specific criteria). When all criteria are evaluated, tally the points for a total at the bottom of each column.

Tasksheet Scoring

	Test		Retest	
Evaluation Items	**Pass**	**Fail**	**Pass**	**Fail**
Task-Specific Evaluation	**(1 pt)**	**(0 pts)**	**(1 pt)**	**(0 pts)**
1. Student accurately identified the grade of each fastener.				
2. Student accurately identified the pitch of each fastener.				
3. Student accurately identified the diameter of each fastener and used the correct units of measurement.				
4. Student accurately identified the length of each fastener and used the correct units of measurement.				
Non-Task-Specific Evaluation	**(0 pts)**	**(−1 pt)**	**(0 pts)**	**(−1 pt)**
Student successfully completed at least three of the non-task-specific steps.				
Student successfully completed all five of the non-task-specific steps.				
Total Score: <total # of points / 4 = %>				

Supervisor/Instructor:

Supervisor/instructor signature _____ Date _____

Comments:

_____

Retest supervisor/instructor signature _____ Date _____

Comments:

_____

CDX Tasksheet Number: 1a1003

Student/Intern Information

Name _____ Date _____ Class _____

Machine, Customer, and Service Information

Machine used for this activity:

Make _____ Model _____

Hours _____ Serial Number _____

Materials Required
- Standard toolkit and other tools as required
- Gears pressed to shafts
- Bearings pressed to hollow shafts
- Bushing pressed in bore
- Bearing cup pressed in bore
- Lip-type seal pressed in bore
- Bearing pressed in bore
- Mechanical two-jaw puller
- Mechanical three-jaw puller
- Step plate
- Mechanical slide hammer
- Bearing cup puller
- Lip-type seal puller
- Push puller
- Centering plate
- Bearing pulling attachment
- Hydraulic puller

Task-Specific Safety Considerations
- Comply with personal and environmental safety practices associated with clothing; eye protection; hand tools; power equipment; proper ventilation; and the handling, storage, and disposal of chemicals/materials in accordance with local, state, and federal safety and environmental regulations.
- Tools allow us to increase our productivity and effectiveness. However, they can also cause severe injury or death if used improperly. Make sure you follow the manufacturer's operation procedures.

▶ TASK Utilize mechanical and hydraulic pullers. **AED** 1a.1

Time off_____

Time on_____

Student Instructions: Read through the entire procedure prior to starting. Prepare your workspace and any tools or parts that may be needed to complete the task. When directed by your supervisor/instructor, begin the procedure to complete the task, and comment or check the box as each step is finished. Track your time on this procedure for later comparison to the standard completion time (i.e., "flat rate" or customer pay time).

Total time_____

© 2021 Jones & Bartlett Learning, LLC, an Ascend Learning Company

Procedure	Step Completed
1. Station #1: Set up a mechanical two-jaw puller as if to safely remove the gear from the shaft. Have your supervisor/instructor verify satisfactory completion of the setup. Supervisor's/instructor's initials: _____	☐
2. Station #2: Set up a mechanical three-jaw puller and step plate as if to safely remove the bearing from the hollow shaft. Have your supervisor/instructor verify satisfactory completion of the setup. Supervisor's/instructor's initials: _____	☐
3. Station #3: Set up a mechanical slide hammer as if to safely remove the bushing from the bore of the housing. Have your supervisor/instructor verify satisfactory completion of these procedures. Supervisor's/instructor's initials: _____	☐
4. Station #4: Set up a bearing cup puller as if to safely remove the bearing cup from the bore of the housing. Have your supervisor/instructor verify satisfactory completion of the setup. Supervisor's/instructor's initials: _____	☐
5. Station #5: Set up a lip-type seal puller as if to safely remove the lip-type seal from the bore of the housing. Have your supervisor/instructor verify satisfactory completion of the setup. Supervisor's/instructor's initials: _____	☐
6. Station #6: Set up a push puller and centering plate as if to safely remove the bearing from the bore of the housing. Have your supervisor/instructor verify satisfactory completion of the setup. Supervisor's/instructor's initials: _____	☐
7. Station #7: Set up a bearing pulling attachment and puller as if to safely remove the bearing from the shaft. Have your supervisor/instructor verify satisfactory completion of the setup. Supervisor's/instructor's initials: _____	☐
8. Station #8: Set up a hydraulic puller as if to safely remove the gear from the shaft. Have your supervisor/instructor verify satisfactory completion of the setup. Supervisor's/instructor's initials: _____	☐

Non-Task-Specific Evaluation	Step Completed
1. Tools and equipment were used as directed and returned in good working order.	☐
2. Complied with all general and task-specific safety standards, including proper use of any personal protective equipment (PPE).	☐
3. Completed the task in an appropriate time frame (recommendation: 1.5 or 2 times the flat rate).	☐
4. Left the workspace clean and orderly.	☐
5. Cared for customer property and returned it undamaged.	☐

Student signature _____ Date _____

Comments:

Have your supervisor/instructor verify satisfactory completion of this procedure, any observations made, and any necessary action(s) recommended.

Evaluation Instructions: The scoring box below is intended to act as a guide for both student and supervisor/instructor. Each criterion listed will help students to understand what is expected of them and help supervisors/instructors to articulate the level of success at a particular task. The scoring is set up to allow a second attempt at each task (see the Test and Retest columns). Scoring is designed only to award students points for task criteria that were completed correctly. Points are lost for failure to complete the employability requirements (see Non-Task-Specific criteria). When all criteria are evaluated, tally the points for a total at the bottom of each column.

Tasksheet Scoring

Evaluation Items	Test		Retest	
	Pass	**Fail**	**Pass**	**Fail**
Task-Specific Evaluation	**(1 pt)**	**(0 pts)**	**(1 pt)**	**(0 pts)**
1. Student accurately and safely set up at least two stations.				
2. Student accurately and safely set up at least four stations.				
3. Student accurately and safely set up at least six stations.				
4. Student accurately and safely set up all eight stations.				
Non-Task-Specific Evaluation	**(0 pts)**	**(−1 pt)**	**(0 pts)**	**(−1 pt)**
Student successfully completed at least three of the non-task-specific steps.				
Student successfully completed all five of the non-task-specific steps.				
Total Score: <total # of points / 4 = %>				

Supervisor/Instructor:

Supervisor/instructor signature _____ Date _____

Comments:

Retest supervisor/instructor signature _____ Date _____

Comments:

CDX Tasksheet Number: 1a1004

Student/Intern Information

Name _____ Date _____ Class _____

Machine, Customer, and Service Information

Machine used for this activity:

Make _____ Model _____

Hours _____ Serial Number _____

Materials Required

- Standard toolkit and other tools as required
- Inside micrometer and master gauge
- Outside micrometer and master gauge
- Depth micrometer and master gauge
- Split ball gauge and master gauge
- Dial bore gauge and master gauge
- Pressure gauge and master gauge tool
- Hydrometer
- Refractometer
- Torque wrench

Task-Specific Safety Considerations

- Comply with personal and environmental safety practices associated with clothing; eye protection; hand tools; power equipment; proper ventilation; and the handling, storage, and disposal of chemicals/materials in accordance with local, state, and federal safety and environmental regulations.
- Tools allow us to increase our productivity and effectiveness. However, they must be used according to the manufacturer's procedures. Failure to follow those procedures can result in serious injury or death.

▶ **TASK** Test operation and calibration of precision hand tools.

Student Instructions: Read through the entire procedure prior to starting. Prepare your workspace and any tools or parts that may be needed to complete the task. When directed by your supervisor/instructor, begin the procedure to complete the task, and comment or check the box as each step is finished. Track your time on this procedure for later comparison to the standard completion time (i.e., "flat rate" or customer pay time).

Time off_____

Time on_____

Total time_____

Procedure	Step Completed
1. Select an inside micrometer. Use a master gauge to test it for proper operation and accurate calibration. Does it operate properly? Yes ☐ No ☐ Is it accurately calibrated? Yes ☐ No ☐	☐
2. Select an outside micrometer. Use a master gauge to test it for proper operation and accurate calibration. Does it operate properly? Yes ☐ No ☐ Is it accurately calibrated? Yes ☐ No ☐	☐
3. Select a depth micrometer. Use a master gauge to test it for proper operation and accurate calibration. Does it operate properly? Yes ☐ No ☐ Is it accurately calibrated? Yes ☐ No ☐	☐
4. Select a split ball gauge. Use a master gauge to test it for proper operation and accurate calibration. Does it operate properly? Yes ☐ No ☐ Is it accurately calibrated? Yes ☐ No ☐	☐
5. Select a dial bore gauge. Use a master gauge to test it for proper operation and accurate calibration. Does it operate properly? Yes ☐ No ☐ Is it accurately calibrated? Yes ☐ No ☐	☐
6. Select a pressure gauge. Use a master gauge to test it for proper operation and accurate calibration. Does it operate properly? Yes ☐ No ☐ Is it accurately calibrated? Yes ☐ No ☐	☐

	Step Completed
7. Select a hydrometer. Use a master gauge to test it for proper operation and accurate calibration. Does it operate properly? Yes ☐ No ☐ Is it accurately calibrated? Yes ☐ No ☐	☐
8. Select a refractometer. Use a master gauge to test it for proper operation and accurate calibration. Does it operate properly? Yes ☐ No ☐ Is it accurately calibrated? Yes ☐ No ☐	☐
9. Select a torque wrench. Use a master gauge to test it for proper operation and accurate calibration. Does it operate properly? Yes ☐ No ☐ Is it accurately calibrated? Yes ☐ No ☐	☐
10. Return any tools you used to their proper location.	☐

Non-Task-Specific Evaluation	Step Completed
1. Tools and equipment were used as directed and returned in good working order.	☐
2. Complied with all general and task-specific safety standards, including proper use of any personal protective equipment (PPE).	☐
3. Completed the task in an appropriate time frame (recommendation: 1.5 or 2 times the flat rate).	☐
4. Left the workspace clean and orderly.	☐
5. Cared for customer property and returned it undamaged.	☐

Student signature _____ Date _____

Comments:

Have your supervisor/instructor verify satisfactory completion of this procedure, any observations made,

and any necessary action(s) recommended.

Evaluation Instructions: The scoring box below is intended to act as a guide for both student and supervisor/instructor. Each criterion listed will help students to understand what is expected of them and help supervisors/instructors to articulate the level of success at a particular task. The scoring is set up to allow a second attempt at each task (see the Test and Retest columns). Scoring is designed only to award students points for task criteria that were completed correctly. Points are lost for failure to complete the employability requirements (see Non-Task-Specific criteria). When all criteria are evaluated, tally the points for a total at the bottom of each column.

Tasksheet Scoring

Evaluation Items	Test		Retest	
	Pass	**Fail**	**Pass**	**Fail**
Task-Specific Evaluation	**(1 pt)**	**(0 pts)**	**(1 pt)**	**(0 pts)**
1. Student correctly tested at least four tools for proper operation.				
2. Student correctly tested all nine tools for proper operation.				
3. Student correctly tested at least four tools for accurate calibration.				
4. Student correctly tested all nine tools for accurate calibration.				
Non-Task-Specific Evaluation	**(0 pts)**	**(−1 pt)**	**(0 pts)**	**(−1 pt)**
Student successfully completed at least three of the non-task-specific steps.				
Student successfully completed all five of the non-task-specific steps.				
Total Score: <total # of points / 4 = %>				

Supervisor/Instructor:

Supervisor/instructor signature _____ Date _____
Comments:

Retest supervisor/instructor signature _____ Date _____
Comments:

CDX Tasksheet Number: 1a1006

Student/Intern Information

Name _____ Date _____ Class _____

Machine, Customer, and Service Information

Machine used for this activity:

Make _____ Model _____

Hours _____ Serial Number _____

Materials Required
- Six standard or metric fasteners chosen by the supervisor/instructor to complete the task
- Torque wrench ft-lb, N·m clicker-style
- Torque wrench ft-lb, N·m dial-style
- Torque wrench in-lb, N·m clicker-style
- Torque wrench in-lb, N·m dial-style
- Angle gauge
- Metric torque chart
- Standard torque chart
- Step method torque procedure
- Engine assembly

Task-Specific Safety Considerations
- Comply with personal and environmental safety practices associated with clothing; eye protection; hand tools; power equipment; proper ventilation; and the handling, storage, and disposal of chemicals/materials in accordance with local, state, and federal safety and environmental regulations.
- Tools allow us to increase our productivity and effectiveness. However, they can also cause severe injury or death if used improperly. Make sure you follow the manufacturer's operation procedures.

▶ TASK Torque and de-torque fasteners to specification. _____ **AED 1a.1**

Time off_____

Time on_____

Student Instructions: Read through the entire procedure prior to starting. Prepare your workspace and any tools or parts that may be needed to complete the task. When directed by your supervisor/instructor, begin the procedure to complete the task, and comment or check the box as each step is finished. Track your time on this procedure for later comparison to the standard completion time (i.e., "flat rate" or customer pay time).

Total time_____

Procedure	Step Completed
1. Using Fastener #1, identify the fastener diameter, grade, threads per inch/pitch, and torque value. Write the values below: Diameter: _____ Grade: _____ Threads per inch/pitch: _____ Torque value: _____	☐
a. Select the correct clicker-style torque wrench, set up the torque fastener to specification, and demonstrate proper torque. Have your supervisor/instructor verify satisfactory completion of these procedures. Supervisor's/instructor's initials: _____	☐
b. De-torque fastener when complete.	☐
2. Using Fastener #2, identify the fastener diameter, grade, threads per inch/pitch, and torque value. Write the values below: Diameter: _____ Grade: _____ Threads per inch/pitch: _____ Torque value: _____	☐
a. Select the correct dial-style torque wrench, set up the torque fastener to specification, and demonstrate proper torque. Have your supervisor/instructor verify satisfactory completion of these procedures. Supervisor's/instructor's initials: _____	☐
b. De-torque fastener when complete.	☐
3. Using Fastener #3, identify the fastener diameter, grade, threads per inch/pitch, and torque value. Write the values below: Diameter: _____ Grade: _____ Threads per inch/pitch: _____ Torque value: _____	☐

a. Select the correct clicker-style torque wrench, set up the torque fastener to specification, and demonstrate proper torque. Have your supervisor/instructor verify satisfactory completion of these procedures. Supervisor's/instructor's initials: _____	☐
b. De-torque fastener when complete.	☐
4. Using Fastener #4, identify the fastener diameter, grade, threads per inch/pitch, and torque value. Write the values below: Diameter: _____ Grade: _____ Threads per inch/pitch: _____ Torque value: _____	☐
a. Select the correct dial-style torque wrench, set up the torque fastener to specification, and demonstrate proper torque. Have your supervisor/instructor verify satisfactory completion of these procedures. Supervisor's/instructor's initials: _____	☐
b. De-torque fastener when complete.	☐
5. Using Fastener #5, follow directions to torque the fastener using the torque angle method.	☐
a. Select the correct torque wrench and angle gauge and demonstrate proper torque procedure. Have your supervisor/instructor verify satisfactory completion of these procedures. Supervisor's/instructor's initials: _____	☐
b. De-torque fastener when complete.	☐
6. Using Fastener #6, follow directions to torque the cylinder head fasteners using the step method torque procedure.	☐
a. Select the correct torque wrench and demonstrate proper torque procedure. Have your supervisor/instructor verify satisfactory completion of these procedures. Supervisor's/instructor's initials: _____	☐
b. De-torque fastener when complete.	☐
7. Return any tools you used to their proper location.	☐

Non-Task-Specific Evaluation	Step Completed
1. Tools and equipment were used as directed and returned in good working order.	☐
2. Complied with all general and task-specific safety standards, including proper use of any personal protective equipment (PPE).	☐
3. Completed the task in an appropriate time frame (recommendation: 1.5 or 2 times the flat rate).	☐
4. Left the workspace clean and orderly.	☐
5. Cared for customer property and returned it undamaged.	☐

Student signature _____ Date _____

Comments:

Have your supervisor/instructor verify satisfactory completion of this procedure, any observations made, and any necessary action(s) recommended.

Evaluation Instructions: The scoring box below is intended to act as a guide for both student and supervisor/instructor. Each criterion listed will help students to understand what is expected of them and help supervisors/instructors to articulate the level of success at a particular task. The scoring is set up to allow a second attempt at each task (see the Test and Retest columns). Scoring is designed only to award students points for task criteria that were completed correctly. Points are lost for failure to complete the employability requirements (see Non-Task-Specific criteria). When all criteria are evaluated, tally the points for a total at the bottom of each column.

Tasksheet Scoring

Evaluation Items	Test		Retest	
	Pass	**Fail**	**Pass**	**Fail**
Task-Specific Evaluation	**(1 pt)**	**(0 pts)**	**(1 pt)**	**(0 pts)**
1. Student correctly identified the diameter, grade, threads per inch/pitch, torque value, and proper torque for Fasteners #1–4.				
2. Student demonstrated the proper use of the torque angle method and the step method torque procedure.				
3. Student chose the proper torque wrench for each fastener.				
4. Student demonstrated proper de-torque for all fasteners.				
Non-Task-Specific Evaluation	**(0 pts)**	**(−1 pt)**	**(0 pts)**	**(−1 pt)**
Student successfully completed at least three of the non-task-specific steps.				
Student successfully completed all five of the non-task-specific steps.				
Total Score: <total # of points / 4 = %>				

CDX Tasksheet Number: 1a1007

Student/Intern Information

Name _____ Date _____ Class _____

Machine, Customer, and Service Information

Machine used for this activity:

Make _____ Model _____

Hours _____ Serial Number _____

Materials Required
- One standard fastener
- One metric fastener
- One standard washer
- One metric washer
- Six additional parts chosen by the supervisor/instructor to complete the task
- Tags numbered 5-9 for labeling parts
- Straight edge (standard and metric)
- Micrometer (standard and metric)
- Caliper (standard and metric)
- Bore gauge (standard and metric)
- Dial indicator (standard and metric)
- Feeler gauge set (standard and metric)

Task-Specific Safety Considerations
- Comply with personal and environmental safety practices associated with clothing; eye protection; hand tools; power equipment; proper ventilation; and the handling, storage, and disposal of chemicals/materials in accordance with local, state, and federal safety and environmental regulations.
- Tools allow us to increase our productivity and effectiveness. However, they can also cause severe injury or death if used improperly. Make sure you follow the manufacturer's operation procedures.

▶ **TASK** Measure parts using precision measuring tools and gauges. **AED** *1a.1*

Time off_____

Time on_____

Student Instructions: Read through the entire procedure prior to starting. Prepare your workspace and any tools or parts that may be needed to complete the task. When directed by your supervisor/instructor, begin the procedure to complete the task, and comment or check the box as each step is finished. Track your time on this procedure for later comparison to the standard completion time (i.e., "flat rate" or customer pay time).

Total time_____

Procedure	Step Completed
1. Select the standard fastener, then take and record the following measurements:	☐
a. Use a straight edge to measure the length to the nearest graduation: _____ "	☐
b. Use a micrometer to measure the diameter to the nearest graduation: _____ "	☐
2. Select the metric fastener, then take and record the following measurements:	☐
a. Use a straight edge to measure the length to the nearest graduation: _____ mm	☐
b. Use a micrometer to measure the diameter to the nearest graduation: _____ mm	☐
3. Select the standard washer, then take and record the following measurements:	☐
a. Use a caliper to measure the outside diameter to the nearest graduation: _____ "	☐
b. Use a caliper to measure the inside diameter to the nearest graduation: _____ "	☐
4. Select the metric washer, then take and record the following measurements:	☐
a. Use a caliper to measure the outside diameter to the nearest graduation: _____ mm	☐
b. Use a caliper to measure the inside diameter to the nearest graduation: _____ mm	☐
5. Select Part #5, then take and record the following measurement:	☐
a. Use a micrometer to measure the inside diameter to the nearest graduation: _____ "	☐
6. Select Part #6, then take and record the following measurement:	☐

a. Use a micrometer to measure the inside diameter to the nearest graduation: _____ mm	☐
7. Select Part #7, then take and record the following measurements:	☐
a. Use a bore gauge to measure the inside diameter to the nearest graduation: _____ "	☐
b. Use a bore gauge to measure the inside diameter to the nearest graduation: _____ mm	☐
8. Select Part #8, then take and record the following measurements:	☐
a. Use a dial indicator to measure the end play to the nearest graduation: _____ "	☐
b. Use a dial indicator to measure the end play to the nearest graduation: _____ mm	☐
9. Select Part #9, then take and record the following measurements:	☐
a. Use a feeler gauge set to measure the clearance to the nearest gauge thickness: _____ "	☐
b. Use a feeler gauge set to measure the clearance to the nearest gauge thickness: _____ mm	☐
10. Return any tools you used to their proper location.	☐

Non-Task-Specific Evaluation	Step Completed
1. Tools and equipment were used as directed and returned in good working order.	☐
2. Complied with all general and task-specific safety standards, including proper use of any personal protective equipment (PPE).	☐
3. Completed the task in an appropriate time frame (recommendation: 1.5 or 2 times the flat rate).	☐
4. Left the workspace clean and orderly.	☐
5. Cared for customer property and returned it undamaged.	☐

Student signature _____ Date _____

Comments:

Have your supervisor/instructor verify satisfactory completion of this procedure, any observations made, and any necessary action(s) recommended.

Evaluation Instructions: The scoring box below is intended to act as a guide for both student and supervisor/instructor. Each criterion listed will help students to understand what is expected of them and help supervisors/instructors to articulate the level of success at a particular task. The scoring is set up to allow a second attempt at each task (see the Test and Retest columns). Scoring is designed only to award students points for task criteria that were completed correctly. Points are lost for failure to complete the employability requirements (see Non-Task-Specific criteria). When all criteria are evaluated, tally the points for a total at the bottom of each column.

Tasksheet Scoring

Evaluation Items	Test		Retest	
	Pass	**Fail**	**Pass**	**Fail**
Task-Specific Evaluation	**(1 pt)**	**(0 pts)**	**(1 pt)**	**(0 pts)**
1. Student correctly measured at least two tools.				
2. Student correctly measured at least four tools.				
3. Student correctly measured at least six tools.				
4. Student correctly measured all nine tools.				
Non-Task-Specific Evaluation	**(0 pts)**	**(−1 pt)**	**(0 pts)**	**(−1 pt)**
Student successfully completed at least three of the non-task-specific steps.				
Student successfully completed all five of the non-task-specific steps.				
Total Score: <total # of points / 4 = %>				

Supervisor/Instructor:

Supervisor/instructor signature _____ Date _____

Comments:

Retest supervisor/instructor signature _____ Date _____

Comments:

CDX Tasksheet Number: 1a1009

Student/Intern Information

Name _____ Date _____ Class _____

Machine, Customer, and Service Information

Machine used for this activity:

Make _____ Model _____

Hours _____ Serial Number _____

Materials Required

- Various machines
- Speed/rpm indicators
- Magnetic/optical tachometers and pulse generators

Task-Specific Safety Considerations

- Comply with personal and environmental safety practices associated with clothing; eye protection; hand tools; power equipment; proper ventilation; and the handling, storage, and disposal of chemicals/materials in accordance with local, state, and federal safety and environmental regulations.
- Tools allow us to increase our productivity and effectiveness. However, they can also cause severe injury or death if used improperly. Make sure you follow the manufacturer's operation procedures.

▶ **TASK** Measure engine speed and pulses per revolution.

AED
1a.1

Time off_____

Time on_____

Total time_____

Student Instructions: Read through the entire procedure prior to starting. Prepare your workspace and any tools or parts that may be needed to complete the task. When directed by your supervisor/instructor, begin the procedure to complete the task, and comment or check the box as each step is finished. Track your time on this procedure for later comparison to the standard completion time (i.e., "flat rate" or customer pay time).

Procedure	Step Completed
1. Using Machine #1, set up an optical tachometer according to the manufacturer's instructions. Measure engine idle speed and record it below. _____	☐

	Step Completed
2. Using Machine #2, set up a magnetic/pulse-type tachometer according to the manufacturer's instructions. Measure engine idle speed and record it below. _____	☐
3. Return any tools you used to their proper location.	☐

Non-Task-Specific Evaluation	Step Completed
1. Tools and equipment were used as directed and returned in good working order.	☐
2. Complied with all general and task-specific safety standards, including proper use of any personal protective equipment (PPE).	☐
3. Completed the task in an appropriate time frame (recommendation: 1.5 or 2 times the flat rate).	☐
4. Left the workspace clean and orderly.	☐
5. Cared for customer property and returned it undamaged.	☐

Student signature _____ Date _____

Comments:

Have your supervisor/instructor verify satisfactory completion of this procedure, any observations made, and any necessary action(s) recommended.

Evaluation Instructions: The scoring box below is intended to act as a guide for both student and supervisor/instructor. Each criterion listed will help students to understand what is expected of them and help supervisors/instructors to articulate the level of success at a particular task. The scoring is set up to allow a second attempt at each task (see the Test and Retest columns). Scoring is designed only to award students points for task criteria that were completed correctly. Points are lost for failure to complete the employability requirements (see Non-Task-Specific criteria). When all criteria are evaluated, tally the points for a total at the bottom of each column.

Tasksheet Scoring

Evaluation Items	Test		Retest	
	Pass	**Fail**	**Pass**	**Fail**
Task-Specific Evaluation	**(1 pt)**	**(0 pts)**	**(1 pt)**	**(0 pts)**
1. Student set up the optical tachometer according to the manufacturer's instructions.				
2. Student set up the magnetic/pulse-type tachometer according to the manufacturer's instructions.				
3. Student properly measured and recorded engine idle speed for Machine #1.				
4. Student properly measured and recorded engine idle speed for Machine #2.				
Non-Task-Specific Evaluation	**(0 pts)**	**(−1 pt)**	**(0 pts)**	**(−1 pt)**
Student successfully completed at least three of the non-task-specific steps.				
Student successfully completed all five of the non-task-specific steps.				
Total Score: <total # of points / 4 = %>				

Supervisor/Instructor:

Supervisor/instructor signature _____ Date _____

Comments:

Retest supervisor/instructor signature _____ Date _____

Comments:

CDX Tasksheet Number: 1a1O1O

Student/Intern Information

Name _____ Date _____ Class _____

Machine, Customer, and Service Information

Machine used for this activity

Make _____ Model _____

Hours _____ Serial Number _____

Materials Required
- Various machines or hydraulic tables
- Pressure/flow gauges and meters, manometers, and vacuum gauges
- Temperature gauges, pyrometers, thermocouples, and infrared thermometers
- Personal protective equipment (PPE)

Task-Specific Safety Considerations
- Comply with personal and environmental safety practices associated with clothing; eye protection; hand tools; power equipment; proper ventilation; and the handling, storage, and disposal of chemicals/materials in accordance with local, state, and federal safety and environmental regulations.
- Tools allow us to increase our productivity and effectiveness. However, they can also cause severe injury or death if used improperly. Make sure you follow the manufacturer's operation procedures.

▶ **TASK** Measure pressure, flows, and temperature. **AED** 1a.1

Time off_____

Time on_____

Total time_____

Student Instructions: Read through the entire procedure prior to starting. Prepare your workspace and any tools or parts that may be needed to complete the task. When directed by your supervisor/instructor, begin the procedure to complete the task, and comment or check the box as each step is finished. Track your time on this procedure for later comparison to the standard completion time (i.e., "flat rate" or customer pay time).

Procedure	Step Completed
1. Using Machine #1, set up a pressure gauge to measure the system pressure designated by your supervisor/instructor. Take and record each of the following measurements:	☐

a. Gauge minor and major graduation reading:
 	
    Minor _____
 	
    Major _____
	☐

b. Gauge minimum and maximum pressure: Minimum _____ Maximum _____	☐
c. Supervisor/instructor-requested pressure measurement: _____ PSI/KPA/bar	☐
2. Using Machine #2, set up a flow gauge to measure the system flow designated by your supervisor/instructor. Take and record each of the following measurements:	☐
a. Gauge minor and major graduation reading: Minor _____ Major _____	☐
b. Gauge minimum and maximum flow: Minimum _____ Maximum _____	☐
c. Supervisor/instructor-requested flow measurement: _____ GPM/LPM	☐
3. Using Machine #3, set up a manometer to measure the water column (WC) designated by your supervisor/instructor. Take and record each of the following measurements:	☐
a. Gauge minor and major graduation reading: Minor _____ Major _____	☐
b. Gauge minimum and maximum WC: Minimum _____ Maximum _____	☐
c. Supervisor/instructor-requested WC: _____ " WC	☐
4. Using Machine #4, set up a vacuum gauge to measure the system vacuum designated by your supervisor/instructor. Take and record each of the following measurements:	☐
a. Gauge minor and major graduation reading: Minor _____ Major _____	☐
b. Gauge minimum and maximum vacuum: Minimum _____ Maximum _____	☐
c. Supervisor/instructor-requested vacuum measurement: _____ "	☐

	Step Completed
5. Using Machine #5, set up a temperature gauge to measure the system temperature designated by your supervisor/instructor. Take and record each of the following measurements:	☐

a. Gauge minimum and maximum temperature:
 	
    Minimum _____
 	
    Maximum _____
	☐

b. Supervisor/instructor-requested temperature measurement: _____ °F	☐
6. Return any tools you used to their proper location.	☐

Non-Task-Specific Evaluation	Step Completed
1. Tools and equipment were used as directed and returned in good working order.	☐
2. Complied with all general and task-specific safety standards, including proper use of any PPE.	☐
3. Completed the task in an appropriate time frame (recommendation: 1.5 or 2 times the flat rate).	☐
4. Left the workspace clean and orderly.	☐
5. Cared for customer property and returned it undamaged.	☐

Student signature _____ Date _____

Comments:

Have your supervisor/instructor verify satisfactory completion of this procedure, any observations made, and any necessary action(s) recommended.

Evaluation Instructions: The scoring box below is intended to act as a guide for both student and supervisor/instructor. Each criterion listed will help students to understand what is expected of them and help supervisors/instructors to articulate the level of success at a particular task. The scoring is set up to allow a second attempt at each task (see the Test and Retest columns). Scoring is designed only to award students points for task criteria that were completed correctly. Points are lost for failure to complete the employability requirements (see Non-Task-Specific criteria). When all criteria are evaluated, tally the points for a total at the bottom of each column.

Tasksheet Scoring

Evaluation Items	Test		Retest	
	Pass	**Fail**	**Pass**	**Fail**
Task-Specific Evaluation	**(1 pt)**	**(0 pts)**	**(1 pt)**	**(0 pts)**
1. Student properly set up the correct gauge/ manometer for each machine.				
2. Student correctly measured the gauge major and minor graduation readings for each applicable machine.				
3. Student correctly measured the applicable minimum and maximum values for each machine.				
4. Student correctly measured the supervisor/ instructor-requested measurement for each machine.				
Non-Task-Specific Evaluation	**(0 pts)**	**(−1 pt)**	**(0 pts)**	**(−1 pt)**
Student successfully completed at least three of the non-task-specific steps.				
Student successfully completed all five of the non-task-specific steps.				
Total Score: <total # of points / 4 = %>				

Supervisor/Instructor:

Supervisor/instructor signature _____ Date _____

Comments:

Retest supervisor/instructor signature _____ Date _____

Comments:

CDX Tasksheet Number: 1a1O11

Student/Intern Information

Name _____ Date _____ Class _____

Machine, Customer, and Service Information

Machine used for this activity

Make _____ Model _____

Hours _____ Serial Number _____

Materials Required
- Various fuel samples
- Various coolant samples
- Various electrolyte samples
- Various batteries for testing electrolyte
- Various hydrometers/refractometers
- Personal protective equipment (PPE)

Task-Specific Safety Considerations
- Comply with personal and environmental safety practices associated with clothing; eye protection; hand tools; power equipment; proper ventilation; and the handling, storage, and disposal of chemicals/materials in accordance with local, state, and federal safety and environmental regulations.
- Tools allow us to increase our productivity and effectiveness. However, they can also cause severe injury or death if used improperly. Make sure you follow the manufacturer's operation procedures.

▶ TASK Measure specific gravity of fuel, coolant, and electrolyte.

AED
1a.1

Time off_____

Time on_____

Total time_____

Student Instructions: Read through the entire procedure prior to starting. Prepare your workspace and any tools or parts that may be needed to complete the task. When directed by your supervisor/instructor, begin the procedure to complete the task, and comment or check the box as each step is finished. Track your time on this procedure for later comparison to the standard completion time (i.e., "flat rate" or customer pay time).

Procedure	Step Completed
1. Using Fuel Sample #1, set up a hydrometer to measure specific gravity and record the reading below: Spec. gravity _____ Temperature _____	☐

2. Using Fuel Sample #2, set up a refractometer to measure specific gravity and record the reading below: Spec. gravity _____ Temperature _____	☐
3. Using Coolant Sample #1, set up a hydrometer to measure specific gravity and record the reading below: Spec. gravity _____ Temperature _____	☐
4. Using Coolant Sample #2, set up a refractometer to measure specific gravity and record the reading below: Spec. gravity _____ Temperature _____	☐
5. Using Electrolyte Sample #1, set up a hydrometer to measure specific gravity and record the reading below: Spec. gravity _____ Temperature _____	☐
6. Using Electrolyte Sample #2, set up a refractometer to measure specific gravity and record the reading below: Spec. gravity _____ Temperature _____	☐
7. Return any tools you used to their proper location.	☐

Non-Task-Specific Evaluation	Step Completed
1. Tools and equipment were used as directed and returned in good working order.	☐
2. Complied with all general and task-specific safety standards, including proper use of any PPE.	☐
3. Completed the task in an appropriate time frame (recommendation: 1.5 or 2 times the flat rate).	☐
4. Left the workspace clean and orderly.	☐
5. Cared for customer property and returned it undamaged.	☐

Student signature _____ Date _____

Comments:

Have your supervisor/instructor verify satisfactory completion of this procedure, any observations made, and any necessary action(s) recommended.

Evaluation Instructions: The scoring box below is intended to act as a guide for both student and supervisor/instructor. Each criterion listed will help students to understand what is expected of them and help supervisors/instructors to articulate the level of success at a particular task. The scoring is set up to allow a second attempt at each task (see the Test and Retest columns). Scoring is designed only to award students points for task criteria that were completed correctly. Points are lost for failure to complete the employability requirements (see Non-Task-Specific criteria). When all criteria are evaluated, tally the points for a total at the bottom of each column.

Tasksheet Scoring

Evaluation Items	Test Pass (1 pt)	Test Fail (0 pts)	Retest Pass (1 pt)	Retest Fail (0 pts)
Task-Specific Evaluation	**(1 pt)**	**(0 pts)**	**(1 pt)**	**(0 pts)**
1. Student properly set up a hydrometer or refractometer for each sample.				
2. Student correctly measured specific gravity and temperature for each fuel sample.				
3. Student correctly measured specific gravity and temperature for each coolant sample.				
4. Student correctly measured specific gravity and temperature for each electrolyte sample.				
Non-Task-Specific Evaluation	**(0 pts)**	**(−1 pt)**	**(0 pts)**	**(−1 pt)**
Student successfully completed at least three of the non-task-specific steps.				
Student successfully completed all five of the non-task-specific steps.				
Total Score: <total # of points / 4 = %>				

Chapter 2: Use of Electric Tools

Learning Objective/Task	CDX Tasksheet Number	AED Reference Number
• Identify basic electric tools by their proper name.	1a2001	AED 1a.2
• Demonstrate the proper use of electric hand tools.	1a2002	AED 1a.2
• Exhibit the safe and proper use of ground fault circuits.	1a2004	AED 1a.2

Materials Required

- 20 basic electric tools chosen by the supervisor/instructor to complete the task
- Tags numbered 1–20 for labeling tools
- Electric drills ($\frac{3}{8}$" chuck and $\frac{1}{2}$" chuck)
- Electric grinders (4" and 6")
- Electric die grinder
- Electric impact wrenches ($\frac{3}{8}$ and $\frac{1}{2}$)
- Electric bench grinder
- Grinding wheels (4" and 6")
- Cut-off wheel (4")
- Strip disc (2")
- Cup brush
- Wire wheel
- Hole saw (1")
- Rotary file
- Screwdriver bits (flat head, Phillips head, and T40 Torx®)
- Five electric tools chosen by the supervisor/instructor to complete the task

Safety Considerations

- Comply with personal and environmental safety practices associated with clothing; eye protection; hand tools; power equipment; proper ventilation; and the handling, storage, and disposal of chemicals/materials in accordance with local, state, and federal safety and environmental regulations.
- Tools allow us to increase our productivity and effectiveness. However, they can also cause severe injury or death if used improperly. Make sure you follow the manufacturer's operation procedures.

CDX Tasksheet Number: 1a2001

Student/Intern Information

Name _____ Date _____ Class _____

Machine, Customer, and Service Information

Machine used for this activity:

Make _____ Model _____

Hours _____ Serial Number _____

Materials Required
- 20 basic electric tools chosen by the supervisor/instructor to complete the task
- Tags numbered 1-20 for labeling tools

Task-Specific Safety Considerations
- Comply with personal and environmental safety practices associated with clothing; eye protection; hand tools; power equipment; proper ventilation; and the handling, storage, and disposal of chemicals/materials in accordance with local, state, and federal safety and environmental regulations.
- Tools allow us to increase our productivity and effectiveness. However, they can also cause severe injury or death if used improperly. Make sure you follow the manufacturer's operation procedures.

▶ **TASK** Identify basic electric tools by their proper name.

AED
1a.2

Time off_____

Time on_____

Total time_____

Student Instructions: Read through the entire procedure prior to starting. Prepare your workspace and any tools or parts that may be needed to complete the task. When directed by your supervisor/instructor, begin the procedure to complete the task, and comment or check the box as each step is finished. Track your time on this procedure for later comparison to the standard completion time (i.e., "flat rate" or customer pay time).

Procedure	Step Completed
1. Select Tool #1 and write its correct name below:	☐
2. Select Tool #2 and write its correct name below:	☐
3. Select Tool #3 and write its correct name below:	☐

4. Select Tool #4 and write its correct name below:	☐
5. Select Tool #5 and write its correct name below:	☐
6. Select Tool #6 and write its correct name below:	☐
7. Select Tool #7 and write its correct name below:	☐
8. Select Tool #8 and write its correct name below:	☐
9. Select Tool #9 and write its correct name below:	☐
10. Select Tool #10 and write its correct name below:	☐
11. Select Tool #11 and write its correct name below:	☐
12. Select Tool #12 and write its correct name below:	☐
13. Select Tool #13 and write its correct name below:	☐
14. Select Tool #14 and write its correct name below:	☐
15. Select Tool #15 and write its correct name below:	☐
16. Select Tool #16 and write its correct name below:	☐
17. Select Tool #17 and write its correct name below:	☐
18. Select Tool #18 and write its correct name below:	☐
19. Select Tool #19 and write its correct name below:	☐
20. Select Tool #20 and write its correct name below:	☐

Non-Task-Specific Evaluation	Step Completed
1. Tools and equipment were used as directed and returned in good working order.	☐
2. Complied with all general and task-specific safety standards, including proper use of any personal protective equipment (PPE).	☐
3. Completed the task in an appropriate time frame (recommendation: 1.5 or 2 times the flat rate).	☐
4. Left the workspace clean and orderly.	☐
5. Cared for customer property and returned it undamaged.	☐

Student signature _____ Date _____

Comments:

Have your supervisor/instructor verify satisfactory completion of this procedure, any observations made, and any necessary action(s) recommended.

Evaluation Instructions: The scoring box below is intended to act as a guide for both student and supervisor/instructor. Each criterion listed will help students to understand what is expected of them and help supervisors/instructors to articulate the level of success at a particular task. The scoring is set up to allow a second attempt at each task (see the Test and Retest columns). Scoring is designed only to award students points for task criteria that were completed correctly. Points are lost for failure to complete the employability requirements (see Non-Task-Specific criteria). When all criteria are evaluated, tally the points for a total at the bottom of each column.

Tasksheet Scoring

	Test		Retest	
Evaluation Items	**Pass**	**Fail**	**Pass**	**Fail**
Task-Specific Evaluation	**(1 pt)**	**(0 pts)**	**(1 pt)**	**(0 pts)**
1. Student correctly identified at least five tools.				
2. Student correctly identified at least 10 tools.				
3. Student correctly identified at least 15 tools.				
4. Student correctly identified all 20 tools.				
Non-Task-Specific Evaluation	**(0 pts)**	**(−1 pt)**	**(0 pts)**	**(−1 pt)**
Student successfully completed at least three of the non-task-specific steps.				
Student successfully completed all five of the non-task-specific steps.				
Total Score: <total # of points / 4 = %>				

Supervisor/Instructor:

Supervisor/instructor signature _____ Date _____

Comments:

Retest supervisor/instructor signature _____ Date _____

Comments:

CDX Tasksheet Number: 1a2002

Student/Intern Information

Name _____ Date _____ Class _____

Machine, Customer, and Service Information

Machine used for this activity:

Make _____ Model _____

Hours _____ Serial Number _____

Materials Required

- Electric drills (³⁄₈" chuck and ¹⁄₂" chuck)
- Electric grinders (4" and 6")
- Electric die grinder
- Electric impact wrenches (³⁄₈" and ¹⁄₂")
- Electric bench grinder
- Grinding wheels (4" and 6")
- Cut-off wheel (4")
- Strip disc (2")
- Cup brush
- Wire wheel
- Hole saw (1")
- Rotary file
- Screwdriver bits (flat head, Phillips head, and T40 Torx®)

Task-Specific Safety Considerations

- Comply with personal and environmental safety practices associated with clothing; eye protection; hand tools; power equipment; proper ventilation; and the handling, storage, and disposal of chemicals/materials in accordance with local, state, and federal safety and environmental regulations.
- Tools allow us to increase our productivity and effectiveness. However, they can also cause severe injury or death if used improperly. Make sure you follow the manufacturer's operation procedures.

▶ **TASK** Demonstrate the proper use of electric hand tools. **AED 1a.2**

Time off_____

Time on_____

Total time_____

Student Instructions: Read through the entire procedure prior to starting. Prepare your workspace and any tools or parts that may be needed to complete the task. When directed by your supervisor/instructor, begin the procedure to complete the task, and comment or check the box as each step is finished. Track your time on this procedure for later comparison to the standard completion time (i.e., "flat rate" or customer pay time).

Procedure	Step Completed
1. Select an electric drill ³⁄₈" chuck and demonstrate its proper use, care and maintenance, and safe operating procedure. Have your supervisor/instructor verify satisfactory completion of these procedures. Supervisor's/instructor's initials: _____	☐
2. Select an electric drill ½" chuck and demonstrate its proper use, care and maintenance, and safe operating procedure. Have your supervisor/instructor verify satisfactory completion of these procedures. Supervisor's/instructor's initials: _____	☐
3. Select a 4" electric grinder and demonstrate its proper use, care and maintenance, and operating procedure. Have your supervisor/instructor verify satisfactory completion of these procedures. Supervisor's/instructor's initials: _____	☐
4. Select a 6" electric grinder and demonstrate its proper use, care and maintenance, and safe operating procedure. Have your supervisor/instructor verify satisfactory completion of these procedures. Supervisor's/instructor's initials: _____	☐
5. Select an electric die grinder and demonstrate its proper use, care and maintenance, and safe operating procedure. Have your supervisor/instructor verify satisfactory completion of these procedures. Supervisor's/instructor's initials: _____	☐
6. Select a ³⁄₈" electric impact wrench and demonstrate its proper use, care and maintenance, and safe operating procedure. Have your supervisor/instructor verify satisfactory completion of these procedures. Supervisor's/instructor's initials: _____	☐
7. Select a ½" electric impact wrench and demonstrate its proper use, care and maintenance, and safe operating procedure. Have your supervisor/instructor verify satisfactory completion of these procedures. Supervisor's/instructor's initials: _____	☐
8. Select an electric bench grinder and demonstrate its proper use, care and maintenance, and safe operating procedure. Have your supervisor/instructor verify satisfactory completion of these procedures. Supervisor's/instructor's initials: _____	☐

9. Select a 4" grinding wheel and demonstrate its proper use, care and maintenance, and safe operating procedure. Have your supervisor/instructor verify satisfactory completion of these procedures. Supervisor's/instructor's initials: _____	☐
10. Select a 6" grinding wheel and demonstrate its proper use, care and maintenance, and safe operating procedure. Have your supervisor/instructor verify satisfactory completion of these procedures. Supervisor's/instructor's initials: _____	☐
11. Select a 4" cut-off wheel and demonstrate its proper use, care and maintenance, and safe operating procedure. Have your supervisor/instructor verify satisfactory completion of these procedures. Supervisor's/instructor's initials: _____	☐
12. Select a 2" strip disc and demonstrate its proper use, care and maintenance, and safe operating procedure. Have your supervisor/instructor verify satisfactory completion of these procedures. Supervisor's/instructor's initials: _____	☐
13. Select a cup brush and demonstrate its proper use, care and maintenance, and safe operating procedure. Have your supervisor/instructor verify satisfactory completion of these procedures. Supervisor's/instructor's initials: _____	☐
14. Select a wire wheel and demonstrate its proper use, care and maintenance, and safe operating procedure. Have your supervisor/instructor verify satisfactory completion of these procedures. Supervisor's/instructor's initials: _____	☐
15. Select a 1" hole saw and demonstrate its proper use, care and maintenance, and safe operating procedure. Have your supervisor/instructor verify satisfactory completion of these procedures. Supervisor's/instructor's initials: _____	☐
16. Select a rotary file and demonstrate its proper use, care and maintenance, and safe operating procedure. Have your supervisor/instructor verify satisfactory completion of these procedures. Supervisor's/instructor's initials: _____	☐

17. Select a flat head screwdriver bit and demonstrate its proper use, care and maintenance, and safe operating procedure. Have your supervisor/instructor verify satisfactory completion of these procedures. Supervisor's/instructor's initials: _____	☐
18. Select a Phillips head screwdriver bit and demonstrate its proper use, care and maintenance, and safe operating procedure. Have your supervisor/instructor verify satisfactory completion of these procedures. Supervisor's/instructor's initials: _____	☐
19. Select a T40 Torx® bit and demonstrate its proper use, care and maintenance, and safe operating procedure. Have your supervisor/instructor verify satisfactory completion of these procedures. Supervisor's/instructor's initials: _____	☐

Non-Task-Specific Evaluation	Step Completed
1. Tools and equipment were used as directed and returned in good working order.	☐
2. Complied with all general and task-specific safety standards, including proper use of any personal protective equipment (PPE).	☐
3. Completed the task in an appropriate time frame (recommendation: 1.5 or 2 times the flat rate).	☐
4. Left the workspace clean and orderly.	☐
5. Cared for customer property and returned it undamaged.	☐

Student signature _____ Date _____

Comments:

Have your supervisor/instructor verify satisfactory completion of this procedure, any observations made,

and any necessary action(s) recommended.

Evaluation Instructions: The scoring box below is intended to act as a guide for both student and supervisor/instructor. Each criterion listed will help students to understand what is expected of them and help supervisors/instructors to articulate the level of success at a particular task. The scoring is set up to allow a second attempt at each task (see the Test and Retest columns). Scoring is designed only to award students points for task criteria that were completed correctly. Points are lost for failure to complete the employability requirements (see Non-Task-Specific criteria). When all criteria are evaluated, tally the points for a total at the bottom of each column.

Tasksheet Scoring

Evaluation Items	Test		Retest	
	Pass	Fail	Pass	Fail
Task-Specific Evaluation	**(1 pt)**	**(0 pts)**	**(1 pt)**	**(0 pts)**
1. Students chose the correct tool each time.				
2. Student correctly demonstrated the proper use of all tools.				
3. Student correctly demonstrated the proper care and maintenance for all tools.				
4. Student correctly demonstrated the proper safe operating procedure for all tools.				
Non-Task-Specific Evaluation	**(0 pts)**	**(−1 pt)**	**(0 pts)**	**(−1 pt)**
Student successfully completed at least three of the non-task-specific steps.				
Student successfully completed all five of the non-task-specific steps.				
Total Score: <total # of points / 4 = %>				

Supervisor/Instructor:

Supervisor/instructor signature _____ Date _____

Comments:

[ ]

Retest supervisor/instructor signature _____ Date _____

Comments:

[ ]

CDX Tasksheet Number: 1a2004

Student/Intern Information

Name _____ Date _____ Class _____

Machine, Customer, and Service Information

Machine used for this activity:

Make _____ Model _____

Hours _____ Serial Number _____

Materials Required
- Five electric tools chosen by the supervisor/instructor to complete the task
- Tags numbered 1–5 for labeling tools

Task-Specific Safety Considerations
- Comply with personal and environmental safety practices associated with clothing; eye protection; hand tools; power equipment; proper ventilation; and the handling, storage, and disposal of chemicals/materials in accordance with local, state, and federal safety and environmental regulations.
- Tools allow us to increase our productivity and effectiveness. However, they can also cause severe injury or death if used improperly. Make sure you follow the manufacturer's operation procedures.

▶ **TASK** Exhibit the safe and proper use of ground fault circuits.

AED
1a.2

Time off_____

Time on_____

Total time_____

Student Instructions: Read through the entire procedure prior to starting. Prepare your workspace and any tools or parts that may be needed to complete the task. When directed by your supervisor/instructor, begin the procedure to complete the task, and comment or check the box as each step is finished. Track your time on this procedure for later comparison to the standard completion time (i.e., "flat rate" or customer pay time).

Procedure	Step Completed
1. Identify Tool #1 and write its name below:	☐
a. Is this tool equipped with the proper ground fault circuit? Yes ☐ No ☐	☐

b. If yes, demonstrate how to properly ensure that the ground fault circuit works. If no, demonstrate how a ground fault circuit can be easily added to the tool for safe operation. Have your supervisor/instructor verify satisfactory demonstration. Supervisor's/instructor's initials: _____	☐
2. Identify Tool #2 and write its name below:	☐
a. Is this tool equipped with the proper ground fault circuit? Yes ☐ No ☐	☐
b. If yes, demonstrate how to properly ensure that the ground fault circuit works. If no, demonstrate how a ground fault circuit can be easily added to the tool for safe operation. Have your supervisor/instructor verify satisfactory demonstration. Supervisor's/instructor's initials: _____	☐
3. Identify Tool #3 and write its name below:	☐
a. Is this tool equipped with the proper ground fault circuit? Yes ☐ No ☐	☐
b. If yes, demonstrate how to properly ensure that the ground fault circuit works. If no, demonstrate how a ground fault circuit can be easily added to the tool for safe operation. Have your supervisor/instructor verify satisfactory demonstration. Supervisor's/instructor's initials: _____	☐
4. Identify Tool #4 and write its name below:	☐
a. Is this tool equipped with the proper ground fault circuit? Yes ☐ No ☐	☐
b. If yes, demonstrate how to properly ensure that the ground fault circuit works. If no, demonstrate how a ground fault circuit can be easily added to the tool for safe operation. Have your supervisor/instructor verify satisfactory demonstration. Supervisor's/instructor's initials: _____	☐
5. Identify Tool #5 and write its name below:	☐
a. Is this tool equipped with the proper ground fault circuit? Yes ☐ No ☐	☐

	Step Completed
b. If yes, demonstrate how to properly ensure that the ground fault circuit works. If no, demonstrate how a ground fault circuit can be easily added to the tool for safe operation. Have your supervisor/instructor verify satisfactory demonstration. Supervisor's/instructor's initials: _____	☐
6. Return any tools you used to their proper location.	☐

Non-Task-Specific Evaluation	Step Completed
1. Tools and equipment were used as directed and returned in good working order.	☐
2. Complied with all general and task-specific safety standards, including proper use of any personal protective equipment (PPE).	☐
3. Completed the task in an appropriate time frame (recommendation: 1.5 or 2 times the flat rate).	☐
4. Left the workspace clean and orderly.	☐
5. Cared for customer property and returned it undamaged.	☐

Student signature _____ Date _____

Comments:

Have your supervisor/instructor verify satisfactory completion of this procedure, any observations made, and any necessary action(s) recommended.

Evaluation Instructions: The scoring box below is intended to act as a guide for both student and supervisor/instructor. Each criterion listed will help students to understand what is expected of them and help supervisors/instructors to articulate the level of success at a particular task. The scoring is set up to allow a second attempt at each task (see the Test and Retest columns). Scoring is designed only to award students points for task criteria that were completed correctly. Points are lost for failure to complete the employability requirements (see Non-Task-Specific criteria). When all criteria are evaluated, tally the points for a total at the bottom of each column.

Taksheet Scoring

Evaluation Items	Test		Retest	
	Pass	**Fail**	**Pass**	**Fail**
Task-Specific Evaluation	**(1 pt)**	**(0 pts)**	**(1 pt)**	**(0 pts)**
1. Student correctly identified all tools by name.				
2. Student correctly identified whether each tool was equipped with the proper ground fault circuit.				
3. Student correctly demonstrated how to properly ensure the ground fault circuit works, where applicable.				
4. Student correctly demonstrated how a ground fault circuit can be easily added to a tool for safe operation, where applicable.				
Non-Task-Specific Evaluation	**(0 pts)**	**(−1 pt)**	**(0 pts)**	**(−1 pt)**
Student successfully completed at least three of the non-task-specific steps.				
Student successfully completed all five of the non-task-specific steps.				
Total Score: <total # of points / 4 = %>				

Supervisor/Instructor:

Supervisor/instructor signature _____ Date _____

Comments:

Retest supervisor/instructor signature _____ Date _____

Comments:

Chapter 3: Use of Air Tools

Learning Objective/Task	CDX Tasksheet Number	AED Reference Number
• Identify basic air tools by their proper name.	1a3001	AED 1a.3
• Demonstrate the proper use of air tools.	1a3002	AED 1a.3

Materials Required

- Nine basic hand tools chosen by the supervisor/instructor to complete the task
- Tags numbered 1-9 for labeling tools
- Air drills ($3/8$" chuck and $1/2$" chuck)
- Air grinders (4" and 6")
- Air die grinder
- Air impact wrenches ($3/8$", $1/2$", $3/4$", and 1")

Safety Considerations

- Comply with personal and environmental safety practices associated with clothing; eye protection; hand tools; power equipment; proper ventilation; and the handling, storage, and disposal of chemicals/materials in accordance with local, state, and federal safety and environmental regulations.
- Tools allow us to increase our productivity and effectiveness. However, they can also cause severe injury or death if used improperly. Make sure you follow the manufacturer's operation procedures.

CDX Tasksheet Number: 1a3001

Student/Intern Information

Name _____ Date _____ Class _____

Machine, Customer, and Service Information

Machine used for this activity:

Make _____ Model _____

Hours _____ Serial Number _____

Materials Required

- Nine basic air tools chosen by the supervisor/instructor to complete the task
- Tags numbered 1–9 for labeling tools

Task-Specific Safety Considerations

- Comply with personal and environmental safety practices associated with clothing; eye protection; hand tools; power equipment; proper ventilation; and the handling, storage, and disposal of chemicals/materials in accordance with local, state, and federal safety and environmental regulations.
- Tools allow us to increase our productivity and effectiveness. However, they can also cause severe injury or death if used improperly. Make sure you follow the manufacturer's operation procedures.

▶ TASK Identify basic air tools by their proper name. **AED** *1a.3*

Time off_____

Student Instructions: Read through the entire procedure prior to starting. Prepare your workspace and any tools or parts that may be needed to complete the task. When directed by your supervisor/instructor, begin the procedure to complete the task, and comment or check the box as each step is finished. Track your time on this procedure for later comparison to the standard completion time (i.e., "flat rate" or customer pay time).

Time on_____

Total time_____

Procedure	Step Completed
1. Select Tool #1 and write its correct name below:	☐
2. Select Tool #2 and write its correct name below:	☐
3. Select Tool #3 and write its correct name below:	☐

	Step Completed
4. Select Tool #4 and write its correct name below:	☐
5. Select Tool #5 and write its correct name below:	☐
6. Select Tool #6 and write its correct name below:	☐
7. Select Tool #7 and write its correct name below:	☐
8. Select Tool #8 and write its correct name below:	☐
9. Select Tool #9 and write its correct name below:	☐

Non-Task-Specific Evaluation	Step Completed
1. Tools and equipment were used as directed and returned in good working order.	☐
2. Complied with all general and task-specific safety standards, including proper use of any personal protective equipment (PPE).	☐
3. Completed the task in an appropriate time frame (recommendation: 1.5 or 2 times the flat rate).	☐
4. Left the workspace clean and orderly.	☐
5. Cared for customer property and returned it undamaged.	☐

Student signature _____ Date _____

Comments:

Have your supervisor/instructor verify satisfactory completion of this procedure, any observations made, and any necessary action(s) recommended.

Evaluation Instructions: The scoring box below is intended to act as a guide for both student and supervisor/instructor. Each criterion listed will help students to understand what is expected of them and help supervisors/instructors to articulate the level of success at a particular task. The scoring is set up to allow a second attempt at each task (see the Test and Retest columns). Scoring is designed only to award students points for task criteria that were completed correctly. Points are lost for failure to complete the employability requirements (see Non-Task-Specific criteria). When all criteria are evaluated, tally the points for a total at the bottom of each column.

Tasksheet Scoring

Evaluation Items	Test		Retest	
	Pass	Fail	Pass	Fail
Task-Specific Evaluation	**(1 pt)**	**(0 pts)**	**(1 pt)**	**(0 pts)**
1. Student correctly identified at least two tools.				
2. Student correctly identified at least four tools.				
3. Student correctly identified at least six tools.				
4. Student correctly identified all nine tools.				
Non-Task-Specific Evaluation	**(0 pts)**	**(−1 pt)**	**(0 pts)**	**(−1 pt)**
Student successfully completed at least three of the non-task-specific steps.				
Student successfully completed all five of the non-task-specific steps.				
Total Score: <total # of points / 4 = %>				

Supervisor/Instructor:

Supervisor/instructor signature _____ Date _____

Comments:

Retest supervisor/instructor signature _____ Date _____

Comments:

CDX Tasksheet Number: 1a3002

Student/Intern Information

Name _____ Date _____ Class _____

Machine, Customer, and Service Information

Machine used for this activity:

Make _____ Model _____

Hours _____ Serial Number _____

Materials Required

- Air drills ($3/8$" chuck and $1/2$" chuck)
- Air grinders (4" and 6")
- Air die grinder
- Air impact wrenches ($3/8$", $1/2$", $3/4$", and 1")

Task-Specific Safety Considerations

- Comply with personal and environmental safety practices associated with clothing; eye protection; hand tools; power equipment; proper ventilation; and the handling, storage, and disposal of chemicals/materials in accordance with local, state, and federal safety and environmental regulations.
- Tools allow us to increase our productivity and effectiveness. However, they can also cause severe injury or death if used improperly. Make sure you follow the manufacturer's operation procedures.

▶ **TASK** Demonstrate the proper use of air tools.

AED
1a.3

Time off_____

Time on_____

Total time_____

Student Instructions: Read through the entire procedure prior to starting. Prepare your workspace and any tools or parts that may be needed to complete the task. When directed by your supervisor/instructor, begin the procedure to complete the task, and comment or check the box as each step is finished. Track your time on this procedure for later comparison to the standard completion time (i.e., "flat rate" or customer pay time).

Procedure	Step Completed
1. Select an air drill $3/8$" chuck and demonstrate its proper use, care and maintenance, and safe operating procedure. Have your supervisor/instructor verify satisfactory completion of these procedures. Supervisor's/instructor's initials: _____	☐

2. Select an air drill $\frac{1}{2}$" chuck and demonstrate its proper use, care and maintenance, and safe operating procedure. Have your supervisor/instructor verify satisfactory completion of these procedures. Supervisor's/instructor's initials: _____	☐
3. Select an air grinder 6" and demonstrate its proper use, care and maintenance, and safe operating procedure. Have your supervisor/instructor verify satisfactory completion of these procedures. Supervisor's/instructor's initials: _____	☐
4. Select an air grinder 4" and demonstrate its proper use, care and maintenance, and safe operating procedure. Have your supervisor/instructor verify satisfactory completion of these procedures. Supervisor's/instructor's initials: _____	☐
5. Select an air die grinder and demonstrate its proper use, care and maintenance, and safe operating procedure. Have your supervisor/instructor verify satisfactory completion of these procedures. Supervisor's/instructor's initials: _____	☐
6. Select an air impact wrench $\frac{3}{8}$" and demonstrate its proper use, care and maintenance, and safe operating procedure. Have your supervisor/instructor verify satisfactory completion of these procedures. Supervisor's/instructor's initials: _____	☐
7. Select an air impact wrench $\frac{1}{2}$" and demonstrate its proper use, care and maintenance, and safe operating procedure. Have your supervisor/instructor verify satisfactory completion of these procedures. Supervisor's/instructor's initials: _____	☐
8. Select an air impact wrench $\frac{3}{4}$" and demonstrate its proper use, care and maintenance, and safe operating procedure. Have your supervisor/instructor verify satisfactory completion of these procedures. Supervisor's/instructor's initials: _____	☐
9. Select an air impact wrench 1" and demonstrate its proper use, care and maintenance, and safe operating procedure. Have your supervisor/instructor verify satisfactory completion of these procedures. Supervisor's/instructor's initials: _____	☐

Non-Task-Specific Evaluation	Step Completed
1. Tools and equipment were used as directed and returned in good working order.	☐
2. Complied with all general and task-specific safety standards, including proper use of any personal protective equipment (PPE).	☐
3. Completed the task in an appropriate time frame (recommendation: 1.5 or 2 times the flat rate).	☐
4. Left the workspace clean and orderly.	☐
5. Cared for customer property and returned it undamaged.	☐

Student signature _____ Date _____

Comments:

Have your supervisor/instructor verify satisfactory completion of this procedure, any observations made, and any necessary action(s) recommended.

Evaluation Instructions: The scoring box below is intended to act as a guide for both student and supervisor/instructor. Each criterion listed will help students to understand what is expected of them and help supervisors/instructors to articulate the level of success at a particular task. The scoring is set up to allow a second attempt at each task (see the Test and Retest columns). Scoring is designed only to award students points for task criteria that were completed correctly. Points are lost for failure to complete the employability requirements (see Non-Task-Specific criteria). When all criteria are evaluated, tally the points for a total at the bottom of each column.

Tasksheet Scoring

	Test		Retest	
Evaluation Items	**Pass**	**Fail**	**Pass**	**Fail**
Task-Specific Evaluation	**(1 pt)**	**(0 pts)**	**(1 pt)**	**(0 pts)**
1. Students chose the correct tool each time.				
2. Student correctly demonstrated the proper use of all tools.				
3. Student correctly demonstrated the proper care and maintenance for all tools.				
4. Student correctly demonstrated the proper safe operating procedure for all tools.				
Non-Task-Specific Evaluation	**(0 pts)**	**(−1 pt)**	**(0 pts)**	**(−1 pt)**
Student successfully completed at least three of the non-task-specific steps.				
Student successfully completed all five of the non-task-specific steps.				
Total Score: <total # of points / 4 = %>				

Supervisor/Instructor:

Supervisor/instructor signature _____ Date _____

Comments:

Retest supervisor/instructor signature _____ Date _____

Comments:

Chapter 4: Use of Hydraulic Tools

Learning Objective/Task	CDX Tasksheet Number	AED Reference Number
• Identify basic hydraulic tools by their name.	1a4001	AED 1a.4
• Demonstrate the proper use of hydraulic tools.	1a4003	AED 1a.4

Materials Required

- Six basic hydraulic tools chosen by the supervisor/instructor to complete the task
- Tags numbered 1-6 for labeling tools
- Hydraulic shop press
- Hydraulic portable press
- Hydraulic spreader
- Hydraulic floor jack
- Hydraulic bottle jack
- Hydraulic porto power

Safety Considerations

- Comply with personal and environmental safety practices associated with clothing; eye protection; hand tools; power equipment; proper ventilation; and the handling, storage, and disposal of chemicals/materials in accordance with local, state, and federal safety and environmental regulations.
- Tools allow us to increase our productivity and effectiveness. However, they can also cause severe injury or death if used improperly. Make sure you follow the manufacturer's operation procedures.

CDX Tasksheet Number: 1a4001

Student/Intern Information

Name _____ Date _____ Class _____

Machine, Customer, and Service Information

Machine used for this activity:

Make _____ Model _____

Hours _____ Serial Number _____

Materials Required

- Six basic hydraulic tools chosen by the supervisor/instructor to complete the task
- Tags numbered 1-6 for labeling tools

Task-Specific Safety Considerations

- Comply with personal and environmental safety practices associated with clothing; eye protection; hand tools; power equipment; proper ventilation; and the handling, storage, and disposal of chemicals/materials in accordance with local, state, and federal safety and environmental regulations.
- Tools allow us to increase our productivity and effectiveness. However, they can also cause severe injury or death if used improperly. Make sure you follow the manufacturer's operation procedures.

▶ TASK Identify basic hydraulic tools by their name.

AED
1a.4

Time off_____

Time on_____

Total time_____

Student Instructions: Read through the entire procedure prior to starting. Prepare your workspace and any tools or parts that may be needed to complete the task. When directed by your supervisor/instructor, begin the procedure to complete the task, and comment or check the box as each step is finished. Track your time on this procedure for later comparison to the standard completion time (i.e., "flat rate" or customer pay time).

Procedure	Step Completed
1. Select Tool #1 and write its correct name below:	☐
2. Select Tool #2 and write its correct name below:	☐
3. Select Tool #3 and write its correct name below:	☐

	Step Completed
4. Select Tool #4 and write its correct name below:	☐
5. Select Tool #5 and write its correct name below:	☐
6. Select Tool #6 and write its correct name below:	☐

Non-Task-Specific Evaluation	**Step Completed**
1. Tools and equipment were used as directed and returned in good working order.	☐
2. Complied with all general and task-specific safety standards, including proper use of any personal protective equipment (PPE).	☐
3. Completed the task in an appropriate time frame (recommendation: 1.5 or 2 times the flat rate).	☐
4. Left the workspace clean and orderly.	☐
5. Cared for customer property and returned it undamaged.	☐

Student signature _____ Date _____

Comments:

Have your supervisor/instructor verify satisfactory completion of this procedure, any observations made, and any necessary action(s) recommended.

Evaluation Instructions: The scoring box below is intended to act as a guide for both student and supervisor/instructor. Each criterion listed will help students to understand what is expected of them and help supervisors/instructors to articulate the level of success at a particular task. The scoring is set up to allow a second attempt at each task (see the Test and Retest columns). Scoring is designed only to award students points for task criteria that were completed correctly. Points are lost for failure to complete the employability requirements (see Non-Task-Specific criteria). When all criteria are evaluated, tally the points for a total at the bottom of each column.

Tasksheet Scoring

Evaluation Items	Test		Retest	
	Pass	Fail	Pass	Fail
Task-Specific Evaluation	**(1 pt)**	**(0 pts)**	**(1 pt)**	**(0 pts)**
1. Student correctly identified at least one tool.				
2. Student correctly identified at least two tools.				
3. Student correctly identified at least four tools.				
4. Student correctly identified all six tools.				
Non-Task-Specific Evaluation	**(0 pts)**	**(−1 pt)**	**(0 pts)**	**(−1 pt)**
Student successfully completed at least three of the non-task-specific steps.				
Student successfully completed all five of the non-task-specific steps.				
Total Score: <total # of points / 4 = %>				

Supervisor/Instructor:

Supervisor/instructor signature _____ Date _____

Comments:

Retest supervisor/instructor signature _____ Date _____

Comments:

CDX Tasksheet Number: 1a4003

Student/Intern Information

Name _____ Date _____ Class _____

Machine, Customer, and Service Information

Machine used for this activity:

Make _____ Model _____

Hours _____ Serial Number _____

Materials Required
- Hydraulic shop press
- Hydraulic portable press
- Hydraulic spreader
- Hydraulic floor jack
- Hydraulic bottle jack
- Hydraulic porto power

Task-Specific Safety Considerations
- Comply with personal and environmental safety practices associated with clothing; eye protection; hand tools; power equipment; proper ventilation; and the handling, storage, and disposal of chemicals/materials in accordance with local, state, and federal safety and environmental regulations.
- Tools allow us to increase our productivity and effectiveness. However, they can also cause severe injury or death if used improperly. Make sure you follow the manufacturer's operation procedures.

▶ **TASK** Demonstrate the proper use of hydraulic tools.

AED
1a.4

Time off_____

Time on_____

Total time_____

Student Instructions: Read through the entire procedure prior to starting. Prepare your workspace and any tools or parts that may be needed to complete the task. When directed by your supervisor/instructor, begin the procedure to complete the task, and comment or check the box as each step is finished. Track your time on this procedure for later comparison to the standard completion time (i.e., "flat rate" or customer pay time).

Procedure	Step Completed
1. Select a hydraulic shop press and demonstrate its proper use, care and maintenance, and safe operating procedure. Have your supervisor/instructor verify satisfactory completion of these procedures. Supervisor's/instructor's initials: _____	☐

2. Select a hydraulic portable press and demonstrate its proper use, care and maintenance, and safe operating procedure. Have your supervisor/ instructor verify satisfactory completion of these procedures. Supervisor's/instructor's initials: _____	☐
3. Select a hydraulic spreader and demonstrate its proper use, care and maintenance, and safe operating procedure. Have your supervisor/ instructor verify satisfactory completion of these procedures. Supervisor's/instructor's initials: _____	☐
4. Select a hydraulic floor jack and demonstrate its proper use, care and maintenance, and safe operating procedure. Have your supervisor/ instructor verify satisfactory completion of these procedures. Supervisor's/instructor's initials: _____	☐
5. Select a hydraulic bottle jack and demonstrate its proper use, care and maintenance, and safe operating procedure. Have your supervisor/ instructor verify satisfactory completion of these procedures. Supervisor's/instructor's initials: _____	☐
6. Select hydraulic porto power and demonstrate its proper use, care and maintenance, and safe operating procedure. Have your supervisor/ instructor verify satisfactory completion of these procedures. Supervisor's/instructor's initials: _____	☐

Non-Task-Specific Evaluation	Step Completed
1. Tools and equipment were used as directed and returned in good working order.	☐
2. Complied with all general and task-specific safety standards, including proper use of any personal protective equipment (PPE).	☐
3. Completed the task in an appropriate time frame (recommendation: 1.5 or 2 times the flat rate).	☐
4. Left the workspace clean and orderly.	☐
5. Cared for customer property and returned it undamaged.	☐

Student signature _____ Date _____

Comments:

Have your supervisor/instructor verify satisfactory completion of this procedure, any observations made,

and any necessary action(s) recommended.

Evaluation Instructions: The scoring box below is intended to act as a guide for both student and supervisor/instructor. Each criterion listed will help students to understand what is expected of them and help supervisors/instructors to articulate the level of success at a particular task. The scoring is set up to allow a second attempt at each task (see the Test and Retest columns). Scoring is designed only to award students points for task criteria that were completed correctly. Points are lost for failure to complete the employability requirements (see Non-Task-Specific criteria). When all criteria are evaluated, tally the points for a total at the bottom of each column.

Tasksheet Scoring

Evaluation Items	Test		Retest	
	Pass	**Fail**	**Pass**	**Fail**
Task-Specific Evaluation	**(1 pt)**	**(0 pts)**	**(1 pt)**	**(0 pts)**
1. Students chose the correct tool each time.				
2. Student correctly demonstrated the proper use of all tools.				
3. Student correctly demonstrated the proper care and maintenance for all tools.				
4. Student correctly demonstrated the proper safe operating procedure for all tools.				
Non-Task-Specific Evaluation	**(0 pts)**	**(−1 pt)**	**(0 pts)**	**(−1 pt)**
Student successfully completed at least three of the non-task-specific steps.				
Student successfully completed all five of the non-task-specific steps.				
Total Score: <total # of points / 4 = %>				

Supervisor/Instructor:

Supervisor/instructor signature _____ Date _____

Comments:

Retest supervisor/instructor signature _____ Date _____

Comments:

Chapter 5: Use of Lifting Equipment

Learning Objective/Task	CDX Tasksheet Number	AED Reference Number
• Identify various types of lifting equipment by their name.	1a5001	AED 1a.5
• Inspect and maintain lifting equipment.	1a5002	AED 1a.5
• Demonstrate the proper use of lifting equipment.	1a5003	AED 1a.5

Materials Required

- Seven different types of lifting equipment chosen by the supervisor/instructor to complete the task
- Tags numbered 1–7 for labeling equipment
- Various equipment/loads to be lifted
- Standard shop lifting equipment
- Manufacturer's guidelines for lifting equipment
- Jack stands
- Hoists (overhead and floor type)
- Hydraulic jacks
- Blocking and cribbing
- Come-a-long (chain and cable type)
- Lifting chains (lifting eyes, links, spreader bars, etc.)
- Slings
- Securing chains
- Tractor lift
- Lifting beam
- Various machines/loads to be lifted

Safety Considerations

- Comply with personal and environmental safety practices associated with clothing; eye protection; hand tools; power equipment; proper ventilation; and the handling, storage, and disposal of chemicals/materials in accordance with local, state, and federal safety and environmental regulations.
- Lifting equipment such as vehicle jacks and stands, vehicle hoists, and engine hoists are important tools that increase productivity and make the job easier. However, they can also cause severe injury or death if used improperly. Make sure you follow the manufacturer's operation procedures. Also, make sure you have your supervisor's/instructor's permission to use any particular type of lifting equipment.

CDX Tasksheet Number: 1a5001

Student/Intern Information

Name _____ Date _____ Class _____

Machine, Customer, and Service Information

Machine used for this activity:

Make _____ Model _____

Hours _____ Serial Number _____

Materials Required

- Seven different types of lifting equipment chosen by the supervisor/instructor to complete the task
- Tags numbered 1-7 for labeling lifting equipment

Task-Specific Safety Considerations

- Comply with personal and environmental safety practices associated with clothing; eye protection; hand tools; power equipment; proper ventilation; and the handling, storage, and disposal of chemicals/materials in accordance with local, state, and federal safety and environmental regulations.
- Lifting equipment such as vehicle jacks and stands, vehicle hoists, and engine hoists are important tools that increase productivity and make the job easier. However, they can also cause severe injury or death if used improperly. Make sure you follow the manufacturer's operation procedures. Also, make sure you have your supervisor's/instructor's permission to use any particular type of lifting equipment.

▶ **TASK** Identify various types of lifting equipment by their name. **AED 1a.5**

Time off_____

Time on_____

Student Instructions: Read through the entire procedure prior to starting. Prepare your workspace and any tools or parts that may be needed to complete the task. When directed by your supervisor/instructor, begin the procedure to complete the task, and comment or check the box as each step is finished. Track your time on this procedure for later comparison to the standard completion time (i.e., "flat rate" or customer pay time).

Total time_____

Procedure	Step Completed
1. Select Lifting Equipment #1 and write its correct name below:	☐
2. Select Lifting Equipment #2 and write its correct name below:	☐

	Step Completed
3. Select Lifting Equipment #3 and write its correct name below:	☐
4. Select Lifting Equipment #4 and write its correct name below:	☐
5. Select Lifting Equipment #5 and write its correct name below:	☐
6. Select Lifting Equipment #6 and write its correct name below:	☐
7. Select Lifting Equipment #7 and write its correct name below:	☐

Non-Task-Specific Evaluation	Step Completed
1. Tools and equipment were used as directed and returned in good working order.	☐
2. Complied with all general and task-specific safety standards, including proper use of any personal protective equipment (PPE).	☐
3. Completed the task in an appropriate time frame (recommendation: 1.5 or 2 times the flat rate).	☐
4. Left the workspace clean and orderly.	☐
5. Cared for customer property and returned it undamaged.	☐

Student signature _____ Date _____

Comments:

Have your supervisor/instructor verify satisfactory completion of this procedure, any observations made, and any necessary action(s) recommended.

Evaluation Instructions: The scoring box below is intended to act as a guide for both student and supervisor/instructor. Each criterion listed will help students to understand what is expected of them and help supervisors/instructors to articulate the level of success at a particular task. The scoring is set up to allow a second attempt at each task (see the Test and Retest columns). Scoring is designed only to award students points for task criteria that were completed correctly. Points are lost for failure to complete the employability requirements (see Non-Task-Specific criteria). When all criteria are evaluated, tally the points for a total at the bottom of each column.

Tasksheet Scoring

Evaluation Items	Test		Retest	
	Pass	**Fail**	**Pass**	**Fail**
Task-Specific Evaluation	**(1 pt)**	**(0 pts)**	**(1 pt)**	**(0 pts)**
1. Student correctly identified at least one piece of lifting equipment.				
2. Student correctly identified at least three pieces of lifting equipment.				
3. Student correctly identified at least five pieces of lifting equipment.				
4. Student correctly identified all seven pieces of lifting equipment.				
Non-Task-Specific Evaluation	**(0 pts)**	**(−1 pt)**	**(0 pts)**	**(−1 pt)**
Student successfully completed at least three of the non-task-specific steps.				
Student successfully completed all five of the non-task-specific steps.				
Total Score: <total # of points / 4 = %>				

Supervisor/Instructor:

Supervisor/instructor signature _____ Date _____

Comments:

Retest supervisor/instructor signature _____ Date _____

Comments:

CDX Tasksheet Number: 1a5002

Student/Intern Information

Name _____ Date _____ Class _____

Machine, Customer, and Service Information

Machine used for this activity:

Make _____ Model _____

Hours _____ Serial Number _____

Materials Required

- Standard shop lifting equipment
- Manufacturer's guidelines for lifting equipment
- Jack stands
- Hoists (overhead and floor type)
- Hydraulic jacks
- Blocking and cribbing
- Come-a-long (chain and cable type)
- Lifting chains (lifting eyes, links, spreader bars, etc.)
- Slings
- Securing chains

Task-Specific Safety Considerations

- Comply with personal and environmental safety practices associated with clothing; eye protection; hand tools; power equipment; proper ventilation; and the handling, storage, and disposal of chemicals/materials in accordance with local, state, and federal safety and environmental regulations.
- Lifting equipment such as vehicle jacks and stands, vehicle hoists, and engine hoists are important tools that increase productivity and make the job easier. However, they can also cause severe injury or death if used improperly. Make sure you follow the manufacturer's operation procedures. Also, make sure you have your supervisor's/instructor's permission to use any particular type of lifting equipment.

▶ **TASK** Inspect and maintain lifting equipment.

Student Instructions: Read through the entire procedure prior to starting. Prepare your workspace and any tools or parts that may be needed to complete the task. When directed by your supervisor/instructor, begin the procedure to complete the task, and comment or check the box as each step is finished. Track your time on this procedure for later comparison to the standard completion time (i.e., "flat rate" or customer pay time).

Time off_____

Time on_____

Total time_____

Procedure	Step Completed
1. Review the manufacturer's guidelines for jack stands.	☐
a. Inspect the jack stands using the manufacturer's guidelines.	☐
i. Are the jack stands safe to use? Yes ☐ No ☐	☐
ii. List any defects found:	☐
b. What is the safe working load (SWL) for the jack stands? (**Note:** If SWL varies on use, list each use, e.g., basket, choker.)	☐
c. List the safe storage procedures for jack stands:	☐
2. Review the manufacturer's guidelines for overhead hoists.	☐
a. Inspect the overhead hoists using the manufacturer's guidelines.	☐
i. Are the overhead hoists safe to use? Yes ☐ No ☐	☐
ii. List any defects found:	☐
b. What is the SWL for the overhead hoists? (**Note:** If SWL varies on use, list each use, e.g., basket, choker.)	☐
c. List the safe storage procedures for overhead hoists:	☐

3. Review the manufacturer's guidelines for floor hoists.	☐
a. Inspect the floor hoists using the manufacturer's guidelines.	☐
i. Are the floor hoists safe to use? Yes ☐ No ☐	☐
ii. List any defects found:	☐
b. What is the SWL for the floor hoists? (**Note:** If SWL varies on use, list each use, e.g., basket, choker.)	☐
c. List the safe storage procedures for floor hoists:	☐
4. Review the manufacturer's guidelines for hydraulic jacks.	☐
a. Inspect the hydraulic jacks using the manufacturer's guidelines.	☐
i. Are the hydraulic jacks safe to use? Yes ☐ No ☐	☐
ii. List any defects found:	☐
b. What is the SWL for the hydraulic jacks? (**Note:** If SWL varies on use, list each use, e.g., basket, choker.)	☐
c. List the safe storage procedures for hydraulic jacks:	☐
5. Review the manufacturer's guidelines for blocking and cribbing.	☐
a. Inspect the blocking and cribbing using the manufacturer's guidelines.	☐
i. Is the blocking and cribbing safe to use? Yes ☐ No ☐	☐

ii. List any defects found:	☐
b. What is the SWL for the blocking and cribbing? (**Note:** If SWL varies on use, list each use, e.g., basket, choker.)	☐
c. List the safe storage procedures for blocking and cribbing:	☐
6. Review the manufacturer's guidelines for a come-a-long chain.	☐
a. Inspect the come-a-long chain using the manufacturer's guidelines.	☐
i. Is the come-a-long chain safe to use? Yes ☐ No ☐	☐
ii. List any defects found:	☐
b. What is the SWL for the come-a-long chain? (**Note:** If SWL varies on use, list each use, e.g., basket, choker.)	☐
c. List the safe storage procedures for a come-a-long chain:	☐
7. Review the manufacturer's guidelines for a come-a-long cable.	☐
a. Inspect the come-a-long cable using the manufacturer's guidelines.	☐
i. Is the come-a-long cable safe to use? Yes ☐ No ☐	☐
ii. List any defects found:	☐

b. What is the SWL for the come-a-long cable? (**Note:** If SWL varies on use, list each use, e.g., basket, choker.)	☐
c. List the safe storage procedures for a come-a-long cable:	☐
8. Review the manufacturer's guidelines for lifting eyes.	☐
a. Inspect the lifting eyes using the manufacturer's guidelines.	☐
i. Are the lifting eyes safe to use? Yes ☐ No ☐	☐
ii. List any defects found:	☐
b. What is the SWL for the lifting eyes? (**Note:** If SWL varies on use, list each use, e.g., basket, choker.)	☐
c. List the safe storage procedures for lifting eyes:	☐
9. Review the manufacturer's guidelines for links.	☐
a. Inspect the links using the manufacturer's guidelines.	☐
i. Are the links safe to use? Yes ☐ No ☐	☐
ii. List any defects found:	☐
b. What is the SWL for the links? (**Note:** If SWL varies on use, list each use, e.g., basket, choker.)	☐

c. List the safe storage procedures for links:	☐
10. Review the manufacturer's guidelines for spreader bars.	☐
a. Inspect the spreader bars using the manufacturer's guidelines.	☐
i. Are the spreader bars safe to use? Yes ☐ No ☐	☐
ii. List any defects found:	☐
b. What is the SWL for the spreader bars? (**Note:** If SWL varies on use, list each use, e.g., basket, choker.)	☐
c. List the safe storage procedures for spreader bars:	☐
11. Review the manufacturer's guidelines for slings.	☐
a. Inspect the slings using the manufacturer's guidelines.	☐
i. Are the slings safe to use? Yes ☐ No ☐	☐
ii. List any defects found:	☐
b. What is the SWL for the slings? (**Note:** If SWL varies on use, list each use, e.g., basket, choker.)	☐
c. List the safe storage procedures for slings:	☐

12. Review the manufacturer's guidelines for securing chains.	☐
a. Inspect the securing chains using the manufacturer's guidelines.	☐
i. Are the securing chains safe to use? Yes ☐ No ☐	☐
ii. List any defects found:	☐
b. What is the SWL for the securing chains? (**Note:** If SWL varies on use, list each use, e.g., basket, choker.)	☐
c. List the safe storage procedures for securing chains:	☐
13. Return any tools you used to their proper location.	☐

Non-Task-Specific Evaluation	Step Completed
1. Tools and equipment were used as directed and returned in good working order.	☐
2. Complied with all general and task-specific safety standards, including proper use of any personal protective equipment (PPE).	☐
3. Completed the task in an appropriate time frame (recommendation: 1.5 or 2 times the flat rate).	☐
4. Left the workspace clean and orderly.	☐
5. Cared for customer property and returned it undamaged.	☐

Student signature _____ Date _____

Comments:

Have your supervisor/instructor verify satisfactory completion of this procedure, any observations made, and any necessary action(s) recommended.

Evaluation Instructions: The scoring box below is intended to act as a guide for both student and supervisor/instructor. Each criterion listed will help students to understand what is expected of them and help supervisors/instructors to articulate the level of success at a particular task. The scoring is set up to allow a second attempt at each task (see the Test and Retest columns). Scoring is designed only to award students points for task criteria that were completed correctly. Points are lost for failure to complete the employability requirements (see Non-Task-Specific criteria). When all criteria are evaluated, tally the points for a total at the bottom of each column.

Tasksheet Scoring

Evaluation Items	Test		Retest	
	Pass	**Fail**	**Pass**	**Fail**
Task-Specific Evaluation	**(1 pt)**	**(0 pts)**	**(1 pt)**	**(0 pts)**
1. Student performed the proper inspection for each piece of equipment.				
2. Student performed the proper care for each piece of equipment.				
3. Student performed the proper maintenance for each piece of equipment.				
4. Student performed the proper storage for each piece of equipment.				
Non-Task-Specific Evaluation	**(0 pts)**	**(−1 pt)**	**(0 pts)**	**(−1 pt)**
Student successfully completed at least three of the non-task-specific steps.				
Student successfully completed all five of the non-task-specific steps.				
Total Score: <total # of points / 4 = %>				

Supervisor/Instructor:

Supervisor/instructor signature _____ Date _____

Comments:

Retest supervisor/instructor signature _____ Date _____

Comments:

CDX Tasksheet Number: 1a5003

Student/Intern Information

Name _____ Date _____ Class _____

Machine, Customer, and Service Information

Machine used for this activity:

Make _____ Model _____

Hours _____ Serial Number _____

Materials Required

- Jack stands
- Hoists (overhead and floor type)
- Hydraulic jacks
- Tractor lift
- Blocking and cribbing
- Lifting chains (lifting eyes, links, spreader bars, etc.)
- Slings
- Securing chains
- Lifting beam
- Various machines/loads to be lifted

Task-Specific Safety Considerations

- Comply with personal and environmental safety practices associated with clothing; eye protection; hand tools; power equipment; proper ventilation; and the handling, storage, and disposal of chemicals/materials in accordance with local, state, and federal safety and environmental regulations.
- Lifting equipment such as vehicle jacks and stands, vehicle hoists, and engine hoists are important tools that increase productivity and make the job easier. However, they can also cause severe injury or death if used improperly. Make sure you follow the manufacturer's operation procedures. Also, make sure you have your supervisor's/instructor's permission to use any particular type of lifting equipment.

▶ **TASK** Demonstrate the proper use of lifting equipment. **AED** 1a.5

Time off_____

Student Instructions: Read through the entire procedure prior to starting. Prepare your workspace and any tools or parts that may be needed to complete the task. When directed by your supervisor/instructor, begin the procedure to complete the task, and comment or check the box as each step is finished. Track your time on this procedure for later comparison to the standard completion time (i.e., "flat rate" or customer pay time).

Time on_____

Total time_____

Procedure	Step Completed
1. Station #1: Lift and secure a machine.	
a. Position the machine safely.	☐
b. Select two jack stands suitable for the machine's weight.	☐
c. Select an equipment jack suitable for the machine's weight.	☐
d. Select a lifting point at one end of the machine.	☐
e. Position lifting equipment to lift one end of the machine.	☐
f. Have your supervisor/instructor verify satisfactory completion of these procedures before you proceed. Supervisor's/instructor's initials: _____	☐
g. Lift the machine and position the jack stands.	☐
h. Lower the jack and the machine onto the jack stands.	☐
i. Inspect the machine and the stands to ensure they are secure.	☐
j. Have your supervisor/instructor verify satisfactory completion of these procedures before you proceed. Supervisor's/instructor's initials: _____	☐
k. Use the equipment jack to raise the machine, remove the jack stands, and lower the machine back to the ground.	☐
l. Return the jack stands to their storage area(s).	☐
2. Station #2: Lift and secure a track-type machine.	
a. Position the machine safely.	☐
b. Select two jack stands suitable for the machine's weight.	☐
c. Select a tractor lift suitable for the machine's weight.	☐
d. Select lifting points at the rear of the machine.	☐
e. Position the tractor lift equipment to lift the rear of the machine.	☐
f. Have your supervisor/instructor verify satisfactory completion of these procedures before you proceed. Supervisor's/instructor's initials: _____	☐
g. Lift the machine and position the jack stands.	☐
h. Lower the machine onto the jack stands.	☐
i. Inspect the machine and the stands to ensure they are secure.	☐

j. Have your supervisor/instructor verify satisfactory completion of these procedures before you proceed. Supervisor's/instructor's initials: _____	☐
k. Use the tractor lift equipment to raise the machine, remove the jack stands, and lower the machine back to ground.	☐
l. Return the tractor lift equipment and jack stands to their storage area(s).	☐
3. Station #3: Lift using a chain hoist and a chain sling.	
a. Determine the weight of the load to be lifted.	☐
b. Rig a chain sling to the load to be lifted.	☐
c. Rig the chain sling to a chain hoist.	☐
d. Raise the chain hoist until all slack is removed from the sling.	☐
e. Have your supervisor/instructor verify satisfactory completion of these procedures before you proceed. Supervisor's/instructor's initials: _____	☐
f. Raise the load no more than 6 inches above the ground.	☐
g. Lower the load to the ground.	☐
h. Return the lift equipment to its storage area.	☐
4. Station #4: Lift using an electric hoist, multibranch chain sling, and shoulder eye bolts.	
a. Determine the weight of the load to be lifted.	☐
b. Rig shoulder eye bolts to the load to be lifted.	☐
c. Rig a chain sling to the load to be lifted.	☐
d. Rig the chain sling to a chain hoist.	☐
e. Raise the chain hoist until all slack is removed from the sling.	☐
f. Have your supervisor/instructor verify satisfactory completion of these procedures before you proceed. Supervisor's/instructor's initials: _____	☐
g. Raise the load no more than 6 inches above the ground.	☐
h. Lower the load to the ground.	☐
i. Return the lift equipment to its storage area.	☐
5. Station #5: Lift using an electric hoist, chain sling, and link brackets.	
a. Determine the weight of the load to be lifted.	☐
b. Rig link brackets to the load to be lifted.	☐

c. Rig a chain sling to the load to be lifted.	☐
d. Rig the chain sling to a chain hoist.	☐
e. Raise the hoist until all slack is removed from the sling.	☐
f. Have your supervisor/instructor verify satisfactory completion of these procedures before you proceed. Supervisor's/instructor's initials: _____	☐
g. Raise the load no more than 6 inches above the ground.	☐
h. Lower the load to the ground.	☐
i. Return the lift equipment to its storage area.	☐
6. Station #6: Lift using an electric hoist, chain sling, and spreader bar.	
a. Determine the weight of the load to be lifted.	☐
b. Rig a chain sling to the load to be lifted.	☐
c. Rig the chain sling to a chain hoist.	☐
d. Rig a spreader bar into position.	☐
e. Raise the hoist until all slack is removed from the sling.	☐
f. Have your supervisor/instructor verify satisfactory completion of these procedures before you proceed. Supervisor's/instructor's initials: _____	☐
g. Raise the load no more than 6 inches above the ground.	☐
h. Lower the load to the ground.	☐
i. Return the lift equipment to its storage area.	☐
7. Station #7: Lift using an engine hoist and a lifting beam.	
a. Determine the weight of the load to be lifted.	☐
b. Rig a lifting beam to the load to be lifted.	☐
c. Raise the hoist until all slack is removed from the lifting beam.	☐
d. Have your supervisor/instructor verify satisfactory completion of these procedures before you proceed. Supervisor's/instructor's initials: _____	☐
e. Raise the load no more than 6 inches above the ground.	☐
f. Lower the load to the ground.	☐
g. Return the lift equipment to its storage area.	☐

8. Station #8: Lift using an electric hoist and a synthetic sling.	
a. Determine the weight of the load to be lifted.	☐
b. Rig a synthetic sling to the load to be lifted.	☐
c. Rig the synthetic sling to a chain hoist.	☐
d. Raise the hoist until all slack is removed from the lifting beam.	☐
e. Have your supervisor/instructor verify satisfactory completion of these procedures before you proceed. Supervisor's/instructor's initials: _____	☐
f. Raise the load no more than 6 inches above the ground.	☐
g. Lower the load to the ground.	☐
h. Return the lift equipment to its storage area.	☐

Non-Task-Specific Evaluation	Step Completed
1. Tools and equipment were used as directed and returned in good working order.	☐
2. Complied with all general and task-specific safety standards, including proper use of any personal protective equipment (PPE).	☐
3. Completed the task in an appropriate time frame (recommendation: 1.5 or 2 times the flat rate).	☐
4. Left the workspace clean and orderly.	☐
5. Cared for customer property and returned it undamaged.	☐

Student signature _____ Date _____

Comments:

Have your supervisor/instructor verify satisfactory completion of this procedure, any observations made,

and any necessary action(s) recommended.

Evaluation Instructions: The scoring box below is intended to act as a guide for both student and supervisor/instructor. Each criterion listed will help students to understand what is expected of them and help supervisors/instructors to articulate the level of success at a particular task. The scoring is set up to allow a second attempt at each task (see the Test and Retest columns). Scoring is designed only to award students points for task criteria that were completed correctly. Points are lost for failure to complete the employability requirements (see Non-Task-Specific criteria). When all criteria are evaluated, tally the points for a total at the bottom of each column.

Tasksheet Scoring

Evaluation Items	Test		Retest	
	Pass	**Fail**	**Pass**	**Fail**
Task-Specific Evaluation	**(1 pt)**	**(0 pts)**	**(1 pt)**	**(0 pts)**
1. Student properly followed the procedure for at least two stations.				
2. Student properly followed the procedure for at least four stations.				
3. Student properly followed the procedure for at least six stations.				
4. Student properly followed the procedure for all eight stations.				
Non-Task-Specific Evaluation	**(0 pts)**	**(−1 pt)**	**(0 pts)**	**(−1 pt)**
Student successfully completed at least three of the non-task-specific steps.				
Student successfully completed all five of the non-task-specific steps.				
Total Score: <total # of points / 4 = %>				

Chapter 6: Use of Various Cleaning Equipment

Learning Objective/Task	CDX Tasksheet Number	AED Reference Number
• Identify the basic cleaning equipment used in our industry.	1a6001	AED 1a.6
• Demonstrate the proper use of cleaning equipment.	1a6002	AED 1a.6
• Identify cleaning solvents and solutions.	1a6004	AED 1a.6
• Locate hazardous materials and their safety data sheets (SDS).	1a6006	AED 1a.6

Materials Required

- Five pieces of basic cleaning equipment chosen by the supervisor/instructor to complete the task
- Tags numbered 1–5 for labeling cleaning equipment across tasks
- Solvent tank parts washer
- Aqueous parts washer cabinet
- Ultrasonic parts washer
- Pressure washer
- Floor scrubber
- Seven different cleaning solvents or solutions chosen by the supervisor/instructor to complete the task
- Brake cleaner
- Degreaser solvent
- Pressure washer cleaning solution
- Safety data sheets (SDS)

Safety Considerations

- Comply with personal and environmental safety practices associated with clothing; eye protection; hand tools; power equipment; proper ventilation; and the handling, storage, and disposal of chemicals/materials in accordance with local, state, and federal safety and environmental regulations.
- Cleaning equipment allows us to increase our productivity and effectiveness. However, it can also cause severe injury or death if used improperly. Make sure you follow the manufacturer's procedures.

CDX Tasksheet Number: 1a6001

Student/Intern Information

Name _____ Date _____ Class _____

Machine, Customer, and Service Information

Machine used for this activity:

Make _____ Model _____

Hours _____ Serial Number _____

Materials Required

- Five pieces of basic cleaning equipment chosen by the supervisor/instructor to complete the task
- Tags numbered 1-5 for labeling cleaning equipment

Task-Specific Safety Considerations

- Comply with personal and environmental safety practices associated with clothing; eye protection; hand tools; power equipment; proper ventilation; and the handling, storage, and disposal of chemicals/materials in accordance with local, state, and federal safety and environmental regulations.
- Cleaning equipment allows us to increase our productivity and effectiveness. However, it can also cause severe injury or death if used improperly. Make sure you follow the manufacturer's procedures.

▶ **TASK** Identify the basic cleaning equipment used in our industry. **AED 1a.6**

Time off _____

Student Instructions: Read through the entire procedure prior to starting. Prepare your workspace and any tools or parts that may be needed to complete the task. When directed by your supervisor/instructor, begin the procedure to complete the task, and comment or check the box as each step is finished. Track your time on this procedure for later comparison to the standard completion time (i.e., "flat rate" or customer pay time).

Time on _____

Total time _____

Procedure	Step Completed
1. Select Cleaning Equipment #1 and write its correct name below:	☐
2. Select Cleaning Equipment #2 and write its correct name below:	☐
3. Select Cleaning Equipment #3 and write its correct name below:	☐

4. Select Cleaning Equipment #4 and write its correct name below:	☐
5. Select Cleaning Equipment #5 and write its correct name below:	☐

Non-Task-Specific Evaluation	Step Completed
1. Tools and equipment were used as directed and returned in good working order.	☐
2. Complied with all general and task-specific safety standards, including proper use of any personal protective equipment (PPE).	☐
3. Completed the task in an appropriate time frame (recommendation: 1.5 or 2 times the flat rate).	☐
4. Left the workspace clean and orderly.	☐
5. Cared for customer property and returned it undamaged.	☐

Student signature _____ Date _____

Comments:

_____

Have your supervisor/instructor verify satisfactory completion of this procedure, any observations made, and any necessary action(s) recommended.

Evaluation Instructions: The scoring box below is intended to act as a guide for both student and supervisor/instructor. Each criterion listed will help students to understand what is expected of them and help supervisors/instructors to articulate the level of success at a particular task. The scoring is set up to allow a second attempt at each task (see the Test and Retest columns). Scoring is designed only to award students points for task criteria that were completed correctly. Points are lost for failure to complete the employability requirements (see Non-Task-Specific criteria). When all criteria are evaluated, tally the points for a total at the bottom of each column.

Tasksheet Scoring

Evaluation Items	Test		Retest	
	Pass	**Fail**	**Pass**	**Fail**
Task-Specific Evaluation	**(1 pt)**	**(0 pts)**	**(1 pt)**	**(0 pts)**
1. Student correctly identified at least one piece of cleaning equipment.				
2. Student correctly identified at least two pieces of cleaning equipment.				
3. Student correctly identified at least three pieces of cleaning equipment.				
4. Student correctly identified all five pieces of cleaning equipment.				
Non-Task-Specific Evaluation	**(0 pts)**	**(−1 pt)**	**(0 pts)**	**(−1 pt)**
Student successfully completed at least three of the non-task-specific steps.				
Student successfully completed all five of the non-task-specific steps.				
Total Score: <total # of points / 4 = %>				

Supervisor/Instructor:

Supervisor/instructor signature _____ Date _____

Comments:

Retest supervisor/instructor signature _____ Date _____

Comments:

CDX Tasksheet Number: 1a6002

Student/Intern Information

Name _____ Date _____ Class _____

Machine, Customer, and Service Information

Machine used for this activity:

Make _____ Model _____

Hours _____ Serial Number _____

> ### Materials Required
> - Solvent tank parts washer
> - Aqueous parts washer cabinet
> - Ultrasonic parts washer
> - Pressure washer
> - Floor scrubber

Task-Specific Safety Considerations

- Comply with personal and environmental safety practices associated with clothing; eye protection; hand tools; power equipment; proper ventilation; and the handling, storage, and disposal of chemicals/materials in accordance with local, state, and federal safety and environmental regulations.
- Cleaning equipment allows us to increase our productivity and effectiveness. However, it can also cause severe injury or death if used improperly. Make sure you follow the manufacturer's procedures.

▶ **TASK** Demonstrate the proper use of cleaning equipment.   **AED** 1a.6

Time off_____

Time on_____

Student Instructions: Read through the entire procedure prior to starting. Prepare your workspace and any tools or parts that may be needed to complete the task. When directed by your supervisor/instructor, begin the procedure to complete the task, and comment or check the box as each step is finished. Track your time on this procedure for later comparison to the standard completion time (i.e., "flat rate" or customer pay time).

Total time_____

Procedure	Step Completed
1. Select a solvent tank parts washer and demonstrate its proper use, care and maintenance, and safe operating procedure. Have your supervisor/instructor verify satisfactory completion of these procedures. Supervisor's/instructor's initials: _____	☐

2. Select an aqueous parts washer cabinet and demonstrate its proper use, care and maintenance, and safe operating procedure. Have your supervisor/instructor verify satisfactory completion of these procedures. Supervisor's/instructor's initials: _____	☐
3. Select an ultrasonic parts washer and demonstrate its proper use, care and maintenance, and safe operating procedure. Have your supervisor/instructor verify satisfactory completion of these procedures. Supervisor's/instructor's initials: _____	☐
4. Select a pressure washer and demonstrate its proper use, care and maintenance, and safe operating procedure. Have your supervisor/instructor verify satisfactory completion of these procedures. Supervisor's/instructor's initials: _____	☐
5. Select a floor scrubber and demonstrate its proper use, care and maintenance, and safe operating procedure. Have your supervisor/instructor verify satisfactory completion of these procedures. Supervisor's/instructor's initials: _____	☐

Non-Task-Specific Evaluation	Step Completed
1. Tools and equipment were used as directed and returned in good working order.	☐
2. Complied with all general and task-specific safety standards, including proper use of any personal protective equipment (PPE).	☐
3. Completed the task in an appropriate time frame (recommendation: 1.5 or 2 times the flat rate).	☐
4. Left the workspace clean and orderly.	☐
5. Cared for customer property and returned it undamaged.	☐

Student signature _____ Date _____

Comments:

Have your supervisor/instructor verify satisfactory completion of this procedure, any observations made,

and any necessary action(s) recommended.

Evaluation Instructions: The scoring box below is intended to act as a guide for both student and supervisor/instructor. Each criterion listed will help students to understand what is expected of them and help supervisors/instructors to articulate the level of success at a particular task. The scoring is set up to allow a second attempt at each task (see the Test and Retest columns). Scoring is designed only to award students points for task criteria that were completed correctly. Points are lost for failure to complete the employability requirements (see Non-Task-Specific criteria). When all criteria are evaluated, tally the points for a total at the bottom of each column.

Tasksheet Scoring

	Test		Retest	
Evaluation Items	**Pass**	**Fail**	**Pass**	**Fail**
Task-Specific Evaluation	**(1 pt)**	**(0 pts)**	**(1 pt)**	**(0 pts)**
1. Student chose the correct piece of cleaning equipment each time.				
2. Student correctly demonstrated the proper use of all cleaning equipment.				
3. Student correctly demonstrated the proper care and maintenance for all cleaning equipment.				
4. Student correctly demonstrated the proper safe operating procedure for all cleaning equipment.				
Non-Task-Specific Evaluation	**(0 pts)**	**(−1 pt)**	**(0 pts)**	**(−1 pt)**
Student successfully completed at least three of the non-task-specific steps.				
Student successfully completed all five of the non-task-specific steps.				
Total Score: <total # of points / 4 = %>				

CDX Tasksheet Number: 1a6004

Student/Intern Information

Name _____ Date _____ Class _____

Machine, Customer, and Service Information

Machine used for this activity:

Make _____ Model _____

Hours _____ Serial Number _____

Materials Required

- Seven different cleaning solvents or solutions chosen by the supervisor/instructor to complete the task
- Tags numbered 1–7 for labeling cleaning solvents/solutions

Task-Specific Safety Considerations

- Comply with personal and environmental safety practices associated with clothing; eye protection; hand tools; power equipment; proper ventilation; and the handling, storage, and disposal of chemicals/materials in accordance with local, state, and federal safety and environmental regulations.
- Cleaning equipment allows us to increase our productivity and effectiveness. However, it can also cause severe injury or death if used improperly. Make sure you follow the manufacturer's procedures.

▶ **TASK** Identify cleaning solvents and solutions.   **AED** 1a.6

Time off _____

Time on _____

Student Instructions: Read through the entire procedure prior to starting. Prepare your workspace and any tools or parts that may be needed to complete the task. When directed by your supervisor/instructor, begin the procedure to complete the task, and comment or check the box as each step is finished. Track your time on this procedure for later comparison to the standard completion time (i.e., "flat rate" or customer pay time).

Total time _____

Procedure	Step Completed
1. Identify Cleaning Solvent/Solution #1 and write its correct name below:	☐
2. Identify Cleaning Solvent/Solution #2 and write its correct name below:	☐
3. Identify Cleaning Solvent/Solution #3 and write its correct name below:	☐

	Step Completed
4. Identify Cleaning Solvent/Solution #4 and write its correct name below:	☐
5. Identify Cleaning Solvent/Solution #5 and write its correct name below:	☐
6. Identify Cleaning Solvent/Solution #6 and write its correct name below:	☐
7. Identify Cleaning Solvent/Solution #7 and write its correct name below:	☐

Non-Task-Specific Evaluation	Step Completed
1. Tools and equipment were used as directed and returned in good working order.	☐
2. Complied with all general and task-specific safety standards, including proper use of any personal protective equipment (PPE).	☐
3. Completed the task in an appropriate time frame (recommendation: 1.5 or 2 times the flat rate).	☐
4. Left the workspace clean and orderly.	☐
5. Cared for customer property and returned it undamaged.	☐

Student signature _____ Date _____

Comments:

Have your supervisor/instructor verify satisfactory completion of this procedure, any observations made,

and any necessary action(s) recommended.

Evaluation Instructions: The scoring box below is intended to act as a guide for both student and supervisor/instructor. Each criterion listed will help students to understand what is expected of them and help supervisors/instructors to articulate the level of success at a particular task. The scoring is set up to allow a second attempt at each task (see the Test and Retest columns). Scoring is designed only to award students points for task criteria that were completed correctly. Points are lost for failure to complete the employability requirements (see Non-Task-Specific criteria). When all criteria are evaluated, tally the points for a total at the bottom of each column.

Tasksheet Scoring

Evaluation Items	Test		Retest	
	Pass	Fail	Pass	Fail
Task-Specific Evaluation	**(1 pt)**	**(0 pts)**	**(1 pt)**	**(0 pts)**
1. Student correctly identified at least one cleaning solvent or solution.				
2. Student correctly identified at least three cleaning solvents or solutions.				
3. Student correctly identified at least five cleaning solvents or solutions.				
4. Student correctly identified all seven cleaning solvents or solutions.				
Non-Task-Specific Evaluation	**(0 pts)**	**(−1 pt)**	**(0 pts)**	**(−1 pt)**
Student successfully completed at least three of the non-task-specific steps.				
Student successfully completed all five of the non-task-specific steps.				
Total Score: <total # of points / 4 = %>				

Supervisor/Instructor:

Supervisor/instructor signature _____ Date _____

Comments:

Retest supervisor/instructor signature _____ Date _____

Comments:

CDX Tasksheet Number: 1a6006

Student/Intern Information

Name _____ Date _____ Class _____

Machine, Customer, and Service Information

Machine used for this activity:

Make _____ Model _____

Hours _____ Serial Number _____

Materials Required
- Program's shop policy and other safety information
- Brake cleaner
- Degreaser solvent
- Pressure washer cleaning solution
- Safety data sheets (SDS)

Task-Specific Safety Considerations
- Comply with personal and environmental safety practices associated with clothing; eye protection; hand tools; power equipment; proper ventilation; and the handling, storage, and disposal of chemicals/materials in accordance with local, state, and federal safety and environmental regulations.
- Cleaning equipment allows us to increase our productivity and effectiveness. However, it can also cause severe injury or death if used improperly. Make sure you follow the manufacturer's procedures.

▶**TASK** Locate hazardous materials and their SDS.

AED
1a.6

Time off_____

Time on_____

Total time_____

Student Instructions: Read through the entire procedure prior to starting. Prepare your workspace and any tools or parts that may be needed to complete the task. When directed by your supervisor/instructor, begin the procedure to complete the task, and comment or check the box as each step is finished. Track your time on this procedure for later comparison to the standard completion time (i.e., "flat rate" or customer pay time).

Procedure	Step Completed
1. Select a brake cleaner, then locate its SDS following shop procedures.	☐
a. List the safety precautions for handling brake cleaner below:	☐

b. Write the brake cleaner's flash point below:	☐
2. Select a degreaser solvent, then locate its SDS following shop procedures.	☐
a. List the handling and storage precautions of degreaser solvent below:	☐
b. List the physical and chemical properties of degreaser solvent below:	☐
c. List the first aid treatment for ingestion of degreaser solvent below:	☐
d. List exposure controls/personal protection below:	☐
3. Select a pressure washer cleaning solution, then locate its SDS following shop procedures.	☐
a. List the first aid treatment for pressure washer cleaning solution in the eyes below:	☐
b. List accidental release measures below:	☐

Non-Task-Specific Evaluation	Step Completed
1. Tools and equipment were used as directed and returned in good working order.	☐
2. Complied with all general and task-specific safety standards, including proper use of any personal protective equipment (PPE).	☐
3. Completed the task in an appropriate time frame (recommendation: 1.5 or 2 times the flat rate).	☐
4. Left the workspace clean and orderly.	☐
5. Cared for customer property and returned it undamaged.	☐

Student signature _____ Date _____

Comments:

Have your supervisor/instructor verify satisfactory completion of this procedure, any observations made,

and any necessary action(s) recommended.

Evaluation Instructions: The scoring box below is intended to act as a guide for both student and supervisor/instructor. Each criterion listed will help students to understand what is expected of them and help supervisors/instructors to articulate the level of success at a particular task. The scoring is set up to allow a second attempt at each task (see the Test and Retest columns). Scoring is designed only to award students points for task criteria that were completed correctly. Points are lost for failure to complete the employability requirements (see Non-Task-Specific criteria). When all criteria are evaluated, tally the points for a total at the bottom of each column.

Tasksheet Scoring

Evaluation Items	Test		Retest	
	Pass	**Fail**	**Pass**	**Fail**
Task-Specific Evaluation	**(1 pt)**	**(0 pts)**	**(1 pt)**	**(0 pts)**
1. Student located each hazardous material and its accompanying SDS.				
2. Student demonstrated an understanding of the SDS for brake cleaner.				
3. Student demonstrated an understanding of the SDS for degreaser solvent.				
4. Student demonstrated an understanding of the SDS for pressure washer cleaning solution.				
Non-Task-Specific Evaluation	**(0 pts)**	**(−1 pt)**	**(0 pts)**	**(−1 pt)**
Student successfully completed at least three of the non-task-specific steps.				
Student successfully completed all five of the non-task-specific steps.				
Total Score: <total # of points / 4 = %>				

Supervisor/Instructor:

Supervisor/instructor signature _____ Date _____

Comments:

Retest supervisor/instructor signature _____ Date _____

Comments:

Chapter 7: Use of Various Fluid Pressure Testing Equipment

Learning Objective/Task	CDX Tasksheet Number	AED Reference Number
• Identify various types of fluid pressure testing equipment by their name.	1a7001	AED 1a.7
• Measure pressure, flows, and temperature.	1a7002	AED 1a.7
• Identify personal protective equipment (PPE) required for the various types of fluid pressure testing equipment.	1a7004a	AED 1a.7
• Demonstrate the use of PPE required for the various types of fluid pressure testing equipment.	1a7004b	AED 1a.7

Materials Required

- Seven types of fluid pressure testing equipment chosen by the supervisor/instructor to complete the task
- Tags numbered 1-7 for labeling equipment
- Seven types of fluid pressure testing equipment and their accessories as chosen by the supervisor/instructor to complete the task
- Standard shop cleaning equipment
- Pressure gauge
- Flowmeter
- Needle valve
- Seven types of PPE for fluid pressure testing equipment chosen by the supervisor/instructor to complete the task
- Hardhat
- Gloves
- Safety glasses
- Face shield
- Goggles
- Hearing protection

Safety Considerations

- Comply with personal and environmental safety practices associated with clothing; eye protection; hand tools; power equipment; proper ventilation; and the handling, storage, and disposal of chemicals/materials in accordance with local, state, and federal safety and environmental regulations.
- Fluid pressure testing equipment allows us to increase our productivity and effectiveness. However, it can also cause severe injury or death if used improperly. Make sure you follow the manufacturer's procedures.

CDX Tasksheet Number: 1a7001

Student/Intern Information

Name _____ Date _____ Class _____

Machine, Customer, and Service Information

Machine used for this activity:

Make _____ Model _____

Hours _____ Serial Number _____

Materials Required

- Seven types of fluid pressure testing equipment chosen by the supervisor/instructor to complete the task
- Tags numbered 1-7 for labeling PPE.

Task-Specific Safety Considerations

- Comply with personal and environmental safety practices associated with clothing; eye protection; hand tools; power equipment; proper ventilation; and the handling, storage, and disposal of chemicals/materials in accordance with local, state, and federal safety and environmental regulations.
- Fluid pressure testing equipment allows us to increase our productivity and effectiveness. However, it can also cause severe injury or death if used improperly. Make sure you follow the manufacturer's procedures.

▶ **TASK** Identify various types of fluid pressure testing equipment by their name.

AED
1a.7

Time off_____

Time on_____

Total time_____

Student Instructions: Read through the entire procedure prior to starting. Prepare your workspace and any tools or parts that may be needed to complete the task. When directed by your supervisor/instructor, begin the procedure to complete the task, and comment or check the box as each step is finished. Track your time on this procedure for later comparison to the standard completion time (i.e., "flat rate" or customer pay time).

Procedure	Step Completed
1. Identify Fluid Pressure Testing Equipment #1 and write its correct name below:	☐
2. Identify Fluid Pressure Testing Equipment #2 and write its correct name below:	☐

	Step Completed
3. Identify Fluid Pressure Testing Equipment #3 and write its correct name below:	☐
4. Identify Fluid Pressure Testing Equipment #4 and write its correct name below:	☐
5. Identify Fluid Pressure Testing Equipment #5 and write its correct name below:	☐
6. Identify Fluid Pressure Testing Equipment #6 and write its correct name below:	☐
7. Identify Fluid Pressure Testing Equipment #7 and write its correct name below:	☐

Non-Task-Specific Evaluation	Step Completed
1. Tools and equipment were used as directed and returned in good working order.	☐
2. Complied with all general and task-specific safety standards, including proper use of any personal protective equipment (PPE).	☐
3. Completed the task in an appropriate time frame (recommendation: 1.5 or 2 times the flat rate).	☐
4. Left the workspace clean and orderly.	☐
5. Cared for customer property and returned it undamaged.	☐

Student signature _____ Date _____

Comments:

Have your supervisor/instructor verify satisfactory completion of this procedure, any observations made, and any necessary action(s) recommended.

Evaluation Instructions: The scoring box below is intended to act as a guide for both student and supervisor/instructor. Each criterion listed will help students to understand what is expected of them and help supervisors/instructors to articulate the level of success at a particular task. The scoring is set up to allow a second attempt at each task (see the Test and Retest columns). Scoring is designed only to award students points for task criteria that were completed correctly. Points are lost for failure to complete the employability requirements (see Non-Task-Specific criteria). When all criteria are evaluated, tally the points for a total at the bottom of each column.

Tasksheet Scoring

Evaluation Items	Test		Retest	
	Pass	**Fail**	**Pass**	**Fail**
Task-Specific Evaluation	**(1 pt)**	**(0 pts)**	**(1 pt)**	**(0 pts)**
1. Student correctly identified at least one piece of fluid pressure testing equipment.				
2. Student correctly identified at least three pieces of fluid pressure testing equipment.				
3. Student correctly identified at least five pieces of fluid pressure testing equipment.				
4. Student correctly identified all seven pieces of fluid pressure testing equipment.				
Non-Task-Specific Evaluation	**(0 pts)**	**(−1 pt)**	**(0 pts)**	**(−1 pt)**
Student successfully completed at least three of the non-task-specific steps.				
Student successfully completed all five of the non-task-specific steps.				
Total Score: <total # of points / 4 = %>				

Supervisor/Instructor:

Supervisor/instructor signature _____ Date _____

Comments:

Retest supervisor/instructor signature _____ Date _____

Comments:

CDX Tasksheet Number: 1a7002

Student/Intern Information

Name _____ Date _____ Class _____

Machine, Customer, and Service Information

Machine used for this activity:

Make _____ Model _____

Hours _____ Serial Number _____

Materials Required

- Seven types of fluid pressure testing equipment and their accessories as chosen by the supervisor/instructor to complete the task
- Tags numbered 1-7 for labeling equipment
- Standard shop cleaning equipment
- Pressure gauge
- Flowmeter
- Needle valve

Task-Specific Safety Considerations

- Comply with personal and environmental safety practices associated with clothing; eye protection; hand tools; power equipment; proper ventilation; and the handling, storage, and disposal of chemicals/materials in accordance with local, state, and federal safety and environmental regulations.
- Fluid pressure testing equipment allows us to increase our productivity and effectiveness. However, it can also cause severe injury or death if used improperly. Make sure you follow the manufacturer's procedures.

▶ **TASK** Measure pressure, flows, and temperature.

Student Instructions: Read through the entire procedure prior to starting. Prepare your workspace and any tools or parts that may be needed to complete the task. When directed by your supervisor/instructor, begin the procedure to complete the task, and comment or check the box as each step is finished. Track your time on this procedure for later comparison to the standard completion time (i.e., "flat rate" or customer pay time).

Time off_____

Time on_____

Total time_____

Procedure	Step Completed
1. Locate Fluid Pressure Testing Equipment #1 and any accessories required. Demonstrate the proper use of the designed application and safe operating procedures. Have your supervisor/instructor verify satisfactory completion of these procedures. Supervisor's/instructor's initials: _____	☐
2. Locate Fluid Pressure Testing Equipment #2 and any accessories required. Demonstrate the proper use of the designed application and safe operating procedures. Have your supervisor/instructor verify satisfactory completion of these procedures. Supervisor's/instructor's initials: _____	☐
3. Locate Fluid Pressure Testing Equipment #3 and any accessories required. Demonstrate the proper use of the designed application and safe operating procedures. Have your supervisor/instructor verify satisfactory completion of these procedures. Supervisor's/instructor's initials: _____	☐
4. Locate Fluid Pressure Testing Equipment #4 and any accessories required. Demonstrate the proper use of the designed application and safe operating procedures. Have your supervisor/instructor verify satisfactory completion of these procedures. Supervisor's/instructor's initials: _____	☐
5. Locate Fluid Pressure Testing Equipment #5 and any accessories required. Demonstrate the proper use of the designed application and safe operating procedures. Have your supervisor/instructor verify satisfactory completion of these procedures. Supervisor's/instructor's initials: _____	☐
6. Locate Fluid Pressure Testing Equipment #6 and any accessories required. Demonstrate the proper use of the designed application and safe operating procedures. Have your supervisor/instructor verify satisfactory completion of these procedures. Supervisor's/instructor's initials: _____	☐
7. Locate Fluid Pressure Testing Equipment #7 and any accessories required. Demonstrate the proper use of the designed application and safe operating procedures. Have your supervisor/instructor verify satisfactory completion of these procedures. Supervisor's/instructor's initials: _____	☐

Non-Task-Specific Evaluation	Step Completed
1. Tools and equipment were used as directed and returned in good working order.	☐
2. Complied with all general and task-specific safety standards, including proper use of any personal protective equipment (PPE).	☐
3. Completed the task in an appropriate time frame (recommendation: 1.5 or 2 times the flat rate).	☐
4. Left the workspace clean and orderly.	☐
5. Cared for customer property and returned it undamaged.	☐

Student signature _____ Date _____

Comments:

Have your supervisor/instructor verify satisfactory completion of this procedure, any observations made, and any necessary action(s) recommended.

Evaluation Instructions: The scoring box below is intended to act as a guide for both student and supervisor/instructor. Each criterion listed will help students to understand what is expected of them and help supervisors/instructors to articulate the level of success at a particular task. The scoring is set up to allow a second attempt at each task (see the Test and Retest columns). Scoring is designed only to award students points for task criteria that were completed correctly. Points are lost for failure to complete the employability requirements (see Non-Task-Specific criteria). When all criteria are evaluated, tally the points for a total at the bottom of each column.

Tasksheet Scoring

	Test		Retest	
Evaluation Items	**Pass**	**Fail**	**Pass**	**Fail**
Task-Specific Evaluation	**(1 pt)**	**(0 pts)**	**(1 pt)**	**(0 pts)**
1. Student correctly demonstrated the proper use of the designed application and safe operating procedures for at least one piece of fluid pressure testing equipment and any accessories.				
2. Student correctly demonstrated the proper use of the designed application and safe operating procedures for at least three pieces of fluid pressure testing equipment and any accessories.				
3. Student correctly demonstrated the proper use of the designed application and safe operating procedures for at least five pieces of fluid pressure testing equipment and any accessories.				
4. Student correctly demonstrated the proper use of the designed application and safe operating procedures for all seven pieces of fluid pressure testing equipment and any accessories.				

Non-Task-Specific Evaluation	(0 pts)	(−1 pt)	(0 pts)	(−1 pt)
Student successfully completed at least three of the non-task-specific steps.				
Student successfully completed all five of the non-task-specific steps.				
Total Score: <total # of points / 4 = %>				

CDX Tasksheet Number: 1a7004a

Student/Intern Information

Name _____ Date _____ Class _____

Machine, Customer, and Service Information

Machine used for this activity:

Make _____ Model _____

Hours _____ Serial Number _____

Materials Required
- Seven types of personal protective equipment (PPE) for fluid pressure testing equipment chosen by the supervisor/instructor to complete the task
- Tags numbered 1-7 for labeling fluid pressure testing equipment

---

Task-Specific Safety Considerations
- Comply with personal and environmental safety practices associated with clothing; eye protection; hand tools; power equipment; proper ventilation; and the handling, storage, and disposal of chemicals/materials in accordance with local, state, and federal safety and environmental regulations.
- Fluid pressure testing equipment allows us to increase our productivity and effectiveness. However, it can also cause severe injury or death if used improperly. Make sure you follow the manufacturer's procedures.

▶ **TASK** Identify PPE required for the various types of fluid pressure testing equipment.

AED
1a.7

Time off_____

Time on_____

Total time_____

Student Instructions: Read through the entire procedure prior to starting. Prepare your workspace and any tools or parts that may be needed to complete the task. When directed by your supervisor/instructor, begin the procedure to complete the task, and comment or check the box as each step is finished. Track your time on this procedure for later comparison to the standard completion time (i.e., "flat rate" or customer pay time).

Procedure	Step Completed
1. Select PPE #1 and write its correct name below:	☐
2. Select PPE #2 and write its correct name below:	☐

	Step Completed
3. Select PPE #3 and write its correct name below:	☐
4. Select PPE #4 and write its correct name below:	☐
5. Select PPE #5 and write its correct name below:	☐
6. Select PPE #6 and write its correct name below:	☐
7. Select PPE #7 and write its correct name below:	☐

Non-Task-Specific Evaluation	Step Completed
1. Tools and equipment were used as directed and returned in good working order.	☐
2. Complied with all general and task-specific safety standards, including proper use of any PPE.	☐
3. Completed the task in an appropriate time frame (recommendation: 1.5 or 2 times the flat rate).	☐
4. Left the workspace clean and orderly.	☐
5. Cared for customer property and returned it undamaged.	☐

Student signature _____ Date _____

Comments:

Have your supervisor/instructor verify satisfactory completion of this procedure, any observations made,

and any necessary action(s) recommended.

Evaluation Instructions: The scoring box below is intended to act as a guide for both student and supervisor/instructor. Each criterion listed will help students to understand what is expected of them and help supervisors/instructors to articulate the level of success at a particular task. The scoring is set up to allow a second attempt at each task (see the Test and Retest columns). Scoring is designed only to award students points for task criteria that were completed correctly. Points are lost for failure to complete the employability requirements (see Non-Task-Specific criteria). When all criteria are evaluated, tally the points for a total at the bottom of each column.

Tasksheet Scoring

Evaluation Items	Test		Retest	
	Pass	**Fail**	**Pass**	**Fail**
Task-Specific Evaluation	**(1 pt)**	**(O pts)**	**(1 pt)**	**(O pts)**
1. Student correctly identified at least one piece of PPE.				
2. Student correctly identified at least three pieces of PPE.				
3. Student correctly identified at least five pieces of PPE.				
4. Student correctly identified all seven pieces of PPE.				
Non-Task-Specific Evaluation	**(O pts)**	**(−1 pt)**	**(O pts)**	**(−1 pt)**
Student successfully completed at least three of the non-task-specific steps.				
Student successfully completed all five of the non-task-specific steps.				
Total Score: <total # of points / 4 = %>				

CDX Tasksheet Number: 1a7004b

Student/Intern Information

Name _____ Date _____ Class _____

Machine, Customer, and Service Information

Machine used for this activity:

Make _____ Model _____

Hours _____ Serial Number _____

Materials Required
- Personal protective equipment (PPE)
  - Hardhat
  - Gloves
  - Safety glasses
  - Face shield
  - Goggles
  - Hearing protection

Task-Specific Safety Considerations
- Comply with personal and environmental safety practices associated with clothing; eye protection; hand tools; power equipment; proper ventilation; and the handling, storage, and disposal of chemicals/materials in accordance with local, state, and federal safety and environmental regulations.
- Fluid pressure testing equipment allows us to increase our productivity and effectiveness. However, it can also cause severe injury or death if used improperly. Make sure you follow the manufacturer's procedures.

▶ TASK Demonstrate the use of PPE required for the various types of fluid pressure testing equipment.

AED
1a.7

Time off_____

Time on_____

Total time_____

Student Instructions: Read through the entire procedure prior to starting. Prepare your workspace and any tools or parts that may be needed to complete the task. When directed by your supervisor/instructor, begin the procedure to complete the task, and comment or check the box as each step is finished. Track your time on this procedure for later comparison to the standard completion time (i.e., "flat rate" or customer pay time).

Procedure	Step Completed
1. Select a hardhat.	☐
a. Inspect the hardhat for proper operation. Does it operate properly? Yes ☐ No ☐	☐

b. Don (put on) the hardhat. Have your supervisor/instructor verify that you did this properly. Supervisor's/instructor's initials: _____	☐
c. Doff (take off) the hardhat. Have your supervisor/instructor verify that you did this properly. Supervisor's/instructor's initials: _____	☐
2. Select a pair of gloves.	☐
a. Inspect the gloves for proper operation. Do they operate properly? Yes ☐ No ☐	☐
b. Don (put on) the gloves. Have your supervisor/instructor verify that you did this properly. Supervisor's/instructor's initials: _____	☐
c. Doff (take off) the gloves. Have your supervisor/instructor verify that you did this properly. Supervisor's/instructor's initials: _____	☐
3. Select a pair of safety glasses.	☐
a. Inspect the glasses for proper operation. Do they operate properly? Yes ☐ No ☐	☐
b. Don (put on) the glasses. Have your supervisor/instructor verify that you did this properly. Supervisor's/instructor's initials: _____	☐
c. Doff (take off) the glasses. Have your supervisor/instructor verify that you did this properly. Supervisor's/instructor's initials: _____	☐
4. Select a face shield.	☐
a. Inspect the face shield for proper operation. Does it operate properly? Yes ☐ No ☐	☐
b. Don (put on) the face shield. Have your supervisor/instructor verify that you did this properly. Supervisor's/instructor's initials: _____	☐
c. Doff (take off) the face shield. Have your supervisor/instructor verify that you did this properly. Supervisor's/instructor's initials: _____	☐

	Step Completed
5. Select a pair of goggles.	☐
a. Inspect the goggles for proper operation. Do they operate properly? Yes ☐ No ☐	☐
b. Don (put on) the goggles. Have your supervisor/instructor verify that you did this properly. Supervisor's/instructor's initials: _____	☐
c. Doff (take off) the goggles. Have your supervisor/instructor verify that you did this properly. Supervisor's/instructor's initials: _____	☐
6. Select hearing protection.	☐
a. Inspect the hearing protection for proper operation. Does it operate properly? Yes ☐ No ☐	☐
b. Don (put on) the hearing protection. Have your supervisor/instructor verify that you did this properly. Supervisor's/instructor's initials: _____	☐
c. Doff (take off) the hearing protection. Have your supervisor/instructor verify that you did this properly. Supervisor's/instructor's initials: _____	☐

Non-Task-Specific Evaluation	Step Completed
1. Tools and equipment were used as directed and returned in good working order.	☐
2. Complied with all general and task-specific safety standards, including proper use of any PPE.	☐
3. Completed the task in an appropriate time frame (recommendation: 1.5 or 2 times the flat rate).	☐
4. Left the workspace clean and orderly.	☐
5. Cared for customer property and returned it undamaged.	☐

Student signature _____ Date _____

Comments:

[ ]

Have your supervisor/instructor verify satisfactory completion of this procedure, any observations made, and any necessary action(s) recommended.

Evaluation Instructions: The scoring box below is intended to act as a guide for both student and supervisor/instructor. Each criterion listed will help students to understand what is expected of them and help supervisors/instructors to articulate the level of success at a particular task. The scoring is set up to allow a second attempt at each task (see the Test and Retest columns). Scoring is designed only to award students points for task criteria that were completed correctly. Points are lost for failure to complete the employability requirements (see Non-Task-Specific criteria). When all criteria are evaluated, tally the points for a total at the bottom of each column.

Tasksheet Scoring

Evaluation Items	Test		Retest	
	Pass	Fail	Pass	Fail
Task-Specific Evaluation	**(1 pt)**	**(0 pts)**	**(1 pt)**	**(0 pts)**
1. Student correctly demonstrated the use of at least one piece of PPE.				
2. Student correctly demonstrated the use of at least two pieces of PPE.				
3. Student correctly demonstrated the use of at least four pieces of PPE.				
4. Student correctly demonstrated the use of all six pieces of PPE.				
Non-Task-Specific Evaluation	**(0 pts)**	**(−1 pt)**	**(0 pts)**	**(−1 pt)**
Student successfully completed at least three of the non-task-specific steps.				
Student successfully completed all five of the non-task-specific steps.				
Total Score: <total # of points / 4 = %>				

Supervisor/Instructor:

Supervisor/instructor signature _____ Date _____

Comments:

Retest supervisor/instructor signature _____ Date _____

Comments:

Chapter 8: Environment of Service Facility

Learning Objective/Task	CDX Tasksheet Number	AED Reference Number
• Identify the various types of exhaust systems used in repair facility.	1a8001	AED 1a.8
• Demonstrate the proper use of exhaust systems.	1a8002	AED 1a.8

Materials Required

- Program's shop policy and other safety information
- Four types of exhaust systems chosen by the supervisor/instructor to complete the task
- Tags numbered 1-4 for labeling the exhaust systems
- Vehicle exhaust system(s)
- Shop ventilation system(s)
- Shop exhaust system equipment

Safety Considerations

- Comply with personal and environmental safety practices associated with clothing; eye protection; hand tools; power equipment; proper ventilation; and the handling, storage, and disposal of chemicals/materials in accordance with local, state, and federal safety and environmental regulations.
- Exhaust system equipment allows us to increase our productivity and effectiveness. However, it can also cause severe injury or death if used improperly. Make sure you follow the manufacturer's procedures.

CDX Tasksheet Number: 1a8001

Student/Intern Information

Name _____ Date _____ Class _____

Machine, Customer, and Service Information

Machine used for this activity:

Make _____ Model _____

Hours _____ Serial Number _____

Materials Required
- Program's shop policy and other safety information
- Four types of exhaust systems chosen by the supervisor/instructor to complete the task
- Tags numbered 1-4 for labeling the exhaust systems

Task-Specific Safety Considerations
- Comply with personal and environmental safety practices associated with clothing; eye protection; hand tools; power equipment; proper ventilation; and the handling, storage, and disposal of chemicals/materials in accordance with local, state, and federal safety and environmental regulations.
- Exhaust system equipment allows us to increase our productivity and effectiveness. However, it can also cause severe injury or death if used improperly. Make sure you follow the manufacturer's procedures.

▶ TASK Identify the various types of exhaust systems used in repair facility. **AED 1a.8**

Time off_____

Time on_____

Student Instructions: Read through the entire procedure prior to starting. Prepare your workspace and any tools or parts that may be needed to complete the task. When directed by your supervisor/instructor, begin the procedure to complete the task, and comment or check the box as each step is finished. Track your time on this procedure for later comparison to the standard completion time (i.e., "flat rate" or customer pay time).

Total time_____

Procedure	Step Completed
1. Identify Exhaust System #1 and write its correct name below:	☐
2. Identify Exhaust System #2 and write its correct name below:	☐

	Step Completed
3. Identify Exhaust System #3 and write its correct name below:	☐
4. Identify Exhaust System #4 and write its correct name below:	☐

Non-Task-Specific Evaluation	Step Completed
1. Tools and equipment were used as directed and returned in good working order.	☐
2. Complied with all general and task-specific safety standards, including proper use of any personal protective equipment (PPE).	☐
3. Completed the task in an appropriate time frame (recommendation: 1.5 or 2 times the flat rate).	☐
4. Left the workspace clean and orderly.	☐
5. Cared for customer property and returned it undamaged.	☐

Student signature _____ Date _____

Comments:

Have your supervisor/instructor verify satisfactory completion of this procedure, any observations made, and any necessary action(s) recommended.

Evaluation Instructions: The scoring box below is intended to act as a guide for both student and supervisor/instructor. Each criterion listed will help students to understand what is expected of them and help supervisors/instructors to articulate the level of success at a particular task. The scoring is set up to allow a second attempt at each task (see the Test and Retest columns). Scoring is designed only to award students points for task criteria that were completed correctly. Points are lost for failure to complete the employability requirements (see Non-Task-Specific criteria). When all criteria are evaluated, tally the points for a total at the bottom of each column.

Tasksheet Scoring

Evaluation Items	Test		Retest	
	Pass	**Fail**	**Pass**	**Fail**
Task-Specific Evaluation	**(1 pt)**	**(O pts)**	**(1 pt)**	**(O pts)**
1. Student correctly identified Exhaust System #1.				
2. Student correctly identified Exhaust System #2.				
3. Student correctly identified Exhaust System #3.				
4. Student correctly identified Exhaust System #4.				
Non–Task-Specific Evaluation	**(O pts)**	**(−1 pt)**	**(O pts)**	**(−1 pt)**
Student successfully completed at least three of the non-task-specific steps.				
Student successfully completed all five of the non-task-specific steps.				
Total Score: <total # of points / 4 = %>				

Supervisor/Instructor:

Supervisor/instructor signature _____ Date _____

Comments:

Retest supervisor/instructor signature _____ Date _____

Comments:

CDX Tasksheet Number: 1a8002

Student/Intern Information

Name _____ Date _____ Class _____

Machine, Customer, and Service Information

Machine used for this activity:

Make _____ Model _____

Hours _____ Serial Number _____

Materials Required
- Program's shop policy and other safety information
- Vehicle exhaust system(s)
- Shop ventilation system(s)
- Shop exhaust system equipment

Task-Specific Safety Considerations
- Comply with personal and environmental safety practices associated with clothing; eye protection; hand tools; power equipment; proper ventilation; and the handling, storage, and disposal of chemicals/materials in accordance with local, state, and federal safety and environmental regulations.
- Exhaust system equipment allows us to increase our productivity and effectiveness. However, it must be used according to the manufacturer's procedures. Failure to follow those procedures can result in serious injury or death.

▶ TASK Demonstrate the proper use of exhaust systems. _____ **AED** *1a.8*

Time off_____

Time on_____

Student Instructions: Read through the entire procedure prior to starting. Prepare your workspace and any tools or parts that may be needed to complete the task. When directed by your supervisor/instructor, begin the procedure to complete the task, and comment or check the box as each step is finished. Track your time on this procedure for later comparison to the standard completion time (i.e., "flat rate" or customer pay time).

Total time_____

Procedure	Step Completed
1. Locate a vehicle exhaust system.	☐
a. Connect shop exhaust system to machine exhaust following shop procedures. Have your supervisor/instructor verify satisfactory completion of these procedures. Supervisor's/instructor's initials: _____	☐

b. Turn on shop exhaust system and start machine following shop procedures. Have your supervisor/instructor verify satisfactory completion of these procedures. Supervisor's/instructor's initials: _____	☐
c. Shut off machine and disconnect shop exhaust system from machine exhaust following shop procedures. Have your supervisor/instructor verify satisfactory completion of these procedures. Supervisor's/instructor's initials: _____	☐
d. Store the exhaust system following shop procedures.	☐
2. Locate the shop ventilation system.	☐
a. Turn on the shop ventilation system following shop procedures. Have your supervisor/instructor verify satisfactory completion of these procedures. Supervisor's/instructor's initials: _____	☐
b. Shut off the shop ventilation system following shop procedures. Have your supervisor/instructor verify satisfactory completion of these procedures. Supervisor's/instructor's initials: _____	☐
3. Locate additional shop ventilation/exhaust systems.	☐
a. Turn on the shop ventilation/exhaust system following shop procedures. Have your supervisor/instructor verify satisfactory completion of these procedures. Supervisor's/instructor's initials: _____	☐
b. Shut off the shop ventilation/exhaust system following shop procedures. Have your supervisor/instructor verify satisfactory completion of these procedures. Supervisor's/instructor's initials: _____	☐

Non-Task-Specific Evaluation	Step Completed
1. Tools and equipment were used as directed and returned in good working order.	☐
2. Complied with all general and task-specific safety standards, including proper use of any personal protective equipment (PPE).	☐
3. Completed the task in an appropriate time frame (recommendation: 1.5 or 2 times the flat rate).	☐
4. Left the workspace clean and orderly.	☐
5. Cared for customer property and returned it undamaged.	☐

Student signature _____ Date _____

Comments:

Have your supervisor/instructor verify satisfactory completion of this procedure, any observations made, and any necessary action(s) recommended.

Evaluation Instructions: The scoring box below is intended to act as a guide for both student and supervisor/instructor. Each criterion listed will help students to understand what is expected of them and help supervisors/instructors to articulate the level of success at a particular task. The scoring is set up to allow a second attempt at each task (see the Test and Retest columns). Scoring is designed only to award students points for task criteria that were completed correctly. Points are lost for failure to complete the employability requirements (see Non-Task-Specific criteria). When all criteria are evaluated, tally the points for a total at the bottom of each column.

Tasksheet Scoring

	Test		Retest	
Evaluation Items	**Pass**	**Fail**	**Pass**	**Fail**
Task-Specific Evaluation	**(1 pt)**	**(0 pts)**	**(1 pt)**	**(0 pts)**
1. Student located the correct exhaust/ ventilation system.				
2. Student demonstrated the proper use of each exhaust/ventilation system.				
3. Student demonstrated the proper care and maintenance of each exhaust/ventilation system.				
4. Student demonstrated the proper safe operating procedure of each exhaust/ventilation system.				
Non-Task-Specific Evaluation	**(0 pts)**	**(−1 pt)**	**(0 pts)**	**(−1 pt)**
Student successfully completed at least three of the non-task-specific steps.				
Student successfully completed all five of the non-task-specific steps.				
Total Score: <total # of points / 4 = %>				

Chapter 9: Machine Identification and Operation

Learning Objective/Task	CDX Tasksheet Number	AED Reference Number
• Identify the various types of construction equipment and forklifts by their proper name.	1a9001	AED 1a.9
• Operate various types of machinery.	1a9002	AED 1a.9
• Recognize hybrid systems and/or machines.	1a9004	AED 1a.9

Materials Required

- 14 various types of construction equipment and forklifts chosen by the supervisor/instructor to complete the task (e.g., excavator, skid steers, backhoes, compaction equipment, paving equipment, crawler- and track-type loader, scraper, crane, scissor lift, forklift and material handler, wheel loader, haul truck, motor grader, trencher, horizontal directional drill, hybrid drive)
- Four types of hybrid systems or machines chosen by the supervisor/instructor to complete the task
- Tags numbered 1-14 for labeling the systems/machines
- Equipment manufacturer's/operator's manual
- Personal protective equipment (PPE)

Safety Considerations

- Comply with personal and environmental safety practices associated with clothing; eye protection; hand tools; power equipment; proper ventilation; and the handling, storage, and disposal of chemicals/materials in accordance with local, state, and federal safety and environmental regulations.
- This task may require test-driving the vehicle on the school grounds. Attempt this task only with full permission from your supervisor/instructor and follow all the guidelines exactly.

CDX Tasksheet Number: 1a9001

Student/Intern Information

Name _____ Date _____ Class _____

Machine, Customer, and Service Information

Machine used for this activity:

Make _____ Model _____

Hours _____ Serial Number _____

Materials Required

- 14 various types of construction equipment and forklifts chosen by the supervisor/ instructor to complete the task
- Tags numbered 1-14 for labeling the machines
- Equipment manufacturer's/operator's manual
- Personal protective equipment (PPE)

Task-Specific Safety Considerations

- Comply with personal and environmental safety practices associated with clothing; eye protection; hand tools; power equipment; proper ventilation; and the handling, storage, and disposal of chemicals/materials in accordance with local, state, and federal safety and environmental regulations.
- This task may require test-driving the vehicle on the school grounds. Attempt this task only with full permission from your supervisor/instructor and follow all the guidelines exactly.

▶ **TASK** Identify the various types of construction equipment and forklifts by their proper name.

AED
1a.9

Time off_____

Time on_____

Total time_____

Student Instructions: Read through the entire procedure prior to starting. Prepare your workspace and any tools or parts that may be needed to complete the task. When directed by your supervisor/instructor, begin the procedure to complete the task, and comment or check the box as each step is finished. Track your time on this procedure for later comparison to the standard completion time (i.e., "flat rate" or customer pay time).

Procedure	Step Completed
1. Identify Machine #1 and write its standard industry name accepted by equipment manufacturers below:	☐

2. Identify Machine #2 and write its standard industry name accepted by equipment manufacturers below:	☐
3. Identify Machine #3 and write its standard industry name accepted by equipment manufacturers below:	☐
4. Identify Machine #4 and write its standard industry name accepted by equipment manufacturers below:	☐
5. Identify Machine #5 and write its standard industry name accepted by equipment manufacturers below:	☐
6. Identify Machine #6 and write its standard industry name accepted by equipment manufacturers below:	☐
7. Identify Machine #7 and write its standard industry name accepted by equipment manufacturers below:	☐
8. Identify Machine #8 and write its standard industry name accepted by equipment manufacturers below:	☐
9. Identify Machine #9 and write its standard industry name accepted by equipment manufacturers below:	☐

10. Identify Machine #10 and write its standard industry name accepted by equipment manufacturers below:	☐
11. Identify Machine #11 and write its standard industry name accepted by equipment manufacturers below:	☐
12. Identify Machine #12 and write its standard industry name accepted by equipment manufacturers below:	☐
13. Identify Machine #13 and write its standard industry name accepted by equipment manufacturers below:	☐
14. Identify Machine #14 and write its standard industry name accepted by equipment manufacturers below:	☐

Non-Task-Specific Evaluation	Step Completed
1. Tools and equipment were used as directed and returned in good working order.	☐
2. Complied with all general and task-specific safety standards, including proper use of any PPE.	☐
3. Completed the task in an appropriate time frame (recommendation: 1.5 or 2 times the flat rate).	☐
4. Left the workspace clean and orderly.	☐
5. Cared for customer property and returned it undamaged.	☐

Student signature _____ Date _____

Comments:

Have your supervisor/instructor verify satisfactory completion of this procedure, any observations made, and any necessary action(s) recommended.

Evaluation Instructions: The scoring box below is intended to act as a guide for both student and supervisor/instructor. Each criterion listed will help students to understand what is expected of them and help supervisors/instructors to articulate the level of success at a particular task. The scoring is set up to allow a second attempt at each task (see the Test and Retest columns). Scoring is designed only to award students points for task criteria that were completed correctly. Points are lost for failure to complete the employability requirements (see Non-Task-Specific criteria). When all criteria are evaluated, tally the points for a total at the bottom of each column.

Tasksheet Scoring

Evaluation Items	Test		Retest	
	Pass	Fail	Pass	Fail
Task-Specific Evaluation	**(1 pt)**	**(0 pts)**	**(1 pt)**	**(0 pts)**
1. Student correctly identified at least three machines.				
2. Student correctly identified at least six machines.				
3. Student correctly identified at least 10 machines.				
4. Student correctly identified all 14 machines.				
Non-Task-Specific Evaluation	**(0 pts)**	**(−1 pt)**	**(0 pts)**	**(−1 pt)**
Student successfully completed at least three of the non-task-specific steps.				
Student successfully completed all five of the non-task-specific steps.				
Total Score: <total # of points / 4 = %>				

Supervisor/Instructor:

Supervisor/instructor signature _____ Date _____

Comments:

Retest supervisor/instructor signature _____ Date _____

Comments:

CDX Tasksheet Number: 1a9002

Student/Intern Information

Name _____ Date _____ Class _____

Machine, Customer, and Service Information

Machine used for this activity:

Make _____ Model _____

Hours _____ Serial Number _____

Materials Required

- 14 various types of construction equipment and forklifts chosen by the supervisor/ instructor to complete the task (e.g., excavator, skid steers, backhoes, compaction equipment, paving equipment, crawler- and track-type loader, scraper, crane, scissor lift, forklift and material handler, wheel loader, haul truck, motor grader, trencher, horizontal directional drill, hybrid drive)
- Equipment manufacturer's/operator's manual
- Personal protective equipment (PPE)

Task-Specific Safety Considerations

- Comply with personal and environmental safety practices associated with clothing; eye protection; hand tools; power equipment; proper ventilation; and the handling, storage, and disposal of chemicals/materials in accordance with local, state, and federal safety and environmental regulations.
- This task may require test-driving the vehicle on the school grounds. Attempt this task only with full permission from your supervisor/instructor and follow all the guidelines exactly.

▶ **TASK** Operate various types of machinery. _____ **AED** 1a.9

Time off_____

Student Instructions: Read through the entire procedure prior to starting. Prepare your workspace and any tools or parts that may be needed to complete the task. When directed by your supervisor/instructor, begin the procedure to complete the task, and comment or check the box as each step is finished. Track your time on this procedure for later comparison to the standard completion time (i.e., "flat rate" or customer pay time).

Time on_____

Total time_____

Procedure	Step Completed
1. Locate Machine #1 in the shop or yard.	☐
a. Find the operator's manual and perform a walk-around inspection. List any defects found during your inspection below. (**Note:** If any defects are found, report them to your supervisor/instructor and *do not operate the machine*.)	☐
b. If no defects are found, operate the machine in the shop or yard under your supervisor's/instructor's supervision and perform the typical functions of the machine as directed by your supervisor/instructor.	☐
c. Once complete, safely park the machine and stow all implements according to the manufacturer's recommendations.	☐
2. Locate Machine #2 in the shop or yard.	☐
a. Find the operator's manual and perform a walk-around inspection. List any defects found during your inspection below. (**Note:** If any defects are found, report them to your supervisor/instructor and *do not operate the machine*.)	☐
b. If no defects are found, operate the machine in the shop or yard under your supervisor's/instructor's supervision and perform the typical functions of the machine as directed by your supervisor/instructor.	☐
c. Once complete, safely park the machine and stow all implements according to the manufacturer's recommendations.	☐
3. Locate Machine #3 in the shop or yard.	☐
a. Find the operator's manual and perform a walk-around inspection. List any defects found during your inspection below. (**Note:** If any defects are found, report them to your supervisor/instructor and *do not operate the machine*.)	☐
b. If no defects are found, operate the machine in the shop or yard under your supervisor's/instructor's supervision and perform the typical functions of the machine as directed by your supervisor/instructor.	☐
c. Once complete, safely park the machine and stow all implements according to the manufacturer's recommendations.	☐

4. Locate Machine #4 in the shop or yard.	☐
a. Find the operator's manual and perform a walk-around inspection. List any defects found during your inspection below. (**Note:** If any defects are found, report them to your supervisor/instructor and *do not operate the machine.*)	☐
b. If no defects are found, operate the machine in the shop or yard under your supervisor's/instructor's supervision and perform the typical functions of the machine as directed by your supervisor/instructor.	☐
c. Once complete, safely park the machine and stow all implements according to the manufacturer's recommendations.	☐
5. Locate Machine #5 in the shop or yard.	☐
a. Find the operator's manual and perform a walk-around inspection. List any defects found during your inspection below. (**Note:** If any defects are found, report them to your supervisor/instructor and *do not operate the machine.*)	☐
b. If no defects are found, operate the machine in the shop or yard under your supervisor's/instructor's supervision and perform the typical functions of the machine as directed by your supervisor/instructor.	☐
c. Once complete, safely park the machine and stow all implements according to the manufacturer's recommendations.	☐
6. Locate Machine #6 in the shop or yard.	☐
a. Find the operator's manual and perform a walk-around inspection. List any defects found during your inspection below. (**Note:** If any defects are found, report them to your supervisor/instructor and *do not operate the machine.*)	☐
b. If no defects are found, operate the machine in the shop or yard under your supervisor's/instructor's supervision and perform the typical functions of the machine as directed by your supervisor/instructor.	☐
c. Once complete, safely park the machine and stow all implements according to the manufacturer's recommendations.	☐

7. Locate Machine #7 in the shop or yard.	☐
a. Find the operator's manual and perform a walk-around inspection. List any defects found during your inspection below. (**Note:** If any defects are found, report them to your supervisor/instructor and *do not operate the machine*.)	☐
b. If no defects are found, operate the machine in the shop or yard under your supervisor's/instructor's supervision and perform the typical functions of the machine as directed by your supervisor/instructor.	☐
c. Once complete, safely park the machine and stow all implements according to the manufacturer's recommendations.	☐
8. Locate Machine #8 in the shop or yard.	☐
a. Find the operator's manual and perform a walk-around inspection. List any defects found during your inspection below. (**Note:** If any defects are found, report them to your supervisor/instructor and *do not operate the machine*.)	☐
b. If no defects are found, operate the machine in the shop or yard under your supervisor's/instructor's supervision and perform the typical functions of the machine as directed by your supervisor/instructor.	☐
c. Once complete, safely park the machine and stow all implements according to the manufacturer's recommendations.	☐
9. Locate Machine #9 in the shop or yard.	☐
a. Find the operator's manual and perform a walk-around inspection. List any defects found during your inspection below. (**Note:** If any defects are found, report them to your supervisor/instructor and *do not operate the machine*.)	☐
b. If no defects are found, operate the machine in the shop or yard under your supervisor's/instructor's supervision and perform the typical functions of the machine as directed by your supervisor/instructor.	☐
c. Once complete, safely park the machine and stow all implements according to the manufacturer's recommendations.	☐

10. Locate Machine #10 in the shop or yard.	☐
a. Find the operator's manual and perform a walk-around inspection. List any defects found during your inspection below. (**Note:** If any defects are found, report them to your supervisor/instructor and *do not operate the machine*.)	☐
b. If no defects are found, operate the machine in the shop or yard under your supervisor's/instructor's supervision and perform the typical functions of the machine as directed by your supervisor/instructor.	☐
c. Once complete, safely park the machine and stow all implements according to the manufacturer's recommendations.	☐
11. Locate Machine #11 in the shop or yard.	☐
a. Find the operator's manual and perform a walk-around inspection. List any defects found during your inspection below. (**Note:** If any defects are found, report them to your supervisor/instructor and *do not operate the machine*.)	☐
b. If no defects are found, operate the machine in the shop or yard under your supervisor's/instructor's supervision and perform the typical functions of the machine as directed by your supervisor/instructor.	☐
c. Once complete, safely park the machine and stow all implements according to the manufacturer's recommendations.	☐
12. Locate Machine #12 in the shop or yard.	☐
a. Find the operator's manual and perform a walk-around inspection. List any defects found during your inspection below. (**Note:** If any defects are found, report them to your supervisor/instructor and *do not operate the machine*.)	☐
b. If no defects are found, operate the machine in the shop or yard under your supervisor's/instructor's supervision and perform the typical functions of the machine as directed by your supervisor/instructor.	☐
c. Once complete, safely park the machine and stow all implements according to the manufacturer's recommendations.	☐

13. Locate Machine #13 in the shop or yard.	☐
a. Find the operator's manual and perform a walk-around inspection. List any defects found during your inspection below. (**Note:** If any defects are found, report them to your supervisor/instructor and *do not operate the machine*.)	☐
b. If no defects are found, operate the machine in the shop or yard under your supervisor's/instructor's supervision and perform the typical functions of the machine as directed by your supervisor/instructor.	☐
c. Once complete, safely park the machine and stow all implements according to the manufacturer's recommendations.	☐
14. Locate Machine #14 in the shop or yard.	☐
a. Find the operator's manual and perform a walk-around inspection. List any defects found during your inspection below. (**Note:** If any defects are found, report them to your supervisor/instructor and *do not operate the machine*.)	☐
b. If no defects are found, operate the machine in the shop or yard under your supervisor's/instructor's supervision and perform the typical functions of the machine as directed by your supervisor/instructor.	☐
c. Once complete, safely park the machine and stow all implements according to the manufacturer's recommendations.	☐

Non-Task-Specific Evaluation	Step Completed
1. Tools and equipment were used as directed and returned in good working order.	☐
2. Complied with all general and task-specific safety standards, including proper use of any PPE.	☐
3. Completed the task in an appropriate time frame (recommendation: 1.5 or 2 times the flat rate).	☐
4. Left the workspace clean and orderly.	☐
5. Cared for customer property and returned it undamaged.	☐

Student signature _____ Date _____

Comments:

Have your supervisor/instructor verify satisfactory completion of this procedure, any observations made,

and any necessary action(s) recommended.

Evaluation Instructions: The scoring box below is intended to act as a guide for both student and supervisor/instructor. Each criterion listed will help students to understand what is expected of them and help supervisors/instructors to articulate the level of success at a particular task. The scoring is set up to allow a second attempt at each task (see the Test and Retest columns). Scoring is designed only to award students points for task criteria that were completed correctly. Points are lost for failure to complete the employability requirements (see Non-Task-Specific criteria). When all criteria are evaluated, tally the points for a total at the bottom of each column.

Tasksheet Scoring

Evaluation Items	Test Pass	Test Fail	Retest Pass	Retest Fail
Task-Specific Evaluation	**(1 pt)**	**(0 pts)**	**(1 pt)**	**(0 pts)**
1. Student demonstrated the proper, safe, and fundamental operation of at least three machines.				
2. Student demonstrated the proper, safe, and fundamental operation of at least six machines.				
3. Student demonstrated the proper, safe, and fundamental operation of at least 10 machines.				
4. Student demonstrated the proper, safe, and fundamental operation of all 14 machines.				
Non-Task-Specific Evaluation	**(0 pts)**	**(−1 pt)**	**(0 pts)**	**(−1 pt)**
Student successfully completed at least three of the non-task-specific steps.				
Student successfully completed all five of the non-task-specific steps.				
Total Score: <total # of points / 4 = %>				

Supervisor/Instructor:

Supervisor/instructor signature _____ Date _____

Comments:

Retest supervisor/instructor signature _____ Date _____

Comments:

CDX Tasksheet Number: 1a9004

Student/Intern Information

Name _____ Date _____ Class _____

Machine, Customer, and Service Information

Machine used for this activity:

Make _____ Model _____

Hours _____ Serial Number _____

Materials Required

- Four types of hybrid systems or machines chosen by the supervisor/instructor to complete the task
- Tags numbered 1–4 for labeling the systems/machines
- Equipment manufacturer's/operator's manual
- Personal protective equipment (PPE)

Task-Specific Safety Considerations

- Comply with personal and environmental safety practices associated with clothing; eye protection; hand tools; power equipment; proper ventilation; and the handling, storage, and disposal of chemicals/materials in accordance with local, state, and federal safety and environmental regulations.
- This task may require test-driving the vehicle on the school grounds. Attempt this task only with full permission from your supervisor/instructor and follow all the guidelines exactly.

▶ **TASK** Recognize hybrid systems and/or machines. **AED 1a.9**

Time off_____

Time on_____

Total time_____

Student Instructions: Read through the entire procedure prior to starting. Prepare your workspace and any tools or parts that may be needed to complete the task. When directed by your supervisor/instructor, begin the procedure to complete the task, and comment or check the box as each step is finished. Track your time on this procedure for later comparison to the standard completion time (i.e., "flat rate" or customer pay time).

Procedure	Step Completed
1. Write the correct name for Machine #1 below:	☐
a. Demonstrate how to recognize that the machine is equipped with a hybrid system.	☐

b. List the steps you took to recognize the system below:	☐
2. Write the correct name for Machine #2 below:	☐
a. Demonstrate how to recognize that the machine is equipped with a hybrid system.	☐
b. List the steps you took to recognize the system below:	☐
3. Write the correct name for Machine #3 below:	☐
a. Demonstrate how to recognize that the machine is equipped with a hybrid system.	☐
b. List the steps you took to recognize the system below:	☐
4. Write the correct name for Machine #4 below:	☐
a. Demonstrate how to recognize that the machine is equipped with a hybrid system.	☐
b. List the steps you took to recognize the system below:	☐

Non-Task-Specific Evaluation	Step Completed
1. Tools and equipment were used as directed and returned in good working order.	☐
2. Complied with all general and task-specific safety standards, including proper use of any PPE.	☐
3. Completed the task in an appropriate time frame (recommendation: 1.5 or 2 times the flat rate).	☐
4. Left the workspace clean and orderly.	☐
5. Cared for customer property and returned it undamaged.	☐

Student signature _____ Date _____

Comments:

Have your supervisor/instructor verify satisfactory completion of this procedure, any observations made,

and any necessary action(s) recommended.

Evaluation Instructions: The scoring box below is intended to act as a guide for both student and supervisor/instructor. Each criterion listed will help students to understand what is expected of them and help supervisors/instructors to articulate the level of success at a particular task. The scoring is set up to allow a second attempt at each task (see the Test and Retest columns). Scoring is designed only to award students points for task criteria that were completed correctly. Points are lost for failure to complete the employability requirements (see Non-Task-Specific criteria). When all criteria are evaluated, tally the points for a total at the bottom of each column.

Tasksheet Scoring

Evaluation Items	Test		Retest	
	Pass	**Fail**	**Pass**	**Fail**
Task-Specific Evaluation	**(1 pt)**	**(0 pts)**	**(1 pt)**	**(0 pts)**
1. Student correctly demonstrated how to recognize that Machine #1 is equipped with a hybrid system.				
2. Student correctly demonstrated how to recognize that Machine #2 is equipped with a hybrid system.				
3. Student correctly demonstrated how to recognize that Machine #3 is equipped with a hybrid system.				
4. Student correctly demonstrated how to recognize that Machine #4 is equipped with a hybrid system.				
Non-Task-Specific Evaluation	**(0 pts)**	**(−1 pt)**	**(0 pts)**	**(−1 pt)**
Student successfully completed at least three of the non-task-specific steps.				
Student successfully completed all five of the non-task-specific steps.				
Total Score: <total # of points / 4 = %>				

Supervisor/Instructor:

Supervisor/instructor signature _____ Date _____

Comments:

Retest supervisor/instructor signature _____ Date _____

Comments:

Chapter 10: Mandated Regulations

Learning Objective/Task	CDX Tasksheet Number	AED Reference Number
• Identify the various types of personal protective equipment (PPE) by their proper name.	1a10001	AED 1a.10
• Demonstrate the use of PPE.	1a10002	AED 1a.10
• Identify the different types of fire extinguishers.	1a10004a	AED 1a.10
• Demonstrate the use of different types of fire extinguishers.	1a10004b	AED 1a.10
• Utilize safety data sheets (SDS) for products.	1a10005	AED 1a.10
• Identify underground utility hazard marking commonly encountered on a job site.	1a10006	AED 1a.10

Materials Required

- 10 types of PPE chosen by the supervisor/instructor to complete the task
- Tags numbered 1-10 for labeling the equipment/extinguishers/shop products
- PPE
- Hardhat
- Pair of gloves
- Safety glasses
- Face shield
- Goggles
- Hearing protection
- Respirator
- Protective clothing
- Fire protection
- Safety shoes
- Seven types of fire extinguishers chosen by the supervisor/instructor to complete the task
- Fire extinguishers (types A, B, C, D, and K)
- Program's shop policy and other safety information
- 12 various shop products that require SDS chosen by the supervisor/instructor to complete the task
- SDS for each product
- Location's/region's utility location protocol

Safety Considerations

- Comply with personal and environmental safety practices associated with clothing; eye protection; hand tools; power equipment; proper ventilation; and the handling, storage, and disposal of chemicals/materials in accordance with local, state, and federal safety and environmental regulations.
- PPE allows us to increase our productivity and effectiveness. However, it can also cause severe injury or death if used improperly. Make sure you follow the manufacturer's procedures.

CDX Tasksheet Number: 1a10001

Student/Intern Information

Name _____ Date _____ Class _____

Machine, Customer, and Service Information

Machine used for this activity:

Make _____ Model _____

Hours _____ Serial Number _____

Materials Required
- 10 types of personal protective equipment (PPE) chosen by the supervisor/instructor to complete the task
- Tags numbered 1–10 for labeling the equipment

Task-Specific Safety Considerations
- Comply with personal and environmental safety practices associated with clothing; eye protection; hand tools; power equipment; proper ventilation; and the handling, storage, and disposal of chemicals/materials in accordance with local, state, and federal safety and environmental regulations.
- PPE allows us to increase our productivity and effectiveness. However, it can also cause severe injury or death if used improperly. Make sure you follow the manufacturer's procedures.

▶ **TASK** Identify the various types of PPE by their proper name. **AED** 1a.10

Time off_____

Time on_____

Student Instructions: Read through the entire procedure prior to starting. Prepare your workspace and any tools or parts that may be needed to complete the task. When directed by your supervisor/instructor, begin the procedure to complete the task, and comment or check the box as each step is finished. Track your time on this procedure for later comparison to the standard completion time (i.e., "flat rate" or customer pay time).

Total time_____

Procedure	Step Completed
1. Identify PPE #1 and write its correct name below:	☐
2. Identify PPE #2 and write its correct name below:	☐
3. Identify PPE #3 and write its correct name below:	☐

	Step Completed
4. Identify PPE #4 and write its correct name below:	☐
5. Identify PPE #5 and write its correct name below:	☐
6. Identify PPE #6 and write its correct name below:	☐
7. Identify PPE #7 and write its correct name below:	☐
8. Identify PPE #8 and write its correct name below:	☐
9. Identify PPE #9 and write its correct name below:	☐
10. Identify PPE #10 and write its correct name below:	☐

Non-Task-Specific Evaluation	Step Completed
1. Tools and equipment were used as directed and returned in good working order.	☐
2. Complied with all general and task-specific safety standards, including proper use of any PPE.	☐
3. Completed the task in an appropriate time frame (recommendation: 1.5 or 2 times the flat rate).	☐
4. Left the workspace clean and orderly.	☐
5. Cared for customer property and returned it undamaged.	☐

Student signature _____ Date _____

Comments:

Have your supervisor/instructor verify satisfactory completion of this procedure, any observations made, and any necessary action(s) recommended.

Evaluation Instructions: The scoring box below is intended to act as a guide for both student and supervisor/instructor. Each criterion listed will help students to understand what is expected of them and help supervisors/instructors to articulate the level of success at a particular task. The scoring is set up to allow a second attempt at each task (see the Test and Retest columns). Scoring is designed only to award students points for task criteria that were completed correctly. Points are lost for failure to complete the employability requirements (see Non-Task-Specific criteria). When all criteria are evaluated, tally the points for a total at the bottom of each column.

Tasksheet Scoring

Evaluation Items	Test		Retest	
	Pass	**Fail**	**Pass**	**Fail**
Task-Specific Evaluation	**(1 pt)**	**(0 pts)**	**(1 pt)**	**(0 pts)**
1. Student correctly identified at least two types of PPE.				
2. Student correctly identified at least four types of PPE.				
3. Student correctly identified at least seven types of PPE.				
4. Student correctly identified all 10 types of PPE.				
Non-Task-Specific Evaluation	**(0 pts)**	**(−1 pt)**	**(0 pts)**	**(−1 pt)**
Student successfully completed at least three of the non-task-specific steps.				
Student successfully completed all five of the non-task-specific steps.				
Total Score: <total # of points / 4 = %>				

Supervisor/Instructor:

Supervisor/instructor signature _____ Date _____

Comments:

Retest supervisor/instructor signature _____ Date _____

Comments:

CDX Tasksheet Number: 1a10002

Student/Intern Information

Name _____ Date _____ Class _____

Machine, Customer, and Service Information

Machine used for this activity:

Make _____ Model _____

Hours _____ Serial Number _____

Materials Required

- Personal protective equipment (PPE):
  - Hardhat
  - Pair of gloves
  - Safety glasses
  - Face shield
  - Goggles
  - Hearing protection
  - Respirator
  - Protective clothing
  - Fire protection
  - Safety shoes

Task-Specific Safety Considerations

- Comply with personal and environmental safety practices associated with clothing; eye protection; hand tools; power equipment; proper ventilation; and the handling, storage, and disposal of chemicals/materials in accordance with local, state, and federal safety and environmental regulations.
- PPE allows us to increase our productivity and effectiveness. However, it can also cause severe injury or death if used improperly. Make sure you follow the manufacturer's procedures.

▶ **TASK** Demonstrate the use of PPE. **AED** 1a.10

Time off_____

Time on_____

Student Instructions: Read through the entire procedure prior to starting. Prepare your workspace and any tools or parts that may be needed to complete the task. When directed by your supervisor/instructor, begin the procedure to complete the task, and comment or check the box as each step is finished. Track your time on this procedure for later comparison to the standard completion time (i.e., "flat rate" or customer pay time).

Total time_____

Procedure	Step Completed
1. Select a hardhat.	☐
a. Inspect the hardhat for proper operation. Does it operate properly? Yes ☐ No ☐	☐
b. Don (put on) the hardhat. Have your supervisor/instructor verify that you did this properly. Supervisor's/instructor's initials: _____	☐
c. Doff (take off) the hardhat. Have your supervisor/instructor verify that you did this properly. Supervisor's/instructor's initials: _____	☐
2. Select a pair of gloves.	☐
a. Inspect the gloves for proper operation. Do they operate properly? Yes ☐ No ☐	☐
b. Don (put on) the gloves. Have your supervisor/instructor verify that you did this properly. Supervisor's/instructor's initials: _____	☐
c. Doff (take off) the gloves. Have your supervisor/instructor verify that you did this properly. Supervisor's/instructor's initials: _____	☐
3. Select a pair of safety glasses.	☐
a. Inspect the glasses for proper operation. Do they operate properly? Yes ☐ No ☐	☐
b. Don (put on) the glasses. Have your supervisor/instructor verify that you did this properly. Supervisor's/instructor's initials: _____	☐
c. Doff (take off) the glasses. Have your supervisor/instructor verify that you did this properly. Supervisor's/instructor's initials: _____	☐
4. Select a face shield.	☐
a. Inspect the face shield for proper operation. Does it operate properly? Yes ☐ No ☐	☐

b. Don (put on) the face shield. Have your supervisor/instructor verify that you did this properly. Supervisor's/instructor's initials: _____	☐
c. Doff (take off) the face shield. Have your supervisor/instructor verify that you did this properly. Supervisor's/instructor's initials: _____	☐
5. Select a pair of goggles.	☐
a. Inspect the goggles for proper operation. Do they operate properly? Yes ☐ No ☐	☐
b. Don (put on) the goggles. Have your supervisor/instructor verify that you did this properly. Supervisor's/instructor's initials: _____	☐
c. Doff (take off) the goggles. Have your supervisor/instructor verify that you did this properly. Supervisor's/instructor's initials: _____	☐
6. Select hearing protection.	☐
a. Inspect the hearing protection for proper operation. Does it operate properly? Yes ☐ No ☐	☐
b. Don (put on) the hearing protection. Have your supervisor/instructor verify that you did this properly. Supervisor's/instructor's initials: _____	☐
c. Doff (take off) the hearing protection. Have your supervisor/instructor verify that you did this properly. Supervisor's/instructor's initials: _____	☐
7. Select a respirator.	☐
a. Inspect the respirator for proper operation. Does it operate properly? Yes ☐ No ☐	☐
b. Don (put on) the respirator. Have your supervisor/instructor verify that you did this properly. Supervisor's/instructor's initials: _____	☐

c. Doff (take off) the respirator. Have your supervisor/instructor verify that you did this properly. Supervisor's/instructor's initials: _____	☐
8. Select protective clothing.	☐
a. Inspect the protective clothing for proper operation. Does it operate properly? Yes ☐ No ☐	☐
b. Don (put on) the protective clothing. Have your supervisor/instructor verify that you did this properly. Supervisor's/instructor's initials: _____	☐
c. Doff (take off) the protective clothing. Have your supervisor/instructor verify that you did this properly. Supervisor's/instructor's initials: _____	☐
9. Select fire protection.	☐
a. Inspect the fire protection for proper operation. Does it operate properly? Yes ☐ No ☐	☐
b. Don (put on) the fire protection. Have your supervisor/instructor verify that you did this properly. Supervisor's/instructor's initials: _____	☐
c. Doff (take off) the fire protection. Have your supervisor/instructor verify that you did this properly. Supervisor's/instructor's initials: _____	☐
10. Select safety shoes.	☐
a. Inspect the safety shoes for proper operation. Do they operate properly? Yes ☐ No ☐	☐
b. Don (put on) the safety shoes. Have your supervisor/instructor verify that you did this properly. Supervisor's/instructor's initials: _____	☐
c. Doff (take off) the safety shoes. Have your supervisor/instructor verify that you did this properly. Supervisor's/instructor's initials: _____	☐

Non-Task-Specific Evaluation	Step Completed
1. Tools and equipment were used as directed and returned in good working order.	☐
2. Complied with all general and task-specific safety standards, including proper use of any PPE.	☐
3. Completed the task in an appropriate time frame (recommendation: 1.5 or 2 times the flat rate).	☐
4. Left the workspace clean and orderly.	☐
5. Cared for customer property and returned it undamaged.	☐

Student signature _____ Date _____

Comments:

Have your supervisor/instructor verify satisfactory completion of this procedure, any observations made, and any necessary action(s) recommended.

Evaluation Instructions: The scoring box below is intended to act as a guide for both student and supervisor/instructor. Each criterion listed will help students to understand what is expected of them and help supervisors/instructors to articulate the level of success at a particular task. The scoring is set up to allow a second attempt at each task (see the Test and Retest columns). Scoring is designed only to award students points for task criteria that were completed correctly. Points are lost for failure to complete the employability requirements (see Non-Task-Specific criteria). When all criteria are evaluated, tally the points for a total at the bottom of each column.

Tasksheet Scoring

Evaluation Items	Test		Retest	
	Pass	Fail	Pass	Fail
Task-Specific Evaluation	**(1 pt)**	**(0 pts)**	**(1 pt)**	**(0 pts)**
1. Student correctly demonstrated the use of at least two types of PPE.				
2. Student correctly demonstrated the use of at least four types of PPE.				
3. Student correctly demonstrated the use of at least seven types of PPE.				
4. Student correctly demonstrated the use of all 10 types of PPE.				
Non-Task-Specific Evaluation	**(0 pts)**	**(−1 pt)**	**(0 pts)**	**(−1 pt)**
Student successfully completed at least three of the non-task-specific steps.				
Student successfully completed all five of the non-task-specific steps.				
Total Score: <total # of points / 4 = %>				

Supervisor/Instructor:

Supervisor/instructor signature _____ Date _____

Comments:

> [blank comment box]

Retest supervisor/instructor signature _____ Date _____

Comments:

> [blank comment box]

CDX Tasksheet Number: 1a10004a

Student/Intern Information

Name _____ Date _____ Class _____

Machine, Customer, and Service Information

Machine used for this activity:

Make _____ Model _____

Hours _____ Serial Number _____

Task-Specific Safety Considerations
- Comply with personal and environmental safety practices associated with clothing; eye protection; hand tools; power equipment; proper ventilation; and the handling, storage, and disposal of chemicals/materials in accordance with local, state, and federal safety and environmental regulations.
- PPE allows us to increase our productivity and effectiveness. However, it can also cause severe injury or death if used improperly. Make sure you follow the manufacturer's procedures.

▶ TASK Identify the different types of fire extinguishers.

AED
1a.10

Time off_____

Time on_____

Total time_____

Student Instructions: Read through the entire procedure prior to starting. Prepare your workspace and any tools or parts that may be needed to complete the task. When directed by your supervisor/instructor, begin the procedure to complete the task, and comment or check the box as each step is finished. Track your time on this procedure for later comparison to the standard completion time (i.e., "flat rate" or customer pay time).

Procedure	Step Completed
1. Select Fire Extinguisher #1 and write its correct name below:	☐
2. Select Fire Extinguisher #2 and write its correct name below:	☐
3. Select Fire Extinguisher #3 and write its correct name below:	☐

	Step Completed
4. Select Fire Extinguisher #4 and write its correct name below:	☐
5. Select Fire Extinguisher #5 and write its correct name below:	☐
6. Select Fire Extinguisher #6 and write its correct name below:	☐
7. Select Fire Extinguisher #7 and write its correct name below:	☐

Non-Task-Specific Evaluation	Step Completed
1. Tools and equipment were used as directed and returned in good working order.	☐
2. Complied with all general and task-specific safety standards, including proper use of any PPE.	☐
3. Completed the task in an appropriate time frame (recommendation: 1.5 or 2 times the flat rate).	☐
4. Left the workspace clean and orderly.	☐
5. Cared for customer property and returned it undamaged.	☐

Student signature _____ Date _____

Comments:

Have your supervisor/instructor verify satisfactory completion of this procedure, any observations made, and any necessary action(s) recommended.

Evaluation Instructions: The scoring box below is intended to act as a guide for both student and supervisor/instructor. Each criterion listed will help students to understand what is expected of them and help supervisors/instructors to articulate the level of success at a particular task. The scoring is set up to allow a second attempt at each task (see the Test and Retest columns). Scoring is designed only to award students points for task criteria that were completed correctly. Points are lost for failure to complete the employability requirements (see Non-Task-Specific criteria). When all criteria are evaluated, tally the points for a total at the bottom of each column.

Tasksheet Scoring

Evaluation Items	Test		Retest	
	Pass	Fail	Pass	Fail
Task-Specific Evaluation	**(1 pt)**	**(0 pts)**	**(1 pt)**	**(0 pts)**
1. Student correctly identified at least one type of fire extinguisher.				
2. Student correctly identified at least three types of fire extinguishers.				
3. Student correctly identified at least five types of fire extinguishers.				
4. Student correctly identified all seven types of fire extinguishers.				
Non-Task-Specific Evaluation	**(0 pts)**	**(−1 pt)**	**(0 pts)**	**(−1 pt)**
Student successfully completed at least three of the non-task-specific steps.				
Student successfully completed all five of the non-task-specific steps.				
Total Score: <total # of points / 4 = %>				

Supervisor/Instructor:

Supervisor/instructor signature _____ Date _____

Comments:

```



```

Retest supervisor/instructor signature _____ Date _____

Comments:

```



```

CDX Tasksheet Number: 1a10004b

Student/Intern Information

Name _____ Date _____ Class _____

Machine, Customer, and Service Information

Machine used for this activity:

Make _____ Model _____

Hours _____ Serial Number _____

Materials Required
- Fire extinguishers (types A, B, C, D, and K)
- Personal protection equipment (PPE)

Task-Specific Safety Considerations
- Comply with personal and environmental safety practices associated with clothing; eye protection; hand tools; power equipment; proper ventilation; and the handling, storage, and disposal of chemicals/materials in accordance with local, state, and federal safety and environmental regulations.
- PPE allows us to increase our productivity and effectiveness. However, it can also cause severe injury or death if used improperly. Make sure you follow the manufacturer's procedures.

▶ TASK Demonstrate the use of different types of fire extinguishers.

AED
1a.10

Time off_____

Time on_____

Total time_____

Student Instructions: Read through the entire procedure prior to starting. Prepare your workspace and any tools or parts that may be needed to complete the task. When directed by your supervisor/instructor, begin the procedure to complete the task, and comment or check the box as each step is finished. Track your time on this procedure for later comparison to the standard completion time (i.e., "flat rate" or customer pay time).

Procedure	Step Completed
1. Select the type of fire extinguisher used to put out fires on combustibles such as wood and paper. Demonstrate its proper use. Have your supervisor/instructor verify satisfactory completion of these procedures. Supervisor's/instructor's initials: _____	☐

2. Select the type of fire extinguisher used to put out fires on flammable liquids such as grease, gasoline, and oil. Demonstrate its proper use. Have your supervisor/instructor verify satisfactory completion of these procedures. Supervisor's/instructor's initials: _____	☐
3. Select the type of fire extinguisher used to put out electrically energized fires. Demonstrate its proper use. Have your supervisor/instructor verify satisfactory completion of these procedures. Supervisor's/instructor's initials: _____	☐
4. Select the type of fire extinguisher used for metal fires. Demonstrate its proper use. Have your supervisor/instructor verify satisfactory completion of these procedures. Supervisor's/instructor's initials: _____	☐
5. Select the type of fire extinguisher used for cooking fires. Demonstrate its proper use. Have your supervisor/instructor verify satisfactory completion of these procedures. Supervisor's/instructor's initials: _____	☐

Non-Task-Specific Evaluation	Step Completed
1. Tools and equipment were used as directed and returned in good working order.	☐
2. Complied with all general and task-specific safety standards, including proper use of any PPE.	☐
3. Completed the task in an appropriate time frame (recommendation: 1.5 or 2 times the flat rate).	☐
4. Left the workspace clean and orderly.	☐
5. Cared for customer property and returned it undamaged.	☐

Student signature _____ Date _____

Comments:

Have your supervisor/instructor verify satisfactory completion of this procedure, any observations made,

and any necessary action(s) recommended.

Evaluation Instructions: The scoring box below is intended to act as a guide for both student and supervisor/instructor. Each criterion listed will help students to understand what is expected of them and help supervisors/instructors to articulate the level of success at a particular task. The scoring is set up to allow a second attempt at each task (see the Test and Retest columns). Scoring is designed only to award students points for task criteria that were completed correctly. Points are lost for failure to complete the employability requirements (see Non-Task-Specific criteria). When all criteria are evaluated, tally the points for a total at the bottom of each column.

Tasksheet Scoring

Evaluation Items	Test		Retest	
	Pass	**Fail**	**Pass**	**Fail**
Task-Specific Evaluation	**(1 pt)**	**(0 pts)**	**(1 pt)**	**(0 pts)**
1. Student selected the correct type of fire extinguisher for at least two of the given scenarios.				
2. Student selected the correct type of fire extinguisher for all five scenarios.				
3. Student correctly demonstrated the use of at least two fire extinguishers.				
4. Student correctly demonstrated the use of all five fire extinguishers.				
Non-Task-Specific Evaluation	**(0 pts)**	**(−1 pt)**	**(0 pts)**	**(−1 pt)**
Student successfully completed at least three of the non-task-specific steps.				
Student successfully completed all five of the non-task-specific steps.				
Total Score: <total # of points / 4 = %>				

Supervisor/Instructor:

Supervisor/instructor signature _____ Date _____

Comments:

Retest supervisor/instructor signature _____ Date _____

Comments:

CDX Tasksheet Number: 1a10005

Student/Intern Information

Name _____ Date _____ Class _____

Machine, Customer, and Service Information

Machine used for this activity:

Make _____ Model _____

Hours _____ Serial Number _____

Materials Required

- Program's shop policy and other safety information
- 12 various shop products that require safety data sheets (SDS) chosen by the supervisor/instructor to complete the task
- SDS for each product
- Personal protection equipment (PPE)

Task-Specific Safety Considerations

- Comply with personal and environmental safety practices associated with clothing; eye protection; hand tools; power equipment; proper ventilation; and the handling, storage, and disposal of chemicals/materials in accordance with local, state, and federal safety and environmental regulations.
- PPE allows us to increase our productivity and effectiveness. However, it can also cause severe injury or death if used improperly. Make sure you follow the manufacturer's procedures.

▶ **TASK** Utilize SDS for products.

AED
1a.10

Time off_____

Time on_____

Total time_____

Student Instructions: Read through the entire procedure prior to starting. Prepare your workspace and any tools or parts that may be needed to complete the task. When directed by your supervisor/instructor, begin the procedure to complete the task, and comment or check the box as each step is finished. Track your time on this procedure for later comparison to the standard completion time (i.e., "flat rate" or customer pay time).

Procedure	Step Completed
1. Using Product #1 and your shop procedure, locate the product's SDS. Using the SDS, locate the product's latest revision date and list it below:	☐

2. Using Product #2 and your shop procedure, locate the product's SDS. Using the SDS, locate the product's correct name and any synonyms and list them below:	☐
3. Using Product #3 and your shop procedure, locate the product's SDS. Using the SDS, locate the specific hazards posed by this product and the precautions you can take to avoid exposure and list them below:	☐
4. Using Product #4 and your shop procedure, locate the product's SDS. If exposure is possible with this product, use the SDS to identify the symptoms of exposure and the proper first aid measures for each exposure route and list them below:	☐
5. Using Product #5 and your shop procedure, locate the product's SDS. If this product is flammable, use the SDS to identify the flammability risks, precautions, and firefighting equipment used to extinguish a fire and list them below:	☐
6. Using Product #6 and your shop procedure, locate the product's SDS. Using the SDS, identify the precautions to take to avoid accidental exposure and list them below:	☐
7. Using Product #7 and your shop procedure, locate the product's SDS. Using the SDS, identify the proper storage and handling techniques associated with the product and list them below:	☐
8. Using Product #8 and your shop procedure, locate the product's SDS. Using the SDS, identify the upper and lower exposure limits and how to prevent exposure in the workplace and list them below:	☐

9. Using Product #9 and your shop procedure, locate the product's SDS. Using the SDS, identify the reactivity of the product and how to prevent it from reacting with other products and list both below:	☐
10. Using Product #10 and your shop procedure, locate the product's SDS. Using the SDS, identify the symptoms to be expected from varying exposure routes and list them below:	☐
11. Using Product #11 and your shop procedure, locate the product's SDS. Using the SDS, identify the proper disposal of the product or its container and list the process below:	☐
12. Using Product #12 and your shop procedure, locate the product's SDS. Using the SDS, identify if the product is harmful to aquatic life and note the details below:	☐

Non-Task-Specific Evaluation	Step Completed
1. Tools and equipment were used as directed and returned in good working order.	☐
2. Complied with all general and task-specific safety standards, including proper use of any PPE.	☐
3. Completed the task in an appropriate time frame (recommendation: 1.5 or 2 times the flat rate).	☐
4. Left the workspace clean and orderly.	☐
5. Cared for customer property and returned it undamaged.	☐

Student signature _____ Date _____

Comments:

Have your supervisor/instructor verify satisfactory completion of this procedure, any observations made, and any necessary action(s) recommended.

Evaluation Instructions: The scoring box below is intended to act as a guide for both student and supervisor/instructor. Each criterion listed will help students to understand what is expected of them and help supervisors/instructors to articulate the level of success at a particular task. The scoring is set up to allow a second attempt at each task (see the Test and Retest columns). Scoring is designed only to award students points for task criteria that were completed correctly. Points are lost for failure to complete the employability requirements (see Non-Task-Specific criteria). When all criteria are evaluated, tally the points for a total at the bottom of each column.

Tasksheet Scoring

Evaluation Items	Test		Retest	
	Pass	Fail	Pass	Fail
Task-Specific Evaluation	**(1 pt)**	**(0 pts)**	**(1 pt)**	**(0 pts)**
1. Student correctly located and identified SDS information for at least three products.				
2. Student correctly located and identified SDS information for at least six products.				
3. Student correctly located and identified SDS information for at least nine products.				
4. Student correctly located and identified SDS information for all 12 products.				
Non-Task-Specific Evaluation	**(0 pts)**	**(−1 pt)**	**(0 pts)**	**(−1 pt)**
Student successfully completed at least three of the non-task-specific steps.				
Student successfully completed all five of the non-task-specific steps.				
Total Score: <total # of points / 4 = %>				

Supervisor/Instructor:

Supervisor/instructor signature _____ Date _____

Comments:

Retest supervisor/instructor signature _____ Date _____

Comments:

CDX Tasksheet Number: 1a10006

Student/Intern Information

Name _____ Date _____ Class _____

Machine, Customer, and Service Information

Machine used for this activity:

Make _____ Model _____

Hours _____ Serial Number _____

Materials Required
- Location's/region's utility location protocol
- Personal protection equipment (PPE)

Task-Specific Safety Considerations
- Comply with personal and environmental safety practices associated with clothing; eye protection; hand tools; power equipment; proper ventilation; and the handling, storage, and disposal of chemicals/materials in accordance with local, state, and federal safety and environmental regulations.
- PPE allows us to increase our productivity and effectiveness. However, it can also cause severe injury or death if used improperly. Make sure you follow the manufacturer's procedures.

▶ **TASK** Identify underground utility hazard marking commonly encountered on a job site.

AED
1a.10

Time off_____

Time on_____

Student Instructions: Read through the entire procedure prior to starting. Prepare your workspace and any tools or parts that may be needed to complete the task. When directed by your supervisor/instructor, begin the procedure to complete the task, and comment or check the box as each step is finished. Track your time on this procedure for later comparison to the standard completion time (i.e., "flat rate" or customer pay time).

Total time_____

Procedure	Step Completed
1. Identify the color code marking for electric power lines, cables, conduit, or lighting cables and write it below:	☐

2. Identify the color code marking for telecommunication, alarm/signal lines, cables, or conduit and write it below:	☐
3. Identify the color code marking for natural gas, oil, steam, petroleum, or other gaseous/flammable material and write it below:	☐
4. Identify the color code marking for sewers and drain lines and write it below:	☐
5. Identify the color code marking for drinking water and write it below:	☐
6. Identify the color code marking for reclaimed water, irrigation, or slurry lines and list it below:	☐
7. Identify the color code marking for temporary survey markings or unknown/unidentified facilities and list it below:	☐
8. Identify the color code marking for proposed excavation limits or routes and list it below:	☐

Non-Task-Specific Evaluation	Step Completed
1. Tools and equipment were used as directed and returned in good working order.	☐
2. Complied with all general and task-specific safety standards, including proper use of any PPE.	☐
3. Completed the task in an appropriate time frame (recommendation: 1.5 or 2 times the flat rate).	☐
4. Left the workspace clean and orderly.	☐
5. Cared for customer property and returned it undamaged.	☐

Student signature _____ Date _____

Comments:

Have your supervisor/instructor verify satisfactory completion of this procedure, any observations made,

and any necessary action(s) recommended.

Evaluation Instructions: The scoring box below is intended to act as a guide for both student and supervisor/instructor. Each criterion listed will help students to understand what is expected of them and help supervisors/instructors to articulate the level of success at a particular task. The scoring is set up to allow a second attempt at each task (see the Test and Retest columns). Scoring is designed only to award students points for task criteria that were completed correctly. Points are lost for failure to complete the employability requirements (see Non-Task-Specific criteria). When all criteria are evaluated, tally the points for a total at the bottom of each column.

Tasksheet Scoring

Evaluation Items	Test		Retest	
	Pass	Fail	Pass	Fail
Task-Specific Evaluation	**(1 pt)**	**(0 pts)**	**(1 pt)**	**(0 pts)**
1. Student correctly identified at least two underground utility hazard markings.				
2. Student correctly identified at least four underground utility hazard markings.				
3. Student correctly identified at least six underground utility hazard markings.				
4. Student correctly identified all eight underground utility hazard markings.				
Non-Task-Specific Evaluation	**(0 pts)**	**(−1 pt)**	**(0 pts)**	**(−1 pt)**
Student successfully completed at least three of the non-task-specific steps.				
Student successfully completed all five of the non-task-specific steps.				
Total Score: <total # of points / 4 = %>				

Chapter 11: Shop and In-Field Practices

Learning Objective/Task	CDX Tasksheet Number	AED Reference Number
• Identify safe work practices in the shop and in-field.	1a11001	AED 1a.11
• Demonstrate safe work practices in the shop or in the field.	1a11002	AED 1a.11
• Demonstrate proper lifting and pulling techniques.	1a11004	AED 1a.11
• Demonstrate proper shop/facility cleanliness/appearance to dealer standards.	1a11005	AED 1a.11
• Identify potential hazards and develop a plan to deal with them.	1a11006	AED 1a.11

Materials Required

- Program's shop policy and other safety information
- Safety data sheets (SDS)
- Personal protective equipment (PPE)
- Items for lifting demonstration (starter, large box, cylinder, etc.)
- Items for pulling/pushing demonstration
- Manufacturer's housekeeping standards
- Shop cleaning equipment and supplies
- Manufacturer's service information

Safety Considerations

- Comply with personal and environmental safety practices associated with clothing; eye protection; hand tools; power equipment; proper ventilation; and the handling, storage, and disposal of chemicals/materials in accordance with local, state, and federal safety and environmental regulations.
- PPE allows us to increase our productivity and effectiveness. However, it can also cause severe injury or death if used improperly. Make sure you follow the manufacturer's procedures.

CDX Tasksheet Number: 1a11001

Student/Intern Information

Name _____ Date _____ Class _____

Machine, Customer, and Service Information

Machine used for this activity:

Make _____ Model _____

Hours _____ Serial Number _____

Materials Required
- Program's shop policy and other safety information
- Safety data sheets (SDS)
- Personal protective equipment (PPE)

Task-Specific Safety Considerations
- Comply with personal and environmental safety practices associated with clothing; eye protection; hand tools; power equipment; proper ventilation; and the handling, storage, and disposal of chemicals/materials in accordance with local, state, and federal safety and environmental regulations.
- PPE allows us to increase our productivity and effectiveness. However, it can also cause severe injury or death if used improperly. Make sure you follow the manufacturer's procedures.

▶ **TASK** Identify safe work practices in the shop and in-field.

AED
1a.11

Time off_____

Time on_____

Total time_____

Student Instructions: Read through the entire procedure prior to starting. Prepare your workspace and any tools or parts that may be needed to complete the task. When directed by your supervisor/instructor, begin the procedure to complete the task, and comment or check the box as each step is finished. Track your time on this procedure for later comparison to the standard completion time (i.e., "flat rate" or customer pay time).

Procedure	Step Completed
1. Locate the shop's general safety rules and procedures and write the location below:	☐

2. Locate the shop's SDS and write the location below:	☐
3. Locate the shop's fire extinguishers and list the locations below:	☐
4. Locate the shop's policy for wearing safety glasses while in the shop and list it below:	☐
5. Locate the shop's policy for operating machines/equipment and list it below:	☐
6. Locate the shop's policy for type of clothing in the shop and list it below:	☐
7. Locate the shop's policy for jewelry in the shop and list it below:	☐
8. Identify the uniform color code system used to designate safety areas in a shop. List each color and its designation below: Color: _____ designates: _____ Color: _____ designates: _____ Color: _____ designates: _____ Color: _____ designates: _____	☐
9. Locate the eyewash stations in your shop and list their locations below:	☐
10. Identify the purpose of the eyewash stations and write it below:	☐

11. Describe the situations when an eyewash station should be used and the proper procedures for its use and list them below:	☐
12. Describe what type of eye injury would not require the use of an eyewash station below:	☐
13. Locate and identify the purpose of evacuation routes and write it below:	☐
14. Identify the hazardous environments in the shop and the actions and procedures that should be taken in an emergency and list them below:	☐
15. Identify the shop's policies regarding the safe disposal of hazardous waste and list them below:	☐

Non-Task-Specific Evaluation	Step Completed
1. Tools and equipment were used as directed and returned in good working order.	☐
2. Complied with all general and task-specific safety standards, including proper use of any PPE.	☐
3. Completed the task in an appropriate time frame (recommendation: 1.5 or 2 times the flat rate).	☐
4. Left the workspace clean and orderly.	☐
5. Cared for customer property and returned it undamaged.	☐

Student signature _____ Date _____

Comments:

Have your supervisor/instructor verify satisfactory completion of this procedure, any observations made, and any necessary action(s) recommended.

Evaluation Instructions: The scoring box below is intended to act as a guide for both student and supervisor/instructor. Each criterion listed will help students to understand what is expected of them and help supervisors/instructors to articulate the level of success at a particular task. The scoring is set up to allow a second attempt at each task (see the Test and Retest columns). Scoring is designed only to award students points for task criteria that were completed correctly. Points are lost for failure to complete the employability requirements (see Non-Task-Specific criteria). When all criteria are evaluated, tally the points for a total at the bottom of each column.

Tasksheet Scoring

	Test		Retest	
Evaluation Items	**Pass**	**Fail**	**Pass**	**Fail**
Task-Specific Evaluation	**(1 pt)**	**(0 pts)**	**(1 pt)**	**(0 pts)**
1. Student correctly located at least half of the named materials/policies/shop areas.				
2. Student correctly located all of the named materials/policies/shop areas.				
3. Student correctly identified at least half of the safe work practices.				
4. Student correctly identified all of the safe work practices.				
Non-Task-Specific Evaluation	**(0 pts)**	**(−1 pt)**	**(0 pts)**	**(−1 pt)**
Student successfully completed at least three of the non-task-specific steps.				
Student successfully completed all five of the non-task-specific steps.				
Total Score: <total # of points / 4 = %>				

Supervisor/Instructor:

Supervisor/instructor signature _____ Date _____

Comments:

| |
| |

Retest supervisor/instructor signature _____ Date _____

Comments:

| |
| |

CDX Tasksheet Number: 1a11002

Student/Intern Information

Name _____ Date _____ Class _____

Machine, Customer, and Service Information

Machine used for this activity:

Make _____ Model _____

Hours _____ Serial Number _____

Materials Required
- Program's shop policy and other safety information
- Safety data sheets (SDS)
- Personal protective equipment (PPE)

Task-Specific Safety Considerations
- Comply with personal and environmental safety practices associated with clothing; eye protection; hand tools; power equipment; proper ventilation; and the handling, storage, and disposal of chemicals/materials in accordance with local, state, and federal safety and environmental regulations.
- PPE allows us to increase our productivity and effectiveness. However, it can also cause severe injury or death if used improperly. Make sure you follow the manufacturer's procedures.

▶ TASK Demonstrate safe work practices in the shop or in the field. **AED 1a.11**

Time off_____

Time on_____

Student Instructions: Read through the entire procedure prior to starting. Prepare your workspace and any tools or parts that may be needed to complete the task. When directed by your supervisor/instructor, begin the procedure to complete the task, and comment or check the box as each step is finished. Track your time on this procedure for later comparison to the standard completion time (i.e., "flat rate" or customer pay time).

Total time_____

Procedure	Step Completed
1. List the shop's general safety procedures for PPE required when performing general duties in the shop or in the field below:	☐

a. Demonstrate the procedures. Have your supervisor/instructor verify satisfactory completion of these procedures. Supervisor's/instructor's initials: _____	☐
2. List the shop's general safety procedures for PPE required when performing welding, torching, and grinding duties in the shop or in the field below:	☐
a. Demonstrate the procedures. Have your supervisor/instructor verify satisfactory completion of these procedures. Supervisor's/instructor's initials: _____	☐
3. List the shop's safety procedures for PPE required when working in dusty conditions in the shop or in the field below:	☐
a. Demonstrate the procedures. Have your supervisor/instructor verify satisfactory completion of these procedures. Supervisor's/instructor's initials: _____	☐
4. List the shop's safety procedures for PPE required when using a bench grinder in the shop or in the field below:	☐
a. Demonstrate the procedures. Have your supervisor/instructor verify satisfactory completion of these procedures. Supervisor's/instructor's initials: _____	☐
5. List the shop's safety procedures for hazard assessment and control for each of the following, then demonstrate the procedures for your supervisor/instructor.	
a. Blocked emergency exits	
i. Shop's safety procedures:	☐
ii. Demonstrate the procedures. Have your supervisor/instructor verify satisfactory completion of these procedures. Supervisor's/instructor's initials: _____	☐

b. Blocked walkways	
i. Shop's safety procedures:	☐
ii. Demonstrate the procedures. Have your supervisor/instructor verify satisfactory completion of these procedures. Supervisor's/instructor's initials: _____	☐
c. Poor safety signage	
i. Shop's safety procedures:	☐
ii. Demonstrate the procedures. Have your supervisor/instructor verify satisfactory completion of these procedures. Supervisor's/instructor's initials: _____	☐
d. Unsafe storage of flammable goods	
i. Shop's safety procedures:	☐
ii. Demonstrate the procedures. Have your supervisor/instructor verify satisfactory completion of these procedures. Supervisor's/instructor's initials: _____	☐
e. Tripping hazards	
i. Shop's safety procedures:	☐
ii. Demonstrate the procedures. Have your supervisor/instructor verify satisfactory completion of these procedures. Supervisor's/instructor's initials: _____	☐
f. Slipping hazards	
i. Shop's safety procedures:	☐

ii. Demonstrate the procedures. Have your supervisor/instructor verify satisfactory completion of these procedures. Supervisor's/instructor's initials: _____	☐
g. Faulty/unsafe equipment	
i. Shop's safety procedures:	☐
ii. Demonstrate the procedures. Have your supervisor/instructor verify satisfactory completion of these procedures. Supervisor's/instructor's initials: _____	
h. Faulty/unsafe tooling	
i. Shop's safety procedures:	☐
ii. Demonstrate the procedures. Have your supervisor/instructor verify satisfactory completion of these procedures. Supervisor's/instructor's initials: _____	☐
i. Missing fire extinguishers	
i. Shop's safety procedures:	☐
ii. Demonstrate the procedures. Have your supervisor/instructor verify satisfactory completion of these procedures. Supervisor's/instructor's initials: _____	☐
j. Clutter	
i. Shop's safety procedures:	☐
ii. Demonstrate the procedures. Have your supervisor/instructor verify satisfactory completion of these procedures. Supervisor's/instructor's initials: _____	☐

k. Spills	
i. Shop's safety procedures:	☐
ii. Demonstrate the procedures. Have your supervisor/instructor verify satisfactory completion of these procedures. Supervisor's/instructor's initials: _____	☐
l. PPE	
i. Shop's safety procedures:	☐
ii. Demonstrate the procedures. Have your supervisor/instructor verify satisfactory completion of these procedures. Supervisor's/instructor's initials: _____	☐

Non-Task-Specific Evaluation	Step Completed
1. Tools and equipment were used as directed and returned in good working order.	☐
2. Complied with all general and task-specific safety standards, including proper use of any PPE.	☐
3. Completed the task in an appropriate time frame (recommendation: 1.5 or 2 times the flat rate).	☐
4. Left the workspace clean and orderly.	☐
5. Cared for customer property and returned it undamaged.	☐

Student signature _____ Date _____

Comments:

Have your supervisor/instructor verify satisfactory completion of this procedure, any observations made,

and any necessary action(s) recommended.

Evaluation Instructions: The scoring box below is intended to act as a guide for both student and supervisor/instructor. Each criterion listed will help students to understand what is expected of them and help supervisors/instructors to articulate the level of success at a particular task. The scoring is set up to allow a second attempt at each task (see the Test and Retest columns). Scoring is designed only to award students points for task criteria that were completed correctly. Points are lost for failure to complete the employability requirements (see Non-Task-Specific criteria). When all criteria are evaluated, tally the points for a total at the bottom of each column.

Tasksheet Scoring

	Test		Retest	
Evaluation Items	**Pass**	**Fail**	**Pass**	**Fail**
Task-Specific Evaluation	**(1 pt)**	**(0 pts)**	**(1 pt)**	**(0 pts)**
1. Student correctly listed the safety procedures for at least eight of the given scenarios.				
2. Student correctly listed the safety procedures for all 16 of the given scenarios.				
3. Student correctly demonstrated the safety procedures for at least eight of the given scenarios.				
4. Student correctly demonstrated the safety procedures for all 16 of the given scenarios.				
Non-Task-Specific Evaluation	**(0 pts)**	**(−1 pt)**	**(0 pts)**	**(−1 pt)**
Student successfully completed at least three of the non-task-specific steps.				
Student successfully completed all five of the non-task-specific steps.				
Total Score: <total # of points / 4 = %>				

Supervisor/Instructor:

Supervisor/instructor signature _____ Date _____

Comments:

Retest supervisor/instructor signature _____ Date _____

Comments:

CDX Tasksheet Number: 1a11004

Student/Intern Information

Name _____ Date _____ Class _____

Machine, Customer, and Service Information

Machine used for this activity:

Make _____ Model _____

Hours _____ Serial Number _____

Materials Required
- Items for lifting demonstration (starter, large box, cylinder, etc.)
- Items for pulling/pushing demonstration
- Personal protective equipment (PPE)

Task-Specific Safety Considerations
- Comply with personal and environmental safety practices associated with clothing; eye protection; hand tools; power equipment; proper ventilation; and the handling, storage, and disposal of chemicals/materials in accordance with local, state, and federal safety and environmental regulations.
- PPE allows us to increase our productivity and effectiveness. However, it can also cause severe injury or death if used improperly. Make sure you follow the manufacturer's procedures.

▶ **TASK** Demonstrate proper lifting and pulling techniques. **AED 1a.11**

Time off_____

Time on_____

Student Instructions: Read through the entire procedure prior to starting. Prepare your workspace and any tools or parts that may be needed to complete the task. When directed by your supervisor/instructor, begin the procedure to complete the task, and comment or check the box as each step is finished. Track your time on this procedure for later comparison to the standard completion time (i.e., "flat rate" or customer pay time).

Total time_____

Procedure	Step Completed
1. Lift a heavy item off the ground and place it on a bench. Have your supervisor/instructor verify satisfactory use of the proper technique. Supervisor's/instructor's initials: _____	☐
2. Lift a heavy item off the ground with a partner. Have your supervisor/instructor verify satisfactory use of the proper technique. Supervisor's/instructor's initials: _____	☐

	Step Completed
3. Push a heavy load. Have your supervisor/instructor verify satisfactory use of the proper technique. Supervisor's/instructor's initials: _____	☐
4. Pull a heavy load. Have your supervisor/instructor verify satisfactory use of the proper technique. Supervisor's/instructor's initials: _____	☐

Non-Task-Specific Evaluation	Step Completed
1. Tools and equipment were used as directed and returned in good working order.	☐
2. Complied with all general and task-specific safety standards, including proper use of any PPE.	☐
3. Completed the task in an appropriate time frame (recommendation: 1.5 or 2 times the flat rate).	☐
4. Left the workspace clean and orderly.	☐
5. Cared for customer property and returned it undamaged.	☐

Student signature _____ Date _____

Comments:

Have your supervisor/instructor verify satisfactory completion of this procedure, any observations made, and any necessary action(s) recommended.

Evaluation Instructions: The scoring box below is intended to act as a guide for both student and supervisor/instructor. Each criterion listed will help students to understand what is expected of them and help supervisors/instructors to articulate the level of success at a particular task. The scoring is set up to allow a second attempt at each task (see the Test and Retest columns). Scoring is designed only to award students points for task criteria that were completed correctly. Points are lost for failure to complete the employability requirements (see Non-Task-Specific criteria). When all criteria are evaluated, tally the points for a total at the bottom of each column.

Tasksheet Scoring

Evaluation Items	Test		Retest	
	Pass	**Fail**	**Pass**	**Fail**
Task-Specific Evaluation	**(1 pt)**	**(0 pts)**	**(1 pt)**	**(0 pts)**
1. Student lifted a heavy item off the ground and placed it on a bench using the proper technique.				
2. Student lifted a heavy item off the ground with a partner using the proper technique.				
3. Student pushed a heavy load using the proper technique.				
4. Student pulled a heavy load using the proper technique.				
Non-Task-Specific Evaluation	**(0 pts)**	**(−1 pt)**	**(0 pts)**	**(−1 pt)**
Student successfully completed at least three of the non-task-specific steps.				
Student successfully completed all five of the non-task-specific steps.				
Total Score: <total # of points / 4 = %>				

Supervisor/Instructor:

Supervisor/instructor signature _____ Date _____

Comments:

Retest supervisor/instructor signature _____ Date _____

Comments:

CDX Tasksheet Number: 1a11005

Student/Intern Information

Name _____ Date _____ Class _____

Machine, Customer, and Service Information

Machine used for this activity:

Make _____ Model _____

Hours _____ Serial Number _____

Materials Required

- Manufacturer's housekeeping standards
- Shop cleaning equipment and supplies
- Personal protective equipment (PPE)

Task-Specific Safety Considerations

- Comply with personal and environmental safety practices associated with clothing; eye protection; hand tools; power equipment; proper ventilation; and the handling, storage, and disposal of chemicals/materials in accordance with local, state, and federal safety and environmental regulations.
- PPE allows us to increase our productivity and effectiveness. However, it can also cause severe injury or death if used improperly. Make sure you follow the manufacturer's procedures.

▶ TASK Demonstrate proper shop/facility cleanliness/appearance to dealer standards.

AED
1a.11

Time off_____

Time on_____

Student Instructions: Read through the entire procedure prior to starting. Prepare your workspace and any tools or parts that may be needed to complete the task. When directed by your supervisor/instructor, begin the procedure to complete the task, and comment or check the box as each step is finished. Track your time on this procedure for later comparison to the standard completion time (i.e., "flat rate" or customer pay time).

Total time_____

Procedure	Step Completed
(**Note:** These tasks require observation of the student over a prolonged period. Your supervisor/instructor will evaluate your performance on a continued basis.)	
1. Wash all machines before entering the shop.	☐
2. Clean shop floors at least daily.	☐
3. Keep walkways clearly marked and clear of obstructions.	☐

	Step Completed
4. Clean liquid spills up immediately.	☐
5. Keep walls, doors, tools, and storage areas clean.	☐
6. Keep any work-in-progress clean and contamination free.	☐
7. Keep wash tanks clean and liquid filtered.	☐
8. Protect components with caps and plugs.	☐
9. Keep hoses, light cords, and extension cords clean and orderly.	☐
10. Filter new oil coming in from bulk tanks.	☐
11. Filter used oil before refilling the machine.	☐
12. Keep parts in packaging until installed.	☐
13. Keep shelves and benches clean and contamination free.	☐
14. Perform fluid sampling as part of services.	☐
15. Perform particle counting for incoming fluids.	☐

Non-Task-Specific Evaluation	Step Completed
1. Tools and equipment were used as directed and returned in good working order.	☐
2. Complied with all general and task-specific safety standards, including proper use of any PPE.	☐
3. Completed the task in an appropriate time frame (recommendation: 1.5 or 2 times the flat rate).	☐
4. Left the workspace clean and orderly.	☐
5. Cared for customer property and returned it undamaged.	☐

Student signature _____ Date _____

Comments:

Have your supervisor/instructor verify satisfactory completion of this procedure, any observations made, and any necessary action(s) recommended.

Evaluation Instructions: The scoring box below is intended to act as a guide for both student and supervisor/instructor. Each criterion listed will help students to understand what is expected of them and help supervisors/instructors to articulate the level of success at a particular task. The scoring is set up to allow a second attempt at each task (see the Test and Retest columns). Scoring is designed only to award students points for task criteria that were completed correctly. Points are lost for failure to complete the employability requirements (see Non-Task-Specific criteria). When all criteria are evaluated, tally the points for a total at the bottom of each column.

Tasksheet Scoring

Evaluation Items	Test		Retest	
	Pass	Fail	Pass	Fail
Task-Specific Evaluation	**(1 pt)**	**(0 pts)**	**(1 pt)**	**(0 pts)**
1. Student demonstrated proper cleanliness/ appearance around the shop for at least three of the listed items.				
2. Student demonstrated proper cleanliness/ appearance around the shop for at least seven of the listed items.				
3. Student demonstrated proper cleanliness/ appearance around the shop for at least 11 of the listed items.				
4. Student demonstrated proper cleanliness/ appearance around the shop for all 15 of the listed items.				
Non-Task-Specific Evaluation	**(0 pts)**	**(−1 pt)**	**(0 pts)**	**(−1 pt)**
Student successfully completed at least three of the non-task-specific steps.				
Student successfully completed all five of the non-task-specific steps.				
Total Score: <total # of points / 4 = %>				

Supervisor/Instructor:

Supervisor/instructor signature _____ Date _____

Comments:

Retest supervisor/instructor signature _____ Date _____

Comments:

CDX Tasksheet Number: 1a11006

Student/Intern Information

Name _____ Date _____ Class _____

Machine, Customer, and Service Information

Machine used for this activity:

Make _____ Model _____

Hours _____ Serial Number _____

Materials Required
- Manufacturer's service information
- Personal protective equipment (PPE)

Task-Specific Safety Considerations
- Comply with personal and environmental safety practices associated with clothing; eye protection; hand tools; power equipment; proper ventilation; and the handling, storage, and disposal of chemicals/materials in accordance with local, state, and federal safety and environmental regulations.
- PPE allows us to increase our productivity and effectiveness safely. However, they must be used according to the manufacturer's procedures. Failure to follow those procedures can result in serious injury or death.

▶ **TASK** Identify potential hazards and develop a plan to deal with them. **AED** *1a.11*

Time off_____

Time on_____

Total time_____

Student Instructions: Read through the entire procedure prior to starting. Prepare your workspace and any tools or parts that may be needed to complete the task. When directed by your supervisor/instructor, begin the procedure to complete the task, and comment or check the box as each step is finished. Track your time on this procedure for later comparison to the standard completion time (i.e., "flat rate" or customer pay time).

Procedure	Step Completed
1. Research a task assigned by your supervisor/instructor using the manufacturer's service information.	☐
2. List the key areas called out in the task that are potentially hazardous below:	☐

	Step Completed
3. List the procedures and tooling/equipment the manufacturer recommends for proper hazard prevention below:	☐
4. Examine the manufacturer's steps and determine whether any additional hazards may need to be addressed and prevented, then list them below:	☐
5. Using the manufacturer's service information and your examination of the hazards of the task, develop a plan to deal with them, and write the plan in your own words below:	☐

Non-Task-Specific Evaluation	Step Completed
1. Tools and equipment were used as directed and returned in good working order.	☐
2. Complied with all general and task-specific safety standards, including proper use of any PPE.	☐
3. Completed the task in an appropriate time frame (recommendation: 1.5 or 2 times the flat rate).	☐
4. Left the workspace clean and orderly.	☐
5. Cared for customer property and returned it undamaged.	☐

Student signature _____ Date _____

Comments:

Have your supervisor/instructor verify satisfactory completion of this procedure, any observations made, and any necessary action(s) recommended.

Evaluation Instructions: The scoring box below is intended to act as a guide for both student and supervisor/instructor. Each criterion listed will help students to understand what is expected of them and help supervisors/instructors to articulate the level of success at a particular task. The scoring is set up to allow a second attempt at each task (see the Test and Retest columns). Scoring is designed only to award students points for task criteria that were completed correctly. Points are lost for failure to complete the employability requirements (see Non-Task-Specific criteria). When all criteria are evaluated, tally the points for a total at the bottom of each column.

Tasksheet Scoring

	Test		Retest	
Evaluation Items	**Pass**	**Fail**	**Pass**	**Fail**
Task-Specific Evaluation	**(1 pt)**	**(0 pts)**	**(1 pt)**	**(0 pts)**
1. Student listed the key areas called out in the task that are potentially hazardous.				
2. Student correctly listed the procedures and tooling/equipment recommended by the manufacturer for proper hazard prevention.				
3. Student correctly examined the manufacturer's steps and determined whether any additional hazards may need to be addressed and prevented.				
4. Student correctly used the manufacturer's service information and their own examination of the hazards of the task to develop a plan to deal with them and documented the plan in their own words.				

Non-Task-Specific Evaluation	(0 pts)	(−1 pt)	(0 pts)	(−1 pt)
Student successfully completed at least three of the non-task-specific steps.				
Student successfully completed all five of the non-task-specific steps.				
Total Score: \<total # of points / 4 = %\>				

Supervisor/Instructor:

Supervisor/instructor signature _____ Date _____

Comments:

Retest supervisor/instructor signature _____ Date _____

Comments:

Chapter 12: Hazard Identification and Prevention

Learning Objective/Task	CDX Tasksheet Number	AED Reference Number
• Demonstrate safe mounting and dismounting practices on construction machinery.	1a12001	AED 1a.12
• Secure loads using the proper types of chains and binders.	1a12002	AED 1a.12
• Perform proper lockout/tagout procedures.	1a12003	AED 1a.12
• Utilize safety data sheets (SDS) and chemical labels.	1a12004	AED 1a.12
• Handle wheel assemblies safely utilizing proper work procedures.	1a12006	AED 1a.12
• Utilize fall protection equipment safely.	1a12007	AED 1a.12

Materials Required

- Three pieces of construction machinery chosen by the supervisor/instructor to complete the task
- Tags numbered 1-3 for labeling machines/equipment
- Manufacturer's service information
- Personal protective equipment (PPE)
- SDS
- Load (designated by supervisor/instructor)
- Tie downs
- Grade 100 binder chain
- Grade 80 binder chain
- Grade 70 binder chain
- Lifting chain
- Binders
- Trailer
- Various machines chosen by the supervisor/instructor to complete the task
- Shop lockout/tagout procedures
- Lockout/tagout equipment
- Various chemicals used in the shop
- Various shop tools and equipment designed for handling wheel assemblies
- Four different pieces of fall protection equipment chosen by the supervisor/instructor to complete the task
- Tethering equipment
- Full body harness

Safety Considerations

- Comply with personal and environmental safety practices associated with clothing; eye protection; hand tools; power equipment; proper ventilation; and the handling, storage, and disposal of chemicals/materials in accordance with local, state, and federal safety and environmental regulations.
- PPE allows us to increase our productivity and effectiveness. However, it can also cause severe injury or death if used improperly. Make sure you follow the manufacturer's procedures.

CDX Tasksheet Number: 1a12001

Student/Intern Information

Name _____ Date _____ Class _____

Machine, Customer, and Service Information

Machine used for this activity:

Make _____ Model _____

Hours _____ Serial Number _____

Materials Required

- Three pieces of construction machinery chosen by the supervisor/instructor to complete the task
- Tags numbered 1–3 for labeling the machines
- Manufacturer's service information
- Personal protective equipment (PPE)

Task-Specific Safety Considerations

- Comply with personal and environmental safety practices associated with clothing; eye protection; hand tools; power equipment; proper ventilation; and the handling, storage, and disposal of chemicals/materials in accordance with local, state, and federal safety and environmental regulations.
- PPE allows us to increase our productivity and effectiveness. However, it can also cause severe injury or death if used improperly. Make sure you follow the manufacturer's procedures.

▶ **TASK** Demonstrate safe mounting and dismounting practices on construction machinery.

AED
1a.12

Time off_____

Time on_____

Student Instructions: Read through the entire procedure prior to starting. Prepare your workspace and any tools or parts that may be needed to complete the task. When directed by your supervisor/instructor, begin the procedure to complete the task, and comment or check the box as each step is finished. Track your time on this procedure for later comparison to the standard completion time (i.e., "flat rate" or customer pay time).

Total time_____

Procedure	Step Completed
1. Locate the manufacturer's operation manual for Machine #1.	☐
a. List the key steps for operation below:	☐

b. Demonstrate safe mounting and dismounting practices. Have your supervisor/instructor verify satisfactory completion of these procedures. Supervisor's/instructor's initials: _____	☐
2. Locate the manufacturer's operation manual for Machine #2.	☐
a. List the key steps for operation below:	☐
b. Demonstrate safe mounting and dismounting practices. Have your supervisor/instructor verify satisfactory completion of these procedures. Supervisor's/instructor's initials: _____	☐
3. Locate the manufacturer's operation manual for Machine #3.	☐
a. List the key steps for operation below:	☐
b. Demonstrate safe mounting and dismounting practices. Have your supervisor/instructor verify satisfactory completion of these procedures. Supervisor's/instructor's initials: _____	☐

Non-Task-Specific Evaluation	Step Completed
1. Tools and equipment were used as directed and returned in good working order.	☐
2. Complied with all general and task-specific safety standards, including proper use of any PPE.	☐
3. Completed the task in an appropriate time frame (recommendation: 1.5 or 2 times the flat rate).	☐
4. Left the workspace clean and orderly.	☐
5. Cared for customer property and returned it undamaged.	☐

Student signature _____ Date _____

Comments:

Have your supervisor/instructor verify satisfactory completion of this procedure, any observations made, and any necessary action(s) recommended.

Evaluation Instructions: The scoring box below is intended to act as a guide for both student and supervisor/instructor. Each criterion listed will help students to understand what is expected of them and help supervisors/instructors to articulate the level of success at a particular task. The scoring is set up to allow a second attempt at each task (see the Test and Retest columns). Scoring is designed only to award students points for task criteria that were completed correctly. Points are lost for failure to complete the employability requirements (see Non-Task-Specific criteria). When all criteria are evaluated, tally the points for a total at the bottom of each column.

Tasksheet Scoring

Evaluation Items	Test		Retest	
	Pass	**Fail**	**Pass**	**Fail**
Task-Specific Evaluation	**(1 pt)**	**(0 pts)**	**(1 pt)**	**(0 pts)**
1. Student correctly listed the key steps for operating each machine.				
2. Student demonstrated safe mounting and dismounting practices on Machine #1.				
3. Student demonstrated safe mounting and dismounting practices on Machine #2.				
4. Student demonstrated safe mounting and dismounting practices on Machine #3.				
Non-Task-Specific Evaluation	**(0 pts)**	**(−1 pt)**	**(0 pts)**	**(−1 pt)**
Student successfully completed at least three of the non-task-specific steps.				
Student successfully completed all five of the non-task-specific steps.				
Total Score: <total # of points / 4 = %>				

Supervisor/Instructor:

Supervisor/instructor signature _____ Date _____

Comments:

Retest supervisor/instructor signature _____ Date _____

Comments:

CDX Tasksheet Number: 1a12002

Student/Intern Information

Name _____ Date _____ Class _____

Machine, Customer, and Service Information

Machine used for this activity:

Make _____ Model _____

Hours _____ Serial Number _____

Materials Required
- Manufacturer's service information
- Personal protective equipment (PPE)
- Load (designated by supervisor/instructor)
- Tie downs
- Grade 100 binder chain
- Grade 80 binder chain
- Grade 70 binder chain
- Lifting chain
- Binders
- Trailer

Task-Specific Safety Considerations
- Comply with personal and environmental safety practices associated with clothing; eye protection; hand tools; power equipment; proper ventilation; and the handling, storage, and disposal of chemicals/materials in accordance with local, state, and federal safety and environmental regulations.
- PPE allows us to increase our productivity and effectiveness. However, it can also cause severe injury or death if used improperly. Make sure you follow the manufacturer's procedures.

▶ **TASK** Secure loads using the proper types of chains and binders. **AED** 1a.12

Time off_____

Student Instructions: Read through the entire procedure prior to starting. Prepare your workspace and any tools or parts that may be needed to complete the task. When directed by your supervisor/instructor, begin the procedure to complete the task, and comment or check the box as each step is finished. Track your time on this procedure for later comparison to the standard completion time (i.e., "flat rate" or customer pay time).

Time on_____

Total time_____

Procedure	Step Completed
1. Determine the gross weight of the load designated by your supervisor/instructor and write the weight below: _____	☐
2. Determine and select the number of tie downs needed for load securement and write the number below: _____	☐
3. Determine and select the type and amount of chain needed for load securement and write them below:	☐
4. Determine and select the types and positions of binders required for load securement and write them below:	☐
5. Secure the load for safe transport. Have your supervisor/instructor verify satisfactory completion of these procedures. Supervisor's/instructor's initials: _____	☐
6. Remove chains and binders and store them in their proper location(s).	☐

Non-Task-Specific Evaluation	Step Completed
1. Tools and equipment were used as directed and returned in good working order.	☐
2. Complied with all general and task-specific safety standards, including proper use of any PPE.	☐
3. Completed the task in an appropriate time frame (recommendation: 1.5 or 2 times the flat rate).	☐
4. Left the workspace clean and orderly.	☐
5. Cared for customer property and returned it undamaged.	☐

Student signature _____ Date _____

Comments:

Have your supervisor/instructor verify satisfactory completion of this procedure, any observations made, and any necessary action(s) recommended.

Evaluation Instructions: The scoring box below is intended to act as a guide for both student and supervisor/instructor. Each criterion listed will help students to understand what is expected of them and help supervisors/instructors to articulate the level of success at a particular task. The scoring is set up to allow a second attempt at each task (see the Test and Retest columns). Scoring is designed only to award students points for task criteria that were completed correctly. Points are lost for failure to complete the employability requirements (see Non-Task-Specific criteria). When all criteria are evaluated, tally the points for a total at the bottom of each column.

Tasksheet Scoring

	Test		Retest	
Evaluation Items	**Pass**	**Fail**	**Pass**	**Fail**
Task-Specific Evaluation	**(1 pt)**	**(0 pts)**	**(1 pt)**	**(0 pts)**
1. Student determined the correct gross weight of the load.				
2. Student determined the correct types/amounts/positions of tie downs, chains, and binders needed for load securement.				
3. Student properly secured the load for safe transport.				
4. Student properly removed the chains and binders and stored them in the correct location(s).				
Non-Task-Specific Evaluation	**(0 pts)**	**(−1 pt)**	**(0 pts)**	**(−1 pt)**
Student successfully completed at least three of the non-task-specific steps.				
Student successfully completed all five of the non-task-specific steps.				
Total Score: <total # of points / 4 = %>				

Supervisor/Instructor:

Supervisor/instructor signature _____ Date _____

Comments:

Retest supervisor/instructor signature _____ Date _____

Comments:

CDX Tasksheet Number: 1a12003

Student/Intern Information

Name _____ Date _____ Class _____

Machine, Customer, and Service Information

Machine used for this activity:

Make _____ Model _____

Hours _____ Serial Number _____

Materials Required

- Personal protective equipment (PPE)
- Manufacturer's service information
- Various machines chosen by the supervisor/instructor to complete the task
- Shop lockout/tagout procedures
- Lockout/tagout equipment

Task-Specific Safety Considerations

- Comply with personal and environmental safety practices associated with clothing; eye protection; hand tools; power equipment; proper ventilation; and the handling, storage, and disposal of chemicals/materials in accordance with local, state, and federal safety and environmental regulations.
- PPE allows us to increase our productivity and effectiveness. However, it can also cause severe injury or death if used improperly. Make sure you follow the manufacturer's procedures.

▶ **TASK** Perform proper lockout/tagout procedures. _____ **AED** 1a.12

Time off_____

Time on_____

Student Instructions: Read through the entire procedure prior to starting. Prepare your workspace and any tools or parts that may be needed to complete the task. When directed by your supervisor/instructor, begin the procedure to complete the task, and comment or check the box as each step is finished. Track your time on this procedure for later comparison to the standard completion time (i.e., "flat rate" or customer pay time).

Total time_____

Procedure	Step Completed
1. List the shop's lockout/tagout procedures below:	☐

2. Explain when lockout/tagout procedures should be used below:	☐
3. Demonstrate the procedure for locking out a machine's electrical system. Have your supervisor/instructor verify satisfactory completion of this procedure. Supervisor's/instructor's initials: _____	☐
4. Demonstrate the procedure for locking out a machine's hydraulic system. Have your supervisor/instructor verify satisfactory completion of this procedure. Supervisor's/instructor's initials: _____	☐
5. Demonstrate the procedure for locking out a machine's articulating joint (steering). Have your supervisor/instructor verify satisfactory completion of this procedure. Supervisor's/instructor's initials: _____	☐
6. Demonstrate the procedure for locking out a machine's hoist system. Have your supervisor/instructor verify satisfactory completion of this procedure. Supervisor's/instructor's initials: _____	☐

Non-Task-Specific Evaluation	Step Completed
1. Tools and equipment were used as directed and returned in good working order.	☐
2. Complied with all general and task-specific safety standards, including proper use of any PPE.	☐
3. Completed the task in an appropriate time frame (recommendation: 1.5 or 2 times the flat rate).	☐
4. Left the workspace clean and orderly.	☐
5. Cared for customer property and returned it undamaged.	☐

Student signature _____ Date _____

Comments:

Have your supervisor/instructor verify satisfactory completion of this procedure, any observations made, and any necessary action(s) recommended.

Evaluation Instructions: The scoring box below is intended to act as a guide for both student and supervisor/instructor. Each criterion listed will help students to understand what is expected of them and help supervisors/instructors to articulate the level of success at a particular task. The scoring is set up to allow a second attempt at each task (see the Test and Retest columns). Scoring is designed only to award students points for task criteria that were completed correctly. Points are lost for failure to complete the employability requirements (see Non-Task-Specific criteria). When all criteria are evaluated, tally the points for a total at the bottom of each column.

Tasksheet Scoring

	Test		Retest	
Evaluation Items	**Pass**	**Fail**	**Pass**	**Fail**
Task-Specific Evaluation	**(1 pt)**	**(0 pts)**	**(1 pt)**	**(0 pts)**
1. Student correctly listed the shop's lockout/tagout procedures.				
2. Student correctly explained when lockout/tagout procedures should be used.				
3. Student correctly demonstrated the procedures for locking out a machine's electrical and hydraulic systems.				
4. Student correctly demonstrated the procedures for locking out a machine's articulating joint and its hoist system.				
Non-Task-Specific Evaluation	**(0 pts)**	**(−1 pt)**	**(0 pts)**	**(−1 pt)**
Student successfully completed at least three of the non-task-specific steps.				
Student successfully completed all five of the non-task-specific steps.				
Total Score: <total # of points / 4 = %>				

Supervisor/Instructor:

Supervisor/instructor signature _____ Date _____

Comments:

Retest supervisor/instructor signature _____ Date _____

Comments:

CDX Tasksheet Number: 1a12004

Student/Intern Information

Name _____ Date _____ Class _____

Machine, Customer, and Service Information

Machine used for this activity:

Make _____ Model _____

Hours _____ Serial Number _____

Materials Required

- Personal protective equipment (PPE)
- Safety data sheets (SDS)
- Various chemicals used in the shop

Task-Specific Safety Considerations

- Comply with personal and environmental safety practices associated with clothing; eye protection; hand tools; power equipment; proper ventilation; and the handling, storage, and disposal of chemicals/materials in accordance with local, state, and federal safety and environmental regulations.
- PPE allows us to increase our productivity and effectiveness. However, it can also cause severe injury or death if used improperly. Make sure you follow the manufacturer's procedures.

▶ **TASK** Utilize SDS and chemical labels. _____ **AED** 1a.12

Time off_____

Time on_____

Student Instructions: Read through the entire procedure prior to starting. Prepare your workspace and any tools or parts that may be needed to complete the task. When directed by your supervisor/instructor, begin the procedure to complete the task, and comment or check the box as each step is finished. Track your time on this procedure for later comparison to the standard completion time (i.e., "flat rate" or customer pay time).

Total time_____

Procedure	Step Completed
1. Identify the hazard communication (HazCom) policy for your shop and list the key steps below:	☐

2. Explain why it is important to understand and follow a HazCom plan in your own words below:	☐
3. Gather six different chemicals used in your shop and identify the SDS symbols for each chemical. List the chemical name, its SDS symbols, and the meanings of the symbols.	☐

a. Chemical name: _____
     SDS symbols:
 	
     Symbol meanings:
	☐

b. Chemical name: _____
     SDS symbols:
 	
     Symbol meanings:
	☐

c. Chemical name: _____
     SDS symbols:
 	
     Symbol meanings:
	☐

d. Chemical name: _____
     SDS symbols:
 	
     Symbol meanings:
	☐

e. Chemical name: _____
     SDS symbols:
 	
     Symbol meanings:
	☐

f. Chemical name: _____
     SDS symbols:
 	
     Symbol meanings:
	☐

4. Return all chemicals and SDS to their proper location(s).	☐

Non-Task-Specific Evaluation	Step Completed
1. Tools and equipment were used as directed and returned in good working order.	☐
2. Complied with all general and task-specific safety standards, including proper use of any PPE.	☐
3. Completed the task in an appropriate time frame (recommendation: 1.5 or 2 times the flat rate).	☐
4. Left the workspace clean and orderly.	☐
5. Cared for customer property and returned it undamaged.	☐

Student signature _____ Date _____

Comments:

Have your supervisor/instructor verify satisfactory completion of this procedure, any observations made, and any necessary action(s) recommended.

Evaluation Instructions: The scoring box below is intended to act as a guide for both student and supervisor/instructor. Each criterion listed will help students to understand what is expected of them and help supervisors/instructors to articulate the level of success at a particular task. The scoring is set up to allow a second attempt at each task (see the Test and Retest columns). Scoring is designed only to award students points for task criteria that were completed correctly. Points are lost for failure to complete the employability requirements (see Non-Task-Specific criteria). When all criteria are evaluated, tally the points for a total at the bottom of each column.

Tasksheet Scoring

Evaluation Items	Test		Retest	
	Pass	Fail	Pass	Fail
Task-Specific Evaluation	**(1 pt)**	**(0 pts)**	**(1 pt)**	**(0 pts)**
1. Student correctly identified and listed the shop's HazCom policy and explained why HazCom plans are necessary.				
2. Student correctly identified the chemical name, its symbols, and their meanings for at least two different chemicals.				
3. Student correctly identified the chemical name, its symbols, and their meanings for at least four different chemicals.				
4. Student correctly identified the chemical name, its symbols, and their meanings for all six chemicals.				
Non-Task-Specific Evaluation	**(0 pts)**	**(−1 pt)**	**(0 pts)**	**(−1 pt)**
Student successfully completed at least three of the non-task-specific steps.				
Student successfully completed all five of the non-task-specific steps.				
Total Score: <total # of points / 4 = %>				

Supervisor/Instructor:

Supervisor/instructor signature _____ Date _____

Comments:

Retest supervisor/instructor signature _____ Date _____

Comments:

CDX Tasksheet Number: 1a12006

Student/Intern Information

Name _____ Date _____ Class _____

Machine, Customer, and Service Information

Machine used for this activity:

Make _____ Model _____

Hours _____ Serial Number _____

Materials Required

- Personal protective equipment (PPE)
- Various machines chosen by the supervisor/instructor to complete the task
- Manufacturer's service information
- Various shop tools and equipment designed for handling wheel assemblies

---

Task-Specific Safety Considerations

- Comply with personal and environmental safety practices associated with clothing; eye protection; hand tools; power equipment; proper ventilation; and the handling, storage, and disposal of chemicals/materials in accordance with local, state, and federal safety and environmental regulations.
- PPE allows us to increase our productivity and effectiveness. However, it can also cause severe injury or death if used improperly. Make sure you follow the manufacturer's procedures.

▶ **TASK** Handle wheel assemblies safely utilizing proper work procedures.

AED
1a.12

Time off_____

Time on_____

Total time_____

Student Instructions: Read through the entire procedure prior to starting. Prepare your workspace and any tools or parts that may be needed to complete the task. When directed by your supervisor/instructor, begin the procedure to complete the task, and comment or check the box as each step is finished. Track your time on this procedure for later comparison to the standard completion time (i.e., "flat rate" or customer pay time).

Procedure	Step Completed
1. Identify the proper work procedures for handling wheel assemblies using the manufacturer's service information for various machines assigned to you by your supervisor/instructor. List the procedures for the various machines below, including tools and equipment that must be used.	

a. Machine: _____ Procedures: Tools/equipment:	☐
b. Machine: _____ Procedures: Tools/equipment:	☐
c. Machine: _____ Procedures: Tools/equipment:	☐
d. Machine: _____ Procedures: Tools/equipment:	☐
e. Machine: _____ Procedures: Tools/equipment:	☐
f. Machine: _____ Procedures: Tools/equipment:	☐
2. Demonstrate the proper work procedures for handling wheel assemblies on a machine assigned by your supervisor/instructor. Have your supervisor/instructor verify satisfactory completion of these procedures. Supervisor's/instructor's initials: _____	☐

Non-Task-Specific Evaluation	Step Completed
1. Tools and equipment were used as directed and returned in good working order.	☐
2. Complied with all general and task-specific safety standards, including proper use of any PPE.	☐
3. Completed the task in an appropriate time frame (recommendation: 1.5 or 2 times the flat rate).	☐
4. Left the workspace clean and orderly.	☐
5. Cared for customer property and returned it undamaged.	☐

Student signature _____ Date _____

Comments:

Have your supervisor/instructor verify satisfactory completion of this procedure, any observations made, and any necessary action(s) recommended.

Evaluation Instructions: The scoring box below is intended to act as a guide for both student and supervisor/instructor. Each criterion listed will help students to understand what is expected of them and help supervisors/instructors to articulate the level of success at a particular task. The scoring is set up to allow a second attempt at each task (see the Test and Retest columns). Scoring is designed only to award students points for task criteria that were completed correctly. Points are lost for failure to complete the employability requirements (see Non-Task-Specific criteria). When all criteria are evaluated, tally the points for a total at the bottom of each column.

Taksheet Scoring

Evaluation Items	Test		Retest	
	Pass	**Fail**	**Pass**	**Fail**
Task-Specific Evaluation	**(1 pt)**	**(0 pts)**	**(1 pt)**	**(0 pts)**
1. Student correctly identified the proper work procedures for handling wheel assemblies for at least two machines.				
2. Student correctly identified the proper work procedures for handling wheel assemblies for at least four machines.				
3. Student correctly identified the proper work procedures for handling wheel assemblies for all six machines.				
4. Student demonstrated the proper work procedures for handling wheel assemblies on their assigned machine.				
Non-Task-Specific Evaluation	**(0 pts)**	**(−1 pt)**	**(0 pts)**	**(−1 pt)**
Student successfully completed at least three of the non-task-specific steps.				
Student successfully completed all five of the non-task-specific steps.				
Total Score: <total # of points / 4 = %>				

Supervisor/Instructor:

Supervisor/instructor signature _____ Date _____

Comments:

_____

Retest supervisor/instructor signature _____ Date _____

Comments:

_____

CDX Tasksheet Number: 1a12007

Student/Intern Information

Name _____ Date _____ Class _____

Machine, Customer, and Service Information

Machine used for this activity:

Make _____ Model _____

Hours _____ Serial Number _____

Materials Required

- Four different pieces of fall protection equipment chosen by the supervisor/instructor to complete the task
- Tags numbered 1-4 for labeling equipment
- Tethering equipment
- Full body harness
- Personal protective equipment (PPE)

Task-Specific Safety Considerations

- Comply with personal and environmental safety practices associated with clothing; eye protection; hand tools; power equipment; proper ventilation; and the handling, storage, and disposal of chemicals/materials in accordance with local, state, and federal safety and environmental regulations.
- PPE allows us to increase our productivity and effectiveness. However, it can also cause severe injury or death if used improperly. Make sure you follow the manufacturer's procedures.

▶ **TASK** Utilize fall protection equipment safely. **AED** 1a.12

Time off_____

Time on_____

Student Instructions: Read through the entire procedure prior to starting. Prepare your workspace and any tools or parts that may be needed to complete the task. When directed by your supervisor/instructor, begin the procedure to complete the task, and comment or check the box as each step is finished. Track your time on this procedure for later comparison to the standard completion time (i.e., "flat rate" or customer pay time).

Total time_____

Procedure	Step Completed
1. Identify the conditions under which fall protection and tethering must be used and list them below:	☐

2. Identify the manufacturer's procedures for donning (putting on) and doffing (taking off) its fall protection equipment along with proper tethering techniques. List them below:	☐
3. Demonstrate proper procedures for using Fall Protection Equipment #1. Have your supervisor/instructor verify satisfactory completion of these procedures. Supervisor's/instructor's initials: _____	☐
4. Demonstrate proper procedures for using Fall Protection Equipment #2. Have your supervisor/instructor verify satisfactory completion of these procedures. Supervisor's/instructor's initials: _____	☐
5. Demonstrate proper procedures for using Fall Protection Equipment #3. Have your supervisor/instructor verify satisfactory completion of these procedures. Supervisor's/instructor's initials: _____	☐
6. Demonstrate proper procedures for using Fall Protection Equipment #4. Have your supervisor/instructor verify satisfactory completion of these procedures. Supervisor's/instructor's initials: _____	☐

Non-Task-Specific Evaluation	Step Completed
1. Tools and equipment were used as directed and returned in good working order.	☐
2. Complied with all general and task-specific safety standards, including proper use of any PPE.	☐
3. Completed the task in an appropriate time frame (recommendation: 1.5 or 2 times the flat rate).	☐
4. Left the workspace clean and orderly.	☐
5. Cared for customer property and returned it undamaged.	☐

Student signature _____ Date _____

Comments:

Have your supervisor/instructor verify satisfactory completion of this procedure, any observations made, and any necessary action(s) recommended.

Evaluation Instructions: The scoring box below is intended to act as a guide for both student and supervisor/instructor. Each criterion listed will help students to understand what is expected of them and help supervisors/instructors to articulate the level of success at a particular task. The scoring is set up to allow a second attempt at each task (see the Test and Retest columns). Scoring is designed only to award students points for task criteria that were completed correctly. Points are lost for failure to complete the employability requirements (see Non-Task-Specific criteria). When all criteria are evaluated, tally the points for a total at the bottom of each column.

Tasksheet Scoring

Evaluation Items	Test		Retest	
	Pass	Fail	Pass	Fail
Task-Specific Evaluation	**(1 pt)**	**(0 pts)**	**(1 pt)**	**(0 pts)**
1. Student correctly identified the conditions under which fall protection and tethering must be used.				
2. Student correctly identified the manufacturer's procedures for fall protection equipment and proper tethering techniques.				
3. Student demonstrated proper procedures for using at least two pieces of fall protection equipment.				
4. Student demonstrated proper procedures for using all four pieces of fall protection equipment.				
Non-Task-Specific Evaluation	**(0 pts)**	**(−1 pt)**	**(0 pts)**	**(−1 pt)**
Student successfully completed at least three of the non-task-specific steps.				
Student successfully completed all five of the non-task-specific steps.				
Total Score: <total # of points / 4 = %>				

Supervisor/Instructor:

Supervisor/instructor signature _____ Date _____

Comments:

Retest supervisor/instructor signature _____ Date _____

Comments:

Chapter 13: Utilize Industry Software and Electronic Communications Systems and Reference Resources

Learning Objective/Task	CDX Tasksheet Number	AED Reference Number
• Utilize computers and related hardware, current software, Internet, and technology.	1b2002	AED 1b.2
• Retrieve specifications, part numbers, bulletins, schematics, and similar types of information and produce reports using manufacturers' software and Internet-based resources.	1b2004	AED 1b.2

Materials Required

- Shop computers with Internet access
- Access to various manufacturers' service information
- Various machines chosen by the supervisor/instructor to complete the tasks
- Machine manufacturer's electronic service tools and equipment
- Personal protective equipment (PPE)
- Printer or ability to send information electronically

Safety Considerations

- Comply with personal and environmental safety practices associated with clothing; eye protection; hand tools; power equipment; proper ventilation; and the handling, storage, and disposal of chemicals/materials in accordance with local, state, and federal safety and environmental regulations.
- PPE allows us to increase our productivity and effectiveness. However, it can also cause severe injury or death if used improperly. Make sure you follow the manufacturer's procedures.

CDX Tasksheet Number: 1b2002

Student/Intern Information

Name _____ Date _____ Class _____

Machine, Customer, and Service Information

Machine used for this activity:

Make _____ Model _____

Hours _____ Serial Number _____

Materials Required

- Shop computers with Internet access
- Access to various manufacturers' service information
- Various machines
- Machine manufacturer's electronic service tools and equipment
- Personal protective equipment (PPE)

Task-Specific Safety Considerations

- Comply with personal and environmental safety practices associated with clothing; eye protection; hand tools; power equipment; proper ventilation; and the handling, storage, and disposal of chemicals/materials in accordance with local, state, and federal safety and environmental regulations.
- PPE allows us to increase our productivity and effectiveness. However, it can also cause severe injury or death if used improperly. Make sure you follow the manufacturer's procedures.

▶ **TASK** Utilize computers and related hardware, current software, Internet, and technology.

AED
1b.2

Time off_____

Time on_____

Total time_____

Student Instructions: Read through the entire procedure prior to starting. Prepare your workspace and any tools or parts that may be needed to complete the task. When directed by your supervisor/instructor, begin the procedure to complete the task, and comment or check the box as each step is finished. Track your time on this procedure for later comparison to the standard completion time (i.e., "flat rate" or customer pay time).

Procedure	Step Completed
1. Machine #1	
a. Using the appropriate electronic service tool(s) and procedures, connect to the machine data bus with the service tool(s) and check for diagnostic codes. List any active, inactive, and historic codes below:	☐
b. Using the manufacturer's website, access the machine's product information and list it below:	☐
c. Using the manufacturer's website, access the machine's safety information and list it below:	☐
2. Machine #2	
a. Using the appropriate electronic service tool(s) and procedures, connect to the machine data bus with the service tool(s) and open the system's monitor screen list. Select a group to monitor and write it below:	☐
b. Using the manufacturer's website, access the machine's product information and list it below:	☐
c. Using the manufacturer's website, access the machine's safety information and list it below:	☐

3. Machine #3	
a. Using the appropriate electronic service tool(s) and procedures, connect to the machine data bus with the service tool(s) and open the component tests screen. List the component tests below:	☐
b. Using the manufacturer's website, access the machine's product information and list it below:	☐
c. Using the manufacturer's website, access the machine's safety information and list it below:	☐

Non-Task-Specific Evaluation	Step Completed
1. Tools and equipment were used as directed and returned in good working order.	☐
2. Complied with all general and task-specific safety standards, including proper use of any PPE.	☐
3. Completed the task in an appropriate time frame (recommendation: 1.5 or 2 times the flat rate).	☐
4. Left the workspace clean and orderly.	☐
5. Cared for customer property and returned it undamaged.	☐

Student signature _____ Date _____

Comments:

Have your supervisor/instructor verify satisfactory completion of this procedure, any observations made, and any necessary action(s) recommended.

Evaluation Instructions: The scoring box below is intended to act as a guide for both student and supervisor/instructor. Each criterion listed will help students to understand what is expected of them and help supervisors/instructors to articulate the level of success at a particular task. The scoring is set up to allow a second attempt at each task (see the Test and Retest columns). Scoring is designed only to award students points for task criteria that were completed correctly. Points are lost for failure to complete the employability requirements (see Non-Task-Specific criteria). When all criteria are evaluated, tally the points for a total at the bottom of each column.

Tasksheet Scoring

Evaluation Items	Test		Retest	
	Pass	Fail	Pass	Fail
Task-Specific Evaluation	**(1 pt)**	**(0 pts)**	**(1 pt)**	**(0 pts)**
1. Student demonstrated the proper use of appropriate electronic service tools and procedures for connecting to each machine's data bus.				
2. Student correctly listed the product and safety information for each machine.				
3. Student correctly listed any active, inactive, and historic codes for Machine #1.				
4. Student correctly identified a group to monitor for Machine #2 and listed the component tests for Machine #3.				
Non-Task-Specific Evaluation	**(0 pts)**	**(−1 pt)**	**(0 pts)**	**(−1 pt)**
Student successfully completed at least three of the non-task-specific steps.				
Student successfully completed all five of the non-task-specific steps.				
Total Score: <total # of points / 4 = %>				

Supervisor/Instructor:

Supervisor/instructor signature _____ Date _____

Comments:

Retest supervisor/instructor signature _____ Date _____

Comments:

CDX Tasksheet Number: 1b2004

Student/Intern Information

Name _____ Date _____ Class _____

Machine, Customer, and Service Information

Machine used for this activity:

Make _____ Model _____

Hours _____ Serial Number _____

Materials Required

- Shop computers with Internet access
- Access to various manufacturers' service information
- Machine chosen by the supervisor/instructor to complete the task
- Printer or ability to send information electronically
- Personal protective equipment (PPE)

Task-Specific Safety Considerations

- Comply with personal and environmental safety practices associated with clothing; eye protection; hand tools; power equipment; proper ventilation; and the handling, storage, and disposal of chemicals/materials in accordance with local, state, and federal safety and environmental regulations.
- PPE allows us to increase our productivity and effectiveness. However, it can also cause severe injury or death if used improperly. Make sure you follow the manufacturer's procedures.

▶ TASK Retrieve specifications, part numbers, bulletins, schematics, and similar types of information and produce reports using manufacturers' software and Internet-based resources.

AED
1b.2

Time off_____

Time on_____

Total time_____

Student Instructions: Read through the entire procedure prior to starting. Prepare your workspace and any tools or parts that may be needed to complete the task. When directed by your supervisor/instructor, begin the procedure to complete the task, and comment or check the box as each step is finished. Track your time on this procedure for later comparison to the standard completion time (i.e., "flat rate" or customer pay time).

Procedure	Step Completed
(**Note:** Any part of this procedure that calls for printing information can be substituted for emailing the information to your supervisor/instructor, if preferred.)	
1. Locate the following part numbers for your assigned machine and write them below.	
a. Air filter Part number: _____	☐
b. Fuel filter Part number: _____	☐
c. Hydraulic filter Part number: _____	☐
d. Seat belt Part number: _____	☐
2. Locate the following service procedures for your machine, print a copy of the procedures, and attach the copies to the back of this document.	
a. Air filter removal and replacement	☐
b. Fuel filter removal and replacement	☐
c. Hydraulic filter removal and replacement	☐
d. Seat belt inspection and maintenance	☐
e. Electrical schematic	☐
f. Machine fluid capacities	☐
3. Locate service bulletins for your machine, print a copy of two bulletins, and attach them to the back of this document.	☐
4. Locate safety bulletins for your machine, print a copy of two bulletins, and attach them to the back of this document.	☐

Non-Task-Specific Evaluation	Step Completed
1. Tools and equipment were used as directed and returned in good working order.	☐
2. Complied with all general and task-specific safety standards, including proper use of any PPE.	☐
3. Completed the task in an appropriate time frame (recommendation: 1.5 or 2 times the flat rate).	☐
4. Left the workspace clean and orderly.	☐
5. Cared for customer property and returned it undamaged.	☐

Student signature _____ Date _____

Comments:

Have your supervisor/instructor verify satisfactory completion of this procedure, any observations made,

and any necessary action(s) recommended.

Evaluation Instructions: The scoring box below is intended to act as a guide for both student and supervisor/instructor. Each criterion listed will help students to understand what is expected of them and help supervisors/instructors to articulate the level of success at a particular task. The scoring is set up to allow a second attempt at each task (see the Test and Retest columns). Scoring is designed only to award students points for task criteria that were completed correctly. Points are lost for failure to complete the employability requirements (see Non-Task-Specific criteria). When all criteria are evaluated, tally the points for a total at the bottom of each column.

Tasksheet Scoring

	Test		Retest	
Evaluation Items	**Pass**	**Fail**	**Pass**	**Fail**
Task-Specific Evaluation	**(1 pt)**	**(0 pts)**	**(1 pt)**	**(0 pts)**
1. Student located the correct part numbers for their assigned machine.				
2. Student located the requested service procedures for their machine and printed or emailed a copy of the procedures.				
3. Student located service bulletins for their machine and printed or emailed a copy of two bulletins.				
4. Student located safety bulletins for their machine and printed or emailed a copy of two bulletins.				
Non-Task-Specific Evaluation	**(0 pts)**	**(−1 pt)**	**(0 pts)**	**(−1 pt)**
Student successfully completed at least three of the non-task-specific steps.				
Student successfully completed all five of the non-task-specific steps.				
Total Score: <total # of points / 4 = %>				

Supervisor/Instructor:

Supervisor/instructor signature _____ Date _____

Comments:

Retest supervisor/instructor signature _____ Date _____

Comments:

Chapter 14: Describe Functions of the Dealership Service Department; Explain Department Goals and Procedures

Learning Objective/Task	CDX Tasksheet Number	AED Reference Number
• Complete work orders/repair orders and other related reports.	1b5004	AED 1b.5

Materials Required

- Machine chosen by the supervisor/instructor to complete the task
- Access to various manufacturers' service and parts information
- Shop computers with Internet access
- Shop service reporting procedure
- Shop service reports
- Shop parts order procedure
- Shop parts order forms
- Personal protective equipment (PPE)

Safety Considerations

- Comply with personal and environmental safety practices associated with clothing; eye protection; hand tools; power equipment; proper ventilation; and the handling, storage, and disposal of chemicals/materials in accordance with local, state, and federal safety and environmental regulations.
- PPE allows us to increase our productivity and effectiveness. However, it can also cause severe injury or death if used improperly. Make sure you follow the manufacturer's procedures.

CDX Tasksheet Number: 1b5004

Student/Intern Information

Name _____ Date _____ Class _____

Machine, Customer, and Service Information

Machine used for this activity:

Make _____ Model _____

Hours _____ Serial Number _____

Materials Required

- Machine chosen by the supervisor/instructor to complete the task
- Access to various manufacturers' service and parts information
- Shop computers with Internet access
- Shop service reporting procedure
- Shop service reports
- Shop parts order procedure
- Shop parts order forms
- Personal protective equipment (PPE)

Task-Specific Safety Considerations

- Comply with personal and environmental safety practices associated with clothing; eye protection; hand tools; power equipment; proper ventilation; and the handling, storage, and disposal of chemicals/materials in accordance with local, state, and federal safety and environmental regulations.
- PPE allows us to increase our productivity and effectiveness. However, it can also cause severe injury or death if used improperly. Make sure you follow the manufacturer's procedures.

▶ TASK Complete work orders/repair orders and other related reports. **AED 1b.5**

Time off_____

Time on_____

Total time_____

Student Instructions: Read through the entire procedure prior to starting. Prepare your workspace and any tools or parts that may be needed to complete the task. When directed by your supervisor/instructor, begin the procedure to complete the task, and comment or check the box as each step is finished. Track your time on this procedure for later comparison to the standard completion time (i.e., "flat rate" or customer pay time).

Procedure	Step Completed
1. Using your supervisor/instructor-assigned machine, complete the customer and machine information section of your shop work order/repair order.	☐

	Step Completed
2. Ask your supervisor/instructor for a customer complaint and complete the customer complaint section of your work order/repair order.	☐
3. Ask your supervisor/instructor for a correction and record it in the correction section of your work order/repair order.	☐
4. Using machine information on the work order/repair order, look up the parts needed to complete the correction of the complaint. Then accurately complete a shop parts order form and attach it to this document.	☐
5. Using machine information on the work order/repair order, look up the necessary troubleshooting and repair procedure for complaint and correction. Complete the cause and correction sections of your work order/repair order as if you performed the tasks.	☐
6. Complete the work order/repair order by adding the parts and supplies you used.	☐

Non-Task-Specific Evaluation	Step Completed
1. Tools and equipment were used as directed and returned in good working order.	☐
2. Complied with all general and task-specific safety standards, including proper use of any PPE.	☐
3. Completed the task in an appropriate time frame (recommendation: 1.5 or 2 times the flat rate).	☐
4. Left the workspace clean and orderly.	☐
5. Cared for customer property and returned it undamaged.	☐

Student signature _____ Date _____

Comments:

Have your supervisor/instructor verify satisfactory completion of this procedure, any observations made, and any necessary action(s) recommended.

Evaluation Instructions: The scoring box below is intended to act as a guide for both student and supervisor/instructor. Each criterion listed will help students to understand what is expected of them and help supervisors/instructors to articulate the level of success at a particular task. The scoring is set up to allow a second attempt at each task (see the Test and Retest columns). Scoring is designed only to award students points for task criteria that were completed correctly. Points are lost for failure to complete the employability requirements (see Non-Task-Specific criteria). When all criteria are evaluated, tally the points for a total at the bottom of each column.

Tasksheet Scoring

Evaluation Items	Test		Retest	
	Pass	Fail	Pass	Fail
Task-Specific Evaluation	**(1 pt)**	**(0 pts)**	**(1 pt)**	**(0 pts)**
1. Student accurately completed the customer and machine information section of the work order/repair order.				
2. Student accurately completed the customer complaint and correction sections of the work order/repair order based on information provided by the supervisor/instructor.				
3. Student accurately completed a shop parts order form and added the parts/supplies used to the work order/repair order.				
4. Student accurately completed the cause and corrections sections of the work order/repair order as if they had performed the necessary repairs/troubleshooting.				
Non-Task-Specific Evaluation	**(0 pts)**	**(−1 pt)**	**(0 pts)**	**(−1 pt)**
Student successfully completed at least three of the non-task-specific steps.				
Student successfully completed all five of the non-task-specific steps.				
Total Score: <total # of points / 4 = %>				

Supervisor/Instructor:

Supervisor/instructor signature _____ Date _____

Comments:

Retest supervisor/instructor signature _____ Date _____

Comments:

Section 2: Electronics/Electrical

Chapter 15: Ohm's Law

Learning Objective/Task	CDX Tasksheet Number	AED Reference Number
• Measure voltage, amperage, and resistance values in series, parallel, and series/parallel DC circuits.	2.2b001	AED 2.2b

Materials Required

- Machine or simulator with electrical circuit concerns
- Equipment manufacturer's workshop manual including schematic wiring diagrams
- Digital volt-ohmmeter (DVOM)
- Ammeter
- Current clamp

Safety Considerations

- This task may require you to measure electrical values. Always ensure that the supervisor/instructor checks test instrument connections prior to connecting power or taking measurements. High current flows can be dangerous; avoid accidental short circuits or grounding a battery's positive connections.
- This task may require operating the equipment on school grounds, which carries severe risks. Attempt this task only with full permission from your supervisor/instructor and follow all the guidelines exactly.
- Lifting equipment such as equipment jacks and stands, vehicle hoists, and engine hoists are important tools that increase productivity and make the job easier. However, they can also cause severe injury or death if used improperly. Make sure you follow the manufacturer's operation procedures. Also make sure you have your supervisor's/instructor's permission to use any type of lifting equipment.
- Comply with personal and environmental safety practices associated with clothing; eye protection; hand tools; power equipment; proper ventilation; and the handling, storage, and disposal of chemicals/materials in accordance with federal, state, and local regulations.

- Always wear the correct protective eyewear and clothing and use the appropriate safety equipment, as well as seat protectors and floor mat protectors.
- Make sure you understand and observe all legislative and personal safety procedures when carrying out practical assignments. If you are unsure of what these are, ask your supervisor/instructor.

CDX Tasksheet Number: 2.2b001

Student/Intern Information

Name _____ Date _____ Class _____

Machine, Customer, and Service Information

Machine used for this activity:

Make _____ Model _____

Hours _____ Serial Number _____

Materials Required

- Machine or simulator with electrical circuit concerns
- Equipment manufacturer's workshop manual including schematic wiring diagrams
- Digital volt-ohmmeter (DVOM)
- Ammeter
- Current clamp

Task-Specific Safety Considerations

- This task may require you to measure electrical values. Always ensure that the supervisor/instructor checks test instrument connections prior to connecting power or taking measurements. High current flows can be dangerous; avoid accidental short circuits or grounding a battery's positive connections.
- This task may require operating the equipment on school grounds, which carries severe risks. Attempt this task only with full permission from your supervisor/instructor and follow all the guidelines exactly.
- Lifting equipment such as equipment jacks and stands, vehicle hoists, and engine hoists are important tools that increase productivity and make the job easier. However, they can also cause severe injury or death if used improperly. Make sure you follow the manufacturer's operation procedures. Also make sure you have your supervisor/instructor's permission to use any type of lifting equipment.
- Comply with personal and environmental safety practices associated with clothing; eye protection; hand tools; power equipment; proper ventilation; and the handling, storage, and disposal of chemicals/materials in accordance with federal, state, and local regulations.
- Always wear the correct protective eyewear and clothing and use the appropriate safety equipment, as well as seat protectors and floor mat protectors.
- Make sure you understand and observe all legislative and personal safety procedures when carrying out practical assignments. If you are unsure of what these are, ask your supervisor/instructor.

▶ **TASK** Measure voltage, amperage, and resistance values in series, parallel, and series/parallel DC circuits.

AED 2.2b

Student Instructions: Read through the entire procedure prior to starting. Prepare your workspace and any tools or parts that may be needed to complete the task. When directed by your supervisor/instructor, begin the procedure to complete the task, and comment or check the box as each step is finished. Track your time on this procedure for later comparison to the standard completion time (i.e., "flat rate" or customer pay time).

Procedure	Step Completed
1. Set up circuits on an electrical simulator in order to measure electrical values with a DVOM and or amp meter (if DVOM amp rating is too low). Ensure these circuits are tied to specific applications on vehicles, not just as classroom bench activities.	☐
2. Connect the training aid as shown in Figure 1, then complete the tasks below. TP6 TP1 TP4 TP5 TP2 TP3 Power source Control switch Load **Figure 1**	☐
a. With the training aid de-energized, verify that the lamp is not illuminated.	☐
b. Using a DVOM, measure the resistance across the switch (TP2–TP3) and record it below: _____ ohms	☐
c. Using a DVOM, measure the resistance across the lamp (TP4–TP5) and record it below: _____ ohms	☐
3. Prepare the DVOM to measure direct current voltage (DCV), then complete the tasks below.	☐
a. Turn the training aid ON and verify that the lamp is illuminated.	☐
b. Using the DVOM, measure the supply voltage (TP1–TP6) and record it below: _____ DCV	☐
c. Using a DVOM, measure the voltage drop across the switch (TP2–TP3) and record it below: _____ DCV	☐

d. Using a DVOM, measure the voltage drop across the lamp (TP4–TP5) and record it below: _____ DCV	☐
e. What type of circuit is shown in Figure 1? Series ☐ Parallel ☐ Series/Parallel ☐	☐
4. Prepare the DVOM to measure direct current amperage (DCA) and complete the following tasks.	☐
a. Turn the power to the training board OFF and disconnect the wire lead at TP2. Connect a DVOM in series at TP2 and measure the current flow in the circuit after the power is turned ON again. Record your measurement below: _____ DCA	☐
b. Using this amperage reading, calculate the total resistance in the circuit and write it below: _____ ohms	☐
c. Turn the power to the training board OFF and disconnect the wire lead at TP6. Using a DVOM, measure the current flow in the circuit. Turn the power to the training board ON and connect the meter leads at the wire lead and TP6. Record your measurement below: _____ DCA	☐
d. Were the two amperage measurements similar? Explain why or why not below:	☐
5. Find a simple series circuit on a machine with a load like a cab interior light and use a DVOM to complete the following tasks.	☐
a. With the circuit de-energized, measure the resistance to ground on the negative side of the load and record it below: _____ ohms	☐
b. With the circuit energized, measure the voltage across the load and record it below: _____ DCV	☐
c. With the circuit energized, measure the amperage flow through the circuit using a clamp-on ammeter and record it below: _____ DCA	☐

6. Connect the training aid as shown in Figure 2 and complete the tasks below. ☐

Figure 2

a. With the training aid in the ON position, verify the lamps are illuminated.	☐
b. Using a DVOM, measure the supply voltage (TP1–TP8) and record it below: _____ DCV	☐
c. Using a DVOM, measure the voltage drop through the switch (TP1–TP4) and record it below: _____ DCV	☐
d. Using the DVOM, measure the voltage drop across the first lamp (TP4–TP5) and record it below: _____ DCV	☐
e. Using the DVOM, measure the voltage drop across the second lamp (TP6–TP7) and record it below: _____ DCV	☐
f. Using the DVOM, measure the voltage drop across both lamps (TP3–TP7) and record it below: _____ DCV	☐
g. What type of circuit is shown above? Series ☐ Parallel ☐ Series/Parallel ☐	☐
7. Turn the power to the training board OFF and disconnect the wire lead at TP2.	☐
a. Using a DVOM, measure the current flow in the circuit. Turn the power to the training board ON and connect the meter leads at the wire lead and TP2 and record your measurement below: _____ DCA	☐
b. Use this amperage measurement to calculate the total resistance in the circuit and record it below: _____ ohms	☐

8. Connect the training aid as shown in Figure 3, then complete the tasks below.	☐

Figure 3

a. Turn the training aid to the OFF position and confirm that the lamps are off.	☐
b. Using a DVOM, measure the resistance (TP1–TP5) and record it below: _____ ohms	☐
c. Using a DVOM, measure the resistance (TP1–TP7) and record it below: _____ ohms	☐
d. With the switch open, use a DVOM to measure the resistance (TP3–TP8) and record it below: _____ ohms	☐
e. What type of circuit is shown above? Series ☐ Parallel ☐ Series/Parallel ☐	☐
9. Turn the training aid ON and ensure the lamps are ON.	☐
a. Using a DVOM, measure the supply voltage and record it below: _____ DCV	☐
b. Using a DVOM, measure the voltage drop at Lamp A and record it below: _____ DCV	☐
c. Using a DVOM, measure the voltage drop at Lamp B and record it below: _____ DCV	☐
d. Using a DVOM, measure the voltage drop between TP2 and TP8 and record it below: _____ DCV	☐
10. Turn the power to the training board OFF and disconnect the wire lead at TP1.	☐
a. Using a DVOM, measure the total current flow in the circuit by putting the meter in series at TP1 and turning the power ON. Record the current flow below: _____ DCA	☐

b. Using a DVOM, measure the current flow in half the circuit by putting the meter in series at TP4 and turning the power ON. Record the current flow below: _____ DCA	☐
c. Turn the power to the training board OFF and disconnect the wire lead at TP6. Using a DVOM, measure the current flow in half the circuit by putting the meter in series at TP6 and turning the power ON. Record the current flow below: _____ DCA	☐
11. With the aid of a schematic, find a parallel electrical circuit on a machine (a pair of work lights, glow plugs, etc.) and measure the following with a DVOM and/or a clamp-on ammeter.	☐
a. With the circuit de-energized, measure the resistance to ground on the negative side of both loads and record below: Load 1: _____ ohms Load 2: _____ ohms	☐
b. With the circuit energized, measure the voltage drop across the loads and record below: Load 1: _____ DCV Load 2: _____ DCV	☐
c. With the circuit energized, measure and record the current flow in the following locations: After the switch: _____ DCA Before Load 1: _____ DCA Before Load 2: _____ DCA	☐
12. Connect the training aid as shown in Figure 4 and complete the tasks below. Figure 4	☐
a. Turn the power supply OFF and confirm the circuit is de-energized.	☐
b. Using a DVOM, measure the resistance of Lamp B and record it below: _____ ohms	☐

c. Using a DVOM, measure the resistance across the switch and record it below: _____ ohms	☐
d. Turn the power supply ON and confirm the lamps are ON.	☐
e. Using a DVOM, measure the supply voltage (VM1) and record it below: _____ DCV	☐
f. Using a DVOM, measure the voltage drop across Lamp B and record it below: _____ DCV	☐
g. Using a DVOM, measure the voltage drop across the second lamp (VM4) and record it below: _____ DCV	☐
h. Using a DVOM, measure and record the voltage drop across the resistance (VM2) and record it below: _____ DCV	☐
i. What type of circuit is shown above? Series ☐ Parallel ☐ Series/Parallel ☐	☐
13. Turn the power to the training board OFF and disconnect the wire lead at the switch.	☐
a. Using a DVOM, measure the total current flow in the circuit by putting the meter in series before the switch and turning the power ON. Record the current flow below: _____ DCA	☐
14. Turn the power to the training board OFF and disconnect the wire lead at Lamp B.	☐
a. Using a DVOM, measure the total current flow in the circuit by putting the meter in series at Lamp B and turning the power ON. Record the current flow below: _____ DCA	☐
15. Turn the power to the training board OFF and disconnect the wire lead at the second lamp.	☐
a. Using a DVOM, measure the total current flow in the circuit by putting the meter in series at the second lamp and turning the power ON. Record the current flow below: _____ DCA	☐

	Step Completed
16. Turn the power to the training board OFF and disconnect the wire lead at the resistor at VM2.	☐
a. Using a DVOM, measure the total current flow in the circuit by putting the meter in series at VM2 and turning the power ON. Record the current flow below: _____ DCA	☐
17. Return the training board to its original condition. Compare the current flow measurements you recorded and discuss with your supervisor/instructor.	☐

Non-Task-Specific Evaluation	Step Completed
1. Tools and equipment were used as directed and returned in good working order.	☐
2. Complied with all general and task-specific safety standards, including proper use of any personal protective equipment (PPE).	☐
3. Completed the task in an appropriate time frame (recommendation: 1.5 or 2 times the flat rate).	☐
4. Left the workspace clean and orderly.	☐
5. Cared for customer property and returned it undamaged.	☐

Student signature _____ Date _____

Comments:

Have your supervisor/instructor verify satisfactory completion of this procedure, any observations made, and any necessary action(s) recommended.

Evaluation Instructions: The scoring box below is intended to act as a guide for both student and supervisor/instructor. Each criterion listed will help students to understand what is expected of them and help supervisors/instructors to articulate the level of success at a particular task. The scoring is set up to allow a second attempt at each task (see the Test and Retest columns). Scoring is designed only to award students points for task criteria that were completed correctly. Points are lost for failure to complete the employability requirements (see Non-Task-Specific criteria). When all criteria are evaluated, tally the points for a total at the bottom of each column.

Tasksheet Scoring

	Test		Retest	
Evaluation Items	**Pass**	**Fail**	**Pass**	**Fail**
Task-Specific Evaluation	**(1 pt)**	**(0 pts)**	**(1 pt)**	**(0 pts)**
1. Student recorded an accurate DVOM measurement for at least three circuits.				
2. Student recorded an accurate DVOM measurement for at least seven circuits.				
3. Student recorded an accurate DVOM measurement for at least 11 circuits.				
4. Student recorded an accurate DVOM measurement for all 15 circuits.				
Non-Task-Specific Evaluation	**(0 pts)**	**(−1 pt)**	**(0 pts)**	**(−1 pt)**
Student successfully completed at least three of the non-task-specific steps.				
Student successfully completed all five of the non-task-specific steps.				
Total Score: <total # of points / 4 = %>				

Supervisor/Instructor:

Supervisor/instructor signature _____ Date _____

Comments:

Retest supervisor/instructor signature _____ Date _____

Comments:

Chapter 16: 12/24 Volt Cranking Circuits

Learning Objective/Task	CDX Tasksheet Number	AED Reference Number
• Diagnose cranking system problems using voltage drops and other diagnostic methods.	2.3c001	AED 2.3c
• Test and determine if replacement is necessary for the following starting system components: conductors, relays/solenoids, and starters.	2.3d001	AED 2.3d

Materials Required

- Engine that cranks but does not start
- Equipment manufacturer's workshop manual, including schematic wiring diagrams
- Machine lifting equipment, if applicable
- Digital volt-ohmmeter (DVOM)
- High current amp meter
- High current amp gauge

Safety Considerations

- This task may require operating the equipment on school grounds, which carries severe risks. Attempt this task only with full permission from your supervisor/instructor and follow all the guidelines exactly.
- Lifting equipment such as vehicle jacks and stands, vehicle hoists, and engine hoists are important tools that increase productivity and make the job easier. However, they can also cause severe injury or death if used improperly. Make sure you follow the manufacturer's operation procedures. Also make sure you have your supervisor's/instructor's permission to use any particular type of lifting equipment.
- Comply with personal and environmental safety practices associated with clothing; eye protection; hand tools; power equipment; proper ventilation; and the handling, storage, and disposal of chemicals/materials in accordance with federal, state, and local regulations.
- Always wear the correct protective eyewear and clothing and use the appropriate safety equipment, as well as seat protectors and floor mat protectors.
- Make sure you understand and observe all legislative and personal safety procedures when carrying out practical assignments. If you are unsure of what these are, ask your supervisor/instructor.

CDX Tasksheet Number: 2.3c001

Student/Intern Information

Name _____ Date _____ Class _____

Machine, Customer, and Service Information

Machine used for this activity:

Make _____ Model _____

Hours _____ Serial Number _____

> ### Materials Required
> - Engine that cranks but does not start
> - Equipment manufacturer's workshop manual, including schematic wiring diagrams
> - Machine lifting equipment, if applicable
> - Digital volt-ohmmeter (DVOM)
> - High current amp meter

Task-Specific Safety Considerations

- This task may require operating the equipment on school grounds, which carries severe risks. Attempt this task only with full permission from your supervisor/instructor and follow all the guidelines exactly.
- Lifting equipment such as vehicle jacks and stands, vehicle hoists, and engine hoists are important tools that increase productivity and make the job easier. However, they can also cause severe injury or death if used improperly. Make sure you follow the manufacturer's operation procedures. Also make sure you have your supervisor's/instructor's permission to use any particular type of lifting equipment.
- Comply with personal and environmental safety practices associated with clothing; eye protection; hand tools; power equipment; proper ventilation; and the handling, storage, and disposal of chemicals/materials in accordance with federal, state, and local regulations.
- Always wear the correct protective eyewear and clothing and use the appropriate safety equipment, as well as seat protectors and floor mat protectors.
- Make sure you understand and observe all legislative and personal safety procedures when carrying out practical assignments. If you are unsure of what these are, ask your supervisor/instructor.

▶ TASK Diagnose cranking system problems using voltage drops and other diagnostic methods.

AED 2.3C

Time off_____

Time on_____

Student Instructions: Read through the entire procedure prior to starting. Prepare your workspace and any tools or parts that may be needed to complete the task. When directed by your supervisor/instructor, begin the procedure to complete the task, and comment or check the box as each step is finished. Track your time on this procedure for later comparison to the standard completion time (i.e., "flat rate" or customer pay time).

Total time_____

Procedure	Step Completed
1. To conduct this test, it is required that the engine cranks but does not start. Follow the manufacturer's recommendations for disabling the engine so that it does not start. The proper use of testing equipment is paramount.	☐
2. Record the steps you will take to prevent the engine from starting while cranking it over:	☐
3. Prepare the DVOM to measure direct current voltage (DCV). Measure the battery voltage at the battery before cranking, during cranking, and at the starter motor while the engine is cranking and record the measurements below. (**Note:** For the last measurement, place the red lead on the main battery terminal of the starter solenoid and the black lead on the ground terminal of the starter motor.)	☐
a. Voltage before cranking: _____ DCV	☐
b. Voltage during cranking: _____ DCV	☐
c. Voltage at the starter during cranking: _____ DCV	☐
d. Are your readings within the manufacturer's specifications? Yes ☐ No ☐	☐
e. If not, briefly describe the repair procedure needed to correct the problem:	☐
f. What condition does excessive voltage drop equate to?	☐
4. Perform the following tasks for the starter high current circuit voltage drop test.	☐
a. Describe where the DVOM leads should be placed to measure voltage drop on the positive side of the circuit:	☐
b. Write the voltage reading during engine cranking: _____ DCV	☐

c. Describe where the DVOM leads should be placed to measure voltage drop on the negative side of the circuit:	☐
d. Write the voltage reading during engine cranking: _____ DCV	☐
e. Are your readings within the manufacturer's specifications? Yes ☐ No ☐	☐
f. If not, then briefly describe the repair procedure needed to correct the problem:	☐
5. Prepare a high current amp meter for use.	☐
a. With the engine being cranked without starting, measure the amount of current flow through the positive high current cable going to the starter. Record the reading during engine cranking below: _____ DCA	☐
b. Write a cause of potential excessive current flow found during this test:	☐
6. List three cranking system problems that could be diagnosed with voltage drop tests and/or amperage flow tests:	☐
7. Return the machine's engine to normal operating condition. Start the machine and verify proper operation of the starting system and engine.	☐
8. Discuss your findings with your supervisor/instructor.	☐

Non-Task-Specific Evaluation	Step Completed
1. Tools and equipment were used as directed and returned in good working order.	☐
2. Complied with all general and task-specific safety standards, including proper use of any personal protective equipment (PPE).	☐
3. Completed the task in an appropriate time frame (recommendation: 1.5 or 2 times the flat rate).	☐
4. Left the workspace clean and orderly.	☐
5. Cared for customer property and returned it undamaged.	☐

Student signature _____ Date _____

Comments:

Have your supervisor/instructor verify satisfactory completion of this procedure, any observations made, and any necessary action(s) recommended.

Evaluation Instructions: The scoring box below is intended to act as a guide for both student and supervisor/instructor. Each criterion listed will help students to understand what is expected of them and help supervisors/instructors to articulate the level of success at a particular task. The scoring is set up to allow a second attempt at each task (see the Test and Retest columns). Scoring is designed only to award students points for task criteria that were completed correctly. Points are lost for failure to complete the employability requirements (see Non-Task-Specific criteria). When all criteria are evaluated, tally the points for a total at the bottom of each column.

Tasksheet Scoring

Evaluation Items	Test		Retest	
	Pass	**Fail**	**Pass**	**Fail**
Task-Specific Evaluation	**(1 pt)**	**(0 pts)**	**(1 pt)**	**(0 pts)**
1. Student correctly described the steps taken to prevent the engine from starting while cranking it over.				
2. Student showed the proper use of a DVOM during voltage drop testing.				
3. Student showed the proper use of an amp meter during amp flow testing.				
4. Student accurately listed three different problems that could be diagnosed with voltage drop testing.				
Non-Task-Specific Evaluation	**(0 pts)**	**(−1 pt)**	**(0 pts)**	**(−1 pt)**
Student successfully completed at least three of the non-task-specific steps.				
Student successfully completed all five of the non-task-specific steps.				
Total Score: <total # of points / 4 = %>				

Supervisor/Instructor:

Supervisor/instructor signature _____ Date _____

Comments:

Retest supervisor/instructor signature _____ Date _____

Comments:

CDX Tasksheet Number: 2.3d001

Student/Intern Information

Name _____ Date _____ Class _____

Machine, Customer, and Service Information

Machine used for this activity:

Make _____ Model _____

Hours _____ Serial Number _____

Materials Required

- Machine (in a safe service state and disabled from starting)
- Equipment manufacturer's workshop manual including schematic wiring diagrams
- Digital volt-ohmmeter (DVOM)
- High current amp gauge
- Machine lifting equipment, if applicable

Task-Specific Safety Considerations

- This task may require operating the equipment on school grounds, which carries severe risks. Attempt this task only with full permission from your supervisor/instructor and follow all the guidelines exactly.
- Lifting equipment such as vehicle jacks and stands, vehicle hoists, and engine hoists are important tools that increase productivity and make the job easier. However, they can also cause severe injury or death if used improperly. Make sure you follow the manufacturer's operation procedures. Also make sure you have your supervisor's/instructor's permission to use any particular type of lifting equipment.
- Comply with personal and environmental safety practices associated with clothing; eye protection; hand tools; power equipment; proper ventilation; and the handling, storage, and disposal of chemicals/materials in accordance with federal, state, and local regulations.
- Always wear the correct protective eyewear and clothing and use the appropriate safety equipment, as well as seat protectors and floor mat protectors.
- Make sure you understand and observe all legislative and personal safety procedures when carrying out practical assignments. If you are unsure of what these are, ask your supervisor/instructor.

▶ **TASK** Test and determine if replacement is necessary for the following starting system components: conductors, relays/solenoids, and starters.

AED 2.3d

Time off_____

Time on_____

Total time_____

Student Instructions: Read through the entire procedure prior to starting. Prepare your workspace and any tools or parts that may be needed to complete the task. When directed by your supervisor/instructor, begin the procedure to complete the task, and comment or check the box as each step is finished. Track your time on this procedure for later comparison to the standard completion time (i.e., "flat rate" or customer pay time).

Procedure	Step Completed
1. Identify the machine manufacturer's steps you will take to prevent the engine from starting while cranking it over and write them below:	☐
2. Locate and identify the service information and specifications needed to evaluate, test, and replace cranking system conductors, relays/solenoids, and starters and list it below:	☐
3. Prepare a DVOM for direct current (DC) voltage testing.	☐
a. Perform a voltage drop test on one of the high current flow (battery) cables going to the machine's starter. Describe this test and record your measurement below:	☐
b. Assume there was an issue with the battery cable and describe how you would evaluate it to determine whether it can be reused or repaired or if replacement is needed:	☐
c. Briefly describe the steps taken to replace the battery cable:	☐
4. Prepare a DVOM for DC voltage testing.	☐
a. Perform a voltage drop test across the high current terminals of either a cranking system relay or solenoid. Describe the steps taken to do this safely and record your measurement below:	☐
b. Assume there was an issue with the relay or solenoid and describe how you would evaluate it to determine whether it can be reused or repaired or if replacement is needed:	☐

c. Are there specifications for resistance values of the relay or solenoid coil(s)? Yes ☐ No ☐	☐
d. Measure the resistance of the relay coil and record it below: _____ ohms	☐
e. Briefly describe the steps taken to replace the relay or solenoid and include any fastener torqueing procedures:	☐
5. Prepare a high current amp gauge for DC amp testing.	☐
a. Perform a starter current draw test while cranking the engine after it has been disabled to start. Describe the steps taken to perform this test below and record your findings:	☐
b. Assume there was an issue with the starter and describe how you would evaluate it to determine whether it can be reused or repaired or if replacement is needed:	☐
c. Remove the starter (use lifting assistance if necessary) and perform a no-load test on it. Briefly describe how this test is performed:	☐
d. List any torque specifications for fasteners related to installation of the starter:	☐
e. Install the starter per the machine manufacturer's recommendations and return the machine to normal operating condition.	☐

Non-Task-Specific Evaluation	Step Completed
1. Tools and equipment were used as directed and returned in good working order.	☐
2. Complied with all general and task-specific safety standards, including proper use of any personal protective equipment (PPE).	☐
3. Completed the task in an appropriate time frame (recommendation: 1.5 or 2 times the flat rate).	☐
4. Left the workspace clean and orderly.	☐
5. Cared for customer property and returned it undamaged.	☐

Student signature _____ Date _____

Comments:

Have your supervisor/instructor verify satisfactory completion of this procedure, any observations made, and any necessary action(s) recommended.

Evaluation Instructions: The scoring box below is intended to act as a guide for both student and supervisor/instructor. Each criterion listed will help students to understand what is expected of them and help supervisors/instructors to articulate the level of success at a particular task. The scoring is set up to allow a second attempt at each task (see the Test and Retest columns). Scoring is designed only to award students points for task criteria that were completed correctly. Points are lost for failure to complete the employability requirements (see Non-Task-Specific criteria). When all criteria are evaluated, tally the points for a total at the bottom of each column.

Tasksheet Scoring

Evaluation Items	Test		Retest	
	Pass	Fail	Pass	Fail
Task-Specific Evaluation	**(1 pt)**	**(0 pts)**	**(1 pt)**	**(0 pts)**
1. Student correctly described the procedure for preventing engine starting during crank system testing and identified the service information and specifications needed to evaluate, test, and replace cranking system conductors, relays/solenoids, and starters.				
2. Student properly demonstrated voltage drop testing on high current cables.				
3. Student properly demonstrated voltage drop testing on relays and solenoids.				
4. Student properly demonstrated starter testing involving current draw and no-load testing.				
Non-Task-Specific Evaluation	**(0 pts)**	**(−1 pt)**	**(0 pts)**	**(−1 pt)**
Student successfully completed at least three of the non-task-specific steps.				
Student successfully completed all five of the non-task-specific steps.				
Total Score: <total # of points / 4 = %>				

Supervisor/Instructor:

Supervisor/instructor signature _____ Date _____

Comments:

Retest supervisor/instructor signature _____ Date _____

Comments:

Chapter 17: 12/24 Volt Charging Circuits

Learning Objective/Task	CDX Tasksheet Number	AED Reference Number
• Diagnose charging system problems using voltage drops and other diagnostic methods.	2.4c001	AED 2.4c
• Test and determine if replacement is necessary for the following charging system components: conductors, alternators, and regulators.	2.4d001	AED 2.4d

Materials Required

- Machine chosen by the supervisor/instructor to complete the task
- Equipment manufacturer's service information, including schematic wiring diagrams
- Machine lifting equipment, if applicable
- Digital volt-ohmmeter (DVOM)
- Battery load tester, if applicable
- Ammeter
- Current clamp

Safety Considerations

- This task may require operating the equipment on school grounds, which carries severe risks. Attempt this task only with full permission from your supervisor/instructor and follow all the guidelines exactly.
- Lifting equipment such as vehicle jacks and stands, vehicle hoists, and engine hoists are important tools that increase productivity and make the job easier. However, they can also cause severe injury or death if used improperly. Make sure you follow the manufacturer's operation procedures. Also make sure you have your supervisor's/instructor's permission to use any particular type of lifting equipment.
- Use extreme caution when working around batteries. Immediately remove any electrolyte that may come in contact with you. Electrolyte is a mixture of sulfuric acid and water. Batteries may produce explosive mixtures of gas containing hydrogen; avoid creating any sparks around batteries. Consult with the shop safety and emergency procedures when working with or around batteries.
- Comply with personal and environmental safety practices associated with clothing; eye protection; hand tools; power equipment; proper ventilation; and the handling, storage, and disposal of chemicals/materials in accordance with federal, state, and local regulations.
- Always wear the correct protective eyewear and clothing and use the appropriate safety equipment, as well as seat protectors and floor mat protectors.
- Make sure you understand and observe all legislative and personal safety procedures when carrying out practical assignments. If you are unsure of what these are, ask your supervisor/instructor.

CDX Tasksheet Number: 2.4c001

Student/Intern Information

Name _____ Date _____ Class _____

Machine, Customer, and Service Information

Machine used for this activity:

Make _____ Model _____

Hours _____ Serial Number _____

Materials Required

- Machine chosen by the supervisor/instructor to complete the task
- Equipment manufacturer's service information, including schematic wiring diagrams
- Machine lifting equipment, if applicable
- Digital volt-ohmmeter (DVOM)
- Battery load tester, if applicable
- Ammeter
- Current clamp

Task-Specific Safety Considerations

- This task may require operating the equipment on school grounds, which carries severe risks. Attempt this task only with full permission from your supervisor/instructor and follow all the guidelines exactly.
- Lifting equipment such as vehicle jacks and stands, vehicle hoists, and engine hoists are important tools that increase productivity and make the job easier. However, they can also cause severe injury or death if used improperly. Make sure you follow the manufacturer's operation procedures. Also make sure you have your supervisor's/instructor's permission to use any particular type of lifting equipment.
- Use extreme caution when working around batteries. Immediately remove any electrolyte that may come in contact with you. Electrolyte is a mixture of sulfuric acid and water. Batteries may produce explosive mixtures of gas containing hydrogen; avoid creating any sparks around batteries. Consult with the shop safety and emergency procedures when working with or around batteries.
- Comply with personal and environmental safety practices associated with clothing; eye protection; hand tools; power equipment; proper ventilation; and the handling, storage, and disposal of chemicals/materials in accordance with federal, state, and local regulations.
- Always wear the correct protective eyewear and clothing and use the appropriate safety equipment, as well as seat protectors and floor mat protectors.
- Make sure you understand and observe all legislative and personal safety procedures when carrying out practical assignments. If you are unsure of what these are, ask your supervisor/instructor.

▶ **TASK** Diagnose charging system problems using voltage drops and other diagnostic methods.

AED
2.4c

Student Instructions: Read through the entire procedure prior to starting. Prepare your workspace and any tools or parts that may be needed to complete the task. When directed by your supervisor/instructor, begin the procedure to complete the task, and comment or check the box as each step is finished. Track your time on this procedure for later comparison to the standard completion time (i.e., "flat rate" or customer pay time).

Procedure	Step Completed
1. Have your supervisor/instructor choose a machine for this task and answer the questions below to describe its charging system.	☐
a. What is the machine's normal operating electrical system voltage and how do you know this?	☐
b. What kind of belt system drives the alternator, and how is tension maintained?	☐
c. How many wires are connected to the alternator, what are their purpose, and where did you get this information?	☐
d. How many batteries are on the machine, and how are they connected?	☐
e. Does the machine have a fuse or breaker for the charging system? Yes ☐ No ☐	☐
f. Is there a voltmeter or ammeter in the cab? Yes ☐ No ☐	☐
g. What indicators are there in the cab to warn the operator of a problem with the charging system?	☐
h. Does the machine have an external voltage regulator? Yes ☐ No ☐	☐

2. Prepare the DVOM to measure direct current voltage (DCV). Measure the battery voltage at the battery under each of the following conditions and record your measurements.	☐
a. Engine OFF with no electrical loads ON _____ DCV	☐
b. Engine OFF after 5 minutes with lights ON _____ DCV	☐
c. Immediately after the engine starts with no electrical loads ON _____ DCV	☐
d. Five minutes after the engine has been running at 1,500 rpm _____ DCV	☐
e. Do your findings indicate a healthy charging system when compared to machine service information and specifications? Yes ☐ No ☐	☐
3. There are three common problems with charging systems: no charging, low charging, and excessive charging. Briefly describe the most likely cause of each problem below:	☐
4. Inspect the alternator belt condition and tension and record your findings below:	☐
a. Are there any other defects found with the alternator such as loose mounting fasteners, loose wires, or guards missing? Yes ☐ No ☐	☐
b. If yes, list the defects below:	☐
5. Perform a charging system output test as per the machine's service information. If no procedure exists, use a battery load tester to put a load on the battery while the engine is running at 2,000 rpm and use an ammeter and DVOM to record the maximum alternator output in amps and volts. (Note: Stay clear of rotating components such as belts, pulleys, and fans.) Record your results below: _____ DCA _____ DCV	☐
a. Do your measurements fall within the machine manufacturer's specifications? Yes ☐ No ☐	☐

6. Charging system problems can be caused by excessive resistance throughout the wiring and connection points between the alternator and the battery. Using a DVOM, perform a voltage drop test between the alternator output and the positive post of the battery.	☐
a. What is the maximum allowable voltage drop for both 12VDC and 24VDC systems when the alternator is at maximum output? _____ DCV _____ DCV	☐
b. What is the voltage drop between the alternator output terminal and the positive post of the battery? _____ DCV	☐
c. Are there any other connection points between the alternator output terminal and the positive post of the battery? Yes ☐ No ☐	☐
d. If yes, describe the connection point and what issues would be caused by a poor connection (loose or dirty connection):	☐
e. Check for continuity to ground at the alternator or to the ground terminal if there is one. Record the measurement below: _____ ohms	☐
7. List three cranking system problems that could be diagnosed with voltage drop tests and/or amperage flow tests:	☐
8. Return the machine to its normal operating condition. Start the machine and verify proper operation of the charging system and engine.	☐
9. Discuss your findings with your supervisor/instructor.	☐

Non-Task-Specific Evaluation	Step Completed
1. Tools and equipment were used as directed and returned in good working order.	☐
2. Complied with all general and task-specific safety standards, including proper use of any personal protective equipment (PPE).	☐
3. Completed the task in an appropriate time frame (recommendation: 1.5 or 2 times the flat rate).	☐
4. Left the workspace clean and orderly.	☐
5. Cared for customer property and returned it undamaged.	☐

Student signature _____ Date _____

Comments:

Have your supervisor/instructor verify satisfactory completion of this procedure, any observations made,

and any necessary action(s) recommended.

Evaluation Instructions: The scoring box below is intended to act as a guide for both student and supervisor/instructor. Each criterion listed will help students to understand what is expected of them and help supervisors/instructors to articulate the level of success at a particular task. The scoring is set up to allow a second attempt at each task (see the Test and Retest columns). Scoring is designed only to award students points for task criteria that were completed correctly. Points are lost for failure to complete the employability requirements (see Non-Task-Specific criteria). When all criteria are evaluated, tally the points for a total at the bottom of each column.

Tasksheet Scoring

Evaluation Items	Test		Retest	
	Pass	**Fail**	**Pass**	**Fail**
Task-Specific Evaluation	**(1 pt)**	**(0 pts)**	**(1 pt)**	**(0 pts)**
1. Student correctly described the machine's charging system.				
2. Student showed the proper use of a DVOM during voltage drop testing and completed alternator output testing correctly and safely.				
3. Student took accurate voltage measurements.				
4. Student correctly identified alternator defects, causes of common alternator problems, and problems that could be diagnosed with voltage drop testing.				
Non-Task-Specific Evaluation	**(0 pts)**	**(−1 pt)**	**(0 pts)**	**(−1 pt)**
Student successfully completed at least three of the non-task-specific steps.				
Student successfully completed all five of the non-task-specific steps.				
Total Score: <total # of points / 4 = %>				

Supervisor/Instructor:

Supervisor/instructor signature _____ Date _____

Comments:

Retest supervisor/instructor signature _____ Date _____

Comments:

CDX Tasksheet Number: 2.4d001

Student/Intern Information

Name _____ Date _____ Class _____

Machine, Customer, and Service Information

Machine used for this activity:

Make _____ Model _____

Hours _____ Serial Number _____

Materials Required

- Machine chosen by the supervisor/instructor to complete the task
- Equipment manufacturer's service information, including schematic wiring diagrams
- Machine lifting equipment, if applicable
- Digital volt-ohmmeter (DVOM)

Task-Specific Safety Considerations

- This task may require operating the equipment on school grounds, which carries severe risks. Attempt this task only with full permission from your supervisor/instructor and follow all the guidelines exactly.
- Lifting equipment such as vehicle jacks and stands, vehicle hoists, and engine hoists are important tools that increase productivity and make the job easier. However, they can also cause severe injury or death if used improperly. Make sure you follow the manufacturer's operation procedures. Also make sure you have your supervisor's/instructor's permission to use any particular type of lifting equipment.
- Comply with personal and environmental safety practices associated with clothing; eye protection; hand tools; power equipment; proper ventilation; and the handling, storage, and disposal of chemicals/materials in accordance with federal, state, and local regulations.
- Always wear the correct protective eyewear and clothing and use the appropriate safety equipment, as well as seat protectors and floor mat protectors.
- Make sure you understand and observe all legislative and personal safety procedures when carrying out practical assignments. If you are unsure of what these are, ask your supervisor/instructor.

▶ TASK Test and determine if replacement is necessary for the following charging system components: conductors, alternators, and regulators.

AED 2.4d

Time off_____

Time on_____

Total time_____

Student Instructions: Read through the entire procedure prior to starting. Prepare your workspace and any tools or parts that may be needed to complete the task. When directed by your supervisor/instructor, begin the procedure to complete the task, and comment or check the box as each step is finished. Track your time on this procedure for later comparison to the standard completion time (i.e., "flat rate" or customer pay time).

Procedure	Step Completed
Caution: When removing and installing components, ensure the machine (or simulator) you are working with is in a safe service state and disabled from starting.	
1. Using a DVOM, perform a voltage drop test on the battery ground cable that goes to the frame. Record your result below and try to find a specification in the machine's service information to compare it to. _____ DCV	☐
a. Does this measurement indicate a good connection to ground? Yes ☐ No ☐	☐
b. Remove the ground cable and inspect it for defects; clean the cable ends, frame, and battery post; and reinstall the ground cable.	☐
2. Using the machine's service information, wiring diagrams, and schematics, troubleshoot the operator complaint below (assume the problem exists). **Complaint:** Alternator is not charging (the warning lamp stays ON).	
a. Using the appropriate service information for the machine you are working with, locate the testing procedure related to this complaint and research the troubleshooting process. List the steps for the tests you will perform and include all diagnostic tooling used:	☐
b. Conduct the diagnostic procedure and report below:	☐
c. Did the test result stay within the range of the manufacturer's specifications? Yes ☐ No ☐	☐
d. Assume the test results indicated a defective alternator. Safely remove and install the alternator. After installation, perform a check to ensure the alternator is operating properly and confirm below. Yes ☐ No ☐	☐
3. Using the machine's service manual, wiring diagrams, and schematics, troubleshoot the operator complaint below. **Complaint:** Alternator low charging (voltmeter reads low)	☐
a. Using the appropriate service information for the machine you are working with, locate the testing procedure related to this complaint and research the troubleshooting process. List the steps for the tests you will perform and include all diagnostic tooling used:	☐

	Step Completed
b. Conduct the diagnostic procedure and report below:	☐
c. Did the test result stay within the range of the manufacturer's specifications? Yes ☐ No ☐	☐
d. Perform an alternator belt adjustment (if possible) according to the machine's service information. List the steps for this procedure below:	☐
4. Does this machine have an external regulator as part of its charging system? Yes ☐ No ☐	☐
a. If yes, list the steps found in the machine's service information to adjust the system voltage level:	☐
5. Return the machine to its normal operating condition and have your supervisor/instructor confirm you did so properly.	☐

Non-Task-Specific Evaluation	Step Completed
1. Tools and equipment were used as directed and returned in good working order.	☐
2. Complied with all general and task-specific safety standards, including proper use of any personal protective equipment (PPE).	☐
3. Completed the task in an appropriate time frame (recommendation: 1.5 or 2 times the flat rate).	☐
4. Left the workspace clean and orderly.	☐
5. Cared for customer property and returned it undamaged.	☐

Student signature _____ Date _____

Comments:

Have your supervisor/instructor verify satisfactory completion of this procedure, any observations made, and any necessary action(s) recommended.

Evaluation Instructions: The scoring box below is intended to act as a guide for both student and supervisor/instructor. Each criterion listed will help students to understand what is expected of them and help supervisors/instructors to articulate the level of success at a particular task. The scoring is set up to allow a second attempt at each task (see the Test and Retest columns). Scoring is designed only to award students points for task criteria that were completed correctly. Points are lost for failure to complete the employability requirements (see Non-Task-Specific criteria). When all criteria are evaluated, tally the points for a total at the bottom of each column.

Tasksheet Scoring

	Test		Retest	
Evaluation Items	**Pass**	**Fail**	**Pass**	**Fail**
Task-Specific Evaluation	**(1 pt)**	**(0 pts)**	**(1 pt)**	**(0 pts)**
1. Student demonstrated proper voltage drop testing on high current cables.				
2. Student correctly followed any service information procedures and specifications needed to diagnose a no-charge alternator complaint.				
3. Student correctly followed any service information procedures and specifications needed to diagnose a low-charge alternator complaint.				
4. Student located and identified the regulator (if applicable).				
Non-Task-Specific Evaluation	**(0 pts)**	**(−1 pt)**	**(0 pts)**	**(−1 pt)**
Student successfully completed at least three of the non-task-specific steps.				
Student successfully completed all five of the non-task-specific steps.				
Total Score: <total # of points / 4 = %>				

Supervisor/Instructor:

Supervisor/instructor signature _____ Date _____

Comments:

Retest supervisor/instructor signature _____ Date _____

Comments:

Chapter 18: Electrical Schematics/Diagrams

Learning Objective/Task	CDX Tasksheet Number	AED Reference Number
• Trace various circuits using wiring schematics/diagrams.	2.6b001	AED 2.6b
• Diagnose machine electrical system faults using schematics/diagrams.	2.6c001	AED 2.6c

Materials Required

- Machine with a simple 12VDC lighting system (no electronics)
- Machine with a simple 24VDC accessory system (no electronics)
- Machine with an electrical control system that uses a relay
- Equipment manufacturer's service information, including schematic wiring diagrams
- Machine lifting equipment, if applicable
- Piece of clear plastic
- Erasable markers
- Digital volt-ohmmeter (DVOM)
- Ammeter
- Current clamp

Safety Considerations

- This task may require operating the equipment on school grounds, which carries severe risks. Attempt this task only with full permission from your supervisor/instructor and follow all the guidelines exactly.
- Lifting equipment such as vehicle jacks and stands, vehicle hoists, and engine hoists are important tools that increase productivity and make the job easier. However, they can also cause severe injury or death if used improperly. Make sure you follow the manufacturer's operation procedures. Also make sure you have your supervisor's/instructor's permission to use any particular type of lifting equipment.
- Comply with personal and environmental safety practices associated with clothing; eye protection; hand tools; power equipment; proper ventilation; and the handling, storage, and disposal of chemicals/materials in accordance with federal, state, and local regulations.
- Always wear the correct protective eyewear and clothing and use the appropriate safety equipment, as well as seat protectors and floor mat protectors.
- Make sure you understand and observe all legislative and personal safety procedures when carrying out practical assignments. If you are unsure of what these are, ask your supervisor/instructor.
- Use extreme caution when working around batteries. Immediately remove any electrolyte that may come in contact with you. Electrolyte is a mixture of sulfuric acid and water. Batteries may produce explosive mixtures of gas containing hydrogen; avoid creating any sparks around batteries. Consult with the shop safety and emergency procedures when working with or around batteries.

CDX Tasksheet Number: 2.6b001

Student/Intern Information

Name _____ Date _____ Class _____

Machine, Customer, and Service Information

Machine used for this activity:

Make _____ Model _____

Hours _____ Serial Number _____

Materials Required

- Machine with a simple 12VDC lighting system (no electronics)
- Machine with a simple 24VDC accessory system (no electronics)
- Machine with an electrical control system that uses a relay
- Equipment manufacturer's service information, including schematic wiring diagrams
- Machine lifting equipment, if applicable
- Piece of clear plastic
- Erasable markers

Task-Specific Safety Considerations

- This task may require operating the equipment on school grounds, which carries severe risks. Attempt this task only with full permission from your supervisor/instructor and follow all the guidelines exactly.
- Lifting equipment such as vehicle jacks and stands, vehicle hoists, and engine hoists are important tools that increase productivity and make the job easier. However, they can also cause severe injury or death if used improperly. Make sure you follow the manufacturer's operation procedures. Also make sure you have your supervisor's/instructor's permission to use any particular type of lifting equipment.
- Comply with personal and environmental safety practices associated with clothing; eye protection; hand tools; power equipment; proper ventilation; and the handling, storage, and disposal of chemicals/materials in accordance with federal, state, and local regulations.
- Always wear the correct protective eyewear and clothing and use the appropriate safety equipment, as well as seat protectors and floor mat protectors.
- Make sure you understand and observe all legislative and personal safety procedures when carrying out practical assignments. If you are unsure of what these are, ask your supervisor/instructor.

▶ TASK Trace various circuits using wiring schematics/diagrams.

AED 2.6b

Time off_____

Time on_____

Student Instructions: Read through the entire procedure prior to starting. Prepare your workspace and any tools or parts that may be needed to complete the task. When directed by your supervisor/instructor, begin the procedure to complete the task, and comment or check the box as each step is finished. Track your time on this procedure for later comparison to the standard completion time (i.e., "flat rate" or customer pay time).

Total time_____

Procedure	Step Completed
(**Note:** For each of the following steps, place a clear sheet of plastic over the machine's schematic and use an erasable marker to trace the named portion of the schematic.)	
1. Choose a machine with a simple 12VDC lighting system (no electronics). Trace the lighting circuit on the machine's schematic. Have your supervisor/instructor verify you did this correctly. Supervisor's/instructor's initials: _____	☐
2. Choose a machine with a simple 24VDC accessory system (no electronics). Trace the accessory circuit on the machine's schematic. Have your supervisor/instructor verify you did this correctly. Supervisor's/instructor's initials: _____	☐
3. Choose a machine with an electrical control system that uses a relay such as a shutoff solenoid for a fuel injection system. Trace the control circuit on the machine's schematic. Have your supervisor/instructor verify you did this correctly. Supervisor's/instructor's initials: _____	☐
4. Trace a machine's starter control system on the machine's schematic. Have your supervisor/instructor verify you did this correctly. Supervisor's/instructor's initials: _____	☐
5. Trace a machine's sensor circuit (part of the machine's electronic control system) on the machine's electrical schematic. Have your supervisor/instructor verify you did this correctly. Supervisor's/instructor's initials: _____	☐

Non-Task-Specific Evaluation	Step Completed
1. Tools and equipment were used as directed and returned in good working order.	☐
2. Complied with all general and task-specific safety standards, including proper use of any personal protective equipment (PPE).	☐
3. Completed the task in an appropriate time frame (recommendation: 1.5 or 2 times the flat rate).	☐
4. Left the workspace clean and orderly.	☐
5. Cared for customer property and returned it undamaged.	☐

Student signature _____ Date _____

Comments:

Have your supervisor/instructor verify satisfactory completion of this procedure, any observations made, and any necessary action(s) recommended.

Evaluation Instructions: The scoring box below is intended to act as a guide for both student and supervisor/instructor. Each criterion listed will help students to understand what is expected of them and help supervisors/instructors to articulate the level of success at a particular task. The scoring is set up to allow a second attempt at each task (see the Test and Retest columns). Scoring is designed only to award students points for task criteria that were completed correctly. Points are lost for failure to complete the employability requirements (see Non-Task-Specific criteria). When all criteria are evaluated, tally the points for a total at the bottom of each column.

Tasksheet Scoring

	Test		Retest	
Evaluation Items	**Pass**	**Fail**	**Pass**	**Fail**
Task-Specific Evaluation	**(1 pt)**	**(0 pts)**	**(1 pt)**	**(0 pts)**
1. Student accurately traced a machine's lighting circuit with labels and current flow correct.				
2. Student accurately traced a machine's accessory circuit with labels and current flow correct.				
3. Student accurately traced a machine's control circuit with labels and current flow correct.				
4. Student accurately traced a machine's starter control circuit and electronic sensor circuit with labels and current flow correct.				
Non-Task-Specific Evaluation	**(0 pts)**	**(−1 pt)**	**(0 pts)**	**(−1 pt)**
Student successfully completed at least three of the non-task-specific steps.				
Student successfully completed all five of the non-task-specific steps.				
Total Score: <total # of points / 4 = %>				

CDX Tasksheet Number: 2.6c001

Student/Intern Information

Name _____ Date _____ Class _____

Machine, Customer, and Service Information

Machine used for this activity:

Make _____ Model _____

Hours _____ Serial Number _____

Materials Required

- Machine chosen by the supervisor/instructor to complete the task
- Equipment manufacturer's service information, including schematic wiring diagrams
- Machine lifting equipment, if applicable
- Digital volt-ohmmeter (DVOM)
- Ammeter
- Current clamp

Task-Specific Safety Considerations

- This task may require operating the equipment on school grounds, which carries severe risks. Attempt this task only with full permission from your supervisor/instructor and follow all the guidelines exactly.
- Lifting equipment such as equipment jacks and stands, hoists, overhead cranes, and engine hoists are important tools that increase productivity and make the job easier. However, they can also cause severe injury or death if used improperly. Make sure you follow the manufacturer's operation procedures. Also make sure you have your supervisor's/instructor's permission to use any type of lifting equipment.
- Use extreme caution when working around batteries. Immediately remove any electrolyte that may come in contact with you. Electrolyte is a mixture of sulfuric acid and water. Batteries may produce explosive mixtures of gas containing hydrogen; avoid creating any sparks around batteries. Consult with the shop safety and emergency procedures when working with or around batteries.
- Comply with personal and environmental safety practices associated with clothing; eye protection; hand tools; power equipment; proper ventilation; and the handling, storage, and disposal of chemicals/materials in accordance with federal, state, and local regulations.
- Always wear the correct protective eyewear and clothing and use the appropriate safety equipment, as well as seat protectors and floor mat protectors.
- Make sure you understand and observe all legislative and personal safety procedures when carrying out practical assignments. If you are unsure of what these are, ask your supervisor/instructor.

▶ **TASK** Diagnose machine electrical system faults using schematics/diagrams.

AED
2.6c

Student Instructions: Read through the entire procedure prior to starting. Prepare your workspace and any tools or parts that may be needed to complete the task. When directed by your supervisor/instructor, begin the procedure to complete the task, and comment or check the box as each step is finished. Track your time on this procedure for later comparison to the standard completion time (i.e., "flat rate" or customer pay time).

Procedure	Step Completed
1. Have your supervisor/instructor choose a machine and assume it has a lighting circuit that is not functioning (have your supervisor/instructor identify which one). Use the machine's electrical schematic to identify the following information.	☐
a. Are there any other circuits that share the same power source (fuse or circuit breaker)? Yes ☐ No ☐	☐
b. If yes, list the other circuits and identify why this is good to know:	☐
c. Does the electrical schematic indicate if the circuit power needs the key turned ON? Yes ☐ No ☐	☐
d. List the wire numbers/colors shown on the schematic for the light circuit power and ground:	☐
e. Using the schematic, demonstrate where you could check for available voltage in this circuit at three locations on the machine. List these locations below:	☐
2. Assume the machine's starting motor will not turn. Use the machine's electrical schematic to identify the following information.	
a. List the wire numbers/colors shown on the schematic for the key switch power supply:	☐

b. Does the machine have a relay between the key switch and the starter? Yes ☐ No ☐	☐
c. If yes, identify where the relay gets its high current power from and if the wire gauge size is indicated on the schematic:	☐
d. Are there any starter interlock devices shown on the schematic? Yes ☐ No ☐	☐
e. Using the schematic, demonstrate where you could check for available voltage in the starter control circuit at three locations on the machine. List these locations below:	☐
3. Assume there is a problem with one of the machine's gauges or operator warning devices. Use the machine's electrical schematic to identify the following information.	
a. List the wire numbers/colors shown on the schematic for the gauge or warning device:	☐
b. Does the gauge or warning device have an engine control module (ECM) as part of its circuit? Yes ☐ No ☐	☐
c. If yes, name where the ECM gets power from:	☐
d. Is there a sender in this circuit that has a low-voltage reference signal? Yes ☐ No ☐	☐
e. Using the electrical schematic, demonstrate where you could check for available voltage or resistance at the sender on the machine. List the location(s) below:	☐

Non-Task-Specific Evaluation	Step Completed
1. Tools and equipment were used as directed and returned in good working order.	☐
2. Complied with all general and task-specific safety standards, including proper use of any personal protective equipment (PPE).	☐
3. Completed the task in an appropriate time frame (recommendation: 1.5 or 2 times the flat rate).	☐
4. Left the workspace clean and orderly.	☐
5. Cared for customer property and returned it undamaged.	☐

Student signature _____ Date _____

Comments:

Have your supervisor/instructor verify satisfactory completion of this procedure, any observations made, and any necessary action(s) recommended.

Evaluation Instructions: The scoring box below is intended to act as a guide for both student and supervisor/instructor. Each criterion listed will help students to understand what is expected of them and help supervisors/instructors to articulate the level of success at a particular task. The scoring is set up to allow a second attempt at each task (see the Test and Retest columns). Scoring is designed only to award students points for task criteria that were completed correctly. Points are lost for failure to complete the employability requirements (see Non-Task-Specific criteria). When all criteria are evaluated, tally the points for a total at the bottom of each column.

Tasksheet Scoring

	Test		Retest	
Evaluation Items	Pass	Fail	Pass	Fail
Task-Specific Evaluation	**(1 pt)**	**(0 pts)**	**(1 pt)**	**(0 pts)**
1. Student correctly answered the questions about each system fault.				
2. Student listed the correct wire numbers/colors shown on the schematic for each specified part.				
3. Student properly identified where to check for available voltage or resistance for each system fault.				
4. Student provided any additional explanations or locations requested for each system fault.				
Non-Task-Specific Evaluation	**(0 pts)**	**(−1 pt)**	**(0 pts)**	**(−1 pt)**
Student successfully completed at least three of the non-task-specific steps.				
Student successfully completed all five of the non-task-specific steps.				
Total Score: <total # of points / 4 = %>				

Supervisor/Instructor:

Supervisor/instructor signature _____ Date _____

Comments:

Retest supervisor/instructor signature _____ Date _____

Comments:

Chapter 19: Diagnostics Systems Troubleshooting

Learning Objective/Task	CDX Tasksheet Number	AED Reference Number
• Diagnose a machine electrical system fault and determine the root cause of failure.	2.8002	AED 2.8
• Use electrical schematics and troubleshooting flow charts to diagnose an electrical system problem.	2.8007	AED 2.8
• Utilize an interactive equipment diagnostic program to find fault codes and diagnose an electrical system fault.	2.8008	AED 2.8
• Create a repair order based on a machine electrical system problem.	2.8009	AED 2.8

Materials Required

- Engine that cranks but does not start
- Equipment manufacturer's service information, including schematic wiring diagrams
- Machine lifting equipment, if applicable
- Digital volt-ohmmeter (DVOM)
- High current amp meter
- Machine chosen by the supervisor/instructor to complete the task
- Ammeter
- Current clamp
- Manufacturer's service software
- Laptop computer
- Communication adapter
- Repair order form

Safety Considerations

- This task may require operating the equipment on school grounds, which carries severe risks. Attempt this task only with full permission from your supervisor/instructor and follow all the guidelines exactly.
- Lifting equipment such as equipment jacks and stands, hoists, overhead cranes, and engine hoists are important tools that increase productivity and make the job easier. However, they can also cause severe injury or death if used improperly. Make sure you follow the manufacturer's operation procedures. Also make sure you have your supervisor's/instructor's permission to use any type of lifting equipment.
- Comply with personal and environmental safety practices associated with clothing; eye protection; hand tools; power equipment; proper ventilation; and the handling, storage, and disposal of chemicals/materials in accordance with federal, state, and local regulations.
- Always wear the correct protective eyewear and clothing and use the appropriate safety equipment, as well as seat protectors and floor mat protectors.

- Make sure you understand and observe all legislative and personal safety procedures when carrying out practical assignments. If you are unsure of what these are, ask your supervisor/instructor.
- Use extreme caution when working around batteries. Immediately remove any electrolyte that may come in contact with you. Electrolyte is a mixture of sulfuric acid and water. Batteries may produce explosive mixtures of gas containing hydrogen; avoid creating any sparks around batteries. Consult with the shop safety and emergency procedures when working with or around batteries.

CDX Tasksheet Number: 2.8002

Student/Intern Information

Name _____ Date _____ Class _____

Machine, Customer, and Service Information

Machine used for this activity:

Make _____ Model _____

Hours _____ Serial Number _____

Materials Required

- Engine that cranks but does not start
- Equipment manufacturer's workshop manual, including schematic wiring diagrams
- Machine lifting equipment, if applicable
- Digital volt-ohmmeter (DVOM)
- High current amp meter

Task-Specific Safety Considerations

- This task may require operating the equipment on school grounds, which carries severe risks. Attempt this task only with full permission from your supervisor/instructor and follow all the guidelines exactly.
- Lifting equipment such as equipment jacks and stands, hoists, overhead cranes, and engine hoists are important tools that increase productivity and make the job easier. However, they can also cause severe injury or death if used improperly. Make sure you follow the manufacturer's operation procedures. Also make sure you have your supervisor's/instructor's permission to use any type of lifting equipment.
- Comply with personal and environmental safety practices associated with clothing; eye protection; hand tools; power equipment; proper ventilation; and the handling, storage, and disposal of chemicals/materials in accordance with federal, state, and local regulations.
- Always wear the correct protective eyewear and clothing and use the appropriate safety equipment, as well as seat protectors and floor mat protectors.
- Make sure you understand and observe all legislative and personal safety procedures when carrying out practical assignments. If you are unsure of what these are, ask your supervisor/instructor.

▶ TASK Diagnose a machine electrical system fault and determine the root cause of failure.

AED 2.8

Time off_____

Time on_____

Student Instructions: Read through the entire procedure prior to starting. Prepare your workspace and any tools or parts that may be needed to complete the task. When directed by your supervisor/instructor, begin the procedure to complete the task, and comment or check the box as each step is finished. Track your time on this procedure for later comparison to the standard completion time (i.e., "flat rate" or customer pay time).

Total time_____

Procedure	Step Completed
Note: Conducting this test requires that the engine cranks but does not start. Follow the manufacturer's recommendations for disabling the engine so that it does not start.	
1. Identify the steps you will take to prevent the engine from starting while cranking it over. Write them below:	☐
2. Are there any external loads that could be causing a slow cranking problem on this machine (hydraulic pumps, clutches engaged, alternator seized, etc.)? If so, list them below:	☐
3. Prepare the DVOM to measure direct current voltage (DCV). Measure the battery voltage for each of the following and record your measurements.	☐
a. Battery voltage before cranking _____ DCV	☐
b. Battery voltage during cranking _____ DCV	☐
c. Voltage at the starter during cranking (**Note:** Place the red lead on the main battery terminal of the starter solenoid and the black lead on the ground terminal of the starter motor.) _____ DCV	☐
d. Are your readings within the manufacturer's specifications? Yes ☐ No ☐	☐
e. If no, briefly describe the repair procedure needed to correct the problem:	☐
f. What condition does excessive voltage drop equate to?	☐
4. Prepare the DVOM to measure DCV. Perform a starter high current circuit voltage drop test on the positive/feed side.	☐

a. Describe where the DVOM leads should be placed to measure voltage drop on the positive side of the circuit:	☐
b. What is the voltage reading during engine cranking? _____ DCV	☐
c. Describe where the DVOM leads should be placed to measure voltage drop on the negative side of the circuit:	☐
d. What is the voltage reading during engine cranking? _____ DCV	☐
e. Are your readings within the manufacturer's specifications? Yes ☐ No ☐	☐
f. If no, briefly describe the repair procedure needed to correct the problem:	☐
5. Prepare a high current amp meter for use. With the engine being cranked without starting, measure the amount of current flow through the positive high current cable going to the starter.	☐
a. What is the amp meter reading during engine cranking? _____ DCA	☐
b. What would be a common cause of excessive current flow found during this test?	☐
6. List three cranking system problems that could be diagnosed with voltage drop tests and/or amperage flow tests:	☐
7. Based on the results of your tests, what would be the most likely cause (root cause) of the slow cranking problem?	☐

	Step Completed
8. Return the machine's engine to normal operating condition. Start the machine and verify proper operation of the starting system and engine.	☐
9. Discuss your findings with your supervisor/instructor.	☐

Non-Task-Specific Evaluation	Step Completed
1. Tools and equipment were used as directed and returned in good working order.	☐
2. Complied with all general and task-specific safety standards, including proper use of any personal protective equipment (PPE).	☐
3. Completed the task in an appropriate time frame (recommendation: 1.5 or 2 times the flat rate).	☐
4. Left the workspace clean and orderly.	☐
5. Cared for customer property and returned it undamaged.	☐

Student signature _____ Date _____

Comments:

Have your supervisor/instructor verify satisfactory completion of this procedure, any observations made, and any necessary action(s) recommended.

Evaluation Instructions: The scoring box below is intended to act as a guide for both student and supervisor/instructor. Each criterion listed will help students to understand what is expected of them and help supervisors/instructors to articulate the level of success at a particular task. The scoring is set up to allow a second attempt at each task (see the Test and Retest columns). Scoring is designed only to award students points for task criteria that were completed correctly. Points are lost for failure to complete the employability requirements (see Non-Task-Specific criteria). When all criteria are evaluated, tally the points for a total at the bottom of each column.

Tasksheet Scoring

Evaluation Items	Test		Retest	
	Pass	**Fail**	**Pass**	**Fail**
Task-Specific Evaluation	**(1 pt)**	**(0 pts)**	**(1 pt)**	**(0 pts)**
1. Student correctly described the steps taken to prevent the engine from starting while cranking it over and identified alternative causes of excessive engine loads.				
2. Student demonstrated the proper use of a DVOM during voltage drop testing.				
3. Student demonstrated the proper use of an amp meter during amp flow testing.				
4. Student listed three different problems that could be diagnosed with voltage drop testing and determined the most likely cause of the slow cranking problem.				
Non-Task-Specific Evaluation	**(0 pts)**	**(−1 pt)**	**(0 pts)**	**(−1 pt)**
Student successfully completed at least three of the non-task-specific steps.				
Student successfully completed all five of the non-task-specific steps.				
Total Score: <total # of points / 4 = %>				

Supervisor/Instructor:

Supervisor/instructor signature _____ Date _____

Comments:

Retest supervisor/instructor signature _____ Date _____

Comments:

CDX Tasksheet Number: 2.8007

Student/Intern Information

Name _____ Date _____ Class _____

Machine, Customer, and Service Information

Machine used for this activity:

Make _____ Model _____

Hours _____ Serial Number _____

Materials Required

- Machine chosen by the supervisor/instructor to complete the task
- Equipment manufacturer's service information, including schematic wiring diagrams
- Machine lifting equipment, if applicable
- Digital volt-ohmmeter (DVOM)
- Ammeter
- Current clamp

Task-Specific Safety Considerations

- This task may require operating the equipment on school grounds, which carries severe risks. Attempt this task only with full permission from your supervisor/instructor and follow all the guidelines exactly.
- Lifting equipment such as equipment jacks and stands, hoists, overhead cranes, and engine hoists are important tools that increase productivity and make the job easier. However, they can also cause severe injury or death if used improperly. Make sure you follow the manufacturer's operation procedures. Also make sure you have your supervisor's/instructor's permission to use any type of lifting equipment.
- Use extreme caution when working around batteries. Immediately remove any electrolyte that may come in contact with you. Electrolyte is a mixture of sulfuric acid and water. Batteries may produce explosive mixtures of gas containing hydrogen; avoid creating any sparks around batteries. Consult with the shop safety and emergency procedures when working with or around batteries.
- Comply with personal and environmental safety practices associated with clothing; eye protection; hand tools; power equipment; proper ventilation; and the handling, storage, and disposal of chemicals/materials in accordance with federal, state, and local regulations.
- Always wear the correct protective eyewear and clothing and use the appropriate safety equipment, as well as seat protectors and floor mat protectors.
- Make sure you understand and observe all legislative and personal safety procedures when carrying out practical assignments. If you are unsure of what these are, ask your supervisor/instructor.

▶ **TASK** Use electrical schematics and troubleshooting flow charts to diagnose an electrical system problem.

AED
2.8

Student Instructions: Read through the entire procedure prior to starting. Prepare your workspace and any tools or parts that may be needed to complete the task. When directed by your supervisor/instructor, begin the procedure to complete the task, and comment or check the box as each step is finished. Track your time on this procedure for later comparison to the standard completion time (i.e., "flat rate" or customer pay time).

Procedure	Step Completed
1. Have your supervisor/instructor choose a machine and assume it has a lighting circuit that is not functioning (have your supervisor/instructor identify which one). Use the machine's electrical schematic to provide the following information.	☐
a. Are there any other circuits that share the same power source (fuse or circuit breaker)? Yes ☐ No ☐	☐
b. If yes, list the other circuits and identify why this is good to know:	☐
c. Does the schematic indicate if the circuit power needs the key turned ON? Yes ☐ No ☐	☐
d. List the wire numbers/colors shown on the schematic for the light power and ground:	☐
e. Using the schematic, demonstrate where you could check for available voltage in this circuit at three locations on the machine. List these locations below:	☐
2. Assume the machine's starting motor will not turn. Use the machine's electrical schematic to identify the following information.	
a. List the wire numbers/colors shown on the schematic for the key switch power supply:	☐

b. Does the machine have a relay between the key switch and the starter? Yes ☐ No ☐	☐
c. If yes, identify where the relay gets its high current power from and if the wire gauge size is indicated on the schematic:	☐
d. Are there any starter interlock devices shown on the schematic? Yes ☐ No ☐	☐
e. Using the schematic, demonstrate where you could check for available voltage in the starter control circuit at three locations on the machine. List the location(s) below:	☐
3. Assume there is a problem with one of the machine's gauges or operator warning devices. Use the machine's electrical schematic to identify the following information.	
a. List the wire numbers/colors shown on the schematic for the gauge or warning device:	☐
b. Does the gauge or warning device have an engine control module (ECM) as part of its circuit? Yes ☐ No ☐	☐
c. If yes, name where the ECM gets power from:	☐
d. Is there a sender in this circuit that has a low voltage reference signal? Yes ☐ No ☐	☐
e. Using the electrical schematic, demonstrate where you could check for available voltage or resistance at the sender on the machine. List the location(s) below:	☐

4. Find a troubleshooting flow chart for an electrical system problem and follow all steps as described to diagnose an issue provided by your instructor. Describe the process and your diagnosis:	☐

Non-Task-Specific Evaluation	Step Completed
1. Tools and equipment were used as directed and returned in good working order.	☐
2. Complied with all general and task-specific safety standards, including proper use of any personal protective equipment (PPE).	☐
3. Completed the task in an appropriate time frame (recommendation: 1.5 or 2 times the flat rate).	☐
4. Left the workspace clean and orderly.	☐
5. Cared for customer property and returned it undamaged.	☐

Student signature _____ Date _____

Comments:

[ ]

Have your supervisor/instructor verify satisfactory completion of this procedure, any observations made,

and any necessary action(s) recommended.

Evaluation Instructions: The scoring box below is intended to act as a guide for both student and supervisor/instructor. Each criterion listed will help students to understand what is expected of them and help supervisors/instructors to articulate the level of success at a particular task. The scoring is set up to allow a second attempt at each task (see the Test and Retest columns). Scoring is designed only to award students points for task criteria that were completed correctly. Points are lost for failure to complete the employability requirements (see Non-Task-Specific criteria). When all criteria are evaluated, tally the points for a total at the bottom of each column.

Tasksheet Scoring

Evaluation Items	Test		Retest	
	Pass	Fail	Pass	Fail
Task-Specific Evaluation	**(1 pt)**	**(0 pts)**	**(1 pt)**	**(0 pts)**
1. Student provided correct information regarding a lighting circuit that is not functioning.				
2. Student provided correct information regarding a starting motor that will not turn.				
3. Student provided correct information regarding a problem with one of the machine's gauges or operator warning devices.				
4. Student correctly described the process for troubleshooting a given problem.				
Non-Task-Specific Evaluation	**(0 pts)**	**(−1 pt)**	**(0 pts)**	**(−1 pt)**
Student successfully completed at least three of the non-task-specific steps.				
Student successfully completed all five of the non-task-specific steps.				
Total Score: <total # of points / 4 = %>				

Supervisor/Instructor:

Supervisor/instructor signature _____ Date _____

Comments:

Retest supervisor/instructor signature _____ Date _____

Comments:

CDX Tasksheet Number: 2.8008

Student/Intern Information

Name _____ Date _____ Class _____

Machine, Customer, and Service Information

Machine used for this activity:

Make _____ Model _____

Hours _____ Serial Number _____

Materials Required
- Machine chosen by the supervisor/instructor to complete the task
- Equipment manufacturer's service information, including schematic wiring diagrams
- Machine lifting equipment, if applicable
- Manufacturer's service software
- Laptop computer
- Communication adapter

Task-Specific Safety Considerations
- This task may require operating the equipment on school grounds, which carries severe risks. Attempt this task only with full permission from your supervisor/instructor and follow all the guidelines exactly.
- Lifting equipment such as equipment jacks and stands, hoists, overhead cranes, and engine hoists are important tools that increase productivity and make the job easier. However, they can also cause severe injury or death if used improperly. Make sure you follow the manufacturer's operation procedures. Also make sure you have your supervisor's/instructor's permission to use any type of lifting equipment.
- Comply with personal and environmental safety practices associated with clothing; eye protection; hand tools; power equipment; proper ventilation; and the handling, storage, and disposal of chemicals/materials in accordance with federal, state, and local regulations.
- Always wear the correct protective eyewear and clothing and use the appropriate safety equipment, as well as seat protectors and floor mat protectors.
- Make sure you understand and observe all legislative and personal safety procedures when carrying out practical assignments. If you are unsure of what these are, ask your supervisor/instructor.

▶ TASK Utilize an interactive equipment diagnostic program to find fault codes and diagnose an electrical system fault.

AED 2.8

Time off_____

Time on_____

Total time_____

Student Instructions: Read through the entire procedure prior to starting. Prepare your workspace and any tools or parts that may be needed to complete the task. When directed by your supervisor/instructor, begin the procedure to complete the task, and comment or check the box as each step is finished. Track your time on this procedure for later comparison to the standard completion time (i.e., "flat rate" or customer pay time).

Procedure	Step Completed
1. Demonstrate how to connect a laptop computer to a machine's electronic communication system. Describe the steps:	☐
2. Describe the steps taken to find active and logged codes on both the machine's display and the laptop:	☐
3. Describe the steps taken to find an interactive diagnostic test that can be performed with the assistance of a laptop and service software:	☐
4. Have your supervisor/instructor put a fault in the machine. Utilize the service software and laptop to help diagnose the problem. Describe the process:	☐
5. Are there any other tools or equipment you would need to find the root cause of the problem? If so, list them below:	☐
6. Return the machine to normal operating condition. Start the machine and verify proper operation of the machine's electrical/electronic system.	☐
7. Discuss your findings with your supervisor/instructor.	☐

Non-Task-Specific Evaluation	Step Completed
1. Tools and equipment were used as directed and returned in good working order.	☐
2. Complied with all general and task-specific safety standards, including proper use of any personal protective equipment (PPE).	☐
3. Completed the task in an appropriate time frame (recommendation: 1.5 or 2 times the flat rate).	☐
4. Left the workspace clean and orderly.	☐
5. Cared for customer property and returned it undamaged.	☐

Student signature _____ Date _____

Comments:

Have your supervisor/instructor verify satisfactory completion of this procedure, any observations made, and any necessary action(s) recommended.

Evaluation Instructions: The scoring box below is intended to act as a guide for both student and supervisor/instructor. Each criterion listed will help students to understand what is expected of them and help supervisors/instructors to articulate the level of success at a particular task. The scoring is set up to allow a second attempt at each task (see the Test and Retest columns). Scoring is designed only to award students points for task criteria that were completed correctly. Points are lost for failure to complete the employability requirements (see Non-Task-Specific criteria). When all criteria are evaluated, tally the points for a total at the bottom of each column.

Tasksheet Scoring

Evaluation Items	Test		Retest	
	Pass	Fail	Pass	Fail
Task-Specific Evaluation	**(1 pt)**	**(0 pts)**	**(1 pt)**	**(0 pts)**
1. Student accurately described the steps for connecting a laptop to a machine's electronic communication system.				
2. Student accurately described the steps for finding active and logged codes.				
3. Student accurately described the steps for finding an interactive diagnostic test.				
4. Student accurately described the process for diagnosing a fault using the service software and a laptop, and identified any additional tools or equipment that would be needed.				
Non-Task-Specific Evaluation	**(0 pts)**	**(−1 pt)**	**(0 pts)**	**(−1 pt)**
Student successfully completed at least three of the non-task-specific steps.				
Student successfully completed all five of the non-task-specific steps.				
Total Score: <total # of points / 4 = %>				

Supervisor/Instructor:

Supervisor/instructor signature _____ Date _____

Comments:

Retest supervisor/instructor signature _____ Date _____

Comments:

CDX Tasksheet Number: 2.8009

Student/Intern Information

Name _____ Date _____ Class _____

Machine, Customer, and Service Information

Machine used for this activity:

Make _____ Model _____

Hours _____ Serial Number _____

Materials Required
- Machine chosen by the supervisor/instructor to complete the task
- Equipment manufacturer's service information, including schematic wiring diagrams
- Machine lifting equipment, if applicable
- Repair order form

Task-Specific Safety Considerations
- This task may require operating the equipment on school grounds, which carries severe risks. Attempt this task only with full permission from your supervisor/instructor and follow all the guidelines exactly.
- Lifting equipment such as equipment jacks and stands, hoists, overhead cranes, and engine hoists are important tools that increase productivity and make the job easier. However, they can also cause severe injury or death if used improperly. Make sure you follow the manufacturer's operation procedures. Also make sure you have your supervisor's/instructor's permission to use any type of lifting equipment.
- Comply with personal and environmental safety practices associated with clothing; eye protection; hand tools; power equipment; proper ventilation; and the handling, storage, and disposal of chemicals/materials in accordance with federal, state, and local regulations.
- Always wear the correct protective eyewear and clothing and use the appropriate safety equipment, as well as seat protectors and floor mat protectors.
- Make sure you understand and observe all legislative and personal safety procedures when carrying out practical assignments. If you are unsure of what these are, ask your supervisor/instructor.

▶ TASK Create a repair order based on a machine electrical system problem.

AED 2.8

Time off _____

Time on _____

Total time _____

Student Instructions: Read through the entire procedure prior to starting. Prepare your workspace and any tools or parts that may be needed to complete the task. When directed by your supervisor/instructor, begin the procedure to complete the task, and comment or check the box as each step is finished. Track your time on this procedure for later comparison to the standard completion time (i.e., "flat rate" or customer pay time).

Procedure	Step Completed
1. Assume your supervisor/instructor is the machine operator and they have given you, the technician, an operational complaint for the machine. Describe the complaint in clear, simple terms:	☐
2. List three questions you would ask the operator in relation to the complaint:	☐
3. Ask the operator (your supervisor/instructor) these questions and note their answers below:	☐
4. Describe how you would verify the operator concern in clear steps:	☐
5. List three possible causes for the operator concern:	☐
6. Describe the troubleshooting steps you would take to determine the most likely cause of the operator's concern:	☐
7. Fill out the repair order form you were provided following the instructions on the form.	☐
8. Return the machine's engine to normal operating condition. Start the machine and verify proper operation of the starting system and engine.	☐
9. Discuss your findings with your supervisor/instructor.	☐

Non-Task-Specific Evaluation	Step Completed
1. Tools and equipment were used as directed and returned in good working order.	☐
2. Complied with all general and task-specific safety standards, including proper use of any personal protective equipment (PPE).	☐
3. Completed the task in an appropriate time frame (recommendation: 1.5 or 2 times the flat rate).	☐
4. Left the workspace clean and orderly.	☐
5. Cared for customer property and returned it undamaged.	☐

Student signature _____ Date _____

Comments:

Have your supervisor/instructor verify satisfactory completion of this procedure, any observations made, and any necessary action(s) recommended.

Evaluation Instructions: The scoring box below is intended to act as a guide for both student and supervisor/instructor. Each criterion listed will help students to understand what is expected of them and help supervisors/instructors to articulate the level of success at a particular task. The scoring is set up to allow a second attempt at each task (see the Test and Retest columns). Scoring is designed only to award students points for task criteria that were completed correctly. Points are lost for failure to complete the employability requirements (see Non-Task-Specific criteria). When all criteria are evaluated, tally the points for a total at the bottom of each column.

Tasksheet Scoring

	Test		Retest	
Evaluation Items	**Pass**	**Fail**	**Pass**	**Fail**
Task-Specific Evaluation	**(1 pt)**	**(0 pts)**	**(1 pt)**	**(0 pts)**
1. Student described the complaint clearly and concisely and accurately described how to verify the operator concern.				
2. Student listed three pertinent questions for the operator and correctly noted the responses.				
3. Student listed three possible causes for the concern and clearly described the applicable troubleshooting steps.				
4. Student accurately completed the repair order.				
Non-Task-Specific Evaluation	**(0 pts)**	**(−1 pt)**	**(0 pts)**	**(−1 pt)**
Student successfully completed at least three of the non-task-specific steps.				
Student successfully completed all five of the non-task-specific steps.				
Total Score: <total # of points / 4 = %>				

Supervisor/Instructor:

Supervisor/instructor signature _____ Date _____

Comments:

Retest supervisor/instructor signature _____ Date _____

Comments:

Chapter 20: Theory and Operation, Hydraulic and Hydrostatic; Pump Identification and Operation

Learning Objective/Task	CDX Tasksheet Number	AED Reference Number
• Disassemble and assemble external and internal hydraulic gear pumps and identify their components.	3.1b001	AED 3.1
• Disassemble and assemble a vane pump and identify its components.	3.1b002	AED 3.1
• Disassemble and assemble hydraulic piston pumps and identify their components.	3.1b003	AED 3.1
• Disassemble and assemble a gear motor and identify its components.	3.1b006	AED 3.1
• Disassemble and assemble a hydraulic vane motor and identify its components.	3.1b007	AED 3.1

Materials Required

- Hydraulic training unit or machine
- Equipment manufacturer's service information, including schematic hydraulic diagrams
- Hydraulic pressure gauges
- Hydraulic spare parts, including fittings, hoses, and fluid
- Manufacturer-specific tools depending on the concern
- Machine lifting equipment, if applicable
- Machine lockout/tagout equipment, if applicable

Safety Considerations

- This task may require operating the equipment on school grounds, which carries severe risks. Attempt this task only with full permission from your supervisor/instructor and follow all the guidelines exactly.
- Lifting equipment such as equipment jacks and stands, hoists, overhead cranes, and engine hoists are important tools that increase productivity and make the job easier. However, they can also cause severe injury or death if used improperly. Make sure you follow the manufacturer's operation procedures. Also make sure you have your supervisor's/instructor's permission to use any type of lifting equipment.
- This task may require you to measure hydraulic pressures. Always ensure that the supervisor/instructor checks test instrument connections prior to connecting power or taking measurements. High fluid pressures can be dangerous; avoid opening hydraulic circuits until system is de-energized.
- Comply with personal and environmental safety practices associated with clothing; eye protection; hand tools; power equipment; proper ventilation; and the handling, storage, and disposal of chemicals/materials in accordance with federal, state, and local regulations.
- Always wear the correct protective eyewear and clothing and use the appropriate safety equipment, as well as seat protectors and floor mat protectors.
- Make sure you understand and observe all legislative and personal safety procedures when carrying out practical assignments. If you are unsure of what these are, ask your supervisor/instructor.

CDX Tasksheet Number: 3.1b001

Student/Intern Information

Name _____ Date _____ Class _____

Machine, Customer, and Service Information

Machine used for this activity:

Make _____ Model _____

Hours _____ Serial Number _____

Materials Required

- Hydraulic training unit or machine
- Equipment manufacturer's service information, including schematic hydraulic diagrams
- Hydraulic pressure gauges
- Hydraulic spare parts, including fittings, hoses, and fluid
- Manufacturer-specific tools depending on the concern
- Machine lifting equipment, if applicable
- Machine lockout/tagout equipment, if applicable

Task-Specific Safety Considerations

- This task may require operating the equipment on school grounds, which carries severe risks. Attempt this task only with full permission from your supervisor/instructor and follow all the guidelines exactly.
- Lifting equipment such as equipment jacks and stands, hoists, overhead cranes, and engine hoists are important tools that increase productivity and make the job easier. However, they can also cause severe injury or death if used improperly. Make sure you follow the manufacturer's operation procedures. Also make sure you have your supervisor's/instructor's permission to use any type of lifting equipment.
- This task may require you to measure hydraulic pressures. Always ensure that the supervisor/instructor checks test instrument connections prior to connecting power or taking measurements. High fluid pressures can be dangerous; avoid opening hydraulic circuits until system is de-energized.
- Comply with personal and environmental safety practices associated with clothing; eye protection; hand tools; power equipment; proper ventilation; and the handling, storage, and disposal of chemicals/materials in accordance with federal, state, and local regulations.
- Always wear the correct protective eyewear and clothing and use the appropriate safety equipment, as well as seat protectors and floor mat protectors.
- Make sure you understand and observe all legislative and personal safety procedures when carrying out practical assignments. If you are unsure of what these are, ask your supervisor/instructor.

▶ **TASK** Disassemble and assemble external and internal hydraulic gear pumps and identify their components.

AED 3.1

Student Instructions: Read through the entire procedure prior to starting. Prepare your workspace and any tools or parts that may be needed to complete the task. When directed by your supervisor/instructor, begin the procedure to complete the task, and comment or check the box as each step is finished. Track your time on this procedure for later comparison to the standard completion time (i.e., "flat rate" or customer pay time).

Procedure	Step Completed
1. Using the manufacturer's service information, disassemble an external gear pump chosen by your supervisor/instructor. List all pump components below:	☐
2. Identify the inlet and outlet ports and describe how you determined this:	☐
3. Describe the path of fluid flow through the pump:	☐
4. Determine whether this pump is designed for right-hand (clockwise) or left-hand (counterclockwise) rotation, and explain how you determined this: Right-hand rotation ☐ Left-hand rotation ☐	☐
5. Reassemble the pump following the manufacturer's service information. Does the pump rotate by hand freely? Yes ☐ No ☐	☐
6. Using the manufacturer's service information, disassemble an internal gear pump chosen by your supervisor/instructor. List all pump components below:	☐

	Step Completed
7. Identify the inlet and outlet ports and describe how you determined this:	☐
8. Describe the path of fluid flow through the pump:	☐
9. Determine whether this pump is designed for right-hand (clockwise) or left-hand (counterclockwise) rotation, and explain how you determined this: Right-hand rotation ☐ Left-hand rotation ☐	☐
10. Reassemble the pump following the manufacturer's service information. Does the pump rotate by hand freely? Yes ☐ No ☐	☐

Non-Task-Specific Evaluation	Step Completed
1. Tools and equipment were used as directed and returned in good working order.	☐
2. Complied with all general and task-specific safety standards, including proper use of any personal protective equipment (PPE).	☐
3. Completed the task in an appropriate time frame (recommendation: 1.5 or 2 times the flat rate).	☐
4. Left the workspace clean and orderly.	☐
5. Cared for customer property and returned it undamaged.	☐

Student signature _____ Date _____

Comments:

Have your supervisor/instructor verify satisfactory completion of this procedure, any observations made, and any necessary action(s) recommended.

Evaluation Instructions: The scoring box below is intended to act as a guide for both student and supervisor/instructor. Each criterion listed will help students to understand what is expected of them and help supervisors/instructors to articulate the level of success at a particular task. The scoring is set up to allow a second attempt at each task (see the Test and Retest columns). Scoring is designed only to award students points for task criteria that were completed correctly. Points are lost for failure to complete the employability requirements (see Non-Task-Specific criteria). When all criteria are evaluated, tally the points for a total at the bottom of each column.

Tasksheet Scoring

Evaluation Items	Test		Retest	
	Pass	Fail	Pass	Fail
Task-Specific Evaluation	**(1 pt)**	**(O pts)**	**(1 pt)**	**(O pts)**
1. Student properly disassembled both the internal and external gear pumps.				
2. Student correctly identified/described all components of the internal gear pump.				
3. Student correctly identified/described all components of the external gear pump.				
4. Student properly reassembled both the internal and external gear pumps.				
Non-Task-Specific Evaluation	**(O pts)**	**(−1 pt)**	**(O pts)**	**(−1 pt)**
Student successfully completed at least three of the non-task-specific steps.				
Student successfully completed all five of the non-task-specific steps.				
Total Score: <total # of points / 4 = %>				

Supervisor/Instructor:

Supervisor/instructor signature _____ Date _____

Comments:

Retest supervisor/instructor signature _____ Date _____

Comments:

CDX Tasksheet Number: 3.1b002

Student/Intern Information

Name _____ Date _____ Class _____

Machine, Customer, and Service Information

Machine used for this activity:

Make _____ Model _____

Hours _____ Serial Number _____

Materials Required

- Hydraulic training unit or machine
- Equipment manufacturer's service information, including schematic hydraulic diagrams
- Hydraulic pressure gauges
- Hydraulic spare parts, including fittings, hoses, and fluid
- Manufacturer-specific tools depending on the concern
- Machine lifting equipment, if applicable
- Machine lockout/tagout equipment, if applicable

Task-Specific Safety Considerations

- This task may require operating the equipment on school grounds, which carries severe risks. Attempt this task only with full permission from your supervisor/instructor and follow all the guidelines exactly.
- Lifting equipment such as equipment jacks and stands, hoists, overhead cranes, and engine hoists are important tools that increase productivity and make the job easier. However, they can also cause severe injury or death if used improperly. Make sure you follow the manufacturer's operation procedures. Also make sure you have your supervisor's/instructor's permission to use any type of lifting equipment.
- This task may require you to measure hydraulic pressures. Always ensure that the supervisor/instructor checks test instrument connections prior to connecting power or taking measurements. High fluid pressures can be dangerous; avoid opening hydraulic circuits until system is de-energized.
- Comply with personal and environmental safety practices associated with clothing; eye protection; hand tools; power equipment; proper ventilation; and the handling, storage, and disposal of chemicals/materials in accordance with federal, state, and local regulations.
- Always wear the correct protective eyewear and clothing and use the appropriate safety equipment, as well as seat protectors and floor mat protectors.
- Make sure you understand and observe all legislative and personal safety procedures when carrying out practical assignments. If you are unsure of what these are, ask your supervisor/instructor.

► **TASK** Disassemble and assemble a vane pump and identify its components.

AED 3.1

Student Instructions: Read through the entire procedure prior to starting. Prepare your workspace and any tools or parts that may be needed to complete the task. When directed by your supervisor/instructor, begin the procedure to complete the task, and comment or check the box as each step is finished. Track your time on this procedure for later comparison to the standard completion time (i.e., "flat rate" or customer pay time).

Procedure	Step Completed
1. Using the manufacturer's service information, disassemble a vane pump chosen by your supervisor/instructor. List all pump components below:	☐
2. Identify the inlet and outlet ports and describe below how you determined this:	☐
3. Describe the path of fluid flow through the pump:	☐
4. Determine whether this pump is designed for right-hand (clockwise) or left-hand (counterclockwise) rotation, and explain how you determined this. Right-hand rotation ☐ Left-hand rotation ☐	☐
5. Is this a balanced or unbalanced vane pump? Explain how you determined this. Balanced ☐ Unbalanced ☐	☐
6. Reassemble the pump following the manufacturer's service information. Does the pump rotate by hand freely? Yes ☐ No ☐	☐

7. Using the manufacturer's service information, disassemble a variable displacement vane pump chosen by your supervisor/instructor. List all pump components below:	☐
8. Identify the inlet and outlet ports and describe below how you determined this:	☐
9. Describe the path of fluid flow through the pump:	☐
10. Determine whether this pump is designed for right-hand (clockwise) or left-hand (counterclockwise) rotation, and explain how you determined this. Right-hand rotation ☐ Left-hand rotation ☐	☐
11. Reassemble the pump following the manufacturer's service information. Does the pump rotate by hand freely? Yes ☐ No ☐	☐

Non-Task-Specific Evaluation	Step Completed
1. Tools and equipment were used as directed and returned in good working order.	☐
2. Complied with all general and task-specific safety standards, including proper use of any personal protective equipment (PPE).	☐
3. Completed the task in an appropriate time frame (recommendation: 1.5 or 2 times the flat rate).	☐
4. Left the workspace clean and orderly.	☐
5. Cared for customer property and returned it undamaged.	☐

Student signature _____ Date _____

Comments:

Have your supervisor/instructor verify satisfactory completion of this procedure, any observations made, and any necessary action(s) recommended.

Evaluation Instructions: The scoring box below is intended to act as a guide for both student and supervisor/instructor. Each criterion listed will help students to understand what is expected of them and help supervisors/instructors to articulate the level of success at a particular task. The scoring is set up to allow a second attempt at each task (see the Test and Retest columns). Scoring is designed only to award students points for task criteria that were completed correctly. Points are lost for failure to complete the employability requirements (see Non-Task-Specific criteria). When all criteria are evaluated, tally the points for a total at the bottom of each column.

Tasksheet Scoring

Evaluation Items	Test		Retest	
	Pass	Fail	Pass	Fail
Task-Specific Evaluation	**(1 pt)**	**(0 pts)**	**(1 pt)**	**(0 pts)**
1. Student properly disassembled both pumps.				
2. Student correctly identified/described all components of the first vane pump.				
3. Student correctly identified/described all components of the variable displacement vane pump.				
4. Student properly reassembled both pumps.				
Non-Task-Specific Evaluation	**(0 pts)**	**(−1 pt)**	**(0 pts)**	**(−1 pt)**
Student successfully completed at least three of the non-task-specific steps.				
Student successfully completed all five of the non-task-specific steps.				
Total Score: <total # of points / 4 = %>				

Supervisor/Instructor:

Supervisor/instructor signature _____ Date _____

Comments:

Retest supervisor/instructor signature _____ Date _____

Comments:

CDX Tasksheet Number: 3.1b003

Student/Intern Information

Name _____ Date _____ Class _____

Machine, Customer, and Service Information

Machine used for this activity:

Make _____ Model _____

Hours _____ Serial Number _____

Materials Required

- Hydraulic training unit or machine
- Equipment manufacturer's service information, including schematic hydraulic diagrams
- Hydraulic pressure gauges
- Hydraulic spare parts, including fittings, hoses, and fluid
- Manufacturer-specific tools depending on the concern
- Machine lifting equipment, if applicable
- Machine lockout/tagout equipment, if applicable

Task-Specific Safety Considerations

- This task may require operating the equipment on school grounds, which carries severe risks. Attempt this task only with full permission from your supervisor/instructor and follow all the guidelines exactly.
- Lifting equipment such as equipment jacks and stands, hoists, overhead cranes, and engine hoists are important tools that increase productivity and make the job easier. However, they can also cause severe injury or death if used improperly. Make sure you follow the manufacturer's operation procedures. Also make sure you have your supervisor's/instructor's permission to use any type of lifting equipment.
- This task may require you to measure hydraulic pressures. Always ensure that the supervisor/instructor checks test instrument connections prior to connecting power or taking measurements. High fluid pressures can be dangerous; avoid opening hydraulic circuits until system is de-energized.
- Comply with personal and environmental safety practices associated with clothing; eye protection; hand tools; power equipment; proper ventilation; and the handling, storage, and disposal of chemicals/materials in accordance with federal, state, and local regulations.
- Always wear the correct protective eyewear and clothing and use the appropriate safety equipment, as well as seat protectors and floor mat protectors.
- Make sure you understand and observe all legislative and personal safety procedures when carrying out practical assignments. If you are unsure of what these are, ask your supervisor/instructor.

▶ **TASK** Disassemble and assemble hydraulic piston pumps and identify their components.

AED
3.1

Student Instructions: Read through the entire procedure prior to starting. Prepare your workspace and any tools or parts that may be needed to complete the task. When directed by your supervisor/instructor, begin the procedure to complete the task, and comment or check the box as each step is finished. Track your time on this procedure for later comparison to the standard completion time (i.e., "flat rate" or customer pay time).

Procedure	Step Completed
1. Using the manufacturer's service information, disassemble an axial piston pump chosen by your supervisor/instructor. List all pump components below:	☐
2. Identify the inlet and outlet ports and describe how you determined this:	☐
3. Describe the path of fluid flow through the pump:	☐
4. Determine whether this pump is designed for right-hand (clockwise) or left-hand (counterclockwise) rotation, and explain how you determined this. Right-hand rotation ☐ Left-hand rotation ☐	☐
5. Determine whether this pump is a fixed or variable displacement pump and explain how you determined this. Fixed displacement ☐ Variable displacement ☐	☐
6. Reassemble the pump following the manufacturer's service information. Does the pump rotate by hand freely? Yes ☐ No ☐	☐

7. Using the manufacturer's service information, disassemble a bent axis piston pump chosen by your supervisor/instructor. List all pump components below:	☐
8. Identify the inlet and outlet ports and describe how you determined this:	☐
9. Describe the path of fluid flow through the pump:	☐
10. Determine whether this pump is designed for right-hand (clockwise) or left-hand (counterclockwise) rotation, and explain how you determined this. Right-hand rotation ☐ Left-hand rotation ☐	☐
11. Determine whether this is a fixed or variable displacement pump and explain how you determined this. Fixed displacement ☐ Variable displacement ☐	☐
12. Reassemble the pump following manufacturer's service information. Does the pump rotate by hand freely? Yes ☐ No ☐	☐

Non-Task-Specific Evaluation	Step Completed
1. Tools and equipment were used as directed and returned in good working order.	☐
2. Complied with all general and task-specific safety standards, including proper use of any personal protective equipment (PPE).	☐
3. Completed the task in an appropriate time frame (recommendation: 1.5 or 2 times the flat rate).	☐
4. Left the workspace clean and orderly.	☐
5. Cared for customer property and returned it undamaged.	☐

Student signature _____ Date _____

Comments:

Have your supervisor/instructor verify satisfactory completion of this procedure, any observations made, and any necessary action(s) recommended.

Evaluation Instructions: The scoring box below is intended to act as a guide for both student and supervisor/instructor. Each criterion listed will help students to understand what is expected of them and help supervisors/instructors to articulate the level of success at a particular task. The scoring is set up to allow a second attempt at each task (see the Test and Retest columns). Scoring is designed only to award students points for task criteria that were completed correctly. Points are lost for failure to complete the employability requirements (see Non-Task-Specific criteria). When all criteria are evaluated, tally the points for a total at the bottom of each column.

Tasksheet Scoring

Evaluation Items	Test		Retest	
	Pass	Fail	Pass	Fail
Task-Specific Evaluation	**(1 pt)**	**(0 pts)**	**(1 pt)**	**(0 pts)**
1. Student properly disassembled both piston pumps.				
2. Student correctly identified/described all components of the axial piston pump.				
3. Student correctly identified/described all components of the bent axis piston pump.				
4. Student properly reassembled both piston pumps.				
Non-Task-Specific Evaluation	**(0 pts)**	**(−1 pt)**	**(0 pts)**	**(−1 pt)**
Student successfully completed at least three of the non-task-specific steps.				
Student successfully completed all five of the non-task-specific steps.				
Total Score: <total # of points / 4 = %>				

Supervisor/Instructor:

Supervisor/instructor signature _____ Date _____

Comments:

Retest supervisor/instructor signature _____ Date _____

Comments:

CDX Tasksheet Number: 3.1b006

Student/Intern Information

Name _____ Date _____ Class _____

Machine, Customer, and Service Information

Machine used for this activity:

Make _____ Model _____

Hours _____ Serial Number _____

Materials Required

- Hydraulic training unit or machine
- Equipment manufacturer's service information, including schematic hydraulic diagrams
- Hydraulic pressure gauges
- Hydraulic spare parts, including fittings, hoses, and fluid
- Manufacturer-specific tools depending on the concern
- Machine lifting equipment, if applicable
- Machine lockout/tagout equipment, if applicable

Task-Specific Safety Considerations

- This task may require operating the equipment on school grounds, which carries severe risks. Attempt this task only with full permission from your supervisor/instructor and follow all the guidelines exactly.
- Lifting equipment such as equipment jacks and stands, hoists, overhead cranes, and engine hoists are important tools that increase productivity and make the job easier. However, they can also cause severe injury or death if used improperly. Make sure you follow the manufacturer's operation procedures. Also make sure you have your supervisor's/instructor's permission to use any type of lifting equipment.
- This task may require you to measure hydraulic pressures. Always ensure that the supervisor/instructor checks test instrument connections prior to connecting power or taking measurements. High fluid pressures can be dangerous; avoid opening hydraulic circuits until system is de-energized.
- Comply with personal and environmental safety practices associated with clothing; eye protection; hand tools; power equipment; proper ventilation; and the handling, storage, and disposal of chemicals/materials in accordance with federal, state, and local regulations.
- Always wear the correct protective eyewear and clothing and use the appropriate safety equipment, as well as seat protectors and floor mat protectors.
- Make sure you understand and observe all legislative and personal safety procedures when carrying out practical assignments. If you are unsure of what these are, ask your supervisor/instructor.

▶ **TASK** Disassemble and assemble a gear motor and identify its components.

AED
3.1

Student Instructions: Read through the entire procedure prior to starting. Prepare your workspace and any tools or parts that may be needed to complete the task. When directed by your supervisor/instructor, begin the procedure to complete the task, and comment or check the box as each step is finished. Track your time on this procedure for later comparison to the standard completion time (i.e., "flat rate" or customer pay time).

Procedure	Step Completed
1. Using the manufacturer's service information, disassemble a gear motor chosen by your supervisor/instructor. List all motor components below:	☐
2. Identify the inlet and outlet ports and describe how you determined this:	☐
3. Describe the path of fluid flow through the motor:	☐
4. Determine whether this motor is designed for right-hand (clockwise) or left-hand (counterclockwise) rotation, and explain how you determined this: Right-hand rotation ☐ Left-hand rotation ☐	☐
5. Reassemble the motor following the manufacturer's service information. Does the motor rotate by hand freely? Yes ☐ No ☐	☐

Non-Task-Specific Evaluation	Step Completed
1. Tools and equipment were used as directed and returned in good working order.	☐
2. Complied with all general and task-specific safety standards, including proper use of any personal protective equipment (PPE).	☐
3. Completed the task in an appropriate time frame (recommendation: 1.5 or 2 times the flat rate).	☐
4. Left the workspace clean and orderly.	☐
5. Cared for customer property and returned it undamaged.	☐

Student signature _____ Date _____

Comments:

Have your supervisor/instructor verify satisfactory completion of this procedure, any observations made, and any necessary action(s) recommended.

Evaluation Instructions: The scoring box below is intended to act as a guide for both student and supervisor/instructor. Each criterion listed will help students to understand what is expected of them and help supervisors/instructors to articulate the level of success at a particular task. The scoring is set up to allow a second attempt at each task (see the Test and Retest columns). Scoring is designed only to award students points for task criteria that were completed correctly. Points are lost for failure to complete the employability requirements (see Non-Task-Specific criteria). When all criteria are evaluated, tally the points for a total at the bottom of each column.

Tasksheet Scoring

Evaluation Items	Test		Retest	
	Pass	**Fail**	**Pass**	**Fail**
Task-Specific Evaluation	**(1 pt)**	**(0 pts)**	**(1 pt)**	**(0 pts)**
1. Student properly disassembled the gear motor.				
2. Student correctly identified/described the motor's ports and path of fluid flow.				
3. Student correctly identified/described whether the motor was designed for right-hand or left-hand rotation.				
4. Student properly reassembled the gear motor.				
Non-Task-Specific Evaluation	**(0 pts)**	**(−1 pt)**	**(0 pts)**	**(−1 pt)**
Student successfully completed at least three of the non-task-specific steps.				
Student successfully completed all five of the non-task-specific steps.				
Total Score: <total # of points / 4 = %>				

Supervisor/Instructor:

Supervisor/instructor signature _____ Date _____

Comments:

| |
| |

Retest supervisor/instructor signature _____ Date _____

Comments:

| |
| |

CDX Tasksheet Number: 3.1b007

Student/Intern Information

Name _____ Date _____ Class _____

Machine, Customer, and Service Information

Machine used for this activity:

Make _____ Model _____

Hours _____ Serial Number _____

Materials Required

- Hydraulic training unit or machine
- Equipment manufacturer's service information, including schematic hydraulic diagrams
- Hydraulic pressure gauges
- Hydraulic spare parts, including fittings, hoses, and fluid
- Manufacturer-specific tools depending on the concern
- Machine lifting equipment, if applicable
- Machine lockout/tagout equipment, if applicable

Task-Specific Safety Considerations

- This task may require operating the equipment on school grounds, which carries severe risks. Attempt this task only with full permission from your supervisor/instructor and follow all the guidelines exactly.
- Lifting equipment such as equipment jacks and stands, hoists, overhead cranes, and engine hoists are important tools that increase productivity and make the job easier. However, they can also cause severe injury or death if used improperly. Make sure you follow the manufacturer's operation procedures. Also make sure you have your supervisor's/instructor's permission to use any type of lifting equipment.
- This task may require you to measure hydraulic pressures. Always ensure that the supervisor/instructor checks test instrument connections prior to connecting power or taking measurements. High fluid pressures can be dangerous; avoid opening hydraulic circuits until system is de-energized.
- Comply with personal and environmental safety practices associated with clothing; eye protection; hand tools; power equipment; proper ventilation; and the handling, storage, and disposal of chemicals/materials in accordance with federal, state, and local regulations.
- Always wear the correct protective eyewear and clothing and use the appropriate safety equipment, as well as seat protectors and floor mat protectors.
- Make sure you understand and observe all legislative and personal safety procedures when carrying out practical assignments. If you are unsure of what these are, ask your supervisor/instructor.

▶ **TASK** Disassemble and assemble a hydraulic vane motor and identify its components.

AED 3.1

Student Instructions: Read through the entire procedure prior to starting. Prepare your workspace and any tools or parts that may be needed to complete the task. When directed by your supervisor/instructor, begin the procedure to complete the task, and comment or check the box as each step is finished. Track your time on this procedure for later comparison to the standard completion time (i.e., "flat rate" or customer pay time).

Procedure	Step Completed
1. Using the manufacturer's service information, disassemble a vane motor chosen by your supervisor/instructor. List all motor components below:	☐
2. Identify the inlet and outlet ports and describe how you determined this:	☐
3. Describe the path of fluid flow through the motor:	☐
4. Determine whether this motor is designed for right-hand (clockwise) or left-hand (counterclockwise) rotation, and explain how you determined this. Right-hand rotation ☐ Left-hand rotation ☐	☐
5. Explain how a vane motor can be reconfigured to operate in the opposite direction when applicable:	☐
6. Reassemble the motor following the manufacturer's service information. Does the motor rotate by hand freely? Yes ☐ No ☐	☐

Non-Task-Specific Evaluation	Step Completed
1. Tools and equipment were used as directed and returned in good working order.	☐
2. Complied with all general and task-specific safety standards, including proper use of any personal protective equipment (PPE).	☐
3. Completed the task in an appropriate time frame (recommendation: 1.5 or 2 times the flat rate).	☐
4. Left the workspace clean and orderly.	☐
5. Cared for customer property and returned it undamaged.	☐

Student signature _____ Date _____

Comments:

Have your supervisor/instructor verify satisfactory completion of this procedure, any observations made, and any necessary action(s) recommended.

Evaluation Instructions: The scoring box below is intended to act as a guide for both student and supervisor/instructor. Each criterion listed will help students to understand what is expected of them and help supervisors/instructors to articulate the level of success at a particular task. The scoring is set up to allow a second attempt at each task (see the Test and Retest columns). Scoring is designed only to award students points for task criteria that were completed correctly. Points are lost for failure to complete the employability requirements (see Non-Task-Specific criteria). When all criteria are evaluated, tally the points for a total at the bottom of each column.

Tasksheet Scoring

Evaluation Items	Test		Retest	
	Pass	**Fail**	**Pass**	**Fail**
Task-Specific Evaluation	**(1 pt)**	**(0 pts)**	**(1 pt)**	**(0 pts)**
1. Student properly disassembled the vane motor.				
2. Student correctly identified/described the motor's ports and path of fluid flow.				
3. Student correctly identified whether the motor was designed for right-hand or left-hand rotation and described how it could be reconfigured when applicable.				
4. Student properly reassembled the gear motor.				
Non-Task-Specific Evaluation	**(0 pts)**	**(−1 pt)**	**(0 pts)**	**(−1 pt)**
Student successfully completed at least three of the non-task-specific steps.				
Student successfully completed all five of the non-task-specific steps.				
Total Score: <total # of points / 4 = %>				

Supervisor/Instructor:

Supervisor/instructor signature _____ Date _____

Comments:

Retest supervisor/instructor signature _____ Date _____

Comments:

Chapter 21: Theory and Operation, Hydraulic and Hydrostatic; Motor Identification and Operation

Learning Objective/Task	CDX Tasksheet Number	AED Reference Number
• Disassemble and assemble hydraulic motors and identify their components.	3.1c001	AED 3.1
• Disassemble and assemble a gerotor motor and identify its components.	3.1c002	AED 3.1

Materials Required

- Hydraulic training unit or machine
- Equipment manufacturer's service information, including schematic hydraulic diagrams
- Hydraulic pressure gauges
- Hydraulic spare parts, including fittings, hoses, and fluid
- Manufacturer-specific tools depending on the concern
- Machine lifting equipment, if applicable
- Machine lockout/tagout equipment, if applicable

Safety Considerations

- This task may require operating the equipment on school grounds, which carries severe risks. Attempt this task only with full permission from your supervisor/instructor and follow all the guidelines exactly.
- Lifting equipment such as equipment jacks and stands, hoists, overhead cranes, and engine hoists are important tools that increase productivity and make the job easier. However, they can also cause severe injury or death if used improperly. Make sure you follow the manufacturer's operation procedures. Also make sure you have your supervisor's/instructor's permission to use any type of lifting equipment.
- This task may require you to measure hydraulic pressures. Always ensure that the supervisor/instructor checks test instrument connections prior to connecting power or taking measurements. High fluid pressures can be dangerous; avoid opening hydraulic circuits until system is de-energized.
- Comply with personal and environmental safety practices associated with clothing; eye protection; hand tools; power equipment; proper ventilation; and the handling, storage, and disposal of chemicals/materials in accordance with federal, state, and local regulations.
- Always wear the correct protective eyewear and clothing and use the appropriate safety equipment, as well as seat protectors and floor mat protectors.
- Make sure you understand and observe all legislative and personal safety procedures when carrying out practical assignments. If you are unsure of what these are, ask your supervisor/instructor.

CDX Tasksheet Number: 3.1c001

Student/Intern Information

Name _____ Date _____ Class _____

Machine, Customer, and Service Information

Machine used for this activity:

Make _____ Model _____

Hours _____ Serial Number _____

Materials Required

- Hydraulic training unit or machine
- Equipment manufacturer's service information, including schematic hydraulic diagrams
- Hydraulic pressure gauges
- Hydraulic spare parts, including fittings, hoses, and fluid
- Manufacturer-specific tools depending on the concern
- Machine lifting equipment, if applicable
- Machine lockout/tagout equipment, if applicable

Task-Specific Safety Considerations

- This task may require operating the equipment on school grounds, which carries severe risks. Attempt this task only with full permission from your supervisor/instructor and follow all the guidelines exactly.
- Lifting equipment such as equipment jacks and stands, hoists, overhead cranes, and engine hoists are important tools that increase productivity and make the job easier. However, they can also cause severe injury or death if used improperly. Make sure you follow the manufacturer's operation procedures. Also make sure you have your supervisor's/instructor's permission to use any type of lifting equipment.
- This task may require you to measure hydraulic pressures. Always ensure that the supervisor/instructor checks test instrument connections prior to connecting power or taking measurements. High fluid pressures can be dangerous; avoid opening hydraulic circuits until system is de-energized.
- Comply with personal and environmental safety practices associated with clothing; eye protection; hand tools; power equipment; proper ventilation; and the handling, storage, and disposal of chemicals/materials in accordance with federal, state, and local regulations.
- Always wear the correct protective eyewear and clothing and use the appropriate safety equipment, as well as seat protectors and floor mat protectors.
- Make sure you understand and observe all legislative and personal safety procedures when carrying out practical assignments. If you are unsure of what these are, ask your supervisor/instructor.

▶ TASK Disassemble and assemble hydraulic motors and identify their components.

Student Instructions: Read through the entire procedure prior to starting. Prepare your workspace and any tools or parts that may be needed to complete the task. When directed by your supervisor/instructor, begin the procedure to complete the task, and comment or check the box as each step is finished. Track your time on this procedure for later comparison to the standard completion time (i.e., "flat rate" or customer pay time).

Procedure	Step Completed
1. Using the manufacturer's service information, disassemble a radial piston motor chosen by your supervisor/instructor. List all motor components below:	☐
2. Identify the inlet and outlet ports and describe how you determined this:	☐
3. Describe the path of fluid flow through the motor:	☐
4. Determine whether this motor is designed for right-hand (clockwise) or left-hand (counterclockwise) rotation, and explain how you determined this. Right-hand rotation ☐ Left-hand rotation ☐	☐
5. Reassemble the motor following the manufacturer's service information. Does the motor rotate by hand freely? Yes ☐ No ☐	☐
6. Using the manufacturer's service information, disassemble an axial piston motor chosen by your supervisor/instructor. List all motor components below:	☐

7. Identify the inlet and outlet ports and describe below how you determined this:	☐
8. Describe the path of fluid flow through the motor:	☐
9. Determine whether this motor is designed for right-hand (clockwise) or left-hand (counterclockwise) rotation, and explain how you determined this. Right-hand rotation ☐ Left-hand rotation ☐	☐
10. Reassemble the motor following the manufacturer's service information. Does the motor rotate by hand freely? Yes ☐ No ☐	☐

Non-Task-Specific Evaluation	Step Completed
1. Tools and equipment were used as directed and returned in good working order.	☐
2. Complied with all general and task-specific safety standards, including proper use of any personal protective equipment (PPE).	☐
3. Completed the task in an appropriate time frame (recommendation: 1.5 or 2 times the flat rate).	☐
4. Left the workspace clean and orderly.	☐
5. Cared for customer property and returned it undamaged.	☐

Student signature _____ Date _____

Comments:

Have your supervisor/instructor verify satisfactory completion of this procedure, any observations made, and any necessary action(s) recommended.

Evaluation Instructions: The scoring box below is intended to act as a guide for both student and supervisor/instructor. Each criterion listed will help students to understand what is expected of them and help supervisors/instructors to articulate the level of success at a particular task. The scoring is set up to allow a second attempt at each task (see the Test and Retest columns). Scoring is designed only to award students points for task criteria that were completed correctly. Points are lost for failure to complete the employability requirements (see Non-Task-Specific criteria). When all criteria are evaluated, tally the points for a total at the bottom of each column.

Tasksheet Scoring

	Test		Retest	
Evaluation Items	**Pass**	**Fail**	**Pass**	**Fail**
Task-Specific Evaluation	**(1 pt)**	**(0 pts)**	**(1 pt)**	**(0 pts)**
1. Student properly disassembled both the radial piston motor and the axial piston motor.				
2. Student correctly identified/described all components of the radial piston motor.				
3. Student correctly identified/described all components of the axial piston motor.				
4. Student properly reassembled both the radial piston motor and the axial piston motor.				
Non-Task-Specific Evaluation	**(0 pts)**	**(−1 pt)**	**(0 pts)**	**(−1 pt)**
Student successfully completed at least three of the non-task-specific steps.				
Student successfully completed all five of the non-task-specific steps.				
Total Score: <total # of points / 4 = %>				

Supervisor/Instructor:

Supervisor/instructor signature _____ Date _____

Comments:

Retest supervisor/instructor signature _____ Date _____

Comments:

CDX Tasksheet Number: 3.1c002

Student/Intern Information

Name _____ Date _____ Class _____

Machine, Customer, and Service Information

Machine used for this activity:

Make _____ Model _____

Hours _____ Serial Number _____

Materials Required

- Hydraulic training unit or machine
- Equipment manufacturer's service information, including schematic hydraulic diagrams
- Hydraulic pressure gauges
- Hydraulic spare parts, including fittings, hoses, and fluid
- Manufacturer-specific tools depending on the concern
- Machine lifting equipment, if applicable
- Machine lockout/tagout equipment, if applicable

Task-Specific Safety Considerations

- This task may require operating the equipment on school grounds, which carries severe risks. Attempt this task only with full permission from your supervisor/instructor and follow all the guidelines exactly.
- Lifting equipment such as equipment jacks and stands, hoists, overhead cranes, and engine hoists are important tools that increase productivity and make the job easier. However, they can also cause severe injury or death if used improperly. Make sure you follow the manufacturer's operation procedures. Also make sure you have your supervisor's/instructor's permission to use any type of lifting equipment.
- This task may require you to measure hydraulic pressures. Always ensure that the supervisor/instructor checks test instrument connections prior to connecting power or taking measurements. High fluid pressures can be dangerous; avoid opening hydraulic circuits until system is de-energized.
- Comply with personal and environmental safety practices associated with clothing; eye protection; hand tools; power equipment; proper ventilation; and the handling, storage, and disposal of chemicals/materials in accordance with federal, state, and local regulations.
- Always wear the correct protective eyewear and clothing and use the appropriate safety equipment, as well as seat protectors and floor mat protectors.
- Make sure you understand and observe all legislative and personal safety procedures when carrying out practical assignments. If you are unsure of what these are, ask your supervisor/instructor.

▶ TASK Disassemble and assemble a gerotor motor and identify its components.

AED
3.1

Student Instructions: Read through the entire procedure prior to starting. Prepare your workspace and any tools or parts that may be needed to complete the task. When directed by your supervisor/instructor, begin the procedure to complete the task, and comment or check the box as each step is finished. Track your time on this procedure for later comparison to the standard completion time (i.e., "flat rate" or customer pay time).

Procedure	Step Completed
1. Using the manufacturer's service information, disassemble a gerotor motor chosen by your supervisor/instructor. List all motor components below:	☐
2. Identify the inlet and outlet ports and describe how you determined this:	☐
3. Describe the path of fluid flow through the motor:	☐
4. Determine whether this motor is designed for right-hand (clockwise) or left-hand (counterclockwise) rotation, and explain how you determined this. Right-hand rotation ☐ Left-hand rotation ☐	☐
5. Reassemble the motor following the manufacturer's service information. Does the motor rotate by hand freely? Yes ☐ No ☐	☐

Non-Task-Specific Evaluation	Step Completed
1. Tools and equipment were used as directed and returned in good working order.	☐
2. Complied with all general and task-specific safety standards, including proper use of any personal protective equipment (PPE).	☐
3. Completed the task in an appropriate time frame (recommendation: 1.5 or 2 times the flat rate).	☐
4. Left the workspace clean and orderly.	☐
5. Cared for customer property and returned it undamaged.	☐

Student signature _____ Date _____

Comments:

> [   ]

Have your supervisor/instructor verify satisfactory completion of this procedure, any observations made, and any necessary action(s) recommended.

Evaluation Instructions: The scoring box below is intended to act as a guide for both student and supervisor/instructor. Each criterion listed will help students to understand what is expected of them and help supervisors/instructors to articulate the level of success at a particular task. The scoring is set up to allow a second attempt at each task (see the Test and Retest columns). Scoring is designed only to award students points for task criteria that were completed correctly. Points are lost for failure to complete the employability requirements (see Non-Task-Specific criteria). When all criteria are evaluated, tally the points for a total at the bottom of each column.

Tasksheet Scoring

Evaluation Items	Test		Retest	
	Pass	Fail	Pass	Fail
Task-Specific Evaluation	**(1 pt)**	**(0 pts)**	**(1 pt)**	**(0 pts)**
1. Student properly disassembled the motor.				
2. Student correctly identified/described the motor's ports and path of fluid flow.				
3. Student correctly identified/described whether the motor was designed for right-hand or left-hand rotation.				
4. Student properly reassembled the motor.				
Non-Task-Specific Evaluation	**(0 pts)**	**(−1 pt)**	**(0 pts)**	**(−1 pt)**
Student successfully completed at least three of the non-task-specific steps.				
Student successfully completed all five of the non-task-specific steps.				
Total Score: <total # of points / 4 = %>				

Supervisor/Instructor:

Supervisor/instructor signature _____ Date _____

Comments:

Retest supervisor/instructor signature _____ Date _____

Comments:

Chapter 22: Cylinder Identification and Operation

Learning Objective/Task	CDX Tasksheet Number	AED Reference Number
• Disassemble and assemble a single-acting hydraulic cylinder.	3.1e002	AED 3.1
• Disassemble and assemble a double-acting hydraulic cylinder.	3.1e004	AED 3.1

Materials Required

- Hydraulic training unit or machine
- Equipment manufacturer's service information, including schematic hydraulic diagrams
- Hydraulic pressure gauges
- Hydraulic spare parts, including fittings, hoses, and fluid
- Manufacturer-specific tools depending on the concern
- Machine lifting equipment, if applicable
- Machine lockout/tagout equipment, if applicable

Safety Considerations

- This task may require operating the equipment on school grounds, which carries severe risks. Attempt this task only with full permission from your supervisor/instructor and follow all the guidelines exactly.
- Lifting equipment such as equipment jacks and stands, hoists, overhead cranes, and engine hoists are important tools that increase productivity and make the job easier. However, they can also cause severe injury or death if used improperly. Make sure you follow the manufacturer's operation procedures. Also make sure you have your supervisor's/instructor's permission to use any type of lifting equipment.
- This task may require you to measure hydraulic pressures. Always ensure that the supervisor/instructor checks test instrument connections prior to connecting power or taking measurements. High fluid pressures can be dangerous; avoid opening hydraulic circuits until system is de-energized.
- Comply with personal and environmental safety practices associated with clothing; eye protection; hand tools; power equipment; proper ventilation; and the handling, storage, and disposal of chemicals/materials in accordance with federal, state, and local regulations.
- Always wear the correct protective eyewear and clothing and use the appropriate safety equipment, as well as seat protectors and floor mat protectors.
- Make sure you understand and observe all legislative and personal safety procedures when carrying out practical assignments. If you are unsure of what these are, ask your supervisor/instructor.

CDX Tasksheet Number: 3.1e002

Student/Intern Information

Name _____ Date _____ Class _____

Machine, Customer, and Service Information

Machine used for this activity:

Make _____ Model _____

Hours _____ Serial Number _____

Materials Required

- Hydraulic training unit or machine
- Equipment manufacturer's service information, including schematic hydraulic diagrams
- Hydraulic pressure gauges
- Hydraulic spare parts, including fittings, hoses, and fluid
- Manufacturer-specific tools depending on the concern
- Machine lifting equipment, if applicable
- Machine lockout/tagout equipment, if applicable

Task-Specific Safety Considerations

- This task may require operating the equipment on school grounds, which carries severe risks. Attempt this task only with full permission from your supervisor/instructor and follow all the guidelines exactly.
- Lifting equipment such as equipment jacks and stands, hoists, overhead cranes, and engine hoists are important tools that increase productivity and make the job easier. However, they can also cause severe injury or death if used improperly. Make sure you follow the manufacturer's operation procedures. Also make sure you have your supervisor's/ instructor's permission to use any type of lifting equipment.
- This task may require you to measure hydraulic pressures. Always ensure that the supervisor/instructor checks test instrument connections prior to connecting power or taking measurements. High fluid pressures can be dangerous; avoid opening hydraulic circuits until system is de-energized.
- Comply with personal and environmental safety practices associated with clothing; eye protection; hand tools; power equipment; proper ventilation; and the handling, storage, and disposal of chemicals/materials in accordance with federal, state, and local regulations.
- Always wear the correct protective eyewear and clothing and use the appropriate safety equipment, as well as seat protectors and floor mat protectors.
- Make sure you understand and observe all legislative and personal safety procedures when carrying out practical assignments. If you are unsure of what these are, ask your supervisor/ instructor.

Time off_____

Time on_____

Total time_____

Student Instructions: Read through the entire procedure prior to starting. Prepare your workspace and any tools or parts that may be needed to complete the task. When directed by your supervisor/instructor, begin the procedure to complete the task, and comment or check the box as each step is finished. Track your time on this procedure for later comparison to the standard completion time (i.e., "flat rate" or customer pay time).

Procedure	Step Completed
1. Disassemble a single-acting hydraulic cylinder. Identify all the parts of the cylinder below:	☐
2. Identify the cylinder's oil port and describe what prevents a vacuum on top of the piston when the rod retracts:	☐
3. Describe the flow of oil through the cylinder as the rod extends and retracts:	☐
4. Reassemble the cylinder and ensure the rod moves freely.	☐

Non-Task-Specific Evaluation	Step Completed
1. Tools and equipment were used as directed and returned in good working order.	☐
2. Complied with all general and task-specific safety standards, including proper use of any personal protective equipment (PPE).	☐
3. Completed the task in an appropriate time frame (recommendation: 1.5 or 2 times the flat rate).	☐
4. Left the workspace clean and orderly.	☐
5. Cared for customer property and returned it undamaged.	☐

Student signature _____ Date _____

Comments:

Have your supervisor/instructor verify satisfactory completion of this procedure, any observations made,

and any necessary action(s) recommended.

Evaluation Instructions: The scoring box below is intended to act as a guide for both student and supervisor/instructor. Each criterion listed will help students to understand what is expected of them and help supervisors/instructors to articulate the level of success at a particular task. The scoring is set up to allow a second attempt at each task (see the Test and Retest columns). Scoring is designed only to award students points for task criteria that were completed correctly. Points are lost for failure to complete the employability requirements (see Non-Task-Specific criteria). When all criteria are evaluated, tally the points for a total at the bottom of each column.

Tasksheet Scoring

	Test		Retest	
Evaluation Items	**Pass**	**Fail**	**Pass**	**Fail**
Task-Specific Evaluation	**(1 pt)**	**(0 pts)**	**(1 pt)**	**(0 pts)**
1. Student correctly identified all cylinder parts.				
2. Student correctly identified the cylinder oil port.				
3. Student accurately described cylinder movement.				
4. Student properly disassembled and reassembled the cylinder.				
Non-Task-Specific Evaluation	**(0 pts)**	**(−1 pt)**	**(0 pts)**	**(−1 pt)**
Student successfully completed at least three of the non-task-specific steps.				
Student successfully completed all five of the non-task-specific steps.				
Total Score: <total # of points / 4 = %>				

Supervisor/Instructor:

Supervisor/instructor signature _____ Date _____

Comments:

Retest supervisor/instructor signature _____ Date _____

Comments:

CDX Tasksheet Number: 3.1e004

Student/Intern Information

Name _____ Date _____ Class _____

Machine, Customer, and Service Information

Machine used for this activity:

Make _____ Model _____

Hours _____ Serial Number _____

Materials Required

- Hydraulic training unit or machine
- Equipment manufacturer's service information, including schematic hydraulic diagrams
- Hydraulic pressure gauges
- Hydraulic spare parts, including fittings, hoses, and fluid
- Manufacturer-specific tools depending on the concern
- Machine lifting equipment, if applicable
- Machine lockout/tagout equipment, if applicable

Task-Specific Safety Considerations

- This task may require operating the equipment on school grounds, which carries severe risks. Attempt this task only with full permission from your supervisor/instructor and follow all the guidelines exactly.
- Lifting equipment such as equipment jacks and stands, hoists, overhead cranes, and engine hoists are important tools that increase productivity and make the job easier. However, they can also cause severe injury or death if used improperly. Make sure you follow the manufacturer's operation procedures. Also make sure you have your supervisor's/instructor's permission to use any type of lifting equipment.
- This task may require you to measure hydraulic pressures. Always ensure that the supervisor/instructor checks test instrument connections prior to connecting power or taking measurements. High fluid pressures can be dangerous; avoid opening hydraulic circuits until system is de-energized.
- Comply with personal and environmental safety practices associated with clothing; eye protection; hand tools; power equipment; proper ventilation; and the handling, storage, and disposal of chemicals/materials in accordance with federal, state, and local regulations.
- Always wear the correct protective eyewear and clothing and use the appropriate safety equipment, as well as seat protectors and floor mat protectors.
- Make sure you understand and observe all legislative and personal safety procedures when carrying out practical assignments. If you are unsure of what these are, ask your supervisor/instructor.

Time off_____

Time on_____

Total time_____

Student Instructions: Read through the entire procedure prior to starting. Prepare your workspace and any tools or parts that may be needed to complete the task. When directed by your supervisor/instructor, begin the procedure to complete the task, and comment or check the box as each step is finished. Track your time on this procedure for later comparison to the standard completion time (i.e., "flat rate" or customer pay time).

Procedure	Step Completed
1. Disassemble a double-acting hydraulic cylinder. Identify all the parts of the cylinder below:	☐
2. Identify the cylinder's oil ports and give an example of where one would be used on a heavy equipment machine:	☐
3. Describe the flow of oil through the cylinder as the rod extends and retracts:	☐
4. Explain which direction of rod movement would create more linear force for the same amount of hydraulic pressure applied:	☐
5. Reassemble the cylinder and ensure the rod moves freely.	☐

Non-Task-Specific Evaluation	Step Completed
1. Tools and equipment were used as directed and returned in good working order.	☐
2. Complied with all general and task-specific safety standards, including proper use of any personal protective equipment (PPE).	☐
3. Completed the task in an appropriate time frame (recommendation: 1.5 or 2 times the flat rate).	☐
4. Left the workspace clean and orderly.	☐
5. Cared for customer property and returned it undamaged.	☐

Student signature _____ Date _____

Comments:

Have your supervisor/instructor verify satisfactory completion of this procedure, any observations made, and any necessary action(s) recommended.

Evaluation Instructions: The scoring box below is intended to act as a guide for both student and supervisor/instructor. Each criterion listed will help students to understand what is expected of them and help supervisors/instructors to articulate the level of success at a particular task. The scoring is set up to allow a second attempt at each task (see the Test and Retest columns). Scoring is designed only to award students points for task criteria that were completed correctly. Points are lost for failure to complete the employability requirements (see Non-Task-Specific criteria). When all criteria are evaluated, tally the points for a total at the bottom of each column.

Tasksheet Scoring

Evaluation Items	Test		Retest	
	Pass	**Fail**	**Pass**	**Fail**
Task-Specific Evaluation	**(1 pt)**	**(0 pts)**	**(1 pt)**	**(0 pts)**
1. Student correctly identified all cylinder parts.				
2. Student correctly identified oil ports and their typical application.				
3. Student accurately explained cylinder movement and direction movement with greater force.				
4. Student properly disassembled and reassembled the cylinder.				
Non-Task-Specific Evaluation	**(0 pts)**	**(−1 pt)**	**(0 pts)**	**(−1 pt)**
Student successfully completed at least three of the non-task-specific steps.				
Student successfully completed all five of the non-task-specific steps.				
Total Score: <total # of points / 4 = %>				

Supervisor/Instructor:

Supervisor/instructor signature _____ Date _____

Comments:

Retest supervisor/instructor signature _____ Date _____

Comments:

Chapter 23: Accumulator Identification and Operation

Learning Objective/Task	CDX Tasksheet Number	AED Reference Number
• Discharge and recharge a hydraulic accumulator following all service information safety practices.	3.1f003	AED 3.1

Materials Required

- Hydraulic training unit or machine
- Equipment manufacturer's service information, including schematic hydraulic diagrams
- Hydraulic pressure gauges
- Hydraulic spare parts, including fittings, hoses, and fluid
- Manufacturer-specific tools depending on the concern
- Machine lifting equipment, if applicable
- Machine lockout/tagout equipment, if applicable

Safety Considerations

- This task may require operating the equipment on school grounds, which carries severe risks. Attempt this task only with full permission from your supervisor/instructor and follow all the guidelines exactly.
- Lifting equipment such as equipment jacks and stands, hoists, overhead cranes, and engine hoists are important tools that increase productivity and make the job easier. However, they can also cause severe injury or death if used improperly. Make sure you follow the manufacturer's operation procedures. Also make sure you have your supervisor's/instructor's permission to use any type of lifting equipment.
- This task may require you to measure hydraulic pressures. Always ensure that the supervisor/instructor checks test instrument connections prior to connecting power or taking measurements. High fluid pressures can be dangerous; avoid opening hydraulic circuits until system is de-energized.
- Comply with personal and environmental safety practices associated with clothing; eye protection; hand tools; power equipment; proper ventilation; and the handling, storage, and disposal of chemicals/materials in accordance with federal, state, and local regulations.
- Always wear the correct protective eyewear and clothing and use the appropriate safety equipment, as well as seat protectors and floor mat protectors.
- Make sure you understand and observe all legislative and personal safety procedures when carrying out practical assignments. If you are unsure of what these are, ask your supervisor/instructor.

CDX Tasksheet Number: 3.1f003

Student/Intern Information

Name _____ Date _____ Class _____

Machine, Customer, and Service Information

Machine used for this activity:

Make _____ Model _____

Hours _____ Serial Number _____

Materials Required

- Hydraulic training unit or machine
- Equipment manufacturer's service information, including schematic hydraulic diagrams
- Hydraulic pressure gauges
- Hydraulic spare parts, including fittings, hoses, and fluid
- Manufacturer-specific tools depending on the concern
- Machine lifting equipment, if applicable
- Machine lockout/tagout equipment, if applicable

Task-Specific Safety Considerations

- This task may require operating the equipment on school grounds, which carries severe risks. Attempt this task only with full permission from your supervisor/instructor and follow all the guidelines exactly.
- Lifting equipment such as equipment jacks and stands, hoists, overhead cranes, and engine hoists are important tools that increase productivity and make the job easier. However, they can also cause severe injury or death if used improperly. Make sure you follow the manufacturer's operation procedures. Also make sure you have your supervisor's/instructor's permission to use any type of lifting equipment.
- This task may require you to measure hydraulic pressures. Always ensure that the supervisor/instructor checks test instrument connections prior to connecting power or taking measurements. High fluid pressures can be dangerous; avoid opening hydraulic circuits until system is de-energized.
- Comply with personal and environmental safety practices associated with clothing; eye protection; hand tools; power equipment; proper ventilation; and the handling, storage, and disposal of chemicals/materials in accordance with federal, state, and local regulations.
- Always wear the correct protective eyewear and clothing and use the appropriate safety equipment, as well as seat protectors and floor mat protectors.
- Make sure you understand and observe all legislative and personal safety procedures when carrying out practical assignments. If you are unsure of what these are, ask your supervisor/instructor.

▶ **TASK** Discharge and recharge a hydraulic accumulator following all service information safety practices.

AED
3.1

Student Instructions: Read through the entire procedure prior to starting. Prepare your workspace and any tools or parts that may be needed to complete the task. When directed by your supervisor/instructor, begin the procedure to complete the task, and comment or check the box as each step is finished. Track your time on this procedure for later comparison to the standard completion time (i.e., "flat rate" or customer pay time).

Procedure	Step Completed
1. Research the hazards and safety precautions that must be understood and followed when working on hydraulic systems using accumulators.	☐
2. List three hazards related to hydraulic accumulators:	☐
3. List three precautions you would take to keep yourself safe when working with accumulators:	☐
4. Demonstrate how to safely obtain and verify zero energy in an accumulator on a machine. List the steps taken to do this safely:	☐
5. Demonstrate how to safely charge an accumulator to specification on a machine. List the steps taken to achieve this:	☐

Non-Task-Specific Evaluation	Step Completed
1. Tools and equipment were used as directed and returned in good working order.	☐
2. Complied with all general and task-specific safety standards, including proper use of any personal protective equipment (PPE).	☐
3. Completed the task in an appropriate time frame (recommendation: 1.5 or 2 times the flat rate).	☐
4. Left the workspace clean and orderly.	☐
5. Cared for customer property and returned it undamaged.	☐

Student signature _____ Date _____

Comments:

Have your supervisor/instructor verify satisfactory completion of this procedure, any observations made, and any necessary action(s) recommended.

Evaluation Instructions: The scoring box below is intended to act as a guide for both student and supervisor/instructor. Each criterion listed will help students to understand what is expected of them and help supervisors/instructors to articulate the level of success at a particular task. The scoring is set up to allow a second attempt at each task (see the Test and Retest columns). Scoring is designed only to award students points for task criteria that were completed correctly. Points are lost for failure to complete the employability requirements (see Non-Task-Specific criteria). When all criteria are evaluated, tally the points for a total at the bottom of each column.

Tasksheet Scoring

Evaluation Items	Test		Retest	
	Pass	**Fail**	**Pass**	**Fail**
Task-Specific Evaluation	**(1 pt)**	**(0 pts)**	**(1 pt)**	**(0 pts)**
1. Student accurately listed three hazards related to accumulators.				
2. Student accurately listed three safety precautions related to accumulators.				
3. Student properly demonstrated safe discharging of an accumulator.				
4. Student properly demonstrated safe charging of an accumulator.				
Non-Task-Specific Evaluation	**(0 pts)**	**(−1 pt)**	**(0 pts)**	**(−1 pt)**
Student successfully completed at least three of the non-task-specific steps.				
Student successfully completed all five of the non-task-specific steps.				
Total Score: <total # of points / 4 = %>				

Supervisor/Instructor:

Supervisor/instructor signature _____ Date _____

Comments:

Retest supervisor/instructor signature _____ Date _____

Comments:

Chapter 24: Fluids, Transfer Components, and Filtering

Learning Objective/Task	CDX Tasksheet Number	AED Reference Number
• Correctly identify different styles of hydraulic fittings and provide torque installation specifications for them.	3.2003	AED 3.2
• Remove, construct, and install a hydraulic hose on a machine.	3.2004	AED 3.2

Materials Required

- Hydraulic training unit or machine
- Equipment manufacturer's service information, including schematic hydraulic diagrams
- 10 hydraulic fittings chosen by the supervisor/instructor to complete the task
- Tags numbered 1–10 for labeling hydraulic fittings
- Hydraulic pressure gauges
- Hydraulic spare parts, including fittings, hoses, and fluid
- Manufacturer-specific tools depending on the concern
- Machine lifting equipment, if applicable
- Machine lockout/tagout equipment, if applicable

Safety Considerations

- This task may require operating the equipment on school grounds, which carries severe risks. Attempt this task only with full permission from your supervisor/instructor and follow all the guidelines exactly.
- Lifting equipment such as equipment jacks and stands, hoists, overhead cranes, and engine hoists are important tools that increase productivity and make the job easier. However, they can also cause severe injury or death if used improperly. Make sure you follow the manufacturer's operation procedures. Also make sure you have your supervisor's/instructor's permission to use any type of lifting equipment.
- This task may require you to measure hydraulic pressures. Always ensure that the supervisor/instructor checks test instrument connections prior to connecting power or taking measurements. High fluid pressures can be dangerous; avoid opening hydraulic circuits until system is de-energized.
- Comply with personal and environmental safety practices associated with clothing; eye protection; hand tools; power equipment; proper ventilation; and the handling, storage, and disposal of chemicals/materials in accordance with federal, state, and local regulations.
- Always wear the correct protective eyewear and clothing and use the appropriate safety equipment, as well as seat protectors and floor mat protectors.
- Make sure you understand and observe all legislative and personal safety procedures when carrying out practical assignments. If you are unsure of what these are, ask your supervisor/instructor.

CDX Tasksheet Number: 3.2003

Student/Intern Information

Name _____ Date _____ Class _____

Machine, Customer, and Service Information

Machine used for this activity:

Make _____ Model _____

Hours _____ Serial Number _____

Materials Required

- Hydraulic training unit or machine
- Equipment manufacturer's service information, including schematic hydraulic diagrams
- 10 hydraulic fittings chosen by the supervisor/instructor to complete the task
- Tags numbered 1–10 for labeling hydraulic fittings

Task-Specific Safety Considerations

- This task may require operating the equipment on school grounds, which carries severe risks. Attempt this task only with full permission from your supervisor/instructor and follow all the guidelines exactly.
- Lifting equipment such as equipment jacks and stands, hoists, overhead cranes, and engine hoists are important tools that increase productivity and make the job easier. However, they can also cause severe injury or death if used improperly. Make sure you follow the manufacturer's operation procedures. Also make sure you have your supervisor's/instructor's permission to use any type of lifting equipment.
- This task may require you to measure hydraulic pressures. Always ensure that the supervisor/instructor checks test instrument connections prior to connecting power or taking measurements. High fluid pressures can be dangerous; avoid opening hydraulic circuits until system is de-energized.
- Comply with personal and environmental safety practices associated with clothing; eye protection; hand tools; power equipment; proper ventilation; and the handling, storage, and disposal of chemicals/materials in accordance with federal, state, and local regulations.
- Always wear the correct protective eyewear and clothing and use the appropriate safety equipment, as well as seat protectors and floor mat protectors.
- Make sure you understand and observe all legislative and personal safety procedures when carrying out practical assignments. If you are unsure of what these are, ask your supervisor/instructor.

▶ **TASK** Correctly identify different styles of hydraulic fittings and provide torque installation specifications for them.

AED 3.2

Student Instructions: Read through the entire procedure prior to starting. Prepare your workspace and any tools or parts that may be needed to complete the task. When directed by your supervisor/instructor, begin the procedure to complete the task, and comment or check the box as each step is finished. Track your time on this procedure for later comparison to the standard completion time (i.e., "flat rate" or customer pay time).

Procedure	Step Completed
1. Identify and provide the requested information for 10 different hydraulic fittings chosen your supervisor/instructor.	
a. Fitting #1 Name _____ Type _____ Size _____ Torque specification _____	☐
b. Fitting #2 Name _____ Type _____ Size _____ Torque specification _____	☐
c. Fitting #3 Name _____ Type _____ Size _____ Torque specification _____	☐
d. Fitting #4 Name _____ Type _____ Size _____ Torque specification _____	☐
e. Fitting #5 Name _____ Type _____ Size _____ Torque specification _____	☐

f. Fitting #6 Name _____ Type _____ Size _____ Torque specification _____	☐
g. Fitting #7 Name _____ Type _____ Size _____ Torque specification _____	☐
h. Fitting #8 Name _____ Type _____ Size _____ Torque specification _____	☐
i. Fitting #9 Name _____ Type _____ Size _____ Torque specification _____	☐
j. Fitting #10 Name _____ Type _____ Size _____ Torque specification _____	☐

Non-Task-Specific Evaluation	Step Completed
1. Tools and equipment were used as directed and returned in good working order.	☐
2. Complied with all general and task-specific safety standards, including proper use of any personal protective equipment (PPE).	☐
3. Completed the task in an appropriate time frame (recommendation: 1.5 or 2 times the flat rate).	☐
4. Left the workspace clean and orderly.	☐
5. Cared for customer property and returned it undamaged.	☐

Student signature _____ Date _____

Comments:

Have your supervisor/instructor verify satisfactory completion of this procedure, any observations made, and any necessary action(s) recommended.

Evaluation Instructions: The scoring box below is intended to act as a guide for both student and supervisor/instructor. Each criterion listed will help students to understand what is expected of them and help supervisors/instructors to articulate the level of success at a particular task. The scoring is set up to allow a second attempt at each task (see the Test and Retest columns). Scoring is designed only to award students points for task criteria that were completed correctly. Points are lost for failure to complete the employability requirements (see Non-Task-Specific criteria). When all criteria are evaluated, tally the points for a total at the bottom of each column.

Tasksheet Scoring

	Test		Retest	
Evaluation Items	**Pass**	**Fail**	**Pass**	**Fail**
Task-Specific Evaluation	**(1 pt)**	**(0 pts)**	**(1 pt)**	**(0 pts)**
1. Student correctly identified the information for at least two hydraulic fittings.				
2. Student correctly identified the information for at least four hydraulic fittings.				
3. Student correctly identified the information for at least seven hydraulic fittings.				
4. Student correctly identified the information for all 10 hydraulic fittings.				
Non-Task-Specific Evaluation	**(0 pts)**	**(−1 pt)**	**(0 pts)**	**(−1 pt)**
Student successfully completed at least three of the non-task-specific steps.				
Student successfully completed all five of the non-task-specific steps.				
Total Score: <total # of points / 4 = %>				

Supervisor/Instructor:

Supervisor/instructor signature _____ Date _____

Comments:

Retest supervisor/instructor signature _____ Date _____

Comments:

CDX Tasksheet Number: 3.2004

Student/Intern Information

Name _____ Date _____ Class _____

Machine, Customer, and Service Information

Machine used for this activity:

Make _____ Model _____

Hours _____ Serial Number _____

Task-Specific Safety Considerations
- This task may require operating the equipment on school grounds, which carries severe risks. Attempt this task only with full permission from your supervisor/instructor and follow all the guidelines exactly.
- Lifting equipment such as equipment jacks and stands, hoists, overhead cranes, and engine hoists are important tools that increase productivity and make the job easier. However, they can also cause severe injury or death if used improperly. Make sure you follow the manufacturer's operation procedures. Also make sure you have your supervisor's/instructor's permission to use any type of lifting equipment.
- Activities may require you to measure hydraulic pressures. Always ensure that the instructor/supervisor checks test instrument connections prior to connecting power or taking measurements. High fluid pressures can be dangerous; avoid opening hydraulic circuits until system is de-energized.
- Comply with personal and environmental safety practices associated with clothing; eye protection; hand tools; power equipment; proper ventilation; and the handling, storage, and disposal of chemicals/materials in accordance with federal, state, and local regulations.
- Always wear the correct protective eyewear and clothing and use the appropriate safety equipment, as well as seat protectors and floor mat protectors.
- Make sure you understand and observe all legislative and personal safety procedures when carrying out practical assignments. If you are unsure of what these are, ask your supervisor/instructor.

▶ **TASK** Remove, construct, and install a hydraulic hose on a machine.

AED
3.2

Student Instructions: Read through the entire procedure prior to starting. Prepare your workspace and any tools or parts that may be needed to complete the task. When directed by your supervisor/instructor, begin the procedure to complete the task, and comment or check the box as each step is finished. Track your time on this procedure for later comparison to the standard completion time (i.e., "flat rate" or customer pay time).

Procedure	Step Completed
1. Identify the hydraulic hose that your supervisor/instructor chose by the circuit it is part of and the maximum system pressure that it will be exposed to:	☐
2. Describe all necessary tooling and equipment needed to remove the hose safely and contain any oil spillage:	☐
3. List three safety precautions to be taken during hose removal:	☐
4. Describe how you would determine whether there was minimal hydraulic pressure in the hose:	☐
5. Remove the hose from the machine and use the STAMPED method to identify and build the hose. Describe the method and/or specification(s) used to crimp the hose ends on properly:	☐
6. Describe the methods used to ensure no contamination entered the machine's hydraulic system:	☐

	Step Completed
7. Install the hose on the machine. Provide the torque specification(s) below:	☐
8. Describe how the hose is sealed to the machine's hydraulic system:	☐
9. Describe how to safely start up the machine and properly check its hydraulic fluid:	☐
10. Return the machine to its normal operating condition.	☐

Non-Task-Specific Evaluation	Step Completed
1. Tools and equipment were used as directed and returned in good working order.	☐
2. Complied with all general and task-specific safety standards, including proper use of any personal protective equipment (PPE).	☐
3. Completed the task in an appropriate time frame (recommendation: 1.5 or 2 times the flat rate).	☐
4. Left the workspace clean and orderly.	☐
5. Cared for customer property and returned it undamaged.	☐

Student signature _____ Date _____

Comments:

Have your supervisor/instructor verify satisfactory completion of this procedure, any observations made, and any necessary action(s) recommended.

Evaluation Instructions: The scoring box below is intended to act as a guide for both student and supervisor/instructor. Each criterion listed will help students to understand what is expected of them and help supervisors/instructors to articulate the level of success at a particular task. The scoring is set up to allow a second attempt at each task (see the Test and Retest columns). Scoring is designed only to award students points for task criteria that were completed correctly. Points are lost for failure to complete the employability requirements (see Non-Task-Specific criteria). When all criteria are evaluated, tally the points for a total at the bottom of each column.

Tasksheet Scoring

Evaluation Items	Test		Retest	
	Pass	**Fail**	**Pass**	**Fail**
Task-Specific Evaluation	**(1 pt)**	**(0 pts)**	**(1 pt)**	**(0 pts)**
1. Student correctly identified the hose, any tooling or equipment needed, and three safety precautions.				
2. Student correctly described the procedure for confirming minimal hydraulic pressure in the hose, the methods for contamination control, the hose sealing method, and how to safely start up the machine and check hydraulic fluid level.				
3. Student correctly removed the hose and assembled the hose using the STAMPED method.				
4. Student performed proper hose installation.				
Non-Task-Specific Evaluation	**(0 pts)**	**(−1 pt)**	**(0 pts)**	**(−1 pt)**
Student successfully completed at least three of the non-task-specific steps.				
Student successfully completed all five of the non-task-specific steps.				
Total Score: <total # of points / 4 = %>				

Supervisor/Instructor:

Supervisor/instructor signature _____ Date _____

Comments:

_____

Retest supervisor/instructor signature _____ Date _____

Comments:

_____

Chapter 25: Maintenance Procedures; Understand the Importance of Maintenance

Learning Objective/Task	CDX Tasksheet Number	AED Reference Number
• Perform a hydraulic system maintenance procedure.	3.3a001	AED 3.3
• Perform new hydraulic hose internal cleaning procedures.	3.3a005	AED 3.3

Materials Required

- Hydraulic training unit or machine
- Equipment manufacturer's service information, including schematic hydraulic diagrams
- Hydraulic pressure gauges
- Hydraulic spare parts, including fittings, hoses, and fluid
- Manufacturer-specific tools depending on the concern
- Machine lifting equipment, if applicable
- Machine lockout/tagout equipment, if applicable
- Personal protective equipment (PPE)

Safety Considerations

- This task may require operating the equipment on school grounds, which carries severe risks. Attempt this task only with full permission from your supervisor/instructor and follow all the guidelines exactly.
- Lifting equipment such as equipment jacks and stands, hoists, overhead cranes, and engine hoists are important tools that increase productivity and make the job easier. However, they can also cause severe injury or death if used improperly. Make sure you follow the manufacturer's operation procedures. Also make sure you have your supervisor's/instructor's permission to use any type of lifting equipment.
- This task may require you to measure hydraulic pressures. Always ensure that the supervisor/instructor checks test instrument connections prior to connecting power or taking measurements. High fluid pressures can be dangerous; avoid opening hydraulic circuits until system is de-energized.
- Comply with personal and environmental safety practices associated with clothing; eye protection; hand tools; power equipment; proper ventilation; and the handling, storage, and disposal of chemicals/materials in accordance with federal, state, and local regulations.
- Always wear the correct protective eyewear and clothing and use the appropriate safety equipment, as well as seat protectors and floor mat protectors.
- Make sure you understand and observe all legislative and personal safety procedures when carrying out practical assignments. If you are unsure of what these are, ask your supervisor/instructor.

CDX Tasksheet Number: 3.3a001

Student/Intern Information

Name _____ Date _____ Class _____

Machine, Customer, and Service Information

Machine used for this activity:

Make _____ Model _____

Hours _____ Serial Number _____

Materials Required

- Hydraulic training unit or machine
- Equipment manufacturer's service information, including schematic hydraulic diagrams
- Hydraulic pressure gauges
- Hydraulic spare parts, including fittings, hoses, and fluid
- Manufacturer-specific tools depending on the concern
- Machine lifting equipment, if applicable
- Machine lockout/tagout equipment, if applicable
- Personal protective equipment (PPE)

Task-Specific Safety Considerations

- This task may require operating the equipment on school grounds, which carries severe risks. Attempt this task only with full permission from your supervisor/instructor and follow all the guidelines exactly.
- Lifting equipment such as equipment jacks and stands, hoists, overhead cranes, and engine hoists are important tools that increase productivity and make the job easier. However, they can also cause severe injury or death if used improperly. Make sure you follow the manufacturer's operation procedures. Also make sure you have your supervisor's/instructor's permission to use any type of lifting equipment.
- This task may require you to measure hydraulic pressures. Always ensure that the supervisor/instructor checks test instrument connections prior to connecting power or taking measurements. High fluid pressures can be dangerous; avoid opening hydraulic circuits until system is de-energized.
- Comply with personal and environmental safety practices associated with clothing; eye protection; hand tools; power equipment; proper ventilation; and the handling, storage, and disposal of chemicals/materials in accordance with federal, state, and local regulations.
- Always wear the correct protective eyewear and clothing and use the appropriate safety equipment, as well as seat protectors and floor mat protectors.
- Make sure you understand and observe all legislative and personal safety procedures when carrying out practical assignments. If you are unsure of what these are, ask your supervisor/instructor.

► TASK Perform a hydraulic system maintenance procedure.

AED
3.3

Student Instructions: Read through the entire procedure prior to starting. Prepare your workspace and any tools or parts that may be needed to complete the task. When directed by your supervisor/instructor, begin the procedure to complete the task, and comment or check the box as each step is finished. Track your time on this procedure for later comparison to the standard completion time (i.e., "flat rate" or customer pay time).

Procedure	Step Completed
1. Describe how to safely prepare the hydraulic machine your supervisor/instructor assigned you for a hydraulic system maintenance procedure:	☐
2. Describe the hydraulic maintenance procedure step by step:	☐
3. List the tools needed to perform the procedure:	☐
4. Name the highest risk to your safety while performing the maintenance procedure:	☐
5. List all of the PPE you would use while performing this procedure:	☐
6. Perform the procedure safely. Describe how you would ensure the machine is in normal operating condition when finished:	☐

Non-Task-Specific Evaluation	Step Completed
1. Tools and equipment were used as directed and returned in good working order.	☐
2. Complied with all general and task-specific safety standards, including proper use of any PPE.	☐
3. Completed the task in an appropriate time frame (recommendation: 1.5 or 2 times the flat rate).	☐
4. Left the workspace clean and orderly.	☐
5. Cared for customer property and returned it undamaged.	☐

Student signature _____ Date _____

Comments:

Have your supervisor/instructor verify satisfactory completion of this procedure, any observations made, and any necessary action(s) recommended.

Evaluation Instructions: The scoring box below is intended to act as a guide for both student and supervisor/instructor. Each criterion listed will help students to understand what is expected of them and help supervisors/instructors to articulate the level of success at a particular task. The scoring is set up to allow a second attempt at each task (see the Test and Retest columns). Scoring is designed only to award students points for task criteria that were completed correctly. Points are lost for failure to complete the employability requirements (see Non-Task-Specific criteria). When all criteria are evaluated, tally the points for a total at the bottom of each column.

Tasksheet Scoring

Evaluation Items	Test		Retest	
	Pass	Fail	Pass	Fail
Task-Specific Evaluation	**(1 pt)**	**(0 pts)**	**(1 pt)**	**(0 pts)**
1. Student correctly described safe machine preparation.				
2. Student correctly described the hydraulic maintenance procedure and the tools needed.				
3. Student identified the highest risk of the procedure as well as the PPE requirements.				
4. Student correctly described how to confirm the machine was ready for normal operation.				
Non-Task-Specific Evaluation	**(0 pts)**	**(−1 pt)**	**(0 pts)**	**(−1 pt)**
Student successfully completed at least three of the non-task-specific steps.				
Student successfully completed all five of the non-task-specific steps.				
Total Score: <total # of points / 4 = %>				

Supervisor/Instructor:

Supervisor/instructor signature _____ Date _____

Comments:

Retest supervisor/instructor signature _____ Date _____

Comments:

CDX Tasksheet Number: 3.3a005

Student/Intern Information

Name _____ Date _____ Class _____

Machine, Customer, and Service Information

Machine used for this activity:

Make _____ Model _____

Hours _____ Serial Number _____

Materials Required

- Hydraulic training unit or machine
- Equipment manufacturer's service information, including schematic hydraulic diagrams
- Hydraulic pressure gauges
- Hydraulic spare parts, including fittings, hoses, and fluid
- Manufacturer-specific tools depending on the concern
- Machine lifting equipment, if applicable
- Machine lockout/tagout equipment, if applicable
- Personal protective equipment (PPE)

Task-Specific Safety Considerations

- This task may require operating the equipment on school grounds, which carries severe risks. Attempt this task only with full permission from your supervisor/instructor and follow all the guidelines exactly.
- Lifting equipment such as equipment jacks and stands, hoists, overhead cranes, and engine hoists are important tools that increase productivity and make the job easier. However, they can also cause severe injury or death if used improperly. Make sure you follow the manufacturer's operation procedures. Also make sure you have your supervisor's/instructor's permission to use any type of lifting equipment.
- This task may require you to measure hydraulic pressures. Always ensure that the supervisor/instructor checks test instrument connections prior to connecting power or taking measurements. High fluid pressures can be dangerous; avoid opening hydraulic circuits until system is de-energized.
- Comply with personal and environmental safety practices associated with clothing; eye protection; hand tools; power equipment; proper ventilation; and the handling, storage, and disposal of chemicals/materials in accordance with federal, state, and local regulations.
- Always wear the correct protective eyewear and clothing and use the appropriate safety equipment, as well as seat protectors and floor mat protectors.
- Make sure you understand and observe all legislative and personal safety procedures when carrying out practical assignments. If you are unsure of what these are, ask your supervisor/instructor.

▶ **TASK** Perform new hydraulic hose internal cleaning procedures.

AED
3.3

Student Instructions: Read through the entire procedure prior to starting. Prepare your workspace and any tools or parts that may be needed to complete the task. When directed by your supervisor/instructor, begin the procedure to complete the task, and comment or check the box as each step is finished. Track your time on this procedure for later comparison to the standard completion time (i.e., "flat rate" or customer pay time).

Procedure	Step Completed
1. Research hydraulic hose cleaning techniques.	☐
2. Describe, step-by-step, the technique for ensuring the inside of a hydraulic hose is clean after it is built:	☐
3. List three possible negative consequences of not performing this procedure:	☐
4. Describe the PPE needed to keep yourself safe when performing this procedure:	☐
5. Demonstrate how to clean the inside of a hydraulic hose properly and safely after it is built. Have your supervisor/instructor verify satisfactory completion of this procedure. Supervisor's/instructor's initials: _____	☐
6. Describe how the hose should be properly stored and/or shipped and handled before installation:	☐

Non-Task-Specific Evaluation	Step Completed
1. Tools and equipment were used as directed and returned in good working order.	☐
2. Complied with all general and task-specific safety standards, including proper use of any PPE.	☐
3. Completed the task in an appropriate time frame (recommendation: 1.5 or 2 times the flat rate).	☐
4. Left the workspace clean and orderly.	☐
5. Cared for customer property and returned it undamaged.	☐

Student signature _____ Date _____

Comments:

Have your supervisor/instructor verify satisfactory completion of this procedure, any observations made,

and any necessary action(s) recommended.

Evaluation Instructions: The scoring box below is intended to act as a guide for both student and supervisor/instructor. Each criterion listed will help students to understand what is expected of them and help supervisors/instructors to articulate the level of success at a particular task. The scoring is set up to allow a second attempt at each task (see the Test and Retest columns). Scoring is designed only to award students points for task criteria that were completed correctly. Points are lost for failure to complete the employability requirements (see Non-Task-Specific criteria). When all criteria are evaluated, tally the points for a total at the bottom of each column.

Tasksheet Scoring

Evaluation Items	Test		Retest	
	Pass	**Fail**	**Pass**	**Fail**
Task-Specific Evaluation	**(1 pt)**	**(0 pts)**	**(1 pt)**	**(0 pts)**
1. Student correctly described the step-by-step technique for cleaning hoses after building them.				
2. Student correctly described three possible consequences of not cleaning hoses and correctly identified PPE requirements.				
3. Student demonstrated proper and safe cleaning of a hydraulic hose.				
4. Student correctly described how to properly store and handle a cleaned hydraulic hose.				
Non-Task-Specific Evaluation	**(0 pts)**	**(−1 pt)**	**(0 pts)**	**(−1 pt)**
Student successfully completed at least three of the non-task-specific steps.				
Student successfully completed all five of the non-task-specific steps.				
Total Score: <total # of points / 4 = %>				

Supervisor/Instructor:

Supervisor/instructor signature _____ Date _____

Comments:

Retest supervisor/instructor signature _____ Date _____

Comments:

Chapter 26: Maintenance Procedures; Fluid Cleanliness

Learning Objective/Task	CDX Tasksheet Number	AED Reference Number
• Perform a fluid sample procedure on a machine.	3.3c002	AED 3.3

Materials Required

- Hydraulic training unit or machine
- Equipment manufacturer's service information, including schematic hydraulic diagrams
- Hydraulic pressure gauges
- Hydraulic spare parts, including fittings, hoses, and fluid
- Manufacturer-specific tools depending on the concern
- Machine lifting equipment, if applicable
- Machine lockout/tagout equipment, if applicable
- Personal protective equipment (PPE)

Safety Considerations

- This task may require operating the equipment on school grounds, which carries severe risks. Attempt this task only with full permission from your supervisor/instructor and follow all the guidelines exactly.
- Lifting equipment such as equipment jacks and stands, hoists, overhead cranes, and engine hoists are important tools that increase productivity and make the job easier. However, they can also cause severe injury or death if used improperly. Make sure you follow the manufacturer's operation procedures. Also make sure you have your supervisor's/instructor's permission to use any type of lifting equipment.
- This task may require you to measure hydraulic pressures. Always ensure that the supervisor/instructor checks test instrument connections prior to connecting power or taking measurements. High fluid pressures can be dangerous; avoid opening hydraulic circuits until system is de-energized.
- Comply with personal and environmental safety practices associated with clothing; eye protection; hand tools; power equipment; proper ventilation; and the handling, storage, and disposal of chemicals/materials in accordance with federal, state, and local regulations.
- Always wear the correct protective eyewear and clothing and use the appropriate safety equipment, as well as seat protectors and floor mat protectors.
- Make sure you understand and observe all legislative and personal safety procedures when carrying out practical assignments. If you are unsure of what these are, ask your supervisor/instructor.

CDX Tasksheet Number: 3.3c002

Student/Intern Information

Name _____ Date _____ Class _____

Machine, Customer, and Service Information

Machine used for this activity:

Make _____ Model _____

Hours _____ Serial Number _____

Materials Required
- Hydraulic training unit or machine
- Equipment manufacturer's service information, including schematic hydraulic diagrams
- Hydraulic pressure gauges
- Hydraulic spare parts, including fittings, hoses, and fluid
- Manufacturer-specific tools depending on the concern
- Machine lifting equipment, if applicable
- Machine lockout/tagout equipment, if applicable
- Personal protective equipment (PPE)

Task-Specific Safety Considerations
- This task may require operating the equipment on school grounds, which carries severe risks. Attempt this task only with full permission from your supervisor/instructor and follow all the guidelines exactly.
- Lifting equipment such as equipment jacks and stands, hoists, overhead cranes, and engine hoists are important tools that increase productivity and make the job easier. However, they can also cause severe injury or death if used improperly. Make sure you follow the manufacturer's operation procedures. Also make sure you have your supervisor's/instructor's permission to use any type of lifting equipment.
- This task may require you to measure hydraulic pressures. Always ensure that the supervisor/instructor checks test instrument connections prior to connecting power or taking measurements. High fluid pressures can be dangerous; avoid opening hydraulic circuits until system is de-energized.
- Comply with personal and environmental safety practices associated with clothing; eye protection; hand tools; power equipment; proper ventilation; and the handling, storage, and disposal of chemicals/materials in accordance with federal, state, and local regulations.
- Always wear the correct protective eyewear and clothing and use the appropriate safety equipment, as well as seat protectors and floor mat protectors.
- Make sure you understand and observe all legislative and personal safety procedures when carrying out practical assignments. If you are unsure of what these are, ask your supervisor/instructor.

▶ **TASK** Perform a fluid sample procedure on a machine.

Student Instructions: Read through the entire procedure prior to starting. Prepare your workspace and any tools or parts that may be needed to complete the task. When directed by your supervisor/instructor, begin the procedure to complete the task, and comment or check the box as each step is finished. Track your time on this procedure for later comparison to the standard completion time (i.e., "flat rate" or customer pay time).

Procedure	Step Completed
1. Research hydraulic fluid sampling methods.	☐
2. List the three possible methods for taking hydraulic fluid samples:	☐
3. Describe the step-by-step method preferred for taking a hydraulic fluid sample and explain why it is preferred:	☐
4. List three possible consequences if a hydraulic fluid sample is not taken properly:	☐
5. Find a machine with a live sample port for its hydraulic system and note its location:	☐
6. List the ideal conditions for the machine and hydraulic fluid to be in for the best sample results:	☐
7. Describe the minimum information that needs to be provided with a hydraulic sample when it is sent to a laboratory:	☐

	Step Completed
8. Obtain a hydraulic fluid sample from a machine using either the live sample method or the vacuum pump method. Ensure all safety precautions (proper PPE, machine service positioning, etc.) are taken when obtaining the sample. Have your supervisor/instructor verify satisfactory completion of this procedure. Supervisor's/instructor's initials: _____	☐
9. Return your machine to its normal operating condition and describe the visual checks needed to confirm this:	☐

Non-Task-Specific Evaluation	Step Completed
1. Tools and equipment were used as directed and returned in good working order.	☐
2. Complied with all general and task-specific safety standards, including proper use of any PPE.	☐
3. Completed the task in an appropriate time frame (recommendation: 1.5 or 2 times the flat rate).	☐
4. Left the workspace clean and orderly.	☐
5. Cared for customer property and returned it undamaged.	☐

Student signature _____ Date _____

Comments:

Have your supervisor/instructor verify satisfactory completion of this procedure, any observations made,

and any necessary action(s) recommended.

Evaluation Instructions: The scoring box below is intended to act as a guide for both student and supervisor/instructor. Each criterion listed will help students to understand what is expected of them and help supervisors/instructors to articulate the level of success at a particular task. The scoring is set up to allow a second attempt at each task (see the Test and Retest columns). Scoring is designed only to award students points for task criteria that were completed correctly. Points are lost for failure to complete the employability requirements (see Non-Task-Specific criteria). When all criteria are evaluated, tally the points for a total at the bottom of each column.

Tasksheet Scoring

Evaluation Items	Test		Retest	
	Pass	Fail	Pass	Fail
Task-Specific Evaluation	**(1 pt)**	**(0 pts)**	**(1 pt)**	**(0 pts)**
1. Student correctly described three possible sampling methods and identified the preferred method.				
2. Student correctly identified three consequences of not sampling correctly.				
3. Student correctly identified the ideal fluid and machine conditions for live sampling as well as the minimum information that should be sent with a sample.				
4. Student obtained a fluid sample safely and described the visual checks required for knowing their machine has been returned to normal operating condition.				
Non-Task-Specific Evaluation	**(0 pts)**	**(−1 pt)**	**(0 pts)**	**(−1 pt)**
Student successfully completed at least three of the non-task-specific steps.				
Student successfully completed all five of the non-task-specific steps.				
Total Score: <total # of points / 4 = %>				

Supervisor/Instructor:

Supervisor/instructor signature _____ Date _____

Comments:

Retest supervisor/instructor signature _____ Date _____

Comments:

Chapter 27: Component Repair and Replacement

Learning Objective/Task	CDX Tasksheet Number	AED Reference Number
• Perform a hydraulic component recondition procedure.	3.4001	AED 3.4

Materials Required

- Hydraulic training unit or machine
- Equipment manufacturer's service information, including schematic hydraulic diagrams
- Hydraulic pressure gauges
- Hydraulic spare parts, including fittings, hoses, and fluid
- Manufacturer-specific tools depending on the concern
- Machine lifting equipment, if applicable
- Machine lockout/tagout equipment, if applicable

Safety Considerations

- This task may require operating the equipment on school grounds, which carries severe risks. Attempt this task only with full permission from your supervisor/instructor and follow all the guidelines exactly.
- Lifting equipment such as equipment jacks and stands, hoists, overhead cranes, and engine hoists are important tools that increase productivity and make the job easier. However, they can also cause severe injury or death if used improperly. Make sure you follow the manufacturer's operation procedures. Also make sure you have your supervisor's/instructor's permission to use any type of lifting equipment.
- This task may require you to measure hydraulic pressures. Always ensure that the instructor/supervisor checks test instrument connections prior to connecting power or taking measurements. High fluid pressures can be dangerous; avoid opening hydraulic circuits until system is de-energized.
- Comply with personal and environmental safety practices associated with clothing; eye protection; hand tools; power equipment; proper ventilation; and the handling, storage, and disposal of chemicals/materials in accordance with federal, state, and local regulations.
- Always wear the correct protective eyewear and clothing and use the appropriate safety equipment, as well as seat protectors and floor mat protectors.
- Make sure you understand and observe all legislative and personal safety procedures when carrying out practical assignments. If you are unsure of what these are, ask your supervisor/instructor.

CDX Tasksheet Number: 3.4001

Student/Intern Information

Name _____ Date _____ Class _____

Machine, Customer, and Service Information

Machine used for this activity:

Make _____ Model _____

Hours _____ Serial Number _____

Materials Required

- Hydraulic training unit or machine
- Equipment manufacturer's service information, including schematic hydraulic diagrams
- Hydraulic pressure gauges
- Hydraulic spare parts, including fittings, hoses, and fluid
- Manufacturer-specific tools depending on the concern
- Machine lifting equipment, if applicable
- Machine lockout/tagout equipment, if applicable

Task-Specific Safety Considerations

- This task may require operating the equipment on school grounds, which carries severe risks. Attempt this task only with full permission from your supervisor/instructor and follow all the guidelines exactly.
- Lifting equipment such as equipment jacks and stands, hoists, overhead cranes, and engine hoists are important tools that increase productivity and make the job easier. However, they can also cause severe injury or death if used improperly. Make sure you follow the manufacturer's operation procedures. Also make sure you have your supervisor's/ instructor's permission to use any type of lifting equipment.
- This task may require you to measure hydraulic pressures. Always ensure that the instructor/supervisor checks test instrument connections prior to connecting power or taking measurements. High fluid pressures can be dangerous; avoid opening hydraulic circuits until system is de-energized.
- Comply with personal and environmental safety practices associated with clothing; eye protection; hand tools; power equipment; proper ventilation; and the handling, storage, and disposal of chemicals/materials in accordance with federal, state, and local regulations.
- Always wear the correct protective eyewear and clothing and use the appropriate safety equipment, as well as seat protectors and floor mat protectors.
- Make sure you understand and observe all legislative and personal safety procedures when carrying out practical assignments. If you are unsure of what these are, ask your supervisor/ instructor.

▶ **TASK** Perform a hydraulic component recondition procedure.

AED
3.4

Student Instructions: Read through the entire procedure prior to starting. Prepare your workspace and any tools or parts that may be needed to complete the task. When directed by your supervisor/instructor, begin the procedure to complete the task, and comment or check the box as each step is finished. Track your time on this procedure for later comparison to the standard completion time (i.e., "flat rate" or customer pay time).

Procedure	Step Completed
1. Research hydraulic gear pump removal and installation.	☐
2. List the step-by-step procedure required to safely remove a gear pump from a machine:	☐
3. Disassemble a gear pump as described in the manufacturer's service information and list the steps below:	☐
4. Thoroughly inspect all pump components and record any defects found below:	☐
5. List all pump components that should be replaced before assembly:	☐
6. Assemble the gear pump as described in the manufacturer's service information and list the steps below:	☐

7. List the step-by-step procedure for safely installing a gear pump on a machine:	☐
8. Describe the safe initial start-up and test procedure after installing a gear pump and before putting a machine back into production:	☐

Non-Task-Specific Evaluation	Step Completed
1. Tools and equipment were used as directed and returned in good working order.	☐
2. Complied with all general and task-specific safety standards, including proper use of any personal protective equipment (PPE).	☐
3. Completed the task in an appropriate time frame (recommendation: 1.5 or 2 times the flat rate).	☐
4. Left the workspace clean and orderly.	☐
5. Cared for customer property and returned it undamaged.	☐

Student signature _____ Date _____

Comments:

Have your supervisor/instructor verify satisfactory completion of this procedure, any observations made, and any necessary action(s) recommended.

Evaluation Instructions: The scoring box below is intended to act as a guide for both student and supervisor/instructor. Each criterion listed will help students to understand what is expected of them and help supervisors/instructors to articulate the level of success at a particular task. The scoring is set up to allow a second attempt at each task (see the Test and Retest columns). Scoring is designed only to award students points for task criteria that were completed correctly. Points are lost for failure to complete the employability requirements (see Non-Task-Specific criteria). When all criteria are evaluated, tally the points for a total at the bottom of each column.

Tasksheet Scoring

Evaluation Items	Test		Retest	
	Pass	**Fail**	**Pass**	**Fail**
Task-Specific Evaluation	**(1 pt)**	**(0 pts)**	**(1 pt)**	**(0 pts)**
1. Student correctly described the step-by-step procedure for removing a gear pump as well as gear pump disassembly.				
2. Student correctly identified and recorded gear pump component defects and pump components requiring replacement.				
3. Student correctly described and recorded gear pump assembly and installation.				
4. Student correctly described safe initial start-up and test procedure.				
Non-Task-Specific Evaluation	**(0 pts)**	**(−1 pt)**	**(0 pts)**	**(−1 pt)**
Student successfully completed at least three of the non-task-specific steps.				
Student successfully completed all five of the non-task-specific steps.				
Total Score: <total # of points / 4 = %>				

Supervisor/Instructor:

Supervisor/instructor signature _____ Date _____

Comments:

Retest supervisor/instructor signature _____ Date _____

Comments:

Chapter 28: Diagnostics Systems and Component Troubleshooting

Learning Objective/Task	CDX Tasksheet Number	AED Reference Number
• Measure hydraulic system pressure, flow, and temperature.	3.6003	AED 3.6
• Diagnose a hydraulic system problem using hydraulic schematics and flow charts.	3.6004	AED 3.6
• Perform hydraulic system operational tests and measurements.	3.6005	AED 3.6
• Perform a troubleshooting procedure on a load sensing hydraulic system.	3.6006	AED 3.6
• Create a repair order based on a machine hydraulic system problem.	3.6007	AED 3.6

Materials Required

- Hydraulic training unit or machine
- Equipment manufacturer's service information, including schematic hydraulic diagrams
- Hydraulic pressure gauges
- Hydraulic spare parts, including fittings, hoses, and fluid
- Manufacturer-specific tools depending on the concern
- Machine lifting equipment, if applicable
- Machine lockout/tagout equipment, if applicable
- Blank repair order

Safety Considerations

- This task may require operating the equipment on school grounds, which carries severe risks. Attempt this task only with full permission from your supervisor/instructor and follow all the guidelines exactly.
- Lifting equipment such as equipment jacks and stands, hoists, overhead cranes, and engine hoists are important tools that increase productivity and make the job easier. However, they can also cause severe injury or death if used improperly. Make sure you follow the manufacturer's operation procedures. Also make sure you have your supervisor's/instructor's permission to use any type of lifting equipment.
- This task may require you to measure hydraulic pressures. Always ensure that the instructor/supervisor checks test instrument connections prior to connecting power or taking measurements. High fluid pressures can be dangerous; avoid opening hydraulic circuits until system is de-energized.
- Comply with personal and environmental safety practices associated with clothing; eye protection; hand tools; power equipment; proper ventilation; and the handling, storage, and disposal of chemicals/materials in accordance with federal, state, and local regulations.

- Always wear the correct protective eyewear and clothing and use the appropriate safety equipment, as well as seat protectors and floor mat protectors.
- Make sure you understand and observe all legislative and personal safety procedures when carrying out practical assignments. If you are unsure of what these are, ask your supervisor/instructor.

CDX Tasksheet Number: 3.6003

Student/Intern Information

Name _____ Date _____ Class _____

Machine, Customer, and Service Information

Machine used for this activity:

Make _____ Model _____

Hours _____ Serial Number _____

Task-Specific Safety Considerations
- This task may require operating the equipment on school grounds, which carries severe risks. Attempt this task only with full permission from your supervisor/instructor and follow all the guidelines exactly.
- Lifting equipment such as equipment jacks and stands, hoists, overhead cranes, and engine hoists are important tools that increase productivity and make the job easier. However, they can also cause severe injury or death if used improperly. Make sure you follow the manufacturer's operation procedures. Also make sure you have your supervisor's/instructor's permission to use any type of lifting equipment.
- This task may require you to measure hydraulic pressures. Always ensure that the instructor/supervisor checks test instrument connections prior to connecting power or taking measurements. High fluid pressures can be dangerous; avoid opening hydraulic circuits until system is de-energized.
- Comply with personal and environmental safety practices associated with clothing; eye protection; hand tools; power equipment; proper ventilation; and the handling, storage, and disposal of chemicals/materials in accordance with federal, state, and local regulations.
- Always wear the correct protective eyewear and clothing and use the appropriate safety equipment, as well as seat protectors and floor mat protectors.
- Make sure you understand and observe all legislative and personal safety procedures when carrying out practical assignments. If you are unsure of what these are, ask your supervisor/instructor.

▶ **TASK** Measure hydraulic system pressure, flow, and temperature.

AED
3.6

Student Instructions: Read through the entire procedure prior to starting. Prepare your workspace and any tools or parts that may be needed to complete the task. When directed by your supervisor/instructor, begin the procedure to complete the task, and comment or check the box as each step is finished. Track your time on this procedure for later comparison to the standard completion time (i.e., "flat rate" or customer pay time).

Procedure	Step Completed
1. Describe how to safely connect an analog pressure gauge to a hydraulic circuit through a pressure tap coupling:	☐
2. List three possible safety hazards related to measuring hydraulic pressure with a gauge:	☐
3. Identify the biggest safety advantage to using a digital pressure gauge and write it below:	☐
4. Following your supervisor's/instructor's guidance and the machine's service information, safely connect a pressure gauge into the main pump pressure circuit.	☐
a. Start the machine and safely measure main pump pressure. Record the maximum pressure measured:	☐
b. Describe how you operated the machine in order to measure the pressure:	☐
5. Describe how to safely connect a flow meter into a hydraulic circuit:	☐

6. List three safety hazards related to measuring hydraulic system flow with a flowmeter:	☐
7. Following your supervisor's/instructor's guidance and the machine's service information, safely connect a flowmeter into a circuit.	☐
a. Start the machine and safely measure hydraulic flow while the circuit is operating. Record the maximum flow measured:	☐
b. Describe how you operated the machine in order to measure the flow:	☐
8. Describe how and where to safely measure hydraulic fluid temperature:	☐
9. Does your machine have a way to display hydraulic fluid temperature electronically? If so, describe it:	☐
10. Safely start and operate the machine's hydraulic system until the hydraulic fluid changes temperature. Record the highest temperature you viewed:	☐

Non-Task-Specific Evaluation	Step Completed
1. Tools and equipment were used as directed and returned in good working order.	☐
2. Complied with all general and task-specific safety standards, including proper use of any personal protective equipment (PPE).	☐
3. Completed the task in an appropriate time frame (recommendation: 1.5 or 2 times the flat rate).	☐
4. Left the workspace clean and orderly.	☐
5. Cared for customer property and returned it undamaged.	☐

Student signature _____ Date _____

Comments:

Have your supervisor/instructor verify satisfactory completion of this procedure, any observations made,

and any necessary action(s) recommended.

Evaluation Instructions: The scoring box below is intended to act as a guide for both student and supervisor/instructor. Each criterion listed will help students to understand what is expected of them and help supervisors/instructors to articulate the level of success at a particular task. The scoring is set up to allow a second attempt at each task (see the Test and Retest columns). Scoring is designed only to award students points for task criteria that were completed correctly. Points are lost for failure to complete the employability requirements (see Non-Task-Specific criteria). When all criteria are evaluated, tally the points for a total at the bottom of each column.

Tasksheet Scoring

Evaluation Items	Test		Retest	
	Pass	Fail	Pass	Fail
Task-Specific Evaluation	**(1 pt)**	**(0 pts)**	**(1 pt)**	**(0 pts)**
1. Student correctly answered all questions about measuring hydraulic system pressure, flow, and temperature.				
2. Student properly described the processes for safely measuring hydraulic system pressure, flow, and temperature.				
3. Student demonstrated how to safely and correctly measure hydraulic system pressure, flow, and temperature.				
4. Student took and recorded accurate measurements for their machine's pressure, flow, and temperature.				
Non-Task-Specific Evaluation	**(0 pts)**	**(−1 pt)**	**(0 pts)**	**(−1 pt)**
Student successfully completed at least three of the non-task-specific steps.				
Student successfully completed all five of the non-task-specific steps.				
Total Score: <total # of points / 4 = %>				

Supervisor/Instructor:

Supervisor/instructor signature _____ Date _____

Comments:

Retest supervisor/instructor signature _____ Date _____

Comments:

CDX Tasksheet Number: 3.6004

Student/Intern Information

Name _____ Date _____ Class _____

Machine, Customer, and Service Information

Machine used for this activity:

Make _____ Model _____

Hours _____ Serial Number _____

Materials Required

- Hydraulic training unit or machine
- Equipment manufacturer's service information, including schematic hydraulic diagrams
- Hydraulic pressure gauges
- Hydraulic spare parts, including fittings, hoses, and fluid
- Manufacturer-specific tools depending on the concern
- Machine lifting equipment, if applicable
- Machine lockout/tagout equipment, if applicable

Task-Specific Safety Considerations

- This task may require operating the equipment on school grounds, which carries severe risks. Attempt this task only with full permission from your supervisor/instructor and follow all the guidelines exactly.
- Lifting equipment such as equipment jacks and stands, hoists, overhead cranes, and engine hoists are important tools that increase productivity and make the job easier. However, they can also cause severe injury or death if used improperly. Make sure you follow the manufacturer's operation procedures. Also make sure you have your supervisor's/instructor's permission to use any type of lifting equipment.
- This task may require you to measure hydraulic pressures. Always ensure that the instructor/supervisor checks test instrument connections prior to connecting power or taking measurements. High fluid pressures can be dangerous; avoid opening hydraulic circuits until system is de-energized.
- Comply with personal and environmental safety practices associated with clothing; eye protection; hand tools; power equipment; proper ventilation; and the handling, storage, and disposal of chemicals/materials in accordance with federal, state, and local regulations.
- Always wear the correct protective eyewear and clothing and use the appropriate safety equipment, as well as seat protectors and floor mat protectors.
- Make sure you understand and observe all legislative and personal safety procedures when carrying out practical assignments. If you are unsure of what these are, ask your supervisor/instructor.

▶ **TASK** Diagnose a hydraulic system problem using hydraulic schematics and flow charts.

AED 3.6

Student Instructions: Read through the entire procedure prior to starting. Prepare your workspace and any tools or parts that may be needed to complete the task. When directed by your supervisor/instructor, begin the procedure to complete the task, and comment or check the box as each step is finished. Track your time on this procedure for later comparison to the standard completion time (i.e., "flat rate" or customer pay time).

Procedure	Step Completed
1. Your supervisor/instructor will assign you a machine and will act as the machine operator. Have your supervisor/instructor provide you with an operational complaint related to the machine's hydraulic system. Simplify and describe the complaint in your own words:	☐
2. List three possible root causes for this complaint:	☐
3. Demonstrate and describe how you would verify whether the complaint is present:	☐
4. Summarize and record the troubleshooting procedure for this complaint using the machine's service information as a guideline:	☐
5. Perform the troubleshooting procedure as described above. Have your supervisor/instructor verify satisfactory completion of this procedure. Supervisor's/instructor's initials: _____	☐
6. List the three most important safety concerns you would have while performing this procedure:	☐

	Step Completed
7. If the troubleshooting guideline was followed, what is the most likely root cause for this complaint?	☐
8. Demonstrate and describe how the machine's hydraulic schematic could be used to help find the root cause of the operator complaint:	☐
9. If the root cause from above was repaired, how would you verify the original complaint was fixed?	☐

Non-Task-Specific Evaluation	Step Completed
1. Tools and equipment were used as directed and returned in good working order.	☐
2. Complied with all general and task-specific safety standards, including proper use of any personal protective equipment (PPE).	☐
3. Completed the task in an appropriate time frame (recommendation: 1.5 or 2 times the flat rate).	☐
4. Left the workspace clean and orderly.	☐
5. Cared for customer property and returned it undamaged.	☐

Student signature _____ Date _____

Comments:

Have your supervisor/instructor verify satisfactory completion of this procedure, any observations made, and any necessary action(s) recommended.

Evaluation Instructions: The scoring box below is intended to act as a guide for both student and supervisor/instructor. Each criterion listed will help students to understand what is expected of them and help supervisors/instructors to articulate the level of success at a particular task. The scoring is set up to allow a second attempt at each task (see the Test and Retest columns). Scoring is designed only to award students points for task criteria that were completed correctly. Points are lost for failure to complete the employability requirements (see Non-Task-Specific criteria). When all criteria are evaluated, tally the points for a total at the bottom of each column.

Tasksheet Scoring

Evaluation Items	Test		Retest	
	Pass	Fail	Pass	Fail
Task-Specific Evaluation	(1 pt)	(0 pts)	(1 pt)	(0 pts)
1. Student accurately simplified and recorded the operator complaint and listed three possible root causes.				
2. Student accurately described and demonstrated the method for confirming the operator complaint is present and accurately summarized the troubleshooting procedure.				
3. Student properly performed the troubleshooting procedure and identified three safety concerns.				
4. Student correctly described/recorded the most likely root cause of the complaint, how to use the machine's hydraulic schematic, and how to verify the problem was corrected.				

Non-Task-Specific Evaluation	(0 pts)	(−1 pt)	(0 pts)	(−1 pt)
Student successfully completed at least three of the non-task-specific steps.				
Student successfully completed all five of the non-task-specific steps.				
Total Score: <total # of points / 4 = %>				

Supervisor/Instructor:

Supervisor/instructor signature _____ Date _____

Comments:

Retest supervisor/instructor signature _____ Date _____

Comments:

CDX Tasksheet Number: 3.6005

Student/Intern Information

Name _____ Date _____ Class _____

Machine, Customer, and Service Information

Machine used for this activity:

Make _____ Model _____

Hours _____ Serial Number _____

Materials Required

- Hydraulic training unit or machine
- Equipment manufacturer's service information, including schematic hydraulic diagrams
- Hydraulic pressure gauges
- Hydraulic spare parts, including fittings, hoses, and fluid
- Manufacturer-specific tools depending on the concern
- Machine lifting equipment, if applicable
- Machine lockout/tagout equipment, if applicable

Task-Specific Safety Considerations

- This task may require operating the equipment on school grounds, which carries severe risks. Attempt this task only with full permission from your supervisor/instructor and follow all the guidelines exactly.
- Lifting equipment such as equipment jacks and stands, hoists, overhead cranes, and engine hoists are important tools that increase productivity and make the job easier. However, they can also cause severe injury or death if used improperly. Make sure you follow the manufacturer's operation procedures. Also make sure you have your supervisor's/instructor's permission to use any type of lifting equipment.
- This task may require you to measure hydraulic pressures. Always ensure that the instructor/supervisor checks test instrument connections prior to connecting power or taking measurements. High fluid pressures can be dangerous; avoid opening hydraulic circuits until system is de-energized.
- Comply with personal and environmental safety practices associated with clothing; eye protection; hand tools; power equipment; proper ventilation; and the handling, storage, and disposal of chemicals/materials in accordance with federal, state, and local regulations.
- Always wear the correct protective eyewear and clothing and use the appropriate safety equipment, as well as seat protectors and floor mat protectors.
- Make sure you understand and observe all legislative and personal safety procedures when carrying out practical assignments. If you are unsure of what these are, ask your supervisor/instructor.

▶ **TASK** Perform hydraulic system operational tests and measurements.

AED
3.6

Student Instructions: Read through the entire procedure prior to starting. Prepare your workspace and any tools or parts that may be needed to complete the task. When directed by your supervisor/instructor, begin the procedure to complete the task, and comment or check the box as each step is finished. Track your time on this procedure for later comparison to the standard completion time (i.e., "flat rate" or customer pay time).

Procedure	Step Completed
1. Describe where you would find the operational check procedures and specifications to confirm that the machine's hydraulic system is performing as it was designed to:	☐
2. List any tooling/equipment needed to perform these checks:	☐
3. List the specifications for hydraulic cycle times on this machine:	☐
4. List the specifications for hydraulic pressures on this machine:	☐
5. Choose one cycle time test to perform. Name it below:	☐
a. Describe how to perform this test safely:	☐
b. What temperature must the hydraulic fluid be?	☐

c. Note your findings after performing the test:	☐
6. Choose one hydraulic pressure test to perform. Name it below:	☐
a. Describe how to perform this test safely:	☐
b. What temperature must the hydraulic fluid be?	☐
c. Note your findings after performing the test:	☐
7. Choose one hydraulic steering or brake pressure or flow test to perform. Name it below:	☐
a. Describe how to perform this test safely:	☐
b. What temperature must the hydraulic fluid be?	☐
c. Note your findings after performing the test:	☐
8. Return your machine to its normal operating condition.	☐

Non-Task-Specific Evaluation	Step Completed
1. Tools and equipment were used as directed and returned in good working order.	☐
2. Complied with all general and task-specific safety standards, including proper use of any personal protective equipment (PPE).	☐
3. Completed the task in an appropriate time frame (recommendation: 1.5 or 2 times the flat rate).	☐
4. Left the workspace clean and orderly.	☐
5. Cared for customer property and returned it undamaged.	☐

Student signature _____ Date _____

Comments:

Have your supervisor/instructor verify satisfactory completion of this procedure, any observations made, and any necessary action(s) recommended.

Evaluation Instructions: The scoring box below is intended to act as a guide for both student and supervisor/instructor. Each criterion listed will help students to understand what is expected of them and help supervisors/instructors to articulate the level of success at a particular task. The scoring is set up to allow a second attempt at each task (see the Test and Retest columns). Scoring is designed only to award students points for task criteria that were completed correctly. Points are lost for failure to complete the employability requirements (see Non-Task-Specific criteria). When all criteria are evaluated, tally the points for a total at the bottom of each column.

Tasksheet Scoring

Evaluation Items	Test		Retest	
	Pass	Fail	Pass	Fail
Task-Specific Evaluation	**(1 pt)**	**(O pts)**	**(1 pt)**	**(O pts)**
1. Student noted the correct location of operational check procedures and specifications, listed the correct tooling/equipment needed to perform operational checks, and noted the correct cycle time and hydraulic pressure specifications for their machine.				
2. Student accurately described and safely performed at least one hydraulic cycle time test method and its results.				
3. Student accurately described and safely performed at least two hydraulic cycle time test methods and their results.				
4. Student accurately described and safely performed all three hydraulic cycle time test methods and their results.				

Non-Task-Specific Evaluation	(0 pts)	(−1 pt)	(0 pts)	(−1 pt)
Student successfully completed at least three of the non-task-specific steps.				
Student successfully completed all five of the non-task-specific steps.				
Total Score: <total # of points / 4 = %>				

Supervisor/Instructor:

Supervisor/instructor signature _____ Date _____

Comments:

Retest supervisor/instructor signature _____ Date _____

Comments:

CDX Tasksheet Number: 3.6006

Student/Intern Information

Name _____ Date _____ Class _____

Machine, Customer, and Service Information

Machine used for this activity:

Make _____ Model _____

Hours _____ Serial Number _____

Materials Required

- Hydraulic training unit or machine
- Equipment manufacturer's service information, including schematic hydraulic diagrams
- Hydraulic pressure gauges
- Hydraulic spare parts, including fittings, hoses, and fluid
- Manufacturer-specific tools depending on the concern
- Machine lifting equipment, if applicable
- Machine lockout/tagout equipment, if applicable

Task-Specific Safety Considerations

- This task may require operating the equipment on school grounds, which carries severe risks. Attempt this task only with full permission from your supervisor/instructor and follow all the guidelines exactly.
- Lifting equipment such as equipment jacks and stands, hoists, overhead cranes, and engine hoists are important tools that increase productivity and make the job easier. However, they can also cause severe injury or death if used improperly. Make sure you follow the manufacturer's operation procedures. Also make sure you have your supervisor's/instructor's permission to use any type of lifting equipment.
- This task may require you to measure hydraulic pressures. Always ensure that the instructor/supervisor checks test instrument connections prior to connecting power or taking measurements. High fluid pressures can be dangerous; avoid opening hydraulic circuits until system is de-energized.
- Comply with personal and environmental safety practices associated with clothing; eye protection; hand tools; power equipment; proper ventilation; and the handling, storage, and disposal of chemicals/materials in accordance with federal, state, and local regulations.
- Always wear the correct protective eyewear and clothing and use the appropriate safety equipment, as well as seat protectors and floor mat protectors.
- Make sure you understand and observe all legislative and personal safety procedures when carrying out practical assignments. If you are unsure of what these are, ask your supervisor/instructor.

▶ **TASK** Perform a troubleshooting procedure on a load sensing hydraulic
system.

AED
3.6

Student Instructions: Read through the entire procedure prior to starting. Prepare your workspace and any tools or parts that may be needed to complete the task. When directed by your supervisor/instructor, begin the procedure to complete the task, and comment or check the box as each step is finished. Track your time on this procedure for later comparison to the standard completion time (i.e., "flat rate" or customer pay time).

Procedure	Step Completed
1. Define the term *load sensing* in relation to hydraulic systems:	☐
2. Briefly describe how load sensing hydraulic systems work and what their main advantage is:	☐
3. Describe where you would find service information for troubleshooting problems related to the machine's load sensing hydraulic system:	☐
4. List the testing and adjusting tools needed for troubleshooting problems related to the machine's load sensing hydraulic system:	☐
5. Safely demonstrate the testing procedure related to a slow hydraulic system complaint. Describe it step-by-step:	☐
6. Describe one adjustment that could be made to correct a slow load sensing hydraulic system complaint:	☐
7. Return the machine to its normal operating condition.	☐

Non-Task-Specific Evaluation	Step Completed
1. Tools and equipment were used as directed and returned in good working order.	☐
2. Complied with all general and task-specific safety standards, including proper use of any personal protective equipment (PPE).	☐
3. Completed the task in an appropriate time frame (recommendation: 1.5 or 2 times the flat rate).	☐
4. Left the workspace clean and orderly.	☐
5. Cared for customer property and returned it undamaged.	☐

Student signature _____ Date _____

Comments:

Have your supervisor/instructor verify satisfactory completion of this procedure, any observations made, and any necessary action(s) recommended.

Evaluation Instructions: The scoring box below is intended to act as a guide for both student and supervisor/instructor. Each criterion listed will help students to understand what is expected of them and help supervisors/instructors to articulate the level of success at a particular task. The scoring is set up to allow a second attempt at each task (see the Test and Retest columns). Scoring is designed only to award students points for task criteria that were completed correctly. Points are lost for failure to complete the employability requirements (see Non-Task-Specific criteria). When all criteria are evaluated, tally the points for a total at the bottom of each column.

Tasksheet Scoring

Evaluation Items	Test		Retest	
	Pass	Fail	Pass	Fail
Task-Specific Evaluation	**(1 pt)**	**(0 pts)**	**(1 pt)**	**(0 pts)**
1. Student defined *load sensing* correctly and accurately described how load sensing works.				
2. Student accurately identified the location of load sensing troubleshooting information and correctly listed testing and adjusting tools needed for troubleshooting load sensing hydraulic systems.				
3. Student safely demonstrated and accurately described load sensing hydraulic system testing.				
4. Student accurately demonstrated and described one adjustment to a load sensing hydraulic system.				
Non-Task-Specific Evaluation	**(0 pts)**	**(−1 pt)**	**(0 pts)**	**(−1 pt)**
Student successfully completed at least three of the non-task-specific steps.				
Student successfully completed all five of the non-task-specific steps.				
Total Score: <total # of points / 4 = %>				

CDX Tasksheet Number: 3.6007

Student/Intern Information

Name _____ Date _____ Class _____

Machine, Customer, and Service Information

Machine used for this activity:

Make _____ Model _____

Hours _____ Serial Number _____

▶ **TASK** Create a repair order based on a machine hydraulic system problem.

AED
3.6

Student Instructions: Read through the entire procedure prior to starting. Prepare your workspace and any tools or parts that may be needed to complete the task. When directed by your supervisor/instructor, begin the procedure to complete the task, and comment or check the box as each step is finished. Track your time on this procedure for later comparison to the standard completion time (i.e., "flat rate" or customer pay time).

Procedure	Step Completed
1. Your supervisor/instructor will assign you a machine and will act as the machine operator. Have your supervisor/instructor provide you with an operational complaint related to the machine's hydraulic system. Simplify and describe the complaint in your own words:	☐
2. List three questions you would ask the operator to gather information about this complaint:	☐
3. Describe where you would find the service information for troubleshooting problems related to this complaint:	☐
4. Describe how you would verify the complaint:	☐
5. Work through the service information troubleshooting procedure and safely find the root cause of the complaint. Describe your procedure:	☐

	Step Completed
6. Assume the root cause of the problem gets repaired. Describe how you would verify that the repair fixed the original complaint:	☐
7. Return the machine to normal operating condition and complete the repair order.	☐

Non-Task-Specific Evaluation	Step Completed
1. Tools and equipment were used as directed and returned in good working order.	☐
2. Complied with all general and task-specific safety standards, including proper use of any personal protective equipment (PPE).	☐
3. Completed the task in an appropriate time frame (recommendation: 1.5 or 2 times the flat rate).	☐
4. Left the workspace clean and orderly.	☐
5. Cared for customer property and returned it undamaged.	☐

Student signature _____ Date _____

Comments:

Have your supervisor/instructor verify satisfactory completion of this procedure, any observations made,

and any necessary action(s) recommended.

Evaluation Instructions: The scoring box below is intended to act as a guide for both student and supervisor/instructor. Each criterion listed will help students to understand what is expected of them and help supervisors/instructors to articulate the level of success at a particular task. The scoring is set up to allow a second attempt at each task (see the Test and Retest columns). Scoring is designed only to award students points for task criteria that were completed correctly. Points are lost for failure to complete the employability requirements (see Non-Task-Specific criteria). When all criteria are evaluated, tally the points for a total at the bottom of each column.

Tasksheet Scoring

Evaluation Items	Test		Retest	
	Pass	**Fail**	**Pass**	**Fail**
Task-Specific Evaluation	**(1 pt)**	**(0 pts)**	**(1 pt)**	**(0 pts)**
1. Student accurately described the operator complaint, listed three questions to ask about the complaint, noted where to find troubleshooting information, and accurately described how to verify the complaint.				
2. Student accurately described and demonstrated the troubleshooting procedure.				
3. Student accurately described how to verify the repair.				
4. Student filled out the repair order completely and legibly and returned the machine to its normal operating condition.				
Non-Task-Specific Evaluation	**(0 pts)**	**(−1 pt)**	**(0 pts)**	**(−1 pt)**
Student successfully completed at least three of the non-task-specific steps.				
Student successfully completed all five of the non-task-specific steps.				
Total Score: <total # of points / 4 = %>				

Supervisor/Instructor:

Supervisor/instructor signature _____ Date _____

Comments:

Retest supervisor/instructor signature _____ Date _____

Comments:

Chapter 29: Theory and Operation; Basic Principles of Power Trains

Learning Objective/Task	CDX Tasksheet Number	AED Reference Number
• Explain power train system power flow.	4.1a001	AED 4.1
• Identify safety concerns.	4.1a002	AED 4.1
• Identify types of gears.	4.1a003	AED 4.1
• Identify types of bearings.	4.1a005	AED 4.1
• Identify bearings and adjust preload.	4.1a006	AED 4.1
• Identify torque converter components.	4.1a007	AED 4.1
• Describe torque converter operation.	4.1a008	AED 4.1
• Test torque converter.	4.1a009	AED 4.1

Materials Required

- Vehicle manufacturer's service information
- Machine or lab fixture chosen by the supervisor/instructor to complete the task
- Manufacturer's workshop materials
- Manufacturer-specific tools, depending on the concern/procedure(s)
- Vehicle/component lifting equipment, if applicable
- Vehicle with possible power transfer concerns

Safety Considerations

- This task may require test driving the vehicle on the school grounds or on a hoist, both of which carry severe risks. Attempt this task only with full permission from your supervisor/instructor and follow all the guidelines exactly.
- Comply with personal and environmental safety practices associated with clothing; eye protection; hand tools; power equipment; proper ventilation; and the handling, storage, and disposal of chemicals/materials in accordance with federal, state, and local regulations.
- Always wear the correct protective eyewear and clothing and use the appropriate safety equipment, as well as fender covers, seat protectors, and floor mat protectors.
- Make sure you understand and observe all legislative and personal safety procedures when carrying out practical assignments. If you are unsure of what these are, ask your supervisor/instructor.
- While working on the vehicle, wheel chocks must be placed on both sides of one set of tires or as directed by your supervisor/instructor.
- When running any vehicles in the shop, make sure you use the shop's exhaust ventilation system to discharge all exhaust gas safely outside.
- Lifting equipment such as vehicle jacks and stands, vehicle hoists, and engine hoists are important tools that increase productivity and make the job easier. However, they can also cause severe injury or death if used improperly. Make sure you follow the manufacturer's operation procedures. Also make sure you have your supervisor's/instructor's permission to use any particular type of lifting equipment.

CDX Tasksheet Number: 4.1a001

Student/Intern Information

Name _____ Date _____ Class _____

Machine, Customer, and Service Information

Machine used for this activity:

Make _____ Model _____

Hours _____ Serial Number _____

Materials Required
- Vehicle manufacturer's service information

Task-Specific Safety Considerations
- This task may require test driving the vehicle on the school grounds or on a hoist, both of which carry severe risks. Attempt this task only with full permission from your supervisor/instructor and follow all the guidelines exactly.
- Comply with personal and environmental safety practices associated with clothing; eye protection; hand tools; power equipment; proper ventilation; and the handling, storage, and disposal of chemicals/materials in accordance with federal, state, and local regulations.
- Always wear the correct protective eyewear and clothing and use the appropriate safety equipment, as well as fender covers, seat protectors, and floor mat protectors.
- Make sure you understand and observe all legislative and personal safety procedures when carrying out practical assignments. If you are unsure of what these are, ask your supervisor/instructor.
- While working on the vehicle, wheel chocks must be placed on both sides of one set of tires or as directed by your supervisor/instructor.
- When running any vehicles in the shop, make sure you use the shop's exhaust ventilation system to discharge all exhaust gas safely outside.

▶ **TASK** Explain power train system power flow. **AED 4.1**

Time off_____

Time on_____

Student Instructions: Read through the entire procedure prior to starting. Prepare your workspace and any tools or parts that may be needed to complete the task. When directed by your supervisor/instructor, begin the procedure to complete the task, and comment or check the box as each step is finished. Track your time on this procedure for later comparison to the standard completion time (i.e., "flat rate" or customer pay time).

Total time_____

Procedure	Step Completed
1. Using available service literature as a guide, list each power train component in order and describe how they relate to one another.	☐
a. Component #1	☐

b. Component #2	☐
c. Component #3	☐
d. Component #4	☐
e. Component #5 (if applicable)	☐
f. Component #6 (if applicable)	☐
g. Component #7 (if applicable)	☐
h. Component #8 (if applicable)	☐
i. Component #9 (if applicable)	☐
j. Component #10 (if applicable)	☐
2. Discuss your findings with your supervisor/instructor.	☐

Non-Task-Specific Evaluation	Step Completed
1. Tools and equipment were used as directed and returned in good working order.	☐
2. Complied with all general and task-specific safety standards, including proper use of any personal protective equipment (PPE).	☐
3. Completed the task in an appropriate time frame (recommendation: 1.5 or 2 times the flat rate).	☐
4. Left the workspace clean and orderly.	☐
5. Cared for customer property and returned it undamaged.	☐

Student signature _____ Date _____

Comments:

Have your supervisor/instructor verify satisfactory completion of this procedure, any observations made, and any necessary action(s) recommended.

Evaluation Instructions: The scoring box below is intended to act as a guide for both student and supervisor/instructor. Each criterion listed will help students to understand what is expected of them and help supervisors/instructors to articulate the level of success at a particular task. The scoring is set up to allow a second attempt at each task (see the Test and Retest columns). Scoring is designed only to award students points for task criteria that were completed correctly. Points are lost for failure to complete the employability requirements (see Non-Task-Specific criteria). When all criteria are evaluated, tally the points for a total at the bottom of each column.

Tasksheet Scoring

	Test		Retest	
Evaluation Items	**Pass**	**Fail**	**Pass**	**Fail**
Task-Specific Evaluation	**(1 pt)**	**(0 pts)**	**(1 pt)**	**(0 pts)**
Student listed at least half of the power train components in the correct order.3				
Student listed all of the power train components in the correct order.				
Student correctly described how at least half of the power train components relate to one another.				
Student correctly described how all of the power train components relate to one another.				
Non-Task-Specific Evaluation	**(0 pts)**	**(−1 pt)**	**(0 pts)**	**(−1 pt)**
Student successfully completed at least three of the non-task-specific steps.				
Student successfully completed all five of the non-task-specific steps.				
Total Score: <total # of points / 4 = %>				

Supervisor/Instructor:

Supervisor/instructor signature _____ Date _____

Comments:

Retest supervisor/instructor signature _____ Date _____

Comments:

CDX Tasksheet Number: 4.1a002

Student/Intern Information

Name _____ Date _____ Class _____

Machine, Customer, and Service Information

Machine used for this activity:

Make _____ Model _____

Hours _____ Serial Number _____

Materials Required
- Vehicle manufacturer's service information

Task-Specific Safety Considerations
- This task may require test driving the vehicle on the school grounds or on a hoist, both of which carry severe risks. Attempt this task only with full permission from your supervisor/instructor and follow all the guidelines exactly.
- Comply with personal and environmental safety practices associated with clothing; eye protection; hand tools; power equipment; proper ventilation; and the handling, storage, and disposal of chemicals/materials in accordance with federal, state, and local regulations.
- Always wear the correct protective eyewear and clothing and use the appropriate safety equipment, as well as fender covers, seat protectors, and floor mat protectors.
- Make sure you understand and observe all legislative and personal safety procedures when carrying out practical assignments. If you are unsure of what these are, ask your supervisor/instructor.
- While working on the vehicle, wheel chocks must be placed on both sides of one set of tires or as directed by your supervisor/instructor.
- When running any vehicles in the shop, make sure you use the shop's exhaust ventilation system to discharge all exhaust gas safely outside.

▶ TASK Identify safety concerns. **AED 4.1**

Time off_____

Time on_____

Student Instructions: Read through the entire procedure prior to starting. Prepare your workspace and any tools or parts that may be needed to complete the task. When directed by your supervisor/instructor, begin the procedure to complete the task, and comment or check the box as each step is finished. Track your time on this procedure for later comparison to the standard completion time (i.e., "flat rate" or customer pay time).

Total time_____

Procedure	Step Completed
1. Using available service literature as a guide, list the personal protective equipment (PPE) required when servicing/repairing a hybrid/electric drive system:	☐

2. Using available service literature as a guide, record the procedure for de-energizing a hybrid/electric drive system:	☐
3. Using available service literature as a guide, record the procedure for preventing the hybrid/electric drive system from generating electricity while being serviced (lockout):	☐
4. Using available service literature as a guide, record the procedure for verifying that potential hazardous voltage is no longer present in a hybrid/electric drive system:	☐
5. Using available service literature as a guide, record the procedure for restoring a hybrid/electric drive system to service:	☐
6. List any special lab/shop requirements when servicing/repairing a hybrid/electric drive system:	☐
7. Discuss your findings with your supervisor/instructor.	☐

Non-Task-Specific Evaluation	Step Completed
1. Tools and equipment were used as directed and returned in good working order.	☐
2. Complied with all general and task-specific safety standards, including proper use of any PPE.	☐
3. Completed the task in an appropriate time frame (recommendation: 1.5 or 2 times the flat rate).	☐
4. Left the workspace clean and orderly.	☐
5. Cared for customer property and returned it undamaged.	☐

Student signature _____ Date _____

Comments:

Have your supervisor/instructor verify satisfactory completion of this procedure, any observations made, and any necessary action(s) recommended.

Evaluation Instructions: The scoring box below is intended to act as a guide for both student and supervisor/instructor. Each criterion listed will help students to understand what is expected of them and help supervisors/instructors to articulate the level of success at a particular task. The scoring is set up to allow a second attempt at each task (see the Test and Retest columns). Scoring is designed only to award students points for task criteria that were completed correctly. Points are lost for failure to complete the employability requirements (see Non-Task-Specific criteria). When all criteria are evaluated, tally the points for a total at the bottom of each column.

Taksheet Scoring

Evaluation Items	Test		Retest	
	Pass	Fail	Pass	Fail
Task-Specific Evaluation	**(1 pt)**	**(0 pts)**	**(1 pt)**	**(0 pts)**
Student listed the correct PPE and any other special lab/shop requirements when working on a hybrid/electric drive system.				
Student properly described the procedure for de-energizing a hybrid/electric drive system.				
Student properly described the procedures for preventing a hybrid/electric drive system from generating electricity when being serviced and verifying that potential hazardous voltage is no longer present.				
Student properly described the procedure for restoring a hybrid/electric drive system to service.				
Non-Task-Specific Evaluation	**(0 pts)**	**(−1 pt)**	**(0 pts)**	**(−1 pt)**
Student successfully completed at least three of the non-task-specific steps.				
Student successfully completed all five of the non-task-specific steps.				
Total Score: <total # of points / 4 = %>				

Supervisor/Instructor:

Supervisor/instructor signature _____ Date _____

Comments:

Retest supervisor/instructor signature _____ Date _____

Comments:

CDX Tasksheet Number: 4.1a003

Student/Intern Information

Name _____ Date _____ Class _____

Machine, Customer, and Service Information

Machine used for this activity:

Make _____ Model _____

Hours _____ Serial Number _____

Materials Required

- Vehicle manufacturer's service information

Task-Specific Safety Considerations

- This task may require test driving the vehicle on the school grounds or on a hoist, both of which carry severe risks. Attempt this task only with full permission from your supervisor/instructor and follow all the guidelines exactly.
- Comply with personal and environmental safety practices associated with clothing; eye protection; hand tools; power equipment; proper ventilation; and the handling, storage, and disposal of chemicals/materials in accordance with federal, state, and local regulations.
- Always wear the correct protective eyewear and clothing and use the appropriate safety equipment, as well as fender covers, seat protectors, and floor mat protectors.
- Make sure you understand and observe all legislative and personal safety procedures when carrying out practical assignments. If you are unsure of what these are, ask your supervisor/instructor.
- While working on the vehicle, wheel chocks must be placed on both sides of one set of tires or as directed by your supervisor/instructor.
- When running any vehicles in the shop, make sure you use the shop's exhaust ventilation system to discharge all exhaust gas safely outside.

▶ **TASK** Identify types of gears.   **AED**
                                                                               4.1

Time off_____

Time on_____

Student Instructions: Read through the entire procedure prior to starting. Prepare your workspace and any tools or parts that may be needed to complete the task. When directed by your supervisor/instructor, begin the procedure to complete the task, and comment or check the box as each step is finished. Track your time on this procedure for later comparison to the standard completion time (i.e., "flat rate" or customer pay time).

Total time_____

Procedure	Step Completed
1. Using available service literature, identify the machine location, function, advantage, and disadvantage of each of the following different types of gears. (**Note:** Lab fixtures/instructional aids may be used for this task.)	

2. Planetary gear set	
a. Machine location	☐
b. Function	☐
c. Advantage	☐
d. Disadvantage	☐
3. Rack and pinion gears	
a. Machine location	☐
b. Function	☐
c. Advantage	☐
d. Disadvantage	☐
4. Worm gears	
a. Machine location	☐
b. Function	☐
c. Advantage	☐

d. Disadvantage	☐
5. Bevel gears	
a. Machine location	☐
b. Function	☐
c. Advantage	☐
d. Disadvantage	☐
6. Herringbone gears	
a. Machine location	☐
b. Function	☐
c. Advantage	☐
d. Disadvantage	☐
7. Helical gears	
a. Machine location	☐
b. Function	☐

c. Advantage	☐
d. Disadvantage	☐
8. Spur gears	
a. Machine location	☐
b. Function	☐
c. Advantage	☐
d. Disadvantage	☐
9. Discuss your findings with your supervisor/instructor.	☐

Non-Task-Specific Evaluations:	Step Completed
1. Tools and equipment were used as directed and returned in good working order.	☐
2. Complied with all general and task-specific safety standards, including proper use of any personal protective equipment (PPE).	☐
3. Completed the task in an appropriate time frame (recommendation: 1.5 or 2 times the flat rate).	☐
4. Left the workspace clean and orderly.	☐
5. Cared for customer property and returned it undamaged.	☐

Student signature _____ Date _____

Comments:

Have your supervisor/instructor verify satisfactory completion of this procedure, any observations made, and any necessary action(s) recommended.

Evaluation Instructions: The scoring box below is intended to act as a guide for both student and supervisor/instructor. Each criterion listed will help students to understand what is expected of them and help supervisors/instructors to articulate the level of success at a particular task. The scoring is set up to allow a second attempt at each task (see the Test and Retest columns). Scoring is designed only to award students points for task criteria that were completed correctly. Points are lost for failure to complete the employability requirements (see Non-Task-Specific criteria). When all criteria are evaluated, tally the points for a total at the bottom of each column.

Tasksheet Scoring

Evaluation Items	Test		Retest	
	Pass	Fail	Pass	Fail
Task-Specific Evaluation	**(1 pt)**	**(0 pts)**	**(1 pt)**	**(0 pts)**
Student correctly identified the machine location of each gear type.				
Student correctly identified the function of each gear type.				
Student correctly identified an advantage of each gear type.				
Student correctly identified a disadvantage of each gear type.				
Non-Task-Specific Evaluation	**(0 pts)**	**(−1 pt)**	**(0 pts)**	**(−1 pt)**
Student successfully completed at least three of the non-task-specific steps.				
Student successfully completed all five of the non-task-specific steps.				
Total Score: <total # of points / 4 = %>				

Supervisor/Instructor:

Supervisor/instructor signature _____ Date _____

Comments:

Retest supervisor/instructor signature _____ Date _____

Comments:

CDX Tasksheet Number: 4.1a005

Student/Intern Information

Name _____ Date _____ Class _____

Machine, Customer, and Service Information

Machine used for this activity:

Make _____ Model _____

Hours _____ Serial Number _____

Materials Required

- Vehicle manufacturer's service information

Task-Specific Safety Considerations

- This task may require test driving the vehicle on the school grounds or on a hoist, both of which carry severe risks. Attempt this task only with full permission from your supervisor/instructor and follow all the guidelines exactly.
- Comply with personal and environmental safety practices associated with clothing; eye protection; hand tools; power equipment; proper ventilation; and the handling, storage, and disposal of chemicals/materials in accordance with federal, state, and local regulations.
- Always wear the correct protective eyewear and clothing and use the appropriate safety equipment, as well as fender covers, seat protectors, and floor mat protectors.
- Make sure you understand and observe all legislative and personal safety procedures when carrying out practical assignments. If you are unsure of what these are, ask your supervisor/instructor.
- While working on the vehicle, wheel chocks must be placed on both sides of one set of tires or as directed by your supervisor/instructor.
- When running any vehicles in the shop, make sure you use the shop's exhaust ventilation system to discharge all exhaust gas safely outside.

▶ TASK Identify types of bearings.

AED
4.1

Time off_____

Time on_____

Student Instructions: Read through the entire procedure prior to starting. Prepare your workspace and any tools or parts that may be needed to complete the task. When directed by your supervisor/instructor, begin the procedure to complete the task, and comment or check the box as each step is finished. Track your time on this procedure for later comparison to the standard completion time (i.e., "flat rate" or customer pay time).

Total time_____

Procedure	Step Completed
1. Using available service literature, identify the machine location, function, advantage, and disadvantage of each of the following different types of bearings. (**Note:** Lab fixtures/instructional aids may be used for this task.)	

2. Friction (plain) bearing	
a. Machine location	☐
b. Function	☐
c. Advantage	☐
d. Disadvantage	☐
3. Friction (plain) spherical bearing	
a. Machine location	☐
b. Function	☐
c. Advantage	☐
d. Disadvantage	☐
4. Ball bearing	
a. Machine location	☐
b. Function	☐
c. Advantage	☐

d. Disadvantage	☐
5. Roller bearing	
a. Machine location	☐
b. Function	☐
c. Advantage	☐
d. Disadvantage	☐
6. Spherical roller bearing	
a. Machine location	☐
b. Function	☐
c. Advantage	☐
d. Disadvantage	☐
7. Tapered roller bearing	
a. Machine location	☐
b. Function	☐

c. Advantage	☐
d. Disadvantage	☐
8. Needle bearing	
a. Machine location	☐
b. Function	☐
c. Advantage	☐
d. Disadvantage	☐
9. Discuss your findings with your supervisor/instructor.	☐

Non-Task-Specific Evaluation	Step Completed
1. Tools and equipment were used as directed and returned in good working order.	☐
2. Complied with all general and task-specific safety standards, including proper use of any personal protective equipment (PPE).	☐
3. Completed the task in an appropriate time frame (recommendation: 1.5 or 2 times the flat rate).	☐
4. Left the workspace clean and orderly.	☐
5. Cared for customer property and returned it undamaged.	☐

Student signature _____ Date _____

Comments:

Have your supervisor/instructor verify satisfactory completion of this procedure, any observations made, and any necessary action(s) recommended.

Evaluation Instructions: The scoring box below is intended to act as a guide for both student and supervisor/instructor. Each criterion listed will help students to understand what is expected of them and help supervisors/instructors to articulate the level of success at a particular task. The scoring is set up to allow a second attempt at each task (see the Test and Retest columns). Scoring is designed only to award students points for task criteria that were completed correctly. Points are lost for failure to complete the employability requirements (see Non-Task-Specific criteria). When all criteria are evaluated, tally the points for a total at the bottom of each column.

Tasksheet Scoring

	Test		Retest	
Evaluation Items	**Pass**	**Fail**	**Pass**	**Fail**
Task-Specific Evaluation	**(1 pt)**	**(0 pts)**	**(1 pt)**	**(0 pts)**
Student correctly identified the machine location of each bearing type.				
Student correctly identified the function of each bearing type.				
Student correctly identified an advantage of each bearing type.				
Student correctly identified a disadvantage of each bearing type.				
Non-Task-Specific Evaluation	**(0 pts)**	**(−1 pt)**	**(0 pts)**	**(−1 pt)**
Student successfully completed at least three of the non-task-specific steps.				
Student successfully completed all five of the non-task-specific steps.				
Total Score: <total # of points / 4 = %>				

Supervisor/Instructor:

Supervisor/instructor signature _____ Date _____

Comments:

Retest supervisor/instructor signature _____ Date _____

Comments:

CDX Tasksheet Number: 4.1a006

Student/Intern Information

Name _____ Date _____ Class _____

Machine, Customer, and Service Information

Machine used for this activity:

Make _____ Model _____

Hours _____ Serial Number _____

Materials Required

- Machine or lab fixture chosen by the supervisor/instructor to complete the task
- Manufacturer's workshop materials
- Manufacturer-specific tools, depending on the concern/procedure(s)
- Vehicle/component lifting equipment, if applicable

Task-Specific Safety Considerations

- This task may require test driving the vehicle on the school grounds or on a hoist, both of which carry severe risks. Attempt this task only with full permission from your supervisor/instructor and follow all the guidelines exactly.
- Lifting equipment such as vehicle jacks and stands, vehicle hoists, and engine hoists are important tools that increase productivity and make the job easier. However, they can also cause severe injury or death if used improperly. Make sure you follow the manufacturer's operation procedures. Also make sure you have your supervisor's/instructor's permission to use any particular type of lifting equipment.
- Comply with personal and environmental safety practices associated with clothing; eye protection; hand tools; power equipment; proper ventilation; and the handling, storage, and disposal of chemicals/materials in accordance with federal, state, and local regulations.
- Always wear the correct protective eyewear and clothing and use the appropriate safety equipment, as well as wheel chocks, fender covers, seat protectors, and floor mat protectors.
- Make sure you understand and observe all legislative and personal safety procedures when carrying out practical assignments. If you are unsure of what these are, ask your supervisor/instructor.

▶ TASK Identify bearings and adjust preload.

Student Instructions: Read through the entire procedure prior to starting. Prepare your workspace and any tools or parts that may be needed to complete the task. When directed by your supervisor/instructor, begin the procedure to complete the task, and comment or check the box as each step is finished. Track your time on this procedure for later comparison to the standard completion time (i.e., "flat rate" or customer pay time).

Time off_____

Time on_____

Total time_____

Procedure	Step Completed
1. Research the various types of bearings used in heavy equipment and list their applications below.	
a. Friction bearing	☐
b. Plain spherical bearing	☐
c. Ball bearing	☐
d. Roller bearing	☐
e. Spherical roller bearing	☐
f. Cylindrical roller bearing	☐
g. Tapered roller bearing	☐
h. Needle bearing	☐
2. Of the bearings used in heavy equipment applications, which require preload adjustment?	☐
3. Using a machine or lab fixture assigned by your supervisor/instructor and its service information, adjust the bearing preload. Have your supervisor/instructor verify satisfactory completion of this procedure. Supervisor's/instructor's initials _____	☐
4. Discuss your findings with your supervisor/instructor.	☐

Non-Task-Specific Evaluation	Step Completed
1. Tools and equipment were used as directed and returned in good working order.	☐
2. Complied with all general and task-specific safety standards, including proper use of any personal protective equipment (PPE).	☐
3. Completed the task in an appropriate time frame (recommendation: 1.5 or 2 times the flat rate).	☐
4. Left the workspace clean and orderly.	☐
5. Cared for customer property and returned it undamaged.	☐

Student signature _____ Date _____

Comments:

Have your supervisor/instructor verify satisfactory completion of this procedure, any observations made, and any necessary action(s) recommended.

Evaluation Instructions: The scoring box below is intended to act as a guide for both student and supervisor/instructor. Each criterion listed will help students to understand what is expected of them and help supervisors/instructors to articulate the level of success at a particular task. The scoring is set up to allow a second attempt at each task (see the Test and Retest columns). Scoring is designed only to award students points for task criteria that were completed correctly. Points are lost for failure to complete the employability requirements (see Non-Task-Specific criteria). When all criteria are evaluated, tally the points for a total at the bottom of each column.

Tasksheet Scoring

	Test		Retest	
Evaluation Items	Pass	Fail	Pass	Fail
Task-Specific Evaluation	**(1 pt)**	**(0 pts)**	**(1 pt)**	**(0 pts)**
Student correctly identified at least four bearing applications.				
Student correctly identified all eight bearing applications.				
Student properly identified bearings requiring preload.				
Student accurately performed bearing preload.				
Non-Task-Specific Evaluation	**(0 pts)**	**(−1 pt)**	**(0 pts)**	**(−1 pt)**
Student successfully completed at least three of the non-task-specific steps.				
Student successfully completed all five of the non-task-specific steps.				
Total Score: <total # of points / 4 = %>				

Supervisor/Instructor:

Supervisor/instructor signature _____ Date _____

Comments:

Retest supervisor/instructor signature _____ Date _____

Comments:

CDX Tasksheet Number: 4.1a007

Student/Intern Information

Name _____ Date _____ Class _____

Machine, Customer, and Service Information

Machine used for this activity:

Make _____ Model _____

Hours _____ Serial Number _____

Materials Required

- Vehicle manufacturer's service information

Task-Specific Safety Considerations

- This task may require test driving the vehicle on the school grounds or on a hoist, both of which carry severe risks. Attempt this task only with full permission from your supervisor/instructor and follow all the guidelines exactly.
- Comply with personal and environmental safety practices associated with clothing; eye protection; hand tools; power equipment; proper ventilation; and the handling, storage, and disposal of chemicals/materials in accordance with federal, state, and local regulations.
- Always wear the correct protective eyewear and clothing and use the appropriate safety equipment, as well as fender covers, seat protectors, and floor mat protectors.
- Make sure you understand and observe all legislative and personal safety procedures when carrying out practical assignments. If you are unsure of what these are, ask your supervisor/instructor.
- While working on the vehicle, wheel chocks must be placed on both sides of one set of tires or as directed by your supervisor/instructor.
- When running any vehicles in the shop, make sure you use the shop's exhaust ventilation system to discharge all exhaust gas safely outside.

▶ **TASK** Identify torque converter components.

AED
4.1

Time off_____

Time on_____

Student Instructions: Read through the entire procedure prior to starting. Prepare your workspace and any tools or parts that may be needed to complete the task. When directed by your supervisor/instructor, begin the procedure to complete the task, and comment or check the box as each step is finished. Track your time on this procedure for later comparison to the standard completion time (i.e., "flat rate" or customer pay time).

Total time_____

Procedure	Step Completed
1. Using available service literature as a guide, list each torque converter component in order and describe how they relate to one another. (**Note:** Lab fixtures/instructional aids may be used for this task.)	
a. Component #1	☐

b. Component #2	☐
c. Component #3	☐
d. Component #4	☐
e. Component #5 (if applicable)	☐
f. Component #6 (if applicable)	☐
g. Component #7 (if applicable)	☐
h. Component #8 (if applicable)	☐
i. Component #9 (if applicable)	☐
j. Component #10 (if applicable)	☐
2. Discuss your findings with your supervisor/instructor.	☐

Non-Task-Specific Evaluation	Step Completed
1. Tools and equipment were used as directed and returned in good working order.	☐
2. Complied with all general and task-specific safety standards, including proper use of any personal protective equipment (PPE).	☐
3. Completed the task in an appropriate time frame (recommendation: 1.5 or 2 times the flat rate).	☐
4. Left the workspace clean and orderly.	☐
5. Cared for customer property and returned it undamaged.	☐

Student signature _____ Date _____

Comments:

Have your supervisor/instructor verify satisfactory completion of this procedure, any observations made, and any necessary action(s) recommended.

Evaluation Instructions: The scoring box below is intended to act as a guide for both student and supervisor/instructor. Each criterion listed will help students to understand what is expected of them and help supervisors/instructors to articulate the level of success at a particular task. The scoring is set up to allow a second attempt at each task (see the Test and Retest columns). Scoring is designed only to award students points for task criteria that were completed correctly. Points are lost for failure to complete the employability requirements (see Non-Task-Specific criteria). When all criteria are evaluated, tally the points for a total at the bottom of each column.

Tasksheet Scoring

	Test		Retest	
Evaluation Items	**Pass**	**Fail**	**Pass**	**Fail**
Task-Specific Evaluation	**(1 pt)**	**(0 pts)**	**(1 pt)**	**(0 pts)**
Student listed at least half of the torque converter components in the correct order.				
Student listed all of the torque converter components in the correct order.				
Student correctly described how at least half of the torque converter components relate to one another.				
Student correctly described how all of the torque converter components relate to one another.				
Non-Task-Specific Evaluation	**(0 pts)**	**(−1 pt)**	**(0 pts)**	**(−1 pt)**
Student successfully completed at least three of the non-task-specific steps.				
Student successfully completed all five of the non-task-specific steps.				
Total Score: <total # of points / 4 = %>				

Supervisor/Instructor:

Supervisor/instructor signature _____ Date _____

Comments:

Retest supervisor/instructor signature _____ Date _____

Comments:

CDX Tasksheet Number: 4.1a008

Student/Intern Information

Name _____ Date _____ Class _____

Machine, Customer, and Service Information

Machine used for this activity:

Make _____ Model _____

Hours _____ Serial Number _____

Materials Required
- Vehicle manufacturer's repair information

Task-Specific Safety Considerations
- This task may require test driving the vehicle on the school grounds or on a hoist, both of which carry severe risks. Attempt this task only with full permission from your supervisor/instructor and follow all the guidelines exactly.
- Comply with personal and environmental safety practices associated with clothing; eye protection; hand tools; power equipment; proper ventilation; and the handling, storage, and disposal of chemicals/materials in accordance with federal, state, and local regulations.
- Always wear the correct protective eyewear and clothing and use the appropriate safety equipment, as well as fender covers, seat protectors, and floor mat protectors.
- Make sure you understand and observe all legislative and personal safety procedures when carrying out practical assignments. If you are unsure of what these are, ask your supervisor/instructor.
- While working on the vehicle, wheel chocks must be placed on both sides of one set of tires or as directed by your supervisor/instructor.
- When running any vehicles in the shop, make sure you use the shop's exhaust ventilation system to discharge all exhaust gas safely outside.

▶ **TASK** Describe torque converter operation.

AED 4.1

Time off_____

Time on_____

Total time_____

Student Instructions: Read through the entire procedure prior to starting. Prepare your workspace and any tools or parts that may be needed to complete the task. When directed by your supervisor/instructor, begin the procedure to complete the task, and comment or check the box as each step is finished. Track your time on this procedure for later comparison to the standard completion time (i.e., "flat rate" or customer pay time).

Procedure	Step Completed
1. Using available service literature as a guide, describe each stage of torque converter operation. (**Note:** Lab fixtures/instructional aids may be used for this task.)	

a. Rotary flow	☐
b. Vortex flow	☐
c. Multiplication phase	☐
d. Stall speed	☐
e. Coupling phase	☐
2. Discuss your findings with your supervisor/instructor.	☐

Non-Task-Specific Evaluation	Step Completed
1. Tools and equipment were used as directed and returned in good working order.	☐
2. Complied with all general and task-specific safety standards, including proper use of any personal protective equipment (PPE).	☐
3. Completed the task in an appropriate time frame (recommendation: 1.5 or 2 times the flat rate).	☐
4. Left the workspace clean and orderly.	☐
5. Cared for customer property and returned it undamaged.	☐

Student signature _____ Date _____

Comments:

Have your supervisor/instructor verify satisfactory completion of this procedure, any observations made, and any necessary action(s) recommended.

Evaluation Instructions: The scoring box below is intended to act as a guide for both student and supervisor/instructor. Each criterion listed will help students to understand what is expected of them and help supervisors/instructors to articulate the level of success at a particular task. The scoring is set up to allow a second attempt at each task (see the Test and Retest columns). Scoring is designed only to award students points for task criteria that were completed correctly. Points are lost for failure to complete the employability requirements (see Non-Task-Specific criteria). When all criteria are evaluated, tally the points for a total at the bottom of each column.

Tasksheet Scoring

	Test		Retest	
Evaluation Items	**Pass**	**Fail**	**Pass**	**Fail**
Task-Specific Evaluation	**(1 pt)**	**(0 pts)**	**(1 pt)**	**(0 pts)**
Student accurately described the rotary flow stage.				
Student accurately described the vortex flow stage.				
Student accurately described the multiplication phase.				
Student accurately described the stall speed stage and the coupling phase.				
Non-Task-Specific Evaluation	**(0 pts)**	**(−1 pt)**	**(0 pts)**	**(−1 pt)**
Student successfully completed at least three of the non-task-specific steps.				
Student successfully completed all five of the non-task-specific steps.				
Total Score: <total # of points / 4 = %>				

Supervisor/Instructor:

Supervisor/instructor signature _____ Date _____

Comments:

Retest supervisor/instructor signature _____ Date _____

Comments:

CDX Tasksheet Number: 4.1a009

Student/Intern Information

Name _____ Date _____ Class _____

Machine, Customer, and Service Information

Machine used for this activity:

Make _____ Model _____

Hours _____ Serial Number _____

Materials Required
- Vehicle with possible power transfer concerns
- Vehicle manufacturer's service information
- Manufacturer-specific tools, depending on the concern

Task-Specific Safety Considerations
- This task may require test driving the vehicle on the school grounds or on a hoist, both of which carry severe risks. Attempt this task only with full permission from your supervisor/instructor and follow all the guidelines exactly.
- Comply with personal and environmental safety practices associated with clothing; eye protection; hand tools; power equipment; proper ventilation; and the handling, storage, and disposal of chemicals/materials in accordance with federal, state, and local regulations.
- Always wear the correct protective eyewear and clothing and use the appropriate safety equipment, as well as fender covers, seat protectors, and floor mat protectors.
- Make sure you understand and observe all legislative and personal safety procedures when carrying out practical assignments. If you are unsure of what these are, ask your supervisor/instructor.
- While working on the vehicle, wheel chocks must be placed on both sides of one set of tires or as directed by your supervisor/instructor.
- When running any vehicles in the shop, make sure you use the shop's exhaust ventilation system to discharge all exhaust gas safely outside.

▶ TASK Test torque converter.

AED 4.1

Time off_____

Time on_____

Student Instructions: Read through the entire procedure prior to starting. Prepare your workspace and any tools or parts that may be needed to complete the task. When directed by your supervisor/instructor, begin the procedure to complete the task, and comment or check the box as each step is finished. Track your time on this procedure for later comparison to the standard completion time (i.e., "flat rate" or customer pay time).

Total time_____

Procedure	Step Completed
(**Note:** Lab fixtures/instructional aids may be used for this task.)	
1. Using available service literature as a guide, describe the process for performing a stall test, then perform the test:	☐
2. Meets the manufacturer's specifications: Yes ☐ No ☐	☐
a. If no, list your recommendations for rectification:	☐
3. Using available service literature as a guide, describe the process for performing a lockup test, then perform the test (if applicable):	☐
4. Meets the manufacturer's specifications: Yes ☐ No ☐	☐
a. If no, list your recommendations for rectification:	☐
5. Discuss your findings with your supervisor/instructor.	☐

Non-Task-Specific Evaluation	Step Completed
1. Tools and equipment were used as directed and returned in good working order.	☐
2. Complied with all general and task-specific safety standards, including proper use of any personal protective equipment (PPE).	☐
3. Completed the task in an appropriate time frame (recommendation: 1.5 or 2 times the flat rate).	☐
4. Left the workspace clean and orderly.	☐
5. Cared for customer property and returned it undamaged.	☐

Student signature _____ Date _____

Comments:

Have your supervisor/instructor verify satisfactory completion of this procedure, any observations made, and any necessary action(s) recommended.

Evaluation Instructions: The scoring box below is intended to act as a guide for both student and supervisor/instructor. Each criterion listed will help students to understand what is expected of them and help supervisors/instructors to articulate the level of success at a particular task. The scoring is set up to allow a second attempt at each task (see the Test and Retest columns). Scoring is designed only to award students points for task criteria that were completed correctly. Points are lost for failure to complete the employability requirements (see Non-Task-Specific criteria). When all criteria are evaluated, tally the points for a total at the bottom of each column.

Tasksheet Scoring

Evaluation Items	Test Pass	Test Fail	Retest Pass	Retest Fail
Task-Specific Evaluation	**(1 pt)**	**(0 pts)**	**(1 pt)**	**(0 pts)**
Student accurately described the process of and properly performed a stall test.				
Student provided accurate recommendations for rectification, if necessary.				
Student accurately described the process of and properly performed a lockup test.				
Student provided accurate recommendations for rectification, if necessary.				
Non-Task-Specific Evaluation	**(0 pts)**	**(−1 pt)**	**(0 pts)**	**(−1 pt)**
Student successfully completed at least three of the non-task-specific steps.				
Student successfully completed all five of the non-task-specific steps.				
Total Score: <total # of points / 4 = %>				

Supervisor/Instructor:

Supervisor/instructor signature _____ Date _____

Comments:

Retest supervisor/instructor signature _____ Date _____

Comments:

Chapter 30: Theory and Operation; Theory and Principles of Manual Transmissions

Learning Objective/Task	CDX Tasksheet Number	AED Reference Number
• Explain a sliding gear transmission power flow.	4.1b001	AED 4.1
• Explain a collar shift transmission power flow.	4.1b002	AED 4.1
• Explain a synchromesh transmission power flow and how components relate to one another.	4.1b003	AED 4.1
• Explain shift controls.	4.1b004	AED 4.1
• Test/troubleshoot transmission.	4.1b005	AED 4.1

Materials Required
• Vehicle manufacturer's service information

Safety Considerations
• This task may require test driving the vehicle on the school grounds or on a hoist, both of which carry severe risks. Attempt this task only with full permission from your supervisor/instructor and follow all the guidelines exactly.
• Comply with personal and environmental safety practices associated with clothing; eye protection; hand tools; power equipment; proper ventilation; and the handling, storage, and disposal of chemicals/materials in accordance with federal, state, and local regulations.
• Always wear the correct protective eyewear and clothing and use the appropriate safety equipment, as well as fender covers, seat protectors, and floor mat protectors.
• Make sure you understand and observe all legislative and personal safety procedures when carrying out practical assignments. If you are unsure of what these are, ask your supervisor/instructor.
• While working on the vehicle, wheel chocks must be placed on both sides of one set of tires or as directed by your supervisor/instructor.
• When running any vehicles in the shop, make sure you use the shop's exhaust ventilation system to discharge all exhaust gas safely outside.

CDX Tasksheet Number: 4.1b001

Student/Intern Information

Name _____ Date _____ Class _____

Machine, Customer, and Service Information

Machine used for this activity:

Make _____ Model _____

Hours _____ Serial Number _____

Materials Required
- Vehicle manufacturer's service information

Task-Specific Safety Considerations
- This task may require test driving the vehicle on the school grounds or on a hoist, both of which carry severe risks. Attempt this task only with full permission from your supervisor/instructor and follow all the guidelines exactly.
- Comply with personal and environmental safety practices associated with clothing; eye protection; hand tools; power equipment; proper ventilation; and the handling, storage, and disposal of chemicals/materials in accordance with federal, state, and local regulations.
- Always wear the correct protective eyewear and clothing and use the appropriate safety equipment, as well as fender covers, seat protectors, and floor mat protectors.
- Make sure you understand and observe all legislative and personal safety procedures when carrying out practical assignments. If you are unsure of what these are, ask your supervisor/instructor.
- While working on the vehicle, wheel chocks must be placed on both sides of one set of tires or as directed by your supervisor/instructor.
- When running any vehicles in the shop, make sure you use the shop's exhaust ventilation system to discharge all exhaust gas safely outside.

▶ **TASK** Explain a sliding gear transmission power flow. **AED 4.1**

Time off_____

Time on_____

Student Instructions: Read through the entire procedure prior to starting. Prepare your workspace and any tools or parts that may be needed to complete the task. When directed by your supervisor/instructor, begin the procedure to complete the task, and comment or check the box as each step is finished. Track your time on this procedure for later comparison to the standard completion time (i.e., "flat rate" or customer pay time).

Total time_____

Procedure	Step Completed
1. Using available service literature as a guide, list each sliding gear transmission component in order and explain how they relate to one another. (**Note:** Lab fixtures/instructional aids may be used for this task.)	

a. Component #1	☐
b. Component #2	☐
c. Component #3	☐
d. Component #4	☐
e. Component #5 (if applicable)	☐
f. Component #6 (if applicable)	☐
g. Component #7 (if applicable)	☐
h. Component #8 (if applicable)	☐
i. Component #9 (if applicable)	☐
j. Component #10 (if applicable)	☐
2. Discuss your findings with your supervisor/instructor.	☐

Non-Task-Specific Evaluation	Step Completed
1. Tools and equipment were used as directed and returned in good working order.	☐
2. Complied with all general and task-specific safety standards, including proper use of any personal protective equipment (PPE).	☐
3. Completed the task in an appropriate time frame (recommendation: 1.5 or 2 times the flat rate).	☐
4. Left the workspace clean and orderly.	☐
5. Cared for customer property and returned it undamaged.	☐

Student signature _____ Date _____

Comments:

Have your supervisor/instructor verify satisfactory completion of this procedure, any observations made, and any necessary action(s) recommended.

Evaluation Instructions: The scoring box below is intended to act as a guide for both student and supervisor/instructor. Each criterion listed will help students to understand what is expected of them and help supervisors/instructors to articulate the level of success at a particular task. The scoring is set up to allow a second attempt at each task (see the Test and Retest columns). Scoring is designed only to award students points for task criteria that were completed correctly. Points are lost for failure to complete the employability requirements (see Non-Task-Specific criteria). When all criteria are evaluated, tally the points for a total at the bottom of each column.

Tasksheet Scoring

	Test		Retest	
Evaluation Items	**Pass**	**Fail**	**Pass**	**Fail**
Task-Specific Evaluation	**(1 pt)**	**(0 pts)**	**(1 pt)**	**(0 pts)**
Student listed at least half of the sliding gear transmission components in the correct order.				
Student listed all of the sliding gear transmission components in the correct order.				
Student correctly described how at least half of the sliding gear transmission components relate to one another.				
Student correctly described how all of the sliding gear transmission components relate to one another.				
Non-Task-Specific Evaluation	**(0 pts)**	**(−1 pt)**	**(0 pts)**	**(−1 pt)**
Student successfully completed at least three of the non-task-specific steps.				
Student successfully completed all five of the non-task-specific steps.				
Total Score: <total # of points / 4 = %>				

Supervisor/Instructor:

Supervisor/instructor signature _____ Date _____

Comments:

Retest supervisor/instructor signature _____ Date _____

Comments:

CDX Tasksheet Number: 4.1b002

Student/Intern Information

Name _____ Date _____ Class _____

Machine, Customer, and Service Information

Machine used for this activity:

Make _____ Model _____

Hours _____ Serial Number _____

Materials Required
- Vehicle manufacturer's service information

Task-Specific Safety Considerations
- This task may require test driving the vehicle on the school grounds or on a hoist, both of which carry severe risks. Attempt this task only with full permission from your supervisor/instructor and follow all the guidelines exactly.
- Comply with personal and environmental safety practices associated with clothing; eye protection; hand tools; power equipment; proper ventilation; and the handling, storage, and disposal of chemicals/materials in accordance with federal, state, and local regulations.
- Always wear the correct protective eyewear and clothing and use the appropriate safety equipment, as well as fender covers, seat protectors, and floor mat protectors.
- Make sure you understand and observe all legislative and personal safety procedures when carrying out practical assignments. If you are unsure of what these are, ask your supervisor/instructor.
- While working on the vehicle, wheel chocks must be placed on both sides of one set of tires or as directed by your supervisor/instructor.
- When running any vehicles in the shop, make sure you use the shop's exhaust ventilation system to discharge all exhaust gas safely outside.

▶ TASK Explain a collar shift transmission power flow. _____ **AED** 4.1

Student Instructions: Read through the entire procedure prior to starting. Prepare your workspace and any tools or parts that may be needed to complete the task. When directed by your supervisor/instructor, begin the procedure to complete the task, and comment or check the box as each step is finished. Track your time on this procedure for later comparison to the standard completion time (i.e., "flat rate" or customer pay time).

Time off_____

Time on_____

Total time_____

Procedure	Step Completed
1. Using available service literature as a guide, list each collar shift transmission component in order and explain how they relate to one another. **(Note: Lab fixtures/instructional aids may be used for this task.)**	

a. Component #1	☐
b. Component #2	☐
c. Component #3	☐
d. Component #4	☐
e. Component #5 (if applicable)	☐
f. Component #6 (if applicable)	☐
g. Component #7 (if applicable)	☐
h. Component #8 (if applicable)	☐
i. Component #9 (if applicable)	☐
j. Component #10 (if applicable)	☐
2. Discuss your findings with your supervisor/instructor.	☐

Non-Task-Specific Evaluation	Step Completed
1. Tools and equipment were used as directed and returned in good working order.	☐
2. Complied with all general and task-specific safety standards, including proper use of any personal protective equipment (PPE).	☐
3. Completed the task in an appropriate time frame (recommendation: 1.5 or 2 times the flat rate).	☐
4. Left the workspace clean and orderly.	☐
5. Cared for customer property and returned it undamaged.	☐

Student signature _____ Date _____

Comments:

Have your supervisor/instructor verify satisfactory completion of this procedure, any observations made, and any necessary action(s) recommended.

Evaluation Instructions: The scoring box below is intended to act as a guide for both student and supervisor/instructor. Each criterion listed will help students to understand what is expected of them and help supervisors/instructors to articulate the level of success at a particular task. The scoring is set up to allow a second attempt at each task (see the Test and Retest columns). Scoring is designed only to award students points for task criteria that were completed correctly. Points are lost for failure to complete the employability requirements (see Non-Task-Specific criteria). When all criteria are evaluated, tally the points for a total at the bottom of each column.

Tasksheet Scoring

Evaluation Items	Test		Retest	
	Pass	Fail	Pass	Fail
Task-Specific Evaluation	**(1 pt)**	**(0 pts)**	**(1 pt)**	**(0 pts)**
Student listed at least half of the collar shift transmission components in the correct order.				
Student listed all of the collar shift transmission components in the correct order.				
Student correctly described how at least half of the collar shift transmission components relate to one another.				
Student correctly described how all of the collar shift transmission components relate to one another.				
Non-Task-Specific Evaluation	**(0 pts)**	**(−1 pt)**	**(0 pts)**	**(−1 pt)**
Student successfully completed at least three of the non-task-specific steps.				
Student successfully completed all five of the non-task-specific steps.				
Total Score: <total # of points / 4 = %>				

Supervisor/Instructor:

Supervisor/instructor signature _____ Date _____

Comments:

Retest supervisor/instructor signature _____ Date _____

Comments:

CDX Tasksheet Number: 4.1b003

Student/Intern Information

Name _____ Date _____ Class _____

Machine, Customer, and Service Information

Machine used for this activity:

Make _____ Model _____

Hours _____ Serial Number _____

Materials Required

- Vehicle manufacturer's service information

Task-Specific Safety Considerations

- This task may require test driving the vehicle on the school grounds or on a hoist, both of which carry severe risks. Attempt this task only with full permission from your supervisor/instructor and follow all the guidelines exactly.
- Comply with personal and environmental safety practices associated with clothing; eye protection; hand tools; power equipment; proper ventilation; and the handling, storage, and disposal of chemicals/materials in accordance with federal, state, and local regulations.
- Always wear the correct protective eyewear and clothing and use the appropriate safety equipment, as well as fender covers, seat protectors, and floor mat protectors.
- Make sure you understand and observe all legislative and personal safety procedures when carrying out practical assignments. If you are unsure of what these are, ask your supervisor/instructor.
- While working on the vehicle, wheel chocks must be placed on both sides of one set of tires or as directed by your supervisor/instructor.
- When running any vehicles in the shop, make sure you use the shop's exhaust ventilation system to discharge all exhaust gas safely outside.

▶ TASK Explain a synchromesh transmission power flow and how components relate to one another.

AED 4.1

Time off_____

Student Instructions: Read through the entire procedure prior to starting. Prepare your workspace and any tools or parts that may be needed to complete the task. When directed by your supervisor/instructor, begin the procedure to complete the task, and comment or check the box as each step is finished. Track your time on this procedure for later comparison to the standard completion time (i.e., "flat rate" or customer pay time).

Time on_____

Total time_____

Procedure	Step Completed
1. Using available service literature as a guide, list each synchromesh transmission component in order and explain how they relate to one another. (**Note:** Lab fixtures/instructional aids may be used for this task.)	

a. Component #1	☐
b. Component #2	☐
c. Component #3	☐
d. Component #4	☐
e. Component #5 (if applicable)	☐
f. Component #6 (if applicable)	☐
g. Component #7 (if applicable)	☐
h. Component #8 (if applicable)	☐
i. Component #9 (if applicable)	☐
j. Component #10 (if applicable)	☐
2. Discuss your findings with your supervisor/instructor.	☐

Non-Task-Specific Evaluation	Step Completed
1. Tools and equipment were used as directed and returned in good working order.	☐
2. Complied with all general and task-specific safety standards, including proper use of any personal protective equipment (PPE).	☐
3. Completed the task in an appropriate time frame (recommendation: 1.5 or 2 times the flat rate).	☐
4. Left the workspace clean and orderly.	☐
5. Cared for customer property and returned it undamaged.	☐

Student signature _____ Date _____

Comments:

Have your supervisor/instructor verify satisfactory completion of this procedure, any observations made,

and any necessary action(s) recommended.

Evaluation Instructions: The scoring box below is intended to act as a guide for both student and supervisor/instructor. Each criterion listed will help students to understand what is expected of them and help supervisors/instructors to articulate the level of success at a particular task. The scoring is set up to allow a second attempt at each task (see the Test and Retest columns). Scoring is designed only to award students points for task criteria that were completed correctly. Points are lost for failure to complete the employability requirements (see Non-Task-Specific criteria). When all criteria are evaluated, tally the points for a total at the bottom of each column.

Tasksheet Scoring

Evaluation Items	Test		Retest	
	Pass	**Fail**	**Pass**	**Fail**
Task-Specific Evaluation	**(1 pt)**	**(0 pts)**	**(1 pt)**	**(0 pts)**
Student listed at least half of the synchromesh transmission components in the correct order.				
Student listed all of the synchromesh transmission components in the correct order.				
Student correctly described how at least half of the synchromesh transmission components relate to one another.				
Student correctly described how all of the synchromesh transmission components relate to one another.				
Non-Task-Specific Evaluation	**(0 pts)**	**(−1 pt)**	**(0 pts)**	**(−1 pt)**
Student successfully completed at least three of the non-task-specific steps.				
Student successfully completed all five of the non-task-specific steps.				
Total Score: <total # of points / 4 = %>				

Supervisor/Instructor:

Supervisor/instructor signature _____ Date _____

Comments:

Retest supervisor/instructor signature _____ Date _____

Comments:

CDX Tasksheet Number: 4.1b004

Student/Intern Information

Name _____ Date _____ Class _____

Machine, Customer, and Service Information

Machine used for this activity:

Make _____ Model _____

Hours _____ Serial Number _____

Materials Required
- Vehicle manufacturer's service information

Task-Specific Safety Considerations
- This task may require test driving the vehicle on the school grounds or on a hoist, both of which carry severe risks. Attempt this task only with full permission from your supervisor/instructor and follow all the guidelines exactly.
- Comply with personal and environmental safety practices associated with clothing; eye protection; hand tools; power equipment; proper ventilation; and the handling, storage, and disposal of chemicals/materials in accordance with federal, state, and local regulations.
- Always wear the correct protective eyewear and clothing and use the appropriate safety equipment, as well as fender covers, seat protectors, and floor mat protectors.
- Make sure you understand and observe all legislative and personal safety procedures when carrying out practical assignments. If you are unsure of what these are, ask your supervisor/instructor.
- While working on the vehicle, wheel chocks must be placed on both sides of one set of tires or as directed by your supervisor/instructor.
- When running any vehicles in the shop, make sure you use the shop's exhaust ventilation system to discharge all exhaust gas safely outside.

▶ TASK Explain shift controls.

Time off _____

Time on _____

Student Instructions: Read through the entire procedure prior to starting. Prepare your workspace and any tools or parts that may be needed to complete the task. When directed by your supervisor/instructor, begin the procedure to complete the task, and comment or check the box as each step is finished. Track your time on this procedure for later comparison to the standard completion time (i.e., "flat rate" or customer pay time).

Total time _____

Procedure	Step Completed
1. Using available service literature as a guide, list the shift controls and explain how they relate to one another. (**Note:** Lab fixtures/instructional aids may be used for this task.)	
a. Component #1	☐
b. Component #2	☐
c. Component #3	☐
d. Component #4	☐
e. Component #5 (if applicable)	☐
f. Component #6 (if applicable)	☐
g. Component #7 (if applicable)	☐
h. Component #8 (if applicable)	☐
i. Component #9 (if applicable)	☐
j. Component #10 (if applicable)	☐
2. Discuss your findings with your supervisor/instructor.	☐

Non-Task-Specific Evaluation	Step Completed
1. Tools and equipment were used as directed and returned in good working order.	☐
2. Complied with all general and task-specific safety standards, including proper use of any personal protective equipment (PPE).	☐
3. Completed the task in an appropriate time frame (recommendation: 1.5 or 2 times the flat rate).	☐
4. Left the workspace clean and orderly.	☐
5. Cared for customer property and returned it undamaged.	☐

Student signature _____ Date _____

Comments:

Have your supervisor/instructor verify satisfactory completion of this procedure, any observations made, and any necessary action(s) recommended.

Evaluation Instructions: The scoring box below is intended to act as a guide for both student and supervisor/instructor. Each criterion listed will help students to understand what is expected of them and help supervisors/instructors to articulate the level of success at a particular task. The scoring is set up to allow a second attempt at each task (see the Test and Retest columns). Scoring is designed only to award students points for task criteria that were completed correctly. Points are lost for failure to complete the employability requirements (see Non-Task-Specific criteria). When all criteria are evaluated, tally the points for a total at the bottom of each column.

Tasksheet Scoring

Evaluation Items	Test		Retest	
	Pass	**Fail**	**Pass**	**Fail**
Task-Specific Evaluation	**(1 pt)**	**(0 pts)**	**(1 pt)**	**(0 pts)**
Student listed at least half of the shift controls in the correct order.				
Student listed all of the shift controls in the correct order.				
Student correctly described how at least half of the shift controls relate to one another.				
Student correctly described how all of the shift controls relate to one another.				
Non-Task-Specific Evaluation	**(0 pts)**	**(−1 pt)**	**(0 pts)**	**(−1 pt)**
Student successfully completed at least three of the non-task-specific steps.				
Student successfully completed all five of the non-task-specific steps.				
Total Score: <total # of points / 4 = %>				

Supervisor/Instructor:

Supervisor/instructor signature _____ Date _____

Comments:

Retest supervisor/instructor signature _____ Date _____

Comments:

CDX Tasksheet Number: 4.1b005

Student/Intern Information

Name _____ Date _____ Class _____

Machine, Customer, and Service Information

Machine used for this activity:

Make _____ Model _____

Hours _____ Serial Number _____

Materials Required

- Vehicle with possible power transfer concerns
- Vehicle manufacturer's service information
- Manufacturer-specific tools, depending on the concern

Task-Specific Safety Considerations

- This task may require test driving the vehicle on the school grounds or on a hoist, both of which carry severe risks. Attempt this task only with full permission from your supervisor/instructor and follow all the guidelines exactly.
- Comply with personal and environmental safety practices associated with clothing; eye protection; hand tools; power equipment; proper ventilation; and the handling, storage, and disposal of chemicals/materials in accordance with federal, state, and local regulations.
- Always wear the correct protective eyewear and clothing and use the appropriate safety equipment, as well as fender covers, seat protectors, and floor mat protectors.
- Make sure you understand and observe all legislative and personal safety procedures when carrying out practical assignments. If you are unsure of what these are, ask your supervisor/instructor.
- While working on the vehicle, wheel chocks must be placed on both sides of one set of tires or as directed by your supervisor/instructor.
- When running any vehicles in the shop, make sure you use the shop's exhaust ventilation system to discharge all exhaust gas safely outside.

▶ **TASK** Test/troubleshoot transmission.   **AED 4.1**

| Time off_____ |
| Time on_____ |
| Total time_____ |

Student Instructions: Read through the entire procedure prior to starting. Prepare your workspace and any tools or parts that may be needed to complete the task. When directed by your supervisor/instructor, begin the procedure to complete the task, and comment or check the box as each step is finished. Track your time on this procedure for later comparison to the standard completion time (i.e., "flat rate" or customer pay time).

Procedure	Step Completed
(**Note:** Lab fixtures/instructional aids may be used for this task.)	
1. Using available service literature as a guide, describe the process for performing a transmission performance test, then perform the test:	☐
a. Meets the manufacturer's specifications: Yes ☐ No ☐	☐
b. If no, list your recommendations for rectification:	☐
2. Using available service literature as a guide, describe the process for checking transmission fluid level, then perform the check:	☐
a. Meets the manufacturer's specifications: Yes ☐ No ☐	☐
b. If no, list your recommendations for rectification:	☐
3. Using available service literature as a guide, describe the process for checking transmission pressures, then perform the check:	☐
a. Meets the manufacturer's specifications: Yes ☐ No ☐	☐
b. If no, list your recommendations for rectification:	☐
4. Using available service literature as a guide, describe the process for checking transmission linkage, then perform the check:	☐

	Step Completed
a. Meets the manufacturer's specifications: Yes ☐ No ☐	☐
b. If no, list your recommendations for rectification:	☐
5. Discuss your findings with your supervisor/instructor.	☐

Non-Task-Specific Evaluation	Step Completed
1. Tools and equipment were used as directed and returned in good working order.	☐
2. Complied with all general and task-specific safety standards, including proper use of any personal protective equipment (PPE).	☐
3. Completed the task in an appropriate time frame (recommendation: 1.5 or 2 times the flat rate).	☐
4. Left the workspace clean and orderly.	☐
5. Cared for customer property and returned it undamaged.	☐

Student signature _____ Date _____

Comments:

Have your supervisor/instructor verify satisfactory completion of this procedure, any observations made, and any necessary action(s) recommended.

Evaluation Instructions: The scoring box below is intended to act as a guide for both student and supervisor/instructor. Each criterion listed will help students to understand what is expected of them and help supervisors/instructors to articulate the level of success at a particular task. The scoring is set up to allow a second attempt at each task (see the Test and Retest columns). Scoring is designed only to award students points for task criteria that were completed correctly. Points are lost for failure to complete the employability requirements (see Non-Task-Specific criteria). When all criteria are evaluated, tally the points for a total at the bottom of each column.

Tasksheet Scoring

	Test		Retest	
Evaluation Items	**Pass**	**Fail**	**Pass**	**Fail**
Task-Specific Evaluation	**(1 pt)**	**(0 pts)**	**(1 pt)**	**(0 pts)**
Student accurately described the process of a transmission performance test, properly performed the test, and listed any recommendations for rectification, if necessary.				
Student accurately described the process for checking transmission fluid level, properly performed the check, and listed any recommendations for rectification, if necessary.				
Student accurately described the process for checking transmission pressures, properly performed the check, and listed any recommendations for rectification, if necessary.				
Student accurately described the process for checking transmission linkage, properly performed the check, and listed any recommendations for rectification, if necessary.				
Non-Task-Specific Evaluation	**(0 pts)**	**(−1 pt)**	**(0 pts)**	**(−1 pt)**
Student successfully completed at least three of the non-task-specific steps.				
Student successfully completed all five of the non-task-specific steps.				
Total Score: <total # of points / 4 = %>				

Supervisor/Instructor:

Supervisor/instructor signature _____ Date _____

Comments:

Retest supervisor/instructor signature _____ Date _____

Comments:

Chapter 31: Theory and Operation; Theory and Principles of Powershift Transmissions

Learning Objective/Task	CDX Tasksheet Number	AED Reference Number
• Explain transmission operation.	4.1c001	AED 4.1

Safety Considerations
• This task may require test driving the vehicle on the school grounds or on a hoist, both of which carry severe risks. Attempt this task only with full permission from your supervisor/instructor and follow all the guidelines exactly.
• Comply with personal and environmental safety practices associated with clothing; eye protection; hand tools; power equipment; proper ventilation; and the handling, storage, and disposal of chemicals/materials in accordance with federal, state, and local regulations.
• Always wear the correct protective eyewear and clothing and use the appropriate safety equipment, as well as fender covers, seat protectors, and floor mat protectors.
• Make sure you understand and observe all legislative and personal safety procedures when carrying out practical assignments. If you are unsure of what these are, ask your supervisor/instructor.
• While working on the vehicle, wheel chocks must be placed on both sides of one set of tires or as directed by your supervisor/instructor.
• When running any vehicles in the shop, make sure you use the shop's exhaust ventilation system to discharge all exhaust gas safely outside.

CDX Tasksheet Number: 4.1c001

Student/Intern Information

Name _____ Date _____ Class _____

Machine, Customer, and Service Information

Machine used for this activity:

Make _____ Model _____

Hours _____ Serial Number _____

Materials Required
- Vehicle manufacturer's service information

Task-Specific Safety Considerations
- This task may require test driving the vehicle on the school grounds or on a hoist, both of which carry severe risks. Attempt this task only with full permission from your supervisor/instructor and follow all the guidelines exactly.
- Comply with personal and environmental safety practices associated with clothing; eye protection; hand tools; power equipment; proper ventilation; and the handling, storage, and disposal of chemicals/materials in accordance with federal, state, and local regulations.
- Always wear the correct protective eyewear and clothing and use the appropriate safety equipment, as well as fender covers, seat protectors, and floor mat protectors.
- Make sure you understand and observe all legislative and personal safety procedures when carrying out practical assignments. If you are unsure of what these are, ask your supervisor/instructor.
- While working on the vehicle, wheel chocks must be placed on both sides of one set of tires or as directed by your supervisor/instructor.
- When running any vehicles in the shop, make sure you use the shop's exhaust ventilation system to discharge all exhaust gas safely outside.

▶ **TASK** Explain transmission operation. _____ **AED** 4.1

Time off_____

Student Instructions: Read through the entire procedure prior to starting. Prepare your workspace and any tools or parts that may be needed to complete the task. When directed by your supervisor/instructor, begin the procedure to complete the task, and comment or check the box as each step is finished. Track your time on this procedure for later comparison to the standard completion time (i.e., "flat rate" or customer pay time).

Time on_____

Total time_____

Procedure	Step Completed
1. Using available service literature as a guide, describe the operation of the internal clutches and planetary gear sets required for each gear. (**Note:** Lab fixtures/instructional aids may be used for this task.)	
a. Gear #1	☐
b. Gear #2	☐
c. Gear #3	☐
d. Gear #4	☐
e. Gear #5 (if applicable)	☐
f. Gear #6 (if applicable)	☐
g. Gear #7 (if applicable)	☐
h. Gear #8 (if applicable)	☐

	Step Completed
i. Reverse gear	☐
j. Neutral	☐
2. Discuss your findings with your supervisor/instructor.	☐

Non-Task-Specific Evaluation	Step Completed
1. Tools and equipment were used as directed and returned in good working order.	☐
2. Complied with all general and task-specific safety standards, including proper use of any personal protective equipment (PPE).	☐
3. Completed the task in an appropriate time frame (recommendation: 1.5 or 2 times the flat rate).	☐
4. Left the workspace clean and orderly.	☐
5. Cared for customer property and returned it undamaged.	☐

Student signature _____ Date _____

Comments:

Have your supervisor/instructor verify satisfactory completion of this procedure, any observations made, and any necessary action(s) recommended.

Evaluation Instructions: The scoring box below is intended to act as a guide for both student and supervisor/instructor. Each criterion listed will help students to understand what is expected of them and help supervisors/instructors to articulate the level of success at a particular task. The scoring is set up to allow a second attempt at each task (see the Test and Retest columns). Scoring is designed only to award students points for task criteria that were completed correctly. Points are lost for failure to complete the employability requirements (see Non-Task-Specific criteria). When all criteria are evaluated, tally the points for a total at the bottom of each column.

Tasksheet Scoring

	Test		Retest	
Evaluation Items	**Pass**	**Fail**	**Pass**	**Fail**
Task-Specific Evaluation	**(1 pt)**	**(0 pts)**	**(1 pt)**	**(0 pts)**
Student provided an accurate description of at least half of the numbered gears.				
Student provided an accurate description of all of the numbered gears.				
Student provided an accurate description of reverse gears.				
Student provided an accurate description of neutral.				
Non-Task-Specific Evaluation	**(0 pts)**	**(−1 pt)**	**(0 pts)**	**(−1 pt)**
Student successfully completed at least three of the non-task-specific steps.				
Student successfully completed all five of the non-task-specific steps.				
Total Score: <total # of points / 4 = %>				

Supervisor/Instructor:

Supervisor/instructor signature _____ Date _____

Comments:

Retest supervisor/instructor signature _____ Date _____

Comments:

Chapter 32: Theory and Operation; Theory and Principles of Clutches

Learning Objective/Task	CDX Tasksheet Number	AED Reference Number
• Test/troubleshoot power shift transmission.	4.1d001	AED 4.1
• Adjust drive pinion bearing preload.	4.1d002a	AED 4.1
• Adjust side bearing endplay and ring gear backlash.	4.1d002b	AED 4.1
• Identify clutch components.	4.1d003	AED 4.1
• Explain clutch operation.	4.1d004	AED 4.1
• Replace single-disc clutch pressure plate and clutch disc.	4.1d005a	AED 4.1
• Replace two-plate clutch pressure plate, clutch discs intermediate plate, and drive pins/lugs.	4.1d005b	AED 4.1
• Explain overrunning clutch operation.	4.1d007	AED 4.1
• Explain magnetic-type clutch operation.	4.1d008	AED 4.1
• Explain modulating clutch operation.	4.1e001	AED 4.1

Materials Required
- Vehicle with possible power transfer concerns
- Vehicle manufacturer's service information
- Manufacturer-specific tools, depending on the concern

Safety Considerations
- This task may require test driving the vehicle on the school grounds or on a hoist, both of which carry severe risks. Attempt this task only with full permission from your supervisor/instructor and follow all the guidelines exactly.
- Comply with personal and environmental safety practices associated with clothing; eye protection; hand tools; power equipment; proper ventilation; and the handling, storage, and disposal of chemicals/materials in accordance with federal, state, and local regulations.
- Always wear the correct protective eyewear and clothing and use the appropriate safety equipment, as well as fender covers, seat protectors, and floor mat protectors.
- Make sure you understand and observe all legislative and personal safety procedures when carrying out practical assignments. If you are unsure of what these are, ask your supervisor/instructor.
- While working on the vehicle, wheel chocks must be placed on both sides of one set of tires or as directed by your supervisor/instructor.
- When running any vehicles in the shop, make sure you use the shop's exhaust ventilation system to discharge all exhaust gas safely outside.
- Lifting equipment such as vehicle jacks and stands, vehicle hoists, and engine hoists are important tools that increase productivity and make the job easier. However, they can also cause severe injury or death if used improperly. Make sure you follow the manufacturer's operation procedures. Also make sure you have your supervisor's/instructor's permission to use any particular type of lifting equipment.

CDX Tasksheet Number: 4.1d001

Student/Intern Information

Name _____ Date _____ Class _____

Machine, Customer, and Service Information

Machine used for this activity:

Make _____ Model _____

Hours _____ Serial Number _____

Materials Required

- Vehicle with possible power transfer concerns
- Vehicle manufacturer's service information
- Manufacturer-specific tools, depending on the concern

Task-Specific Safety Considerations

- This task may require test driving the vehicle on the school grounds or on a hoist, both of which carry severe risks. Attempt this task only with full permission from your supervisor/instructor and follow all the guidelines exactly.
- Comply with personal and environmental safety practices associated with clothing; eye protection; hand tools; power equipment; proper ventilation; and the handling, storage, and disposal of chemicals/materials in accordance with federal, state, and local regulations.
- Always wear the correct protective eyewear and clothing and use the appropriate safety equipment, as well as fender covers, seat protectors, and floor mat protectors.
- Make sure you understand and observe all legislative and personal safety procedures when carrying out practical assignments. If you are unsure of what these are, ask your supervisor/instructor.
- While working on the vehicle, wheel chocks must be placed on both sides of one set of tires or as directed by your supervisor/instructor.
- When running any vehicles in the shop, make sure you use the shop's exhaust ventilation system to discharge all exhaust gas safely outside.

▶ **TASK** Test/troubleshoot power shift transmission. _____ **AED** 4.1

Time off_____

Time on_____

Student Instructions: Read through the entire procedure prior to starting. Prepare your workspace and any tools or parts that may be needed to complete the task. When directed by your supervisor/instructor, begin the procedure to complete the task, and comment or check the box as each step is finished. Track your time on this procedure for later comparison to the standard completion time (i.e., "flat rate" or customer pay time).

Total time_____

Procedure	Step Completed
1. Using available service literature as a guide, describe the process of performing a power shift performance test, then perform the test:	☐
a. Meets the manufacturer's specifications: Yes ☐ No ☐	☐
b. If no, list your recommendations for rectification:	☐
2. Using available service literature as a guide, describe the process of checking a power shift transmission fluid level, then perform the check:	☐
a. Meets the manufacturer's specifications: Yes ☐ No ☐	☐
b. If no, list your recommendations for rectification:	☐
3. Using available service literature as a guide, describe the process for checking power shift transmission pressures, then perform the check:	☐
a. Meets the manufacturer's specifications: Yes ☐ No ☐	☐
b. If no, list your recommendations for rectification:	☐
4. Using available service literature as a guide, describe the process for checking power shift transmission, then perform the check:	☐

	Step Completed
a. Meets the manufacturer's specifications: Yes ☐ No ☐	☐
b. If no, list your recommendations for rectification:	☐
5. Using available service literature as a guide, describe the process for checking power shift transmission clutch, then perform the check:	☐
a. Meets the manufacturer's specifications: Yes ☐ No ☐	☐
b. If no, list your recommendations for rectification:	☐
6. Discuss your findings with your supervisor/instructor.	☐

Non-Task-Specific Evaluation	Step Completed
1. Tools and equipment were used as directed and returned in good working order.	☐
2. Complied with all general and task-specific safety standards, including proper use of any personal protective equipment (PPE).	☐
3. Completed the task in an appropriate time frame (recommendation: 1.5 or 2 times the flat rate).	☐
4. Left the workspace clean and orderly.	☐
5. Cared for customer property and returned it undamaged.	☐

Student signature _____ Date _____

Comments:

Have your supervisor/instructor verify satisfactory completion of this procedure, any observations made, and any necessary action(s) recommended.

Evaluation Instructions: The scoring box below is intended to act as a guide for both student and supervisor/instructor. Each criterion listed will help students to understand what is expected of them and help supervisors/instructors to articulate the level of success at a particular task. The scoring is set up to allow a second attempt at each task (see the Test and Retest columns). Scoring is designed only to award students points for task criteria that were completed correctly. Points are lost for failure to complete the employability requirements (see Non-Task-Specific criteria). When all criteria are evaluated, tally the points for a total at the bottom of each column.

Tasksheet Scoring

Evaluation Items	Test		Retest	
	Pass	Fail	Pass	Fail
Task-Specific Evaluation	**(1 pt)**	**(0 pts)**	**(1 pt)**	**(0 pts)**
Student accurately described the process of a power shift performance test, properly performed the test, and listed any recommendations for rectification, if necessary.				
Student accurately described the process for checking a power shift transmission fluid level, properly performed the check, and listed any recommendations for rectification, if necessary.				
Student accurately described the process for checking power shift transmission pressures, properly performed the check, and listed any recommendations for rectification, if necessary.				
Student accurately described the processes for checking power shift transmission linkage and power shift transmission clutch, properly performed the checks, and listed any recommendations for rectification, if necessary.				

Non-Task-Specific Evaluation	(0 pts)	(−1 pt)	(0 pts)	(−1 pt)
Student successfully completed at least three of the non-task-specific steps.				
Student successfully completed all five of the non-task-specific steps.				
Total Score: <total # of points / 4 = %>				

Supervisor/Instructor:

Supervisor/instructor signature _____ Date _____

Comments:

Retest supervisor/instructor signature _____ Date _____

Comments:

CDX Tasksheet Number: 4.1d002a

Student/Intern Information

Name _____ Date _____ Class _____

Machine, Customer, and Service Information

Machine used for this activity:

Make _____ Model _____

Hours _____ Serial Number _____

Materials Required

- Vehicle with possible drive axle concerns
- Vehicle manufacturer's service information
- Manufacturer-specific tools, depending on the concern

Task-Specific Safety Considerations

- This task may require test driving the vehicle on the school grounds or on a hoist, both of which carry severe risks. Attempt this task only with full permission from your supervisor/instructor and follow all the guidelines exactly.
- Comply with personal and environmental safety practices associated with clothing; eye protection; hand tools; power equipment; proper ventilation; and the handling, storage, and disposal of chemicals/materials in accordance with federal, state, and local regulations.
- Always wear the correct protective eyewear and clothing and use the appropriate safety equipment, as well as fender covers, seat protectors, and floor mat protectors.
- Make sure you understand and observe all legislative and personal safety procedures when carrying out practical assignments. If you are unsure of what these are, ask your supervisor/instructor.
- While working on the vehicle, wheel chocks must be placed on both sides of one set of tires or as directed by your supervisor/instructor.
- When running any vehicles in the shop, make sure you use the shop's exhaust ventilation system to discharge all exhaust gas safely outside.

▶ TASK Adjust drive pinion bearing preload. _____ **AED** *4.1*

Time off_____

Student Instructions: Read through the entire procedure prior to starting. Prepare your workspace and any tools or parts that may be needed to complete the task. When directed by your supervisor/instructor, begin the procedure to complete the task, and comment or check the box as each step is finished. Track your time on this procedure for later comparison to the standard completion time (i.e., "flat rate" or customer pay time).

Time on_____

Total time_____

Procedure	Step Completed
1. Research the procedure and specifications for measuring and adjusting drive pinion bearing preload in the appropriate manufacturer's service information.	☐
a. Record the manufacturer's specified drive pinion preload: _____ in-lb/Nm	☐
b. Ensure the pinion bearing preload is precisely set by steel shims.	☐
2. Install the pinion bearings and support flange. Once the pinion bearings are installed, the bearing preload is set.	☐
3. Support the pinion under a press. Then, using a correctly sized sleeve, press on the outer bearing inner race. Increase the press load to the amount recommended in the overhaul manual, typically about 10-20 tons (9.079-18.159 tons).	☐
4. Tie a length of string to one of the cage mounting holes and wrap the string around the pinion cage several times. Attach a pull scale that reads in pounds or kilograms to the other end of the string. In a steady motion, start rotating the cage by hand and keep it rotating by pulling the scale.	☐
5. Record the force required to keep the cage rotating (NOT the force required to start it rotating) below:	☐
6. Multiply the pounds or kilograms pulled by the radius of the cage where the string was attached. This will indicate the rotating torque of the pinion in inch-pounds or kilograms per centimeter. Typical settings are between 15 and 30 in-lb (17 and 34 kg-cm). Always check the original equipment manufacturer's manual for the correct specification.	☐
7. Return the vehicle to its beginning condition and return any tools you used to their proper locations.	☐
8. Discuss your findings with your supervisor/instructor.	☐

Non-Task-Specific Evaluation	Step Completed
1. Tools and equipment were used as directed and returned in good working order.	☐
2. Complied with all general and task-specific safety standards, including proper use of any personal protective equipment (PPE).	☐
3. Completed the task in an appropriate time frame (recommendation: 1.5 or 2 times the flat rate).	☐
4. Left the workspace clean and orderly.	☐
5. Cared for customer property and returned it undamaged.	☐

Student signature _____ Date _____

Comments:

Have your supervisor/instructor verify satisfactory completion of this procedure, any observations made, and any necessary action(s) recommended.

Evaluation Instructions: The scoring box below is intended to act as a guide for both student and supervisor/instructor. Each criterion listed will help students to understand what is expected of them and help supervisors/instructors to articulate the level of success at a particular task. The scoring is set up to allow a second attempt at each task (see the Test and Retest columns). Scoring is designed only to award students points for task criteria that were completed correctly. Points are lost for failure to complete the employability requirements (see Non-Task-Specific criteria). When all criteria are evaluated, tally the points for a total at the bottom of each column.

Tasksheet Scoring

Evaluation Items	Test		Retest	
	Pass	Fail	Pass	Fail
Task-Specific Evaluation	**(1 pt)**	**(0 pts)**	**(1 pt)**	**(0 pts)**
Student used the manufacturer's service information to research the procedure and find the correct specifications.				
Student properly adjusted the drive pinion bearing preload.				
Student recorded the correct force required to keep the cage rotating.				
Student determined the correct rotating torque.				
Non-Task-Specific Evaluation	**(0 pts)**	**(−1 pt)**	**(0 pts)**	**(−1 pt)**
Student successfully completed at least three of the non-task-specific steps.				
Student successfully completed all five of the non-task-specific steps.				
Total Score: <total # of points / 4 = %>				

Supervisor/Instructor:

Supervisor/instructor signature _____ Date _____

Comments:

Retest supervisor/instructor signature _____ Date _____

Comments:

CDX Tasksheet Number: 4.1d002b

Student/Intern Information

Name _____ Date _____ Class _____

Machine, Customer, and Service Information

Machine used for this activity:

Make _____ Model _____

Hours _____ Serial Number _____

Materials Required

- Vehicle with possible drive axle concerns
- Vehicle manufacturer's service information
- Manufacturer-specific tools, depending on the concern

Task-Specific Safety Considerations

- This task may require test driving the vehicle on the school grounds or on a hoist, both of which carry severe risks. Attempt this task only with full permission from your supervisor/instructor and follow all the guidelines exactly.
- Comply with personal and environmental safety practices associated with clothing; eye protection; hand tools; power equipment; proper ventilation; and the handling, storage, and disposal of chemicals/materials in accordance with federal, state, and local regulations.
- Always wear the correct protective eyewear and clothing and use the appropriate safety equipment, as well as fender covers, seat protectors, and floor mat protectors.
- Make sure you understand and observe all legislative and personal safety procedures when carrying out practical assignments. If you are unsure of what these are, ask your supervisor/instructor.
- While working on the vehicle, wheel chocks must be placed on both sides of one set of tires or as directed by your supervisor/instructor.
- When running any vehicles in the shop, make sure you use the shop's exhaust ventilation system to discharge all exhaust gas safely outside.

▶ TASK Adjust side bearing endplay and ring gear backlash. **AED 4.1**

Time off_____

Time on_____

Student Instructions: Read through the entire procedure prior to starting. Prepare your workspace and any tools or parts that may be needed to complete the task. When directed by your supervisor/instructor, begin the procedure to complete the task, and comment or check the box as each step is finished. Track your time on this procedure for later comparison to the standard completion time (i.e., "flat rate" or customer pay time).

Total time_____

Procedure	Step Completed
1. Make sure all components are clean and free of any dirt or debris that could cause a false reading and adjustment.	☐
2. Install the ring gear into the differential housing with the bearing races. Prior to this action, the pinion should have been installed and adjusted as necessary.	☐
3. Install the main bearing caps onto the housing and thread the bolts through the caps and into the housing.	☐
4. Thread the side bearing adjusters into the bearing caps (see Figure 1).	☐
5. Torque the bolts to the proper manufacturer's specification.	☐
a. Record the torque specification: _____ft-lb/Nm	☐
6. Thread the side bearing adjusters into the caps until they make contact with the side bearings, allowing for some backlash play to be present.	☐
7. Attach a dial indicator base to the differential case housing and the dial pointer onto one of the ring gear teeth (see Figure 2).	☐

8. Utilizing a spanner wrench or equivalent, rotate one of the side bearing adjusters until the backlash starts to change (see Figure 3). 	☐
9. Always alternate the side bearing adjusters to keep the ring gear stable in the housing.	☐
10. Zero out the dial indicator.	☐
11. Rock the ring gear back and forth to achieve a reading on the dial indicator.	☐

a. Record the reading on the indicator and compare it to the manufacturer's specification:
    Reading _____ in/mm
    Specification _____ in/mm
	☐

12. Depending on the type of differential, record the procedure from the manufacturer's service manual to correct and bring the reading into specification:	☐
13. Return the vehicle to its beginning condition and return any tools you used to their proper locations.	☐
14. Discuss your findings with your supervisor/instructor.	☐

Non-Task-Specific Evaluation	Step Completed
1. Tools and equipment were used as directed and returned in good working order.	☐
2. Complied with all general and task-specific safety standards, including proper use of any personal protective equipment (PPE).	☐
3. Completed the task in an appropriate time frame (recommendation: 1.5 or 2 times the flat rate).	☐
4. Left the workspace clean and orderly.	☐
5. Cared for customer property and returned it undamaged.	☐

Student signature _____ Date _____

Comments:

[ ]

Have your supervisor/instructor verify satisfactory completion of this procedure, any observations made, and any necessary action(s) recommended.

Evaluation Instructions: The scoring box below is intended to act as a guide for both student and supervisor/instructor. Each criterion listed will help students to understand what is expected of them and help supervisors/instructors to articulate the level of success at a particular task. The scoring is set up to allow a second attempt at each task (see the Test and Retest columns). Scoring is designed only to award students points for task criteria that were completed correctly. Points are lost for failure to complete the employability requirements (see Non-Task-Specific criteria). When all criteria are evaluated, tally the points for a total at the bottom of each column.

Tasksheet Scoring

Evaluation Items	Test		Retest	
	Pass	**Fail**	**Pass**	**Fail**
Task-Specific Evaluation	**(1 pt)**	**(0 pts)**	**(1 pt)**	**(0 pts)**
Student properly installed ring gears and main bearing caps.				
Student properly threaded the side bearing adjusters and torqued the bolts to the proper manufacturer's specification.				
Student properly measured ring gear backlash.				
Student properly adjusted the reading to specification and recorded the procedure correctly.				
Non-Task-Specific Evaluation	**(0 pts)**	**(−1 pt)**	**(0 pts)**	**(−1 pt)**
Student successfully completed at least three of the non-task-specific steps.				
Student successfully completed all five of the non-task-specific steps.				
Total Score: <total # of points / 4 = %>				

Supervisor/Instructor:

Supervisor/instructor signature _____ Date _____

Comments:

Retest supervisor/instructor signature _____ Date _____

Comments:

CDX Tasksheet Number: 4.1d003

Student/Intern Information

Name _____ Date _____ Class _____

Machine, Customer, and Service Information

Machine used for this activity:

Make _____ Model _____

Hours _____ Serial Number _____

Materials Required
- Vehicle manufacturer's service information

Task-Specific Safety Considerations
- This task may require test driving the vehicle on the school grounds or on a hoist, both of which carry severe risks. Attempt this task only with full permission from your supervisor/instructor and follow all the guidelines exactly.
- Comply with personal and environmental safety practices associated with clothing; eye protection; hand tools; power equipment; proper ventilation; and the handling, storage, and disposal of chemicals/materials in accordance with federal, state, and local regulations.
- Always wear the correct protective eyewear and clothing and use the appropriate safety equipment, as well as fender covers, seat protectors, and floor mat protectors.
- Make sure you understand and observe all legislative and personal safety procedures when carrying out practical assignments. If you are unsure of what these are, ask your supervisor/instructor.
- While working on the vehicle, wheel chocks must be placed on both sides of one set of tires or as directed by your supervisor/instructor.
- When running any vehicles in the shop, make sure you use the shop's exhaust ventilation system to discharge all exhaust gas safely outside.

▶ **TASK** Identify clutch components.   **AED** 4.1

Time off_____

Student Instructions: Read through the entire procedure prior to starting. Prepare your workspace and any tools or parts that may be needed to complete the task. When directed by your supervisor/instructor, begin the procedure to complete the task, and comment or check the box as each step is finished. Track your time on this procedure for later comparison to the standard completion time (i.e., "flat rate" or customer pay time).

Time on_____

Total time_____

Procedure	Step Completed
1. Using available service literature as a guide, describe the function and application(s) for each of the following clutch components. (**Note:** Lab fixtures/instructional aids may be used for this task.)	
a. Single disc clutch	☐
b. Multiple disc clutch	☐
c. Flywheel	☐
d. Pilot bearing	☐
e. Release bearing	☐
f. Pressure plate	☐
g. Intermediate plate	☐
h. Input shaft	☐

	Step Completed
i. Button (ceramic) clutch	☐
j. Solid (organic) clutch	☐
2. Discuss your findings with your supervisor/instructor.	☐

Non-Task-Specific Evaluation	Step Completed
1. Tools and equipment were used as directed and returned in good working order.	☐
2. Complied with all general and task-specific safety standards, including proper use of any personal protective equipment (PPE).	☐
3. Completed the task in an appropriate time frame (recommendation: 1.5 or 2 times the flat rate).	☐
4. Left the workspace clean and orderly.	☐
5. Cared for customer property and returned it undamaged.	☐

Student signature _____ Date _____

Comments:

_____

Have your supervisor/instructor verify satisfactory completion of this procedure, any observations made, and any necessary action(s) recommended.

Evaluation Instructions: The scoring box below is intended to act as a guide for both student and supervisor/instructor. Each criterion listed will help students to understand what is expected of them and help supervisors/instructors to articulate the level of success at a particular task. The scoring is set up to allow a second attempt at each task (see the Test and Retest columns). Scoring is designed only to award students points for task criteria that were completed correctly. Points are lost for failure to complete the employability requirements (see Non-Task-Specific criteria). When all criteria are evaluated, tally the points for a total at the bottom of each column.

Tasksheet Scoring

Evaluation Items	Test		Retest	
	Pass	**Fail**	**Pass**	**Fail**
Task-Specific Evaluation	**(1 pt)**	**(0 pts)**	**(1 pt)**	**(0 pts)**
Student accurately described the function and application(s) of at least two clutch components.				
Student accurately described the function and application(s) of at least four clutch components.				
Student accurately described the function and application(s) of at least seven clutch components.				
Student accurately described the function and application(s) of all 10 clutch components.				
Non-Task-Specific Evaluation	**(0 pts)**	**(−1 pt)**	**(0 pts)**	**(−1 pt)**
Student successfully completed at least three of the non-task-specific steps.				
Student successfully completed all five of the non-task-specific steps.				
Total Score: <total # of points / 4 = %>				

Supervisor/Instructor:

Supervisor/instructor signature _____ Date _____

Comments:

Retest supervisor/instructor signature _____ Date _____

Comments:

CDX Tasksheet Number: 4.1d004

Student/Intern Information

Name _____ Date _____ Class _____

Machine, Customer, and Service Information

Machine used for this activity:

Make _____ Model _____

Hours _____ Serial Number _____

Materials Required
- Vehicle manufacturer's service information

Task-Specific Safety Considerations
- This task may require test driving the vehicle on the school grounds or on a hoist, both of which carry severe risks. Attempt this task only with full permission from your supervisor/instructor and follow all the guidelines exactly.
- Comply with personal and environmental safety practices associated with clothing; eye protection; hand tools; power equipment; proper ventilation; and the handling, storage, and disposal of chemicals/materials in accordance with federal, state, and local regulations.
- Always wear the correct protective eyewear and clothing and use the appropriate safety equipment, as well as fender covers, seat protectors, and floor mat protectors.
- Make sure you understand and observe all legislative and personal safety procedures when carrying out practical assignments. If you are unsure of what these are, ask your supervisor/instructor.
- While working on the vehicle, wheel chocks must be placed on both sides of one set of tires or as directed by your supervisor/instructor.
- When running any vehicles in the shop, make sure you use the shop's exhaust ventilation system to discharge all exhaust gas safely outside.

▶ TASK Explain clutch operation.   **AED 4.1**

Time off_____

Time on_____

Student Instructions: Read through the entire procedure prior to starting. Prepare your workspace and any tools or parts that may be needed to complete the task. When directed by your supervisor/instructor, begin the procedure to complete the task, and comment or check the box as each step is finished. Track your time on this procedure for later comparison to the standard completion time (i.e., "flat rate" or customer pay time).

Total time_____

Procedure	Step Completed
1. Using available service literature as a guide, describe the operation of the individual components and power flow of the following clutch types. (**Note:** Lab fixtures/instructional aids may be used for this task.)	
a. Single disc clutch	☐
b. Multiple disc clutch	☐
c. Wet disc(s) clutch	☐
2. Discuss your findings with your supervisor/instructor.	☐

Non-Task-Specific Evaluation	Step Completed
1. Tools and equipment were used as directed and returned in good working order.	☐
2. Complied with all general and task-specific safety standards, including proper use of any personal protective equipment (PPE).	☐
3. Completed the task in an appropriate time frame (recommendation: 1.5 or 2 times the flat rate).	☐
4. Left the workspace clean and orderly.	☐
5. Cared for customer property and returned it undamaged.	☐

Student signature _____ Date _____

Comments:

Have your supervisor/instructor verify satisfactory completion of this procedure, any observations made,

and any necessary action(s) recommended.

Evaluation Instructions: The scoring box below is intended to act as a guide for both student and supervisor/instructor. Each criterion listed will help students to understand what is expected of them and help supervisors/instructors to articulate the level of success at a particular task. The scoring is set up to allow a second attempt at each task (see the Test and Retest columns). Scoring is designed only to award students points for task criteria that were completed correctly. Points are lost for failure to complete the employability requirements (see Non-Task-Specific criteria). When all criteria are evaluated, tally the points for a total at the bottom of each column.

Tasksheet Scoring

Evaluation Items	Test		Retest	
	Pass	**Fail**	**Pass**	**Fail**
Task-Specific Evaluation	**(1 pt)**	**(0 pts)**	**(1 pt)**	**(0 pts)**
Student used the manufacturer's service information.				
Student accurately described the operation of the individual components and the power flow of single disc clutches.				
Student accurately described the operation of the individual components and the power flow of multiple disc clutches.				
Student accurately described the operation of the individual components and the power flow of wet disc(s) clutches.				
Non-Task-Specific Evaluation	**(0 pts)**	**(−1 pt)**	**(0 pts)**	**(−1 pt)**
Student successfully completed at least three of the non-task-specific steps.				
Student successfully completed all five of the non-task-specific steps.				
Total Score: <total # of points / 4 = %>				

Supervisor/Instructor:

Supervisor/instructor signature _____ Date _____

Comments:

Retest supervisor/instructor signature _____ Date _____

Comments:

CDX Tasksheet Number: 4.1d005a

Student/Intern Information

Name _____ Date _____ Class _____

Machine, Customer, and Service Information

Machine used for this activity:

Make _____ Model _____

Hours _____ Serial Number _____

Materials Required

- Vehicle with possible clutch concerns
- Vehicle manufacturer's service information
- Manufacturer-specific tools, depending on the concern

Task-Specific Safety Considerations

- This task may require test driving the vehicle on the school grounds or on a hoist, both of which carry severe risks. Attempt this task only with full permission from your supervisor/instructor and follow all the guidelines exactly.
- Comply with personal and environmental safety practices associated with clothing; eye protection; hand tools; power equipment; proper ventilation; and the handling, storage, and disposal of chemicals/materials in accordance with federal, state, and local regulations.
- Always wear the correct protective eyewear and clothing and use the appropriate safety equipment, as well as fender covers, seat protectors, and floor mat protectors.
- Make sure you understand and observe all legislative and personal safety procedures when carrying out practical assignments. If you are unsure of what these are, ask your supervisor/instructor.
- While working on the vehicle, wheel chocks must be placed on both sides of one set of tires or as directed by your supervisor/instructor.
- When running any vehicles in the shop, make sure you use the shop's exhaust ventilation system to discharge all exhaust gas safely outside.
- Lifting equipment such as vehicle jacks and stands, vehicle hoists, and engine hoists are important tools that increase productivity and make the job easier. However, they can also cause severe injury or death if used improperly. Make sure you follow the manufacturer's operation procedures. Also make sure you have your supervisor's/instructor's permission to use any particular type of lifting equipment.

▶ TASK Replace single-disc clutch pressure plate and clutch disc. **AED 4.1**

Time off _____

Time on _____

Student Instructions: Read through the entire procedure prior to starting. Prepare your workspace and any tools or parts that may be needed to complete the task. When directed by your supervisor/instructor, begin the procedure to complete the task, and comment or check the box as each step is finished. Track your time on this procedure for later comparison to the standard completion time (i.e., "flat rate" or customer pay time).

Total time _____

Procedure	Step Completed
1. Reference the manufacturer's service information for procedures to inspect, adjust, and replace the single-disc clutch pressure plate and clutch disc. You are looking specifically for the proper clutch pedal height, the proper clutch pedal free-play, and the procedure for making adjustments.	☐
a. Following the specified procedure, inspect the clutch linkage parts for damage, wear, or bent or missing components. Look for signs of binding, looseness, and excessive wear.	☐
b. Start with the clutch pedal assembly and inspect all components inside the cab. It is a good practice to operate the clutch pedal while you are inspecting the components to observe any looseness or binding.	☐
c. Check the clutch linkage components under the cab for the same signs as the components inside the cab.	☐
d. Measure the clutch pedal height and record it below: _____"	☐
i. Clutch pedal height is normally measured from the floor pan to the top of the clutch pedal pad with the clutch pedal released.	☐
ii. Make sure there are no floor mats or other obstructions that will affect the operation of the pedal.	☐
iii. Compare your reading with the manufacturer's specifications. Determine any necessary actions to correct any fault and describe them below:	☐
e. Measure the clutch pedal free-play and record it below: _____"	☐
i. Pedal free-play is normally measured from the top of the pedal at rest to where all play is taken up between the pedal and the pressure plate. This can be felt by hand or by foot.	☐
ii. Perform any adjustments needed, following the manufacturer's procedure.	☐
f. Start the vehicle and depress the clutch. The clutch should engage at the proper height and have the proper free-play.	☐
i. Make a gear selection to ensure the gears do not clash going into mesh.	☐
ii. While in gear, slowly release the clutch and see how far the clutch pedal must travel before the clutch starts to engage in forward motion.	☐
iii. If it is not within the manufacturer's specifications, determine any necessary actions to correct any fault and describe them below:	☐

2. Removing the manual transmission and clutch	
a. Remove the transmission shift lever and shift tower.	☐
i. Cover the opening of the transmission with a suitable device to prevent the ingress of any contaminants.	☐
b. Remove the driveshaft and mark the location of the drive and driven yokes so they can be realigned upon reinstallation.	☐
i. If the transmission has a removable slip yoke connecting it to the driveshaft, it may be advisable to drain the transmission fluid or use a dummy slip yoke to avoid fluid spills.	☐
ii. If separating a slip yoke, always mark the location of the two halves so they can be reassembled correctly.	☐
c. Disconnect the air supply and electrical connections from the transmission.	☐
i. If the clutch linkage has more than one possible mounting hole in the cross-shaft lever, mark the location and remove the linkage.	☐
ii. If the clutch has a hydraulic actuating system, remove the slave valve and support it by ties or wire.	☐
d. Support the transmission with a suitable jack. Note that the jack must have the correct attachments so that the transmission can be supported at its normal inclination. Use a safety chain to secure the transmission to the jack.	☐
e. Remove the transmission frame supports. Remove the bolts securing the transmission to the flywheel housing. Pull the transmission straight back.	☐
i. Use extreme caution to ensure the transmission does not hang down from the input shaft, as this could result in damage to the transmission and/or clutch discs.	☐
ii. Lower the jack and move the transmission out of the work area. Remove the clutch brake if equipped.	☐
iii. Inspect the clutch release fork and cross-shaft for wear and smooth operation.	☐
f. Before removing the clutch, inspect it to determine the type.	☐
i. An Eaton Solo® self-adjusting clutch, a SACH's Twin XTend™, or a Meritor AutoJust™ clutch will need to have shipping bolts installed before removal.	☐
ii. Failure to install the shipping bolts can lead to adjust mechanism damage and/or pressure plate warping.	☐
g. Install a clutch alignment tool to hold the disc(s) centered. If an alignment tool is unavailable, use an old input shaft.	☐
i. If using a clutch jack, use the alignment tool that comes with the jack. Clutches can weigh in excess of 175 lb (79.38 kg), so it is advisable to use a clutch jack to take the weight of the clutch. Also beware of pinch hazards as the clutch is being removed.	☐

h. On Eaton Solo®, SACH's Twin XTend™, or Meritor AutoJust™ clutches, install the four shipping bolts in the holes provided. Consult documentation from the original equipment manufacturer for the locations and sizes. Tighten bolts until they make contact, then turn one more turn.	☐
i. On all other clutches, use a clutch yoke tool to pull the release bearing back and install two ⅝" (1.6 cm) or larger wooden shipping blocks to remove the spring pressure from the pressure plate. Failure to do so may cause pressure plate warping.	☐
ii. Use a safety chain to secure the clutch to the jack.	☐
i. Remove the top two clutch-attaching bolts and replace them with guide studs. (**Note:** You can purchase guide studs or you can cut the top off a long bolt of the correct size and thread for the particular clutch you are working on and cut a slot in the end to accept a flat-tipped screwdriver.)	☐
j. Remove the rest of the attaching bolts following a crisscross pattern. If the clutch is not being replaced, mark the cover and the flywheel so the clutch can be reinstalled in the same location.	☐
k. Pry the clutch back on the guide studs and remove with the clutch jack.	☐
i. On a 14" (35.6 cm) clutch with a pot-style flywheel, the front friction disc and intermediate plate will likely stay in the flywheel, but be careful that they do not fall out. Use caution when you remove them from the flywheel.	☐
3. Inspect the removed clutch carefully for signs of abuse, such as abnormal overheating, burst clutch facing, cracked friction disc hubs, and excess wear on the release bearing wear pads. All of these signs can indicate clutch abuse. If any of these signs are present, make sure that the driver is notified so as not to repeat the failure.	☐
a. If the flywheel is to be sent for resurfacing, remove it now. Use guide studs in the top two flywheel-attaching bolt positions and use caution to avoid pinching when removing.	☐
b. Remove the pilot bearing using a driver or puller.	☐
4. Installing a single-disc clutch	
a. Install a new pilot bearing. Always replace the pilot bearing when replacing the clutch; the cost of replacing it is very small compared to the work required to replace it if it fails at a later date.	☐
b. Check that the clutch friction disc fits into the flywheel recess and does not contact the attaching bolts.	☐
c. Install two guide studs in the top two clutch-attaching holes. Test fit the clutch friction disc into the flywheel recess using the clutch alignment tool to center the disc.	☐
d. Clutch friction discs are stamped with either "flywheel side" or "pressure plate side" indications, so be sure to install the discs in the correct orientation.	☐
e. Install a clutch alignment tool through the clutch cover and install the disc on the tool splines.	☐

f. Slide the alignment tool through the clutch cover and the clutch disc. Then install the disc and the clutch cover/pressure plate assembly using the previously installed guide pins.	☐
g. To support the cover assembly, be sure the pilot of the alignment tool enters the pilot bearing bore.	☐
h. Install six attaching bolts in the open clutch-attaching holes until they are finger tight (tightened by hand without using a tool).	☐
i. Remove the guide studs and replace them with the other two attaching bolts until they are finger tight.	☐
i. Use an appropriate tool to tighten the bolts in a crisscross pattern, starting with one of the bottom bolts.	☐
ii. When all bolts are tight, torque them to the manufacturer's specification, using a crisscross pattern and starting with one of the bottom bolts.	☐
j. Once the plate is tightened, the alignment tool can be removed, as the clamped pressure plate will hold the friction disc(s) in place.	☐
k. Run the alignment tool into and out of mesh with the splines in the disc and the pilot bearing bore to ensure it does not hang up. That final check ensures that the transmission input shaft will slide easily into place.	☐
i. Some medium-duty push-type coil spring clutches may have wooden shipping blocks installed between the release levers and the clutch cover.	☐
ii. These blocks will be loosened as the clutch cover is tightened to the flywheel.	☐
iii. If they do not fall out by themselves, make sure you remove these blocks after installing the clutch cover.	☐
5. Reinstalling the transmission and adjusting the clutch	
a. In reverse order of disassembly, reinstall the transmission, then the flywheel housing bolts, then the frame supports, then the air and electrical connections, then the drive shaft, and, finally, the shift tower and shift lever. Adjust the clutch to the manufacturer's specifications.	☐
6. Return the vehicle to its beginning condition, and return any tools you used to their proper locations	☐
7. Discuss your findings with your supervisor/instructor.	☐

Non-Task-Specific Evaluation	Step Completed
1. Tools and equipment were used as directed and returned in good working order.	☐
2. Complied with all general and task-specific safety standards, including proper use of any personal protective equipment (PPE).	☐
3. Completed the task in an appropriate time frame (recommendation: 1.5 or 2 times the flat rate).	☐
4. Left the workspace clean and orderly.	☐
5. Cared for customer property and returned it undamaged.	☐

Student signature _____ Date _____

Comments:

Have your supervisor/instructor verify satisfactory completion of this procedure, any observations made, and any necessary action(s) recommended.

Evaluation Instructions: The scoring box below is intended to act as a guide for both student and supervisor/instructor. Each criterion listed will help students to understand what is expected of them and help supervisors/instructors to articulate the level of success at a particular task. The scoring is set up to allow a second attempt at each task (see the Test and Retest columns). Scoring is designed only to award students points for task criteria that were completed correctly. Points are lost for failure to complete the employability requirements (see Non-Task-Specific criteria). When all criteria are evaluated, tally the points for a total at the bottom of each column.

Tasksheet Scoring

Evaluation Items	Test		Retest	
	Pass	**Fail**	**Pass**	**Fail**
Task-Specific Evaluation	**(1 pt)**	**(0 pts)**	**(1 pt)**	**(0 pts)**
Student properly inspected the single-disc clutch pressure plate and clutch disc.				
Student properly removed the manual transmission and clutch and noted any signs of clutch abuse.				
Student properly installed the single-disc clutch.				
Student properly reinstalled the transmission and adjusted the clutch.				
Non-Task-Specific Evaluation	**(0 pts)**	**(−1 pt)**	**(0 pts)**	**(−1 pt)**
Student successfully completed at least three of the non-task-specific steps.				
Student successfully completed all five of the non-task-specific steps.				
Total Score: <total # of points / 4 = %>				

Supervisor/Instructor:

Supervisor/instructor signature _____ Date _____

Comments:

Retest supervisor/instructor signature _____ Date _____

Comments:

CDX Tasksheet Number: 4.1d005b

Student/Intern Information

Name _____ Date _____ Class _____

Machine, Customer, and Service Information

Machine used for this activity:

Make _____ Model _____

Hours _____ Serial Number _____

Task-Specific Safety Considerations
- This task may require test driving the vehicle on the school grounds or on a hoist, both of which carry severe risks. Attempt this task only with full permission from your supervisor/instructor and follow all the guidelines exactly.
- Comply with personal and environmental safety practices associated with clothing; eye protection; hand tools; power equipment; proper ventilation; and the handling, storage, and disposal of chemicals/materials in accordance with federal, state, and local regulations.
- Always wear the correct protective eyewear and clothing and use the appropriate safety equipment, as well as fender covers, seat protectors, and floor mat protectors.
- Make sure you understand and observe all legislative and personal safety procedures when carrying out practical assignments. If you are unsure of what these are, ask your supervisor/instructor.
- While working on the vehicle, wheel chocks must be placed on both sides of one set of tires or as directed by your supervisor/instructor.
- When running any vehicles in the shop, make sure you use the shop's exhaust ventilation system to discharge all exhaust gas safely outside.
- Lifting equipment such as vehicle jacks and stands, vehicle hoists, and engine hoists are important tools that increase productivity and make the job easier. However, they can also cause severe injury or death if used improperly. Make sure you follow the manufacturer's operation procedures. Also make sure you have your supervisor's/instructor's permission to use any particular type of lifting equipment.

▶ **TASK** Replace two-plate clutch pressure plate, clutch discs intermediate plate, and drive pins/lugs.

AED 4.1

Time off_____

Student Instructions: Read through the entire procedure prior to starting. Prepare your workspace and any tools or parts that may be needed to complete the task. When directed by your supervisor/instructor, begin the procedure to complete the task, and comment or check the box as each step is finished. Track your time on this procedure for later comparison to the standard completion time (i.e., "flat rate" or customer pay time).

Time on_____

Total time_____

Procedure	Step Completed
1. Reference the manufacturer's service information for procedures to inspect, adjust, and replace the two-plate clutch pressure plate, clutch discs intermediate plate, and drive pins/lugs.	☐
a. Following the specified procedure, inspect the clutch linkage parts for damage, wear, or bent or missing components. Look for signs of binding, looseness, and excessive wear.	☐
b. Remove the clutch bell housing inspection cover. Bump the engine over until the clutch adjusting mechanism is in line with the opening.	☐
c. Insert a 0.010" feeler gauge between the clutch brake and the transmission front bearing cover. Have an assistant depress the clutch pedal as far as it will go while you clamp the feeler gauge.	☐
d. Have your assistant measure and record the distance the clutch pedal is from the floor of the cab.	☐
i. Tell the assistant to slowly let the pedal up until you can pull the feeler gauge from between the clutch brake and the bearing cover. Then tell them to stop and measure the pedal distance from the floor again.	☐
ii. The difference between the two measurements is the clutch brake squeeze dimension. It should be between 0.5" and 1" (1.27–2.54 cm).	☐
iii. If this dimension is correct, a linkage adjustment is not required. (A linkage adjustment is very rarely required on a pull-type clutch.)	☐
e. Check the distance between the back of the release bearing and the clutch brake.	☐
i. This release bearing free travel dimension should be approximately 0.5" (1.27 cm). As the clutch disc wears, that dimension will increase.	☐
f. To adjust the clutch for wear and reduce the release bearing-free travel dimension, have an assistant hold the clutch pedal down to release the clutch clamp load.	☐
i. Use a wrench to push down on the quick-adjust bolt, if equipped, and turn the bolt clockwise 1/2" turn.	☐
ii. Then let the pedal up and recheck the release bearing-free travel dimension as you did previously. Always ensure that the quick-adjust bolt returns to the out (locked) position after adjustment is complete.	☐
iii. If the clutch does not have a quick-adjust bolt, remove the lock strap and turn the large adjusting ring clockwise one notch at a time while your assistant holds the clutch pedal down. Then recheck the dimension.	☐
g. After correcting the release bearing free travel dimension to be 0.5" (1.27 cm), check that the clearance between the release fork fingers and the contact patches on the release bearing is 1/8" (3.175 mm).	☐
i. This dimension gets smaller as the clutch disc wears and will have gotten larger as the release bearing free travel dimension is corrected for wear.	☐

ii. If this dimension is not correct and the release bearing free travel is correct, then a linkage adjustment may be required. (**Note:** Be aware that increasing the fork-to-bearing clearance by adjusting the linkage will decrease the clutch brake squeeze dimension and vice versa.)	☐
h. Lubricate the release bearing until lubricant purges out the back of the bearing sleeve onto the input shaft. Reinstall the inspection cover.	☐
i. Measure and record the pedal-free travel in the cab. (**Note:** Some hydraulic actuation systems will have little or no pedal-free travel.)	☐
ii. This measurement is the normal pedal-free travel. Inform the driver to have the clutch readjusted when this dimension decreases by half.	☐
2. Removing the manual transmission and clutch	
a. Remove the transmission shift lever and shift tower.	☐
i. Cover the opening of the transmission with a suitable device to prevent the ingress of any contaminants.	☐
b. Remove the driveshaft and mark the location of the drive and driven yokes so they can be realigned upon reinstallation.	☐
i. If the transmission has a removable slip yoke connecting it to the driveshaft, it may be advisable to drain the transmission fluid or use a dummy slip yoke to avoid fluid spills.	☐
ii. If separating a slip yoke, always mark the location of the two halves so they can be reassembled correctly.	☐
c. Disconnect the air supply and electrical connections from the transmission.	☐
i. If the clutch linkage has more than one possible mounting hole in the cross-shaft lever, mark the location and remove the linkage.	☐
ii. If the clutch has a hydraulic actuating system, remove the slave valve and support it by ties or wire.	☐
d. Support the transmission with a suitable jack. Note that the jack must have the correct attachments so that the transmission can be supported at its normal inclination. Use a safety chain to secure the transmission to the jack.	☐
e. Remove the transmission frame supports. Remove the bolts securing the transmission to the flywheel housing. Pull the transmission straight back.	☐
i. Use extreme caution to ensure the transmission does not hang down from the input shaft, as this could result in damage to the transmission and/or clutch discs.	☐
ii. Lower the jack and move the transmission out of the work area. Remove the clutch brake if equipped.	☐
iii. Inspect the clutch release fork and cross-shaft for wear and smooth operation.	☐

f. Before removing the clutch, inspect it to determine the type.	☐
i. An Eaton Solo® self-adjusting clutch, a SACH's Twin XTend™, or a Meritor AutoJust™ clutch will need to have shipping bolts installed before removal.	☐
ii. Failure to install the shipping bolts can lead to adjust mechanism damage and/or warping of the pressure plate.	☐
g. Install a clutch alignment tool to hold the disc(s) centered. If an alignment tool is unavailable, use an old input shaft.	☐
i. If using a clutch jack, use the alignment tool that comes with the jack. Clutches can weigh in excess of 175 lb (79.38 kg), so it is advisable to use a clutch jack to take the weight of the clutch. Also beware of pinch hazards as the clutch is being removed.	☐
h. Remove the top two clutch-attaching bolts and replace them with guide studs. (**Note:** You can purchase guide studs or you can cut the top off a long bolt of the correct size and thread for the particular clutch you are working on and cut a slot in the end to accept a flat-tipped screwdriver.)	☐
i. Remove the rest of the attaching bolts following a crisscross pattern. If the clutch is not being replaced, mark the cover and the flywheel so the clutch can be reinstalled in the same location.	☐
j. Pry the clutch back on the guide studs and remove with the clutch jack.	☐
3. Inspect the removed clutch carefully for signs of abuse, such as abnormal overheating, burst clutch facing, cracked friction disc hubs, and excess wear on the release bearing wear pads. All of these signs can indicate clutch abuse. If any of these signs are present, make sure that the driver is notified so as not to repeat the failure.	☐
a. If the flywheel is to be sent for resurfacing, remove it now. Use guide studs in the top two flywheel-attaching bolt positions and use caution to avoid pinching when removing.	☐
b. Remove the pilot bearing using a driver or puller.	☐
4. Installing a dual disc clutch	
a. Install a new pilot bearing. Always replace the pilot bearing when replacing the clutch; the cost of replacing it is very small compared to the work required to replace it if it fails at a later date.	☐
b. Check that the clutch friction disc fits into the flywheel recess and does not contact the attaching bolts.	☐
c. Install two guide studs in the top two clutch-attaching holes. Test fit the clutch friction disc into the flywheel recess using the clutch alignment tool to center the disc. If the fit is proper, proceed with assembly. If there is interference, make needed corrections.	☐
d. Install the correct alignment spline on the jack, then install the release bearing and clutch cover over the alignment spline.	☐
e. When installing the rear friction disc on the alignment spline, make sure the side stamped "pressure plate" goes toward the clutch cover.	☐

f. Install the intermediate plate and check that it moves smoothly into and out of the clutch cover drive slots.	☐
g. Install the front friction disc with the side marked "flywheel" toward the engine flywheel.	☐
h. Using the jack, raise the complete clutch into position and slide the clutch cover over the two guide studs, ensuring that the alignment tool pilot enters the pilot bearing bore in the flywheel.	☐
i. Install six attaching bolts in the open attaching holes and tighten them until they are finger tight (tightened by hand without using a tool). Remove the guide studs and replace them with the other two attaching bolts, again, until they are finger tight.	☐
i. Use an appropriate tool to tighten the bolts in a crisscross pattern starting with one of the bottom bolts. When all bolts are tight, torque them to the manufacturer's specification, using a crisscross pattern and starting with one of the bottom bolts.	☐
ii. Make sure that the wooden shipping blocks fall out. If they do not, use a release bearing pulling tool to move the bearing until they do.	☐
j. Once the plate is tightened, the alignment tool and jack can be removed, as the clamped pressure plate will hold the friction disc(s) in place.	☐
k. Run the alignment tool into and out of mesh with the splines in the disc and the pilot bearing bore to ensure it does not hang up. That final check ensures that the transmission input shaft will slide easily into place.	☐
5. Reinstalling the transmission and adjusting the clutch	
a. In reverse order of disassembly, reinstall the transmission, then the flywheel housing bolts, then the frame supports, then the air and electrical connections, then the drive shaft, and, finally, the shift tower and shift lever. Adjust the clutch to the manufacturer's specifications.	☐
6. Return the vehicle to its beginning condition, and return any tools you used to their proper locations.	☐
7. Discuss your findings with your supervisor/instructor.	☐

Non-Task-Specific Evaluation	Step Completed
1. Tools and equipment were used as directed and returned in good working order.	☐
2. Complied with all general and task-specific safety standards, including proper use of any personal protective equipment (PPE).	☐
3. Completed the task in an appropriate time frame (recommendation: 1.5 or 2 times the flat rate).	☐
4. Left the workspace clean and orderly.	☐
5. Cared for customer property and returned it undamaged.	☐

Student signature _____ Date _____

Comments:

Have your supervisor/instructor verify satisfactory completion of this procedure, any observations made, and any necessary action(s) recommended.

Evaluation Instructions: The scoring box below is intended to act as a guide for both student and supervisor/instructor. Each criterion listed will help students to understand what is expected of them and help supervisors/instructors to articulate the level of success at a particular task. The scoring is set up to allow a second attempt at each task (see the Test and Retest columns). Scoring is designed only to award students points for task criteria that were completed correctly. Points are lost for failure to complete the employability requirements (see Non-Task-Specific criteria). When all criteria are evaluated, tally the points for a total at the bottom of each column.

Tasksheet Scoring

Evaluation Items	Test Pass	Test Fail	Retest Pass	Retest Fail
Task-Specific Evaluation	**(1 pt)**	**(0 pts)**	**(1 pt)**	**(0 pts)**
Student properly inspected the two-plate clutch pressure plate, clutch discs intermediate plate, and drive pins/lugs.				
Student properly removed the manual transmission and the clutch and noted any signs of clutch abuse.				
Student properly installed the dual-disc clutch.				
Student properly reinstalled the transmission and adjusted the clutch.				
Non–Task-Specific Evaluation	**(0 pts)**	**(−1 pt)**	**(0 pts)**	**(−1 pt)**
Student successfully completed at least three of the non-task-specific steps.				
Student successfully completed all five of the non-task-specific steps.				
Total Score: <total # of points / 4 = %>				

Supervisor/Instructor:

Supervisor/instructor signature _____ Date _____

Comments:

Retest supervisor/instructor signature _____ Date _____

Comments:

CDX Tasksheet Number: 4.1d007

Student/Intern Information

Name _____ Date _____ Class _____

Machine, Customer, and Service Information

Machine used for this activity:

Make _____ Model _____

Hours _____ Serial Number _____

Materials Required
- Vehicle manufacturer's service information

Task-Specific Safety Considerations
- This task may require test driving the vehicle on the school grounds or on a hoist, both of which carry severe risks. Attempt this task only with full permission from your supervisor/instructor and follow all the guidelines exactly.
- Comply with personal and environmental safety practices associated with clothing; eye protection; hand tools; power equipment; proper ventilation; and the handling, storage, and disposal of chemicals/materials in accordance with federal, state, and local regulations.
- Always wear the correct protective eyewear and clothing and use the appropriate safety equipment, as well as fender covers, seat protectors, and floor mat protectors.
- Make sure you understand and observe all legislative and personal safety procedures when carrying out practical assignments. If you are unsure of what these are, ask your supervisor/instructor.
- While working on the vehicle, wheel chocks must be placed on both sides of one set of tires or as directed by your supervisor/instructor.
- When running any vehicles in the shop, make sure you use the shop's exhaust ventilation system to discharge all exhaust gas safely outside.

▶ **TASK** Explain overrunning clutch operation.   **AED 4.1**

Time off_____

Student Instructions: Read through the entire procedure prior to starting. Prepare your workspace and any tools or parts that may be needed to complete the task. When directed by your supervisor/instructor, begin the procedure to complete the task, and comment or check the box as each step is finished. Track your time on this procedure for later comparison to the standard completion time (i.e., "flat rate" or customer pay time).

Time on_____

Total time_____

Procedure	Step Completed
(**Note:** Lab fixtures/instructional aids may be used for this task.)	
1. Using available service literature as a guide, describe the individual components of an overrunning clutch in order of operation.	
a. Component #1	☐
b. Component #2	☐
c. Component #3	☐
d. Component #4	☐
e. Component #5 (if applicable)	☐
f. Component #6 (if applicable)	☐
g. Component #7 (if applicable)	☐
h. Component #8 (if applicable)	☐

i. Component #9 (if applicable)	☐
j. Component #10 (if applicable)	☐
2. Using available service literature as a guide, describe the power flow of an overrunning clutch:	☐
3. Describe the application(s) of an overrunning clutch:	☐
4. Discuss your findings with your supervisor/instructor.	☐

Non-Task-Specific Evaluation	Step Completed
1. Tools and equipment were used as directed and returned in good working order.	☐
2. Complied with all general and task-specific safety standards, including proper use of any personal protective equipment (PPE).	☐
3. Completed the task in an appropriate time frame (recommendation: 1.5 or 2 times the flat rate).	☐
4. Left the workspace clean and orderly.	☐
5. Cared for customer property and returned it undamaged.	☐

Student signature _____ Date _____

Comments:

Have your supervisor/instructor verify satisfactory completion of this procedure, any observations made,

and any necessary action(s) recommended.

Evaluation Instructions: The scoring box below is intended to act as a guide for both student and supervisor/instructor. Each criterion listed will help students to understand what is expected of them and help supervisors/instructors to articulate the level of success at a particular task. The scoring is set up to allow a second attempt at each task (see the Test and Retest columns). Scoring is designed only to award students points for task criteria that were completed correctly. Points are lost for failure to complete the employability requirements (see Non-Task-Specific criteria). When all criteria are evaluated, tally the points for a total at the bottom of each column.

Tasksheet Scoring

	Test		Retest	
Evaluation Items	**Pass**	**Fail**	**Pass**	**Fail**
Task-Specific Evaluation	**(1 pt)**	**(O pts)**	**(1 pt)**	**(O pts)**
Student correctly listed the individual components of an overrunning clutch in order of operation.				
Student accurately described the individual components of an overrunning clutch.				
Student accurately described the power flow of an overrunning clutch.				
Student accurately described the application(s) of an overrunning clutch.				
Non-Task-Specific Evaluation	**(O pts)**	**(−1 pt)**	**(O pts)**	**(−1 pt)**
Student successfully completed at least three of the non-task-specific steps.				
Student successfully completed all five of the non-task-specific steps.				
Total Score: <total # of points / 4 = %>				

CDX Tasksheet Number: 4.1d008

Student/Intern Information

Name _____ Date _____ Class _____

Machine, Customer, and Service Information

Machine used for this activity:

Make _____ Model _____

Hours _____ Serial Number _____

Materials Required
- Vehicle manufacturer's service information

Task-Specific Safety Considerations
- This task may require test driving the vehicle on the school grounds or on a hoist, both of which carry severe risks. Attempt this task only with full permission from your supervisor/instructor and follow all the guidelines exactly.
- Comply with personal and environmental safety practices associated with clothing; eye protection; hand tools; power equipment; proper ventilation; and the handling, storage, and disposal of chemicals/materials in accordance with federal, state, and local regulations.
- Always wear the correct protective eyewear and clothing and use the appropriate safety equipment, as well as fender covers, seat protectors, and floor mat protectors.
- Make sure you understand and observe all legislative and personal safety procedures when carrying out practical assignments. If you are unsure of what these are, ask your supervisor/instructor.
- While working on the vehicle, wheel chocks must be placed on both sides of one set of tires or as directed by your supervisor/instructor.
- When running any vehicles in the shop, make sure you use the shop's exhaust ventilation system to discharge all exhaust gas safely outside.

▶ TASK Explain magnetic-type clutch operation. **AED** 4.1

Time off_____

Time on_____

Student Instructions: Read through the entire procedure prior to starting. Prepare your workspace and any tools or parts that may be needed to complete the task. When directed by your supervisor/instructor, begin the procedure to complete the task, and comment or check the box as each step is finished. Track your time on this procedure for later comparison to the standard completion time (i.e., "flat rate" or customer pay time).

Total time_____

Procedure	Step Completed
(**Note:** Lab fixtures/instructional aids may be used for this task.)	
1. Using available service literature as a guide, describe the individual components of a magnetic-type clutch in order of operation.	
a. Component #1	☐
b. Component #2	☐
c. Component #3	☐
d. Component #4	☐
e. Component #5 (if applicable)	☐
f. Component #6 (if applicable)	☐
g. Component #7 (if applicable)	☐
h. Component #8 (if applicable)	☐
i. Component #9 (if applicable)	☐

	Step Completed
j. Component #10 (if applicable)	☐
2. Using available service literature as a guide, describe the power flow of a magnetic-type clutch:	☐
3. Describe the application(s) of a magnetic-type clutch:	☐
4. Discuss your findings with your supervisor/instructor.	☐

Non-Task-Specific Evaluation	Step Completed
1. Tools and equipment were used as directed and returned in good working order.	☐
2. Complied with all general and task-specific safety standards, including proper use of any personal protective equipment (PPE).	☐
3. Completed the task in an appropriate time frame (recommendation: 1.5 or 2 times the flat rate).	☐
4. Left the workspace clean and orderly.	☐
5. Cared for customer property and returned it undamaged.	☐

Student signature _____ Date _____

Comments:

Have your supervisor/instructor verify satisfactory completion of this procedure, any observations made, and any necessary action(s) recommended.

Evaluation Instructions: The scoring box below is intended to act as a guide for both student and supervisor/instructor. Each criterion listed will help students to understand what is expected of them and help supervisors/instructors to articulate the level of success at a particular task. The scoring is set up to allow a second attempt at each task (see the Test and Retest columns). Scoring is designed only to award students points for task criteria that were completed correctly. Points are lost for failure to complete the employability requirements (see Non-Task-Specific criteria). When all criteria are evaluated, tally the points for a total at the bottom of each column.

Tasksheet Scoring

Evaluation Items	Test		Retest	
	Pass	**Fail**	**Pass**	**Fail**
Task-Specific Evaluation	**(1 pt)**	**(0 pts)**	**(1 pt)**	**(0 pts)**
Student correctly listed the individual components of a magnetic-type clutch in order of operation.				
Student accurately described the individual components of a magnetic-type clutch.				
Student accurately described the power flow of a magnetic-type clutch.				
Student accurately described the application(s) of a magnetic-type clutch.				
Non-Task-Specific Evaluation	**(0 pts)**	**(−1 pt)**	**(0 pts)**	**(−1 pt)**
Student successfully completed at least three of the non-task-specific steps.				
Student successfully completed all five of the non-task-specific steps.				
Total Score: <total # of points / 4 = %>				

Supervisor/Instructor:

Supervisor/instructor signature _____ Date _____

Comments:

```

```

Retest supervisor/instructor signature _____ Date _____

Comments:

```

```

CDX Tasksheet Number: 4.1e001

Student/Intern Information

Name _____ Date _____ Class _____

Machine, Customer, and Service Information

Machine used for this activity:

Make _____ Model _____

Hours _____ Serial Number _____

Materials Required
- Vehicle manufacturer's service information

Task-Specific Safety Considerations
- This task may require test driving the vehicle on the school grounds or on a hoist, both of which carry severe risks. Attempt this task only with full permission from your supervisor/instructor and follow all the guidelines exactly.
- Comply with personal and environmental safety practices associated with clothing; eye protection; hand tools; power equipment; proper ventilation; and the handling, storage, and disposal of chemicals/materials in accordance with federal, state, and local regulations.
- Always wear the correct protective eyewear and clothing and use the appropriate safety equipment, as well as fender covers, seat protectors, and floor mat protectors.
- Make sure you understand and observe all legislative and personal safety procedures when carrying out practical assignments. If you are unsure of what these are, ask your supervisor/instructor.
- While working on the vehicle, wheel chocks must be placed on both sides of one set of tires or as directed by your supervisor/instructor.
- When running any vehicles in the shop, make sure you use the shop's exhaust ventilation system to discharge all exhaust gas safely outside.

▶ **TASK** Explain modulating clutch operation. **AED 4.1**

Time off_____

Student Instructions: Read through the entire procedure prior to starting. Prepare your workspace and any tools or parts that may be needed to complete the task. When directed by your supervisor/instructor, begin the procedure to complete the task, and comment or check the box as each step is finished. Track your time on this procedure for later comparison to the standard completion time (i.e., "flat rate" or customer pay time).

Time on_____

Total time_____

Procedure	Step Completed
1. Using available service literature as a guide, describe the individual components of a modulating-type clutch in order of operation.	
a. Component #1	☐
b. Component #2	☐
c. Component #3	☐
d. Component #4	☐
e. Component #5 (if applicable)	☐
f. Component #6 (if applicable)	☐
g. Component #7 (if applicable)	☐
h. Component #8 (if applicable)	☐

	Step Completed
i. Component #9 (if applicable)	☐
j. Component #10 (if applicable)	☐
2. Using available service literature as a guide, describe the power flow of a modulating-type clutch:	☐
3. Describe the application(s) of a modulating-type clutch:	☐
4. Discuss your findings with your supervisor/instructor.	☐

Non-Task-Specific Evaluation	Step Completed
1. Tools and equipment were used as directed and returned in good working order.	☐
2. Complied with all general and task-specific safety standards, including proper use of any personal protective equipment (PPE).	☐
3. Completed the task in an appropriate time frame (recommendation: 1.5 or 2 times the flat rate).	☐
4. Left the workspace clean and orderly.	☐
5. Cared for customer property and returned it undamaged.	☐

Student signature _____ Date _____

Comments:

Have your supervisor/instructor verify satisfactory completion of this procedure, any observations made,

and any necessary action(s) recommended.

Evaluation Instructions: The scoring box below is intended to act as a guide for both student and supervisor/instructor. Each criterion listed will help students to understand what is expected of them and help supervisors/instructors to articulate the level of success at a particular task. The scoring is set up to allow a second attempt at each task (see the Test and Retest columns). Scoring is designed only to award students points for task criteria that were completed correctly. Points are lost for failure to complete the employability requirements (see Non-Task-Specific criteria). When all criteria are evaluated, tally the points for a total at the bottom of each column.

Tasksheet Scoring

Evaluation Items	Test		Retest	
	Pass	**Fail**	**Pass**	**Fail**
Task-Specific Evaluation	**(1 pt)**	**(0 pts)**	**(1 pt)**	**(0 pts)**
Student correctly listed the individual components of a modulating-type clutch in order of operation.				
Student accurately described the individual components of a modulating-type clutch.				
Student accurately described the power flow of a modulating-type clutch.				
Student accurately described the application(s) of a modulating-type clutch.				
Non-Task-Specific Evaluation	**(0 pts)**	**(−1 pt)**	**(0 pts)**	**(−1 pt)**
Student successfully completed at least three of the non-task-specific steps.				
Student successfully completed all five of the non-task-specific steps.				
Total Score: <total # of points / 4 = %>				

Supervisor/Instructor:

Supervisor/instructor signature _____ Date _____

Comments:

Retest supervisor/instructor signature _____ Date _____

Comments:

Chapter 33: Theory and Principles of Hydrostatic Transmissions

Learning Objective/Task	CDX Tasksheet Number	AED Reference Number
• Perform hydrostatic calibration procedure.	4.1f004	AED 4.1

Materials Required
- Vehicle with possible hydrostatic drive concerns
- Vehicle manufacturer's service information and/or component manufacturer's manuals
- Manufacturer-specific tools, depending on the concern

Safety Considerations
- This task may require test driving the vehicle on the school grounds or on a hoist, both of which carry severe risks. Attempt this task only with full permission from your supervisor/instructor and follow all the guidelines exactly.
- Comply with personal and environmental safety practices associated with clothing; eye protection; hand tools; power equipment; proper ventilation; and the handling, storage, and disposal of chemicals/materials in accordance with federal, state, and local regulations.
- Always wear the correct protective eyewear and clothing and use the appropriate safety equipment, as well as fender covers, seat protectors, and floor mat protectors.
- Make sure you understand and observe all legislative and personal safety procedures when carrying out practical assignments. If you are unsure of what these are, ask your supervisor/instructor.
- While working on the vehicle, wheel chocks must be placed on both sides of one set of tires or as directed by your supervisor/instructor.
- When running any vehicles in the shop, make sure you use the shop's exhaust ventilation system to discharge all exhaust gas safely outside.

CDX Tasksheet Number: 4.1f004

Student/Intern Information

Name _____ Date _____ Class _____

Machine, Customer, and Service Information

Machine used for this activity:

Make _____ Model _____

Hours _____ Serial Number _____

Materials Required
- Vehicle with possible hydrostatic drive concerns
- Vehicle manufacturer's service information and/or component manufacturer's manuals
- Manufacturer-specific tools, depending on the concern

Task-Specific Safety Considerations
- This task may require test driving the vehicle on the school grounds or on a hoist, both of which carry severe risks. Attempt this task only with full permission from your supervisor/instructor and follow all the guidelines exactly.
- Comply with personal and environmental safety practices associated with clothing; eye protection; hand tools; power equipment; proper ventilation; and the handling, storage, and disposal of chemicals/materials in accordance with federal, state, and local regulations.
- Always wear the correct protective eyewear and clothing and use the appropriate safety equipment, as well as fender covers, seat protectors, and floor mat protectors.
- Make sure you understand and observe all legislative and personal safety procedures when carrying out practical assignments. If you are unsure of what these are, ask your supervisor/instructor.
- While working on the vehicle, wheel chocks must be placed on both sides of one set of tires or as directed by your supervisor/instructor.
- When running any vehicles in the shop, make sure you use the shop's exhaust ventilation system to discharge all exhaust gas safely outside.

▶ TASK Perform hydrostatic calibration procedure. _____ **AED** 4.1

Student Instructions: Read through the entire procedure prior to starting. Prepare your workspace and any tools or parts that may be needed to complete the task. When directed by your supervisor/instructor, begin the procedure to complete the task, and comment or check the box as each step is finished. Track your time on this procedure for later comparison to the standard completion time (i.e., "flat rate" or customer pay time).

Time off_____

Time on_____

Total time_____

Procedure	Step Completed
1. Reference the manufacturer's repair information and/or component manufacturer's manuals for procedures to calibrate system.	☐
2. Warm the hydraulic fluid to at least 130° F.	☐
3. Turn the ignition ON but do not start the machine.	☐
4. Move the left joystick to farthest left and forward position and hold.	☐
5. Press the "Press to Operate" button.	☐
6. Move the left joystick to the back and right and hold.	☐
7. Press the "Press to Operate" button.	☐
8. Allow the joystick to return to neutral. After three beeps, start the engine and move to high idle.	☐
9. Move the joystick to full forward and hold.	☐
a. The wheels will rotate slightly forward up to five times, then rotate at full speed, and then stop.	☐
10. Release the joystick when you hear a beep.	☐
11. Move the joystick to full reverse and hold.	☐
a. The wheels will rotate slightly rearward up to five times, then rotate at full speed, and then stop.	☐
12. Release the joystick when you hear a beep. Calibration is now complete.	☐
13. Discuss your findings with your supervisor/instructor.	☐

Non-Task-Specific Evaluation	Step Completed
1. Tools and equipment were used as directed and returned in good working order.	☐
2. Complied with all general and task-specific safety standards, including proper use of any personal protective equipment (PPE).	☐
3. Completed the task in an appropriate time frame (recommendation: 1.5 or 2 times the flat rate).	☐
4. Left the workspace clean and orderly.	☐
5. Cared for customer property and returned it undamaged.	☐

Student signature _____ Date _____

Comments:

Have your supervisor/instructor verify satisfactory completion of this procedure, any observations made, and any necessary action(s) recommended.

Evaluation Instructions: The scoring box below is intended to act as a guide for both student and supervisor/instructor. Each criterion listed will help students to understand what is expected of them and help supervisors/instructors to articulate the level of success at a particular task. The scoring is set up to allow a second attempt at each task (see the Test and Retest columns). Scoring is designed only to award students points for task criteria that were completed correctly. Points are lost for failure to complete the employability requirements (see Non-Task-Specific criteria). When all criteria are evaluated, tally the points for a total at the bottom of each column.

Tasksheet Scoring

	Test		Retest	
Evaluation Items	**Pass**	**Fail**	**Pass**	**Fail**
Task-Specific Evaluation	**(1 pt)**	**(0 pts)**	**(1 pt)**	**(0 pts)**
Student used the manufacturer's repair information.				
Student held the joystick in the correct position for each step.				
Student waited for the correct signal (i.e., hearing a beep, wheels rotating) before moving on to the next step.				
Student accurately performed the full calibration process as directed by the supervisor/instructor.				
Non-Task-Specific Evaluation	**(0 pts)**	**(−1 pt)**	**(0 pts)**	**(−1 pt)**
Student successfully completed at least three of the non-task-specific steps.				
Student successfully completed all five of the non-task-specific steps.				
Total Score: <total # of points / 4 = %>				

Supervisor/Instructor:

Supervisor/instructor signature _____ Date _____

Comments:

Retest supervisor/instructor signature _____ Date _____

Comments:

Chapter 34: Driveshaft Function and Construction

Learning Objective/Task	CDX Tasksheet Number	AED Reference Number
• Identify driveshaft components.	4.2a001a	AED 4.2
• Adjust the driveline angles.	4.2a001b	AED 4.2
• Identify drivetrain failures.	4.2a001c	AED 4.2

Materials Required
- Manufacturer's workshop materials
- Manufacturer-specific tools, depending on the concern/procedure(s)
- Vehicle/component lifting equipment, if applicable

Safety Considerations
- This task may require test driving the vehicle on the school grounds or on a hoist, both of which carry severe risks. Attempt this task only with full permission from your supervisor/instructor and follow all the guidelines exactly.
- Lifting equipment such as vehicle jacks and stands, vehicle hoists, and engine hoists are important tools that increase productivity and make the job easier. However, they can also cause severe injury or death if used improperly. Make sure you follow the manufacturer's operation procedures. Also make sure you have your supervisor's/instructor's permission to use any particular type of lifting equipment.
- Comply with personal and environmental safety practices associated with clothing; eye protection; hand tools; power equipment; proper ventilation; and the handling, storage, and disposal of chemicals/materials in accordance with federal, state, and local regulations.
- Always wear the correct protective eyewear and clothing and use the appropriate safety equipment, as well as wheel chocks, fender covers, seat protectors, and floor mat protectors.
- Make sure you understand and observe all legislative and personal safety procedures when carrying out practical assignments. If you are unsure of what these are, ask your supervisor/instructor.

CDX Tasksheet Number: 4.2a001a

Student/Intern Information

Name _____ Date _____ Class _____

Machine, Customer, and Service Information

Machine used for this activity:

Make _____ Model _____

Hours _____ Serial Number _____

> ## Materials Required
> - Manufacturer's workshop materials
> - Manufacturer-specific tools, depending on the concern/procedure(s)
> - Vehicle/component lifting equipment, if applicable

Task-Specific Safety Considerations

- This task may require test driving the vehicle on the school grounds or on a hoist, both of which carry severe risks. Attempt this task only with full permission from your supervisor/instructor and follow all the guidelines exactly.
- Lifting equipment such as vehicle jacks and stands, vehicle hoists, and engine hoists are important tools that increase productivity and make the job easier. However, they can also cause severe injury or death if used improperly. Make sure you follow the manufacturer's operation procedures. Also make sure you have your supervisor's/instructor's permission to use any particular type of lifting equipment.
- Comply with personal and environmental safety practices associated with clothing; eye protection; hand tools; power equipment; proper ventilation; and the handling, storage, and disposal of chemicals/materials in accordance with federal, state, and local regulations.
- Always wear the correct protective eyewear and clothing and use the appropriate safety equipment, as well as wheel chocks, fender covers, seat protectors, and floor mat protectors.
- Make sure you understand and observe all legislative and personal safety procedures when carrying out practical assignments. If you are unsure of what these are, ask your supervisor/instructor.

▶ **TASK** Identify driveshaft components. **AED 4.2**

Time off_____

Time on_____

Student Instructions: Read through the entire procedure prior to starting. Prepare your workspace and any tools or parts that may be needed to complete the task. When directed by your supervisor/instructor, begin the procedure to complete the task, and comment or check the box as each step is finished. Track your time on this procedure for later comparison to the standard completion time (i.e., "flat rate" or customer pay time).

Total time_____

Procedure	Step Completed
1. Identify the following driveshaft components that have been labeled and displayed by your supervisor/instructor and describe their function.	
a. Tube	☐
b. Tube yoke	☐
c. End yoke	☐
d. Flange yoke	☐
e. Slip joint	☐
f. Coupling shaft	☐
g. Universal joint	☐
h. Pillow block	☐
2. Discuss your findings with your supervisor/instructor.	☐

Non-Task-Specific Evaluation	Step Completed
1. Tools and equipment were used as directed and returned in good working order.	☐
2. Complied with all general and task-specific safety standards, including proper use of any personal protective equipment (PPE).	☐
3. Completed the task in an appropriate time frame (recommendation: 1.5 or 2 times the flat rate).	☐
4. Left the workspace clean and orderly.	☐
5. Cared for customer property and returned it undamaged.	☐

Student signature _____ Date _____

Comments:

Have your supervisor/instructor verify satisfactory completion of this procedure, any observations made, and any necessary action(s) recommended.

Evaluation Instructions: The scoring box below is intended to act as a guide for both student and supervisor/instructor. Each criterion listed will help students to understand what is expected of them and help supervisors/instructors to articulate the level of success at a particular task. The scoring is set up to allow a second attempt at each task (see the Test and Retest columns). Scoring is designed only to award students points for task criteria that were completed correctly. Points are lost for failure to complete the employability requirements (see Non-Task-Specific criteria). When all criteria are evaluated, tally the points for a total at the bottom of each column.

Tasksheet Scoring

Evaluation Items	Test		Retest	
	Pass	**Fail**	**Pass**	**Fail**
Task-Specific Evaluation	**(1 pt)**	**(0 pts)**	**(1 pt)**	**(0 pts)**
Student correctly identified at least four drive-shaft components.				
Student correctly identified all eight driveshaft components.				
Student properly described the functions of at least four driveshaft components.				
Student properly described the functions of all eight driveshaft components.				
Non-Task-Specific Evaluation	**(0 pts)**	**(−1 pt)**	**(0 pts)**	**(−1 pt)**
Student successfully completed at least three of the non-task-specific steps.				
Student successfully completed all five of the non-task-specific steps.				
Total Score: <total # of points / 4 = %>				

CDX Tasksheet Number: 4.2a001b

Student/Intern Information

Name _____ Date _____ Class _____

Machine, Customer, and Service Information

Machine used for this activity:

Make _____ Model _____

Hours _____ Serial Number _____

Materials Required
- Manufacturer's workshop materials
- Manufacturer-specific tools, depending on the concern/procedure(s)
- Vehicle/component lifting equipment, if applicable

Task-Specific Safety Considerations
- This task may require test driving the vehicle on the school grounds or on a hoist, both of which carry severe risks. Attempt this task only with full permission from your supervisor/instructor and follow all the guidelines exactly.
- Lifting equipment such as vehicle jacks and stands, vehicle hoists, and engine hoists are important tools that increase productivity and make the job easier. However, they can also cause severe injury or death if used improperly. Make sure you follow the manufacturer's operation procedures. Also make sure you have your supervisor's/instructor's permission to use any particular type of lifting equipment.
- Comply with personal and environmental safety practices associated with clothing; eye protection; hand tools; power equipment; proper ventilation; and the handling, storage, and disposal of chemicals/materials in accordance with federal, state, and local regulations.
- Always wear the correct protective eyewear and clothing and use the appropriate safety equipment, as well as wheel chocks, fender covers, seat protectors, and floor mat protectors.
- Make sure you understand and observe all legislative and personal safety procedures when carrying out practical assignments. If you are unsure of what these are, ask your supervisor/instructor.

▶ **TASK** Adjust the driveline angles.   **AED 4.2**

Time off_____

Time on_____

Student Instructions: Read through the entire procedure prior to starting. Prepare your workspace and any tools or parts that may be needed to complete the task. When directed by your supervisor/instructor, begin the procedure to complete the task, and comment or check the box as each step is finished. Track your time on this procedure for later comparison to the standard completion time (i.e., "flat rate" or customer pay time).

Total time_____

Procedure	Step Completed
1. Check the driveshaft for balance. List your observation(s):	☐
2. Check the driveshaft for phasing. List your observation(s):	☐
3. Measure driveshaft runout and record below: _____ in/mm	☐
4. Measure the following driveline angles.	
a. Front _____ degrees	☐
b. Center (if specified) _____ degrees	☐
c. Rear _____ degrees	☐
5. Discuss your findings with your supervisor/instructor.	☐

Non-Task-Specific Evaluation	Step Completed
1. Tools and equipment were used as directed and returned in good working order.	☐
2. Complied with all general and task-specific safety standards, including proper use of any personal protective equipment (PPE).	☐
3. Completed the task in an appropriate time frame (recommendation: 1.5 or 2 times the flat rate).	☐
4. Left the workspace clean and orderly.	☐
5. Cared for customer property and returned it undamaged.	☐

Student signature _____ Date _____

Comments:

Have your supervisor/instructor verify satisfactory completion of this procedure, any observations made,

and any necessary action(s) recommended.

Evaluation Instructions: The scoring box below is intended to act as a guide for both student and supervisor/instructor. Each criterion listed will help students to understand what is expected of them and help supervisors/instructors to articulate the level of success at a particular task. The scoring is set up to allow a second attempt at each task (see the Test and Retest columns). Scoring is designed only to award students points for task criteria that were completed correctly. Points are lost for failure to complete the employability requirements (see Non-Task-Specific criteria). When all criteria are evaluated, tally the points for a total at the bottom of each column.

Tasksheet Scoring

Evaluation Items	Test		Retest	
	Pass	**Fail**	**Pass**	**Fail**
Task-Specific Evaluation	**(1 pt)**	**(0 pts)**	**(1 pt)**	**(0 pts)**
Student accurately checked the driveshaft for balance and noted any observations.				
Student accurately checked the driveshaft for phasing and noted any observations.				
Student accurately measured driveshaft runout.				
Student accurately measured all three drive-line angles.				
Non-Task-Specific Evaluation	**(0 pts)**	**(−1 pt)**	**(0 pts)**	**(−1 pt)**
Student successfully completed at least three of the non-task-specific steps.				
Student successfully completed all five of the non-task-specific steps.				
Total Score: <total # of points / 4 = %>				

Supervisor/Instructor:

Supervisor/instructor signature _____ Date _____

Comments:

Retest supervisor/instructor signature _____ Date _____

Comments:

CDX Tasksheet Number: 4.2a001c

Student/Intern Information

Name _____ Date _____ Class _____

Machine, Customer, and Service Information

Machine used for this activity:

Make _____ Model _____

Hours _____ Serial Number _____

Materials Required
- Manufacturer's workshop materials
- Manufacturer-specific tools, depending on the concern/procedure(s)
- Vehicle/component lifting equipment, if applicable

Task-Specific Safety Considerations
- This task may require test driving the vehicle on the school grounds or on a hoist, both of which carry severe risks. Attempt this task only with full permission from your supervisor/instructor and follow all the guidelines exactly.
- Lifting equipment such as vehicle jacks and stands, vehicle hoists, and engine hoists are important tools that increase productivity and make the job easier. However, they can also cause severe injury or death if used improperly. Make sure you follow the manufacturer's operation procedures. Also make sure you have your supervisor's/instructor's permission to use any particular type of lifting equipment.
- Comply with personal and environmental safety practices associated with clothing; eye protection; hand tools; power equipment; proper ventilation; and the handling, storage, and disposal of chemicals/materials in accordance with federal, state, and local regulations.
- Always wear the correct protective eyewear and clothing and use the appropriate safety equipment, as well as wheel chocks, fender covers, seat protectors, and floor mat protectors.
- Make sure you understand and observe all legislative and personal safety procedures when carrying out practical assignments. If you are unsure of what these are, ask your supervisor/instructor.

▶ **TASK** Identify drivetrain failures.

Time off_____

Student Instructions: Read through the entire procedure prior to starting. Prepare your workspace and any tools or parts that may be needed to complete the task. When directed by your supervisor/instructor, begin the procedure to complete the task, and comment or check the box as each step is finished. Track your time on this procedure for later comparison to the standard completion time (i.e., "flat rate" or customer pay time).

Time on_____

Total time_____

Procedure	Step Completed
1. Identify various drivetrain failures using parts assigned to you by your supervisor/instructor.	
a. Vibration	☐
b. Brinelling and false brinelling	☐
c. Spalling or galling	☐
d. Universal joint fractures and breakage	☐
e. Accelerated wear	☐
f. Twisted tubing	☐
g. Pillow block failure	☐
2. Discuss your findings with your supervisor/instructor.	☐

Non-Task-Specific Evaluation	Step Completed
1. Tools and equipment were used as directed and returned in good working order.	☐
2. Complied with all general and task-specific safety standards, including proper use of any personal protective equipment (PPE).	☐
3. Completed the task in an appropriate time frame (recommendation: 1.5 or 2 times the flat rate).	☐
4. Left the workspace clean and orderly.	☐
5. Cared for customer property and returned it undamaged.	☐

Student signature _____ Date _____

Comments:

Have your supervisor/instructor verify satisfactory completion of this procedure, any observations made,

and any necessary action(s) recommended.

Evaluation Instructions: The scoring box below is intended to act as a guide for both student and supervisor/instructor. Each criterion listed will help students to understand what is expected of them and help supervisors/instructors to articulate the level of success at a particular task. The scoring is set up to allow a second attempt at each task (see the Test and Retest columns). Scoring is designed only to award students points for task criteria that were completed correctly. Points are lost for failure to complete the employability requirements (see Non-Task-Specific criteria). When all criteria are evaluated, tally the points for a total at the bottom of each column.

Tasksheet Scoring

Evaluation Items	Test		Retest	
	Pass	**Fail**	**Pass**	**Fail**
Task-Specific Evaluation	**(1 pt)**	**(0 pts)**	**(1 pt)**	**(0 pts)**
Student correctly identified at least one drivetrain failure.				
Student correctly identified at least three drivetrain failures.				
Student correctly identified at least five drivetrain failures.				
Student correctly identified all seven drivetrain failures.				
Non-Task-Specific Evaluation	**(0 pts)**	**(−1 pt)**	**(0 pts)**	**(−1 pt)**
Student successfully completed at least three of the non-task-specific steps.				
Student successfully completed all five of the non-task-specific steps.				
Total Score: <total # of points / 4 = %>				

Supervisor/Instructor:

Supervisor/instructor signature _____ Date _____

Comments:

Retest supervisor/instructor signature _____ Date _____

Comments:

Chapter 35: Theory and Principles of Differentials

Learning Objective/Task	CDX Tasksheet Number	AED Reference Number
• Identify differential components.	4.2b001a	AED 4.2
• Describe power flow through a differential.	4.2b001b	AED 4.2
• Identify differential components.	4.2b002a	AED 4.2
• Describe power flow through a locking differential.	4.2b002b	AED 4.2
• Install differential carrier assembly.	4.2b003a	AED 4.2
• Repair differential case assembly.	4.2b003b	AED 4.2
• Repair differential carrier.	4.2b003c	AED 4.2
• Repair differential carrier.	4.2b003d	AED 4.2
• Adjust ring gear runout.	4.2b003e	AED 4.2
• Adjust drive pinion depth.	4.2b003g	AED 4.2
• Adjust side bearing preload and ring gear backlash.	4.2b003h	AED 4.2
• Adjust ring gear and pinion tooth contact pattern.	4.2b003i	AED 4.2
• Adjust ring gear thrust block/screw.	4.2b003j	AED 4.2
• Describe differential failures.	4.2b004	AED 4.2

Materials Required

- Manufacturer's workshop materials
- Various differential components
- Various differential cutaways
- Various components of a controlled traction or locking differential and a no-spin differential
- Vehicle with possible drive axle concerns
- Vehicle manufacturer's service information
- Component manufacturers' manuals
- Manufacturer-specific tools, depending on the concern

Safety Considerations

- This task may require test driving the vehicle on the school grounds or on a hoist, both of which carry severe risks. Attempt this task only with full permission from your supervisor/instructor and follow all the guidelines exactly.
- Lifting equipment such as vehicle jacks and stands, vehicle hoists, and engine hoists are important tools that increase productivity and make the job easier. However, they can also cause severe injury or death if used improperly. Make sure you follow the manufacturer's operation procedures. Also make sure you have your supervisor's/instructor's permission to use any particular type of lifting equipment.

- Comply with personal and environmental safety practices associated with clothing; eye protection; hand tools; power equipment; proper ventilation; and the handling, storage, and disposal of chemicals/materials in accordance with federal, state, and local regulations.
- Always wear the correct protective eyewear and clothing and use the appropriate safety equipment, as well as wheel chocks, fender covers, seat protectors, and floor mat protectors.
- Make sure you understand and observe all legislative and personal safety procedures when carrying out practical assignments. If you are unsure of what these are, ask your supervisor/instructor.
- While working on the vehicle, wheel chocks must be placed on both sides of one set of tires or as directed by your supervisor/instructor.
- When running any vehicles in the shop, make sure you use the shop's exhaust ventilation system to discharge all exhaust gas safely outside.

CDX Tasksheet Number: 4.2b001a

Student/Intern Information

Name _____ Date _____ Class _____

Machine, Customer, and Service Information

Machine used for this activity:

Make _____ Model _____

Hours _____ Serial Number _____

Materials Required
- Manufacturer's workshop materials
- Various differential components

Task-Specific Safety Considerations
- This task may require test driving the vehicle on the school grounds or on a hoist, both of which carry severe risks. Attempt this task only with full permission from your supervisor/instructor and follow all the guidelines exactly.
- Lifting equipment such as vehicle jacks and stands, vehicle hoists, and engine hoists are important tools that increase productivity and make the job easier. However, they can also cause severe injury or death if used improperly. Make sure you follow the manufacturer's operation procedures. Also make sure you have your supervisor's/instructor's permission to use any particular type of lifting equipment.
- Comply with personal and environmental safety practices associated with clothing; eye protection; hand tools; power equipment; proper ventilation; and the handling, storage, and disposal of chemicals/materials in accordance with federal, state, and local regulations.
- Always wear the correct protective eyewear and clothing and use the appropriate safety equipment, as well as wheel chocks, fender covers, seat protectors, and floor mat protectors.
- Make sure you understand and observe all legislative and personal safety procedures when carrying out practical assignments. If you are unsure of what these are, ask your supervisor/instructor.

▶ **TASK** Identify differential components.

AED 4.2

Time off_____

Time on_____

Student Instructions: Read through the entire procedure prior to starting. Prepare your workspace and any tools or parts that may be needed to complete the task. When directed by your supervisor/instructor, begin the procedure to complete the task, and comment or check the box as each step is finished. Track your time on this procedure for later comparison to the standard completion time (i.e., "flat rate" or customer pay time).

Total time_____

Procedure	Step Completed
1. Identify the following components that have been labeled and displayed by your supervisor/instructor and describe their function.	
a. Plain bevel gears	☐
b. Spiral bevel gears	☐
c. Pinion gear	☐
d. Crown or ring gear	☐
e. Hypoid gears	☐
f. Amboid gears	☐
g. Differential case	☐
h. Removable carrier housing	☐
i. Integral carrier housing	☐

j. Differential cross or spider	☐
k. Differential pinion or spider gears	☐
l. Side gears	☐
2. Discuss your findings with your supervisor/instructor.	☐

Non-Task-Specific Evaluation	Step Completed
1. Tools and equipment were used as directed and returned in good working order.	☐
2. Complied with all general and task-specific safety standards, including proper use of any personal protective equipment (PPE).	☐
3. Completed the task in an appropriate time frame (recommendation: 1.5 or 2 times the flat rate).	☐
4. Left the workspace clean and orderly.	☐
5. Cared for customer property and returned it undamaged.	☐

Student signature _____ Date _____

Comments:

Have your supervisor/instructor verify satisfactory completion of this procedure, any observations made, and any necessary action(s) recommended.

Evaluation Instructions: The scoring box below is intended to act as a guide for both student and supervisor/instructor. Each criterion listed will help students to understand what is expected of them and help supervisors/instructors to articulate the level of success at a particular task. The scoring is set up to allow a second attempt at each task (see the Test and Retest columns). Scoring is designed only to award students points for task criteria that were completed correctly. Points are lost for failure to complete the employability requirements (see Non-Task-Specific criteria). When all criteria are evaluated, tally the points for a total at the bottom of each column.

Tasksheet Scoring

	Test		Retest	
Evaluation Items	**Pass**	**Fail**	**Pass**	**Fail**
Task-Specific Evaluation	**(1 pt)**	**(0 pts)**	**(1 pt)**	**(0 pts)**
Student correctly identified at least six differential components.				
Student correctly identified all 12 differential components.				
Student correctly identified the functions of at least six differential components.				
Student correctly identified the functions of all 12 differential components.				
Non-Task-Specific Evaluation	**(0 pts)**	**(−1 pt)**	**(0 pts)**	**(−1 pt)**
Student successfully completed at least three of the non-task-specific steps.				
Student successfully completed all five of the non-task-specific steps.				
Total Score: <total # of points / 4 = %>				

Supervisor/Instructor:

Supervisor/instructor signature _____ Date _____

Comments:

Retest supervisor/instructor signature _____ Date _____

Comments:

CDX Tasksheet Number: 4.2b001b

Student/Intern Information

Name _____ Date _____ Class _____

Machine, Customer, and Service Information

Machine used for this activity:

Make _____ Model _____

Hours _____ Serial Number _____

Materials Required
- Manufacturer's workshop materials
- Various differential cutaways

Task-Specific Safety Considerations
- This task may require test driving the vehicle on the school grounds or on a hoist, both of which carry severe risks. Attempt this task only with full permission from your supervisor/instructor and follow all the guidelines exactly.
- Lifting equipment such as vehicle jacks and stands, vehicle hoists, and engine hoists are important tools that increase productivity and make the job easier. However, they can also cause severe injury or death if used improperly. Make sure you follow the manufacturer's operation procedures. Also make sure you have your supervisor/instructor's permission to use any particular type of lifting equipment.
- Comply with personal and environmental safety practices associated with clothing; eye protection; hand tools; power equipment; proper ventilation; and the handling, storage, and disposal of chemicals/materials in accordance with federal, state, and local regulations.
- Always wear the correct protective eyewear and clothing and use the appropriate safety equipment, as well as wheel chocks, fender covers, seat protectors, and floor mat protectors.
- Make sure you understand and observe all legislative and personal safety procedures when carrying out practical assignments. If you are unsure of what these are, ask your supervisor/instructor.

▶ **TASK** Describe power flow through a differential. _____

Student Instructions: Read through the entire procedure prior to starting. Prepare your workspace and any tools or parts that may be needed to complete the task. When directed by your supervisor/instructor, begin the procedure to complete the task, and comment or check the box as each step is finished. Track your time on this procedure for later comparison to the standard completion time (i.e., "flat rate" or customer pay time).

Time off_____

Time on_____

Total time_____

Procedure	Step Completed
1. Using a differential cutaway, describe how power flows through the differential, starting with the input shaft and ending at the axle shafts.	
a. Power flow driving straight	☐
b. Power flow driving through a turn	☐
2. Using a differential with power divider cutaway, describe how power flows through the differential and power divider, starting with the input shaft and ending at the axle shafts and the through shaft.	
a. Power flow driving straight	☐
b. Power flow driving through a turn	☐
c. Power flow driving front and rear axle at different speeds	☐
3. Discuss your findings with your supervisor/instructor.	☐

Non-Task-Specific Evaluation	Step Completed
1. Tools and equipment were used as directed and returned in good working order.	☐
2. Complied with all general and task-specific safety standards, including proper use of any personal protective equipment (PPE).	☐
3. Completed the task in an appropriate time frame (recommendation: 1.5 or 2 times the flat rate).	☐
4. Left the workspace clean and orderly.	☐
5. Cared for customer property and returned it undamaged.	☐

Student signature _____ Date _____

Comments:

Have your supervisor/instructor verify satisfactory completion of this procedure, any observations made,

and any necessary action(s) recommended.

Evaluation Instructions: The scoring box below is intended to act as a guide for both student and supervisor/instructor. Each criterion listed will help students to understand what is expected of them and help supervisors/instructors to articulate the level of success at a particular task. The scoring is set up to allow a second attempt at each task (see the Test and Retest columns). Scoring is designed only to award students points for task criteria that were completed correctly. Points are lost for failure to complete the employability requirements (see Non-Task-Specific criteria). When all criteria are evaluated, tally the points for a total at the bottom of each column.

Tasksheet Scoring

Evaluation Items	Test		Retest	
	Pass	Fail	Pass	Fail
Task-Specific Evaluation	**(1 pt)**	**(0 pts)**	**(1 pt)**	**(0 pts)**
Student correctly described how power flows through the differential driving straight.				
Student correctly described how power flows through the differential driving through a turn.				
Student correctly described how power flows through the differential and power divider driving straight and through a turn.				
Student correctly described how power flows through the differential and power divider driving front and rear axle at different speeds.				
Non-Task-Specific Evaluation	**(0 pts)**	**(−1 pt)**	**(0 pts)**	**(−1 pt)**
Student successfully completed at least three of the non-task-specific steps.				
Student successfully completed all five of the non-task-specific steps.				
Total Score: <total # of points / 4 = %>				

CDX Tasksheet Number: 4.2b002a

Student/Intern Information

Name _____ Date _____ Class _____

Machine, Customer, and Service Information

Machine used for this activity:

Make _____ Model _____

Hours _____ Serial Number _____

Materials Required

- Manufacturer's workshop materials
- Various components of a controlled traction or locking differential and a no-spin differential

---

Task-Specific Safety Considerations

- This task may require test driving the vehicle on the school grounds or on a hoist, both of which carry severe risks. Attempt this task only with full permission from your supervisor/instructor and follow all the guidelines exactly.
- Lifting equipment such as vehicle jacks and stands, vehicle hoists, and engine hoists are important tools that increase productivity and make the job easier. However, they can also cause severe injury or death if used improperly. Make sure you follow the manufacturer's operation procedures. Also make sure you have your supervisor's/instructor's permission to use any particular type of lifting equipment.
- Comply with personal and environmental safety practices associated with clothing; eye protection; hand tools; power equipment; proper ventilation; and the handling, storage, and disposal of chemicals/materials in accordance with federal, state, and local regulations.
- Always wear the correct protective eyewear and clothing and use the appropriate safety equipment, as well as wheel chocks, fender covers, seat protectors, and floor mat protectors.
- Make sure you understand and observe all legislative and personal safety procedures when carrying out practical assignments. If you are unsure of what these are, ask your supervisor/instructor.

▶ TASK Identify differential components.

AED 4.2

Time off_____

Time on_____

Student Instructions: Read through the entire procedure prior to starting. Prepare your workspace and any tools or parts that may be needed to complete the task. When directed by your supervisor/instructor, begin the procedure to complete the task, and comment or check the box as each step is finished. Track your time on this procedure for later comparison to the standard completion time (i.e., "flat rate" or customer pay time).

Total time_____

Procedure	Step Completed
1. Identify the following components of a controlled traction or locking differential that have been labeled and displayed by your supervisor/instructor and describe their function.	
a. Shift fork	☐
b. Sliding sleeve	☐
c. Axle shaft	☐
d. Compression spring	☐
e. Clutch pack	☐
f. Center housing	☐
g. Side gear	☐
2. Identify the following components of a no-spin differential that have been labeled and displayed by your supervisor/instructor and describe their function.	
a. Side gear	☐

	Step Completed
b. Spring retainer	☐
c. Spring	☐
d. Clutch assembly	☐
e. Spider assembly	☐
3. Discuss your findings with your supervisor/instructor.	☐

Non-Task-Specific Evaluation	Step Completed
1. Tools and equipment were used as directed and returned in good working order.	☐
2. Complied with all general and task-specific safety standards, including proper use of any personal protective equipment (PPE).	☐
3. Completed the task in an appropriate time frame (recommendation: 1.5 or 2 times the flat rate).	☐
4. Left the workspace clean and orderly.	☐
5. Cared for customer property and returned it undamaged.	☐

Student signature _____ Date _____

Comments:

Have your supervisor/instructor verify satisfactory completion of this procedure, any observations made,

and any necessary action(s) recommended.

Evaluation Instructions: The scoring box below is intended to act as a guide for both student and supervisor/instructor. Each criterion listed will help students to understand what is expected of them and help supervisors/instructors to articulate the level of success at a particular task. The scoring is set up to allow a second attempt at each task (see the Test and Retest columns). Scoring is designed only to award students points for task criteria that were completed correctly. Points are lost for failure to complete the employability requirements (see Non-Task-Specific criteria). When all criteria are evaluated, tally the points for a total at the bottom of each column.

Tasksheet Scoring

	Test		Retest	
Evaluation Items	**Pass**	**Fail**	**Pass**	**Fail**
Task-Specific Evaluation	**(1 pt)**	**(0 pts)**	**(1 pt)**	**(0 pts)**
Student correctly identified at least three controlled traction/locking differential components.				
Student correctly identified all seven controlled traction/locking differential components.				
Student correctly identified at least two no-spin differential components.				
Student correctly identified all five no-spin differential components.				
Non-Task-Specific Evaluation	**(0 pts)**	**(−1 pt)**	**(0 pts)**	**(−1 pt)**
Student successfully completed at least three of the non-task-specific steps.				
Student successfully completed all five of the non-task-specific steps.				
Total Score: <total # of points / 4 = %>				

Supervisor/Instructor:

Supervisor/instructor signature _____ Date _____

Comments:

Retest supervisor/instructor signature _____ Date _____

Comments:

CDX Tasksheet Number: 4.2b002b

> ### Materials Required
> - Manufacturer's workshop materials
> - Locking differential cutaway

Task-Specific Safety Considerations
- This task may require test driving the vehicle on the school grounds or on a hoist, both of which carry severe risks. Attempt this task only with full permission from your supervisor/instructor and follow all the guidelines exactly.
- Lifting equipment such as vehicle jacks and stands, vehicle hoists, and engine hoists are important tools that increase productivity and make the job easier. However, they can also cause severe injury or death if used improperly. Make sure you follow the manufacturer's operation procedures. Also make sure you have your supervisor's/instructor's permission to use any particular type of lifting equipment.
- Comply with personal and environmental safety practices associated with clothing; eye protection; hand tools; power equipment; proper ventilation; and the handling, storage, and disposal of chemicals/materials in accordance with federal, state, and local regulations.
- Always wear the correct protective eyewear and clothing and use the appropriate safety equipment, as well as wheel chocks, fender covers, seat protectors, and floor mat protectors.
- Make sure you understand and observe all legislative and personal safety procedures when carrying out practical assignments. If you are unsure of what these are, ask your supervisor/instructor.

▶ TASK Describe power flow through a locking differential. _____ **AED 4.2**

Time off_____

Time on_____

Student Instructions: Read through the entire procedure prior to starting. Prepare your workspace and any tools or parts that may be needed to complete the task. When directed by your supervisor/instructor, begin the procedure to complete the task, and comment or check the box as each step is finished. Track your time on this procedure for later comparison to the standard completion time (i.e., "flat rate" or customer pay time).

Total time_____

Procedure	Step Completed
1. Using a locking differential cutaway, describe how power flows through the differential, starting with the input shaft and ending at the axle shafts.	
a. Power flow driving straight	☐
b. Power flow driving through a turn	☐
c. Power flow driving on a split-coefficient surface	☐
2. Discuss your findings with your supervisor/instructor.	☐

Non-Task-Specific Evaluation	Step Completed
1. Tools and equipment were used as directed and returned in good working order.	☐
2. Complied with all general and task-specific safety standards, including proper use of any personal protective equipment (PPE).	☐
3. Completed the task in an appropriate time frame (recommendation: 1.5 or 2 times the flat rate).	☐
4. Left the workspace clean and orderly.	☐
5. Cared for customer property and returned it undamaged.	☐

Student signature _____ Date _____

Comments:

Have your supervisor/instructor verify satisfactory completion of this procedure, any observations made, and any necessary action(s) recommended.

Evaluation Instructions: The scoring box below is intended to act as a guide for both student and supervisor/instructor. Each criterion listed will help students to understand what is expected of them and help supervisors/instructors to articulate the level of success at a particular task. The scoring is set up to allow a second attempt at each task (see the Test and Retest columns). Scoring is designed only to award students points for task criteria that were completed correctly. Points are lost for failure to complete the employability requirements (see Non-Task-Specific criteria). When all criteria are evaluated, tally the points for a total at the bottom of each column.

Tasksheet Scoring

Evaluation Items	Test		Retest	
	Pass	Fail	Pass	Fail
Task-Specific Evaluation	**(1 pt)**	**(0 pts)**	**(1 pt)**	**(0 pts)**
Student correctly described each power flow starting with the input shaft and ending at the axle shafts.				
Student correctly described the power flow driving straight.				
Student correctly described the power flow driving through a turn.				
Student correctly described the power flow driving on a split-coefficient surface.				
Non-Task-Specific Evaluation	**(0 pts)**	**(−1 pt)**	**(0 pts)**	**(−1 pt)**
Student successfully completed at least three of the non-task-specific steps.				
Student successfully completed all five of the non-task-specific steps.				
Total Score: <total # of points / 4 = %>				

Supervisor/Instructor:

Supervisor/instructor signature _____ Date _____

Comments:

Retest supervisor/instructor signature _____ Date _____

Comments:

CDX Tasksheet Number: 4.2b003a

Student/Intern Information

Name _____ Date _____ Class _____

Machine, Customer, and Service Information

Machine used for this activity:

Make _____ Model _____

Hours _____ Serial Number _____

Materials Required

- Vehicle with possible drive axle concerns
- Vehicle manufacturer's service information
- Component manufacturers' manuals
- Manufacturer-specific tools, depending on the concern

Task-Specific Safety Considerations

- This task may require test driving the vehicle on the school grounds or on a hoist, both of which carry severe risks. Attempt this task only with full permission from your supervisor/instructor and follow all the guidelines exactly.
- Lifting equipment such as vehicle jacks and stands, vehicle hoists, and engine hoists are important tools that increase productivity and make the job easier. However, they can also cause severe injury or death if used improperly. Make sure you follow the manufacturer's operation procedures. Also make sure you have your supervisor's/instructor's permission to use any particular type of lifting equipment.
- Comply with personal and environmental safety practices associated with clothing; eye protection; hand tools; power equipment; proper ventilation; and the handling, storage, and disposal of chemicals/materials in accordance with federal, state, and local regulations.
- Always wear the correct protective eyewear and clothing and use the appropriate safety equipment, as well as fender covers, seat protectors, and floor mat protectors.
- Make sure you understand and observe all legislative and personal safety procedures when carrying out practical assignments. If you are unsure of what these are, ask your supervisor/instructor.
- While working on the vehicle, wheel chocks must be placed on both sides of one set of tires or as directed by your supervisor/instructor.
- When running any vehicles in the shop, make sure you use the shop's exhaust ventilation system to discharge all exhaust gas safely outside.

▶ TASK Install differential carrier assembly.   **AED** 4.2

Student Instructions: Read through the entire procedure prior to starting. Prepare your workspace and any tools or parts that may be needed to complete the task. When directed by your supervisor/instructor, begin the procedure to complete the task, and comment or check the box as each step is finished. Track your time on this procedure for later comparison to the standard completion time (i.e., "flat rate" or customer pay time).

Time off_____

Time on_____

Total time_____

Procedure	Step Completed
1. Reference the manufacturer's service information and/or component manufacturer's manuals for procedures to remove and replace the differential carrier assembly.	☐
2. Support the vehicle on stands at a sufficient level that allows enough room to work beneath it. Remove the differential carrier without interference from the frame and/or suspension.	☐
3. Remove the driveshaft from the drive axle and ensure it is sufficiently out of the way to allow for the removal of the differential carrier.	☐
4. Drain the axle fluid into a suitable container. The fluid can be an important indicator of the axle's condition. Look for evidence of metal contamination (indicating extreme wear) and sludge (usually caused by overheating or lack of lubricant).	☐
5. Loosen the nuts holding the axles in place at the wheel hub until they are holding by one or two threads. Leave them in place to stop the axle stud locating wedges from flying off.	☐
6. Using a large brass drift and a hammer, strike the axle flanges to loosen the tapered locating wedges in the axles. These steel wedges center the axle shaft as it is bolted to the wheel hub.	☐
7. Remove the nuts, wedges, and axles. Mark the axles as either right or left.	☐
8. Support the differential carrier with a suitable floor jack and platform designed for the purpose. Restrain the front of the differential carrier to the jack. The rear side of the carrier is much heavier than the front and will try to roll off as it is removed. Before removing the differential carrier–attaching bolts, ensure the carrier is securely supported.	☐
9. Remove the differential carrier retaining cap screws or stud nuts, leaving the top two loose to hold the weight while the carrier mounting flange is loosened.	☐
10. Loosen the differential carrier-to-housing mounting flange by either (a) using a pry bar in the pry slots on the flange or (b) moving the front of the housing back and forth.	☐
11. Remove the top two retainers, pull the differential carrier forward, and lower it to the floor.	☐
12. Mount the differential carrier in a suitable stand for overhaul.	☐
13. When reinstalling, clean the axle housing interior with rags and a mild solvent to remove any metal particles. Clean the flange mounting surface of all old gasket material.	☐
14. Run a new bead of silicone gasket compound or install a new gasket. Install the differential carrier by reversing the removal process.	☐
15. Install both axle shafts with a new gasket—installing the locating wedges and nuts. Torque the nuts to the correct specification.	☐

	Step Completed
16. Connect all air lines. Fill the axle with the correct lubricant until it is level with the fill hole. Lift the right side of the vehicle 6″ or more for 1 minute. Then lower the right side and lift the left side for the same amount of time. Lower the left side and let the vehicle sit for 1 minute. Recheck and top off lubricant as necessary. This procedure ensures that the wheel hubs have a sufficient level of lubricant and that the level in the drive axle housing is correct.	☐
17. Return the vehicle to its beginning condition and return any tools you used to their proper locations.	☐
18. Discuss your findings with your supervisor/instructor.	☐

Non-Task-Specific Evaluation	Step Completed
1. Tools and equipment were used as directed and returned in good working order.	☐
2. Complied with all general and task-specific safety standards, including proper use of any personal protective equipment (PPE).	☐
3. Completed the task in an appropriate time frame (recommendation: 1.5 or 2 times the flat rate).	☐
4. Left the workspace clean and orderly.	☐
5. Cared for customer property and returned it undamaged.	☐

Student signature _____ Date _____

Comments:

```



```

Have your supervisor/instructor verify satisfactory completion of this procedure, any observations made,

and any necessary action(s) recommended.

Evaluation Instructions: The scoring box below is intended to act as a guide for both student and supervisor/instructor. Each criterion listed will help students to understand what is expected of them and help supervisors/instructors to articulate the level of success at a particular task. The scoring is set up to allow a second attempt at each task (see the Test and Retest columns). Scoring is designed only to award students points for task criteria that were completed correctly. Points are lost for failure to complete the employability requirements (see Non-Task–Specific criteria). When all criteria are evaluated, tally the points for a total at the bottom of each column.

Tasksheet Scoring

Evaluation Items	Test		Retest	
	Pass	Fail	Pass	Fail
Task-Specific Evaluation	**(1 pt)**	**(0 pts)**	**(1 pt)**	**(0 pts)**
Student used the manufacturer's service information.				
Student properly removed the differential carrier assembly.				
Student properly reinstalled the differential carrier assembly.				
Student performed all necessary checks throughout the procedure, including looking for evidence of metal contamination/sludge and rechecking lubricant.				
Non-Task-Specific Evaluation	**(0 pts)**	**(−1 pt)**	**(0 pts)**	**(−1 pt)**
Student successfully completed at least three of the non-task-specific steps.				
Student successfully completed all five of the non-task-specific steps.				
Total Score: <total # of points / 4 = %>				

Supervisor/Instructor:

Supervisor/instructor signature _____ Date _____

Comments:

Retest supervisor/instructor signature _____ Date _____

Comments:

CDX Tasksheet Number: 4.2b003b

Student/Intern Information

Name _____ Date _____ Class _____

Machine, Customer, and Service Information

Machine used for this activity:

Make _____ Model _____

Hours _____ Serial Number _____

Materials Required

- Vehicle with possible drive axle concerns
- Vehicle manufacturer's service information
- Manufacturer-specific tools, depending on the concern

Task-Specific Safety Considerations

- This task may require test driving the vehicle on the school grounds or on a hoist, both of which carry severe risks. Attempt this task only with full permission from your supervisor/instructor and follow all the guidelines exactly.
- Comply with personal and environmental safety practices associated with clothing; eye protection; hand tools; power equipment; proper ventilation; and the handling, storage, and disposal of chemicals/materials in accordance with federal, state, and local regulations.
- Always wear the correct protective eyewear and clothing and use the appropriate safety equipment, as well as fender covers, seat protectors, and floor mat protectors.
- Make sure you understand and observe all legislative and personal safety procedures when carrying out practical assignments. If you are unsure of what these are, ask your supervisor/instructor.
- While working on the vehicle, wheel chocks must be placed on both sides of one set of tires or as directed by your supervisor/instructor.
- When running any vehicles in the shop, make sure you use the shop's exhaust ventilation system to discharge all exhaust gas safely outside.

> **TASK** Repair differential case assembly. _____ **AED** 4.2

Time off_____

Time on_____

Student Instructions: Read through the entire procedure prior to starting. Prepare your workspace and any tools or parts that may be needed to complete the task. When directed by your supervisor/instructor, begin the procedure to complete the task, and comment or check the box as each step is finished. Track your time on this procedure for later comparison to the standard completion time (i.e., "flat rate" or customer pay time).

Total time_____

Procedure	Step Completed
1. Reference the appropriate workshop manual to inspect the differential case assembly, including spider gears, cross-shaft, side gears, thrust washers, case halves, and bearings.	☐
2. Disassemble the differential case.	☐
a. Place the differential case on the bench with the flange side down. Mark the differential case halves with a punch so that they can be reassembled in the correct position. Remove the differential case cap screws.	☐
b. Remove the plain half of the differential case. The plain half of the differential case is opposite the crown gear side. It may be necessary to lightly tap the case to separate the two halves.	☐
c. Remove the thrust washer and right-hand side gear. Then remove the cross, spider gears, and their thrust washers together. Remove each spider gear and thrust washer.	☐
d. Remove the left side gear and thrust washer and check the running surfaces of the differential case and the side gears for wear.	☐
3. Clean and carefully examine all of the components, looking for any signs of wear or damage.	☐
a. Inspect all parts for steps or grooving caused by wear. Look for any pitting or cracks on gear contact areas.	☐
b. Check the teeth of the crown, pinion, and differential gears for excessive wear, pitting, and/or spalling at the contact areas.	☐
c. Check for nicks or burrs on mating surfaces, and inspect all cap screws for bends, cracks, or thread damage.	☐
4. Return the vehicle to its beginning condition and return any tools you used to their proper locations.	☐
5. Discuss your findings with your supervisor/instructor.	☐

Non-Task-Specific Evaluation	Step Completed
1. Tools and equipment were used as directed and returned in good working order.	☐
2. Complied with all general and task-specific safety standards, including proper use of any personal protective equipment (PPE).	☐
3. Completed the task in an appropriate time frame (recommendation: 1.5 or 2 times the flat rate).	☐
4. Left the workspace clean and orderly.	☐
5. Cared for customer property and returned it undamaged.	☐

Student signature _____ Date _____

Comments:

Have your supervisor/instructor verify satisfactory completion of this procedure, any observations made, and any necessary action(s) recommended.

Evaluation Instructions: The scoring box below is intended to act as a guide for both student and supervisor/instructor. Each criterion listed will help students to understand what is expected of them and help supervisors/instructors to articulate the level of success at a particular task. The scoring is set up to allow a second attempt at each task (see the Test and Retest columns). Scoring is designed only to award students points for task criteria that were completed correctly. Points are lost for failure to complete the employability requirements (see Non-Task-Specific criteria). When all criteria are evaluated, tally the points for a total at the bottom of each column.

Tasksheet Scoring

Evaluation Items	Test		Retest	
	Pass	**Fail**	**Pass**	**Fail**
Task-Specific Evaluation	**(1 pt)**	**(0 pts)**	**(1 pt)**	**(0 pts)**
Student used the manufacturer's service information.				
Student properly disassembled the differential case.				
Student properly marked any necessary parts for reassembly.				
Student properly cleaned the components and examined them for any signs of wear or damage.				
Non-Task-Specific Evaluation	**(0 pts)**	**(−1 pt)**	**(0 pts)**	**(−1 pt)**
Student successfully completed at least three of the non-task-specific steps.				
Student successfully completed all five of the non-task-specific steps.				
Total Score: <total # of points / 4 = %>				

Supervisor/Instructor:

Supervisor/instructor signature _____ Date _____

Comments:

_____

Retest supervisor/instructor signature _____ Date _____

Comments:

_____

CDX Tasksheet Number: 4.2b003c

Student/Intern Information

Name _____ Date _____ Class _____

Machine, Customer, and Service Information

Machine used for this activity:

Make _____ Model _____

Hours _____ Serial Number _____

Materials Required

- Vehicle with possible drive axle concerns
- Vehicle manufacturer's service information
- Manufacturer-specific tools, depending on the concern

Task-Specific Safety Considerations

- This task may require test driving the vehicle on the school grounds or on a hoist, both of which carry severe risks. Attempt this task only with full permission from your supervisor/instructor and follow all the guidelines exactly.
- Comply with personal and environmental safety practices associated with clothing; eye protection; hand tools; power equipment; proper ventilation; and the handling, storage, and disposal of chemicals/materials in accordance with federal, state, and local regulations.
- Always wear the correct protective eyewear and clothing and use the appropriate safety equipment, as well as fender covers, seat protectors, and floor mat protectors.
- Make sure you understand and observe all legislative and personal safety procedures when carrying out practical assignments. If you are unsure of what these are, ask your supervisor/instructor.
- While working on the vehicle, wheel chocks must be placed on both sides of one set of tires or as directed by your supervisor/instructor.
- When running any vehicles in the shop, make sure you use the shop's exhaust ventilation system to discharge all exhaust gas safely outside.

▶ **TASK** Repair differential carrier. _____ **AED 4.2**

Time off_____

Time on_____

Student Instructions: Read through the entire procedure prior to starting. Prepare your workspace and any tools or parts that may be needed to complete the task. When directed by your supervisor/instructor, begin the procedure to complete the task, and comment or check the box as each step is finished. Track your time on this procedure for later comparison to the standard completion time (i.e., "flat rate" or customer pay time).

Total time_____

Procedure	Step Completed
1. Reference the appropriate manufacturer's service information to inspect differential carrier housing and caps, side bearing bores, and pilot (spigot, pocket) bearing bore.	☐
2. Clean and carefully examine all of the components, looking for any signs of wear or damage.	☐
3. Check the bore in the differential carrier that supports the pinion spigot bearing and check the side bearings for unusual wear.	☐
4. Inspect all parts for steps and grooving caused by wear. Scuffing, deformation, or discoloration can be signs of excessive heat in the axle, usually caused by lubrication issues—either low lubricant level or the wrong type of lubricant.	☐
5. Return the vehicle to its beginning condition and return any tools you used to their proper locations.	☐
6. Discuss your findings with your supervisor/instructor.	☐

Non-Task-Specific Evaluation	Step Completed
1. Tools and equipment were used as directed and returned in good working order.	☐
2. Complied with all general and task-specific safety standards, including proper use of any personal protective equipment (PPE).	☐
3. Completed the task in an appropriate time frame (recommendation: 1.5 or 2 times the flat rate).	☐
4. Left the workspace clean and orderly.	☐
5. Cared for customer property and returned it undamaged.	☐

Student signature _____ Date _____

Comments:

Have your supervisor/instructor verify satisfactory completion of this procedure, any observations made,

and any necessary action(s) recommended.

Evaluation Instructions: The scoring box below is intended to act as a guide for both student and supervisor/instructor. Each criterion listed will help students to understand what is expected of them and help supervisors/instructors to articulate the level of success at a particular task. The scoring is set up to allow a second attempt at each task (see the Test and Retest columns). Scoring is designed only to award students points for task criteria that were completed correctly. Points are lost for failure to complete the employability requirements (see Non-Task-Specific criteria). When all criteria are evaluated, tally the points for a total at the bottom of each column.

Tasksheet Scoring

Evaluation Items	Test		Retest	
	Pass	Fail	Pass	Fail
Task-Specific Evaluation	**(1 pt)**	**(O pts)**	**(1 pt)**	**(O pts)**
Student used the manufacturer's service information.				
Student properly cleaned all components.				
Student properly checked all components for wear.				
Student properly inspected all parts for signs of excessive heat.				
Non-Task-Specific Evaluation	**(O pts)**	**(−1 pt)**	**(O pts)**	**(−1 pt)**
Student successfully completed at least three of the non-task-specific steps.				
Student successfully completed all five of the non-task-specific steps.				
Total Score: <total # of points / 4 = %>				

Supervisor/Instructor:

Supervisor/instructor signature _____ Date _____

Comments:

Retest supervisor/instructor signature _____ Date _____

Comments:

CDX Tasksheet Number: 4.2b003d

Student/Intern Information

Name _____ Date _____ Class _____

Machine, Customer, and Service Information

Machine used for this activity:

Make _____ Model _____

Hours _____ Serial Number _____

Materials Required

- Vehicle with possible drive axle concerns
- Vehicle manufacturer's service information
- Manufacturer-specific tools, depending on the concern

Task-Specific Safety Considerations

- This task may require test driving the vehicle on the school grounds or on a hoist, both of which carry severe risks. Attempt this task only with full permission from your supervisor/instructor and follow all the guidelines exactly.
- Comply with personal and environmental safety practices associated with clothing; eye protection; hand tools; power equipment; proper ventilation; and the handling, storage, and disposal of chemicals/materials in accordance with federal, state, and local regulations.
- Always wear the correct protective eyewear and clothing and use the appropriate safety equipment, as well as fender covers, seat protectors, and floor mat protectors.
- Make sure you understand and observe all legislative and personal safety procedures when carrying out practical assignments. If you are unsure of what these are, ask your supervisor/instructor.
- While working on the vehicle, wheel chocks must be placed on both sides of one set of tires or as directed by your supervisor/instructor.
- When running any vehicles in the shop, make sure you use the shop's exhaust ventilation system to discharge all exhaust gas safely outside.

▶ TASK Repair differential carrier.

AED 4.2

Time off_____

Time on_____

Student Instructions: Read through the entire procedure prior to starting. Prepare your workspace and any tools or parts that may be needed to complete the task. When directed by your supervisor/instructor, begin the procedure to complete the task, and comment or check the box as each step is finished. Track your time on this procedure for later comparison to the standard completion time (i.e., "flat rate" or customer pay time).

Total time_____

Procedure	Step Completed
1. Reference the manufacturer's service information to inspect and replace ring and drive pinion gears, spacers, sleeves, bearing cages, and bearings.	☐
2. Check the teeth of the crown, pinion, and differential gears for excessive wear, pitting, and/or spalling at the contact areas.	☐
3. Inspect all machined surfaces of the cast iron parts of the differential carrier and pinion cage for cracks and/or scoring or obvious wear.	☐
4. Check for nicks or burrs on mating surfaces, and inspect all cap screws for bends, cracks, or thread damage.	☐
5. Return the vehicle to its beginning condition and return any tools you used to their proper locations.	☐
6. Discuss your findings with your supervisor/instructor.	☐

Non-Task-Specific Evaluation	Step Completed
1. Tools and equipment were used as directed and returned in good working order.	☐
2. Complied with all general and task-specific safety standards, including proper use of any personal protective equipment (PPE).	☐
3. Completed the task in an appropriate time frame (recommendation: 1.5 or 2 times the flat rate).	☐
4. Left the workspace clean and orderly.	☐
5. Cared for customer property and returned it undamaged.	☐

Student signature _____ Date _____

Comments:

Have your supervisor/instructor verify satisfactory completion of this procedure, any observations made, and any necessary action(s) recommended.

Evaluation Instructions: The scoring box below is intended to act as a guide for both student and supervisor/instructor. Each criterion listed will help students to understand what is expected of them and help supervisors/instructors to articulate the level of success at a particular task. The scoring is set up to allow a second attempt at each task (see Test and Retest columns). Scoring is designed only to award students points for task criteria that were completed correctly. Points are lost for failure to complete the employability requirements (see Non-Task-Specific criteria). When all criteria are evaluated, tally the points for a total at the bottom of each column.

Tasksheet Scoring

Evaluation Items	Test		Retest	
	Pass	**Fail**	**Pass**	**Fail**
Task-Specific Evaluation	**(1 pt)**	**(0 pts)**	**(1 pt)**	**(0 pts)**
Student used the manufacturer's service information.				
Student properly inspected the teeth of the crown, pinion, and differential gears.				
Student properly inspected all machined surfaces of the cast iron parts of the differential carrier and pinion cage.				
Student properly inspected all mating surfaces and cap screws.				
Non-Task-Specific Evaluation	**(0 pts)**	**(−1 pt)**	**(0 pts)**	**(−1 pt)**
Student successfully completed at least three of the non-task-specific steps.				
Student successfully completed all five of the non-task-specific steps.				
Total Score: <total # of points / 4 = %>				

Supervisor/Instructor:

Supervisor/instructor signature _____ Date _____

Comments:

Retest supervisor/instructor signature _____ Date _____

Comments:

CDX Tasksheet Number: 4.2b003e

Student/Intern Information

Name _____ Date _____ Class _____

Machine, Customer, and Service Information

Machine used for this activity:

Make _____ Model _____

Hours _____ Serial Number _____

Materials Required

- Vehicle with possible drive axle concerns
- Vehicle manufacturer's repair information
- Manufacturer-specific tools, depending on the concern

Task-Specific Safety Considerations

- This task may require test driving the vehicle on the school grounds or on a hoist, both of which carry severe risks. Attempt this task only with full permission from your supervisor/instructor and follow all the guidelines exactly.
- Comply with personal and environmental safety practices associated with clothing; eye protection; hand tools; power equipment; proper ventilation; and the handling, storage, and disposal of chemicals/materials in accordance with federal, state, and local regulations.
- Always wear the correct protective eyewear and clothing and use the appropriate safety equipment, as well as fender covers, seat protectors, and floor mat protectors.
- Make sure you understand and observe all legislative and personal safety procedures when carrying out practical assignments. If you are unsure of what these are, ask your supervisor/instructor.
- While working on the vehicle, wheel chocks must be placed on both sides of one set of tires or as directed by your supervisor/instructor.
- When running any vehicles in the shop, make sure you use the shop's exhaust ventilation system to discharge all exhaust gas safely outside.

▶ TASK Adjust ring gear runout. **AED 4.2**

Time off_____

Time on_____

Student Instructions: Read through the entire procedure prior to starting. Prepare your workspace and any tools or parts that may be needed to complete the task. When directed by your supervisor/instructor, begin the procedure to complete the task, and comment or check the box as each step is finished. Track your time on this procedure for later comparison to the standard completion time (i.e., "flat rate" or customer pay time).

Total time_____

Procedure	Step Completed
1. Research the procedure and specifications for inspecting and measuring ring gear runout in the appropriate service information.	☐
a. Record the manufacturer's specified maximum ring gear runout below: _____ in/mm	☐
2. Using a dial indicator, measure the ring gear runout by attaching a dial indicator base to the differential case (a mechanical clamp or a magnetic base) _____ in/mm	☐
3. Attach the dial pointer to the ring gear outer flat edge (see Figure 1). **(Note:** Make sure the ring gear outer surface is clean and free of anything that could result in a false reading.) 	☐
4. Zero the dial indicator out.	☐
5. Obtain a ratchet and a socket to mount on the front of the pinion gear retaining nut.	☐
6. Rotate the pinion slowly in the direction of drive to obtain a reading.	☐
7. Record the reading below: _____ ft-lb/Nm	☐
a. Meets manufacturer's specifications? Yes ☐ No ☐	☐
b. If any adjustments are necessary, consult the manufacturer's service manuals and record the procedure below:	☐
8. Return the vehicle to its beginning condition and return any tools you used to their proper locations.	☐
9. Discuss your findings with your supervisor/instructor.	☐

Non-Task-Specific Evaluation	Step Completed
1. Tools and equipment were used as directed and returned in good working order.	☐
2. Complied with all general and task-specific safety standards, including proper use of any personal protective equipment (PPE).	☐
3. Completed the task in an appropriate time frame (recommendation: 1.5 or 2 times the flat rate).	☐
4. Left the workspace clean and orderly.	☐
5. Cared for customer property and returned it undamaged.	☐

Student signature _____ Date _____

Comments:

Have your supervisor/instructor verify satisfactory completion of this procedure, any observations made, and any necessary action(s) recommended.

Evaluation Instructions: The scoring box below is intended to act as a guide for both student and supervisor/instructor. Each criterion listed will help students to understand what is expected of them and help supervisors/instructors to articulate the level of success at a particular task. The scoring is set up to allow a second attempt at each task (see the Test and Retest columns). Scoring is designed only to award students points for task criteria that were completed correctly. Points are lost for failure to complete the employability requirements (see Non-Task-Specific criteria). When all criteria are evaluated, tally the points for a total at the bottom of each column.

Tasksheet Scoring

Evaluation Items	Test		Retest	
	Pass	Fail	Pass	Fail
Task-Specific Evaluation	**(1 pt)**	**(0 pts)**	**(1 pt)**	**(0 pts)**
Student properly measured the ring gear runout.				
Student properly attached the dial pointer.				
Student obtained an accurate reading.				
Student made any necessary adjustments.				
Non-Task-Specific Evaluation	**(0 pts)**	**(−1 pt)**	**(0 pts)**	**(−1 pt)**
Student successfully completed at least three of the non-task-specific steps.				
Student successfully completed all five of the non-task-specific steps.				
Total Score: <total # of points / 4 = %>				

Supervisor/Instructor:

Supervisor/instructor signature _____ Date _____

Comments:

Retest supervisor/instructor signature _____ Date _____

Comments:

CDX Tasksheet Number: 4.2b003g

Student/Intern Information

Name _____ Date _____ Class _____

Machine, Customer, and Service Information

Machine used for this activity:

Make _____ Model _____

Hours _____ Serial Number _____

Materials Required
- Vehicle with possible drive axle concerns
- Vehicle manufacturer's repair information
- Manufacturer-specific tools, depending on the concern

Task-Specific Safety Considerations
- This task may require test driving the vehicle on the school grounds or on a hoist, both of which carry severe risks. Attempt this task only with full permission from your supervisor/instructor and follow all the guidelines exactly.
- Comply with personal and environmental safety practices associated with clothing; eye protection; hand tools; power equipment; proper ventilation; and the handling, storage, and disposal of chemicals/materials in accordance with federal, state, and local regulations.
- Always wear the correct protective eyewear and clothing and use the appropriate safety equipment, as well as fender covers, seat protectors, and floor mat protectors.
- Make sure you understand and observe all legislative and personal safety procedures when carrying out practical assignments. If you are unsure of what these are, ask your supervisor/instructor.
- While working on the vehicle, wheel chocks must be placed on both sides of one set of tires or as directed by your supervisor/instructor.
- When running any vehicles in the shop, make sure you use the shop's exhaust ventilation system to discharge all exhaust gas safely outside.

▶ TASK Adjust drive pinion depth.

AED 4.2

Time off_____

Student Instructions: Read through the entire procedure prior to starting. Prepare your workspace and any tools or parts that may be needed to complete the task. When directed by your supervisor/instructor, begin the procedure to complete the task, and comment or check the box as each step is finished. Track your time on this procedure for later comparison to the standard completion time (i.e., "flat rate" or customer pay time).

Time on_____

Total time_____

Procedure	Step Completed
1. Research the procedure and specifications to measure and adjust drive pinion depth in the manufacturer's service information.	☐
2. Make sure all components are free from dirt or debris that could cause premature wear or failure.	☐
3. Place the pinion gear into the differential housing with the bearings installed. (**Note:** Pay attention to the etching number on the bottom of the pinion drive gear; compare to the old one.)	☐
a. Record the number that is etched on the bottom of the pinion drive gear for future reference: _____	☐
b. Prior to this, all bearing races should have been replaced along with the new bearings.	☐
c. If there were shims under one of the races, paying attention to the thickness of the shims, these should also have been reinstalled. (**Note:** The thickness of the shims will determine how far the pinion will be sitting into the ring gear. Adjust as necessary. If pinion housing is separate from the differential case, measure old shims and replace as necessary.)	☐
4. Utilizing a pinion depth gauge, measure and record the actual depth reading _____ in/mm (**Note:** The purpose of measuring drive pinion depth is to ensure that the drive gear is in perfect alignment with the ring gear and is in correct contact with the ring gear teeth.)	☐
a. Meets manufacturer's specifications? Yes ☐ No ☐	☐
b. If adjustments are necessary, follow the steps to bring the pinion to manufacturer's specification.	☐
5. Return the vehicle to its beginning condition and return any tools you used to their proper locations.	☐
6. Discuss your findings with your supervisor/instructor.	☐

Non-Task-Specific Evaluation	Step Completed
1. Tools and equipment were used as directed and returned in good working order.	☐
2. Complied with all general and task-specific safety standards, including proper use of any personal protective equipment (PPE).	☐
3. Completed the task in an appropriate time frame (recommendation: 1.5 or 2 times the flat rate).	☐
4. Left the workspace clean and orderly.	☐
5. Cared for customer property and returned it undamaged.	☐

Student signature _____ Date _____

Comments:

Have your supervisor/instructor verify satisfactory completion of this procedure, any observations made,

and any necessary action(s) recommended.

Evaluation Instructions: The scoring box below is intended to act as a guide for both student and supervisor/instructor. Each criterion listed will help students to understand what is expected of them and help supervisors/instructors to articulate the level of success at a particular task. The scoring is set up to allow a second attempt at each task (see the Test and Retest columns). Scoring is designed only to award students points for task criteria that were completed correctly. Points are lost for failure to complete the employability requirements (see Non-Task-Specific criteria). When all criteria are evaluated, tally the points for a total at the bottom of each column.

Tasksheet Scoring

Evaluation Items	Test		Retest	
	Pass	**Fail**	**Pass**	**Fail**
Task-Specific Evaluation	**(1 pt)**	**(0 pts)**	**(1 pt)**	**(0 pts)**
Student ensured all components were clean and showed no signs of wear or failure.				
Student properly placed the pinion gear into the differential housing.				
Student accurately measured the actual pinion depth reading and properly made any necessary adjustments to the pinion depth.				
Student ensured all components were clean and showed no signs of wear or failure.				
Non-Task-Specific Evaluation	**(0 pts)**	**(−1 pt)**	**(0 pts)**	**(−1 pt)**
Student successfully completed at least three of the non-task-specific steps.				
Student successfully completed all five of the non-task-specific steps.				
Total Score: <total # of points / 4 = %>				

CDX Tasksheet Number: 4.2b003h

Student/Intern Information

Name _____ Date _____ Class _____

Machine, Customer, and Service Information

Machine used for this activity:

Make _____ Model _____

Hours _____ Serial Number _____

Materials Required
- Vehicle with possible drive axle concerns
- Vehicle manufacturer's service information
- Manufacturer-specific tools, depending on the concern

Task-Specific Safety Considerations
- This task may require test driving the vehicle on the school grounds or on a hoist, both of which carry severe risks. Attempt this task only with full permission from your supervisor/instructor and follow all the guidelines exactly.
- Comply with personal and environmental safety practices associated with clothing; eye protection; hand tools; power equipment; proper ventilation; and the handling, storage, and disposal of chemicals/materials in accordance with federal, state, and local regulations.
- Always wear the correct protective eyewear and clothing and use the appropriate safety equipment, as well as fender covers, seat protectors, and floor mat protectors.
- Make sure you understand and observe all legislative and personal safety procedures when carrying out practical assignments. If you are unsure of what these are, ask your supervisor/instructor.
- While working on the vehicle, wheel chocks must be placed on both sides of one set of tires or as directed by your supervisor/instructor.
- When running any vehicles in the shop, make sure you use the shop's exhaust ventilation system to discharge all exhaust gas safely outside.

▶ TASK Adjust side bearing preload and ring gear backlash. **AED 4.2**

Time off_____

Student Instructions: Read through the entire procedure prior to starting. Prepare your workspace and any tools or parts that may be needed to complete the task. When directed by your supervisor/instructor, begin the procedure to complete the task, and comment or check the box as each step is finished. Track your time on this procedure for later comparison to the standard completion time (i.e., "flat rate" or customer pay time).

Time on_____

Total time_____

Procedure	Step Completed
1. Make sure all components are clean and free of dirt or debris that could cause a false reading and adjustment.	☐
2. Install the ring gear into the differential housing with the bearing races. Prior to this action, the pinion should have been installed and adjusted as necessary.	☐
3. Install the main bearing caps onto the housing and thread the bolts through the caps and into the housing.	☐
4. Thread the side bearing adjusters into the bearing caps (see Figure 1).	☐
5. Torque the bolts to the proper manufacturer's specification.	☐
a. Record the torque specification: _____ ft-lb/Nm	☐
6. Thread the side bearing adjusters into the caps until they make contact with the side bearings, allowing for some backlash play to be present.	☐
7. Attach a dial indicator base to the differential case housing and the dial pointer onto one of the ring gear teeth (see Figure 2).	☐

8. Utilizing a spanner wrench or equivalent, rotate one of the side bearing adjusters until the backlash starts to change (see Figure 3). 	☐
9. Always alternate the side bearing adjusters to keep the ring gear stable in the housing.	☐
10. Zero out the dial indicator.	☐
11. Rock the ring gear back and forth to achieve a reading on the dial indicator.	☐
a. Record the reading on the indicator and compare it to the manufacturer's specification: _____ in/mm	☐
12. Depending on the type of differential, record the procedure from the manufacturer's service manual to correct and bring the reading into specification:	☐
13. Return the vehicle to its beginning condition and return any tools you used to their proper locations.	☐
14. Discuss your findings with your supervisor/instructor.	☐

Non-Task-Specific Evaluation	Step Completed
1. Tools and equipment were used as directed and returned in good working order.	☐
2. Complied with all general and task-specific safety standards, including proper use of any personal protective equipment (PPE).	☐
3. Completed the task in an appropriate time frame (recommendation: 1.5 or 2 times the flat rate).	☐
4. Left the workspace clean and orderly.	☐
5. Cared for customer property and returned it undamaged.	☐

Student signature _____ Date _____

Comments:

Have your supervisor/instructor verify satisfactory completion of this procedure, any observations made, and any necessary action(s) recommended.

Evaluation Instructions: The scoring box below is intended to act as a guide for both student and supervisor/instructor. Each criterion listed will help students to understand what is expected of them and help supervisors/instructors to articulate the level of success at a particular task. The scoring is set up to allow a second attempt at each task (see the Test and Retest columns). Scoring is designed only to award students points for task criteria that were completed correctly. Points are lost for failure to complete the employability requirements (see Non-Task-Specific criteria). When all criteria are evaluated, tally the points for a total at the bottom of each column.

Tasksheet Scoring

Evaluation Items	Test		Retest	
	Pass	Fail	Pass	Fail
Task-Specific Evaluation	**(1 pt)**	**(0 pts)**	**(1 pt)**	**(0 pts)**
Student properly installed the ring gear and main bearing caps.				
Student properly attached the dial pointer.				
Student obtained an accurate reading on the dial indicator.				
Student made any necessary adjustments to bring the reading to specification and recorded the procedure to do so.				
Non-Task-Specific Evaluation	**(0 pts)**	**(−1 pt)**	**(0 pts)**	**(−1 pt)**
Student successfully completed at least three of the non-task-specific steps.				
Student successfully completed all five of the non-task-specific steps.				
Total Score: <total # of points / 4 = %>				

Supervisor/Instructor:

Supervisor/instructor signature _____ Date _____

Comments:

Retest supervisor/instructor signature _____ Date _____

Comments:

CDX Tasksheet Number: 4.2b003i

Student/Intern Information

Name _____ Date _____ Class _____

Machine, Customer, and Service Information

Machine used for this activity:

Make _____ Model _____

Hours _____ Serial Number _____

Materials Required

- Vehicle with possible drive axle concerns
- Vehicle manufacturer's service information
- Manufacturer-specific tools, depending on the concern

Task-Specific Safety Considerations

- This task may require test driving the vehicle on the school grounds or on a hoist, both of which carry severe risks. Attempt this task only with full permission from your supervisor/instructor and follow all the guidelines exactly.
- Comply with personal and environmental safety practices associated with clothing; eye protection; hand tools; power equipment; proper ventilation; and the handling, storage, and disposal of chemicals/materials in accordance with federal, state, and local regulations.
- Always wear the correct protective eyewear and clothing and use the appropriate safety equipment, as well as fender covers, seat protectors, and floor mat protectors.
- Make sure you understand and observe all legislative and personal safety procedures when carrying out practical assignments. If you are unsure of what these are, ask your supervisor/instructor.
- While working on the vehicle, wheel chocks must be placed on both sides of one set of tires or as directed by your supervisor/instructor.
- When running any vehicles in the shop, make sure you use the shop's exhaust ventilation system to discharge all exhaust gas safely outside.

▶ **TASK** Adjust ring gear and pinion tooth contact pattern. **AED 4.2**

Time off_____

Time on_____

Student Instructions: Read through the entire procedure prior to starting. Prepare your workspace and any tools or parts that may be needed to complete the task. When directed by your supervisor/instructor, begin the procedure to complete the task, and comment or check the box as each step is finished. Track your time on this procedure for later comparison to the standard completion time (i.e., "flat rate" or customer pay time).

Total time_____

Procedure	Step Completed
1. Upon overhaul of the differential, it is necessary to check tooth contact patterns to assess if all parts are in their proper positions and adjusted correctly.	☐
2. Mount the differential in an overhaul stand with the ring gear (crown gear) facing the top.	☐
3. Using a tube of Prussian blue or equivalent, paint six to eight of the ring gear (crown gear) teeth.	☐
4. Utilizing a ratchet and socket on the pinion gear retainer nut, slowly rotate the ring gear to the drive side direction one full turn or 360 degrees.	☐
5. Rotate the ring in the reverse direction a full turn or 360 degrees. (**Note:** It may be wise to wedge a piece of wood or equivalent between the ring gear and the carrier housing to create a drag on the ring gear, simulating a drive condition.)	☐
6. Compare the gear tooth pattern to the chart shown in Figure 1.	☐

7.

Pattern too close to heel

Pattern too close to toe

Pattern too close to tooth root

Pattern too close to top land

Procedure	Step Completed
7. If the gear tooth patterns do not match the chart, use the manufacturer's workshop manual to record the procedure for adjusting and/or correcting the pattern to specification. Record the procedure below:	☐

	Step Completed
8. Return the vehicle to its beginning condition and return any tools you used to their proper locations.	☐
9. Discuss your findings with your supervisor/instructor.	☐

Non-Task-Specific Evaluation	Step Completed
1. Tools and equipment were used as directed and returned in good working order.	☐
2. Complied with all general and task-specific safety standards, including proper use of any personal protective equipment (PPE).	☐
3. Completed the task in an appropriate time frame (recommendation: 1.5 or 2 times the flat rate).	☐
4. Left the workspace clean and orderly.	☐
5. Cared for customer property and returned it undamaged.	☐

Student signature _____ Date _____

Comments:

Have your supervisor/instructor verify satisfactory completion of this procedure, any observations made, and any necessary action(s) recommended.

Evaluation Instructions: The scoring box below is intended to act as a guide for both student and supervisor/instructor. Each criterion listed will help students to understand what is expected of them and help supervisors/instructors to articulate the level of success at a particular task. The scoring is set up to allow a second attempt at each task (see the Test and Retest columns). Scoring is designed only to award students points for task criteria that were completed correctly. Points are lost for failure to complete the employability requirements (see Non-Task-Specific criteria). When all criteria are evaluated, tally the points for a total at the bottom of each column.

Tasksheet Scoring

Evaluation Items	Test		Retest	
	Pass	**Fail**	**Pass**	**Fail**
Task-Specific Evaluation	**(1 pt)**	**(0 pts)**	**(1 pt)**	**(0 pts)**
Student correctly painted the ring gear teeth.				
Student accurately rotated the ring gear and the ring.				
Student accurately compared the tooth patterns to the chart.				
Student accurately made any adjustments/corrections and recorded the procedure to do so.				
Non-Task-Specific Evaluation	**(0 pts)**	**(−1 pt)**	**(0 pts)**	**(−1 pt)**
Student successfully completed at least three of the non-task-specific steps.				
Student successfully completed all five of the non-task-specific steps.				
Total Score: <total # of points / 4 = %>				

Supervisor/Instructor:

Supervisor/instructor signature _____ Date _____

Comments:

Retest supervisor/instructor signature _____ Date _____

Comments:

CDX Tasksheet Number: 4.2b003j

Student/Intern Information

Name _____ Date _____ Class _____

Machine, Customer, and Service Information

Machine used for this activity:

Make _____ Model _____

Hours _____ Serial Number _____

Materials Required

- Vehicle with possible drive axle concerns
- Vehicle manufacturer's repair information
- Manufacturer-specific tools, depending on the concern

Task-Specific Safety Considerations

- This task may require test driving the vehicle on the school grounds or on a hoist, both of which carry severe risks. Attempt this task only with full permission from your supervisor/instructor and follow all the guidelines exactly.
- Comply with personal and environmental safety practices associated with clothing; eye protection; hand tools; power equipment; proper ventilation; and the handling, storage, and disposal of chemicals/materials in accordance with federal, state, and local regulations.
- Always wear the correct protective eyewear and clothing and use the appropriate safety equipment, as well as fender covers, seat protectors, and floor mat protectors.
- Make sure you understand and observe all legislative and personal safety procedures when carrying out practical assignments. If you are unsure of what these are, ask your supervisor/instructor.
- While working on the vehicle, wheel chocks must be placed on both sides of one set of tires or as directed by your supervisor/instructor.
- When running any vehicles in the shop, make sure you use the shop's exhaust ventilation system to discharge all exhaust gas safely outside.

▶ **TASK** Adjust ring gear thrust block/screw. _____ **AED** 4.2

Time off_____

Time on_____

Student Instructions: Read through the entire procedure prior to starting. Prepare your workspace and any tools or parts that may be needed to complete the task. When directed by your supervisor/instructor, begin the procedure to complete the task, and comment or check the box as each step is finished. Track your time on this procedure for later comparison to the standard completion time (i.e., "flat rate" or customer pay time).

Total time_____

Procedure	Step Completed
(**Note:** Some of the differential carriers do not come with a thrust block adjuster.)	
1. Mount the carrier assembly in the overhaul stand with the back surface of the ring gear (crown gear) toward the top.	☐
2. Install the thrust block on the back side of the ring gear (crown gear). The thrust block must be on center between the backside of the ring gear (crown gear) and the differential case.	☐
3. Turn the ring gear (crown gear) until the thrust block and the hole for the thrust screw and the carrier housing are lined up.	☐
4. Thread the thrust screw lock nut onto the thrust screw about halfway down the threads.	☐
5. Thread the thrust screw into the carrier housing until the thrust screw makes contact with the backside of the ring gear (crown gear) or thrust block.	☐
6. Unscrew the thrust screw one half turn, or 180 degrees.	☐
7. Tighten the thrust screw lock nut to manufacturer's specifications (see Figure 1). Record the torque specification: _____ ft-lb. (Nm)	☐
8. If adjustment is not within specification, record the procedure that is outlined in the manufacturer's workshop manual to correct the problem:	☐
9. Return the vehicle to its beginning condition and return any tools you used to their proper locations.	☐
10. Discuss your findings with your supervisor/instructor.	☐

Non-Task-Specific Evaluation	Step Completed
1. Tools and equipment were used as directed and returned in good working order.	☐
2. Complied with all general and task-specific safety standards, including proper use of any personal protective equipment (PPE).	☐
3. Completed the task in an appropriate time frame (recommendation: 1.5 or 2 times the flat rate).	☐
4. Left the workspace clean and orderly.	☐
5. Cared for customer property and returned it undamaged.	☐

Student signature _____ Date _____

Comments:

Have your supervisor/instructor verify satisfactory completion of this procedure, any observations made,

and any necessary action(s) recommended.

Evaluation Instructions: The scoring box below is intended to act as a guide for both student and supervisor/instructor. Each criterion listed will help students to understand what is expected of them and help supervisors/instructors to articulate the level of success at a particular task. The scoring is set up to allow a second attempt at each task (see the Test and Retest columns). Scoring is designed only to award students points for task criteria that were completed correctly. Points are lost for failure to complete the employability requirements (see Non-Task-Specific criteria). When all criteria are evaluated, tally the points for a total at the bottom of each column.

Tasksheet Scoring

Evaluation Items	Test		Retest	
	Pass	**Fail**	**Pass**	**Fail**
Task-Specific Evaluation	**(1 pt)**	**(0 pts)**	**(1 pt)**	**(0 pts)**
Student properly installed the thrust block.				
Student properly torqued the thrust screw lock nut to specification.				
Student made any necessary adjustments and recorded the procedure for doing so.				
Student properly installed the thrust block.				
Non-Task-Specific Evaluation	**(0 pts)**	**(−1 pt)**	**(0 pts)**	**(−1 pt)**
Student successfully completed at least three of the non-task-specific steps.				
Student successfully completed all five of the non-task-specific steps.				
Total Score: <total # of points / 4 = %>				

Supervisor/Instructor:

Supervisor/instructor signature _____ Date _____

Comments:

_____

Retest supervisor/instructor signature _____ Date _____

Comments:

_____

CDX Tasksheet Number: 4.2b004

Student/Intern Information

Name _____ Date _____ Class _____

Machine, Customer, and Service Information

Machine used for this activity:

Make _____ Model _____

Hours _____ Serial Number _____

Materials Required
- Manufacturer's workshop materials

Task-Specific Safety Considerations
- This task may require test driving the vehicle on the school grounds or on a hoist, both of which carry severe risks. Attempt this task only with full permission from your supervisor/instructor and follow all the guidelines exactly.
- Lifting equipment such as vehicle jacks and stands, vehicle hoists, and engine hoists are important tools that increase productivity and make the job easier. However, they can also cause severe injury or death if used improperly. Make sure you follow the manufacturer's operation procedures. Also make sure you have your supervisor's/instructor's permission to use any particular type of lifting equipment.
- Comply with personal and environmental safety practices associated with clothing; eye protection; hand tools; power equipment; proper ventilation; and the handling, storage, and disposal of chemicals/materials in accordance with federal, state, and local regulations.
- Always wear the correct protective eyewear and clothing and use the appropriate safety equipment, as well as wheel chocks, fender covers, seat protectors, and floor mat protectors.
- Make sure you understand and observe all legislative and personal safety procedures when carrying out practical assignments. If you are unsure of what these are, ask your supervisor/instructor.

▶ **TASK** Describe differential failures. **AED 4.2**

Time off_____

Time on_____

Student Instructions: Read through the entire procedure prior to starting. Prepare your workspace and any tools or parts that may be needed to complete the task. When directed by your supervisor/instructor, begin the procedure to complete the task, and comment or check the box as each step is finished. Track your time on this procedure for later comparison to the standard completion time (i.e., "flat rate" or customer pay time).

Total time_____

Procedure	Step Completed
1. Identify the failures shown below and the cause for each.	
a. Failure type: Common cause: 	☐

b. Failure type:

☐

Common cause:

c. Failure type:

☐

Common cause:

d. Failure type:	☐
Common cause:	
2. Discuss your findings with your supervisor/instructor.	☐

Non-Task-Specific Evaluation	Step Completed
1. Tools and equipment were used as directed and returned in good working order.	☐
2. Complied with all general and task-specific safety standards, including proper use of any personal protective equipment (PPE).	☐
3. Completed the task in an appropriate time frame (recommendation: 1.5 or 2 times the flat rate).	☐
4. Left the workspace clean and orderly.	☐
5. Cared for customer property and returned it undamaged.	☐

Student signature _____ Date _____

Comments:

Have your supervisor/instructor verify satisfactory completion of this procedure, any observations made,

and any necessary action(s) recommended.

Evaluation Instructions: The scoring box below is intended to act as a guide for both student and supervisor/instructor. Each criterion listed will help students to understand what is expected of them and help supervisors/instructors to articulate the level of success at a particular task. The scoring is set up to allow a second attempt at each task (see the Test and Retest columns). Scoring is designed only to award students points for task criteria that were completed correctly. Points are lost for failure to complete the employability requirements (see Non-Task-Specific criteria). When all criteria are evaluated, tally the points for a total at the bottom of each column.

Tasksheet Scoring

	Test		Retest	
Evaluation Items	**Pass**	**Fail**	**Pass**	**Fail**
Task-Specific Evaluation	**(1 pt)**	**(0 pts)**	**(1 pt)**	**(0 pts)**
Student correctly identified at least two differential failures.				
Student correctly identified all four differential failures.				
Student correctly identified at least two failure causes.				
Student correctly identified all four failure causes.				
Non-Task-Specific Evaluation	**(0 pts)**	**(−1 pt)**	**(0 pts)**	**(−1 pt)**
Student successfully completed at least three of the non-task-specific steps.				
Student successfully completed all five of the non-task-specific steps.				
Total Score: <total # of points / 4 = %>				

Chapter 36: Theory and Principles of Final Drives

Learning Objective/Task	CDX Tasksheet Number	AED Reference Number
• Describe final drive components.	4.2c001	AED 4.2
• Install planetary drive assembly.	4.2c002a	AED 4.2
• Change oil in chain drive.	4.2c002b	AED 4.2

Materials Required

- Manufacturer's workshop materials
- Vehicle manufacturer's service information
- Component manufacturer's manuals
- Manufacturer-specific tools, depending on the concern

Safety Considerations

- This task may require test driving the vehicle on the school grounds or on a hoist, both of which carry severe risks. Attempt this task only with full permission from your supervisor/instructor and follow all the guidelines exactly.
- Comply with personal and environmental safety practices associated with clothing; eye protection; hand tools; power equipment; proper ventilation; and the handling, storage, and disposal of chemicals/materials in accordance with federal, state, and local regulations.
- Always wear the correct protective eyewear and clothing and use the appropriate safety equipment, as well as wheel chocks, fender covers, seat protectors, and floor mat protectors.
- Make sure you understand and observe all legislative and personal safety procedures when carrying out practical assignments. If you are unsure of what these are, ask your supervisor/instructor.
- Lifting equipment such as vehicle jacks and stands, vehicle hoists, and engine hoists are important tools that increase productivity and make the job easier. However, they can also cause severe injury or death if used improperly. Make sure you follow the manufacturer's operation procedures. Also make sure you have your supervisor's/instructor's permission to use any particular type of lifting equipment.
- While working on the vehicle, wheel chocks must be placed on both sides of one set of tires or as directed by your supervisor/instructor.
- When running any vehicles in the shop, make sure you use the shop's exhaust ventilation system to discharge all exhaust gas safely outside.

CDX Tasksheet Number: 4.2c001

Student/Intern Information

Name _____ Date _____ Class _____

Machine, Customer, and Service Information

Machine used for this activity:

Make _____ Model _____

Hours _____ Serial Number _____

Materials Required
- Manufacturer's workshop materials

Task-Specific Safety Considerations
- This task may require test driving the vehicle on the school grounds or on a hoist, both of which carry severe risks. Attempt this task only with full permission from your supervisor/ instructor and follow all the guidelines exactly.
- Comply with personal and environmental safety practices associated with clothing; eye protection; hand tools; power equipment; proper ventilation; and the handling, storage, and disposal of chemicals/materials in accordance with federal, state, and local regulations.
- Always wear the correct protective eyewear and clothing and use the appropriate safety equipment, as well as wheel chocks, fender covers, seat protectors, and floor mat protectors.
- Make sure you understand and observe all legislative and personal safety procedures when carrying out practical assignments. If you are unsure of what these are, ask your supervisor/ instructor.

▶ **TASK** Describe final drive components. **AED** 4.2

Time off_____

Time on_____

Student Instructions: Read through the entire procedure prior to starting. Prepare your workspace and any tools or parts that may be needed to complete the task. When directed by your supervisor/instructor, begin the procedure to complete the task, and comment or check the box as each step is finished. Track your time on this procedure for later comparison to the standard completion time (i.e., "flat rate" or customer pay time).

Total time_____

Procedure	Step Completed
1. Identify the following components of a final drive that have been labeled and displayed by your supervisor/instructor and describe their function.	
a. Pinion-type final drive	☐

b. Bull and pinion final drive	☐
c. Double-reduction pinion and bull final drive	☐
d. Planetary final drive	☐
e. Double- and multiple-reduction planetary final drive	☐
f. Chain-type final drive	☐
2. Discuss your findings with your supervisor/instructor.	☐

Non-Task-Specific Evaluation	Step Completed
1. Tools and equipment were used as directed and returned in good working order.	☐
2. Complied with all general and task-specific safety standards, including proper use of any personal protective equipment (PPE).	☐
3. Completed the task in an appropriate time frame (recommendation: 1.5 or 2 times the flat rate).	☐
4. Left the workspace clean and orderly.	☐
5. Cared for customer property and returned it undamaged.	☐

Student signature _____ Date _____

Comments:

Have your supervisor/instructor verify satisfactory completion of this procedure, any observations made,

and any necessary action(s) recommended.

Evaluation Instructions: The scoring box below is intended to act as a guide for both student and supervisor/instructor. Each criterion listed will help students to understand what is expected of them and help supervisors/instructors to articulate the level of success at a particular task. The scoring is set up to allow a second attempt at each task (see the Test and Retest columns). Scoring is designed only to award students points for task criteria that were completed correctly. Points are lost for failure to complete the employability requirements (see Non-Task-Specific criteria). When all criteria are evaluated, tally the points for a total at the bottom of each column.

Tasksheet Scoring

Evaluation Items	Test		Retest	
	Pass	**Fail**	**Pass**	**Fail**
Task-Specific Evaluation	**(1 pt)**	**(O pts)**	**(1 pt)**	**(O pts)**
Student correctly identified at least three final drive components.				
Student correctly identified all six final drive components.				
Student correctly identified the functions of at least three final drive components.				
Student correctly identified the functions of all six final drive components.				
Non-Task-Specific Evaluation	**(O pts)**	**(−1 pt)**	**(O pts)**	**(−1 pt)**
Student successfully completed at least three of the non-task-specific steps.				
Student successfully completed all five of the non-task-specific steps.				
Total Score: <total # of points / 4 = %>				

Supervisor/Instructor:

Supervisor/instructor signature _____ Date _____

Comments:

_____

Retest supervisor/instructor signature _____ Date _____

Comments:

_____

CDX Tasksheet Number: 4.2c002a

Student/Intern Information

Name _____ Date _____ Class _____

Machine, Customer, and Service Information

Machine used for this activity:

Make _____ Model _____

Hours _____ Serial Number _____

Materials Required

- Vehicle with possible final drive concerns
- Vehicle manufacturer's service information and/or component manufacturer's manuals
- Manufacturer-specific tools, depending on the concern

Task-Specific Safety Considerations

- This task may require test driving the vehicle on the school grounds or on a hoist, both of which carry severe risks. Attempt this task only with full permission from your supervisor/instructor and follow all the guidelines exactly.
- Lifting equipment such as vehicle jacks and stands, vehicle hoists, and engine hoists are important tools that increase productivity and make the job easier. However, they can also cause severe injury or death if used improperly. Make sure you follow the manufacturer's operation procedures. Also make sure you have your supervisor's/instructor's permission to use any particular type of lifting equipment.
- Comply with personal and environmental safety practices associated with clothing; eye protection; hand tools; power equipment; proper ventilation; and the handling, storage, and disposal of chemicals/materials in accordance with federal, state, and local regulations.
- Always wear the correct protective eyewear and clothing and use the appropriate safety equipment, as well as fender covers, seat protectors, and floor mat protectors.
- Make sure you understand and observe all legislative and personal safety procedures when carrying out practical assignments. If you are unsure of what these are, ask your supervisor/instructor.
- While working on the vehicle, wheel chocks must be placed on both sides of one set of tires or as directed by your supervisor/instructor.
- When running any vehicles in the shop, make sure you use the shop's exhaust ventilation system to discharge all exhaust gas safely outside.

▶ **TASK** Install planetary drive assembly. _____ **AED** 4.2

Time off_____

Time on_____

Student Instructions: Read through the entire procedure prior to starting. Prepare your workspace and any tools or parts that may be needed to complete the task. When directed by your supervisor/instructor, begin the procedure to complete the task, and comment or check the box as each step is finished. Track your time on this procedure for later comparison to the standard completion time (i.e., "flat rate" or customer pay time).

Total time_____

Procedure	Step Completed
1. Reference the manufacturer's service information and/or component manufacturer's manuals for procedures to remove and replace planetary final assembly.	☐
2. Remove the guard to access the parking brake lines.	☐
3. Disconnect the parking brake lines and cap all fittings.	☐
4. Remove the parking brake manifold from the frame.	☐
5. Remove the bolts that hold the bottom of the final drive case to the frame.	☐
6. Remove the two bolts on opposite sides of the top of the final drive case and install guide studs at least 6 in (15 cm) long.	☐
7. Remove sprocket segments to gain clearance from the track roller.	☐
8. Attach a sling and lifting device to the final drive to take the weight of the drive.	☐
9. Remove the remaining bolts attaching the final drive case and install forcing screws into the appropriate threaded holes in the case.	☐
10. Using the forcing screws, move the case away from the frame.	☐
11. Following the manufacturer's procedures, repair the final drive.	☐
12. When reinstalling, clean the frame mounts with rags and a mild solvent to remove any metal particles. Clean the flange mounting surface of all old gasket material.	☐
13. Install the differential carrier by reversing the removal process.	☐
14. Connect all park brake lines. Fill the final drive with the correct lubricant until it is level with the fill hole. Recheck and top up lubricant as necessary.	☐
15. Return the machine to its beginning condition and return any tools you used to their proper locations.	☐
16. Discuss your findings with your supervisor/instructor.	☐

Non-Task-Specific Evaluation	Step Completed
1. Tools and equipment were used as directed and returned in good working order.	☐
2. Complied with all general and task-specific safety standards, including proper use of any personal protective equipment (PPE).	☐
3. Completed the task in an appropriate time frame (recommendation: 1.5 or 2 times the flat rate).	☐
4. Left the workspace clean and orderly.	☐
5. Cared for customer property and returned it undamaged.	☐

Student signature _____ Date _____

Comments:

Have your supervisor/instructor verify satisfactory completion of this procedure, any observations made,

and any necessary action(s) recommended.

Evaluation Instructions: The scoring box below is intended to act as a guide for both student and supervisor/instructor. Each criterion listed will help students to understand what is expected of them and help supervisors/instructors to articulate the level of success at a particular task. The scoring is set up to allow a second attempt at each task (see the Test and Retest columns). Scoring is designed only to award students points for task criteria that were completed correctly. Points are lost for failure to complete the employability requirements (see Non-Task-Specific criteria). When all criteria are evaluated, tally the points for a total at the bottom of each column.

Tasksheet Scoring

Evaluation Items	Test		Retest	
	Pass	**Fail**	**Pass**	**Fail**
Task-Specific Evaluation	**(1 pt)**	**(0 pts)**	**(1 pt)**	**(0 pts)**
Student properly removed the final drive.				
Student properly repaired the final drive.				
Student properly reinstalled the final drive.				
Student properly filled and rechecked the lubricant.				
Non-Task-Specific Evaluation	**(0 pts)**	**(−1 pt)**	**(0 pts)**	**(−1 pt)**
Student successfully completed at least three of the non-task-specific steps.				
Student successfully completed all five of the non-task-specific steps.				
Total Score: <total # of points / 4 = %>				

Supervisor/Instructor:

Supervisor/instructor signature _____ Date _____

Comments:

Retest supervisor/instructor signature _____ Date _____

Comments:

CDX Tasksheet Number: 4.2c002b

Student/Intern Information

Name _____ Date _____ Class _____

Machine, Customer, and Service Information

Machine used for this activity:

Make _____ Model _____

Hours _____ Serial Number _____

Materials Required

- Vehicle with possible final drive concerns
- Vehicle manufacturer's service information and/or component manufacturer's manuals
- Manufacturer-specific tools, depending on the concern

Task-Specific Safety Considerations

- This task may require test driving the vehicle on the school grounds or on a hoist, both of which carry severe risks. Attempt this task only with full permission from your supervisor/instructor and follow all the guidelines exactly.
- Comply with personal and environmental safety practices associated with clothing; eye protection; hand tools; power equipment; proper ventilation; and the handling, storage, and disposal of chemicals/materials in accordance with federal, state, and local regulations.
- Always wear the correct protective eyewear and clothing and use the appropriate safety equipment, as well as fender covers, seat protectors, and floor mat protectors.
- Make sure you understand and observe all legislative and personal safety procedures when carrying out practical assignments. If you are unsure of what these are, ask your supervisor/instructor.
- While working on the vehicle, wheel chocks must be placed on both sides of one set of tires or as directed by your supervisor/instructor.
- When running any vehicles in the shop, make sure you use the shop's exhaust ventilation system to discharge all exhaust gas safely outside.

▶ **TASK** Change oil in chain drive.

AED 4.2

Time off_____

Student Instructions: Read through the entire procedure prior to starting. Prepare your workspace and any tools or parts that may be needed to complete the task. When directed by your supervisor/instructor, begin the procedure to complete the task, and comment or check the box as each step is finished. Track your time on this procedure for later comparison to the standard completion time (i.e., "flat rate" or customer pay time).

Time on_____

Total time_____

Procedure	Step Completed
1. Reference the manufacturer's service information and/or component manufacturer's manuals for procedures to remove and replace planetary final assembly.	☐
2. Operate the machine long enough to warm the oil.	☐
3. Place a suitable drain pan under the drain plug. Note that the drive can contain as much as 17–21 gallons (64.4–79.5 liters) of lubricant.	☐
4. Remove the drain plug and oil check plug and allow the lubricant to drain.	☐
5. Check the lubricant closely for signs of metal wear, contamination, and/or sludge. It may be necessary to flush the housing with diesel if contamination exists.	☐
6. Clean the area around one of the cover plates and remove.	☐
7. Clean and replace the drain plug. Fill the case through the removed cover plate to the correct level with the recommended lubricant. Clean and install the level check plug.	☐
8. Clean and reinstall the cover plate.	☐
9. Operate the machine long enough to circulate the oil. Oil level should be at the bottom of the level check plug hole. Adjust the oil level as necessary.	☐
10. Return the machine to its beginning condition and return any tools you used to their proper locations.	☐
11. Discuss your findings with your supervisor/instructor.	☐

Non-Task-Specific Evaluation	Step Completed
1. Tools and equipment were used as directed and returned in good working order.	☐
2. Complied with all general and task-specific safety standards, including proper use of any personal protective equipment (PPE).	☐
3. Completed the task in an appropriate time frame (recommendation: 1.5 or 2 times the flat rate).	☐
4. Left the workspace clean and orderly.	☐
5. Cared for customer property and returned it undamaged.	☐

Student signature _____ Date _____

Comments:

Have your supervisor/instructor verify satisfactory completion of this procedure, any observations made,

and any necessary action(s) recommended.

Evaluation Instructions: The scoring box below is intended to act as a guide for both student and supervisor/instructor. Each criterion listed will help students to understand what is expected of them and help supervisors/instructors to articulate the level of success at a particular task. The scoring is set up to allow a second attempt at each task (see the Test and Retest columns). Scoring is designed only to award students points for task criteria that were completed correctly. Points are lost for failure to complete the employability requirements (see Non-Task-Specific criteria). When all criteria are evaluated, tally the points for a total at the bottom of each column.

Tasksheet Scoring

Evaluation Items	Test		Retest	
	Pass	**Fail**	**Pass**	**Fail**
Task-Specific Evaluation	**(1 pt)**	**(0 pts)**	**(1 pt)**	**(0 pts)**
Student properly drained the lubricant.				
Student properly checked the lubricant and flushed the housing if necessary.				
Student properly cleaned and replaced/reinstalled the drain plug and the cover plate.				
Student properly checked the oil level and adjusted if necessary.				
Non-Task-Specific Evaluation	**(0 pts)**	**(−1 pt)**	**(0 pts)**	**(−1 pt)**
Student successfully completed at least three of the non-task-specific steps.				
Student successfully completed all five of the non-task-specific steps.				
Total Score: <total # of points / 4 = %>				

Supervisor/Instructor:

Supervisor/instructor signature _____ Date _____

Comments:

Retest supervisor/instructor signature _____ Date _____

Comments:

Chapter 37: Fundamental Theory of Hydraulic and Pneumatic Braking Systems

Learning Objective/Task	CDX Tasksheet Number	AED Reference Number
• Test brake system.	4.3001a	AED 4.3
• Inspect brake system.	4.3001b	AED 4.3
• Bleed brake system.	4.3001c	AED 4.3
• Describe brake components of an external dry braking system.	4.3002a	AED 4.3
• Describe brake components of an internal wet braking system.	4.3002b	AED 4.3

Materials Required

- Vehicle with possible brake concerns
- Vehicle manufacturer's service information
- Component manufacturer's manuals
- Manufacturer-specific tools, depending on the concern

Safety Considerations

- This task may require test driving the vehicle on the school grounds or on a hoist, both of which carry severe risks. Attempt this task only with full permission from your supervisor/instructor and follow all the guidelines exactly.
- Comply with personal and environmental safety practices associated with clothing; eye protection; hand tools; power equipment; proper ventilation; and the handling, storage, and disposal of chemicals/materials in accordance with federal, state, and local regulations.
- Always wear the correct protective eyewear and clothing and use the appropriate safety equipment, as well as fender covers, seat protectors, and floor mat protectors.
- Make sure you understand and observe all legislative and personal safety procedures when carrying out practical assignments. If you are unsure of what these are, ask your supervisor/instructor.
- While working on the vehicle, wheel chocks must be placed on both sides of one set of tires or as directed by your supervisor/instructor.
- When running any vehicles in the shop, make sure you use the shop's exhaust ventilation system to discharge all exhaust gas safely outside.

CDX Tasksheet Number: 4.3001a

Student/Intern Information

Name _____ Date _____ Class _____

Machine, Customer, and Service Information

Machine used for this activity:

Make _____ Model _____

Hours _____ Serial Number _____

Materials Required

- Vehicle with possible brake concerns
- Vehicle manufacturer's service information and/or component manufacturer's manuals
- Manufacturer-specific tools, depending on the concern

Task-Specific Safety Considerations

- This task may require test driving the vehicle on the school grounds or on a hoist, both of which carry severe risks. Attempt this task only with full permission from your supervisor/instructor and follow all the guidelines exactly.
- Comply with personal and environmental safety practices associated with clothing; eye protection; hand tools; power equipment; proper ventilation; and the handling, storage, and disposal of chemicals/materials in accordance with federal, state, and local regulations.
- Always wear the correct protective eyewear and clothing and use the appropriate safety equipment, as well as fender covers, seat protectors, and floor mat protectors.
- Make sure you understand and observe all legislative and personal safety procedures when carrying out practical assignments. If you are unsure of what these are, ask your supervisor/instructor.
- While working on the vehicle, wheel chocks must be placed on both sides of one set of tires or as directed by your supervisor/instructor.
- When running any vehicles in the shop, make sure you use the shop's exhaust ventilation system to discharge all exhaust gas safely outside.

▶ TASK Test brake system.

Time off_____

Time on_____

Student Instructions: Read through the entire procedure prior to starting. Prepare your workspace and any tools or parts that may be needed to complete the task. When directed by your supervisor/instructor, begin the procedure to complete the task, and comment or check the box as each step is finished. Track your time on this procedure for later comparison to the standard completion time (i.e., "flat rate" or customer pay time).

Total time_____

Procedure	Step Completed
1. Reference the manufacturer's service information and/or component manufacturer's manuals for procedures to test the braking system.	☐
2. If the machine is equipped with a power shift transmission, do the following:	
a. Put the machine in the highest speed range and forward or reverse.	☐
b. Apply the service brake and slowly increase engine rpm to high idle. The machine should not move.	☐
3. If the machine is equipped with a hydrostatic drivetrain, do the following:	
a. Disable the parking brake release.	☐
b. Try to move the machine with the park brake applied. (**Note:** Some machines should be left at low idle, and some may require high idle. The machine should not move.)	☐
4. If the machine is equipped with a driveline parking brake, do the following:	
a. Apply the parking brake.	☐
b. Try to move the machine in high range. The machine should not move.	☐
5. If the machine is equipped with reverse modulated spring applied brakes, do the following:	
a. Depress the brake pedal fully.	☐
b. Try to move the machine; it should not move.	☐
6. Discuss your findings with your supervisor/instructor.	☐

Non-Task-Specific Evaluation	Step Completed
1. Tools and equipment were used as directed and returned in good working order.	☐
2. Complied with all general and task-specific safety standards, including proper use of any personal protective equipment (PPE).	☐
3. Completed the task in an appropriate time frame (recommendation: 1.5 or 2 times the flat rate).	☐
4. Left the workspace clean and orderly.	☐
5. Cared for customer property and returned it undamaged.	☐

Student signature _____ Date _____

Comments:

Have your supervisor/instructor verify satisfactory completion of this procedure, any observations made, and any necessary action(s) recommended.

Evaluation Instructions: The scoring box below is intended to act as a guide for both student and supervisor/instructor. Each criterion listed will help students to understand what is expected of them and help supervisors/instructors to articulate the level of success at a particular task. The scoring is set up to allow a second attempt at each task (see the Test and Retest columns). Scoring is designed only to award students points for task criteria that were completed correctly. Points are lost for failure to complete the employability requirements (see Non-Task-Specific criteria). When all criteria are evaluated, tally the points for a total at the bottom of each column.

Tasksheet Scoring

Evaluation Items	Test		Retest	
	Pass	Fail	Pass	Fail
Task-Specific Evaluation	**(1 pt)**	**(0 pts)**	**(1 pt)**	**(0 pts)**
Student properly tested the braking system for vehicles with a power shift transmission.				
Student properly tested the braking system for vehicles with a hydrostatic drivetrain.				
Student properly tested the braking system for vehicles with a driveline parking brake.				
Student properly tested the braking system for vehicles with reverse modulated spring applied brakes.				
Non-Task-Specific Evaluation	**(0 pts)**	**(−1 pt)**	**(0 pts)**	**(−1 pt)**
Student successfully completed at least three of the non-task-specific steps.				
Student successfully completed all five of the non-task-specific steps.				
Total Score: <total # of points / 4 = %>				

Supervisor/Instructor:

Supervisor/instructor signature _____ Date _____

Comments:

Retest supervisor/instructor signature _____ Date _____

Comments:

CDX Tasksheet Number: 4.3001b

Student/Intern Information

Name _____ Date _____ Class _____

Machine, Customer, and Service Information

Machine used for this activity:

Make _____ Model _____

Hours _____ Serial Number _____

Materials Required

- Vehicle with possible brake concerns
- Vehicle manufacturer's service information and/or component manufacturer's manuals
- Manufacturer-specific tools, depending on the concern

Task-Specific Safety Considerations

- This task may require test driving the vehicle on the school grounds or on a hoist, both of which carry severe risks. Attempt this task only with full permission from your supervisor/instructor and follow all the guidelines exactly.
- Comply with personal and environmental safety practices associated with clothing; eye protection; hand tools; power equipment; proper ventilation; and the handling, storage, and disposal of chemicals/materials in accordance with federal, state, and local regulations.
- Always wear the correct protective eyewear and clothing and use the appropriate safety equipment, as well as fender covers, seat protectors, and floor mat protectors.
- Make sure you understand and observe all legislative and personal safety procedures when carrying out practical assignments. If you are unsure of what these are, ask your supervisor/instructor.
- While working on the vehicle, wheel chocks must be placed on both sides of one set of tires or as directed by your supervisor/instructor.
- When running any vehicles in the shop, make sure you use the shop's exhaust ventilation system to discharge all exhaust gas safely outside.

▶ TASK Inspect brake system. **AED 4.3**

Time off_____

Time on_____

Student Instructions: Read through the entire procedure prior to starting. Prepare your workspace and any tools or parts that may be needed to complete the task. When directed by your supervisor/instructor, begin the procedure to complete the task, and comment or check the box as each step is finished. Track your time on this procedure for later comparison to the standard completion time (i.e., "flat rate" or customer pay time).

Total time_____

Procedure	Step Completed
1. Reference the manufacturer's service information and/or component manufacturer's manuals for procedures to inspect the braking system.	☐
2. Check the fluid level. This could involve looking at a sight glass, pulling a dipstick, or looking into a reservoir.	☐
3. Check the fluid condition. There should be no visible air, and the fluid should appear clear with no burnt smell.	☐
4. Check the brake system malfunction warning system. This could involve turning the key and looking for a warning light or pushing a button or toggle switch.	☐
5. Check for fault codes related to the braking system.	☐
6. Check the system for fluid leaks.	☐
7. Check for damaged seals or boots at the caliper wheel cylinders.	☐
8. Check for proper operation of the service brake system.	☐
9. Check for proper operation of the parking brake system.	☐
10. Perform a visual inspection of the controls of the braking system.	☐
11. Check for proper operation or damage of the brake lights.	☐
12. Check the brake cooling system for proper operation.	☐
13. Check for any unusual or excessive wear of friction materials, drums, or rotors.	☐
14. Check for loose or missing covers around the foundation brakes.	☐
15. Discuss your findings with your supervisor/instructor.	☐

Non-Task-Specific Evaluation	Step Completed
1. Tools and equipment were used as directed and returned in good working order.	☐
2. Complied with all general and task-specific safety standards, including proper use of any personal protective equipment (PPE).	☐
3. Completed the task in an appropriate time frame (recommendation: 1.5 or 2 times the flat rate).	☐
4. Left the workspace clean and orderly.	☐
5. Cared for customer property and returned it undamaged.	☐

Student signature _____ Date _____

Comments:

Have your supervisor/instructor verify satisfactory completion of this procedure, any observations made, and any necessary action(s) recommended.

Evaluation Instructions: The scoring box below is intended to act as a guide for both student and supervisor/instructor. Each criterion listed will help students to understand what is expected of them and help supervisors/instructors to articulate the level of success at a particular task. The scoring is set up to allow a second attempt at each task (see the Test and Retest columns). Scoring is designed only to award students points for task criteria that were completed correctly. Points are lost for failure to complete the employability requirements (see Non-Task-Specific criteria). When all criteria are evaluated, tally the points for a total at the bottom of each column.

Tasksheet Scoring

	Test		Retest	
Evaluation Items	**Pass**	**Fail**	**Pass**	**Fail**
Task-Specific Evaluation	**(1 pt)**	**(0 pts)**	**(1 pt)**	**(0 pts)**
Student properly checked the fluid level and condition and checked the system for leaks.				
Student properly checked for related fault codes, damaged seals or boots, and signs of wear.				
Student properly performed a visual inspection of the controls and checked for loose or missing covers around the foundation breaks.				
Student properly checked the malfunction warning system, service brake system, parking brake system, and brake cooling system for proper operation.				
Non-Task-Specific Evaluation	**(0 pts)**	**(−1 pt)**	**(0 pts)**	**(−1 pt)**
Student successfully completed at least three of the non-task-specific steps.				
Student successfully completed all five of the non-task-specific steps.				
Total Score: <total # of points / 4 = %>				

Supervisor/Instructor:

Supervisor/instructor signature _____ Date _____

Comments:

Retest supervisor/instructor signature _____ Date _____

Comments:

CDX Tasksheet Number: 4.3001c

Student/Intern Information

Name _____ Date _____ Class _____

Machine, Customer, and Service Information

Machine used for this activity:

Make _____ Model _____

Hours _____ Serial Number _____

Materials Required

- Vehicle with possible brake concerns
- Vehicle manufacturer's service information and/or component manufacturer's manuals
- Manufacturer-specific tools, depending on the concern

Task-Specific Safety Considerations

- This task may require test driving the vehicle on the school grounds or on a hoist, both of which carry severe risks. Attempt this task only with full permission from your supervisor/instructor and follow all the guidelines exactly.
- Comply with personal and environmental safety practices associated with clothing; eye protection; hand tools; power equipment; proper ventilation; and the handling, storage, and disposal of chemicals/materials in accordance with federal, state, and local regulations.
- Always wear the correct protective eyewear and clothing and use the appropriate safety equipment, as well as fender covers, seat protectors, and floor mat protectors.
- Make sure you understand and observe all legislative and personal safety procedures when carrying out practical assignments. If you are unsure of what these are, ask your supervisor/instructor.
- While working on the vehicle, wheel chocks must be placed on both sides of one set of tires or as directed by your supervisor/instructor.
- When running any vehicles in the shop, make sure you use the shop's exhaust ventilation system to discharge all exhaust gas safely outside.

▶ **TASK** Bleed brake system. **AED** 4.3

Time off_____

Time on_____

Student Instructions: Read through the entire procedure prior to starting. Prepare your workspace and any tools or parts that may be needed to complete the task. When directed by your supervisor/instructor, begin the procedure to complete the task, and comment or check the box as each step is finished. Track your time on this procedure for later comparison to the standard completion time (i.e., "flat rate" or customer pay time).

Total time_____

Procedure	Step Completed
1. Reference the manufacturer's service information and/or component manufacturer's manuals for procedures to bleed the braking system.	☐
2. Ask an assistant to slowly push the brake pedal down.	☐
3. Start with the bleeder screw that is the farthest from the master cylinder.	
a. Attach a clear bleeder hose to the bleeder screw and insert the other end of the tube into a clear plastic container.	☐
b. Open the bleeder screw one-quarter to one-half turn (90–180 degrees).	☐
4. Observe any old brake fluid and air bubbles coming out of the bleeder screw.	☐
5. When the brake fluid stream stops, close the bleeder screw lightly. Have your assistant slowly release the pedal; this allows the master cylinder to pull a fresh charge of brake fluid from the reservoir.	☐
6. Repeat the previous steps until there is no more air coming out of the bleeder screw. Remove the plastic hose and tighten the bleeder screw to the manufacturer's specifications. (**Note:** Be sure that you do not bleed the system so much that the reservoir runs dry and admits air into the system. Top off the reservoir often.)	☐
7. Repeat this procedure for each of the wheel brakes, moving closer to the master cylinder until all the air is removed and the brake pedal is not spongy.	☐
8. Start the engine and check for proper operation of the braking system.	☐
9. Check the brake cooling system for proper operation.	☐
10. Check for any unusual or excessive wear of friction materials, drums, or rotors.	☐
11. Check for loose or missing covers around the foundation brakes.	☐
12. Discuss your findings with your supervisor/instructor.	☐

Non-Task-Specific Evaluation	Step Completed
1. Tools and equipment were used as directed and returned in good working order.	☐
2. Complied with all general and task-specific safety standards, including proper use of any personal protective equipment (PPE).	☐
3. Completed the task in an appropriate time frame (recommendation: 1.5 or 2 times the flat rate).	☐
4. Left the workspace clean and orderly.	☐
5. Cared for customer property and returned it undamaged.	☐

Student signature _____ Date _____

Comments:

Have your supervisor/instructor verify satisfactory completion of this procedure, any observations made, and any necessary action(s) recommended.

Evaluation Instructions: The scoring box below is intended to act as a guide for both student and supervisor/instructor. Each criterion listed will help students to understand what is expected of them and help supervisors/instructors to articulate the level of success at a particular task. The scoring is set up to allow a second attempt at each task (see the Test and Retest columns). Scoring is designed only to award students points for task criteria that were completed correctly. Points are lost for failure to complete the employability requirements (see Non-Task-Specific criteria). When all criteria are evaluated, tally the points for a total at the bottom of each column.

Tasksheet Scoring

Evaluation Items	Test		Retest	
	Pass	**Fail**	**Pass**	**Fail**
Task-Specific Evaluation	**(1 pt)**	**(0 pts)**	**(1 pt)**	**(0 pts)**
Student properly bled each of the wheel brakes in the correct order.				
Student properly checked for brake operation.				
Student properly checked the brake cooling system.				
Student properly checked for any signs of wear and for any loose or missing covers.				
Non-Task-Specific Evaluation	**(0 pts)**	**(−1 pt)**	**(0 pts)**	**(−1 pt)**
Student successfully completed at least three of the non-task-specific steps.				
Student successfully completed all five of the non-task-specific steps.				
Total Score: <total # of points / 4 = %>				

Supervisor/Instructor:

Supervisor/instructor signature _____ Date _____

Comments:

Retest supervisor/instructor signature _____ Date _____

Comments:

CDX Tasksheet Number: 4.3002a

Student/Intern Information

Name _____ Date _____ Class _____

Machine, Customer, and Service Information

Machine used for this activity:

Make _____ Model _____

Hours _____ Serial Number _____

Materials Required
- Vehicle manufacturer's service information

Task-Specific Safety Considerations
- This task may require test driving the vehicle on the school grounds or on a hoist, both of which carry severe risks. Attempt this task only with full permission from your supervisor/instructor and follow all the guidelines exactly.
- Comply with personal and environmental safety practices associated with clothing; eye protection; hand tools; power equipment; proper ventilation; and the handling, storage, and disposal of chemicals/materials in accordance with federal, state, and local regulations.
- Always wear the correct protective eyewear and clothing and use the appropriate safety equipment, as well as fender covers, seat protectors, and floor mat protectors.
- Make sure you understand and observe all legislative and personal safety procedures when carrying out practical assignments. If you are unsure of what these are, ask your supervisor/instructor.
- While working on the vehicle, wheel chocks must be placed on both sides of one set of tires or as directed by your supervisor/instructor.
- When running any vehicles in the shop, make sure you use the shop's exhaust ventilation system to discharge all exhaust gas safely outside.

▶ **TASK** Describe brake components of an external dry braking system.　**AED 4.3**

Time off_____

Time on_____

Student Instructions: Read through the entire procedure prior to starting. Prepare your workspace and any tools or parts that may be needed to complete the task. When directed by your supervisor/instructor, begin the procedure to complete the task, and comment or check the box as each step is finished. Track your time on this procedure for later comparison to the standard completion time (i.e., "flat rate" or customer pay time).

Total time_____

Procedure	Step Completed
1. With your supervisor/instructor present, use available service literature as a guide to identify the following components of an external dry braking system. (**Note:** Lab fixtures/instructional aids may be used for this task.)	
a. Air	☐
b. Hydraulic	☐
c. Disc	☐
d. Drum	☐
e. Pad	☐
f. Shoe	☐
g. Caliper	☐
h. Wheel cylinder	☐
i. Air brake chamber	☐
j. Slack adjuster	☐
k. Master cylinder	☐
l. Air treadle valve	☐
m. Brake booster	☐
n. Nonboosted	☐
2. Describe the function of valves in an air (pneumatic) brake system and their relationship to one another:	☐
3. Describe the function of valves in a hydraulic brake system and their relationship to one another:	☐
4. Discuss your findings with your supervisor/instructor.	☐

Non-Task-Specific Evaluation	Step Completed
1. Tools and equipment were used as directed and returned in good working order.	☐
2. Complied with all general and task-specific safety standards, including proper use of any personal protective equipment (PPE).	☐
3. Completed the task in an appropriate time frame (recommendation: 1.5 or 2 times the flat rate).	☐
4. Left the workspace clean and orderly.	☐
5. Cared for customer property and returned it undamaged.	☐

Student signature _____ Date _____

Comments:

Have your supervisor/instructor verify satisfactory completion of this procedure, any observations made, and any necessary action(s) recommended.

Evaluation Instructions: The scoring box below is intended to act as a guide for both student and supervisor/instructor. Each criterion listed will help students to understand what is expected of them and help supervisors/instructors to articulate the level of success at a particular task. The scoring is set up to allow a second attempt at each task (see the Test and Retest columns). Scoring is designed only to award students points for task criteria that were completed correctly. Points are lost for failure to complete the employability requirements (see Non-Task-Specific criteria). When all criteria are evaluated, tally the points for a total at the bottom of each column.

Tasksheet Scoring

Evaluation Items	Test		Retest	
	Pass	Fail	Pass	Fail
Task-Specific Evaluation	**(1 pt)**	**(O pts)**	**(1 pt)**	**(O pts)**
Student correctly identified at least seven of the external dry braking system components.				
Student correctly identified all 14 of the external dry braking system components.				
Student accurately described the function of valves in an air (pneumatic) brake system and their relationship to one another.				
Student accurately described the function of valves in a hydraulic brake system and their relationship to one another.				
Non-Task-Specific Evaluation	**(O pts)**	**(−1 pt)**	**(O pts)**	**(−1 pt)**
Student successfully completed at least three of the non-task-specific steps.				
Student successfully completed all five of the non-task-specific steps.				
Total Score: <total # of points / 4 = %>				

Supervisor/Instructor:

Supervisor/instructor signature _____ Date _____

Comments:

Retest supervisor/instructor signature _____ Date _____

Comments:

CDX Tasksheet Number: 4.3002b

Student/Intern Information

Name _____ Date _____ Class _____

Machine, Customer, and Service Information

Machine used for this activity:

Make _____ Model _____

Hours _____ Serial Number _____

Materials Required
- Vehicle manufacturer's service information

Task-Specific Safety Considerations
- This task may require test driving the vehicle on the school grounds or on a hoist, both of which carry severe risks. Attempt this task only with full permission from your supervisor/instructor and follow all the guidelines exactly.
- Comply with personal and environmental safety practices associated with clothing; eye protection; hand tools; power equipment; proper ventilation; and the handling, storage, and disposal of chemicals/materials in accordance with federal, state, and local regulations.
- Always wear the correct protective eyewear and clothing and use the appropriate safety equipment, as well as fender covers, seat protectors, and floor mat protectors.
- Make sure you understand and observe all legislative and personal safety procedures when carrying out practical assignments. If you are unsure of what these are, ask your supervisor/instructor.
- While working on the vehicle, wheel chocks must be placed on both sides of one set of tires or as directed by your supervisor/instructor.
- When running any vehicles in the shop, make sure you use the shop's exhaust ventilation system to discharge all exhaust gas safely outside.

▶ TASK Describe brake components of an internal wet braking system. **AED 4.3**

Time off_____

Time on_____

Student Instructions: Read through the entire procedure prior to starting. Prepare your workspace and any tools or parts that may be needed to complete the task. When directed by your supervisor/instructor, begin the procedure to complete the task, and comment or check the box as each step is finished. Track your time on this procedure for later comparison to the standard completion time (i.e., "flat rate" or customer pay time).

Total time_____

Procedure	Step Completed
1. With your supervisor/instructor present, use available service literature as a guide to identify the following components of an internal wet braking system. (**Note:** Lab fixtures/instructional aids may be used for this task.)	
a. Friction disc	☐
b. Spacer plate	☐
c. Primary piston	☐
d. Secondary piston	☐
e. Parking brake spring	☐
f. Brake valve	☐
g. Accumulator	☐
2. Describe the function of valves in an internal wet braking system and their relationship to one another:	☐
3. Discuss your findings with your supervisor/instructor.	☐

Non-Task-Specific Evaluation	Step Completed
1. Tools and equipment were used as directed and returned in good working order.	☐
2. Complied with all general and task-specific safety standards, including proper use of any personal protective equipment (PPE).	☐
3. Completed the task in an appropriate time frame (recommendation: 1.5 or 2 times the flat rate).	☐
4. Left the workspace clean and orderly.	☐
5. Cared for customer property and returned it undamaged.	☐

Student signature _____ Date _____

Comments:

Have your supervisor/instructor verify satisfactory completion of this procedure, any observations made, and any necessary action(s) recommended.

Evaluation Instructions: The scoring box below is intended to act as a guide for both student and supervisor/instructor. Each criterion listed will help students to understand what is expected of them and help supervisors/instructors to articulate the level of success at a particular task. The scoring is set up to allow a second attempt at each task (see the Test and Retest columns). Scoring is designed only to award students points for task criteria that were completed correctly. Points are lost for failure to complete the employability requirements (see Non-Task-Specific criteria). When all criteria are evaluated, tally the points for a total at the bottom of each column.

Tasksheet Scoring

Evaluation Items	Test		Retest	
	Pass	Fail	Pass	Fail
Task-Specific Evaluation	**(1 pt)**	**(0 pts)**	**(1 pt)**	**(0 pts)**
Student correctly identified at least three of the internal wet braking system components.				
Student correctly identified all seven of the internal wet braking system components.				
Student accurately described the function of valves in an internal wet braking system.				
Student accurately described the relationship between valves in an internal wet braking system.				
Non-Task-Specific Evaluation	**(0 pts)**	**(−1 pt)**	**(0 pts)**	**(−1 pt)**
Student successfully completed at least three of the non-task-specific steps.				
Student successfully completed all five of the non-task-specific steps.				
Total Score: <total # of points / 4 = %>				

Supervisor/Instructor:

Supervisor/instructor signature _____ Date _____

Comments:

Retest supervisor/instructor signature _____ Date _____

Comments:

Chapter 38: Understanding Maintenance Practices in Power Trains

Learning Objective/Task	CDX Tasksheet Number	AED Reference Number
• Clean component(s) when replaced.	4.4002	AED 4.4
• Remove oil sample.	4.4003	AED 4.4

Materials Required
- Vehicle with possible power transfer concerns
- Vehicle manufacturer's service information
- Manufacturer-specific tools, depending on the concern

Safety Considerations
- This task may require test driving the vehicle on the school grounds or on a hoist, both of which carry severe risks. Attempt this task only with full permission from your supervisor/instructor and follow all the guidelines exactly.
- Comply with personal and environmental safety practices associated with clothing; eye protection; hand tools; power equipment; proper ventilation; and the handling, storage, and disposal of chemicals/materials in accordance with federal, state, and local regulations.
- Always wear the correct protective eyewear and clothing and use the appropriate safety equipment, as well as fender covers, seat protectors, and floor mat protectors.
- Make sure you understand and observe all legislative and personal safety procedures when carrying out practical assignments. If you are unsure of what these are, ask your supervisor/instructor.
- While working on the vehicle, wheel chocks must be placed on both sides of one set of tires or as directed by your supervisor/instructor.
- When running any vehicles in the shop, make sure you use the shop's exhaust ventilation system to discharge all exhaust gas safely outside.

CDX Tasksheet Number: 4.4002

Student/Intern Information

Name _____ Date _____ Class _____

Machine, Customer, and Service Information

Machine used for this activity:

Make _____ Model _____

Hours _____ Serial Number _____

Materials Required

- Vehicle with possible power transfer concerns
- Vehicle manufacturer's service information
- Manufacturer-specific tools, depending on the concern

Task-Specific Safety Considerations

- This task may require test driving the vehicle on the school grounds or on a hoist, both of which carry severe risks. Attempt this task only with full permission from your supervisor/instructor and follow all the guidelines exactly.
- Comply with personal and environmental safety practices associated with clothing; eye protection; hand tools; power equipment; proper ventilation; and the handling, storage, and disposal of chemicals/materials in accordance with federal, state, and local regulations.
- Always wear the correct protective eyewear and clothing and use the appropriate safety equipment, as well as fender covers, seat protectors, and floor mat protectors.
- Make sure you understand and observe all legislative and personal safety procedures when carrying out practical assignments. If you are unsure of what these are, ask your supervisor/instructor.
- While working on the vehicle, wheel chocks must be placed on both sides of one set of tires or as directed by your supervisor/instructor.
- When running any vehicles in the shop, make sure you use the shop's exhaust ventilation system to discharge all exhaust gas safely outside.

▶ **TASK** Clean component(s) when replaced. **AED 4.4**

Time off_____

Time on_____

Student Instructions: Read through the entire procedure prior to starting. Prepare your workspace and any tools or parts that may be needed to complete the task. When directed by your supervisor/instructor, begin the procedure to complete the task, and comment or check the box as each step is finished. Track your time on this procedure for later comparison to the standard completion time (i.e., "flat rate" or customer pay time).

Total time_____

Procedure	Step Completed
(**Note:** Lab fixtures/instructional aids may be used for this task.)	
1. Using available service literature as a guide, describe the procedure for flushing the transmission oil after failure and for replacing the oil:	☐
2. Using the procedure described above, flush and refill the transmission oil.	☐
a. Was the procedure successful? Yes ☐ No ☐	☐
b. If no, list your recommendations for rectification:	☐
c. Record the oil capacity: _____ quarts/L	☐
d. Record the oil viscosity: _____	☐
3. Using available service literature as a guide, describe the procedure for flushing the drive axle/final drive(s) oil after failure and for replacing the oil:	☐
4. Using the procedure described above, flush and refill the drive axle/final drive(s) oil.	☐
a. Was the procedure successful? Yes ☐ No ☐	☐
b. If no, list your recommendations for rectification:	☐
c. Record the oil capacity: _____ quarts/L	☐
d. Record the oil viscosity: _____	☐
5. Using available service literature as a guide, describe the procedure for flushing the hydraulic oil after a component failure and for replacing the oil:	☐
6. Using the procedure described above, flush and refill the hydraulic oil.	☐
a. Was the procedure successful? Yes ☐ No ☐	☐

	Step Completed
b. If no, list your recommendations for rectification:	☐
c. Record the oil capacity: _____ quarts/L	☐
d. Record the oil viscosity: _____	☐
7. Discuss your findings with your supervisor/instructor.	☐

Non-Task-Specific Evaluation	Step Completed
1. Tools and equipment were used as directed and returned in good working order.	☐
2. Complied with all general and task-specific safety standards, including proper use of any personal protective equipment (PPE).	☐
3. Completed the task in an appropriate time frame (recommendation: 1.5 or 2 times the flat rate).	☐
4. Left the workspace clean and orderly.	☐
5. Cared for customer property and returned it undamaged.	☐

Student signature _____ Date _____

Comments:

Have your supervisor/instructor verify satisfactory completion of this procedure, any observations made, and any necessary action(s) recommended.

Evaluation Instructions: The scoring box below is intended to act as a guide for both student and supervisor/instructor. Each criterion listed will help students to understand what is expected of them and help supervisors/instructors to articulate the level of success at a particular task. The scoring is set up to allow a second attempt at each task (see the Test and Retest columns). Scoring is designed only to award students points for task criteria that were completed correctly. Points are lost for failure to complete the employability requirements (see Non-Task-Specific criteria). When all criteria are evaluated, tally the points for a total at the bottom of each column.

Tasksheet Scoring

	Test		Retest	
Evaluation Items	**Pass**	**Fail**	**Pass**	**Fail**
Task-Specific Evaluation	**(1 pt)**	**(0 pts)**	**(1 pt)**	**(0 pts)**
Student properly flushed and replaced the transmission oil after failure and described the procedure accurately.				
Student properly flushed and replaced the drive axle/final drive(s) oil after failure and described the procedure accurately.				
Student properly flushed and replaced the hydraulic oil after a component failure and described the procedure accurately.				
Student accurately listed recommendations for rectification when necessary.				
Non-Task-Specific Evaluation	**(0 pts)**	**(−1 pt)**	**(0 pts)**	**(−1 pt)**
Student successfully completed at least three of the non-task-specific steps.				
Student successfully completed all five of the non-task-specific steps.				
Total Score: <total # of points / 4 = %>				

Supervisor/Instructor:

Supervisor/instructor signature _____ Date _____

Comments:

Retest supervisor/instructor signature _____ Date _____

Comments:

CDX Tasksheet Number: 4.4003

Student/Intern Information

Name _____ Date _____ Class _____

Machine, Customer, and Service Information

Machine used for this activity:

Make _____ Model _____

Hours _____ Serial Number _____

Materials Required
- Vehicle with possible power transfer concerns
- Vehicle manufacturer's service information
- Manufacturer-specific tools, depending on the concern

Task-Specific Safety Considerations
- This task may require test driving the vehicle on the school grounds or on a hoist, both of which carry severe risks. Attempt this task only with full permission from your supervisor/instructor and follow all the guidelines exactly.
- Comply with personal and environmental safety practices associated with clothing; eye protection; hand tools; power equipment; proper ventilation; and the handling, storage, and disposal of chemicals/materials in accordance with federal, state, and local regulations.
- Always wear the correct protective eyewear and clothing and use the appropriate safety equipment, as well as fender covers, seat protectors, and floor mat protectors.
- Make sure you understand and observe all legislative and personal safety procedures when carrying out practical assignments. If you are unsure of what these are, ask your supervisor/instructor.
- While working on the vehicle, wheel chocks must be placed on both sides of one set of tires or as directed by your supervisor/instructor.
- When running any vehicles in the shop, make sure you use the shop's exhaust ventilation system to discharge all exhaust gas safely outside.

▶ **TASK** Remove oil sample. **AED 4.4**

Time off_____

Time on_____

Student Instructions: Read through the entire procedure prior to starting. Prepare your workspace and any tools or parts that may be needed to complete the task. When directed by your supervisor/instructor, begin the procedure to complete the task, and comment or check the box as each step is finished. Track your time on this procedure for later comparison to the standard completion time (i.e., "flat rate" or customer pay time).

Total time_____

Procedure	Step Completed
(**Note:** Lab fixtures/instructional aids may be used for this task.)	
1. Using available service literature as a guide, describe the procedure for drawing an engine oil sample using each of the following methods.	
a. Vacuum extraction	☐
b. Sampling valve	☐
2. Using one of the procedures described above, take an engine oil sample and record the required information below.	☐
a. Machine hours _____ hours	☐
b. Hours on engine oil _____ hours	☐
c. Filter(s) changed? Yes ☐ No ☐	☐
d. Engine oil changed at the time of the sample? Yes ☐ No ☐	☐
e. Oil viscosity _____	☐
3. Using available service literature as a guide, describe the procedure for drawing a transmission oil sample using each of the following methods.	
a. Vacuum extraction	☐
b. Sampling valve	☐
4. Using one of the procedures described above, take a transmission oil sample and record the required information below.	☐
a. Machine hours _____ hours	☐
b. Hours on transmission oil _____ hours	☐
c. Filter(s) changed? Yes ☐ No ☐	☐
d. Transmission oil changed at the time of the sample? Yes ☐ No ☐	☐
e. Oil viscosity _____	☐

5. Using available service literature as a guide, describe the procedure for drawing a hydraulic oil sample using each of the following methods.	
a. Vacuum extraction	☐
b. Sampling valve	☐
6. Using one of the procedures described above, take a hydraulic oil sample and record the required information below.	☐
a. Machine hours _____ hours	☐
b. Hours on hydraulic oil _____ hours	☐
c. Filter(s) changed? Yes ☐ No ☐	☐
d. Hydraulic oil changed at the time of the sample? Yes ☐ No ☐	☐
e. Oil viscosity _____	☐
7. Using available service literature as a guide, describe the procedure for drawing a coolant sample using each of the following methods.	
a. Vacuum extraction	☐
b. Sampling valve	☐
8. Using one of the procedures described above, take a coolant sample and record the required information below.	☐
a. Machine hours _____ hours	☐
b. Hours on engine coolant _____ hours	☐
c. Filter(s) changed? Yes ☐ No ☐	☐
d. Coolant changed at the time of the sample? Yes ☐ No ☐	☐
e. Coolant type _____	☐

	Step Completed
9. Using available service literature as a guide, describe the procedure for drawing a drive axle/final drive(s) oil sample using each of the following methods.	
a. Vacuum extraction	☐
b. A method other than vacuum extraction	☐
10. Using one of the procedures described above, take a drive axle/final drive(s) oil sample and record the required information below.	☐
a. Machine hours _____ hours	☐
b. Hours on drive axle/final drive(s) oil _____ hours	☐
c. Filter(s) changed? Yes ☐ No ☐	☐
d. Drive axle/final drive(s) oil changed at the time of the sample? Yes ☐ No ☐	☐
e. Oil viscosity _____	☐
11. Discuss your findings with your supervisor/instructor.	☐

Non-Task-Specific Evaluation	Step Completed
1. Tools and equipment were used as directed and returned in good working order.	☐
2. Complied with all general and task-specific safety standards, including proper use of any personal protective equipment (PPE).	☐
3. Completed the task in an appropriate time frame (recommendation: 1.5 or 2 times the flat rate).	☐
4. Left the workspace clean and orderly.	☐
5. Cared for customer property and returned it undamaged.	☐

Student signature _____ Date _____

Comments:

Have your supervisor/instructor verify satisfactory completion of this procedure, any observations made, and any necessary action(s) recommended.

Evaluation Instructions: The scoring box below is intended to act as a guide for both student and supervisor/instructor. Each criterion listed will help students to understand what is expected of them and help supervisors/instructors to articulate the level of success at a particular task. The scoring is set up to allow a second attempt at each task (see the Test and Retest columns). Scoring is designed only to award students points for task criteria that were completed correctly. Points are lost for failure to complete the employability requirements (see Non-Task-Specific criteria). When all criteria are evaluated, tally the points for a total at the bottom of each column.

Tasksheet Scoring

Evaluation Items	Test		Retest	
	Pass	Fail	Pass	Fail
Task-Specific Evaluation	**(1 pt)**	**(0 pts)**	**(1 pt)**	**(0 pts)**
Student accurately described how to take a sample of each oil type using vacuum extraction.				
Student accurately described how to take a sample of each oil type using a sampling valve (or other method).				
Student took a sample of each oil type correctly.				
Student accurately recorded the information about each oil sample.				
Non-Task-Specific Evaluation	**(0 pts)**	**(−1 pt)**	**(0 pts)**	**(−1 pt)**
Student successfully completed at least three of the non-task-specific steps.				
Student successfully completed all five of the non-task-specific steps.				
Total Score: <total # of points / 4 = %>				

Supervisor/Instructor:

Supervisor/instructor signature _____ Date _____

Comments:

Retest supervisor/instructor signature _____ Date _____

Comments:

Chapter 39: Power Train Schematics and Flow Diagrams

Learning Objective/Task	CDX Tasksheet Number	AED Reference Number
• Identify powertrain symbols.	4.5001	AED 4.5

Materials Required
• Vehicle manufacturer's service information

Safety Considerations
- This task may require test driving the vehicle on the school grounds or on a hoist, both of which carry severe risks. Attempt this task only with full permission from your supervisor/instructor and follow all the guidelines exactly.
- Comply with personal and environmental safety practices associated with clothing; eye protection; hand tools; power equipment; proper ventilation; and the handling, storage, and disposal of chemicals/materials in accordance with federal, state, and local regulations.
- Always wear the correct protective eyewear and clothing and use the appropriate safety equipment, as well as fender covers, seat protectors, and floor mat protectors.
- Make sure you understand and observe all legislative and personal safety procedures when carrying out practical assignments. If you are unsure of what these are, ask your supervisor/instructor.
- While working on the vehicle, wheel chocks must be placed on both sides of one set of tires or as directed by your supervisor/instructor.
- When running any vehicles in the shop, make sure you use the shop's exhaust ventilation system to discharge all exhaust gas safely outside.

CDX Tasksheet Number: 4.5001

Student/Intern Information

Name _____ Date _____ Class _____

Machine, Customer, and Service Information

Machine used for this activity:

Make _____ Model _____

Hours _____ Serial Number _____

Materials Required

- Vehicle manufacturer's service information

Task-Specific Safety Considerations

- This task may require test driving the vehicle on the school grounds or on a hoist, both of which carry severe risks. Attempt this task only with full permission from your supervisor/instructor and follow all the guidelines exactly.
- Comply with personal and environmental safety practices associated with clothing; eye protection; hand tools; power equipment; proper ventilation; and the handling, storage, and disposal of chemicals/materials in accordance with federal, state, and local regulations.
- Always wear the correct protective eyewear and clothing and use the appropriate safety equipment, as well as fender covers, seat protectors, and floor mat protectors.
- Make sure you understand and observe all legislative and personal safety procedures when carrying out practical assignments. If you are unsure of what these are, ask your supervisor/instructor.
- While working on the vehicle, wheel chocks must be placed on both sides of one set of tires or as directed by your supervisor/instructor.
- When running any vehicles in the shop, make sure you use the shop's exhaust ventilation system to discharge all exhaust gas safely outside.

▶ **TASK** Identify powertrain symbols.

AED 4.5

Time off_____

Time on_____

Total time_____

Student Instructions: Read through the entire procedure prior to starting. Prepare your workspace and any tools or parts that may be needed to complete the task. When directed by your supervisor/instructor, begin the procedure to complete the task, and comment or check the box as each step is finished. Track your time on this procedure for later comparison to the standard completion time (i.e., "flat rate" or customer pay time).

Procedure	Step Completed
1. Identify the following electrical symbols.	
a.	☐
b.	☐
c.	☐
d.	☐
e.	☐
f.	☐
2. Identify the following pneumatic symbols.	
a.	☐
b.	☐
c.	☐
d.	☐

e.	☐
f.	☐
3. Identify the following hydraulic symbols.	
a.	☐
b.	☐
c.	☐
d.	☐
e.	☐
f.	☐
4. Identify the following powertrain symbols.	
a.	☐

b.	☐
c.	☐
d.	☐
e.	☐
f.	☐
5. Discuss your findings with your supervisor/instructor.	☐

Non-Task-Specific Evaluation	Step Completed
1. Tools and equipment were used as directed and returned in good working order.	☐
2. Complied with all general and task-specific safety standards, including proper use of any personal protective equipment (PPE).	☐
3. Completed the task in an appropriate time frame (recommendation: 1.5 or 2 times the flat rate).	☐
4. Left the workspace clean and orderly.	☐
5. Cared for customer property and returned it undamaged.	☐

Student signature _____ Date _____

Comments:

Have your supervisor/instructor verify satisfactory completion of this procedure, any observations made,

and any necessary action(s) recommended.

Evaluation Instructions: The scoring box below is intended to act as a guide for both student and supervisor/instructor. Each criterion listed will help students to understand what is expected of them and help supervisors/instructors to articulate the level of success at a particular task. The scoring is set up to allow a second attempt at each task (see the Test and Retest columns). Scoring is designed only to award students points for task criteria that were completed correctly. Points are lost for failure to complete the employability requirements (see Non-Task-Specific criteria). When all criteria are evaluated, tally the points for a total at the bottom of each column.

Tasksheet Scoring

	Test		Retest	
Evaluation Items	**Pass**	**Fail**	**Pass**	**Fail**
Task-Specific Evaluation	**(1 pt)**	**(0 pts)**	**(1 pt)**	**(0 pts)**
Student correctly identified all of the electrical symbols.				
Student correctly identified all of the pneumatic symbols.				
Student correctly identified all of the hydraulic symbols.				
Student correctly identified all of the powertrain symbols.				
Non-Task-Specific Evaluation	**(0 pts)**	**(−1 pt)**	**(0 pts)**	**(−1 pt)**
Student successfully completed at least three of the non-task-specific steps.				
Student successfully completed all five of the non-task-specific steps.				
Total Score: <total # of points / 4 = %>				

Supervisor/Instructor:

Supervisor/instructor signature _____ Date _____

Comments:

Retest supervisor/instructor signature _____ Date _____

Comments:

Chapter 40: Troubleshooting and Failure Analysis

Learning Objective/Task	CDX Tasksheet Number	AED Reference Number
• Identify part failures.	4.6002	AED 4.6
• Replace oil and filter service.	4.6004	AED 4.6
• Fill out technical work order.	4.6005	AED 4.6

Materials Required
- Vehicle manufacturer's service information
- Vehicle with possible powertrain concern
- Vehicle with possible power transfer concerns
- Engine manufacturer's workshop materials
- Manufacturer-specific tools, depending on the concern/procedure(s)
- Vehicle/component lifting equipment, if applicable

Safety Considerations
- This task may require test driving the vehicle on the school grounds or on a hoist, both of which carry severe risks. Attempt this task only with full permission from your supervisor/instructor and follow all the guidelines exactly.
- Comply with personal and environmental safety practices associated with clothing; eye protection; hand tools; power equipment; proper ventilation; and the handling, storage, and disposal of chemicals/materials in accordance with federal, state, and local regulations.
- Always wear the correct protective eyewear and clothing and use the appropriate safety equipment, as well as fender covers, seat protectors, and floor mat protectors.
- Make sure you understand and observe all legislative and personal safety procedures when carrying out practical assignments. If you are unsure of what these are, ask your supervisor/instructor.
- While working on the vehicle, wheel chocks must be placed on both sides of one set of tires or as directed by your supervisor/instructor.
- When running any vehicles in the shop, make sure you use the shop's exhaust ventilation system to discharge all exhaust gas safely outside.
- Lifting equipment such as vehicle jacks and stands, vehicle hoists, and engine hoists are important tools that increase productivity and make the job easier. However, they can also cause severe injury or death if used improperly. Make sure you follow the manufacturer's operation procedures. Also make sure you have your supervisor's/instructor's permission to use any particular type of lifting equipment.

CDX Tasksheet Number: 4.6002

Student/Intern Information

Name _____ Date _____ Class _____

Machine, Customer, and Service Information

Machine used for this activity:

Make _____ Model _____

Hours _____ Serial Number _____

Materials Required
- Vehicle manufacturer's service information

Task-Specific Safety Considerations
- This task may require test driving the vehicle on the school grounds or on a hoist, both of which carry severe risks. Attempt this task only with full permission from your supervisor/instructor and follow all the guidelines exactly.
- Comply with personal and environmental safety practices associated with clothing; eye protection; hand tools; power equipment; proper ventilation; and the handling, storage, and disposal of chemicals/materials in accordance with federal, state, and local regulations.
- Always wear the correct protective eyewear and clothing and use the appropriate safety equipment, as well as fender covers, seat protectors, and floor mat protectors.
- Make sure you understand and observe all legislative and personal safety procedures when carrying out practical assignments. If you are unsure of what these are, ask your supervisor/instructor.
- While working on the vehicle, wheel chocks must be placed on both sides of one set of tires or as directed by your supervisor/instructor.
- When running any vehicles in the shop, make sure you use the shop's exhaust ventilation system to discharge all exhaust gas safely outside.

▶ **TASK** Identify part failures.　　　　　　　　　　　　　　**AED** 4.6

Time off_____

Time on_____

Student Instructions: Read through the entire procedure prior to starting. Prepare your workspace and any tools or parts that may be needed to complete the task. When directed by your supervisor/instructor, begin the procedure to complete the task, and comment or check the box as each step is finished. Track your time on this procedure for later comparison to the standard completion time (i.e., "flat rate" or customer pay time).

Total time_____

Procedure	Step Completed
1. Describe a creep failure:	☐
a. Give an example of a creep failure:	☐
2. Describe an erosion failure:	☐
a. Give an example of an erosion failure:	☐
3. Describe a fretting failure:	☐
a. Give an example of a fretting failure:	☐
4. Describe a corrosion failure:	☐
a. Give an example of a corrosion failure:	☐

5. Describe an overload failure:	☐
a. Give an example of an overload failure:	☐
6. Describe a fatigue failure:	☐
a. Give an example of a fatigue failure:	☐
7. Describe a ductile failure:	☐
a. Give an example of a ductile failure:	☐
8. Describe a brittle failure:	☐
a. Give an example of a brittle failure:	☐
9. Describe a brinelling failure:	☐
a. Give an example of a brinelling failure:	☐

	Step Completed
10. Describe a contamination failure:	☐
a. Give an example of a contamination failure:	☐
11. Discuss your findings with your supervisor/instructor.	☐

Non-Task-Specific Evaluation	Step Completed
1. Tools and equipment were used as directed and returned in good working order.	☐
2. Complied with all general and task-specific safety standards, including proper use of any personal protective equipment (PPE).	☐
3. Completed the task in an appropriate time frame (recommendation: 1.5 or 2 times the flat rate).	☐
4. Left the workspace clean and orderly.	☐
5. Cared for customer property and returned it undamaged.	☐

Student signature _____ Date _____

Comments:

Have your supervisor/instructor verify satisfactory completion of this procedure, any observations made, and any necessary action(s) recommended.

Evaluation Instructions: The scoring box below is intended to act as a guide for both student and supervisor/instructor. Each criterion listed will help students to understand what is expected of them and help supervisors/instructors to articulate the level of success at a particular task. The scoring is set up to allow a second attempt at each task (see the Test and Retest columns). Scoring is designed only to award students points for task criteria that were completed correctly. Points are lost for failure to complete the employability requirements (see Non-Task-Specific criteria). When all criteria are evaluated, tally the points for a total at the bottom of each column.

Tasksheet Scoring

	Test		Retest	
Evaluation Items	**Pass**	**Fail**	**Pass**	**Fail**
Task-Specific Evaluation	**(1 pt)**	**(0 pts)**	**(1 pt)**	**(0 pts)**
Student accurately described at least five of the failure types.				
Student accurately described all 10 of the failure types.				
Student provided a correct example of at least five of the failure types.				
Student provided a correct example of all 10 of the failure types.				
Non-Task-Specific Evaluation	**(0 pts)**	**(−1 pt)**	**(0 pts)**	**(−1 pt)**
Student successfully completed at least three of the non-task-specific steps.				
Student successfully completed all five of the non-task-specific steps.				
Total Score: <total # of points / 4 = %>				

Supervisor/Instructor:

Supervisor/instructor signature _____ Date _____

Comments:

Retest supervisor/instructor signature _____ Date _____

Comments:

CDX Tasksheet Number: 4.6004

Student/Intern Information

Name _____ Date _____ Class _____

Machine, Customer, and Service Information

Machine used for this activity:

Make _____ Model _____

Hours _____ Serial Number _____

Materials Required
- Vehicle with possible powertrain concern
- Engine manufacturer's workshop materials
- Manufacturer-specific tools, depending on the concern/procedure(s)
- Vehicle/component lifting equipment, if applicable

Task-Specific Safety Considerations
- This task may require test driving the vehicle on the school grounds or on a hoist, both of which carry severe risks. Attempt this task only with full permission from your supervisor/instructor and follow all the guidelines exactly.
- Lifting equipment such as vehicle jacks and stands, vehicle hoists, and engine hoists are important tools that increase productivity and make the job easier. However, they can also cause severe injury or death if used improperly. Make sure you follow the manufacturer's operation procedures. Also make sure you have your supervisor's/instructor's permission to use any particular type of lifting equipment.
- Comply with personal and environmental safety practices associated with clothing; eye protection; hand tools; power equipment; proper ventilation; and the handling, storage, and disposal of chemicals/materials in accordance with federal, state, and local regulations.
- Always wear the correct protective eyewear and clothing and use the appropriate safety equipment, as well as wheel chocks, fender covers, seat protectors, and floor mat protectors.
- Make sure you understand and observe all legislative and personal safety procedures when carrying out practical assignments. If you are unsure of what these are, ask your supervisor/instructor.

▶ TASK Replace oil and filter service.

AED
4.6

Time off_____

Time on_____

Student Instructions: Read through the entire procedure prior to starting. Prepare your workspace and any tools or parts that may be needed to complete the task. When directed by your supervisor/instructor, begin the procedure to complete the task, and comment or check the box as each step is finished. Track your time on this procedure for later comparison to the standard completion time (i.e., "flat rate" or customer pay time).

Total time_____

Note: This tasksheet may require the student to check the condition of miscellaneous vehicle fluids, some of which may be flammable and could damage the environment or cause health problems if not handled properly. Observe all safety precautions and follow local regulations for the proper disposal of fluids.

Procedure	Step Completed
1. While referencing the manufacturer's workshop materials, record the proper oil type and quantity for the vehicle.	
a. Type	☐
b. Quantity _____ quarts/L	☐
2. Using the proper equipment, drain the oil and remove the filter(s). Place in proper container(s) for disposal.	☐
3. Install new filter(s).	☐
4. While referencing the manufacturer's workshop materials, determine how much oil is to be added to bring the oil level from the ADD mark to the FULL mark on the oil dipstick. _____ quarts/L/gallons	☐
5. Fill with the appropriate amount of oil minus the amount of oil needed to bring the level from the ADD to the FULL mark on the oil dipstick. (**Note:** This is the procedure to determine the proper calibration of the oil dipstick.)	☐
6. Allow a sufficient amount of time for the oil to drain into the oil pan, then check the oil level on the dipstick. (**Note:** The level should be at the ADD mark on the dipstick.)	☐
a. Meets the manufacturer's specifications: Yes ☐ No ☐	☐
b. If no, list your recommendations for rectification:	☐
7. Add the appropriate amount of oil to bring the level from the ADD mark to the FULL mark on the oil dipstick.	☐
8. Allow a sufficient amount of time for the oil to drain into the oil pan, then check the oil level on the dipstick. (**Note:** The level should be at the FULL mark on the dipstick.)	☐
a. Meets the manufacturer's specifications: Yes ☐ No ☐	☐
b. If no, list your recommendations for rectification:	☐
9. Discuss your findings with your supervisor/instructor.	☐

Non-Task-Specific Evaluation	Step Completed
1. Tools and equipment were used as directed and returned in good working order.	☐
2. Complied with all general and task-specific safety standards, including proper use of any personal protective equipment (PPE).	☐
3. Completed the task in an appropriate time frame (recommendation: 1.5 or 2 times the flat rate).	☐
4. Left the workspace clean and orderly.	☐
5. Cared for customer property and returned it undamaged.	☐

Student signature _____ Date _____

Comments:

Have your supervisor/instructor verify satisfactory completion of this procedure, any observations made, and any necessary action(s) recommended.

Evaluation Instructions: The scoring box below is intended to act as a guide for both student and supervisor/instructor. Each criterion listed will help students to understand what is expected of them and help supervisors/instructors to articulate the level of success at a particular task. The scoring is set up to allow a second attempt at each task (see the Test and Retest columns). Scoring is designed only to award students points for task criteria that were completed correctly. Points are lost for failure to complete the employability requirements (see Non-Task-Specific criteria). When all criteria are evaluated, tally the points for a total at the bottom of each column.

Tasksheet Scoring

Evaluation Items	Test Pass (1 pt)	Test Fail (0 pts)	Retest Pass (1 pt)	Retest Fail (0 pts)
Task-Specific Evaluation	**(1 pt)**	**(0 pts)**	**(1 pt)**	**(0 pts)**
Student properly drained the oil and removed the filters.				
Student added the correct amount of oil and later verified the level was at the ADD mark.				
Student added the correct amount of oil and later verified the level was at the FULL mark.				
Student accurately noted any necessary rectifications.				
Non-Task-Specific Evaluation	**(0 pts)**	**(−1 pt)**	**(0 pts)**	**(−1 pt)**
Student successfully completed at least three of the non-task-specific steps.				
Student successfully completed all five of the non-task-specific steps.				
Total Score: <total # of points / 4 = %>				

CDX Tasksheet Number: 4.6005

Student/Intern Information

Name _____ Date _____ Class _____

Machine, Customer, and Service Information

Machine used for this activity:

Make _____ Model _____

Hours _____ Serial Number _____

Materials Required

- Vehicle with possible power transfer concerns
- Vehicle manufacturer's service information
- Manufacturer-specific tools, depending on the concern

Task-Specific Safety Considerations

- This task may require test driving the vehicle on the school grounds or on a hoist, both of which carry severe risks. Attempt this task only with full permission from your supervisor/instructor and follow all the guidelines exactly.
- Comply with personal and environmental safety practices associated with clothing; eye protection; hand tools; power equipment; proper ventilation; and the handling, storage, and disposal of chemicals/materials in accordance with federal, state, and local regulations.
- Always wear the correct protective eyewear and clothing and use the appropriate safety equipment, as well as fender covers, seat protectors, and floor mat protectors.
- Make sure you understand and observe all legislative and personal safety procedures when carrying out practical assignments. If you are unsure of what these are, ask your supervisor/instructor.
- While working on the vehicle, wheel chocks must be placed on both sides of one set of tires or as directed by your supervisor/instructor.
- When running any vehicles in the shop, make sure you use the shop's exhaust ventilation system to discharge all exhaust gas safely outside.

▶ TASK Fill out technical work order.

AED 4.6

Time off_____

Time on_____

Student Instructions: Read through the entire procedure prior to starting. Prepare your workspace and any tools or parts that may be needed to complete the task. When directed by your supervisor/instructor, begin the procedure to complete the task, and comment or check the box as each step is finished. Track your time on this procedure for later comparison to the standard completion time (i.e., "flat rate" or customer pay time).

Total time_____

Procedure	Step Completed
1. Have your supervisor/instructor assign you a fault. Troubleshoot and repair the fault using the 3 Cs (complaint, cause, and correction).	☐
2. List the machine information below.	☐
a. Make	☐
b. Model	☐
c. Serial number	☐
3. Complaint	
a. Clearly describe the machine fault/malfunction:	☐
b. Using available service literature as a guide, describe the steps for troubleshooting the fault/malfunction:	☐
c. Using available service literature as a guide, repair the fault/malfunction.	☐
4. Cause	
a. Clearly describe the cause of the fault/malfunction:	☐
5. Correction	
a. Clearly describe the steps involved in correcting the fault/malfunction:	☐
6. Discuss your findings with your supervisor/instructor.	☐

Non-Task-Specific Evaluation	Step Completed
1. Tools and equipment were used as directed and returned in good working order.	☐
2. Complied with all general and task-specific safety standards, including proper use of any personal protective equipment (PPE).	☐
3. Completed the task in an appropriate time frame (recommendation: 1.5 or 2 times the flat rate).	☐
4. Left the workspace clean and orderly.	☐
5. Cared for customer property and returned it undamaged.	☐

Student signature _____ Date _____

Comments:

Have your supervisor/instructor verify satisfactory completion of this procedure, any observations made, and any necessary action(s) recommended.

Evaluation Instructions: The scoring box below is intended to act as a guide for both student and supervisor/instructor. Each criterion listed will help students to understand what is expected of them and help supervisors/instructors to articulate the level of success at a particular task. The scoring is set up to allow a second attempt at each task (see the Test and Retest columns). Scoring is designed only to award students points for task criteria that were completed correctly. Points are lost for failure to complete the employability requirements (see Non-Task-Specific criteria). When all criteria are evaluated, tally the points for a total at the bottom of each column.

Tasksheet Scoring

Evaluation Items	Test		Retest	
	Pass	Fail	Pass	Fail
Task-Specific Evaluation	**(1 pt)**	**(0 pts)**	**(1 pt)**	**(0 pts)**
Student accurately described the complaint and how to troubleshoot the fault/malfunction.				
Student properly repaired the fault/malfunction.				
Student accurately described the cause of the fault/malfunction.				
Student accurately described how to correct the fault/malfunction.				
Non-Task-Specific Evaluation	**(0 pts)**	**(−1 pt)**	**(0 pts)**	**(−1 pt)**
Student successfully completed at least three of the non-task-specific steps.				
Student successfully completed all five of the non-task-specific steps.				
Total Score: <total # of points / 4 = %>				

Section 5: Diesel Engines

Chapter 41: Theory and Operation

Learning Objective/Task	CDX Tasksheet Number	AED Reference Number
• Test preheater system and controls.	5.2010	AED 5.2
• Determine engine rotation.	5.2011	AED 5.2
• Adjust valve clearances and injector settings.	5.2013	AED 5.2
• Inspect cooling system components (water pump, hoses, and clamps).	5.2015a	AED 5.2
• Inspect cooling system components (radiator and recovery tanks).	5.2015b	AED 5.2
• Inspect cooling system components: thermostatic cooling fan system (hydraulic, pneumatic, and electronic) and fan shroud.	5.2015c	AED 5.2
• Inspect oil pump, drives, inlet pipes, and pick-up screens.	5.2017a	AED 5.2
• Inspect oil pressure regulator valve(s), bypass and pressure relief valve(s), oil thermostat, and filters.	5.2017b	AED 5.2
• Inspect engine oil level, condition, and consumption.	5.2018a	AED 5.2
• Perform oil and filter service.	5.2018b	AED 5.2

• Discuss knowledge of the fuel system.	5.2019	AED 5.2
• Test common rail fuel systems.	5.2020	AED 5.2
• Inspect exhaust after-treatment system.	5.2021a	AED 5.2
• Inspect the emission control system.	5.2021b	AED 5.2

Materials Required

- Vehicle with possible engine concern
- Engine manufacturer's workshop materials
- Manufacturer-specific tools, depending on the concern/procedure(s)
- Vehicle/component lifting equipment, if applicable

Safety Considerations

- This task may require test driving the vehicle on the school grounds or on a hoist, both of which carry severe risks. Attempt this task only with full permission from your supervisor/instructor and follow all the guidelines exactly.
- Lifting equipment such as vehicle jacks and stands, vehicle hoists, and engine hoists are important tools that increase productivity and make the job easier. However, they can also cause severe injury or death if used improperly. Make sure you follow the manufacturer's operation procedures. Also make sure you have your supervisor's/instructor's permission to use any particular type of lifting equipment.
- Comply with personal and environmental safety practices associated with clothing; eye protection; hand tools; power equipment; proper ventilation; and the handling, storage, and disposal of chemicals/materials in accordance with federal, state, and local regulations.
- Always wear the correct protective eyewear and clothing and use the appropriate safety equipment, as well as wheel chocks, fender covers, seat protectors, and floor mat protectors.
- Make sure you understand and observe all legislative and personal safety procedures when carrying out practical assignments. If you are unsure of what these are, ask your supervisor/instructor.

CDX Tasksheet Number: 5.2010

Student/Intern Information

Name _____ Date _____ Class _____

Machine, Customer, and Service Information

Machine used for this activity:

Make _____ Model _____

Hours _____ Serial Number _____

Materials Required
- Vehicle with possible engine concern
- Engine manufacturer's workshop materials
- Manufacturer-specific tools, depending on the concern/procedure(s)
- Vehicle/component lifting equipment, if applicable

Task-Specific Safety Considerations
- This task may require test driving the vehicle on the school grounds or on a hoist, both of which carry severe risks. Attempt this task only with full permission from your supervisor/instructor and follow all the guidelines exactly.
- Lifting equipment such as vehicle jacks and stands, vehicle hoists, and engine hoists are important tools that increase productivity and make the job easier. However, they can also cause severe injury or death if used improperly. Make sure you follow the manufacturer's operation procedures. Also make sure you have your supervisor's/instructor's permission to use any particular type of lifting equipment.
- Comply with personal and environmental safety practices associated with clothing; eye protection; hand tools; power equipment; proper ventilation; and the handling, storage, and disposal of chemicals/materials in accordance with federal, state, and local regulations.
- Always wear the correct protective eyewear and clothing and use the appropriate safety equipment, as well as wheel chocks, fender covers, seat protectors, and floor mat protectors.
- Make sure you understand and observe all legislative and personal safety procedures when carrying out practical assignments. If you are unsure of what these are, ask your supervisor/instructor.

▶ **TASK** Test preheater system and controls.

AED 5.2

Time off_____

Time on_____

Total time_____

Student Instructions: Read through the entire procedure prior to starting. Prepare your workspace and any tools or parts that may be needed to complete the task. When directed by your supervisor/instructor, begin the procedure to complete the task, and comment or check the box as each step is finished. Track your time on this procedure for later comparison to the standard completion time (i.e., "flat rate" or customer pay time).

Note: This tasksheet may require the student to check the condition of miscellaneous vehicle fluids, some of which may be flammable and could damage the environment or cause health problems if not handled properly. Observe all safety precautions and follow local regulations for the proper disposal of fluids.

Procedure	Step Completed
1. Reference the manufacturer's workshop materials and identify the type of air induction system heating device:	☐
2. While referencing the manufacturer's workshop materials, inspect the air induction system heating device for missing, loose, or damaged components.	☐
a. Note any problems you found below:	☐
b. If problems exist, list your recommendations for rectification:	☐
3. While referencing the manufacturer's workshop materials, inspect the air induction system heating device wiring and controls for damaged wiring and connections.	☐
a. Note any problems you found below:	☐
b. If problems exist, list your recommendations for rectification:	☐
4. While referencing the manufacturer's workshop materials and using the appropriate electronic service tool (EST), record any air induction system heating device codes:	☐
5. If directed by your supervisor/instructor and while referencing the manufacturer's workshop materials, repair any active air induction system heating device codes.	☐
a. Meets the manufacturer's specifications: Yes ☐ No ☐	☐

b. If no, list your recommendations for rectification:	☐
6. While referencing the manufacturer's workshop materials and using the appropriate EST, perform a grid heater override test (if equipped).	☐
a. Meets the manufacturer's specifications: Yes ☐ No ☐	☐
b. If no, list your recommendations for rectification:	☐
7. Remove all electrical connections from the glow plugs (if equipped). Using a test light with an incandescent bulb, connect the alligator clip to source voltage and touch the probe end of the test light to the electrical connection on each glow plug. The test light should illuminate when touched to each connection at the glow plug (not the glow plug electrical harness). Any glow plug that does not illuminate the test light is open and needs to be replaced. (**Note:** This test can only be done with a test light with an incandescent bulb.)	☐
a. Record the test result for each glow plug:	☐
8. If directed by your supervisor/instructor and while referencing the manufacturer's workshop materials, replace any defective glow plug(s).	☐
a. Meets the manufacturer's specifications: Yes ☐ No ☐	☐
b. If no, list your recommendations for rectification:	☐
9. Discuss your findings with your supervisor/instructor.	☐

Non-Task-Specific Evaluation	Step Completed
1. Tools and equipment were used as directed and returned in good working order.	☐
2. Complied with all general and task-specific safety standards, including proper use of any personal protective equipment (PPE).	☐
3. Completed the task in an appropriate time frame (recommendation: 1.5 or 2 times the flat rate).	☐
4. Left the workspace clean and orderly.	☐
5. Cared for customer property and returned it undamaged.	☐

Student signature _____ Date _____

Comments:

Have your supervisor/instructor verify satisfactory completion of this procedure, any observations made, and any necessary action(s) recommended.

Evaluation Instructions: The scoring box below is intended to act as a guide for both student and supervisor/instructor. Each criterion listed will help students to understand what is expected of them and help supervisors/instructors to articulate the level of success at a particular task. The scoring is set up to allow a second attempt at each task (see the Test and Retest columns). Scoring is designed only to award students points for task criteria that were completed correctly. Points are lost for failure to complete the employability requirements (see Non-Task-Specific criteria). When all criteria are evaluated, tally the points for a total at the bottom of each column.

Tasksheet Scoring

Evaluation Items	Test		Retest	
	Pass	**Fail**	**Pass**	**Fail**
Task-Specific Evaluation	**(1 pt)**	**(0 pts)**	**(1 pt)**	**(0 pts)**
Student accurately identified the air induction system heating device, then properly inspected the device and its wiring and controls.				
Student properly retrieved, diagnosed, and repaired any active air induction system heating device codes.				
Student properly performed a grid heater override test.				
Student properly tested and repaired all glow plugs.				
Non-Task-Specific Evaluation	**(0 pts)**	**(−1 pt)**	**(0 pts)**	**(−1 pt)**
Student successfully completed at least three of the non-task-specific steps.				
Student successfully completed all five of the non-task-specific steps.				
Total Score: <total # of points / 4 = %>				

Supervisor/Instructor:

Supervisor/instructor signature _____ Date _____

Comments:

Retest supervisor/instructor signature _____ Date _____

Comments:

CDX Tasksheet Number: 5.2011

Student/Intern Information

Name _____ Date _____ Class _____

Machine, Customer, and Service Information

Machine used for this activity:

Make _____ Model _____

Hours _____ Serial Number _____

Materials Required
- Vehicle with possible engine concern
- Engine manufacturer's workshop materials
- Manufacturer-specific tools, depending on the concern/procedure(s)
- Vehicle/component lifting equipment, if applicable

Task-Specific Safety Considerations
- This task may require test driving the vehicle on the school grounds or on a hoist, both of which carry severe risks. Attempt this task only with full permission from your supervisor/instructor and follow all the guidelines exactly.
- Lifting equipment such as vehicle jacks and stands, vehicle hoists, and engine hoists are important tools that increase productivity and make the job easier. However, they can also cause severe injury or death if used improperly. Make sure you follow the manufacturer's operation procedures. Also make sure you have your supervisor's/instructor's permission to use any particular type of lifting equipment.
- Comply with personal and environmental safety practices associated with clothing; eye protection; hand tools; power equipment; proper ventilation; and the handling, storage, and disposal of chemicals/materials in accordance with federal, state, and local regulations.
- Always wear the correct protective eyewear and clothing and use the appropriate safety equipment, as well as wheel chocks, fender covers, seat protectors, and floor mat protectors.
- Make sure you understand and observe all legislative and personal safety procedures when carrying out practical assignments. If you are unsure of what these are, ask your supervisor/instructor.

▶ TASK Determine engine rotation.

Time off_____

Time on_____

Student Instructions: Read through the entire procedure prior to starting. Prepare your workspace and any tools or parts that may be needed to complete the task. When directed by your supervisor/instructor, begin the procedure to complete the task, and comment or check the box as each step is finished. Track your time on this procedure for later comparison to the standard completion time (i.e., "flat rate" or customer pay time).

Total time_____

Note: This tasksheet may require the student to check the condition of miscellaneous vehicle fluids, some of which may be flammable and could damage the environment or cause health problems if not handled properly. Observe all safety precautions and follow local regulations for the proper disposal of fluids.

Procedure	Step Completed
1. Describe the order of the four-stroke combustion cycle, referencing piston movement and valve positioning:	☐
2. Describe what is meant by engine rotation being either clockwise (CW) or counterclockwise (CCW):	☐
3. Describe what is meant by "valve overlap":	☐
a. Describe why valve overlap is crucial for engine positioning:	☐
4. What is the firing order for an inline six-cylinder engine?	☐
5. Describe what is meant by a "companion" cylinder and identify the companion cylinders on an inline six-cylinder engine:	☐
6. Select an inline six-cylinder assembled engine in the lab with the valves correctly adjusted and the flywheel exposed.	☐
7. Remove a valve cover and identify the intake and exhaust rocker levers.	☐
8. Referencing a shop manual or the original equipment manufacturer's service information, use the valve overlap of the companion cylinder to position the engine at top dead center (TDC) for Cylinder 1. (**Note:** The use of timing pins and aligning markers on the front engine dampener, flywheel, or accessory drive pulley are just a few of the ways TDC can be identified; however, this task involves valve overlap.)	☐
a. With Cylinder 1 at TDC, do the rocker levers have clearance? Yes ☐ No ☐	☐

	Step Completed
b. With Cylinder 1 at TDC, do its companion cylinder rocker levers have clearance? Yes ☐ No ☐	☐
c. Is the engine positioned properly for Cylinder 1 at TDC? Yes ☐ No ☐	☐
9. Taking notice of the engine rotation as CW or CCW, rotate the engine while watching the companion cylinder of the next cylinder in the firing order. Stop rotating when valve overlap occurs.	☐
a. Overlap should occur after a 120-degree or one-third rotation of the flywheel. Did the companion cylinder go into the valve overlap? Yes ☐ No ☐	☐
b. If yes, then the engine was rotated in the proper direction. If no, reverse the direction to establish proper engine rotation.	☐
10. Discuss your findings with your supervisor/instructor.	☐

Non-Task-Specific Evaluation	Step Completed
1. Tools and equipment were used as directed and returned in good working order.	☐
2. Complied with all general and task-specific safety standards, including proper use of any personal protective equipment (PPE).	☐
3. Completed the task in an appropriate time frame (recommendation: 1.5 or 2 times the flat rate).	☐
4. Left the workspace clean and orderly.	☐
5. Cared for customer property and returned it undamaged.	☐

Student signature _____ Date _____

Comments:

Have your supervisor/instructor verify satisfactory completion of this procedure, any observations made,

and any necessary action(s) recommended.

Evaluation Instructions: The scoring box below is intended to act as a guide for both student and supervisor/instructor. Each criterion listed will help students to understand what is expected of them and help supervisors/instructors to articulate the level of success at a particular task. The scoring is set up to allow a second attempt at each task (see the Test and Retest columns). Scoring is designed only to award students points for task criteria that were completed correctly. Points are lost for failure to complete the employability requirements (see Non-Task-Specific criteria). When all criteria are evaluated, tally the points for a total at the bottom of each column.

Tasksheet Scoring

Evaluation Items	Test		Retest	
	Pass	Fail	Pass	Fail
Task-Specific Evaluation	**(1 pt)**	**(0 pts)**	**(1 pt)**	**(0 pts)**
Student accurately described the four-stroke cycle and CW and CCW rotation.				
Student accurately described valve overlap.				
Student accurately described firing order and companion cylinder.				
Student established proper engine rotation with valve overlap.				
Non-Task-Specific Evaluation	**(0 pts)**	**(−1 pt)**	**(0 pts)**	**(−1 pt)**
Student successfully completed at least three of the non-task-specific steps.				
Student successfully completed all five of the non-task-specific steps.				
Total Score: <total # of points / 4 = %>				

Supervisor/Instructor:

Supervisor/instructor signature _____ Date _____

Comments:

Retest supervisor/instructor signature _____ Date _____

Comments:

CDX Tasksheet Number: 5.2013

Student/Intern Information

Name _____ Date _____ Class _____

Machine, Customer, and Service Information

Machine used for this activity:

Make _____ Model _____

Hours _____ Serial Number _____

Materials Required

- Vehicle with possible engine concern
- Engine manufacturer's workshop materials
- Manufacturer-specific tools, depending on the concern/procedure(s)
- Vehicle/component lifting equipment, if applicable

Task-Specific Safety Considerations

- This task may require test driving the vehicle on the school grounds or on a hoist, both of which carry severe risks. Attempt this task only with full permission from your supervisor/instructor and follow all the guidelines exactly.
- Lifting equipment such as vehicle jacks and stands, vehicle hoists, and engine hoists are important tools that increase productivity and make the job easier. However, they can also cause severe injury or death if used improperly. Make sure you follow the manufacturer's operation procedures. Also make sure you have your supervisor's/instructor's permission to use any particular type of lifting equipment.
- Comply with personal and environmental safety practices associated with clothing; eye protection; hand tools; power equipment; proper ventilation; and the handling, storage, and disposal of chemicals/materials in accordance with federal, state, and local regulations.
- Always wear the correct protective eyewear and clothing and use the appropriate safety equipment, as well as wheel chocks, fender covers, seat protectors, and floor mat protectors.
- Make sure you understand and observe all legislative and personal safety procedures when carrying out practical assignments. If you are unsure of what these are, ask your supervisor/instructor.

▶ **TASK** Adjust valve clearances and injector settings.

Time off_____

Student Instructions: Read through the entire procedure prior to starting. Prepare your workspace and any tools or parts that may be needed to complete the task. When directed by your supervisor/instructor, begin the procedure to complete the task, and comment or check the box as each step is finished. Track your time on this procedure for later comparison to the standard completion time (i.e., "flat rate" or customer pay time).

Time on_____

Total time_____

Note: This tasksheet may require the student to check the condition of miscellaneous vehicle fluids, some of which may be flammable and could damage the environment or cause health problems if not handled properly. Observe all safety precautions and follow local regulations for the proper disposal of fluids.

Procedure	Step Completed
1. Reference the manufacturer's workshop materials and provide the following information.	☐
a. List the steps involved in adjusting valve bridges (crossheads):	☐
b. Determine what safety precautions must be observed when adjusting the valve bridges (crossheads):	☐
2. Following the procedures listed above, and while referencing the manufacturer's workshop materials, adjust the valve bridges (crossheads).	☐
a. Meets the manufacturer's specifications: Yes ☐ No ☐	☐
b. If no, list your recommendations for any rectifications:	☐
3. Reference the manufacturer's workshop materials and provide the following information.	☐
a. List the steps involved in adjusting the injectors:	☐
b. Determine what safety precautions must be observed when adjusting the injectors:	☐
4. Following the procedures listed above, and while referencing the manufacturer's workshop materials, adjust the injectors.	☐
a. Meets the manufacturer's specifications: Yes ☐ No ☐	☐
b. If no, list your recommendations for any rectifications:	☐
5. Reference the manufacturer's workshop materials and provide the following information.	☐

	Step Completed
a. List the steps involved in adjusting the valves:	☐
b. Determine what safety precautions must be observed when adjusting the valves:	☐
6. Following the procedures listed above, and while referencing the manufacturer's workshop materials, adjust the valves.	☐
a. Meets the manufacturer's specifications: Yes ☐ No ☐	☐
b. If no, list your recommendations for any rectifications:	☐
7. Reinstall all removed components undamaged and in working order.	☐
8. Discuss your findings with your supervisor/instructor.	☐

Non-Task-Specific Evaluation	Step Completed
1. Tools and equipment were used as directed and returned in good working order.	☐
2. Complied with all general and task-specific safety standards, including proper use of any personal protective equipment (PPE).	☐
3. Completed the task in an appropriate time frame (recommendation: 1.5 or 2 times the flat rate).	☐
4. Left the workspace clean and orderly.	☐
5. Cared for customer property and returned it undamaged.	☐

Student signature _____ Date _____

Comments:

Have your supervisor/instructor verify satisfactory completion of this procedure, any observations made, and any necessary action(s) recommended.

Evaluation Instructions: The scoring box below is intended to act as a guide for both student and supervisor/instructor. Each criterion listed will help students to understand what is expected of them and help supervisors/instructors to articulate the level of success at a particular task. The scoring is set up to allow a second attempt at each task (see the Test and Retest columns). Scoring is designed only to award students points for task criteria that were completed correctly. Points are lost for failure to complete the employability requirements (see Non-Task-Specific criteria). When all criteria are evaluated, tally the points for a total at the bottom of each column.

Tasksheet Scoring

Evaluation Items	Test		Retest	
	Pass	Fail	Pass	Fail
Task-Specific Evaluation	**(1 pt)**	**(0 pts)**	**(1 pt)**	**(0 pts)**
Student properly adjusted the valve bridges to the manufacturer's specification.				
Student properly adjusted the injectors to the manufacturer's specification.				
Student properly adjusted the valves to the manufacturer's specification.				
Student properly reinstalled all removed components.				
Non-Task-Specific Evaluation	**(0 pts)**	**(−1 pt)**	**(0 pts)**	**(−1 pt)**
Student successfully completed at least three of the non-task-specific steps.				
Student successfully completed all five of the non-task-specific steps.				
Total Score: <total # of points / 4 = %>				

CDX Tasksheet Number: 5.2015a

Student/Intern Information

Name _____ Date _____ Class _____

Machine, Customer, and Service Information

Machine used for this activity:

Make _____ Model _____

Hours _____ Serial Number _____

Materials Required

- Vehicle with possible engine concern
- Engine manufacturer's workshop materials
- Manufacturer-specific tools, depending on the concern/procedure(s)
- Vehicle/component lifting equipment, if applicable

Task-Specific Safety Considerations

- This task may require test driving the vehicle on the school grounds or on a hoist, both of which carry severe risks. Attempt this task only with full permission from your supervisor/instructor and follow all the guidelines exactly.
- Lifting equipment such as vehicle jacks and stands, vehicle hoists, and engine hoists are important tools that increase productivity and make the job easier. However, they can also cause severe injury or death if used improperly. Make sure you follow the manufacturer's operation procedures. Also make sure you have your supervisor's/instructor's permission to use any particular type of lifting equipment.
- Comply with personal and environmental safety practices associated with clothing; eye protection; hand tools; power equipment; proper ventilation; and the handling, storage, and disposal of chemicals/materials in accordance with federal, state, and local regulations.
- Always wear the correct protective eyewear and clothing and use the appropriate safety equipment, as well as wheel chocks, fender covers, seat protectors, and floor mat protectors.
- Make sure you understand and observe all legislative and personal safety procedures when carrying out practical assignments. If you are unsure of what these are, ask your supervisor/instructor.

▶ TASK Inspect cooling system components (water pump, hoses, and clamps).

AED 5.2

Time off_____

Time on_____

Student Instructions: Read through the entire procedure prior to starting. Prepare your workspace and any tools or parts that may be needed to complete the task. When directed by your supervisor/instructor, begin the procedure to complete the task, and comment or check the box as each step is finished. Track your time on this procedure for later comparison to the standard completion time (i.e., "flat rate" or customer pay time).

Total time_____

Note: This tasksheet may require the student to check the condition of miscellaneous vehicle fluids, some of which may be flammable and could damage the environment or cause health problems if not handled properly. Observe all safety precautions and follow local regulations for the proper disposal of fluids.

Procedure	Step Completed
1. Reference the manufacturer's workshop materials and check and inspect the water pump for leaks. Be sure to look closely at the weep hole in the bottom of the pump for dried coolant residue. Always replace upon engine overhaul.	☐
a. Meets the manufacturer's specifications: Yes ☐ No ☐	☐
b. If no, list your recommendations for rectification:	☐
2. Check and inspect all hoses for leaks, damage, swelling, or soft spots.	☐
a. Meets the manufacturer's specifications: Yes ☐ No ☐	☐
b. If no, list your recommendations for rectification:	☐
3. Check all hose clamps for proper tightness/damage.	☐
a. Meets the manufacturer's specifications: Yes ☐ No ☐	☐
b. If no, list your recommendations for rectification:	☐
4. If directed by your supervisor/instructor, replace the water pump, hoses, and/or clamps.	☐
5. Discuss your findings with your supervisor/instructor.	☐

Non-Task-Specific Evaluation	Step Completed
1. Tools and equipment were used as directed and returned in good working order.	☐
2. Complied with all general and task-specific safety standards, including proper use of any personal protective equipment (PPE).	☐
3. Completed the task in an appropriate time frame (recommendation: 1.5 or 2 times the flat rate).	☐
4. Left the workspace clean and orderly.	☐
5. Cared for customer property and returned it undamaged.	☐

Student signature _____ Date _____

Comments:

Have your supervisor/instructor verify satisfactory completion of this procedure, any observations made, and any necessary action(s) recommended.

Evaluation Instructions: The scoring box below is intended to act as a guide for both student and supervisor/instructor. Each criterion listed will help students to understand what is expected of them and help supervisors/instructors to articulate the level of success at a particular task. The scoring is set up to allow a second attempt at each task (see the Test and Retest columns). Scoring is designed only to award students points for task criteria that were completed correctly. Points are lost for failure to complete the employability requirements (see Non-Task-Specific criteria). When all criteria are evaluated, tally the points for a total at the bottom of each column.

Tasksheet Scoring

	Test		Retest	
Evaluation Items	**Pass**	**Fail**	**Pass**	**Fail**
Task-Specific Evaluation	**(1 pt)**	**(0 pts)**	**(1 pt)**	**(0 pts)**
Student properly inspected the water pump.				
Student properly inspected the cooling system hoses.				
Student properly inspected the coolant system hose clamps.				
Student properly replaced the water pump, hoses, and/or clamps.				
Non-Task-Specific Evaluation	**(0 pts)**	**(−1 pt)**	**(0 pts)**	**(−1 pt)**
Student successfully completed at least three of the non-task-specific steps.				
Student successfully completed all five of the non-task-specific steps.				
Total Score: <total # of points / 4 = %>				

Supervisor/Instructor:

Supervisor/instructor signature _____ Date _____

Comments:

Retest supervisor/instructor signature _____ Date _____

Comments:

CDX Tasksheet Number: 5.2015b

Student/Intern Information

Name _____ Date _____ Class _____

Machine, Customer, and Service Information

Machine used for this activity:

Make _____ Model _____

Hours _____ Serial Number _____

Materials Required
- Vehicle with possible engine concern
- Engine manufacturer's workshop materials
- Manufacturer-specific tools, depending on the concern/procedure(s)
- Vehicle/component lifting equipment, if applicable

Task-Specific Safety Considerations
- This task may require test driving the vehicle on the school grounds or on a hoist, both of which carry severe risks. Attempt this task only with full permission from your supervisor/instructor and follow all the guidelines exactly.
- Lifting equipment such as vehicle jacks and stands, vehicle hoists, and engine hoists are important tools that increase productivity and make the job easier. However, they can also cause severe injury or death if used improperly. Make sure you follow the manufacturer's operation procedures. Also make sure you have your supervisor's/instructor's permission to use any particular type of lifting equipment.
- Comply with personal and environmental safety practices associated with clothing; eye protection; hand tools; power equipment; proper ventilation; and the handling, storage, and disposal of chemicals/materials in accordance with federal, state, and local regulations.
- Always wear the correct protective eyewear and clothing and use the appropriate safety equipment, as well as wheel chocks, fender covers, seat protectors, and floor mat protectors.
- Make sure you understand and observe all legislative and personal safety procedures when carrying out practical assignments. If you are unsure of what these are, ask your supervisor/instructor.

▶ **TASK** Inspect cooling system components (radiator and recovery tanks). **AED 5.2**

Time off_____

Time on_____

Student Instructions: Read through the entire procedure prior to starting. Prepare your workspace and any tools or parts that may be needed to complete the task. When directed by your supervisor/instructor, begin the procedure to complete the task, and comment or check the box as each step is finished. Track your time on this procedure for later comparison to the standard completion time (i.e., "flat rate" or customer pay time).

Total time_____

Note: This tasksheet may require the student to check the condition of miscellaneous vehicle fluids, some of which may be flammable and could damage the environment or cause health problems if not handled properly. Observe all safety precautions and follow local regulations for the proper disposal of fluids.

Procedure	Step Completed
1. Inspect the radiator and recovery tanks for signs of leakage.	☐
a. Meets the manufacturer's specifications: Yes ☐ No ☐	☐
b. If no, list your recommendations for rectification:	☐
2. Inspect radiator mounts for loose, missing, or damaged components.	☐
a. Meets the manufacturer's specifications: Yes ☐ No ☐	☐
b. If no, list your recommendations for rectification:	☐
3. Reference the manufacturer's workshop materials and record the cooling system pressure cap rating: _____ psi/kPa	☐
4. Test the pressure cap.	☐
a. Meets the manufacturer's specifications: Yes ☐ No ☐	☐
b. If no, list your recommendations for rectification:	☐
5. Reference the manufacturer's workshop materials and record the manufacturer's pressure recommendation for pressure testing the cooling system: _____ psi/kPa	☐
6. Pressure test the cooling system.	☐
a. Meets the manufacturer's specifications: Yes ☐ No ☐	☐

	Step Completed
b. If no, list your recommendations for rectification:	☐
7. Start the engine and bring it to operating temperature. Using an infrared thermometer, check the radiator core in multiple locations for hot/cold areas.	☐
a. Meets the manufacturer's specifications: Yes ☐ No ☐	☐
b. If no, list your recommendations for rectification:	☐
8. Discuss your findings with your supervisor/instructor.	☐

Non-Task-Specific Evaluation	Step Completed
1. Tools and equipment were used as directed and returned in good working order.	☐
2. Complied with all general and task-specific safety standards, including proper use of any personal protective equipment (PPE).	☐
3. Completed the task in an appropriate time frame (recommendation: 1.5 or 2 times the flat rate).	☐
4. Left the workspace clean and orderly.	☐
5. Cared for customer property and returned it undamaged.	☐

Student signature _____ Date _____

Comments:

Have your supervisor/instructor verify satisfactory completion of this procedure, any observations made,

and any necessary action(s) recommended.

Evaluation Instructions: The scoring box below is intended to act as a guide for both student and supervisor/instructor. Each criterion listed will help students to understand what is expected of them and help supervisors/instructors to articulate the level of success at a particular task. The scoring is set up to allow a second attempt at each task (see the Test and Retest columns). Scoring is designed only to award students points for task criteria that were completed correctly. Points are lost for failure to complete the employability requirements (see Non-Task-Specific criteria). When all criteria are evaluated, tally the points for a total at the bottom of each column.

Tasksheet Scoring

Evaluation Items	Test		Retest	
	Pass	Fail	Pass	Fail
Task-Specific Evaluation	**(1 pt)**	**(0 pts)**	**(1 pt)**	**(0 pts)**
Student properly inspected the radiator and recovery tank.				
Student properly inspected the radiator mounts and brackets.				
Student properly tested the cooling system pressure cap and properly performed the cooling system pressure test.				
Student properly inspected the radiator for hot and cold spots.				
Non-Task-Specific Evaluation	**(0 pts)**	**(−1 pt)**	**(0 pts)**	**(−1 pt)**
Student successfully completed at least three of the non-task-specific steps.				
Student successfully completed all five of the non-task-specific steps.				
Total Score: <total # of points / 4 = %>				

Supervisor/Instructor:

Supervisor/instructor signature _____ Date _____

Comments:

Retest supervisor/instructor signature _____ Date _____

Comments:

CDX Tasksheet Number: 5.2015c

Student/Intern Information

Name _____ Date _____ Class _____

Machine, Customer, and Service Information

Machine used for this activity:

Make _____ Model _____

Hours _____ Serial Number _____

Materials Required

- Vehicle with possible engine concern
- Engine manufacturer's workshop materials
- Manufacturer-specific tools, depending on the concern/procedure(s)
- Vehicle/component lifting equipment, if applicable

Task-Specific Safety Considerations

- This task may require test driving the vehicle on the school grounds or on a hoist, both of which carry severe risks. Attempt this task only with full permission from your supervisor/instructor and follow all the guidelines exactly.
- Lifting equipment such as vehicle jacks and stands, vehicle hoists, and engine hoists are important tools that increase productivity and make the job easier. However, they can also cause severe injury or death if used improperly. Make sure you follow the manufacturer's operation procedures. Also make sure you have your supervisor's/instructor's permission to use any particular type of lifting equipment.
- Comply with personal and environmental safety practices associated with clothing; eye protection; hand tools; power equipment; proper ventilation; and the handling, storage, and disposal of chemicals/materials in accordance with federal, state, and local regulations.
- Always wear the correct protective eyewear and clothing and use the appropriate safety equipment, as well as wheel chocks, fender covers, seat protectors, and floor mat protectors.
- Make sure you understand and observe all legislative and personal safety procedures when carrying out practical assignments. If you are unsure of what these are, ask your supervisor/instructor.

▶TASK Inspect cooling system components: thermostatic cooling fan system (hydraulic, pneumatic, and electronic) and fan shroud.

AED 5.2

Time off_____

Time on_____

Total time_____

Student Instructions: Read through the entire procedure prior to starting. Prepare your workspace and any tools or parts that may be needed to complete the task. When directed by your supervisor/instructor, begin the procedure to complete the task, and comment or check the box as each step is finished. Track your time on this procedure for later comparison to the standard completion time (i.e., "flat rate" or customer pay time).

Note: This tasksheet may require the student to check the condition of miscellaneous vehicle fluids, some of which may be flammable and could damage the environment or cause health problems if not handled properly. Observe all safety precautions and follow local regulations for the proper disposal of fluids.

Procedure	Step Completed
1. Reference the manufacturer's workshop materials and provide the following information about the cooling fan drive.	☐
a. Identify the type of cooling fan drive (viscous, hydraulic, pneumatic, electric, or Visctronic®):	☐
b. List items of concern for the applicable fan drive:	☐
2. Inspect the fan drive for loose, missing, or damaged components.	☐
a. Meets the manufacturer's specifications: Yes ☐ No ☐	☐
b. If no, list your recommendations for rectification:	☐
3. Inspect the engine cooling fan for loose, missing, or damaged blades/mounting.	☐
a. Meets the manufacturer's specifications: Yes ☐ No ☐	☐
b. If no, list your recommendations for rectification:	☐
4. Inspect the radiator shroud for loose, missing, or damaged components.	☐
a. Meets the manufacturer's specifications: Yes ☐ No ☐	☐

	Step Completed
b. If no, list your recommendations for rectification:	☐
5. Start the engine and use the appropriate electronic service tool (EST) to command the cooling fan to engage.	☐
a. Meets the manufacturer's specifications: Yes ☐ No ☐	☐
b. If no, list your recommendations for rectification:	☐
6. If directed by your supervisor/instructor, remove/reinstall the fan drive.	☐
7. Discuss your findings with your supervisor/instructor.	☐

Non-Task-Specific Evaluation	Step Completed
1. Tools and equipment were used as directed and returned in good working order.	☐
2. Complied with all general and task-specific safety standards, including proper use of any personal protective equipment (PPE).	☐
3. Completed the task in an appropriate time frame (recommendation: 1.5 or 2 times the flat rate).	☐
4. Left the workspace clean and orderly.	☐
5. Cared for customer property and returned it undamaged.	☐

Student signature _____ Date _____

Comments:

Have your supervisor/instructor verify satisfactory completion of this procedure, any observations made,

and any necessary action(s) recommended.

Evaluation Instructions: The scoring box below is intended to act as a guide for both student and supervisor/instructor. Each criterion listed will help students to understand what is expected of them and help supervisors/instructors to articulate the level of success at a particular task. The scoring is set up to allow a second attempt at each task (see the Test and Retest columns). Scoring is designed only to award students points for task criteria that were completed correctly. Points are lost for failure to complete the employability requirements (see Non-Task-Specific criteria). When all criteria are evaluated, tally the points for a total at the bottom of each column.

Tasksheet Scoring

Evaluation Items	Test		Retest	
	Pass	Fail	Pass	Fail
Task-Specific Evaluation	**(1 pt)**	**(0 pts)**	**(1 pt)**	**(0 pts)**
Student properly identified and inspected the fan drive.				
Student properly inspected the cooling fan.				
Student properly inspected the fan shroud.				
Student used the EST properly to engage the fan drive.				
Non-Task-Specific Evaluation	**(0 pts)**	**(−1 pt)**	**(0 pts)**	**(−1 pt)**
Student successfully completed at least three of the non-task-specific steps.				
Student successfully completed all five of the non-task-specific steps.				
Total Score: <total # of points / 4 = %>				

CDX Tasksheet Number: 5.2017a

Student/Intern Information

Name _____ Date _____ Class _____

Machine, Customer, and Service Information

Machine used for this activity:

Make _____ Model _____

Hours _____ Serial Number _____

Materials Required

- Vehicle with possible engine concern
- Engine manufacturer's workshop materials
- Manufacturer-specific tools, depending on the concern/procedure(s)
- Vehicle/component lifting equipment, if applicable

Task-Specific Safety Considerations

- This task may require test driving the vehicle on the school grounds or on a hoist, both of which carry severe risks. Attempt this task only with full permission from your supervisor/instructor and follow all the guidelines exactly.
- Lifting equipment such as vehicle jacks and stands, vehicle hoists, and engine hoists are important tools that increase productivity and make the job easier. However, they can also cause severe injury or death if used improperly. Make sure you follow the manufacturer's operation procedures. Also make sure you have your supervisor's/instructor's permission to use any particular type of lifting equipment.
- Comply with personal and environmental safety practices associated with clothing; eye protection; hand tools; power equipment; proper ventilation; and the handling, storage, and disposal of chemicals/materials in accordance with federal, state, and local regulations.
- Always wear the correct protective eyewear and clothing and use the appropriate safety equipment, as well as wheel chocks, fender covers, seat protectors, and floor mat protectors.
- Make sure you understand and observe all legislative and personal safety procedures when carrying out practical assignments. If you are unsure of what these are, ask your supervisor/instructor.

▶ TASK Inspect oil pump, drives, inlet pipes, and pick-up screens. **AED 5.2**

Time off_____

Time on_____

Student Instructions: Read through the entire procedure prior to starting. Prepare your workspace and any tools or parts that may be needed to complete the task. When directed by your supervisor/instructor, begin the procedure to complete the task, and comment or check the box as each step is finished. Track your time on this procedure for later comparison to the standard completion time (i.e., "flat rate" or customer pay time).

Total time_____

Note: This tasksheet may require the student to check the condition of miscellaneous vehicle fluids, some of which may be flammable and could damage the environment or cause health problems if not handled properly. Observe all safety precautions and follow local regulations for the proper disposal of fluids.

Procedure	Step Completed
1. Reference the manufacturer's workshop materials and list the type of oil pump (e.g., gear, gerotor):	☐
2. While referencing the manufacturer's workshop materials, disassemble oil pump, clean and inspect for wear/damage.	☐
a. Note any areas of wear/damage below:	☐
b. If any wear/damage exists, list your recommendations for rectification:	☐
3. Reference the manufacturer's workshop materials and note the specification for the gear to pump body end clearance: _____ in/mm	☐
a. Measure the gear to pump body end clearance and record your measurement below: _____ in/mm	☐
b. Meets the manufacturer's specifications: Yes ☐ No ☐	☐
c. If no, list your recommendations for rectification:	☐
4. Reference the manufacturer's workshop materials and note the specification for gear inner tip clearance: _____ in/mm	☐
a. Measure the gear inner tip clearance and record your measurement below: _____ in/mm	☐
b. Meets the manufacturer's specifications: Yes ☐ No ☐	☐
c. If no, list your recommendations for rectification:	☐

5. While referencing the manufacturer's workshop materials, check the pressure regulator bore and piston for wear/damage.	☐
a. Note any areas of wear/damage below:	☐
b. If any wear/damage exists, list your recommendations for rectification:	☐
6. Reference the manufacturer's workshop materials and note the specification for bore measurement: _____ in/mm	☐
a. Measure the bore and record your measurement below: _____ in/mm	☐
b. Meets the manufacturer's specifications: Yes ☐ No ☐	☐
c. If no, list your recommendations for rectification:	☐
7. Reference the manufacturer's workshop materials and note the specification for piston measurement: _____ in/mm	☐
a. Measure the piston and record your measurement below: _____ in/mm	☐
b. Meets the manufacturer's specifications: Yes ☐ No ☐	☐
c. If no, list your recommendations for rectification:	☐
8. While referencing the manufacturer's workshop materials, reassemble the oil pump. Place the oil pump in a clean plastic bag until it is installed on the engine. Apply a coating of lithium grease to all rotating components during assembly.	☐
9. While referencing the manufacturer's workshop materials, inspect the oil pick-up tube for damage (e.g., cracks, broken mounts).	☐

	Step Completed
a. Note any areas of wear/damage below:	☐
b. If any wear/damage exists, list your recommendations for rectification:	☐
10. While referencing the manufacturer's workshop materials, describe the effects of machine operating angle on the lubrication system:	☐
11. Discuss your findings with your supervisor/instructor.	☐

Non-Task-Specific Evaluation	Step Completed
1. Tools and equipment were used as directed and returned in good working order.	☐
2. Complied with all general and task-specific safety standards, including proper use of any personal protective equipment (PPE).	☐
3. Completed the task in an appropriate time frame (recommendation: 1.5 or 2 times the flat rate).	☐
4. Left the workspace clean and orderly.	☐
5. Cared for customer property and returned it undamaged.	☐

Student signature _____ Date _____

Comments:

Have your supervisor/instructor verify satisfactory completion of this procedure, any observations made,

and any necessary action(s) recommended.

Evaluation Instructions: The scoring box below is intended to act as a guide for both student and supervisor/instructor. Each criterion listed will help students to understand what is expected of them and help supervisors/instructors to articulate the level of success at a particular task. The scoring is set up to allow a second attempt at each task (see the Test and Retest columns). Scoring is designed only to award students points for task criteria that were completed correctly. Points are lost for failure to complete the employability requirements (see Non-Task-Specific criteria). When all criteria are evaluated, tally the points for a total at the bottom of each column.

Tasksheet Scoring

Evaluation Items	Test		Retest	
	Pass	**Fail**	**Pass**	**Fail**
Task-Specific Evaluation	**(1 pt)**	**(0 pts)**	**(1 pt)**	**(0 pts)**
Student correctly identified the type of oil pump and properly inspected it.				
Student properly inspected the oil pump end clearance and the oil pump tip clearance.				
Student properly cleaned and reassembled the oil pick pump.				
Student properly inspected the oil pick-up tube and screen.				
Non-Task-Specific Evaluation	**(0 pts)**	**(−1 pt)**	**(0 pts)**	**(−1 pt)**
Student successfully completed at least three of the non-task-specific steps.				
Student successfully completed all five of the non-task-specific steps.				
Total Score: <total # of points / 4 = %>				

Supervisor/Instructor:

Supervisor/instructor signature _____ Date _____

Comments:

Retest supervisor/instructor signature _____ Date _____

Comments:

CDX Tasksheet Number: 5.2017b

Student/Intern Information

Name _____ Date _____ Class _____

Machine, Customer, and Service Information

Machine used for this activity:

Make _____ Model _____

Hours _____ Serial Number _____

> ### Materials Required
> - Vehicle with possible engine concern
> - Engine manufacturer's workshop materials
> - Manufacturer-specific tools, depending on the concern/procedure(s)
> - Vehicle/component lifting equipment, if applicable

Task-Specific Safety Considerations

- This task may require test driving the vehicle on the school grounds or on a hoist, both of which carry severe risks. Attempt this task only with full permission from your supervisor/instructor and follow all the guidelines exactly.
- Lifting equipment such as vehicle jacks and stands, vehicle hoists, and engine hoists are important tools that increase productivity and make the job easier. However, they can also cause severe injury or death if used improperly. Make sure you follow the manufacturer's operation procedures. Also make sure you have your supervisor's/instructor's permission to use any particular type of lifting equipment.
- Comply with personal and environmental safety practices associated with clothing; eye protection; hand tools; power equipment; proper ventilation; and the handling, storage, and disposal of chemicals/materials in accordance with federal, state, and local regulations.
- Always wear the correct protective eyewear and clothing and use the appropriate safety equipment, as well as wheel chocks, fender covers, seat protectors, and floor mat protectors.
- Make sure you understand and observe all legislative and personal safety procedures when carrying out practical assignments. If you are unsure of what these are, ask your supervisor/instructor.

▶ TASK Inspect oil pressure regulator valve(s), bypass and pressure relief valve(s), oil thermostat, and filters.

AED 5.2

Time off_____

Time on_____

Student Instructions: Read through the entire procedure prior to starting. Prepare your workspace and any tools or parts that may be needed to complete the task. When directed by your supervisor/instructor, begin the procedure to complete the task, and comment or check the box as each step is finished. Track your time on this procedure for later comparison to the standard completion time (i.e., "flat rate" or customer pay time).

Total time_____

Note: This tasksheet may require the student to check the condition of miscellaneous vehicle fluids, some of which may be flammable and could damage the environment or cause health problems if not handled properly. Observe all safety precautions and follow local regulations for the proper disposal of fluids.

Procedure	Step Completed
1. Reference the manufacturer's workshop materials and inspect the external oil pressure regulator bore and piston for wear/damage.	☐
a. Note any areas of wear/damage below:	☐
b. If any wear/damage exists, list your recommendations for rectification:	☐
2. Reference the manufacturer's workshop materials and inspect the oil pressure bypass valve and piston for wear/damage.	☐
a. Note any areas of wear/damage below:	☐
b. If any wear/damage exists, list your recommendations for rectification:	☐
3. Reference the manufacturer's workshop materials and inspect the pressure relief valve and piston for wear/damage.	☐
a. Note any areas of wear/damage below:	☐
b. If any wear/damage exists, list your recommendations for rectification:	☐
4. Reference the manufacturer's workshop materials and inspect the oil cooler thermostat for wear/damage.	☐
a. Note any areas of wear/damage below:	☐

	Step Completed
b. If any wear/damage exists, list your recommendations for rectification:	☐
5. Remove the oil filter and use the appropriate tools to remove the filter media. Use **extreme** caution; cut edges on filter canister are extremely sharp. Cut a section of the media loose from the core and place it in a clean rag. Using a shop vice, squeeze the oil out of the filter media. Inspect the filter media for metal particles/contamination and record your findings below:	☐
6. Reference the manufacturer's workshop materials and describe the effects of machine operating angle on the lubrication system:	☐
7. Discuss your findings with your supervisor/instructor.	☐

Non-Task-Specific Evaluation	Step Completed
1. Tools and equipment were used as directed and returned in good working order.	☐
2. Complied with all general and task-specific safety standards, including proper use of any personal protective equipment (PPE).	☐
3. Completed the task in an appropriate time frame (recommendation: 1.5 or 2 times the flat rate).	☐
4. Left the workspace clean and orderly.	☐
5. Cared for customer property and returned it undamaged.	☐

Student signature _____ Date _____

Comments:

Have your supervisor/instructor verify satisfactory completion of this procedure, any observations made,

and any necessary action(s) recommended.

Evaluation Instructions: The scoring box below is intended to act as a guide for both student and supervisor/instructor. Each criterion listed will help students to understand what is expected of them and help supervisors/instructors to articulate the level of success at a particular task. The scoring is set up to allow a second attempt at each task (see the Test and Retest columns). Scoring is designed only to award students points for task criteria that were completed correctly. Points are lost for failure to complete the employability requirements (see Non-Task-Specific criteria). When all criteria are evaluated, tally the points for a total at the bottom of each column.

Tasksheet Scoring

Evaluation Items	Test		Retest	
	Pass	**Fail**	**Pass**	**Fail**
Task-Specific Evaluation	**(1 pt)**	**(0 pts)**	**(1 pt)**	**(0 pts)**
Student properly inspected the external oil pressure regulator bore and piston.				
Student properly inspected the oil pressure bypass valve and piston.				
Student properly inspected the oil pressure relief valve and piston.				
Student properly inspected the oil cooler thermostat and the oil filter.				
Non-Task-Specific Evaluation	**(0 pts)**	**(−1 pt)**	**(0 pts)**	**(−1 pt)**
Student successfully completed at least three of the non-task-specific steps.				
Student successfully completed all five of the non-task-specific steps.				
Total Score: <total # of points / 4 = %>				

Supervisor/Instructor:

Supervisor/instructor signature _____ Date _____

Comments:

Retest supervisor/instructor signature _____ Date _____

Comments:

CDX Tasksheet Number: 5.2018a

Student/Intern Information

Name _____ Date _____ Class _____

Machine, Customer, and Service Information

Machine used for this activity:

Make _____ Model _____

Hours _____ Serial Number _____

Materials Required
- Vehicle with possible engine concern
- Engine manufacturer's workshop materials
- Manufacturer-specific tools, depending on the concern/procedure(s)
- Vehicle/component lifting equipment, if applicable

Task-Specific Safety Considerations
- This task may require test driving the vehicle on the school grounds or on a hoist, both of which carry severe risks. Attempt this task only with full permission from your supervisor/instructor and follow all the guidelines exactly.
- Lifting equipment such as vehicle jacks and stands, vehicle hoists, and engine hoists are important tools that increase productivity and make the job easier. However, they can also cause severe injury or death if used improperly. Make sure you follow the manufacturer's operation procedures. Also make sure you have your supervisor's/instructor's permission to use any particular type of lifting equipment.
- Comply with personal and environmental safety practices associated with clothing; eye protection; hand tools; power equipment; proper ventilation; and the handling, storage, and disposal of chemicals/materials in accordance with federal, state, and local regulations.
- Always wear the correct protective eyewear and clothing and use the appropriate safety equipment, as well as wheel chocks, fender covers, seat protectors, and floor mat protectors.
- Make sure you understand and observe all legislative and personal safety procedures when carrying out practical assignments. If you are unsure of what these are, ask your supervisor/instructor.

▶ TASK Inspect engine oil level, condition, and consumption.

Time off_____

Time on_____

Student Instructions: Read through the entire procedure prior to starting. Prepare your workspace and any tools or parts that may be needed to complete the task. When directed by your supervisor/instructor, begin the procedure to complete the task, and comment or check the box as each step is finished. Track your time on this procedure for later comparison to the standard completion time (i.e., "flat rate" or customer pay time).

Total time_____

Note: This tasksheet may require the student to check the condition of miscellaneous vehicle fluids, some of which may be flammable and could damage the environment or cause health problems if not handled properly. Observe all safety precautions and follow local regulations for the proper disposal of fluids.

Procedure	Step Completed
1. While referencing the manufacturer's workshop materials, check the engine oil level.	☐
a. Meets the manufacturer's specifications: Yes ☐ No ☐	☐
b. If no, list your recommendations for rectification:	☐
2. Using the proper equipment, take an engine oil sample. Record all information needed for analysis:	☐
3. While referencing the manufacturer's workshop materials, determine the conditions for conducting a proper oil consumption test:	☐
4. Discuss the effects that oil levels (over and under) might have, with reference to performance and longevity of the engine:	☐
5. Discuss your findings with your supervisor/instructor.	☐

Non-Task-Specific Evaluation	Step Completed
1. Tools and equipment were used as directed and returned in good working order.	☐
2. Complied with all general and task-specific safety standards, including proper use of any personal protective equipment (PPE).	☐
3. Completed the task in an appropriate time frame (recommendation: 1.5 or 2 times the flat rate).	☐
4. Left the workspace clean and orderly.	☐
5. Cared for customer property and returned it undamaged.	☐

Student signature _____ Date _____

Comments:

Have your supervisor/instructor verify satisfactory completion of this procedure, any observations made,

and any necessary action(s) recommended.

Evaluation Instructions: The scoring box below is intended to act as a guide for both student and supervisor/instructor. Each criterion listed will help students to understand what is expected of them and help supervisors/instructors to articulate the level of success at a particular task. The scoring is set up to allow a second attempt at each task (see the Test and Retest columns). Scoring is designed only to award students points for task criteria that were completed correctly. Points are lost for failure to complete the employability requirements (see Non-Task-Specific criteria). When all criteria are evaluated, tally the points for a total at the bottom of each column.

Tasksheet Scoring

Evaluation Items	Test		Retest	
	Pass	**Fail**	**Pass**	**Fail**
Task-Specific Evaluation	**(1 pt)**	**(0 pts)**	**(1 pt)**	**(0 pts)**
Student properly checked the engine oil level.				
Student properly took an engine oil sample.				
Student accurately recorded information about the engine oil consumption test.				
Student accurately described the effects that oil levels (over and under) might have on an engine.				
Non-Task-Specific Evaluation	**(0 pts)**	**(−1 pt)**	**(0 pts)**	**(−1 pt)**
Student successfully completed at least three of the non-task-specific steps.				
Student successfully completed all five of the non-task-specific steps.				
Total Score: <total # of points / 4 = %>				

Supervisor/Instructor:

Supervisor/instructor signature _____ Date _____

Comments:

[ ]

Retest supervisor/instructor signature _____ Date _____

Comments:

[ ]

CDX Tasksheet Number: 5.2018b

Student/Intern Information

Name _____ Date _____ Class _____

Machine, Customer, and Service Information

Machine used for this activity:

Make _____ Model _____

Hours _____ Serial Number _____

Materials Required

- Vehicle with possible engine concern
- Engine manufacturer's workshop materials
- Manufacturer-specific tools, depending on the concern/procedure(s)
- Vehicle/component lifting equipment, if applicable

Task-Specific Safety Considerations

- This task may require test driving the vehicle on the school grounds or on a hoist, both of which carry severe risks. Attempt this task only with full permission from your supervisor/instructor and follow all the guidelines exactly.
- Lifting equipment such as vehicle jacks and stands, vehicle hoists, and engine hoists are important tools that increase productivity and make the job easier. However, they can also cause severe injury or death if used improperly. Make sure you follow the manufacturer's operation procedures. Also make sure you have your supervisor's/instructor's permission to use any particular type of lifting equipment.
- Comply with personal and environmental safety practices associated with clothing; eye protection; hand tools; power equipment; proper ventilation; and the handling, storage, and disposal of chemicals/materials in accordance with federal, state, and local regulations.
- Always wear the correct protective eyewear and clothing and use the appropriate safety equipment, as well as wheel chocks, fender covers, seat protectors, and floor mat protectors.
- Make sure you understand and observe all legislative and personal safety procedures when carrying out practical assignments. If you are unsure of what these are, ask your supervisor/instructor.

▶ TASK Change engine oil and filter. **AED 5.2**

Time off_____

Time on_____

Student Instructions: Read through the entire procedure prior to starting. Prepare your workspace and any tools or parts that may be needed to complete the task. When directed by your supervisor/instructor, begin the procedure to complete the task, and comment or check the box as each step is finished. Track your time on this procedure for later comparison to the standard completion time (i.e., "flat rate" or customer pay time).

Total time_____

Note: This tasksheet may require the student to check the condition of miscellaneous vehicle fluids, some of which may be flammable and could damage the environment or cause health problems if not handled properly. Observe all safety precautions and follow local regulations for the proper disposal of fluids.

Procedure	Step Completed
1. Reference the manufacturer's workshop materials and record the proper engine oil type and quantity.	☐
a. Type	☐
b. Quantity _____ quarts/L/gallons	☐
2. Using the proper equipment, drain the engine oil and remove the filter(s). Place them in proper container(s) for disposal.	☐
3. Install new filter(s).	☐
4. While referencing the manufacturer's workshop materials, determine how much oil should be added to bring the oil level from the ADD mark to the FULL mark on the engine oil dipstick. Record it below: _____ quarts/L/gallons	☐
5. Fill the engine with the appropriate amount of engine oil minus the amount of oil needed to bring the level from the ADD to the FULL mark on the engine oil dipstick. (**Note:** This procedure determines the proper calibration of the engine oil dipstick.)	☐
6. Allow a sufficient amount of time for the engine oil to drain into the engine oil pan, then check the oil level on the dipstick. The level should be at the ADD mark on the dipstick.	☐
a. Meets the manufacturer's specifications: Yes ☐ No ☐	☐
b. If no, list your recommendations for rectification:	☐
7. Add the appropriate amount of engine oil to bring the level from the ADD mark to the FULL mark on the engine oil dipstick.	☐
8. Allow a sufficient amount of time for the engine oil to drain into the engine oil pan, then check the oil level on the dipstick. The level should be to the FULL mark on the dipstick.	☐
a. Meets the manufacturer's specifications: Yes ☐ No ☐	☐
b. If no, list your recommendations for rectification:	☐

	Step Completed
9. Discuss the effects that oil levels (over and under) might have, with reference to performance and longevity of the engine:	☐
10. Discuss your findings with your supervisor/instructor.	☐

Non-Task-Specific Evaluation	Step Completed
1. Tools and equipment were used as directed and returned in good working order.	☐
2. Complied with all general and task-specific safety standards, including proper use of any personal protective equipment (PPE).	☐
3. Completed the task in an appropriate time frame (recommendation: 1.5 or 2 times the flat rate).	☐
4. Left the workspace clean and orderly.	☐
5. Cared for customer property and returned it undamaged.	☐

Student signature _____ Date _____

Comments:

Have your supervisor/instructor verify satisfactory completion of this procedure, any observations made, and any necessary action(s) recommended.

Evaluation Instructions: The scoring box below is intended to act as a guide for both student and supervisor/instructor. Each criterion listed will help students to understand what is expected of them and help supervisors/instructors to articulate the level of success at a particular task. The scoring is set up to allow a second attempt at each task (see the Test and Retest columns). Scoring is designed only to award students points for task criteria that were completed correctly. Points are lost for failure to complete the employability requirements (see Non-Task-Specific criteria). When all criteria are evaluated, tally the points for a total at the bottom of each column.

Tasksheet Scoring

Evaluation Items	Test		Retest	
	Pass	**Fail**	**Pass**	**Fail**
Task-Specific Evaluation	**(1 pt)**	**(0 pts)**	**(1 pt)**	**(0 pts)**
Student properly drained and placed the engine oil in suitable containers for disposal.				
Student properly changed the engine oil filter(s).				
Student properly checked the engine oil dipstick calibration.				
Student accurately described the effects that oil levels (over and under) might have on an engine.				
Non-Task-Specific Evaluation	**(0 pts)**	**(−1 pt)**	**(0 pts)**	**(−1 pt)**
Student successfully completed at least three of the non-task-specific steps.				
Student successfully completed all five of the non-task-specific steps.				
Total Score: <total # of points / 4 = %>				

Supervisor/Instructor:

Supervisor/instructor signature _____ Date _____

Comments:

Retest supervisor/instructor signature _____ Date _____

Comments:

CDX Tasksheet Number: 5.2019

Student/Intern Information

Name _____ Date _____ Class _____

Machine, Customer, and Service Information

Machine used for this activity:

Make _____ Model _____

Hours _____ Serial Number _____

Materials Required

- Vehicle with possible engine concern
- Engine manufacturer's workshop materials
- Manufacturer-specific tools, depending on the concern/procedure(s)
- Vehicle/component lifting equipment, if applicable

Task-Specific Safety Considerations

- This task may require test driving the vehicle on the school grounds or on a hoist, both of which carry severe risks. Attempt this task only with full permission from your supervisor/instructor and follow all the guidelines exactly.
- Lifting equipment such as vehicle jacks and stands, vehicle hoists, and engine hoists are important tools that increase productivity and make the job easier. However, they can also cause severe injury or death if used improperly. Make sure you follow the manufacturer's operation procedures. Also make sure you have your supervisor's/instructor's permission to use any particular type of lifting equipment.
- Comply with personal and environmental safety practices associated with clothing; eye protection; hand tools; power equipment; proper ventilation; and the handling, storage, and disposal of chemicals/materials in accordance with federal, state, and local regulations.
- Always wear the correct protective eyewear and clothing and use the appropriate safety equipment, as well as wheel chocks, fender covers, seat protectors, and floor mat protectors.
- Make sure you understand and observe all legislative and personal safety procedures when carrying out practical assignments. If you are unsure of what these are, ask your supervisor/instructor.

▶ **TASK** Discuss knowledge of the fuel system. **AED 5.2**

Time off_____

Time on_____

Student Instructions: Read through the entire procedure prior to starting. Prepare your workspace and any tools or parts that may be needed to complete the task. When directed by your supervisor/instructor, begin the procedure to complete the task, and comment or check the box as each step is finished. Track your time on this procedure for later comparison to the standard completion time (i.e., "flat rate" or customer pay time).

Total time_____

Note: This tasksheet may require the student to check the condition of miscellaneous vehicle fluids, some of which may be flammable and could damage the environment or cause health problems if not handled properly. Observe all safety precautions and follow local regulations for the proper disposal of fluids.

Procedure	Step Completed
1. While researching different manufacturers, explain the operation of an indirect diesel fuel injection (IDI) system:	☐
a. Manufacturer type	☐
b. Special service precautions	☐
c. Disadvantages	☐
2. While researching different manufacturers, explain the operation of a multiple plunger diesel fuel injection system:	☐
a. Manufacturer type	☐
b. Special service precautions	☐
c. Disadvantages	☐
3. While researching different manufacturers, explain the operation of a mechanical distributor diesel fuel injection system:	☐

a. Manufacturer type	☐
b. Special service precautions	☐
c. Disadvantages	☐
4. While researching different manufacturers, explain the operation of an electronic distributor diesel fuel injection system:	☐
a. Manufacturer type	☐
b. Special service precautions	☐
c. Disadvantages	☐
5. While researching different manufacturers, explain the operation of an electronic unit injector (EUI) diesel fuel injection system:	☐
a. Manufacturer type	☐

b. Special service precautions	☐
c. Disadvantages	☐
6. While researching different manufacturers, explain the operation of a hydraulic electronic unit injector (HEUI) diesel fuel injection system:	☐
a. Manufacturer type	☐
b. Special service precautions	☐
c. Disadvantages	☐
7. While researching different manufacturers, explain the operation of a unit injector diesel fuel injection system:	☐
a. Manufacturer type	☐
b. Special service precautions	☐

c. Disadvantages	☐
8. While researching different manufacturers, explain the operation of a common rail diesel fuel injection system:	☐
a. Manufacturer type	☐
b. Special service precautions	☐
c. Disadvantages	☐
9. Describe some of the common characteristics that the above fuel injection systems have:	☐
10. Discuss your findings with your supervisor/instructor.	☐

Non-Task-Specific Evaluation	Step Completed
1. Tools and equipment were used as directed and returned in good working order.	☐
2. Complied with all general and task-specific safety standards, including proper use of any personal protective equipment (PPE).	☐
3. Completed the task in an appropriate time frame (recommendation: 1.5 or 2 times the flat rate).	☐
4. Left the workspace clean and orderly.	☐
5. Cared for customer property and returned it undamaged.	☐

Student signature _____ Date _____

Comments:

Have your supervisor/instructor verify satisfactory completion of this procedure, any observations made, and any necessary action(s) recommended.

Evaluation Instructions: The scoring box below is intended to act as a guide for both student and supervisor/instructor. Each criterion listed will help students to understand what is expected of them and help supervisors/instructors to articulate the level of success at a particular task. The scoring is set up to allow a second attempt at each task (see the Test and Retest columns). Scoring is designed only to award students points for task criteria that were completed correctly. Points are lost for failure to complete the employability requirements (see Non-Task-Specific criteria). When all criteria are evaluated, tally the points for a total at the bottom of each column.

Tasksheet Scoring

Evaluation Items	Test		Retest	
	Pass	**Fail**	**Pass**	**Fail**
Task-Specific Evaluation	**(1 pt)**	**(0 pts)**	**(1 pt)**	**(0 pts)**
Student accurately explained the operation of at least two of the fuel systems.				
Student accurately explained the operation of at least five of the fuel systems.				
Student accurately explained the operation of all eight of the fuel systems.				
Student accurately explained common characteristics among the different systems.				
Non-Task-Specific Evaluation	**(0 pts)**	**(−1 pt)**	**(0 pts)**	**(−1 pt)**
Student successfully completed at least three of the non-task-specific steps.				
Student successfully completed all five of the non-task-specific steps.				
Total Score: <total # of points / 4 = %>				

Supervisor/Instructor:

Supervisor/instructor signature _____ Date _____

Comments:

Retest supervisor/instructor signature _____ Date _____

Comments:

CDX Tasksheet Number: 5.2020

Student/Intern Information

Name _____ Date _____ Class _____

Machine, Customer, and Service Information

Machine used for this activity:

Make _____ Model _____

Hours _____ Serial Number _____

Materials Required
- Vehicle with possible engine concern
- Engine manufacturer's workshop materials
- Manufacturer-specific tools, depending on the concern/procedure(s)
- Vehicle/component lifting equipment, if applicable

Task-Specific Safety Considerations
- This task may require test driving the vehicle on the school grounds or on a hoist, both of which carry severe risks. Attempt this task only with full permission from your supervisor/instructor and follow all the guidelines exactly.
- Lifting equipment such as vehicle jacks and stands, vehicle hoists, and engine hoists are important tools that increase productivity and make the job easier. However, they can also cause severe injury or death if used improperly. Make sure you follow the manufacturer's operation procedures. Also make sure you have your supervisor's/instructor's permission to use any particular type of lifting equipment.
- Comply with personal and environmental safety practices associated with clothing; eye protection; hand tools; power equipment; proper ventilation; and the handling, storage, and disposal of chemicals/materials in accordance with federal, state, and local regulations.
- Always wear the correct protective eyewear and clothing and use the appropriate safety equipment, as well as wheel chocks, fender covers, seat protectors, and floor mat protectors.
- Make sure you understand and observe all legislative and personal safety procedures when carrying out practical assignments. If you are unsure of what these are, ask your supervisor/instructor.

▶ **TASK** Test common rail fuel systems.

Time off_____

Student Instructions: Read through the entire procedure prior to starting. Prepare your workspace and any tools or parts that may be needed to complete the task. When directed by your supervisor/instructor, begin the procedure to complete the task, and comment or check the box as each step is finished. Track your time on this procedure for later comparison to the standard completion time (i.e., "flat rate" or customer pay time).

Time on_____

Total time_____

Note: This tasksheet may require the student to check the condition of miscellaneous vehicle fluids, some of which may be flammable and could damage the environment or cause health problems if not handled properly. Observe all safety precautions and follow local regulations for the proper disposal of fluids.

Procedure	Step Completed
1. While referencing the manufacturer's workshop materials, inspect the high-pressure fuel system for damage, leaks, and proper securement.	☐
a. List any problems you found below:	☐
b. If problems exist, list your recommendations for rectification:	☐
2. While referencing the manufacturer's workshop materials, list all precautions to take for the following situations.	
a. Before servicing the high-pressure fuel system:	☐
b. While servicing the high-pressure fuel system:	☐
3. While referencing the manufacturer's workshop materials, list all safety precautions when servicing the high-pressure fuel system:	☐
4. While referencing the manufacturer's workshop materials, list the inspection procedure for high-pressure fuel lines below, then perform the inspection:	☐
a. Meets the manufacturer's specifications: Yes ☐ No ☐	☐
b. If no, list your recommendations for rectification:	☐

5. While referencing the manufacturer's workshop materials, list the inspection procedure for the fuel pressure relief valve below, then perform the inspection:	☐
a. Meets the manufacturer's specifications: Yes ☐ No ☐	☐
b. If no, list your recommendations for rectification:	☐
6. While referencing the manufacturer's workshop materials, list the inspection procedure for the fuel injector feed tubes below, then perform the inspection:	☐
a. Meets the manufacturer's specifications: Yes ☐ No ☐	☐
b. If no, list your recommendations for rectification:	☐
7. While referencing the manufacturer's workshop materials, list the procedure for performing a high-pressure system leak-down test below, then perform the test.	☐
a. Meets the manufacturer's specifications: Yes ☐ No ☐	☐
b. If no, list your recommendations for rectification:	☐
8. While referencing the manufacturer's workshop materials, list the procedure for performing a high-pressure fuel pump return flow test below, then perform the test.	☐

a. Meets the manufacturer's specifications: Yes ☐ No ☐	☐
b. If no, list your recommendations for rectification:	☐
9. While referencing the manufacturer's workshop materials, list the procedure for performing a high-pressure injector return flow test below, then perform the test.	☐
a. Meets the manufacturer's specifications: Yes ☐ No ☐	☐
b. If no, list your recommendations for rectification:	☐
10. While referencing the manufacturer's workshop materials, list the procedure for performing a high-pressure fuel pump performance test below, then perform the test:	☐
a. Meets the manufacturer's specifications: Yes ☐ No ☐	☐
b. If no, list your recommendations for rectification:	☐
11. While referencing the manufacturer's workshop materials, list the procedure for performing a high-pressure injector return flow isolation test below, then perform the test.	☐
a. Meets the manufacturer's specifications: Yes ☐ No ☐	☐
b. If no, list your recommendations for rectification:	☐

	Step Completed
12. While referencing the manufacturer's workshop materials, list the procedure for performing a fuel pressure relief valve return flow test below, then perform the test:	☐
a. Meets the manufacturer's specifications: Yes ☐ No ☐	☐
b. If no, list your recommendations for rectification:	☐
13. Discuss your findings with your supervisor/instructor.	☐

Non-Task-Specific Evaluation	Step Completed
1. Tools and equipment were used as directed and returned in good working order.	☐
2. Complied with all general and task-specific safety standards, including proper use of any personal protective equipment (PPE).	☐
3. Completed the task in an appropriate time frame (recommendation: 1.5 or 2 times the flat rate).	☐
4. Left the workspace clean and orderly.	☐
5. Cared for customer property and returned it undamaged.	☐

Student signature _____ Date _____

Comments:

Have your supervisor/instructor verify satisfactory completion of this procedure, any observations made, and any necessary action(s) recommended.

Evaluation Instructions: The scoring box below is intended to act as a guide for both student and supervisor/instructor. Each criterion listed will help students to understand what is expected of them and help supervisors/instructors to articulate the level of success at a particular task. The scoring is set up to allow a second attempt at each task (see the Test and Retest columns). Scoring is designed only to award students points for task criteria that were completed correctly. Points are lost for failure to complete the employability requirements (see Non-Task-Specific criteria). When all criteria are evaluated, tally the points for a total at the bottom of each column.

Tasksheet Scoring

Evaluation Items	Test		Retest	
	Pass	**Fail**	**Pass**	**Fail**
Task-Specific Evaluation	**(1 pt)**	**(0 pts)**	**(1 pt)**	**(0 pts)**
Student accurately described how to perform each of the inspections/tests.				
Student properly performed each inspection.				
Student properly performed each test.				
Student accurately listed rectifications for any problems found.				
Non-Task-Specific Evaluation	**(0 pts)**	**(−1 pt)**	**(0 pts)**	**(−1 pt)**
Student successfully completed at least three of the non-task-specific steps.				
Student successfully completed all five of the non-task-specific steps.				
Total Score: <total # of points / 4 = %>				

Supervisor/Instructor:

Supervisor/instructor signature _____ Date _____

Comments:

Retest supervisor/instructor signature _____ Date _____

Comments:

CDX Tasksheet Number: 5.2021a

Student/Intern Information

Name _____ Date _____ Class _____

Machine, Customer, and Service Information

Machine used for this activity:

Make _____ Model _____

Hours _____ Serial Number _____

Task-Specific Safety Considerations

- This task may require test driving the vehicle on the school grounds or on a hoist, both of which carry severe risks. Attempt this task only with full permission from your supervisor/instructor and follow all the guidelines exactly.
- Lifting equipment such as vehicle jacks and stands, vehicle hoists, and engine hoists are important tools that increase productivity and make the job easier. However, they can also cause severe injury or death if used improperly. Make sure you follow the manufacturer's operation procedures. Also make sure you have your supervisor's/instructor's permission to use any particular type of lifting equipment.
- Comply with personal and environmental safety practices associated with clothing; eye protection; hand tools; power equipment; proper ventilation; and the handling, storage, and disposal of chemicals/materials in accordance with federal, state, and local regulations.
- Always wear the correct protective eyewear and clothing and use the appropriate safety equipment, as well as wheel chocks, fender covers, seat protectors, and floor mat protectors.
- Make sure you understand and observe all legislative and personal safety procedures when carrying out practical assignments. If you are unsure of what these are, ask your supervisor/instructor.

▶ **TASK** Inspect exhaust after-treatment system.

Time off_____

Time on_____

Student Instructions: Read through the entire procedure prior to starting. Prepare your workspace and any tools or parts that may be needed to complete the task. When directed by your supervisor/instructor, begin the procedure to complete the task, and comment or check the box as each step is finished. Track your time on this procedure for later comparison to the standard completion time (i.e., "flat rate" or customer pay time).

Total time_____

Note: This tasksheet may require the student to check the condition of miscellaneous vehicle fluids, some of which may be flammable and could damage the environment or cause health problems if not handled properly. Observe all safety precautions and follow local regulations for the proper disposal of fluids.

Procedure	Step Completed
1. While referencing the manufacturer's workshop materials, inspect the exhaust manifold for missing, loose, or damaged components.	☐
a. Meets the manufacturer's specifications: Yes ☐ No ☐	☐
b. If no, list your recommendations for rectification:	☐
2. While referencing the manufacturer's workshop materials, inspect the exhaust manifold gaskets/sections for signs of leakage or damage.	☐
a. Meets the manufacturer's specifications: Yes ☐ No ☐	☐
b. If no, list your recommendations for rectification:	☐
3. While referencing the manufacturer's workshop materials, record the procedure and torque specification(s) for tightening the exhaust manifold bolts, then check the exhaust manifold bolt torque.	☐
a. Meets the manufacturer's specifications: Yes ☐ No ☐	☐
b. If no, list your recommendations for rectification:	☐
4. While referencing the manufacturer's workshop materials, inspect the exhaust gas recirculation (EGR) cooler for missing, loose, or damaged components.	☐
a. Meets the manufacturer's specifications: Yes ☐ No ☐	☐
b. If no, list your recommendations for rectification:	☐

5. While referencing the manufacturer's workshop materials, record the procedure for performing an on-engine EGR cooler coolant strip test, then perform the test.	☐
a. Meets the manufacturer's specifications: Yes ☐ No ☐	☐
b. If no, list your recommendations for rectification:	☐
6. While referencing the manufacturer's workshop materials, record the procedure for performing an EGR cooler pressure test, then perform the test.	☐
a. Meets the manufacturer's specifications: Yes ☐ No ☐	☐
b. If no, list your recommendations for rectification:	☐
7. While referencing the manufacturer's workshop materials, inspect the exhaust pipe and muffler for leaks; proper routing; and missing, loose, or damaged components.	☐
a. Meets the manufacturer's specifications: Yes ☐ No ☐	☐
b. If no, list your recommendations for rectification:	☐
8. While referencing the manufacturer's workshop materials, inspect the after-treatment system for leaks and missing, loose, or damaged components.	☐
a. Meets the manufacturer's specifications: Yes ☐ No ☐	☐
b. If no, list your recommendations for rectification:	☐

9. While referencing the manufacturer's workshop materials, record the procedure for removing and inspecting the after-treatment selective catalytic reduction (SCR) catalyst.	☐
a. Remove the SCR catalyst, inspect it, then reinstall it.	☐
b. Meets the manufacturer's specifications: Yes ☐ No ☐	☐
c. If no, list your recommendations for rectification:	☐
10. While referencing the manufacturer's workshop materials, record the procedure for removing and inspecting the diesel particulate filter (DPF).	☐
a. Remove the DPF, inspect it, then reinstall it.	☐
b. Meets the manufacturer's specifications: Yes ☐ No ☐	☐
c. If no, list your recommendations for rectification:	☐
11. Describe the effect of emission components on Environmental Protection Agency (EPA) and California Air Resources Board (CARB) regulations:	☐
12. Discuss your findings with your supervisor/instructor.	☐

Non-Task-Specific Evaluation	Step Completed
1. Tools and equipment were used as directed and returned in good working order.	☐
2. Complied with all general and task-specific safety standards, including proper use of any personal protective equipment (PPE).	☐
3. Completed the task in an appropriate time frame (recommendation: 1.5 or 2 times the flat rate).	☐
4. Left the workspace clean and orderly.	☐
5. Cared for customer property and returned it undamaged.	☐

Student signature _____ Date _____

Comments:

Have your supervisor/instructor verify satisfactory completion of this procedure, any observations made, and any necessary action(s) recommended.

Evaluation Instructions: The scoring box below is intended to act as a guide for both student and supervisor/instructor. Each criterion listed will help students to understand what is expected of them and help supervisors/instructors to articulate the level of success at a particular task. The scoring is set up to allow a second attempt at each task (see the Test and Retest columns). Scoring is designed only to award students points for task criteria that were completed correctly. Points are lost for failure to complete the employability requirements (see Non-Task-Specific criteria). When all criteria are evaluated, tally the points for a total at the bottom of each column.

Tasksheet Scoring

Evaluation Items	Test		Retest	
	Pass	**Fail**	**Pass**	**Fail**
Task-Specific Evaluation	**(1 pt)**	**(0 pts)**	**(1 pt)**	**(0 pts)**
Student accurately described how to perform each of the inspections/tests.				
Student properly performed each inspection.				
Student properly performed each test.				
Student properly removed, inspected, and reinstalled the SCR catalyst and DPF.				
Non-Task-Specific Evaluation	**(0 pts)**	**(−1 pt)**	**(0 pts)**	**(−1 pt)**
Student successfully completed at least three of the non-task-specific steps.				
Student successfully completed all five of the non-task-specific steps.				
Total Score: <total # of points / 4 = %>				

Supervisor/Instructor:

Supervisor/instructor signature _____ Date _____

Comments:

Retest supervisor/instructor signature _____ Date _____

Comments:

CDX Tasksheet Number: 5.2021b

Student/Intern Information

Name _____ Date _____ Class _____

Machine, Customer, and Service Information

Machine used for this activity:

Make _____ Model _____

Hours _____ Serial Number _____

Materials Required
- Vehicle with possible engine concern
- Engine manufacturer's workshop materials
- Manufacturer-specific tools, depending on the concern/procedure(s)
- Vehicle/component lifting equipment, if applicable

Task-Specific Safety Considerations
- This task may require test driving the vehicle on the school grounds or on a hoist, both of which carry severe risks. Attempt this task only with full permission from your supervisor/instructor and follow all the guidelines exactly.
- Lifting equipment such as vehicle jacks and stands, vehicle hoists, and engine hoists are important tools that increase productivity and make the job easier. However, they can also cause severe injury or death if used improperly. Make sure you follow the manufacturer's operation procedures. Also make sure you have your supervisor's/instructor's permission to use any particular type of lifting equipment.
- Comply with personal and environmental safety practices associated with clothing; eye protection; hand tools; power equipment; proper ventilation; and the handling, storage, and disposal of chemicals/materials in accordance with federal, state, and local regulations.
- Always wear the correct protective eyewear and clothing and use the appropriate safety equipment, as well as wheel chocks, fender covers, seat protectors, and floor mat protectors.
- Make sure you understand and observe all legislative and personal safety procedures when carrying out practical assignments. If you are unsure of what these are, ask your supervisor/instructor.

▶ TASK Inspect the emission control system.

AED 5.2

Time off_____

Time on_____

Student Instructions: Read through the entire procedure prior to starting. Prepare your workspace and any tools or parts that may be needed to complete the task. When directed by your supervisor/instructor, begin the procedure to complete the task, and comment or check the box as each step is finished. Track your time on this procedure for later comparison to the standard completion time (i.e., "flat rate" or customer pay time).

Total time_____

Note: This tasksheet may require the student to check the condition of miscellaneous vehicle fluids, some of which may be flammable and could damage the environment or cause health problems if not handled properly. Observe all safety precautions and follow local regulations for the proper disposal of fluids.

Procedure	Step Completed
1. While referencing the manufacturer's workshop materials and using the appropriate electronic service tool (EST), record any after-treatment codes:	☐
2. While referencing the manufacturer's workshop materials, inspect the exhaust aftertreatment system for missing, loose, or damaged components.	☐
a. Note any problems you found below:	☐
b. If problems exist, list your recommendations for rectification:	☐
3. If equipped and while referencing the manufacturer's workshop materials, inspect the aftertreatment fuel injector connections for signs of fuel (and coolant, if equipped) leakage.	☐
a. Note any problems you found below:	☐
b. If problems exist, list your recommendations for rectification:	☐
4. While referencing the manufacturer's workshop materials, record the procedure for removing and inspecting the aftertreatment fuel injector (if equipped):	☐
5. If directed by your supervisor/instructor and while referencing the manufacturer's workshop materials, remove, inspect, and reinstall the aftertreatment fuel injector.	☐
a. Meets the manufacturer's specifications: Yes ☐ No ☐	☐

b. If no, list your recommendations for rectification:	☐
6. While referencing the manufacturer's workshop materials, record the procedure for removing and inspecting the aftertreatment selective catalytic reduction (SCR) catalyst:	☐
7. If directed by your supervisor/instructor and while referencing the manufacturer's workshop materials, remove, inspect, and reinstall the aftertreatment SCR catalyst.	☐
a. Meets the manufacturer's specifications: Yes ☐ No ☐	☐
b. If no, list your recommendations for rectification:	☐
8. While referencing the manufacturer's workshop materials, record the procedure for removing and inspecting the diesel particulate filter (DPF):	☐
9. If directed by your supervisor/instructor and while referencing the manufacturer's workshop materials, remove, inspect, and reinstall the DPF.	☐
a. Meets the manufacturer's specifications: Yes ☐ No ☐	☐
b. If no, list your recommendations for rectification:	☐
10. While referencing the manufacturer's workshop materials, inspect the diesel exhaust fluid (DEF) reservoir, lines, and connections for missing, loose, or damaged components.	☐
a. Note any problems you found below:	☐

b. If problems exist, list your recommendations for rectification:	☐
11. While referencing the manufacturer's workshop materials, record the procedure for removing, inspecting, and reinstalling the aftertreatment decomposition tube:	☐
12. If directed by your supervisor/instructor and while referencing the manufacturer's workshop materials, remove, inspect, and reinstall the aftertreatment decomposition tube.	☐
a. Meets the manufacturer's specifications: Yes ☐ No ☐	☐
b. If no, list your recommendations for rectification:	☐
13. While referencing the manufacturer's workshop materials and using the appropriate EST, record any aftertreatment codes that may have become active after the aftertreatment components were removed, inspected, and reinstalled:	☐
14. If directed by your supervisor/instructor and while referencing the manufacturer's workshop materials, repair any active aftertreatment codes.	☐
15. While referencing the manufacturer's workshop materials, record the procedure and any special precautions for performing a stationary regeneration:	☐
16. If directed by your supervisor/instructor and while referencing the manufacturer's workshop materials, perform a stationary regeneration.	☐
a. Meets the manufacturer's specifications: Yes ☐ No ☐	☐
b. If no, list your recommendations for rectification:	☐

	Step Completed
17. Describe the effect of the emission components on Environmental Protection Agency (EPA) and California Air Resources Board (CARB) regulations:	☐
18. Discuss your findings with your supervisor/instructor.	☐

Non-Task-Specific Evaluation	Step Completed
1. Tools and equipment were used as directed and returned in good working order.	☐
2. Complied with all general and task-specific safety standards, including proper use of any personal protective equipment (PPE).	☐
3. Completed the task in an appropriate time frame (recommendation: 1.5 or 2 times the flat rate).	☐
4. Left the workspace clean and orderly.	☐
5. Cared for customer property and returned it undamaged.	☐

Student signature _____ Date _____

Comments:

Have your supervisor/instructor verify satisfactory completion of this procedure, any observations made, and any necessary action(s) recommended.

Evaluation Instructions: The scoring box below is intended to act as a guide for both student and supervisor/instructor. Each criterion listed will help students to understand what is expected of them and help supervisors/instructors to articulate the level of success at a particular task. The scoring is set up to allow a second attempt at each task (see the Test and Retest columns). Scoring is designed only to award students points for task criteria that were completed correctly. Points are lost for failure to complete the employability requirements (see Non-Task-Specific criteria). When all criteria are evaluated, tally the points for a total at the bottom of each column.

Tasksheet Scoring

	Test		Retest	
Evaluation Items	**Pass**	**Fail**	**Pass**	**Fail**
Task-Specific Evaluation	**(1 pt)**	**(0 pts)**	**(1 pt)**	**(0 pts)**
Student properly performed all inspections.				
Student properly removed, inspected, and reinstalled the aftertreatment fuel injector, SCR catalyst, DPF, and decomposition tube.				
Student properly diagnosed and repaired any active aftertreatment codes.				
Student properly performed stationary regeneration.				
Non-Task-Specific Evaluation	**(0 pts)**	**(−1 pt)**	**(0 pts)**	**(−1 pt)**
Student successfully completed at least three of the non-task-specific steps.				
Student successfully completed all five of the non-task-specific steps.				
Total Score: <total # of points / 4 = %>				

Supervisor/Instructor:

Supervisor/instructor signature _____ Date _____

Comments:

Retest supervisor/instructor signature _____ Date _____

Comments:

Chapter 42: Maintenance Practices; Understanding Industry and OEM Planned Maintenance Procedures

Learning Objective/Task	CDX Tasksheet Number	AED Reference Number
• Locate maintenance specifications.	5.3001	AED 5.3
• Take oil sample.	5.3003a	AED 5.3
• Take coolant sample.	5.3003b	AED 5.3
• Take fuel sample.	5.3003c	AED 5.3
• Inspect oil filter.	5.3005	AED 5.3
• Check operation of all accessories.	5.3006	AED 5.3

Materials Required

- Vehicle with possible engine concern
- Vehicle manufacturer's service information
- Engine manufacturer's workshop materials
- Manufacturer-specific tools, depending on the concern/procedure(s)
- Vehicle/component lifting equipment, if applicable

Safety Considerations

- This task may require test driving the vehicle on the school grounds or on a hoist, both of which carry severe risks. Attempt this task only with full permission from your supervisor/instructor and follow all the guidelines exactly.
- Lifting equipment such as vehicle jacks and stands, vehicle hoists, and engine hoists are important tools that increase productivity and make the job easier. However, they can also cause severe injury or death if used improperly. Make sure you follow the manufacturer's operation procedures. Also make sure you have your supervisor's/instructor's permission to use any particular type of lifting equipment.
- Comply with personal and environmental safety practices associated with clothing; eye protection; hand tools; power equipment; proper ventilation; and the handling, storage, and disposal of chemicals/materials in accordance with federal, state, and local regulations.
- Always wear the correct protective eyewear and clothing and use the appropriate safety equipment, as well as fender covers, seat protectors, and floor mat protectors.
- Make sure you understand and observe all legislative and personal safety procedures when carrying out practical assignments. If you are unsure of what these are, ask your supervisor/instructor.
- While working on the vehicle, wheel chocks must be placed on both sides of one set of tires or as directed by your supervisor/instructor.
- When running any vehicles in the shop, make sure you use the shop's exhaust ventilation system to discharge all exhaust gas safely outside.

CDX Tasksheet Number: 5.3001

Student/Intern Information

Name _____ Date _____ Class _____

Machine, Customer, and Service Information

Machine used for this activity:

Make _____ Model _____

Hours _____ Serial Number _____

Task-Specific Safety Considerations

- This task may require test driving the vehicle on the school grounds or on a hoist, both of which carry severe risks. Attempt this task only with full permission from your supervisor/instructor and follow all the guidelines exactly.
- Comply with personal and environmental safety practices associated with clothing; eye protection; hand tools; power equipment; proper ventilation; and the handling, storage, and disposal of chemicals/materials in accordance with federal, state, and local regulations.
- Always wear the correct protective eyewear and clothing and use the appropriate safety equipment, as well as fender covers, seat protectors, and floor mat protectors.
- Make sure you understand and observe all legislative and personal safety procedures when carrying out practical assignments. If you are unsure of what these are, ask your supervisor/instructor.
- While working on the vehicle, wheel chocks must be placed on both sides of one set of tires or as directed by your supervisor/instructor.

▶ **TASK** Locate maintenance specifications. _____ **AED** 5.3

Time off _____

Student Instructions: Read through the entire procedure prior to starting. Prepare your workspace and any tools or parts that may be needed to complete the task. When directed by your supervisor/instructor, begin the procedure to complete the task, and comment or check the box as each step is finished. Track your time on this procedure for later comparison to the standard completion time (i.e., "flat rate" or customer pay time).

Time on _____

Total time _____

Procedure	Step Completed
1. Research the vehicle's service information, including fluid specification, vehicle service history, service precautions, and technical service bulletins (TSBs).	☐
2. Identify the fluid type for the respective vehicle:	☐
3. What type of oil does the manufacturer call for?	☐
4. What service history can be found for the vehicle?	☐
a. Are there any service precautions listed for the vehicle? Yes ☐ No ☐	☐
b. If so, what are the service precautions listed?	☐
c. Are there any TSBs listed for the vehicle? Yes ☐ No ☐	☐
d. If so, what TSBs are listed?	☐
5. Return the vehicle to its beginning condition and return any tools you used to their proper locations.	☐
6. Discuss your findings with your supervisor/instructor.	☐

Non-Task-Specific Evaluation	Step Completed
1. Tools and equipment were used as directed and returned in good working order.	☐
2. Complied with all general and task-specific safety standards, including proper use of any personal protective equipment (PPE).	☐
3. Completed the task in an appropriate time frame (recommendation: 1.5 or 2 times the flat rate).	☐
4. Left the workspace clean and orderly.	☐
5. Cared for customer property and returned it undamaged.	☐

Student signature _____ Date _____

Comments:

Have your supervisor/instructor verify satisfactory completion of this procedure, any observations made,

and any necessary action(s) recommended.

Evaluation Instructions: The scoring box below is intended to act as a guide for both student and supervisor/instructor. Each criterion listed will help students to understand what is expected of them and help supervisors/instructors to articulate the level of success at a particular task. The scoring is set up to allow a second attempt at each task (see the Test and Retest columns). Scoring is designed only to award students points for task criteria that were completed correctly. Points are lost for failure to complete the employability requirements (see Non-Task-Specific criteria). When all criteria are evaluated, tally the points for a total at the bottom of each column.

Tasksheet Scoring

Evaluation Items	Test		Retest	
	Pass	Fail	Pass	Fail
Task-Specific Evaluation	**(1 pt)**	**(0 pts)**	**(1 pt)**	**(0 pts)**
Student correctly identified the fluid type.				
Student correctly identified the oil type.				
Student correctly identified the service precautions, if any, that existed for the vehicle.				
Student correctly identified the TSBs, if any, that existed for the vehicle.				
Non-Task-Specific Evaluation	**(0 pts)**	**(−1 pt)**	**(0 pts)**	**(−1 pt)**
Student successfully completed at least three of the non-task-specific steps.				
Student successfully completed all five of the non-task-specific steps.				
Total Score: <total # of points / 4 = %>				

Supervisor/Instructor:

Supervisor/instructor signature _____ Date _____

Comments:

Retest supervisor/instructor signature _____ Date _____

Comments:

CDX Tasksheet Number: 5.3003a

Student/Intern Information

Name _____ Date _____ Class _____

Machine, Customer, and Service Information

Machine used for this activity:

Make _____ Model _____

Hours _____ Serial Number _____

Materials Required

- Vehicle with possible engine concern
- Engine manufacturer's workshop materials
- Manufacturer-specific tools, depending on the concern/procedure(s)
- Vehicle/component lifting equipment, if applicable

Task-Specific Safety Considerations

- This task may require test driving the vehicle on the school grounds or on a hoist, both of which carry severe risks. Attempt this task only with full permission from your supervisor/instructor and follow all the guidelines exactly.
- Lifting equipment such as vehicle jacks and stands, vehicle hoists, and engine hoists are important tools that increase productivity and make the job easier. However, they can also cause severe injury or death if used improperly. Make sure you follow the manufacturer's operation procedures. Also make sure you have your supervisor's/instructor's permission to use any particular type of lifting equipment.
- Comply with personal and environmental safety practices associated with clothing; eye protection; hand tools; power equipment; proper ventilation; and the handling, storage, and disposal of chemicals/materials in accordance with federal, state, and local regulations.
- Always wear the correct protective eyewear and clothing and use the appropriate safety equipment, as well as wheel chocks, fender covers, seat protectors, and floor mat protectors.
- Make sure you understand and observe all legislative and personal safety procedures when carrying out practical assignments. If you are unsure of what these are, ask your supervisor/instructor.

▶ **TASK** Take oil sample. **AED 5.3**

Time off_____

Time on_____

Student Instructions: Read through the entire procedure prior to starting. Prepare your workspace and any tools or parts that may be needed to complete the task. When directed by your supervisor/instructor, begin the procedure to complete the task, and comment or check the box as each step is finished. Track your time on this procedure for later comparison to the standard completion time (i.e., "flat rate" or customer pay time).

Total time_____

Note: This tasksheet may require the student to check the condition of miscellaneous vehicle fluids, some of which may be flammable and could damage the environment or cause health problems if not handled properly. Observe all safety precautions and follow local regulations for the proper disposal of fluids.

Procedure	Step Completed
1. While referencing the manufacturer's workshop materials, check the engine oil level.	☐
a. Meets the manufacturer's specifications: Yes ☐ No ☐	☐
b. If no, list your recommendations for rectification:	☐
2. While referencing the manufacturer's workshop materials, identify the proper conditions for conducting an oil consumption test.	☐
3. Discuss your findings with your supervisor/instructor.	☐

Non-Task-Specific Evaluation	Step Completed
1. Tools and equipment were used as directed and returned in good working order.	☐
2. Complied with all general and task-specific safety standards, including proper use of any personal protective equipment (PPE).	☐
3. Completed the task in an appropriate time frame (recommendation: 1.5 or 2 times the flat rate).	☐
4. Left the workspace clean and orderly.	☐
5. Cared for customer property and returned it undamaged.	☐

Student signature _____ Date _____

Comments:

Have your supervisor/instructor verify satisfactory completion of this procedure, any observations made, and any necessary action(s) recommended.

Evaluation Instructions: The scoring box below is intended to act as a guide for both student and supervisor/instructor. Each criterion listed will help students to understand what is expected of them and help supervisors/instructors to articulate the level of success at a particular task. The scoring is set up to allow a second attempt at each task (see the Test and Retest columns). Scoring is designed only to award students points for task criteria that were completed correctly. Points are lost for failure to complete the employability requirements (see Non-Task-Specific criteria). When all criteria are evaluated, tally the points for a total at the bottom of each column.

Tasksheet Scoring

Evaluation Items	Test		Retest	
	Pass	Fail	Pass	Fail
Task-Specific Evaluation	**(1 pt)**	**(0 pts)**	**(1 pt)**	**(0 pts)**
Student used the manufacturer's workshop materials.				
Student properly checked the engine oil level.				
Student accurately noted any necessary rectifications.				
Student accurately identified the proper conditions for conducting an oil consumption test.				
Non-Task-Specific Evaluation	**(0 pts)**	**(−1 pt)**	**(0 pts)**	**(−1 pt)**
Student successfully completed at least three of the non-task-specific steps.				
Student successfully completed all five of the non-task-specific steps.				
Total Score: <total # of points / 4 = %>				

Supervisor/Instructor:

Supervisor/instructor signature _____ Date _____

Comments:

Retest supervisor/instructor signature _____ Date _____

Comments:

CDX Tasksheet Number: 5.3003b

Student/Intern Information

Name _____ Date _____ Class _____

Machine, Customer, and Service Information

Machine used for this activity:

Make _____ Model _____

Hours _____ Serial Number _____

Materials Required
- Vehicle with possible engine concern
- Engine manufacturer's workshop materials
- Manufacturer-specific tools, depending on the concern/procedure(s)
- Vehicle/component lifting equipment, if applicable

Task-Specific Safety Considerations
- This task may require test driving the vehicle on the school grounds or on a hoist, both of which carry severe risks. Attempt this task only with full permission from your supervisor/instructor and follow all the guidelines exactly.
- Lifting equipment such as vehicle jacks and stands, vehicle hoists, and engine hoists are important tools that increase productivity and make the job easier. However, they can also cause severe injury or death if used improperly. Make sure you follow the manufacturer's operation procedures. Also make sure you have your supervisor's/instructor's permission to use any particular type of lifting equipment.
- Comply with personal and environmental safety practices associated with clothing; eye protection; hand tools; power equipment; proper ventilation; and the handling, storage, and disposal of chemicals/materials in accordance with federal, state, and local regulations.
- Always wear the correct protective eyewear and clothing and use the appropriate safety equipment, as well as wheel chocks, fender covers, seat protectors, and floor mat protectors.
- Make sure you understand and observe all legislative and personal safety procedures when carrying out practical assignments. If you are unsure of what these are, ask your supervisor/instructor.

▶ TASK Take coolant sample. **AED 5.3**

Time off_____

Time on_____

Student Instructions: Read through the entire procedure prior to starting. Prepare your workspace and any tools or parts that may be needed to complete the task. When directed by your supervisor/instructor, begin the procedure to complete the task, and comment or check the box as each step is finished. Track your time on this procedure for later comparison to the standard completion time (i.e., "flat rate" or customer pay time).

Total time_____

Note: This tasksheet may require the student to check the condition of miscellaneous vehicle fluids, some of which may be flammable and could damage the environment or cause health problems if not handled properly. Observe all safety precautions and follow local regulations for the proper disposal of fluids.

Procedure	Step Completed
1. Reference the manufacturer's workshop materials and identify the proper engine coolant type, level, condition, and consumption.	☐
a. Coolant type:	☐
b. Coolant quantity: _____ quarts/gallons	☐
c. Cooling system pressure cap: _____ psi/kPa	☐
2. Check the coolant level.	☐
a. Meets the manufacturer's specifications: Yes ☐ No ☐	☐
b. If no, list your recommendations for rectification:	☐
3. Pressure test the cooling system pressure cap and record the results: _____ psi/kPa	☐
a. Meets the manufacturer's specifications: Yes ☐ No ☐	☐
b. If no, list your recommendations for rectification:	☐
4. Pressure test the cooling system.	☐
a. Meets the manufacturer's specifications: Yes ☐ No ☐	☐
b. If no, list your recommendations for rectification:	☐
5. Retrieve a coolant sample for analysis.	☐
6. Test the coolant for proper freeze protection.	☐
a. Meets the manufacturer's specifications: Yes ☐ No ☐	☐

b. If no, list your recommendations for rectification:	☐
7. Test the coolant for proper additive package concentration.	☐
a. Meets the manufacturer's specifications: Yes ☐ No ☐	☐
b. If no, list your recommendations for rectification:	☐
8. Test the cooling system for proper pH.	☐
a. Meets the manufacturer's specifications: Yes ☐ No ☐	☐
b. If no, list your recommendations for rectification:	☐
9. Reference the manufacturer's workshop materials and list the possible causes for excessive coolant consumption:	☐
10. Discuss your findings with your supervisor/instructor.	☐

Non-Task-Specific Evaluation	Step Completed
1. Tools and equipment were used as directed and returned in good working order.	☐
2. Complied with all general and task-specific safety standards, including proper use of any personal protective equipment (PPE).	☐
3. Completed the task in an appropriate time frame (recommendation: 1.5 or 2 times the flat rate).	☐
4. Left the workspace clean and orderly.	☐
5. Cared for customer property and returned it undamaged.	☐

Student signature _____ Date _____

Comments:

Have your supervisor/instructor verify satisfactory completion of this procedure, any observations made, and any necessary action(s) recommended.

© 2021 Jones & Bartlett Learning, LLC, an Ascend Learning Company

840 Maintenance Practices; Understanding Industry and OEM Planned Maintenance Procedures

Evaluation Instructions: The scoring box below is intended to act as a guide for both student and supervisor/instructor. Each criterion listed will help students to understand what is expected of them and help supervisors/instructors to articulate the level of success at a particular task. The scoring is set up to allow a second attempt at each task (see the Test and Retest columns). Scoring is designed only to award students points for task criteria that were completed correctly. Points are lost for failure to complete the employability requirements (see Non-Task-Specific criteria). When all criteria are evaluated, tally the points for a total at the bottom of each column.

Tasksheet Scoring

Evaluation Items	Test		Retest	
	Pass	Fail	Pass	Fail
Task-Specific Evaluation	**(1 pt)**	**(0 pts)**	**(1 pt)**	**(0 pts)**
Student properly checked the coolant level and the cooling system pressure cap.				
Student properly performed the cooling system pressure test and properly retrieved a coolant sample.				
Student accurately checked the coolant for proper freeze protection and proper additive package concentration.				
Student accurately checked the cooling system for proper pH and accurately listed possible causes of excessive coolant consumption.				
Non-Task-Specific Evaluation	**(0 pts)**	**(−1 pt)**	**(0 pts)**	**(−1 pt)**
Student successfully completed at least three of the non-task-specific steps.				
Student successfully completed all five of the non-task-specific steps.				
Total Score: <total # of points / 4 = %>				

Supervisor/Instructor:

Supervisor/instructor signature _____ Date _____

Comments:

Retest supervisor/instructor signature _____ Date _____

Comments:

CDX Tasksheet Number: 5.3003c

Student/Intern Information

Name _____ Date _____ Class _____

Machine, Customer, and Service Information

Machine used for this activity:

Make _____ Model _____

Hours _____ Serial Number _____

Materials Required

- Vehicle with possible engine concern
- Engine manufacturer's workshop materials
- Manufacturer-specific tools, depending on the concern/procedure(s)
- Vehicle/component lifting equipment, if applicable

Task-Specific Safety Considerations

- This task may require test driving the vehicle on the school grounds or on a hoist, both of which carry severe risks. Attempt this task only with full permission from your supervisor/instructor and follow all the guidelines exactly.
- Lifting equipment such as vehicle jacks and stands, vehicle hoists, and engine hoists are important tools that increase productivity and make the job easier. However, they can also cause severe injury or death if used improperly. Make sure you follow the manufacturer's operation procedures. Also make sure you have your supervisor's/instructor's permission to use any particular type of lifting equipment.
- Comply with personal and environmental safety practices associated with clothing; eye protection; hand tools; power equipment; proper ventilation; and the handling, storage, and disposal of chemicals/materials in accordance with federal, state, and local regulations.
- Always wear the correct protective eyewear and clothing and use the appropriate safety equipment, as well as wheel chocks, fender covers, seat protectors, and floor mat protectors.
- Make sure you understand and observe all legislative and personal safety procedures when carrying out practical assignments. If you are unsure of what these are, ask your supervisor/instructor.

▶ TASK Take fuel sample. **AED 5.3**

Time off_____

Time on_____

Student Instructions: Read through the entire procedure prior to starting. Prepare your workspace and any tools or parts that may be needed to complete the task. When directed by your supervisor/instructor, begin the procedure to complete the task, and comment or check the box as each step is finished. Track your time on this procedure for later comparison to the standard completion time (i.e., "flat rate" or customer pay time).

Total time_____

Note: This tasksheet may require the student to check the condition of miscellaneous vehicle fluids, some of which may be flammable and could damage the environment or cause health problems if not handled properly. Observe all safety precautions and follow local regulations for the proper disposal of fluids.

Procedure	Step Completed
1. While referencing the manufacturer's workshop materials, record the fuel level as it is shown on the manufacturer's electronic fuel gauge:	☐
2. Manually check the fuel level. Insert a clean yard stick or some other instrument into the fuel tank and compare the level with the manufacturer's electronic fuel gauge.	☐
a. Meets the manufacturer's specifications: Yes ☐ No ☐	☐
b. If no, list your recommendations for rectification:	☐
3. While referencing the manufacturer's workshop materials, draw off a clean fuel sample for testing.	☐
a. Meets the manufacturer's specifications: Yes ☐ No ☐	☐
b. If no, list your recommendations for rectification:	☐
4. Record the procedure for using a water test paste to check the fuel supply for contamination, then perform the test.	☐
a. Meets the manufacturer's specifications: Yes ☐ No ☐	☐
b. If no, list your recommendations for rectification:	☐
5. Discuss your findings with your supervisor/instructor.	☐

Non-Task-Specific Evaluation	Step Completed
1. Tools and equipment were used as directed and returned in good working order.	☐
2. Complied with all general and task-specific safety standards, including proper use of any personal protective equipment (PPE).	☐
3. Completed the task in an appropriate time frame (recommendation: 1.5 or 2 times the flat rate).	☐
4. Left the workspace clean and orderly.	☐
5. Cared for customer property and returned it undamaged.	☐

Student signature _____ Date _____

Comments:

Have your supervisor/instructor verify satisfactory completion of this procedure, any observations made,

and any necessary action(s) recommended.

Evaluation Instructions: The scoring box below is intended to act as a guide for both student and supervisor/instructor. Each criterion listed will help students to understand what is expected of them and help supervisors/instructors to articulate the level of success at a particular task. The scoring is set up to allow a second attempt at each task (see the Test and Retest columns). Scoring is designed only to award students points for task criteria that were completed correctly. Points are lost for failure to complete the employability requirements (see Non-Task-Specific criteria). When all criteria are evaluated, tally the points for a total at the bottom of each column.

Tasksheet Scoring

Evaluation Items	Test		Retest	
	Pass	Fail	Pass	Fail
Task-Specific Evaluation	**(1 pt)**	**(0 pts)**	**(1 pt)**	**(0 pts)**
Student properly checked the fuel system level using the manufacturer's electronic fuel gauge.				
Student properly checked the fuel system level and compared it to the electronic fuel system gauge.				
Student properly obtained a fuel system sample for testing.				
Student properly tested the fuel system storage tank for water contamination.				
Non-Task-Specific Evaluation	**(0 pts)**	**(−1 pt)**	**(0 pts)**	**(−1 pt)**
Student successfully completed at least three of the non-task-specific steps.				
Student successfully completed all five of the non-task-specific steps.				
Total Score: <total # of points / 4 = %>				

Supervisor/Instructor:

Supervisor/instructor signature _____ Date _____

Comments:

Retest supervisor/instructor signature _____ Date _____

Comments:

CDX Tasksheet Number: 5.3005

Student/Intern Information

Name _____ Date _____ Class _____

Machine, Customer, and Service Information

Machine used for this activity:

Make _____ Model _____

Hours _____ Serial Number _____

Materials Required

- Vehicle with possible engine concern
- Engine manufacturer's workshop materials
- Manufacturer-specific tools, depending on the concern/procedure(s)
- Vehicle/component lifting equipment, if applicable

Task-Specific Safety Considerations

- This task may require test driving the vehicle on the school grounds or on a hoist, both of which carry severe risks. Attempt this task only with full permission from your supervisor/instructor and follow all the guidelines exactly.
- Lifting equipment such as vehicle jacks and stands, vehicle hoists, and engine hoists are important tools that increase productivity and make the job easier. However, they can also cause severe injury or death if used improperly. Make sure you follow the manufacturer's operation procedures. Also make sure you have your supervisor's/instructor's permission to use any particular type of lifting equipment.
- Comply with personal and environmental safety practices associated with clothing; eye protection; hand tools; power equipment; proper ventilation; and the handling, storage, and disposal of chemicals/materials in accordance with federal, state, and local regulations.
- Always wear the correct protective eyewear and clothing and use the appropriate safety equipment, as well as wheel chocks, fender covers, seat protectors, and floor mat protectors.
- Make sure you understand and observe all legislative and personal safety procedures when carrying out practical assignments. If you are unsure of what these are, ask your supervisor/instructor.

▶ TASK Inspect oil filter.

AED 5.3

Time off_____

Time on_____

Student Instructions: Read through the entire procedure prior to starting. Prepare your workspace and any tools or parts that may be needed to complete the task. When directed by your supervisor/instructor, begin the procedure to complete the task, and comment or check the box as each step is finished. Track your time on this procedure for later comparison to the standard completion time (i.e., "flat rate" or customer pay time).

Total time_____

Note: This tasksheet may require the student to check the condition of miscellaneous vehicle fluids, some of which may be flammable and could damage the environment or cause health problems if not handled properly. Observe all safety precautions and follow local regulations for the proper disposal of fluids.

Procedure	Step Completed
1. While referencing the manufacturer's workshop materials, inspect the external oil pressure regulator bore and piston for wear/damage.	☐
a. Note any problems you found below:	☐
b. If problems exist, list your recommendations for rectification:	☐
2. While referencing the manufacturer's workshop materials, inspect the oil pressure bypass valve and piston for wear/damage.	☐
a. Note any problems you found below:	☐
b. If problems exist, list your recommendations for rectification:	☐
3. While referencing the manufacturer's workshop materials, inspect the pressure relief valve and piston for wear/damage.	☐
a. Note any problems you found below:	☐
b. If problems exist, list your recommendations for rectification:	☐
4. While referencing the manufacturer's workshop materials, inspect the oil cooler thermostat.	☐
a. Meets the manufacturer's specifications: Yes ☐　No ☐	☐
b. If no, list your recommendations for rectification:	☐

	Step Completed
5. Remove the oil filter and use the appropriate tools to remove the filter media. Use **extreme** caution; cut edges on the filter canister are extremely sharp. Cut a section of the media loose from the core and place it in a clean rag. Using a shop vice, squeeze the oil out of the filter media. Inspect the filter media for metal particles/contamination and record any findings:	☐
6. Discuss your findings with your supervisor/instructor.	☐

Non-Task-Specific Evaluation	Step Completed
1. Tools and equipment were used as directed and returned in good working order.	☐
2. Complied with all general and task-specific safety standards, including proper use of any personal protective equipment (PPE).	☐
3. Completed the task in an appropriate time frame (recommendation: 1.5 or 2 times the flat rate).	☐
4. Left the workspace clean and orderly.	☐
5. Cared for customer property and returned it undamaged.	☐

Student signature _____ Date _____

Comments:

Have your supervisor/instructor verify satisfactory completion of this procedure, any observations made,

and any necessary action(s) recommended.

Evaluation Instructions: The scoring box below is intended to act as a guide for both student and supervisor/instructor. Each criterion listed will help students to understand what is expected of them and help supervisors/instructors to articulate the level of success at a particular task. The scoring is set up to allow a second attempt at each task (see the Test and Retest columns). Scoring is designed only to award students points for task criteria that were completed correctly. Points are lost for failure to complete the employability requirements (see Non-Task-Specific criteria). When all criteria are evaluated, tally the points for a total at the bottom of each column.

Tasksheet Scoring

Evaluation Items	Test		Retest	
	Pass	**Fail**	**Pass**	**Fail**
Task-Specific Evaluation	**(1 pt)**	**(0 pts)**	**(1 pt)**	**(0 pts)**
Student properly inspected the external oil pressure regulator bore and piston.				
Student properly inspected the oil pressure bypass valve and piston.				
Student properly inspected the oil pressure relief valve and piston.				
Student properly inspected the oil cooler thermostat and the oil filter.				
Non-Task-Specific Evaluation	**(0 pts)**	**(−1 pt)**	**(0 pts)**	**(−1 pt)**
Student successfully completed at least three of the non-task-specific steps.				
Student successfully completed all five of the non-task-specific steps.				
Total Score: <total # of points / 4 = %>				

Supervisor/Instructor:

Supervisor/instructor signature _____ Date _____

Comments:

```



```

Retest supervisor/instructor signature _____ Date _____

Comments:

```



```

CDX Tasksheet Number: 5.3006

Student/Intern Information

Name _____ Date _____ Class _____

Machine, Customer, and Service Information

Machine used for this activity:

Make _____ Model _____

Hours _____ Serial Number _____

> ## Materials Required
> - Vehicle with possible engine concern
> - Vehicle manufacturer's service information
> - Manufacturer-specific tools, depending on the concern/procedure(s)

Task-Specific Safety Considerations
- This task may require test driving the vehicle on the school grounds or on a hoist, both of which carry severe risks. Attempt this task only with full permission from your supervisor/instructor and follow all the guidelines exactly.
- Comply with personal and environmental safety practices associated with clothing; eye protection; hand tools; power equipment; proper ventilation; and the handling, storage, and disposal of chemicals/materials in accordance with federal, state, and local regulations.
- Always wear the correct protective eyewear and clothing and use the appropriate safety equipment, as well as fender covers, seat protectors, and floor mat protectors.
- Make sure you understand and observe all legislative and personal safety procedures when carrying out practical assignments. If you are unsure of what these are, ask your supervisor/instructor.
- While working on the vehicle, wheel chocks must be placed on both sides of one set of tires or as directed by your supervisor/instructor.
- When running any vehicles in the shop, make sure you use the shop's exhaust ventilation system to discharge all exhaust gas safely outside.

▶ TASK Check operation of all accessories. **AED 5.3**

Time off_____

Time on_____

Student Instructions: Read through the entire procedure prior to starting. Prepare your workspace and any tools or parts that may be needed to complete the task. When directed by your supervisor/instructor, begin the procedure to complete the task, and comment or check the box as each step is finished. Track your time on this procedure for later comparison to the standard completion time (i.e., "flat rate" or customer pay time).

Total time_____

Procedure	Step Completed
1. Check all accessory devices fitted and ensure that they are activating and working in accordance with the manufacturer's specifications.	☐
a. For example, is the driver's navigational assistance screen operating as described in the workshop materials? Yes ☐ No ☐	☐
b. If no, list the problem(s) and your recommendation(s):	☐
c. Systematically test additional accessories and record your findings:	☐
2. Return the vehicle to its beginning condition and return any tools you used to their proper locations.	☐
3. Discuss your findings with your supervisor/instructor.	☐

Non-Task-Specific Evaluation	Step Completed
1. Tools and equipment were used as directed and returned in good working order.	☐
2. Complied with all general and task-specific safety standards, including proper use of any personal protective equipment (PPE).	☐
3. Completed the task in an appropriate time frame (recommendation: 1.5 or 2 times the flat rate).	☐
4. Left the workspace clean and orderly.	☐
5. Cared for customer property and returned it undamaged.	☐

Student signature _____ Date _____

Comments:

Have your supervisor/instructor verify satisfactory completion of this procedure, any observations made,

and any necessary action(s) recommended.

Evaluation Instructions: The scoring box below is intended to act as a guide for both student and supervisor/instructor. Each criterion listed will help students to understand what is expected of them and help supervisors/instructors to articulate the level of success at a particular task. The scoring is set up to allow a second attempt at each task (see the Test and Retest columns). Scoring is designed only to award students points for task criteria that were completed correctly. Points are lost for failure to complete the employability requirements (see Non-Task-Specific criteria). When all criteria are evaluated, tally the points for a total at the bottom of each column.

Tasksheet Scoring

	Test		Retest	
Evaluation Items	Pass	Fail	Pass	Fail
Task-Specific Evaluation	**(1 pt)**	**(0 pts)**	**(1 pt)**	**(0 pts)**
Student used the manufacturer's service information.				
Student properly checked all accessory devices.				
Student accurately listed any problems.				
Student accurately listed any necessary recommendations.				
Non-Task-Specific Evaluation	**(0 pts)**	**(−1 pt)**	**(0 pts)**	**(−1 pt)**
Student successfully completed at least three of the non-task-specific steps.				
Student successfully completed all five of the non-task-specific steps.				
Total Score: <total # of points / 4 = %>				

Supervisor/Instructor:

Supervisor/instructor signature _____ Date _____

Comments:

Retest supervisor/instructor signature _____ Date _____

Comments:

Chapter 43: Component Repair; Understanding Proper Component Repair Procedures

Learning Objective/Task	CDX Tasksheet Number	AED Reference Number
• Inspect valve train components.	5.4001	AED 5.4
• Install water pump and hoses.	5.4003	AED 5.4

Materials Required

- Vehicle with possible engine concern(s)
- Engine manufacturer's workshop materials
- Manufacturer-specific tools, depending on the concern(s)/procedure(s)
- Vehicle/component lifting equipment, if applicable

Safety Considerations

- This task may require test driving the vehicle on the school grounds or on a hoist, both of which carry severe risks. Attempt this task only with full permission from your supervisor/instructor and follow all the guidelines exactly.
- Lifting equipment such as vehicle jacks and stands, vehicle hoists, and engine hoists are important tools that increase productivity and make the job easier. However, they can also cause severe injury or death if used improperly. Make sure you follow the manufacturer's operation procedures. Also make sure you have your supervisor's/instructor's permission to use any particular type of lifting equipment.
- Comply with personal and environmental safety practices associated with clothing; eye protection; hand tools; power equipment; proper ventilation; and the handling, storage, and disposal of chemicals/materials in accordance with federal, state, and local regulations.
- Always wear the correct protective eyewear and clothing and use the appropriate safety equipment, as well as wheel chocks, fender covers, seat protectors, and floor mat protectors.
- Make sure you understand and observe all legislative and personal safety procedures when carrying out practical assignments. If you are unsure of what these are, ask your supervisor/instructor.

CDX Tasksheet Number: 5.4001

Student/Intern Information

Name _____ Date _____ Class _____

Machine, Customer, and Service Information

Machine used for this activity:

Make _____ Model _____

Hours _____ Serial Number _____

Materials Required
- Vehicle with possible engine concern(s)
- Engine manufacturer's workshop materials
- Manufacturer-specific tools, depending on the concern(s)/procedure(s)
- Vehicle/component lifting equipment, if applicable

Task-Specific Safety Considerations
- This task may require test driving the vehicle on the school grounds or on a hoist, both of which carry severe risks. Attempt this task only with full permission from your supervisor/instructor and follow all the guidelines exactly.
- Lifting equipment such as vehicle jacks and stands, vehicle hoists, and engine hoists are important tools that increase productivity and make the job easier. However, they can also cause severe injury or death if used improperly. Make sure you follow the manufacturer's operation procedures. Also make sure you have your supervisor's/instructor's permission to use any particular type of lifting equipment.
- Comply with personal and environmental safety practices associated with clothing; eye protection; hand tools; power equipment; proper ventilation; and the handling, storage, and disposal of chemicals/materials in accordance with federal, state, and local regulations.
- Always wear the correct protective eyewear and clothing and use the appropriate safety equipment, as well as wheel chocks, fender covers, seat protectors, and floor mat protectors.
- Make sure you understand and observe all legislative and personal safety procedures when carrying out practical assignments. If you are unsure of what these are, ask your supervisor/instructor.

▶ TASK Inspect valve train components.

Time off_____

Student Instructions: Read through the entire procedure prior to starting. Prepare your workspace and any tools or parts that may be needed to complete the task. When directed by your supervisor/instructor, begin the procedure to complete the task, and comment or check the box as each step is finished. Track your time on this procedure for later comparison to the standard completion time (i.e., "flat rate" or customer pay time).

Time on_____

Total time_____

Note: This tasksheet may require the student to check the condition of miscellaneous vehicle fluids, some of which may be flammable and could damage the environment or cause health problems if not handled properly. Observe all safety precautions and follow local regulations for the proper disposal of fluids.

Procedure	Step Completed
1. While referencing the appropriate manufacturer's workshop materials, inspect the following valve train components.	
a. Camshaft/lobes Serviceable ☐ Repairable ☐ Unserviceable ☐	☐
b. Cam followers Serviceable ☐ Repairable ☐ Unserviceable ☐	☐
c. Bucket tappets Serviceable ☐ Repairable ☐ Unserviceable ☐	☐
d. Adjusting shims Serviceable ☐ Repairable ☐ Unserviceable ☐	☐
e. Rockers Serviceable ☐ Repairable ☐ Unserviceable ☐	☐
f. Camshaft gear(s) Serviceable ☐ Repairable ☐ Unserviceable ☐	☐
g. Camshaft retaining caps Serviceable ☐ Repairable ☐ Unserviceable ☐	☐
h. Timing belt/chains(s) Serviceable ☐ Repairable ☐ Unserviceable ☐	☐
i. Rocker shafts Serviceable ☐ Repairable ☐ Unserviceable ☐	☐
j. Rocker shaft bushings Serviceable ☐ Repairable ☐ Unserviceable ☐	☐
2. Test the following valve springs for compressed height and tension and record below.	
a. Cylinder #1 Intake valve(s) _____ in/mm Tension _____ ft-lb/Nm	☐
b. Cylinder #1 Exhaust valve(s) _____ in/mm Tension _____ ft-lb/Nm	☐
c. Cylinder #2 Intake valve(s) _____ in/mm Tension _____ ft-lb/Nm	☐
d. Cylinder #2 Exhaust valve(s) _____ in/mm Tension _____ ft-lb/Nm	☐

e. Cylinder #3
 	
     Intake valve(s) _____ in/mm
 	
     Tension _____ ft-lb/Nm
	☐

f. Cylinder #3
 	
     Exhaust valve(s) _____ in/mm
 	
     Tension _____ ft-lb/Nm
	☐

g. Cylinder #4
 	
     Intake valve(s) _____ in/mm
 	
     Tension _____ ft-lb/Nm
	☐

h. Cylinder #4
 	
     Exhaust valve(s) _____ in/mm
 	
     Tension _____ ft-lb/Nm
	☐

i. Cylinder #5
 	
     Intake valve(s) _____ in/mm
 	
     Tension _____ ft-lb/Nm
	☐

j. Cylinder #5
 	
     Exhaust valve(s) _____ in/mm
 	
     Tension _____ ft-lb/Nm
	☐

k. Cylinder #6
 	
     Intake valve(s) _____ in/mm
 	
     Tension _____ ft-lb/Nm
	☐

l. Cylinder #6
 	
     Exhaust valve(s) _____ in/mm
 	
     Tension _____ ft-lb/Nm
	☐

3. List any component that does not meet the manufacturer's specifications:	☐
4. List your recommendations for rectification of any areas of concern.	☐
5. Reinstall all removed components undamaged and in working order unless teardown is to continue.	☐
6. Discuss your findings with your supervisor/instructor.	☐

Non-Task-Specific Evaluation	Step Completed
1. Tools and equipment were used as directed and returned in good working order.	☐
2. Complied with all general and task-specific safety standards, including proper use of any personal protective equipment (PPE).	☐
3. Completed the task in an appropriate time frame (recommendation: 1.5 or 2 times the flat rate).	☐
4. Left the workspace clean and orderly.	☐
5. Cared for customer property and returned it undamaged.	☐

Student signature _____ Date _____

Comments:

Have your supervisor/instructor verify satisfactory completion of this procedure, any observations made, and any necessary action(s) recommended.

Evaluation Instructions: The scoring box below is intended to act as a guide for both student and supervisor/instructor. Each criterion listed will help students to understand what is expected of them and help supervisors/instructors to articulate the level of success at a particular task. The scoring is set up to allow a second attempt at each task (see the Test and Retest columns). Scoring is designed only to award students points for task criteria that were completed correctly. Points are lost for failure to complete the employability requirements (see Non-Task-Specific criteria). When all criteria are evaluated, tally the points for a total at the bottom of each column.

Tasksheet Scoring

Evaluation Items	Test		Retest	
	Pass	**Fail**	**Pass**	**Fail**
Task-Specific Evaluation	**(1 pt)**	**(0 pts)**	**(1 pt)**	**(0 pts)**
Student properly inspected the valve train components.				
Student properly inspected and tested the valve springs for height and tension.				
Student accurately listed the areas of concern and recommendations for any rectification.				
Student reinstalled all removed components undamaged and in working order unless teardown was to continue.				
Non-Task-Specific Evaluation	**(0 pts)**	**(−1 pt)**	**(0 pts)**	**(−1 pt)**
Student successfully completed at least three of the non-task-specific steps.				
Student successfully completed all five of the non-task-specific steps.				
Total Score: <total # of points / 4 = %>				

Supervisor/Instructor:

Supervisor/instructor signature _____ Date _____

Comments:

Retest supervisor/instructor signature _____ Date _____

Comments:

CDX Tasksheet Number: 5.4003

Student/Intern Information

Name _____ Date _____ Class _____

Machine, Customer, and Service Information

Machine used for this activity:

Make _____ Model _____

Hours _____ Serial Number _____

Materials Required
- Vehicle with possible engine concern(s)
- Engine manufacturer's workshop materials
- Manufacturer-specific tools, depending on the concern(s)/procedure(s)
- Vehicle/component lifting equipment, if applicable

Task-Specific Safety Considerations
- This task may require test driving the vehicle on the school grounds or on a hoist, both of which carry severe risks. Attempt this task only with full permission from your supervisor/instructor and follow all the guidelines exactly.
- Lifting equipment such as vehicle jacks and stands, vehicle hoists, and engine hoists are important tools that increase productivity and make the job easier. However, they can also cause severe injury or death if used improperly. Make sure you follow the manufacturer's operation procedures. Also make sure you have your supervisor's/instructor's permission to use any particular type of lifting equipment.
- Comply with personal and environmental safety practices associated with clothing; eye protection; hand tools; power equipment; proper ventilation; and the handling, storage, and disposal of chemicals/materials in accordance with federal, state, and local regulations.
- Always wear the correct protective eyewear and clothing and use the appropriate safety equipment, as well as wheel chocks, fender covers, seat protectors, and floor mat protectors.
- Make sure you understand and observe all legislative and personal safety procedures when carrying out practical assignments. If you are unsure of what these are, ask your supervisor/instructor.

▶ TASK Install water pump and hoses.

AED 5.4

Time off_____

Time on_____

Total time_____

Student Instructions: Read through the entire procedure prior to starting. Prepare your workspace and any tools or parts that may be needed to complete the task. When directed by your supervisor/instructor, begin the procedure to complete the task, and comment or check the box as each step is finished. Track your time on this procedure for later comparison to the standard completion time (i.e., "flat rate" or customer pay time).

Note: This tasksheet may require the student to check the condition of miscellaneous vehicle fluids, some of which may be flammable and could damage the environment or cause health problems if not handled properly. Observe all safety precautions and follow local regulations for the proper disposal of fluids.

Procedure	Step Completed
1. Reference the manufacturer's workshop materials and check and inspect the water pump for leaks. Look closely at the weep hole in the bottom of the pump for dried coolant residue. Always replace upon engine overhaul.	☐
a. Note any problems you found below:	☐
b. If problems exist, list your recommendations for rectification:	☐
2. Check and inspect all hoses for leaks, damage, swelling, or soft spots.	☐
a. Note any problems you found below:	☐
b. If problems exist, list your recommendations for rectification:	☐
3. If directed by your supervisor/instructor, replace the water pump, hoses, and/or clamps.	☐
4. Discuss your findings with your supervisor/instructor.	☐

Non-Task-Specific Evaluation	Step Completed
1. Tools and equipment were used as directed and returned in good working order.	☐
2. Complied with all general and task-specific safety standards, including proper use of any personal protective equipment (PPE).	☐
3. Completed the task in an appropriate time frame (recommendation: 1.5 or 2 times the flat rate).	☐
4. Left the workspace clean and orderly.	☐
5. Cared for customer property and returned it undamaged.	☐

Student signature _____ Date _____

Comments:

Have your supervisor/instructor verify satisfactory completion of this procedure, any observations made,

and any necessary action(s) recommended.

Evaluation Instructions: The scoring box below is intended to act as a guide for both student and supervisor/instructor. Each criterion listed will help students to understand what is expected of them and help supervisors/instructors to articulate the level of success at a particular task. The scoring is set up to allow a second attempt at each task (see the Test and Retest columns). Scoring is designed only to award students points for task criteria that were completed correctly. Points are lost for failure to complete the employability requirements (see Non-Task-Specific criteria). When all criteria are evaluated, tally the points for a total at the bottom of each column.

Tasksheet Scoring

Evaluation Items	Test		Retest	
	Pass	Fail	Pass	Fail
Task-Specific Evaluation	**(1 pt)**	**(0 pts)**	**(1 pt)**	**(0 pts)**
Student properly inspected the water pump.				
Student properly inspected the cooling system hoses.				
Student accurately listed recommendations for any rectifications.				
Student properly replaced the water pump, hoses, and/or clamps if directed by their supervisor/instructor.				
Non-Task-Specific Evaluation	**(0 pts)**	**(−1 pt)**	**(0 pts)**	**(−1 pt)**
Student successfully completed at least three of the non-task-specific steps.				
Student successfully completed all five of the non-task-specific steps.				
Total Score: <total # of points / 4 = %>				

Supervisor/Instructor:

Supervisor/instructor signature _____ Date _____

Comments:

Retest supervisor/instructor signature _____ Date _____

Comments:

Chapter 44: Engine Subsystems; Engine Identification of External Components

Learning Objective/Task	CDX Tasksheet Number	AED Reference Number
• Inspect external engine components.	5.5a001	AED 5.5
• Identify engine vibration problems.	5.5a002	AED 5.5
• Inspect and test exhaust aftertreatment devices.	5.5a003	AED 5.5

Materials Required

- Vehicle with possible engine concern
- Engine manufacturer's workshop materials
- Manufacturer-specific tools, depending on the concern/procedure(s)
- Vehicle/component lifting equipment, if applicable

Safety Considerations

- This task may require test driving the vehicle on the school grounds or on a hoist, both of which carry severe risks. Attempt this task only with full permission from your supervisor/instructor and follow all the guidelines exactly.
- Lifting equipment such as vehicle jacks and stands, vehicle hoists, and engine hoists are important tools that increase productivity and make the job easier. However, they can also cause severe injury or death if used improperly. Make sure you follow the manufacturer's operation procedures. Also make sure you have your supervisor's/instructor's permission to use any particular type of lifting equipment.
- Comply with personal and environmental safety practices associated with clothing; eye protection; hand tools; power equipment; proper ventilation; and the handling, storage, and disposal of chemicals/materials in accordance with federal, state, and local regulations.
- Always wear the correct protective eyewear and clothing and use the appropriate safety equipment, as well as wheel chocks, fender covers, seat protectors, and floor mat protectors.
- Make sure you understand and observe all legislative and personal safety procedures when carrying out practical assignments. If you are unsure of what these are, ask your supervisor/instructor.

CDX Tasksheet Number: 5.5a001

Student/Intern Information

Name _____ Date _____ Class _____

Machine, Customer, and Service Information

Machine used for this activity:

Make _____ Model _____

Hours _____ Serial Number _____

Materials Required

- Vehicle with possible engine concern
- Engine manufacturer's workshop materials
- Manufacturer-specific tools, depending on the concern/procedure(s)
- Vehicle/component lifting equipment, if applicable

Task-Specific Safety Considerations

- This task may require test driving the vehicle on the school grounds or on a hoist, both of which carry severe risks. Attempt this task only with full permission from your supervisor/instructor and follow all the guidelines exactly.
- Lifting equipment such as vehicle jacks and stands, vehicle hoists, and engine hoists are important tools that increase productivity and make the job easier. However, they can also cause severe injury or death if used improperly. Make sure you follow the manufacturer's operation procedures. Also make sure you have your supervisor's/instructor's permission to use any particular type of lifting equipment.
- Comply with personal and environmental safety practices associated with clothing; eye protection; hand tools; power equipment; proper ventilation; and the handling, storage, and disposal of chemicals/materials in accordance with federal, state, and local regulations.
- Always wear the correct protective eyewear and clothing and use the appropriate safety equipment, as well as wheel chocks, fender covers, seat protectors, and floor mat protectors.
- Make sure you understand and observe all legislative and personal safety procedures when carrying out practical assignments. If you are unsure of what these are, ask your supervisor/instructor.

▶ **TASK** Inspect external engine components. **AED 5.5**

Time off _____

Time on _____

Student Instructions: Read through the entire procedure prior to starting. Prepare your workspace and any tools or parts that may be needed to complete the task. When directed by your supervisor/instructor, begin the procedure to complete the task, and comment or check the box as each step is finished. Track your time on this procedure for later comparison to the standard completion time (i.e., "flat rate" or customer pay time).

Total time _____

Note: This tasksheet may require the student to check the condition of miscellaneous vehicle fluids, some of which may be flammable and could damage the environment or cause health problems if not handled properly. Observe all safety precautions and follow local regulations for the proper disposal of fluids.

Procedure	Step Completed
1. While referencing the manufacturer's workshop materials, inspect the exhaust manifold and determine any needed action.	☐
a. Meets the manufacturer's specifications: Yes ☐ No ☐	☐
b. If no, list your recommendations for rectification:	☐
2. While referencing the manufacturer's workshop materials, inspect the exhaust piping for missing, loose, or damaged components.	☐
a. Meets the manufacturer's specifications: Yes ☐ No ☐	☐
b. If no, list your recommendations for rectification:	☐
3. While referencing the manufacturer's workshop materials, check the mufflers and mounting hardware.	☐
a. Meets the manufacturer's specifications: Yes ☐ No ☐	☐
b. If no, list your recommendations for rectification:	☐
4. Discuss your findings with your supervisor/instructor.	☐

Non-Task-Specific Evaluation	Step Completed
1. Tools and equipment were used as directed and returned in good working order.	☐
2. Complied with all general and task-specific safety standards, including proper use of any personal protective equipment (PPE).	☐
3. Completed the task in an appropriate time frame (recommendation: 1.5 or 2 times the flat rate).	☐
4. Left the workspace clean and orderly.	☐
5. Cared for customer property and returned it undamaged.	☐

Student signature _____ Date _____

Comments:

Have your supervisor/instructor verify satisfactory completion of this procedure, any observations made, and any necessary action(s) recommended.

Evaluation Instructions: The scoring box below is intended to act as a guide for both student and supervisor/instructor. Each criterion listed will help students to understand what is expected of them and help supervisors/instructors to articulate the level of success at a particular task. The scoring is set up to allow a second attempt at each task (see the Test and Retest columns). Scoring is designed only to award students points for task criteria that were completed correctly. Points are lost for failure to complete the employability requirements (see Non-Task-Specific criteria). When all criteria are evaluated, tally the points for a total at the bottom of each column.

Tasksheet Scoring

Evaluation Items	Test		Retest	
	Pass	Fail	Pass	Fail
Task-Specific Evaluation	**(1 pt)**	**(0 pts)**	**(1 pt)**	**(0 pts)**
Student properly inspected the exhaust manifold.				
Student properly inspected the exhaust piping.				
Student properly inspected the mufflers and mounting hardware.				
Student accurately listed any necessary rectifications.				
Non-Task-Specific Evaluation	**(0 pts)**	**(−1 pt)**	**(0 pts)**	**(−1 pt)**
Student successfully completed at least three of the non-task-specific steps.				
Student successfully completed all five of the non-task-specific steps.				
Total Score: <total # of points / 4 = %>				

Supervisor/Instructor:

Supervisor/instructor signature _____ Date _____

Comments:

Retest supervisor/instructor signature _____ Date _____

Comments:

CDX Tasksheet Number: 5.5a002

Student/Intern Information

Name _____ Date _____ Class _____

Machine, Customer, and Service Information

Machine used for this activity:

Make _____ Model _____

Hours _____ Serial Number _____

> **Materials Required**
> - Vehicle with possible engine concern
> - Engine manufacturer's workshop materials
> - Manufacturer-specific tools, depending on the concern/procedure(s)
> - Vehicle/component lifting equipment, if applicable

Task-Specific Safety Considerations
- This task may require test driving the vehicle on the school grounds or on a hoist, both of which carry severe risks. Attempt this task only with full permission from your supervisor/instructor and follow all the guidelines exactly.
- Lifting equipment such as vehicle jacks and stands, vehicle hoists, and engine hoists are important tools that increase productivity and make the job easier. However, they can also cause severe injury or death if used improperly. Make sure you follow the manufacturer's operation procedures. Also make sure you have your supervisor's/instructor's permission to use any particular type of lifting equipment.
- Comply with personal and environmental safety practices associated with clothing; eye protection; hand tools; power equipment; proper ventilation; and the handling, storage, and disposal of chemicals/materials in accordance with federal, state, and local regulations.
- Always wear the correct protective eyewear and clothing and use the appropriate safety equipment, as well as wheel chocks, fender covers, seat protectors, and floor mat protectors.
- Make sure you understand and observe all legislative and personal safety procedures when carrying out practical assignments. If you are unsure of what these are, ask your supervisor/instructor.

▶ TASK Identify engine vibration problems.   **AED 5.5**

Time off_____

Time on_____

Student Instructions: Read through the entire procedure prior to starting. Prepare your workspace and any tools or parts that may be needed to complete the task. When directed by your supervisor/instructor, begin the procedure to complete the task, and comment or check the box as each step is finished. Track your time on this procedure for later comparison to the standard completion time (i.e., "flat rate" or customer pay time).

Total time_____

Note: This tasksheet may require the student to check the condition of miscellaneous vehicle fluids, some of which may be flammable and could damage the environment or cause health problems if not handled properly. Observe all safety precautions and follow local regulations for the proper disposal of fluids.

Procedure	Step Completed
1. Start the engine and bring it to operating temperature.	☐
a. List any hard starting problems (e.g., extended cranking):	☐
2. With the engine running at operating temperature, record the following.	
a. Idle rpm _____ rpm	☐
b. Governed rpm (high idle) _____ rpm	☐
3. Record excessive vibrations at each of the following. (**Note:** If the vehicle has automatic transmission, engage the air conditioning.)	
a. Idle rpm _____ rpm	☐
b. Governed rpm with clutch disengaged _____ rpm	☐
c. Governed rpm with clutch engaged _____ rpm	☐
4. List possible causes for excessive vibrations:	☐
a. Determine what action is required for an engine's excessive vibrations:	☐
5. Return the vehicle to its beginning condition and return any tools you used to their proper locations.	☐
6. Discuss your findings with your supervisor/instructor.	☐

Non-Task-Specific Evaluation	Step Completed
1. Tools and equipment were used as directed and returned in good working order.	☐
2. Complied with all general and task-specific safety standards, including proper use of any personal protective equipment (PPE).	☐
3. Completed the task in an appropriate time frame (recommendation: 1.5 or 2 times the flat rate).	☐
4. Left the workspace clean and orderly.	☐
5. Cared for customer property and returned it undamaged.	☐

Student signature _____ Date _____

Comments:

Have your supervisor/instructor verify satisfactory completion of this procedure, any observations made,

and any necessary action(s) recommended.

Evaluation Instructions: The scoring box below is intended to act as a guide for both student and supervisor/instructor. Each criterion listed will help students to understand what is expected of them and help supervisors/instructors to articulate the level of success at a particular task. The scoring is set up to allow a second attempt at each task (see the Test and Retest columns). Scoring is designed only to award students points for task criteria that were completed correctly. Points are lost for failure to complete the employability requirements (see Non-Task-Specific criteria). When all criteria are evaluated, tally the points for a total at the bottom of each column.

Tasksheet Scoring

Evaluation Items	Test		Retest	
	Pass	**Fail**	**Pass**	**Fail**
Task-Specific Evaluation	**(1 pt)**	**(0 pts)**	**(1 pt)**	**(0 pts)**
Student properly started the engine, brought it to operating temperature, and listed hard starting problems.				
Student properly recorded idle and governed rpm with the engine at operating temperature.				
Student properly observed and recorded unusual vibrations at idle and governed rpm (clutch/air conditioning).				
Student accurately listed possible causes for excessive vibrations.				
Non-Task-Specific Evaluation	**(0 pts)**	**(−1 pt)**	**(0 pts)**	**(−1 pt)**
Student successfully completed at least three of the non-task-specific steps.				
Student successfully completed all five of the non-task-specific steps.				
Total Score: <total # of points / 4 = %>				

Supervisor/Instructor:

Supervisor/instructor signature _____ Date _____

Comments:

Retest supervisor/instructor signature _____ Date _____

Comments:

CDX Tasksheet Number: 5.5a003

Student/Intern Information

Name _____ Date _____ Class _____

Machine, Customer, and Service Information

Machine used for this activity:

Make _____ Model _____

Hours _____ Serial Number _____

> ### Materials Required
> - Vehicle with possible engine concern
> - Engine manufacturer's workshop materials
> - Manufacturer-specific tools, depending on the concern/procedure(s)
> - Vehicle/component lifting equipment, if applicable

Task-Specific Safety Considerations

- This task may require test driving the vehicle on the school grounds or on a hoist, both of which carry severe risks. Attempt this task only with full permission from your supervisor/instructor and follow all the guidelines exactly.
- Lifting equipment such as vehicle jacks and stands, vehicle hoists, and engine hoists are important tools that increase productivity and make the job easier. However, they can also cause severe injury or death if used improperly. Make sure you follow the manufacturer's operation procedures. Also make sure you have your supervisor's/instructor's permission to use any particular type of lifting equipment.
- Comply with personal and environmental safety practices associated with clothing; eye protection; hand tools; power equipment; proper ventilation; and the handling, storage, and disposal of chemicals/materials in accordance with federal, state, and local regulations.
- Always wear the correct protective eyewear and clothing and use the appropriate safety equipment, as well as wheel chocks, fender covers, seat protectors, and floor mat protectors.
- Make sure you understand and observe all legislative and personal safety procedures when carrying out practical assignments. If you are unsure of what these are, ask your supervisor/instructor.

▶ **TASK** Inspect and test exhaust after-treatment devices. **AED 5.5**

Time off_____

Time on_____

Student Instructions: Read through the entire procedure prior to starting. Prepare your workspace and any tools or parts that may be needed to complete the task. When directed by your supervisor/instructor, begin the procedure to complete the task, and comment or check the box as each step is finished. Track your time on this procedure for later comparison to the standard completion time (i.e., "flat rate" or customer pay time).

Total time_____

Note: This tasksheet may require the student to check the condition of miscellaneous vehicle fluids, some of which may be flammable and could damage the environment or cause health problems if not handled properly. Observe all safety precautions and follow local regulations for the proper disposal of fluids.

Procedure	Step Completed
1. While referencing the manufacturer's workshop materials and using the appropriate electronic service tool (EST), record any aftertreatment codes.	☐
2. While referencing the manufacturer's workshop materials, inspect the exhaust aftertreatment system for missing, loose, or damaged components.	☐
a. Meets the manufacturer's specifications: Yes ☐ No ☐	☐
b. If no, list your recommendations for rectification:	☐
3. If equipped and while referencing the manufacturer's workshop materials, inspect the aftertreatment fuel injector connections for signs of fuel (and coolant, if equipped) leakage.	☐
a. Meets the manufacturer's specifications: Yes ☐ No ☐	☐
b. If no, list your recommendations for rectification:	☐
4. While referencing the manufacturer's workshop materials, record the procedure for removing and inspecting the aftertreatment fuel injector (if equipped):	☐
5. If directed by your supervisor/instructor and while referencing the manufacturer's workshop materials, remove, inspect, and reinstall the aftertreatment fuel injector.	☐
a. Meets the manufacturer's specifications: Yes ☐ No ☐	☐
b. If no, list your recommendations for rectification:	☐

6. While referencing the manufacturer's workshop materials, record the procedure for removing and inspecting the aftertreatment selective catalytic reduction (SCR) catalyst:	☐
7. If directed by your supervisor/instructor and while referencing the manufacturer's workshop materials, remove, inspect, and reinstall the aftertreatment SCR catalyst.	☐
a. Meets the manufacturer's specifications: Yes ☐ No ☐	☐
b. If no, list your recommendations for rectification:	☐
8. While referencing the manufacturer's workshop materials, record the procedure for removing and inspecting the diesel particulate filter (DPF).	☐
9. If directed by your supervisor/instructor and while referencing the manufacturer's workshop materials, remove, inspect, and reinstall the DPF.	☐
a. Meets the manufacturer's specifications: Yes ☐ No ☐	☐
b. If no, list your recommendations for rectification:	☐
10. While referencing the manufacturer's workshop materials, inspect the diesel exhaust fluid (DEF) reservoir, lines, and connections for missing, loose, or damaged components.	☐
a. Meets the manufacturer's specifications: Yes ☐ No ☐	☐
b. If no, list your recommendations for rectification:	☐
11. While referencing the manufacturer's workshop materials, record the procedure for removing, inspecting, and reinstalling the aftertreatment decomposition tube:	☐

12. If directed by your supervisor/instructor and while referencing the manufacturer's workshop materials, remove, inspect, and reinstall the aftertreatment decomposition tube.	☐
a. Meets the manufacturer's specifications: Yes ☐ No ☐	☐
b. If no, list your recommendations for rectification:	☐
13. While referencing the manufacturer's workshop materials and using the appropriate EST, check for any aftertreatment codes that may have become active after the aftertreatment components were removed, inspected, and reinstalled. Record them below:	☐
14. If directed by your supervisor/instructor and while referencing the manufacturer's workshop materials, repair any active aftertreatment code(s).	☐
a. Meets the manufacturer's specifications: Yes ☐ No ☐	☐
b. If no list the recommendations for rectification:	☐
15. While referencing the manufacturer's workshop materials, record the procedure and any special precautions for performing a stationary regeneration:	☐
16. If directed by your supervisor/instructor and while referencing the manufacturer's workshop materials, perform a stationary regeneration.	☐
a. Meets the manufacturer's specifications: Yes ☐ No ☐	☐
b. If no, list your recommendations for rectification:	☐
17. Discuss your findings with your supervisor/instructor.	☐

Non-Task-Specific Evaluation	Step Completed
1. Tools and equipment were used as directed and returned in good working order.	☐
2. Complied with all general and task-specific safety standards, including proper use of any personal protective equipment (PPE).	☐
3. Completed the task in an appropriate time frame (recommendation: 1.5 or 2 times the flat rate).	☐
4. Left the workspace clean and orderly.	☐
5. Cared for customer property and returned it undamaged.	☐

Student signature _____ Date _____

Comments:

Have your supervisor/instructor verify satisfactory completion of this procedure, any observations made, and any necessary action(s) recommended.

Evaluation Instructions: The scoring box below is intended to act as a guide for both student and supervisor/instructor. Each criterion listed will help students to understand what is expected of them and help supervisors/instructors to articulate the level of success at a particular task. The scoring is set up to allow a second attempt at each task (see the Test and Retest columns). Scoring is designed only to award students points for task criteria that were completed correctly. Points are lost for failure to complete the employability requirements (see Non-Task-Specific criteria). When all criteria are evaluated, tally the points for a total at the bottom of each column.

Tasksheet Scoring

Evaluation Items	Test		Retest	
	Pass	Fail	Pass	Fail
Task-Specific Evaluation	**(1 pt)**	**(0 pts)**	**(1 pt)**	**(0 pts)**
Student properly inspected all aftertreatment components and reinstalled when applicable.				
Student accurately listed any necessary rectifications for any components out of specification.				
Student properly retrieved and repaired any aftertreatment codes.				
Student properly recorded and performed a stationary regeneration.				
Non-Task-Specific Evaluation	**(0 pts)**	**(−1 pt)**	**(0 pts)**	**(−1 pt)**
Student successfully completed at least three of the non-task-specific steps.				
Student successfully completed all five of the non-task-specific steps.				
Total Score: <total # of points / 4 = %>				

Supervisor/Instructor:

Supervisor/instructor signature _____ Date _____

Comments:

Retest supervisor/instructor signature _____ Date _____

Comments:

Chapter 45: Engine Subsystems; Understanding Internal Engine Components

Learning Objective/Task	CDX Tasksheet Number	AED Reference Number
• Repair cylinder head.	5.5b001	AED 5.5
• Inspect all internal components.	5.5b002	AED 5.5
• Install cylinder liners.	5.5b003	AED 5.5
• Install main bearings.	5.5b004	AED 5.5
• Adjust valve clearances and injector settings.	5.5b005a	AED 5.5
• Install timing gear train.	5.5b005b	AED 5.5

Materials Required

- Vehicle with possible engine concern
- Engine manufacturer's workshop materials
- Manufacturer-specific tools, depending on the concern/procedure(s)
- Vehicle/component lifting equipment, if applicable

Safety Considerations

- This task may require test driving the vehicle on the school grounds or on a hoist, both of which carry severe risks. Attempt this task only with full permission from your supervisor/instructor and follow all the guidelines exactly.
- Lifting equipment such as vehicle jacks and stands, vehicle hoists, and engine hoists are important tools that increase productivity and make the job easier. However, they can also cause severe injury or death if used improperly. Make sure you follow the manufacturer's operation procedures. Also make sure you have your supervisor's/instructor's permission to use any particular type of lifting equipment.
- Comply with personal and environmental safety practices associated with clothing; eye protection; hand tools; power equipment; proper ventilation; and the handling, storage, and disposal of chemicals/materials in accordance with federal, state, and local regulations.
- Always wear the correct protective eyewear and clothing and use the appropriate safety equipment, as well as wheel chocks, fender covers, seat protectors, and floor mat protectors.
- Make sure you understand and observe all legislative and personal safety procedures when carrying out practical assignments. If you are unsure of what these are, ask your supervisor/instructor.

CDX Tasksheet Number: 5.5b001

Student/Intern Information

Name _____ Date _____ Class _____

Machine, Customer, and Service Information

Machine used for this activity:

Make _____ Model _____

Hours _____ Serial Number _____

Task-Specific Safety Considerations

- This task may require test driving the vehicle on the school grounds or on a hoist, both of which carry severe risks. Attempt this task only with full permission from your supervisor/instructor and follow all the guidelines exactly.
- Lifting equipment such as vehicle jacks and stands, vehicle hoists, and engine hoists are important tools that increase productivity and make the job easier. However, they can also cause severe injury or death if used improperly. Make sure you follow the manufacturer's operation procedures. Also make sure you have your supervisor's/instructor's permission to use any particular type of lifting equipment.
- Comply with personal and environmental safety practices associated with clothing; eye protection; hand tools; power equipment; proper ventilation; and the handling, storage, and disposal of chemicals/materials in accordance with federal, state, and local regulations.
- Always wear the correct protective eyewear and clothing and use the appropriate safety equipment, as well as wheel chocks, fender covers, seat protectors, and floor mat protectors.
- Make sure you understand and observe all legislative and personal safety procedures when carrying out practical assignments. If you are unsure of what these are, ask your supervisor/instructor.

▶ **TASK** Repair cylinder head.

AED 5.5

Time off_____

Time on_____

Student Instructions: Read through the entire procedure prior to starting. Prepare your workspace and any tools or parts that may be needed to complete the task. When directed by your supervisor/instructor, begin the procedure to complete the task, and comment or check the box as each step is finished. Track your time on this procedure for later comparison to the standard completion time (i.e., "flat rate" or customer pay time).

Total time_____

Note: This tasksheet may require the student to check the condition of miscellaneous vehicle fluids, some of which may be flammable and could damage the environment or cause health problems if not handled properly. Observe all safety precautions and follow local regulations for the proper disposal of fluids.

Procedure	Step Completed
1. Reference the appropriate manufacturer's workshop materials.	☐
2. Determine the type of crack detection process(es) that your workshop utilizes and respond below.	☐
a. Magnetic particle inspection Yes ☐ No ☐	☐
b. Penetrating dyes Yes ☐ No ☐	☐
c. Pressure testing Yes ☐ No ☐	☐
d. Vacuum testing Yes ☐ No ☐	☐
e. Ultrasonic testing Yes ☐ No ☐	☐
f. If none of the above, describe the method that your workshop uses:	☐

g. Outsource testing and repairs
 	
    Yes ☐ No ☐
 	
    If yes, describe the procedure used below:
	☐

3. Reference the manufacturer's workshop materials for information about inspecting the cylinder head for cracks/damage.	☐
a. List the procedure for inspecting the cylinder head for cracks/damage:	☐
b. List the safety precautions that must be observed during the inspection:	☐

4. Discuss these procedures and precautions with your supervisor/instructor. Determine what method of testing should be carried out, and name it below:	☐
5. If directed by your supervisor/instructor, commence inspecting the cylinder head. Follow the procedure listed above and reference the manufacturer's workshop materials.	☐
a. Meets the manufacturer's specifications: Yes ☐ No ☐	☐
b. If no, list the areas with cracks/damage and your recommendations for any rectifications:	☐
6. Reference the manufacturer's workshop materials for information about checking the cylinder head for warpage.	☐
a. List the steps involved in checking the cylinder head for warpage:	☐
b. List the safety precautions that must be observed when checking the cylinder head for warpage:	☐
7. Following the procedure listed above, and while referencing the manufacturer's workshop materials, check for any warpage of the cylinder head mating surfaces.	☐
a. Meets the manufacturer's specifications: Yes ☐ No ☐	☐
b. If no, list your recommendations for any rectifications:	☐
8. Referring to the manufacturer's workshop materials, check the condition of the passages and inspect the core/expansion and gallery plugs.	☐
a. Meets the manufacturer's specifications: Yes ☐ No ☐	☐

	Step Completed
b. If no, list the areas of concern and your recommendations for any rectifications:	☐
9. Reinstall all removed components undamaged and in working order unless teardown is to continue.	☐
10. Discuss your findings with your supervisor/instructor.	☐

Non-Task-Specific Evaluation	Step Completed
1. Tools and equipment were used as directed and returned in good working order.	☐
2. Complied with all general and task-specific safety standards, including proper use of any personal protective equipment (PPE).	☐
3. Completed the task in an appropriate time frame (recommendation: 1.5 or 2 times the flat rate).	☐
4. Left the workspace clean and orderly.	☐
5. Cared for customer property and returned it undamaged.	☐

Student signature _____ Date _____

Comments:

Have your supervisor/instructor verify satisfactory completion of this procedure, any observations made, and any necessary action(s) recommended.

Evaluation Instructions: The scoring box below is intended to act as a guide for both student and supervisor/instructor. Each criterion listed will help students to understand what is expected of them and help supervisors/instructors to articulate the level of success at a particular task. The scoring is set up to allow a second attempt at each task (see the Test and Retest columns). Scoring is designed only to award students points for task criteria that were completed correctly. Points are lost for failure to complete the employability requirements (see Non-Task-Specific criteria). When all criteria are evaluated, tally the points for a total at the bottom of each column.

Tasksheet Scoring

Evaluation Items	Test		Retest	
	Pass	Fail	Pass	Fail
Task-Specific Evaluation	**(1 pt)**	**(0 pts)**	**(1 pt)**	**(0 pts)**
Student accurately determined the type of crack detection process(es) that their workshop utilizes.				
Student accurately recorded the procedure for each inspection/check and its safety precautions.				
Student properly performed each inspection/check.				
Student accurately noted any necessary rectifications and properly reinstalled all removed components.				
Non-Task-Specific Evaluation	**(0 pts)**	**(−1 pt)**	**(0 pts)**	**(−1 pt)**
Student successfully completed at least three of the non-task-specific steps.				
Student successfully completed all five of the non-task-specific steps.				
Total Score: <total # of points / 4 = %>				

Supervisor/Instructor:

Supervisor/instructor signature _____ Date _____

Comments:

Retest supervisor/instructor signature _____ Date _____

Comments:

CDX Tasksheet Number: 5.5b002

Student/Intern Information

Name _____ Date _____ Class _____

Machine, Customer, and Service Information

Machine used for this activity:

Make _____ Model _____

Hours _____ Serial Number _____

Materials Required

- Vehicle with possible engine concern
- Engine manufacturer's workshop materials
- Manufacturer-specific tools, depending on the concern/procedure(s)
- Vehicle/component lifting equipment, if applicable

Task-Specific Safety Considerations

- This task may require test driving the vehicle on the school grounds or on a hoist, both of which carry severe risks. Attempt this task only with full permission from your supervisor/instructor and follow all the guidelines exactly.
- Lifting equipment such as vehicle jacks and stands, vehicle hoists, and engine hoists are important tools that increase productivity and make the job easier. However, they can also cause severe injury or death if used improperly. Make sure you follow the manufacturer's operation procedures. Also make sure you have your supervisor's/instructor's permission to use any particular type of lifting equipment.
- Comply with personal and environmental safety practices associated with clothing; eye protection; hand tools; power equipment; proper ventilation; and the handling, storage, and disposal of chemicals/materials in accordance with federal, state, and local regulations.
- Always wear the correct protective eyewear and clothing and use the appropriate safety equipment, as well as wheel chocks, fender covers, seat protectors, and floor mat protectors.
- Make sure you understand and observe all legislative and personal safety procedures when carrying out practical assignments. If you are unsure of what these are, ask your supervisor/instructor.

▶ TASK Inspect all internal components.

Time off_____

Student Instructions: Read through the entire procedure prior to starting. Prepare your workspace and any tools or parts that may be needed to complete the task. When directed by your supervisor/instructor, begin the procedure to complete the task, and comment or check the box as each step is finished. Track your time on this procedure for later comparison to the standard completion time (i.e., "flat rate" or customer pay time).

Time on_____

Total time_____

Note: This tasksheet may require the student to check the condition of miscellaneous vehicle fluids, some of which may be flammable and could damage the environment or cause health problems if not handled properly. Observe all safety precautions and follow local regulations for the proper disposal of fluids.

Procedure	Step Completed
1. Reference the manufacturer's workshop materials for information about disassembling an engine assembly.	☐
a. List the procedures and any special tooling needed to disassemble an engine assembly:	☐
b. Determine what safety precautions must be observed during the disassembly:	☐
2. Discuss these procedures and safety precautions with your supervisor/instructor. Record any special instructions below:	☐
a. If available, mount the engine to an engine rebuild stand. (**Note:** Drain the engine oil and coolant and steam clean/pressure wash the engine if needed before installing on the stand.)	☐
3. Using the proper tools and procedures, disassemble the engine. (**Note:** Store all fasteners in labeled storage trays/bins. Store any component that may contain oil or other fluids in a manner that will prevent spillage on the workshop floor. This is a safety requirement.)	☐
4. Before removing the connecting rod caps, mark their locations and positions.	☐
5. Inspect the cylinder liner/bore for a wear ridge at the top of the piston travel.	☐
a. Record your findings:	☐
b. Record your method for removing the wear ridge:	☐
6. Remove the piston/connecting rod assemblies and store them in a safe location. (**Note:** Install the correct connecting rod cap onto the connecting rod immediately after removing it from the engine.)	☐

7. Remove the flywheel and the flywheel housing from the engine.	☐
8. Remove the front timing cover from the engine.	☐
9. Remove the main bearing caps. (**Note:** Mark the positions of the crankshaft main bearing caps before removal.)	☐
10. Carefully remove the crankshaft from the engine and store it in a safe location. Note that damage can occur if the crankshaft is stored laying down; store it in an upright position. (**Hint:** Reinstall the flywheel onto the crankshaft to help keep it in an upright position for storage.)	☐
11. Reinstall the crankshaft main bearing caps onto the engine.	☐
12. Using the correct tooling, remove the cylinder liners (if applicable). (**Note:** Damage can occur if the liners are not stored in an upright position.)	☐
13. While observing all lifting safety precautions, transport the disassembled block and disassembled components to the designated cleaning bay.	☐
14. Clean and dry the engine block and all the related components. Have your supervisor/instructor verify satisfactory cleanliness. Supervisor's/instructor's initials: _____	☐
15. Remount the clean engine block to the engine rebuild stand.	☐
16. Lay out all the components in an orderly manner to assist in reassembly.	☐
17. Reference the manufacturer's workshop materials and list the procedure for measuring mating surfaces for warpage:	☐
18. Following the procedure listed above, and while referencing the manufacturer's workshop materials, measure the mating surfaces for warpage.	☐
a. Meets the manufacturer's specifications: Yes ☐ No ☐	☐
b. If no, list the procedure(s) for rectification:	☐
19. Referring to the manufacturer's workshop materials, check the condition of passages, core/expansion, and gallery plugs; inspect threaded holes, studs, dowel pins, and bolts for serviceability.	☐

	Step Completed
a. Meets the manufacturer's specifications: Yes ☐ No ☐	☐
b. If no, list the procedure(s) for rectification:	☐
20. Discuss your findings with your supervisor/instructor.	☐

Non-Task-Specific Evaluation	Step Completed
1. Tools and equipment were used as directed and returned in good working order.	☐
2. Complied with all general and task-specific safety standards, including proper use of any personal protective equipment (PPE).	☐
3. Completed the task in an appropriate time frame (recommendation: 1.5 or 2 times the flat rate).	☐
4. Left the workspace clean and orderly.	☐
5. Cared for customer property and returned it undamaged.	☐

Student signature _____ Date _____

Comments:

Have your supervisor/instructor verify satisfactory completion of this procedure, any observations made, and any necessary action(s) recommended.

Evaluation Instructions: The scoring box below is intended to act as a guide for both student and supervisor/instructor. Each criterion listed will help students to understand what is expected of them and help supervisors/instructors to articulate the level of success at a particular task. The scoring is set up to allow a second attempt at each task (see the Test and Retest columns). Scoring is designed only to award students points for task criteria that were completed correctly. Points are lost for failure to complete the employability requirements (see Non-Task-Specific criteria). When all criteria are evaluated, tally the points for a total at the bottom of each column.

Tasksheet Scoring

Evaluation Items	Test		Retest	
	Pass	**Fail**	**Pass**	**Fail**
Task-Specific Evaluation	**(1 pt)**	**(0 pts)**	**(1 pt)**	**(0 pts)**
Student sorted and labeled small parts and fasteners during disassembly.				
Student properly cleaned all components and laid them out in a neat and orderly manner.				
Student used the proper tools and techniques to check surfaces for warpage.				
Student properly inspected threaded holes, dowel pins, core/expansion plugs, and plugs.				
Non-Task-Specific Evaluation	**(0 pts)**	**(−1 pt)**	**(0 pts)**	**(−1 pt)**
Student successfully completed at least three of the non-task-specific steps.				
Student successfully completed all five of the non-task-specific steps.				
Total Score: <total # of points / 4 = %>				

Supervisor/Instructor:

Supervisor/instructor signature _____ Date _____

Comments:

Retest supervisor/instructor signature _____ Date _____

Comments:

CDX Tasksheet Number: 5.5b003

Student/Intern Information

Name _____ Date _____ Class _____

Machine, Customer, and Service Information

Machine used for this activity:

Make _____ Model _____

Hours _____ Serial Number _____

Materials Required
- Vehicle with possible engine concern
- Engine manufacturer's workshop materials
- Manufacturer-specific tools, depending on the concern/procedure(s)
- Vehicle/component lifting equipment, if applicable

Task-Specific Safety Considerations
- This task may require test driving the vehicle on the school grounds or on a hoist, both of which carry severe risks. Attempt this task only with full permission from your supervisor/instructor and follow all the guidelines exactly.
- Lifting equipment such as vehicle jacks and stands, vehicle hoists, and engine hoists are important tools that increase productivity and make the job easier. However, they can also cause severe injury or death if used improperly. Make sure you follow the manufacturer's operation procedures. Also make sure you have your supervisor's/instructor's permission to use any particular type of lifting equipment.
- Comply with personal and environmental safety practices associated with clothing; eye protection; hand tools; power equipment; proper ventilation; and the handling, storage, and disposal of chemicals/materials in accordance with federal, state, and local regulations.
- Always wear the correct protective eyewear and clothing and use the appropriate safety equipment, as well as wheel chocks, fender covers, seat protectors, and floor mat protectors.
- Make sure you understand and observe all legislative and personal safety procedures when carrying out practical assignments. If you are unsure of what these are, ask your supervisor/instructor.

▶ TASK Install cylinder liners. **AED 5.5**

Time off_____

Time on_____

Student Instructions: Read through the entire procedure prior to starting. Prepare your workspace and any tools or parts that may be needed to complete the task. When directed by your supervisor/instructor, begin the procedure to complete the task, and comment or check the box as each step is finished. Track your time on this procedure for later comparison to the standard completion time (i.e., "flat rate" or customer pay time).

Total time_____

Note: This tasksheet may require the student to check the condition of miscellaneous vehicle fluids, some of which may be flammable and could damage the environment or cause health problems if not handled properly. Observe all safety precautions and follow local regulations for the proper disposal of fluids.

Procedure	Step Completed
1. Referring to the manufacturer's workshop materials, inspect and measure liners/cylinder walls for wear and damage. Then record the specifications below.	☐
a. Cylinder diameter _____ in/mm	☐
b. Cylinder taper _____ in/mm	☐
c. Cylinder out-of-round _____ in/mm	☐
d. Minimum wall thickness _____ in/mm	☐
2. Visually inspect the liners/cylinder walls (e.g., for pitting, cracks).	☐
a. Meets the manufacturer's specifications: Yes ☐ No ☐	☐
b. If no, list your recommendations for rectification:	☐
3. Referring to the manufacturer's workshop materials and using the correct recommended tools, measure and record the reading for each engine's liners/cylinder walls. Record your findings below.	

a. Engine #1
 	
   Diameter (top) _____ in/mm
 	
   Diameter at 90 degrees (top) _____ in/mm
 	
   Diameter (bottom) _____ in/mm
 	
   Diameter at 90 degrees (bottom) _____ in/mm
 	
   Taper _____ in/mm
 	
   Out-of-round _____ in/mm
	☐

b. Engine #2
 	
   Diameter (top) _____ in/mm
 	
   Diameter at 90 degrees (top) _____ in/mm
 	
   Diameter (bottom) _____ in/mm
 	
   Diameter at 90 degrees (bottom) _____ in/mm
 	
   Taper _____ in/mm
 	
   Out-of-round _____ in/mm
	☐

c. Engine #3	☐
Diameter (top) _____ in/mm	
Diameter at 90 degrees (top) _____ in/mm	
Diameter (bottom) _____ in/mm	
Diameter at 90 degrees (bottom) _____ in/mm	
Taper _____ in/mm	
Out-of-round _____ in/mm	
d. Engine #4	☐
Diameter (top) _____ in/mm	
Diameter at 90 degrees (top) _____ in/mm	
Diameter (bottom) _____ in/mm	
Diameter at 90 degrees (bottom) _____ in/mm	
Taper _____ in/mm	
Out-of-round _____ in/mm	
e. Engine #5	☐
Diameter (top) _____ in/mm	
Diameter at 90 degrees (top) _____ in/mm	
Diameter (bottom) _____ in/mm	
Diameter at 90 degrees (bottom) _____ in/mm	
Taper _____ in/mm	
Out-of-round _____ in/mm	
f. Engine #6	☐
Diameter (top) _____ in/mm	
Diameter at 90 degrees (top) _____ in/mm	
Diameter (bottom) _____ in/mm	
Diameter at 90 degrees (bottom) _____ in/mm	
Taper _____ in/mm	
Out-of-round _____ in/mm	
4. Meets the manufacturer's specifications: Yes ☐ No ☐	☐
a. If no, list your recommendations for rectification:	☐

5. Reference the manufacturer's workshop materials. Record the procedure for checking liner height (protrusion):	☐
6. Reference the manufacturer's workshop materials. Record the manufacturer's specification for liner height (protrusion): _____in/mm	☐
7. Install cylinder liners and record the liner height (protrusion) for each engine.	☐

a. Engine #1
   Liner height (protrusion)
 	
   _____in/mm
	☐

b. Engine #2
   Liner height (protrusion)
 	
   _____in/mm
	☐

c. Engine #3
   Liner height (protrusion)
 	
   _____in/mm
	☐

d. Engine #4
   Liner height (protrusion)
 	
   _____in/mm
	☐

e. Engine #5
   Liner height (protrusion)
 	
   _____in/mm
	☐

f. Engine #6
   Liner height (protrusion)
 	
   _____in/mm
	☐

8. Meets the manufacturer's specifications: Yes ☐ No ☐	☐
a. If no, list your recommendations for rectification:	☐
9. Discuss your findings with your supervisor/instructor.	☐

Non-Task-Specific Evaluation	Step Completed
1. Tools and equipment were used as directed and returned in good working order.	☐
2. Complied with all general and task-specific safety standards, including proper use of any personal protective equipment (PPE).	☐
3. Completed the task in an appropriate time frame (recommendation: 1.5 or 2 times the flat rate).	☐
4. Left the workspace clean and orderly.	☐
5. Cared for customer property and returned it undamaged.	☐

Student signature _____ Date _____

Comments:

Have your supervisor/instructor verify satisfactory completion of this procedure, any observations made, and any necessary action(s) recommended.

Evaluation Instructions: The scoring box below is intended to act as a guide for both student and supervisor/instructor. Each criterion listed will help students to understand what is expected of them and help supervisors/instructors to articulate the level of success at a particular task. The scoring is set up to allow a second attempt at each task (see the Test and Retest columns). Scoring is designed only to award students points for task criteria that were completed correctly. Points are lost for failure to complete the employability requirements (see Non-Task-Specific criteria). When all criteria are evaluated, tally the points for a total at the bottom of each column.

Tasksheet Scoring

	Test		Retest	
Evaluation Items	**Pass**	**Fail**	**Pass**	**Fail**
Task-Specific Evaluation	**(1 pt)**	**(0 pts)**	**(1 pt)**	**(0 pts)**
Student properly inspected cylinder condition and diameter.				
Student properly inspected cylinder taper and out-of-round.				
Student properly installed cylinder liners.				
Student properly checked cylinder liner height (protrusion).				
Non-Task-Specific Evaluation	**(0 pts)**	**(−1 pt)**	**(0 pts)**	**(−1 pt)**
Student successfully completed at least three of the non-task-specific steps.				
Student successfully completed all five of the non-task-specific steps.				
Total Score: <total # of points / 4 = %>				

Supervisor/Instructor:

Supervisor/instructor signature _____ Date _____

Comments:

Retest supervisor/instructor signature _____ Date _____

Comments:

CDX Tasksheet Number: 5.5b004

Student/Intern Information

Name _____ Date _____ Class _____

Machine, Customer, and Service Information

Machine used for this activity:

Make _____ Model _____

Hours _____ Serial Number _____

Materials Required

- Vehicle with possible engine concern
- Engine manufacturer's workshop materials
- Manufacturer-specific tools, depending on the concern/procedure(s)
- Vehicle/component lifting equipment, if applicable

Task-Specific Safety Considerations

- This task may require test driving the vehicle on the school grounds or on a hoist, both of which carry severe risks. Attempt this task only with full permission from your supervisor/instructor and follow all the guidelines exactly.
- Lifting equipment such as vehicle jacks and stands, vehicle hoists, and engine hoists are important tools that increase productivity and make the job easier. However, they can also cause severe injury or death if used improperly. Make sure you follow the manufacturer's operation procedures. Also make sure you have your supervisor's/instructor's permission to use any particular type of lifting equipment.
- Comply with personal and environmental safety practices associated with clothing; eye protection; hand tools; power equipment; proper ventilation; and the handling, storage, and disposal of chemicals/materials in accordance with federal, state, and local regulations.
- Always wear the correct protective eyewear and clothing and use the appropriate safety equipment, as well as wheel chocks, fender covers, seat protectors, and floor mat protectors.
- Make sure you understand and observe all legislative and personal safety procedures when carrying out practical assignments. If you are unsure of what these are, ask your supervisor/instructor.

▶ TASK Install main bearings. **AED 5.5**

Time off_____

Time on_____

Student Instructions: Read through the entire procedure prior to starting. Prepare your workspace and any tools or parts that may be needed to complete the task. When directed by your supervisor/instructor, begin the procedure to complete the task, and comment or check the box as each step is finished. Track your time on this procedure for later comparison to the standard completion time (i.e., "flat rate" or customer pay time).

Total time_____

Note: This tasksheet may require the student to check the condition of miscellaneous vehicle fluids, some of which may be flammable and could damage the environment or cause health problems if not handled properly. Observe all safety precautions and follow local regulations for the proper disposal of fluids.

Procedure	Step Completed
1. Reference the manufacturer's workshop materials regarding inspecting the main bearings for wear patterns and damage, replacing the bearings as needed, checking the bearing clearances, and checking/correcting the crankshaft end play.	☐
a. List the steps involved in the processes listed above:	☐
b. Determine the safety precautions that must be observed during these processes:	☐
2. Following the procedures listed above, and while referencing the manufacturer's workshop materials, inspect the main bearings for wear patterns and damage.	☐
a. Note any problems you found below:	☐
b. If problems exist, list your recommendations for rectification:	☐
3. Referring to the manufacturer's workshop materials and using the correct recommended tools, measure and record the reading for each crankshaft main bearing clearance. Record your findings below. Manufacturer's specification: _____ in/mm	☐
a. #1 _____ in/mm	☐
b. #2 _____ in/mm	☐
c. #3 _____ in/mm	☐
d. #4 _____ in/mm	☐
e. #5 _____ in/mm	☐

f. #6 _____ in/mm	☐
g. #7 _____ in/mm	☐
4. Meets the manufacturer's specifications: Yes ☐ No ☐	☐
a. If no, list your recommendations for rectification:	☐
5. While referring to the manufacturer's workshop materials, install the crankshaft and torque main bearing caps. (**Note:** The crankshaft should turn by hand after installation. If it does not, remove the crankshaft and check for any misaligned bearings or contamination.)	☐
a. Manufacturer's torque specification/procedure:	☐
6. While referring to the manufacturer's workshop materials, measure the crankshaft end play. Manufacturer's specification: _____ in/mm	☐
7. Actual crankshaft end play: _____ in/mm	☐
a. Meets the manufacturer's specifications: Yes ☐ No ☐	☐
b. If no, list your recommendations for rectification:	☐
8. Discuss your findings with your supervisor/instructor.	☐

Non-Task-Specific Evaluation	Step Completed
1. Tools and equipment were used as directed and returned in good working order.	☐
2. Complied with all general and task-specific safety standards, including proper use of any personal protective equipment (PPE).	☐
3. Completed the task in an appropriate time frame (recommendation: 1.5 or 2 times the flat rate).	☐
4. Left the workspace clean and orderly.	☐
5. Cared for customer property and returned it undamaged.	☐

Student signature _____ Date _____

Comments:

[ ]

Have your supervisor/instructor verify satisfactory completion of this procedure, any observations made,

and any necessary action(s) recommended.

Evaluation Instructions: The scoring box below is intended to act as a guide for both student and supervisor/instructor. Each criterion listed will help students to understand what is expected of them and help supervisors/instructors to articulate the level of success at a particular task. The scoring is set up to allow a second attempt at each task (see the Test and Retest columns). Scoring is designed only to award students points for task criteria that were completed correctly. Points are lost for failure to complete the employability requirements (see Non-Task-Specific criteria). When all criteria are evaluated, tally the points for a total at the bottom of each column.

Tasksheet Scoring

Evaluation Items	Test		Retest	
	Pass	Fail	Pass	Fail
Task-Specific Evaluation	**(1 pt)**	**(0 pts)**	**(1 pt)**	**(0 pts)**
Student properly inspected the bearings.				
Student properly checked the crankshaft main bearing clearance.				
Student properly installed/torqued the crankshaft.				
Student properly checked the crankshaft end play.				
Non-Task-Specific Evaluation	**(0 pts)**	**(−1 pt)**	**(0 pts)**	**(−1 pt)**
Student successfully completed at least three of the non-task-specific steps.				
Student successfully completed all five of the non-task-specific steps.				
Total Score: <total # of points / 4 = %>				

Supervisor/Instructor:

Supervisor/instructor signature _____ Date _____

Comments:

Retest supervisor/instructor signature _____ Date _____

Comments:

CDX Tasksheet Number: 5.5b005a

Student/Intern Information

Name _____ Date _____ Class _____

Machine, Customer, and Service Information

Machine used for this activity:

Make _____ Model _____

Hours _____ Serial Number _____

Materials Required
- Vehicle with possible engine concern
- Engine manufacturer's workshop materials
- Manufacturer-specific tools, depending on the concern/procedure(s)
- Vehicle/component lifting equipment, if applicable

Task-Specific Safety Considerations
- This task may require test driving the vehicle on the school grounds or on a hoist, both of which carry severe risks. Attempt this task only with full permission from your supervisor/instructor and follow all the guidelines exactly.
- Lifting equipment such as vehicle jacks and stands, vehicle hoists, and engine hoists are important tools that increase productivity and make the job easier. However, they can also cause severe injury or death if used improperly. Make sure you follow the manufacturer's operation procedures. Also make sure you have your supervisor's/instructor's permission to use any particular type of lifting equipment.
- Comply with personal and environmental safety practices associated with clothing; eye protection; hand tools; power equipment; proper ventilation; and the handling, storage, and disposal of chemicals/materials in accordance with federal, state, and local regulations.
- Always wear the correct protective eyewear and clothing and use the appropriate safety equipment, as well as wheel chocks, fender covers, seat protectors, and floor mat protectors.
- Make sure you understand and observe all legislative and personal safety procedures when carrying out practical assignments. If you are unsure of what these are, ask your supervisor/instructor.

▶ **TASK** Adjust valve clearances and injector settings. **AED 5.5**

Time off_____

Time on_____

Student Instructions: Read through the entire procedure prior to starting. Prepare your workspace and any tools or parts that may be needed to complete the task. When directed by your supervisor/instructor, begin the procedure to complete the task, and comment or check the box as each step is finished. Track your time on this procedure for later comparison to the standard completion time (i.e., "flat rate" or customer pay time).

Total time_____

Note: This tasksheet may require the student to check the condition of miscellaneous vehicle fluids, some of which may be flammable and could damage the environment or cause health problems if not handled properly. Observe all safety precautions and follow local regulations for the proper disposal of fluids.

Procedure	Step Completed
1. Reference the manufacturer's workshop materials for information about adjusting valve bridges (crossheads).	☐
a. List the steps involved in adjusting valve bridges (crossheads):	☐
b. Determine what safety precautions must be observed when adjusting valve bridges (crossheads):	☐
2. Following the procedures listed above, and while referencing the manufacturer's workshop materials, adjust the valve bridges (crossheads).	☐
a. Meets the manufacturer's specifications: Yes ☐ No ☐	☐
b. If no, list your recommendations for any rectifications:	☐
3. Reference the manufacturer's workshop materials for information about adjusting the injectors.	☐
a. List the steps involved in adjusting the injectors:	☐
b. Determine what safety precautions must be observed when adjusting the injectors:	☐
4. Following the procedures listed above, and while referencing the manufacturer's workshop materials, adjust the injectors.	☐
a. Meets the manufacturer's specifications: Yes ☐ No ☐	☐
b. If no, list your recommendations for any rectifications:	☐

	Step Completed
5. Reference the manufacturer's workshop materials for information about adjusting the valves.	☐
a. List the steps involved in adjusting the valves:	☐
b. Determine what safety precautions must be observed when adjusting the valves:	☐
6. Following the procedures listed above, and while referencing the manufacturer's workshop materials, adjust the valves.	☐
a. Meets the manufacturer's specifications: Yes ☐ No ☐	☐
b. If no, list your recommendations for any rectifications:	☐
7. Reinstall all removed components undamaged and in working order unless teardown is to continue.	☐
8. Discuss your findings with your supervisor/instructor.	☐

Non-Task-Specific Evaluation	Step Completed
1. Tools and equipment were used as directed and returned in good working order.	☐
2. Complied with all general and task-specific safety standards, including proper use of any personal protective equipment (PPE).	☐
3. Completed the task in an appropriate time frame (recommendation: 1.5 or 2 times the flat rate).	☐
4. Left the workspace clean and orderly.	☐
5. Cared for customer property and returned it undamaged.	☐

Student signature _____ Date _____

Comments:

Have your supervisor/instructor verify satisfactory completion of this procedure, any observations made, and any necessary action(s) recommended.

Evaluation Instructions: The scoring box below is intended to act as a guide for both student and supervisor/instructor. Each criterion listed will help students to understand what is expected of them and help supervisors/instructors to articulate the level of success at a particular task. The scoring is set up to allow a second attempt at each task (see the Test and Retest columns). Scoring is designed only to award students points for task criteria that were completed correctly. Points are lost for failure to complete the employability requirements (see Non-Task-Specific criteria). When all criteria are evaluated, tally the points for a total at the bottom of each column.

Tasksheet Scoring

	Test		Retest	
Evaluation Items	**Pass**	**Fail**	**Pass**	**Fail**
Task-Specific Evaluation	**(1 pt)**	**(0 pts)**	**(1 pt)**	**(0 pts)**
Student adjusted valve bridges to the manufacturer's specification.				
Student adjusted injectors to the manufacturer's specification.				
Student adjusted valves to the manufacturer's specification.				
Student reinstalled all removed components undamaged and in working order unless teardown is to continue.				
Non-Task-Specific Evaluation	**(0 pts)**	**(−1 pt)**	**(0 pts)**	**(−1 pt)**
Student successfully completed at least three of the non-task-specific steps.				
Student successfully completed all five of the non-task-specific steps.				
Total Score: <total # of points / 4 = %>				

Supervisor/Instructor:

Supervisor/instructor signature _____ Date _____

Comments:

Retest supervisor/instructor signature _____ Date _____

Comments:

CDX Tasksheet Number: 5.5b005b

Student/Intern Information

Name _____ Date _____ Class _____

Machine, Customer, and Service Information

Machine used for this activity:

Make _____ Model _____

Hours _____ Serial Number _____

Materials Required

- Vehicle with possible engine concern
- Engine manufacturer's workshop materials
- Manufacturer-specific tools, depending on the concern/procedure(s)
- Vehicle/component lifting equipment, if applicable

Task-Specific Safety Considerations

- This task may require test driving the vehicle on the school grounds or on a hoist, both of which carry severe risks. Attempt this task only with full permission from your supervisor/instructor and follow all the guidelines exactly.
- Lifting equipment such as vehicle jacks and stands, vehicle hoists, and engine hoists are important tools that increase productivity and make the job easier. However, they can also cause severe injury or death if used improperly. Make sure you follow the manufacturer's operation procedures. Also make sure you have your supervisor's/instructor's permission to use any particular type of lifting equipment.
- Comply with personal and environmental safety practices associated with clothing; eye protection; hand tools; power equipment; proper ventilation; and the handling, storage, and disposal of chemicals/materials in accordance with federal, state, and local regulations.
- Always wear the correct protective eyewear and clothing and use the appropriate safety equipment, as well as wheel chocks, fender covers, seat protectors, and floor mat protectors.
- Make sure you understand and observe all legislative and personal safety procedures when carrying out practical assignments. If you are unsure of what these are, ask your supervisor/instructor.

▶ TASK Install timing gear train.   **AED** 5.5

Time off_____

Time on_____

Student Instructions: Read through the entire procedure prior to starting. Prepare your workspace and any tools or parts that may be needed to complete the task. When directed by your supervisor/instructor, begin the procedure to complete the task, and comment or check the box as each step is finished. Track your time on this procedure for later comparison to the standard completion time (i.e., "flat rate" or customer pay time).

Total time_____

Note: This tasksheet may require the student to check the condition of miscellaneous vehicle fluids, some of which may be flammable and could damage the environment or cause health problems if not handled properly. Observe all safety precautions and follow local regulations for the proper disposal of fluids.

Procedure	Step Completed
1. While referring to the manufacturer's workshop materials, inspect all timing components (for excessive wear, pitting, worn bushings, etc.) and record any findings below:	☐
2. While referencing the manufacturer's workshop materials, install the gear train. Once installed, have your supervisor/instructor verify correct timing. Supervisor's/instructor's initials: _____	☐
3. Referring to the manufacturer's workshop materials and using the correct recommended tools, measure and record the timing gear backlash: _____ in/mm	☐
a. Meets the manufacturer's specifications: Yes ☐ No ☐	☐
b. If no, list your recommendations for rectification:	☐
4. Discuss your findings with your supervisor/instructor.	☐

Non-Task-Specific Evaluation	Step Completed
1. Tools and equipment were used as directed and returned in good working order.	☐
2. Complied with all general and task-specific safety standards, including proper use of any personal protective equipment (PPE).	☐
3. Completed the task in an appropriate time frame (recommendation: 1.5 or 2 times the flat rate).	☐
4. Left the workspace clean and orderly.	☐
5. Cared for customer property and returned it undamaged.	☐

Student signature _____ Date _____

Comments:

Have your supervisor/instructor verify satisfactory completion of this procedure, any observations made,

and any necessary action(s) recommended.

Evaluation Instructions: The scoring box below is intended to act as a guide for both student and supervisor/instructor. Each criterion listed will help students to understand what is expected of them and help supervisors/instructors to articulate the level of success at a particular task. The scoring is set up to allow a second attempt at each task (see the Test and Retest columns). Scoring is designed only to award students points for task criteria that were completed correctly. Points are lost for failure to complete the employability requirements (see Non-Task-Specific criteria). When all criteria are evaluated, tally the points for a total at the bottom of each column.

Tasksheet Scoring

	Test		Retest	
Evaluation Items	**Pass**	**Fail**	**Pass**	**Fail**
Task-Specific Evaluation	**(1 pt)**	**(0 pts)**	**(1 pt)**	**(0 pts)**
Student used the manufacturer's workshop materials.				
Student properly inspected the timing components.				
Student properly installed the timing components.				
Student properly checked/set the timing gear backlash.				
Non-Task-Specific Evaluation	**(0 pts)**	**(−1 pt)**	**(0 pts)**	**(−1 pt)**
Student successfully completed at least three of the non-task-specific steps.				
Student successfully completed all five of the non-task-specific steps.				
Total Score: <total # of points / 4 = %>				

Supervisor/Instructor:

Supervisor/instructor signature _____ Date _____

Comments:

Retest supervisor/instructor signature _____ Date _____

Comments:

Chapter 46: Identify Hydraulic System Components

Learning Objective/Task	CDX Tasksheet Number	AED Reference Number
• Identify hydraulic system components.	5.5b006	AED 5.5
• Repair preheater system.	5.5b007	AED 5.5

Materials Required
- Vehicle with possible engine concerns
- Vehicle manufacturer's service information
- Manufacturer-specific tools, depending on the concern/procedure(s)

Safety Considerations
- This task may require test driving the vehicle on the school grounds or on a hoist, both of which carry severe risks. Attempt this task only with full permission from your supervisor/instructor and follow all the guidelines exactly.
- Lifting equipment such as vehicle jacks and stands, vehicle hoists, and engine hoists are important tools that increase productivity and make the job easier. However, they can also cause severe injury or death if used improperly. Make sure you follow the manufacturer's operation procedures. Also make sure you have your supervisor's/instructor's permission to use any particular type of lifting equipment.
- Comply with personal and environmental safety practices associated with clothing; eye protection; hand tools; power equipment; proper ventilation; and the handling, storage, and disposal of chemicals/materials in accordance with federal, state, and local regulations.
- Always wear the correct protective eyewear and clothing and use the appropriate safety equipment, as well as wheel chocks, fender covers, seat protectors, and floor mat protectors.
- Make sure you understand and observe all legislative and personal safety procedures when carrying out practical assignments. If you are unsure of what these are, ask your supervisor/instructor.
- While working on the vehicle, wheel chocks must be placed on both sides of one set of tires or as directed by your supervisor/instructor.
- When running any vehicles in the shop, make sure you use the shop's exhaust ventilation system to discharge all exhaust gas safely outside.

CDX Tasksheet Number: 5.5b006

Student/Intern Information

Name _____ Date _____ Class _____

Machine, Customer, and Service Information

Machine used for this activity:

Make _____ Model _____

Hours _____ Serial Number _____

Materials Required

- Vehicle with possible engine concerns
- Vehicle manufacturer's service information
- Manufacturer-specific tools, depending on the concern/procedure(s)

Task-Specific Safety Considerations

- This task may require test driving the vehicle on the school grounds or on a hoist, both of which carry severe risks. Attempt this task only with full permission from your supervisor/instructor and follow all the guidelines exactly.
- Comply with personal and environmental safety practices associated with clothing; eye protection; hand tools; power equipment; proper ventilation; and the handling, storage, and disposal of chemicals/materials in accordance with federal, state, and local regulations.
- Always wear the correct protective eyewear and clothing and use the appropriate safety equipment, as well as fender covers, seat protectors, and floor mat protectors.
- Make sure you understand and observe all legislative and personal safety procedures when carrying out practical assignments. If you are unsure of what these are, ask your supervisor/instructor.
- While working on the vehicle, wheel chocks must be placed on both sides of one set of tires or as directed by your supervisor/instructor.
- When running any vehicles in the shop, make sure you use the shop's exhaust ventilation system to discharge all exhaust gas safely outside.

▶ **TASK** Identify hydraulic system components. _____ **AED 5.5**

Time off_____

Student Instructions: Read through the entire procedure prior to starting. Prepare your workspace and any tools or parts that may be needed to complete the task. When directed by your supervisor/instructor, begin the procedure to complete the task, and comment or check the box as each step is finished. Track your time on this procedure for later comparison to the standard completion time (i.e., "flat rate" or customer pay time).

Time on_____

Total time_____

Procedure	Step Completed
1. Reference the manufacturer's service information for the correct schematic layout and locations of the hydraulic system components.	
a. Locate and identify the hydraulic pump:	☐
b. Locate and identify the hydraulic reservoir and filtration components:	☐
c. Locate and identify the hydraulic control valves:	☐
d. Locate and identify the hydraulic actuators (single-acting, double-acting, multistage, telescopic, and motors):	☐
2. Service filters and breathers.	
a. With the system shut down, operate the levers to relieve system pressure.	☐
b. Clean the area around the filter.	☐
c. Remove the old filter.	☐
d. Clean the filter housing (if it is a cartridge-type filter).	☐
e. Install a new filter and tighten it to the manufacturer's specifications.	☐
f. Operate the system and check for leaks.	☐
3. Return the vehicle to its beginning condition and return any tools you used to their proper locations.	☐
4. Discuss your findings with your supervisor/instructor.	☐

Non-Task-Specific Evaluation	Step Completed
1. Tools and equipment were used as directed and returned in good working order.	☐
2. Complied with all general and task-specific safety standards, including proper use of any personal protective equipment (PPE).	☐
3. Completed the task in an appropriate time frame (recommendation: 1.5 or 2 times the flat rate).	☐
4. Left the workspace clean and orderly.	☐
5. Cared for customer property and returned it undamaged.	☐

Student signature _____ Date _____

Comments:

Have your supervisor/instructor verify satisfactory completion of this procedure, any observations made,

and any necessary action(s) recommended.

Evaluation Instructions: The scoring box below is intended to act as a guide for both student and supervisor/instructor. Each criterion listed will help students to understand what is expected of them and help supervisors/instructors to articulate the level of success at a particular task. The scoring is set up to allow a second attempt at each task (see the Test and Retest columns). Scoring is designed only to award students points for task criteria that were completed correctly. Points are lost for failure to complete the employability requirements (see Non-Task-Specific criteria). When all criteria are evaluated, tally the points for a total at the bottom of each column.

Tasksheet Scoring

	Test		Retest	
Evaluation Items	**Pass**	**Fail**	**Pass**	**Fail**
Task-Specific Evaluation	**(1 pt)**	**(0 pts)**	**(1 pt)**	**(0 pts)**
Student used the manufacturer's service information.				
Student accurately identified each hydraulic system component.				
Student properly removed and cleaned the filter.				
Student properly reinstalled the filter.				
Non-Task-Specific Evaluation	**(0 pts)**	**(−1 pt)**	**(0 pts)**	**(−1 pt)**
Student successfully completed at least three of the non-task-specific steps.				
Student successfully completed all five of the non-task-specific steps.				
Total Score: <total # of points / 4 = %>				

Supervisor/Instructor:

Supervisor/instructor signature _____ Date _____

Comments:

Retest supervisor/instructor signature _____ Date _____

Comments:

CDX Tasksheet Number: 5.5b007

Student/Intern Information

Name _____ Date _____ Class _____

Machine, Customer, and Service Information

Machine used for this activity:

Make _____ Model _____

Hours _____ Serial Number _____

Materials Required

- Vehicle with possible engine concern
- Engine manufacturer's workshop materials
- Manufacturer-specific tools, depending on the concern/procedure(s)
- Vehicle/component lifting equipment, if applicable

Task-Specific Safety Considerations

- This task may require test driving the vehicle on the school grounds or on a hoist, both of which carry severe risks. Attempt this task only with full permission from your supervisor/instructor and follow all the guidelines exactly.
- Lifting equipment such as vehicle jacks and stands, vehicle hoists, and engine hoists are important tools that increase productivity and make the job easier. However, they can also cause severe injury or death if used improperly. Make sure you follow the manufacturer's operation procedures. Also make sure you have your supervisor's/instructor's permission to use any particular type of lifting equipment.
- Comply with personal and environmental safety practices associated with clothing; eye protection; hand tools; power equipment; proper ventilation; and the handling, storage, and disposal of chemicals/materials in accordance with federal, state, and local regulations.
- Always wear the correct protective eyewear and clothing and use the appropriate safety equipment, as well as wheel chocks, fender covers, seat protectors, and floor mat protectors.
- Make sure you understand and observe all legislative and personal safety procedures when carrying out practical assignments. If you are unsure of what these are, ask your supervisor/instructor.

▶ **TASK** Repair preheater system. _____ **AED 5.5**

Time off_____

Time on_____

Student Instructions: Read through the entire procedure prior to starting. Prepare your workspace and any tools or parts that may be needed to complete the task. When directed by your supervisor/instructor, begin the procedure to complete the task, and comment or check the box as each step is finished. Track your time on this procedure for later comparison to the standard completion time (i.e., "flat rate" or customer pay time).

Total time_____

Note: This tasksheet may require the student to check the condition of miscellaneous vehicle fluids, some of which may be flammable and could damage the environment or cause health problems if not handled properly. Observe all safety precautions and follow local regulations for the proper disposal of fluids.

Procedure	Step Completed
1. Reference the manufacturer's workshop materials and identify the type of air induction system heating device:	☐
2. While referencing the manufacturer's workshop materials, inspect the wiring and controls in the air induction system heating device for any damage.	☐
a. Note any problems you found below:	☐
b. If problems exist, list your recommendations for rectification:	☐
3. While referencing the manufacturer's workshop materials, list the steps to replace the heater grid:	☐
4. If directed by your supervisor/instructor, remove and replace the heater grid.	☐
a. Meets the manufacturer's specifications: Yes ☐ No ☐	☐
b. If no, list your recommendations for rectification:	☐
5. If directed by your supervisor/instructor and while referencing the manufacturer's workshop materials, replace any defective glow plug(s).	☐
a. Meets the manufacturer's specifications: Yes ☐ No ☐	☐
b. If no, list your recommendations for rectification:	☐
6. Discuss your findings with your supervisor/instructor.	☐

Non-Task-Specific Evaluation	Step Completed
1. Tools and equipment were used as directed and returned in good working order.	☐
2. Complied with all general and task-specific safety standards, including proper use of any personal protective equipment (PPE).	☐
3. Completed the task in an appropriate time frame (recommendation: 1.5 or 2 times the flat rate).	☐
4. Left the workspace clean and orderly.	☐
5. Cared for customer property and returned it undamaged.	☐

Student signature _____ Date _____

Comments:

Have your supervisor/instructor verify satisfactory completion of this procedure, any observations made, and any necessary action(s) recommended.

Evaluation Instructions: The scoring box below is intended to act as a guide for both student and supervisor/instructor. Each criterion listed will help students to understand what is expected of them and help supervisors/instructors to articulate the level of success at a particular task. The scoring is set up to allow a second attempt at each task (see the Test and Retest columns). Scoring is designed only to award students points for task criteria that were completed correctly. Points are lost for failure to complete the employability requirements (see Non-Task-Specific criteria). When all criteria are evaluated, tally the points for a total at the bottom of each column.

Tasksheet Scoring

Evaluation Items	Test		Retest	
	Pass	Fail	Pass	Fail
Task-Specific Evaluation	**(1 pt)**	**(0 pts)**	**(1 pt)**	**(0 pts)**
Student accurately identified the air induction system heating device, then properly inspected the device's wiring and connections.				
Student accurately listed the steps for replacing the heater grid.				
Student properly removed and replaced the heater grid if directed by their supervisor/instructor.				
Student properly replaced any defective glow plugs if directed by their supervisor/instructor.				
Non-Task-Specific Evaluation	**(0 pts)**	**(−1 pt)**	**(0 pts)**	**(−1 pt)**
Student successfully completed at least three of the non-task-specific steps.				
Student successfully completed all five of the non-task-specific steps.				
Total Score: <total # of points / 4 = %>				

Chapter 47: Fuel and Governing Systems, Mechanical and Electronic Systems; Understanding Basic Fuel Systems

Learning Objective/Task	CDX Tasksheet Number	AED Reference Number
• Inspect fuel tanks.	5.6a002	AED 5.6
• Measure fuel level and condition.	5.6a003	AED 5.6
• Test fuel supply and return systems.	5.6a004	AED 5.6
• Prime and bleed fuel system.	5.6a005	AED 5.6
• Install fuel transfer (lift) pump.	5.6a006	AED 5.6
• Repair misfiring cylinders.	5.6a007	AED 5.6
• Test high-pressure injection pump and system.	5.6a008	AED 5.6

Materials Required

- Vehicle with possible engine concern
- Engine manufacturer's workshop materials
- Manufacturer-specific tools, depending on the concern/procedure(s)
- Vehicle/component lifting equipment, if applicable

Safety Considerations

- This task may require test driving the vehicle on the school grounds or on a hoist, both of which carry severe risks. Attempt this task only with full permission from your supervisor/instructor and follow all the guidelines exactly.
- Lifting equipment such as vehicle jacks and stands, vehicle hoists, and engine hoists are important tools that increase productivity and make the job easier. However, they can also cause severe injury or death if used improperly. Make sure you follow the manufacturer's operation procedures. Also make sure you have your supervisor's/instructor's permission to use any particular type of lifting equipment.
- Comply with personal and environmental safety practices associated with clothing; eye protection; hand tools; power equipment; proper ventilation; and the handling, storage, and disposal of chemicals/materials in accordance with federal, state, and local regulations.
- Always wear the correct protective eyewear and clothing and use the appropriate safety equipment, as well as wheel chocks, fender covers, seat protectors, and floor mat protectors.
- Make sure you understand and observe all legislative and personal safety procedures when carrying out practical assignments. If you are unsure of what these are, ask your supervisor/instructor.

CDX Tasksheet Number: 5.6a002

Student/Intern Information

Name _____ Date _____ Class _____

Machine, Customer, and Service Information

Machine used for this activity:

Make _____ Model _____

Hours _____ Serial Number _____

Materials Required
- Vehicle with possible engine concern
- Engine manufacturer's workshop materials
- Manufacturer-specific tools, depending on the concern/procedure(s)
- Vehicle/component lifting equipment, if applicable

Task-Specific Safety Considerations
- This task may require test driving the vehicle on the school grounds or on a hoist, both of which carry severe risks. Attempt this task only with full permission from your supervisor/instructor and follow all the guidelines exactly.
- Lifting equipment such as vehicle jacks and stands, vehicle hoists, and engine hoists are important tools that increase productivity and make the job easier. However, they can also cause severe injury or death if used improperly. Make sure you follow the manufacturer's operation procedures. Also make sure you have your supervisor's/instructor's permission to use any particular type of lifting equipment.
- Comply with personal and environmental safety practices associated with clothing; eye protection; hand tools; power equipment; proper ventilation; and the handling, storage, and disposal of chemicals/materials in accordance with federal, state, and local regulations.
- Always wear the correct protective eyewear and clothing and use the appropriate safety equipment, as well as wheel chocks, fender covers, seat protectors, and floor mat protectors.
- Make sure you understand and observe all legislative and personal safety procedures when carrying out practical assignments. If you are unsure of what these are, ask your supervisor/instructor.

▶ TASK Inspect fuel tanks. **AED 5.6**

Time off _____

Student Instructions: Read through the entire procedure prior to starting. Prepare your workspace and any tools or parts that may be needed to complete the task. When directed by your supervisor/instructor, begin the procedure to complete the task, and comment or check the box as each step is finished. Track your time on this procedure for later comparison to the standard completion time (i.e., "flat rate" or customer pay time).

Time on _____

Total time _____

Note: This tasksheet may require the student to check the condition of miscellaneous vehicle fluids, some of which may be flammable and could damage the environment or cause health problems if not handled properly. Observe all safety precautions and follow local regulations for the proper disposal of fluids.

Procedure	Step Completed
1. While referencing the manufacturer's workshop materials, inspect the fuel tank for any signs of structural damage or leakage.	☐
a. Note any problems you found below:	☐
b. If problems exist, list your recommendations for rectification:	☐
2. While referencing the manufacturer's workshop materials, inspect the fuel tank cap/vents for signs of damage or blockage.	☐
a. Note any problems you found below:	☐
b. If problems exist, list your recommendations for rectification:	☐
3. While referencing the manufacturer's workshop materials, inspect the fuel tank mounts for any signs of damage (e.g., loose bolts, damaged straps, missing/damaged strap isolators, damaged/loose frame mounts).	☐
a. Note any problems you found below:	☐
b. If problems exist, list your recommendations for rectification:	☐
4. While referencing the manufacturer's workshop materials, measure and record the fuel tank strap torque: _____ lb/Nm	☐
a. Meets the manufacturer's specifications: Yes ☐ No ☐	☐

b. If no, list your recommendations for rectification:	☐
5. While referencing the manufacturer's workshop materials, measure and record the fuel tank mount bolt torque: _____ lb/Nm	☐
a. Meets the manufacturer's specifications: Yes ☐ No ☐	☐
b. If no, list your recommendations for rectification:	☐
6. While referencing the manufacturer's workshop materials, inspect the fuel tank valves for signs of leakage and proper operation.	☐
a. Note any problems you found below:	☐
b. If problems exist, list your recommendations for rectification:	☐
7. While referencing the manufacturer's workshop materials, inspect the fuel tank for missing or damaged filter screens.	☐
a. Note any problems you found below:	☐
b. If problems exist, list your recommendations for rectification:	☐
8. While referencing the manufacturer's workshop materials, inspect the fuel tank crossover line/pipe (if applicable) for leaks, damage, and proper securement.	☐
a. Note any problems you found below:	☐

	Step Completed
b. If problems exist, list your recommendations for rectification:	☐
9. While referencing the manufacturer's workshop materials, inspect the fuel supply and return lines for damage, leaks, and proper securement.	☐
a. Note any problems you found below:	☐
b. If problems exist, list your recommendations for rectification:	☐
10. Discuss your findings with your supervisor/instructor.	☐

Non-Task-Specific Evaluation	Step Completed
1. Tools and equipment were used as directed and returned in good working order.	☐
2. Complied with all general and task-specific safety standards, including proper use of any personal protective equipment (PPE).	☐
3. Completed the task in an appropriate time frame (recommendation: 1.5 or 2 times the flat rate).	☐
4. Left the workspace clean and orderly.	☐
5. Cared for customer property and returned it undamaged.	☐

Student signature _____ Date _____

Comments:

Have your supervisor/instructor verify satisfactory completion of this procedure, any observations made, and any necessary action(s) recommended.

Evaluation Instructions: The scoring box below is intended to act as a guide for both student and supervisor/instructor. Each criterion listed will help students to understand what is expected of them and help supervisors/instructors to articulate the level of success at a particular task. The scoring is set up to allow a second attempt at each task (see the Test and Retest columns). Scoring is designed only to award students points for task criteria that were completed correctly. Points are lost for failure to complete the employability requirements (see Non-Task-Specific criteria). When all criteria are evaluated, tally the points for a total at the bottom of each column.

Tasksheet Scoring

	Test		Retest	
Evaluation Items	**Pass**	**Fail**	**Pass**	**Fail**
Task-Specific Evaluation	**(1 pt)**	**(0 pts)**	**(1 pt)**	**(0 pts)**
Student properly inspected/checked at least three of the named components.				
Student properly inspected/checked all seven of the named components.				
Student properly measured the fuel tank strap and mount torque.				
Student accurately listed recommendations for necessary rectifications.				
Non-Task-Specific Evaluation	**(0 pts)**	**(−1 pt)**	**(0 pts)**	**(−1 pt)**
Student successfully completed at least three of the non-task-specific steps.				
Student successfully completed all five of the non-task-specific steps.				
Total Score: <total # of points / 4 = %>				

© 2021 Jones & Bartlett Learning, LLC, an Ascend Learning Company

CDX Tasksheet Number: 5.6a003

Student/Intern Information

Name _____ Date _____ Class _____

Machine, Customer, and Service Information

Machine used for this activity:

Make _____ Model _____

Hours _____ Serial Number _____

Materials Required
- Vehicle with possible engine concern
- Engine manufacturer's workshop materials
- Manufacturer-specific tools, depending on the concern/procedure(s)
- Vehicle/component lifting equipment, if applicable

Task-Specific Safety Considerations
- This task may require test driving the vehicle on the school grounds or on a hoist, both of which carry severe risks. Attempt this task only with full permission from your supervisor/instructor and follow all the guidelines exactly.
- Lifting equipment such as vehicle jacks and stands, vehicle hoists, and engine hoists are important tools that increase productivity and make the job easier. However, they can also cause severe injury or death if used improperly. Make sure you follow the manufacturer's operation procedures. Also make sure you have your supervisor's/instructor's permission to use any particular type of lifting equipment.
- Comply with personal and environmental safety practices associated with clothing; eye protection; hand tools; power equipment; proper ventilation; and the handling, storage, and disposal of chemicals/materials in accordance with federal, state, and local regulations.
- Always wear the correct protective eyewear and clothing and use the appropriate safety equipment, as well as wheel chocks, fender covers, seat protectors, and floor mat protectors.
- Make sure you understand and observe all legislative and personal safety procedures when carrying out practical assignments. If you are unsure of what these are, ask your supervisor/instructor.

▶ TASK Measure fuel level and condition. **AED 5.6**

Time off_____

Time on_____

Student Instructions: Read through the entire procedure prior to starting. Prepare your workspace and any tools or parts that may be needed to complete the task. When directed by your supervisor/instructor, begin the procedure to complete the task, and comment or check the box as each step is finished. Track your time on this procedure for later comparison to the standard completion time (i.e., "flat rate" or customer pay time).

Total time_____

Note: This tasksheet may require the student to check the condition of miscellaneous vehicle fluids, some of which may be flammable and could damage the environment or cause health problems if not handled properly. Observe all safety precautions and follow local regulations for the proper disposal of fluids.

Procedure	Step Completed
1. While referencing the manufacturer's workshop materials, record the fuel level as it is shown on the manufacturer's electronic fuel gauge: _____	☐
2. Manually check the fuel level. Insert a clean yard stick or similar instrument into the fuel tank and compare the level to that shown on the manufacturer's electronic fuel gauge.	☐
a. Meets the manufacturer's specifications: Yes ☐ No ☐	☐
b. If no, list your recommendations for rectification:	☐
3. While referencing the manufacturer's workshop materials, draw off a clean fuel sample for testing.	☐
a. Meets the manufacturer's specifications: Yes ☐ No ☐	☐
b. If no, list your recommendations for rectification:	☐
4. Record the procedure for using a water test paste to check the fuel supply for contamination, then perform the test:	☐
a. Meets the manufacturer's specifications: Yes ☐ No ☐	☐
b. If no, list your recommendations for rectification:	☐
5. Discuss your findings with your supervisor/instructor.	☐

Non-Task-Specific Evaluation	Step Completed
1. Tools and equipment were used as directed and returned in good working order.	☐
2. Complied with all general and task-specific safety standards, including proper use of any personal protective equipment (PPE).	☐
3. Completed the task in an appropriate time frame (recommendation: 1.5 or 2 times the flat rate).	☐
4. Left the workspace clean and orderly.	☐
5. Cared for customer property and returned it undamaged.	☐

Student signature _____ Date _____

Comments:

Have your supervisor/instructor verify satisfactory completion of this procedure, any observations made, and any necessary action(s) recommended.

Evaluation Instructions: The scoring box below is intended to act as a guide for both student and supervisor/instructor. Each criterion listed will help students to understand what is expected of them and help supervisors/instructors to articulate the level of success at a particular task. The scoring is set up to allow a second attempt at each task (see the Test and Retest columns). Scoring is designed only to award students points for task criteria that were completed correctly. Points are lost for failure to complete the employability requirements (see Non-Task-Specific criteria). When all criteria are evaluated, tally the points for a total at the bottom of each column.

Tasksheet Scoring

	Test		Retest	
Evaluation Items	**Pass**	**Fail**	**Pass**	**Fail**
Task-Specific Evaluation	**(1 pt)**	**(0 pts)**	**(1 pt)**	**(0 pts)**
Student properly checked the fuel system level.				
Student properly checked the fuel system level and compared it with the electronic fuel system gauge.				
Student properly obtained a fuel system sample for testing.				
Student properly tested the fuel system storage tank for water contamination.				
Non-Task-Specific Evaluation	**(0 pts)**	**(−1 pt)**	**(0 pts)**	**(−1 pt)**
Student successfully completed at least three of the non-task-specific steps.				
Student successfully completed all five of the non-task-specific steps.				
Total Score: <total # of points / 4 = %>				

Supervisor/Instructor:

Supervisor/instructor signature _____ Date _____

Comments:

Retest supervisor/instructor signature _____ Date _____

Comments:

CDX Tasksheet Number: 5.6a004

Student/Intern Information

Name _____ Date _____ Class _____

Machine, Customer, and Service Information

Machine used for this activity:

Make _____ Model _____

Hours _____ Serial Number _____

Materials Required
- Vehicle with possible engine concern
- Engine manufacturer's workshop materials
- Manufacturer-specific tools, depending on the concern/procedure(s)
- Vehicle/component lifting equipment, if applicable

Task-Specific Safety Considerations
- This task may require test driving the vehicle on the school grounds or on a hoist, both of which carry severe risks. Attempt this task only with full permission from your supervisor/instructor and follow all the guidelines exactly.
- Lifting equipment such as vehicle jacks and stands, vehicle hoists, and engine hoists are important tools that increase productivity and make the job easier. However, they can also cause severe injury or death if used improperly. Make sure you follow the manufacturer's operation procedures. Also make sure you have your supervisor's/instructor's permission to use any particular type of lifting equipment.
- Comply with personal and environmental safety practices associated with clothing; eye protection; hand tools; power equipment; proper ventilation; and the handling, storage, and disposal of chemicals/materials in accordance with federal, state, and local regulations.
- Always wear the correct protective eyewear and clothing and use the appropriate safety equipment, as well as wheel chocks, fender covers, seat protectors, and floor mat protectors.
- Make sure you understand and observe all legislative and personal safety procedures when carrying out practical assignments. If you are unsure of what these are, ask your supervisor/instructor.

▶ **TASK** Test fuel supply and return systems. **AED 5.6**

Time off_____

Time on_____

Student Instructions: Read through the entire procedure prior to starting. Prepare your workspace and any tools or parts that may be needed to complete the task. When directed by your supervisor/instructor, begin the procedure to complete the task, and comment or check the box as each step is finished. Track your time on this procedure for later comparison to the standard completion time (i.e., "flat rate" or customer pay time).

Total time_____

Note: This tasksheet may require the student to check the condition of miscellaneous vehicle fluids, some of which may be flammable and could damage the environment or cause health problems if not handled properly. Observe all safety precautions and follow local regulations for the proper disposal of fluids.

Procedure	Step Completed
1. While referencing the manufacturer's workshop materials, inspect the fuel supply and return lines for damage, leaks, and proper securement.	☐
a. Note any problems you found below:	☐
b. If problems exist, list your recommendations for rectification:	☐
2. While referencing the manufacturer's workshop materials, record the procedure for performing an air in fuel system test for the supply side, then perform the test:	☐
a. Meets the manufacturer's specifications: Yes ☐ No ☐	☐
b. If no, list your recommendations for rectification:	☐
3. While referencing the manufacturer's workshop materials, record the procedure for performing a low-pressure supply pump flow test, then perform the test:	☐
a. Record the results of the test below: _____ GPM	☐
b. Meets the manufacturer's specifications: Yes ☐ No ☐	☐
c. If no, list your recommendations for rectification:	☐
4. While referencing the manufacturer's workshop materials, record the procedure for performing a low-pressure supply pump pressure test, then perform the test:	☐

	Step Completed
a. Record the results of the test below: _____ psi/kPa	☐
b. Meets the manufacturer's specifications: Yes ☐ No ☐	☐
c. If no, list your recommendations for rectification:	☐
5. While referencing the manufacturer's workshop materials, record the procedure for performing a fuel drain line restriction test, then perform the test:	☐
a. Record the results of the test below: _____ mm/in-Hg	☐
b. Meets the manufacturer's specifications: Yes ☐ No ☐	☐
c. If no, list your recommendations for rectification:	☐
6. Discuss your findings with your supervisor/instructor.	☐

Non-Task-Specific Evaluation	Step Completed
1. Tools and equipment were used as directed and returned in good working order.	☐
2. Complied with all general and task-specific safety standards, including proper use of any personal protective equipment (PPE).	☐
3. Completed the task in an appropriate time frame (recommendation: 1.5 or 2 times the flat rate).	☐
4. Left the workspace clean and orderly.	☐
5. Cared for customer property and returned it undamaged.	☐

Student signature _____ Date _____

Comments:

Have your supervisor/instructor verify satisfactory completion of this procedure, any observations made, and any necessary action(s) recommended.

Evaluation Instructions: The scoring box below is intended to act as a guide for both student and supervisor/instructor. Each criterion listed will help students to understand what is expected of them and help supervisors/instructors to articulate the level of success at a particular task. The scoring is set up to allow a second attempt at each task (see the Test and Retest columns). Scoring is designed only to award students points for task criteria that were completed correctly. Points are lost for failure to complete the employability requirements (see Non-Task-Specific criteria). When all criteria are evaluated, tally the points for a total at the bottom of each column.

Tasksheet Scoring

	Test		Retest	
Evaluation Items	**Pass**	**Fail**	**Pass**	**Fail**
Task-Specific Evaluation	**(1 pt)**	**(0 pts)**	**(1 pt)**	**(0 pts)**
Student properly inspected the fuel supply and return lines.				
Student properly performed the air in fuel system test for the supply side.				
Student properly performed the low-pressure supply pump flow test and the low-pressure supply pump pressure test.				
Student properly performed the fuel drain line restriction test.				
Non-Task-Specific Evaluation	**(0 pts)**	**(−1 pt)**	**(0 pts)**	**(−1 pt)**
Student successfully completed at least three of the non-task-specific steps.				
Student successfully completed all five of the non-task-specific steps.				
Total Score: <total # of points / 4 = %>				

Supervisor/Instructor:

Supervisor/instructor signature _____ Date _____

Comments:

Retest supervisor/instructor signature _____ Date _____

Comments:

CDX Tasksheet Number: 5.6a005

Student/Intern Information

Name _____ Date _____ Class _____

Machine, Customer, and Service Information

Machine used for this activity:

Make _____ Model _____

Hours _____ Serial Number _____

Task-Specific Safety Considerations

- This task may require test driving the vehicle on the school grounds or on a hoist, both of which carry severe risks. Attempt this task only with full permission from your supervisor/instructor and follow all the guidelines exactly.
- Lifting equipment such as vehicle jacks and stands, vehicle hoists, and engine hoists are important tools that increase productivity and make the job easier. However, they can also cause severe injury or death if used improperly. Make sure you follow the manufacturer's operation procedures. Also make sure you have your supervisor's/instructor's permission to use any particular type of lifting equipment.
- Comply with personal and environmental safety practices associated with clothing; eye protection; hand tools; power equipment; proper ventilation; and the handling, storage, and disposal of chemicals/materials in accordance with federal, state, and local regulations.
- Always wear the correct protective eyewear and clothing and use the appropriate safety equipment, as well as wheel chocks, fender covers, seat protectors, and floor mat protectors.
- Make sure you understand and observe all legislative and personal safety procedures when carrying out practical assignments. If you are unsure of what these are, ask your supervisor/instructor.

▶ **TASK** Prime and bleed fuel system.   **AED** 5.6

Time off_____

Student Instructions: Read through the entire procedure prior to starting. Prepare your workspace and any tools or parts that may be needed to complete the task. When directed by your supervisor/instructor, begin the procedure to complete the task, and comment or check the box as each step is finished. Track your time on this procedure for later comparison to the standard completion time (i.e., "flat rate" or customer pay time).

Time on_____

Total time_____

Note: This tasksheet may require the student to check the condition of miscellaneous vehicle fluids, some of which may be flammable and could damage the environment or cause health problems if not handled properly. Observe all safety precautions and follow local regulations for the proper disposal of fluids.

Procedure	Step Completed
1. While referencing the manufacturer's workshop materials, inspect the fuel filter(s) and mounts for damage, leaks, and proper securement.	☐
a. Note any problems you found below:	☐
b. If problems exist, list your recommendations for rectification:	☐
2. While referencing the manufacturer's workshop materials, close the fuel supply valve(s), start the engine, and allow the engine to run out of fuel. (**Note:** This is done to allow students to learn the proper procedure for bleeding the air from a fuel system.)	☐
3. While referencing the manufacturer's workshop materials, remove the fuel filter(s), drain the filters in an appropriate container for proper disposal, then install new filter(s).	☐
4. While referencing the manufacturer's workshop materials, record the procedure for bleeding air from the fuel system:	☐
5. While referencing the manufacturer's workshop materials, bleed the air from the fuel system.	☐
a. Meets the manufacturer's specifications: Yes ☐ No ☐	☐
b. If no, list your recommendations for rectification:	☐
6. While referencing the manufacturer's workshop materials, start the engine and bring it up to operating temperature. (**Note:** Do *not* crank engine for more than 30 seconds and wait at least 2 minutes between cranking attempts.)	☐
a. Meets the manufacturer's specifications: Yes ☐ No ☐	☐

	Step Completed
b. If no, list your recommendations for rectification:	☐
7. While referencing the manufacturer's workshop materials, inspect the new fuel filters for signs of leakage.	☐
a. Note any problems you found below:	☐
b. If problems exist, list your recommendations for rectification:	☐
8. Discuss your findings with your supervisor/instructor.	☐

Non-Task-Specific Evaluation	Step Completed
1. Tools and equipment were used as directed and returned in good working order.	☐
2. Complied with all general and task-specific safety standards, including proper use of any personal protective equipment (PPE).	☐
3. Completed the task in an appropriate time frame (recommendation: 1.5 or 2 times the flat rate).	☐
4. Left the workspace clean and orderly.	☐
5. Cared for customer property and returned it undamaged.	☐

Student signature _____ Date _____

Comments:

Have your supervisor/instructor verify satisfactory completion of this procedure, any observations made, and any necessary action(s) recommended.

Evaluation Instructions: The scoring box below is intended to act as a guide for both student and supervisor/instructor. Each criterion listed will help students to understand what is expected of them and help supervisors/instructors to articulate the level of success at a particular task. The scoring is set up to allow a second attempt at each task (see the Test and Retest columns). Scoring is designed only to award students points for task criteria that were completed correctly. Points are lost for failure to complete the employability requirements (see Non-Task-Specific criteria). When all criteria are evaluated, tally the points for a total at the bottom of each column.

Tasksheet Scoring

Evaluation Items	Test		Retest	
	Pass	Fail	Pass	Fail
Task-Specific Evaluation	**(1 pt)**	**(0 pts)**	**(1 pt)**	**(0 pts)**
Student properly inspected fuel filter(s) and mounts.				
Student properly closed the fuel supply valve(s), allowing the engine to run out of fuel.				
Student properly replaced the filters.				
Student properly bled air from the fuel system and inspected the new filter(s) for leaks.				
Non-Task-Specific Evaluation	**(0 pts)**	**(−1 pt)**	**(0 pts)**	**(−1 pt)**
Student successfully completed at least three of the non-task-specific steps.				
Student successfully completed all five of the non-task-specific steps.				
Total Score: <total # of points / 4 = %>				

Supervisor/Instructor:

Supervisor/instructor signature _____ Date _____

Comments:

Retest supervisor/instructor signature _____ Date _____

Comments:

CDX Tasksheet Number: 5.6a006

Student/Intern Information

Name _____ Date _____ Class _____

Machine, Customer, and Service Information

Machine used for this activity:

Make _____ Model _____

Hours _____ Serial Number _____

Materials Required
- Vehicle with possible engine concern
- Engine manufacturer's workshop materials
- Manufacturer-specific tools, depending on the concern/procedure(s)
- Vehicle/component lifting equipment, if applicable

Task-Specific Safety Considerations
- This task may require test driving the vehicle on the school grounds or on a hoist, both of which carry severe risks. Attempt this task only with full permission from your supervisor/instructor and follow all the guidelines exactly.
- Lifting equipment such as vehicle jacks and stands, vehicle hoists, and engine hoists are important tools that increase productivity and make the job easier. However, they can also cause severe injury or death if used improperly. Make sure you follow the manufacturer's operation procedures. Also make sure you have your supervisor's/instructor's permission to use any particular type of lifting equipment.
- Comply with personal and environmental safety practices associated with clothing; eye protection; hand tools; power equipment; proper ventilation; and the handling, storage, and disposal of chemicals/materials in accordance with federal, state, and local regulations.
- Always wear the correct protective eyewear and clothing and use the appropriate safety equipment, as well as wheel chocks, fender covers, seat protectors, and floor mat protectors.
- Make sure you understand and observe all legislative and personal safety procedures when carrying out practical assignments. If you are unsure of what these are, ask your supervisor/instructor.

▶ **TASK** Install fuel transfer (lift) pump.

AED 5.6

Time off_____

Student Instructions: Read through the entire procedure prior to starting. Prepare your workspace and any tools or parts that may be needed to complete the task. When directed by your supervisor/instructor, begin the procedure to complete the task, and comment or check the box as each step is finished. Track your time on this procedure for later comparison to the standard completion time (i.e., "flat rate" or customer pay time).

Time on_____

Total time_____

Note: This tasksheet may require the student to check the condition of miscellaneous vehicle fluids, some of which may be flammable and could damage the environment or cause health problems if not handled properly. Observe all safety precautions and follow local regulations for the proper disposal of fluids.

Procedure	Step Completed
1. While referencing the manufacturer's workshop materials, inspect the fuel supply and return lines for damage, leaks, and proper securement.	☐
a. Note any problems you found below:	☐
b. If problems exist, list your recommendations for rectification:	☐
2. While referencing the manufacturer's workshop materials, inspect the engine control module cooling plate for proper mounting, damage, or signs of leakage.	☐
a. Note any problems you found below:	☐
b. If problems exist, list your recommendations for rectification:	☐
3. While referencing the manufacturer's workshop materials, inspect the water fuel separator/primary fuel filter for proper mounting, damage, or signs of leakage.	☐
a. Meets the manufacturer's specifications: Yes ☐ No ☐	☐
b. If no, list your recommendations for rectification:	☐
4. While referencing the manufacturer's workshop materials, drain any water from the water fuel separator and properly dispose of it.	☐
5. While referencing the manufacturer's workshop materials, disconnect the wiring harness from the water fuel separator and observe the operation of the water in fuel light. If the light does not come on with the harness disconnected, place a jumper wire across the harness connections and observe the operation of the water in fuel light. (**Note:** For wiring harnesses other than a two-wire harness/connector, refer to the manufacturer's workshop materials/wiring diagram(s) for proper testing.)	☐

a. Meets the manufacturer's specifications: Yes ☐ No ☐	☐
b. If no, list your recommendations for rectification:	☐
6. While referencing the manufacturer's workshop materials, inspect the fuel cooler for proper mounting, damage, or signs of leakage.	☐
a. Note any problems you found below:	☐
b. If problems exist, list your recommendations for rectification:	☐
7. While referencing the manufacturer's workshop materials, record the procedure for performing a fuel heater test, then perform the test:	☐
a. Meets the manufacturer's specifications: Yes ☐ No ☐	☐
b. If no, list your recommendations for rectification:	☐
8. While referencing the manufacturer's workshop materials, inspect the electric/mechanical fuel transfer/lift pump for proper mounting, damage, or signs of leakage.	☐
a. Note any problems you found below:	☐
b. If problems exist, list your recommendations for rectification:	☐
9. While referencing the manufacturer's workshop materials, remove the manual transfer/lift pump and inspect the pump drive for damage. (**Note:** This procedure is for engines with mechanical lift pumps only.)	☐
a. Note any problems you found below:	☐

b. If problems exist, list your recommendations for rectification:	☐
10. While referencing the manufacturer's workshop materials, record the procedure for performing a transfer/lift pump flow rate test, then perform the test:	☐
a. Meets the manufacturer's specifications: Yes ☐ No ☐	☐
b. If no, list your recommendations for rectification:	☐
11. While referencing the manufacturer's workshop materials, record the procedure for performing a transfer/lift pump pressure test, then perform the test:	☐
a. Meets the manufacturer's specifications: Yes ☐ No ☐	☐
b. If no, list your recommendations for rectification:	☐
12. Discuss your findings with your supervisor/instructor.	☐

Non-Task-Specific Evaluation	Step Completed
1. Tools and equipment were used as directed and returned in good working order.	☐
2. Complied with all general and task-specific safety standards, including proper use of any personal protective equipment (PPE).	☐
3. Completed the task in an appropriate time frame (recommendation: 1.5 or 2 times the flat rate).	☐
4. Left the workspace clean and orderly.	☐
5. Cared for customer property and returned it undamaged.	☐

Student signature _____ Date _____

Comments:

Have your supervisor/instructor verify satisfactory completion of this procedure, any observations made, and any necessary action(s) recommended.

Evaluation Instructions: The scoring box below is intended to act as a guide for both student and supervisor/instructor. Each criterion listed will help students to understand what is expected of them and help supervisors/instructors to articulate the level of success at a particular task. The scoring is set up to allow a second attempt at each task (see the Test and Retest columns). Scoring is designed only to award students points for task criteria that were completed correctly. Points are lost for failure to complete the employability requirements (see Non-Task-Specific criteria). When all criteria are evaluated, tally the points for a total at the bottom of each column.

Tasksheet Scoring

	Test		Retest	
Evaluation Items	**Pass**	**Fail**	**Pass**	**Fail**
Task-Specific Evaluation	**(1 pt)**	**(0 pts)**	**(1 pt)**	**(0 pts)**
Student properly inspected all components.				
Student accurately described the procedure and properly performed the fuel heater test.				
Student accurately described the procedure and properly performed the fuel transfer/lift pump flow rate test.				
Student accurately described the procedure and properly performed the fuel transfer/lift pump pressure test.				
Non-Task-Specific Evaluation	**(0 pts)**	**(−1 pt)**	**(0 pts)**	**(−1 pt)**
Student successfully completed at least three of the non-task-specific steps.				
Student successfully completed all five of the non-task-specific steps.				
Total Score: <total # of points / 4 = %>				

Supervisor/Instructor:

Supervisor/instructor signature _____ Date _____

Comments:

Retest supervisor/instructor signature _____ Date _____

Comments:

CDX Tasksheet Number: 5.6a007

Student/Intern Information

Name _____ Date _____ Class _____

Machine, Customer, and Service Information

Machine used for this activity:

Make _____ Model _____

Hours _____ Serial Number _____

> ### Materials Required
> - Vehicle with possible engine concern
> - Engine manufacturer's workshop materials
> - Manufacturer-specific tools, depending on the concern/procedure(s)
> - Vehicle/component lifting equipment, if applicable

Task-Specific Safety Considerations

- This task may require test driving the vehicle on the school grounds or on a hoist, both of which carry severe risks. Attempt this task only with full permission from your supervisor/instructor and follow all the guidelines exactly.
- Lifting equipment such as vehicle jacks and stands, vehicle hoists, and engine hoists are important tools that increase productivity and make the job easier. However, they can also cause severe injury or death if used improperly. Make sure you follow the manufacturer's operation procedures. Also make sure you have your supervisor's/instructor's permission to use any particular type of lifting equipment.
- Comply with personal and environmental safety practices associated with clothing; eye protection; hand tools; power equipment; proper ventilation; and the handling, storage, and disposal of chemicals/materials in accordance with federal, state, and local regulations.
- Always wear the correct protective eyewear and clothing and use the appropriate safety equipment, as well as wheel chocks, fender covers, seat protectors, and floor mat protectors.
- Make sure you understand and observe all legislative and personal safety procedures when carrying out practical assignments. If you are unsure of what these are, ask your supervisor/instructor.

▶ TASK Repair misfiring cylinders.

AED 5.6

Time off_____

Time on_____

Student Instructions: Read through the entire procedure prior to starting. Prepare your workspace and any tools or parts that may be needed to complete the task. When directed by your supervisor/instructor, begin the procedure to complete the task, and comment or check the box as each step is finished. Track your time on this procedure for later comparison to the standard completion time (i.e., "flat rate" or customer pay time).

Total time_____

Note: This tasksheet may require the student to check the condition of miscellaneous vehicle fluids, some of which may be flammable and could damage the environment or cause health problems if not handled properly. Observe all safety precautions and follow local regulations for the proper disposal of fluids.

Procedure	Step Completed
1. Start the engine and observe warning lights and gauges.	☐
a. List any warning lights (other than low air) that come on and stay on after the engine is started: (**Note:** The low air light should go out after the vehicle's air system has reached 60 psi.)	☐
b. Check the operation of all vehicle electrical accessories.	☐
2. List any electrical accessory that fails to operate or operates in an erratic manner:	☐
3. Using a diagnostic tool or an on-board diagnostic system, extract the engine monitoring information and record it below:	☐
a. Are there any fault codes listed in the diagnostic tester? Yes ☐ No ☐	☐
b. If yes, list the codes:	☐
4. Using the diagnostic tool's testing function, perform a cylinder cutoff test and record the engine rpm for each of the following.	☐
a. Drop Cylinder 1 _____ rpm	☐
b. Drop Cylinder 2 _____ rpm	☐
c. Drop Cylinder 3 _____ rpm	☐
d. Drop Cylinder 4 _____ rpm	☐
e. Drop Cylinder 5 _____ rpm	☐

	Step Completed
f. Drop Cylinder 6 _____ rpm	☐
5. Reference the vehicle manufacturer's specifications.	☐
a. Are all the results within the manufacturer's specifications? Yes ☐ No ☐	☐
b. If no, list the results that are outside the manufacturer's specifications:	☐
6. If directed by your supervisor/instructor, do the following.	☐
a. Clear any stored codes.	☐
b. When possible, investigate and rectify any of the "out of specifications" that you recorded.	☐
7. Return the vehicle to its beginning condition and return any tools you used to their proper locations.	☐
8. Discuss your findings with your supervisor/instructor.	☐

Non-Task-Specific Evaluation	Step Completed
1. Tools and equipment were used as directed and returned in good working order.	☐
2. Complied with all general and task-specific safety standards, including proper use of any personal protective equipment (PPE).	☐
3. Completed the task in an appropriate time frame (recommendation: 1.5 or 2 times the flat rate).	☐
4. Left the workspace clean and orderly.	☐
5. Cared for customer property and returned it undamaged.	☐

Student signature _____ Date _____

Comments:

Have your supervisor/instructor verify satisfactory completion of this procedure, any observations made, and any necessary action(s) recommended.

Evaluation Instructions: The scoring box below is intended to act as a guide for both student and supervisor/instructor. Each criterion listed will help students to understand what is expected of them and help supervisors/instructors to articulate the level of success at a particular task. The scoring is set up to allow a second attempt at each task (see the Test and Retest columns). Scoring is designed only to award students points for task criteria that were completed correctly. Points are lost for failure to complete the employability requirements (see Non-Task-Specific criteria). When all criteria are evaluated, tally the points for a total at the bottom of each column.

Tasksheet Scoring

Evaluation Items	Test		Retest	
	Pass	**Fail**	**Pass**	**Fail**
Task-Specific Evaluation	**(1 pt)**	**(0 pts)**	**(1 pt)**	**(0 pts)**
Student properly observed warning lights and gauges and checked the operation of all electrical accessories.				
Student properly extracted and recorded the engine monitoring information.				
Student properly performed a cylinder cutoff test and recorded the results for each drop cylinder.				
Student accurately listed any results that did not meet the manufacturer's specifications and rectified them if instructed by their supervisor/instructor.				
Non-Task-Specific Evaluation	**(0 pts)**	**(−1 pt)**	**(0 pts)**	**(−1 pt)**
Student successfully completed at least three of the non-task-specific steps.				
Student successfully completed all five of the non-task-specific steps.				
Total Score: <total # of points / 4 = %>				

CDX Tasksheet Number: 5.6a008

Student/Intern Information

Name _____ Date _____ Class _____

Machine, Customer, and Service Information

Machine used for this activity:

Make _____ Model _____

Hours _____ Serial Number _____

Materials Required

- Vehicle with possible engine concern
- Engine manufacturer's workshop materials
- Manufacturer-specific tools, depending on the concern/procedure(s)
- Vehicle/component lifting equipment, if applicable

Task-Specific Safety Considerations

- This task may require test driving the vehicle on the school grounds or on a hoist, both of which carry severe risks. Attempt this task only with full permission from your supervisor/instructor and follow all the guidelines exactly.
- Lifting equipment such as vehicle jacks and stands, vehicle hoists, and engine hoists are important tools that increase productivity and make the job easier. However, they can also cause severe injury or death if used improperly. Make sure you follow the manufacturer's operation procedures. Also make sure you have your supervisor's/instructor's permission to use any particular type of lifting equipment.
- Comply with personal and environmental safety practices associated with clothing; eye protection; hand tools; power equipment; proper ventilation; and the handling, storage, and disposal of chemicals/materials in accordance with federal, state, and local regulations.
- Always wear the correct protective eyewear and clothing and use the appropriate safety equipment, as well as wheel chocks, fender covers, seat protectors, and floor mat protectors.
- Make sure you understand and observe all legislative and personal safety procedures when carrying out practical assignments. If you are unsure of what these are, ask your supervisor/instructor.

▶ **TASK** Test high-pressure injection pump and system. **AED 5.6**

Time off_____

Time on_____

Student Instructions: Read through the entire procedure prior to starting. Prepare your workspace and any tools or parts that may be needed to complete the task. When directed by your supervisor/instructor, begin the procedure to complete the task, and comment or check the box as each step is finished. Track your time on this procedure for later comparison to the standard completion time (i.e., "flat rate" or customer pay time).

Total time_____

Note: This tasksheet may require the student to check the condition of miscellaneous vehicle fluids, some of which may be flammable and could damage the environment or cause health problems if not handled properly. Observe all safety precautions and follow local regulations for the proper disposal of fluids.

Procedure	Step Completed
1. While referencing the manufacturer's workshop materials, inspect the high-pressure fuel system for damage, leaks, and proper securement.	☐
a. Note any problems you found below:	☐
b. If problems exist, list your recommendations for rectification:	☐
2. While referencing the manufacturer's workshop materials, list all special precautions to be used before servicing the high-pressure fuel system:	☐
3. While referencing the manufacturer's workshop materials, list all safety precautions to be used while servicing the high-pressure fuel system:	☐
4. While referencing the manufacturer's workshop materials, list the inspection procedure for high-pressure fuel lines, then perform the inspection:	☐
a. Meets the manufacturer's specifications: Yes ☐ No ☐	☐
b. If no, list your recommendations for rectification:	☐
5. While referencing the manufacturer's workshop materials, list the inspection procedure for the fuel pressure relief valve, then perform the inspection:	☐

a. Meets the manufacturer's specifications: Yes ☐ No ☐	☐
b. If no, list your recommendations for rectification:	☐
6. While referencing the manufacturer's workshop materials, list the inspection procedure for the fuel injector feed tubes, then perform the inspection:	☐
a. Meets the manufacturer's specifications: Yes ☐ No ☐	☐
b. If no, list your recommendations for rectification:	☐
7. While referencing the manufacturer's workshop materials, record the procedure for performing a high-pressure system leak-down test, then perform the test:	☐
a. Meets the manufacturer's specifications: Yes ☐ No ☐	☐
b. If no, list your recommendations for rectification:	☐
8. While referencing the manufacturer's workshop materials, record the procedure for performing a high-pressure fuel pump return flow test, then perform the test:	☐
a. Meets the manufacturer's specifications: Yes ☐ No ☐	☐
b. If no, list your recommendations for rectification:	☐

9. While referencing the manufacturer's workshop materials, record the procedure for performing a high-pressure injector return flow test, then perform the test:	☐
a. Meets the manufacturer's specifications: Yes ☐ No ☐	☐
b. If no, list your recommendations for rectification:	☐
10. While referencing the manufacturer's workshop materials, record the procedure for performing a high-pressure fuel pump performance test, then perform the test:	☐
a. Meets the manufacturer's specifications: Yes ☐ No ☐	☐
b. If no, list your recommendations for rectification:	☐
11. While referencing the manufacturer's workshop materials, record the procedure for performing a high-pressure injector return flow isolation test, then perform the test:	☐
a. Meets the manufacturer's specifications: Yes ☐ No ☐	☐
b. If no, list your recommendations for rectification:	☐

	Step Completed
12. While referencing the manufacturer's workshop materials, record the procedure for performing a fuel pressure relief valve return flow test, then perform the test:	☐
a. Meets the manufacturer's specifications: Yes ☐ No ☐	☐
b. If no, list your recommendations for rectification:	☐
13. Discuss your findings with your supervisor/instructor.	☐

Non-Task-Specific Evaluation	Step Completed
1. Tools and equipment were used as directed and returned in good working order.	☐
2. Complied with all general and task-specific safety standards, including proper use of any personal protective equipment (PPE).	☐
3. Completed the task in an appropriate time frame (recommendation: 1.5 or 2 times the flat rate).	☐
4. Left the workspace clean and orderly.	☐
5. Cared for customer property and returned it undamaged.	☐

Student signature _____ Date _____

Comments:

Have your supervisor/instructor verify satisfactory completion of this procedure, any observations made, and any necessary action(s) recommended.

Evaluation Instructions: The scoring box below is intended to act as a guide for both student and supervisor/instructor. Each criterion listed will help students to understand what is expected of them and help supervisors/instructors to articulate the level of success at a particular task. The scoring is set up to allow a second attempt at each task (see the Test and Retest columns). Scoring is designed only to award students points for task criteria that were completed correctly. Points are lost for failure to complete the employability requirements (see Non-Task-Specific criteria). When all criteria are evaluated, tally the points for a total at the bottom of each column.

Tasksheet Scoring

	Test		Retest	
Evaluation Items	**Pass**	**Fail**	**Pass**	**Fail**
Task-Specific Evaluation	**(1 pt)**	**(0 pts)**	**(1 pt)**	**(0 pts)**
Student accurately described the precautions and procedures for inspecting/testing various parts of the high-pressure fuel system.				
Student properly inspected/tested at least half of the different areas of the fuel system.				
Student properly inspected/tested all of the different areas of the fuel system.				
Student accurately listed recommendations for necessary rectifications.				
Non-Task-Specific Evaluation	**(0 pts)**	**(−1 pt)**	**(0 pts)**	**(−1 pt)**
Student successfully completed at least three of the non-task-specific steps.				
Student successfully completed all five of the non-task-specific steps.				
Total Score: <total # of points / 4 = %>				

Chapter 48: Fuel and Governing Systems, Mechanical and Electronic Systems; Understanding Governor Fundamentals

Learning Objective/Task	CDX Tasksheet Number	AED Reference Number
• Troubleshoot electronic governors.	5.6b004	AED 5.6
• Test engine sensors.	5.6b005	AED 5.6

Materials Required

- Vehicle with possible engine concern
- Vehicle manufacturer's workshop materials
- Manufacturer-specific tools, depending on the concern/procedure(s)
- Vehicle/component lifting equipment, if applicable
- Digital multimeter (DMM)

Safety Considerations

- This task may require test driving the vehicle on the school grounds or on a hoist, both of which carry severe risks. Attempt this task only with full permission from your supervisor/instructor and follow all the guidelines exactly.
- Lifting equipment such as vehicle jacks and stands, vehicle hoists, and engine hoists are important tools that increase productivity and make the job easier. However, they can also cause severe injury or death if used improperly. Make sure you follow the manufacturer's operation procedures. Also make sure you have your supervisor's/instructor's permission to use any particular type of lifting equipment.
- Comply with personal and environmental safety practices associated with clothing; eye protection; hand tools; power equipment; proper ventilation; and the handling, storage, and disposal of chemicals/materials in accordance with federal, state, and local regulations.
- Always wear the correct protective eyewear and clothing and use the appropriate safety equipment, as well as wheel chocks, fender covers, seat protectors, and floor mat protectors.
- Make sure you understand and observe all legislative and personal safety procedures when carrying out practical assignments. If you are unsure of what these are, ask your supervisor/instructor.

CDX Tasksheet Number: 5.6b004

Student/Intern Information

Name _____ Date _____ Class _____

Machine, Customer, and Service Information

Machine used for this activity:

Make _____ Model _____

Hours _____ Serial Number _____

Materials Required

- Vehicle with possible engine concern
- Vehicle manufacturer's workshop materials
- Manufacturer-specific tools, depending on the concern/procedure(s)
- Vehicle/component lifting equipment, if applicable

Task-Specific Safety Considerations

- This task may require test driving the vehicle on the school grounds or on a hoist, both of which carry severe risks. Attempt this task only with full permission from your supervisor/instructor and follow all the guidelines exactly.
- Lifting equipment such as vehicle jacks and stands, vehicle hoists, and engine hoists are important tools that increase productivity and make the job easier. However, they can also cause severe injury or death if used improperly. Make sure you follow the manufacturer's operation procedures. Also make sure you have your supervisor's/instructor's permission to use any particular type of lifting equipment.
- Comply with personal and environmental safety practices associated with clothing; eye protection; hand tools; power equipment; proper ventilation; and the handling, storage, and disposal of chemicals/materials in accordance with federal, state, and local regulations.
- Always wear the correct protective eyewear and clothing and use the appropriate safety equipment, as well as wheel chocks, fender covers, seat protectors, and floor mat protectors.
- Make sure you understand and observe all legislative and personal safety procedures when carrying out practical assignments. If you are unsure of what these are, ask your supervisor/instructor.

▶ TASK Troubleshoot electronic governors.

Time off_____

Student Instructions: Read through the entire procedure prior to starting. Prepare your workspace and any tools or parts that may be needed to complete the task. When directed by your supervisor/instructor, begin the procedure to complete the task, and comment or check the box as each step is finished. Track your time on this procedure for later comparison to the standard completion time (i.e., "flat rate" or customer pay time).

Time on_____

Total time_____

Note: This tasksheet may require the student to check the condition of miscellaneous vehicle fluids, some of which may be flammable and could damage the environment or cause health problems if not handled properly. Observe all safety precautions and follow local regulations for the proper disposal of fluids.

Procedure	Step Completed
1. Start the engine and observe warning lights and gauges.	☐
a. List any warning lights (other than low air) that come on and stay on after the engine is started. (**Note:** The low air light should go out after the vehicle's air system has reached 60 psi.)	☐
2. Check the operation of all vehicle electrical accessories.	☐
a. List any electrical accessory that fails to operate or operates in an erratic manner:	☐
3. Using a diagnostic tool or an on-board diagnostic system, extract the engine monitoring information and record it below:	☐
a. Are there any fault codes listed in the diagnostic tester? Yes ☐ No ☐	☐
b. If yes, list the codes:	☐
4. Using the diagnostic tools monitoring function, record the following.	
a. Engine rpm _____ rpm	☐
b. Engine temperature _____ degrees	☐
c. Throttle position percentage at idle _____ %	☐
d. Throttle position voltage at governed rpm _____ volts	☐
e. Key-on time (HH/MM/SS) _____	☐
f. Total idle time (HH/MM/SS) _____	☐
g. Gallons of fuel used at idle _____ gallons	☐

	Step Completed
h. Turbo speed at governed rpm _____ rpm	☐
i. Number of diesel particulate filter regenerations _____	☐
j. Exhaust system temperature _____ degrees	☐
5. Reference the vehicle manufacturer's specifications.	☐
a. Are all the results within the manufacturer's specifications? Yes ☐ No ☐	☐
b. If no, list the results that are outside the manufacturer's specifications:	☐
6. When possible, investigate and rectify any of the "out of specifications" that you recorded.	☐
7. Return the vehicle to its beginning condition and return any tools you used to their proper locations.	☐
8. Discuss your findings with your supervisor/instructor.	☐

Non-Task-Specific Evaluation	Step Completed
1. Tools and equipment were used as directed and returned in good working order.	☐
2. Complied with all general and task-specific safety standards, including proper use of any personal protective equipment (PPE).	☐
3. Completed the task in an appropriate time frame (recommendation: 1.5 or 2 times the flat rate).	☐
4. Left the workspace clean and orderly.	☐
5. Cared for customer property and returned it undamaged.	☐

Student signature _____ Date _____

Comments:

Have your supervisor/instructor verify satisfactory completion of this procedure, any observations made,

and any necessary action(s) recommended.

Evaluation Instructions: The scoring box below is intended to act as a guide for both student and supervisor/instructor. Each criterion listed will help students to understand what is expected of them and help supervisors/instructors to articulate the level of success at a particular task. The scoring is set up to allow a second attempt at each task (see the Test and Retest columns). Scoring is designed only to award students points for task criteria that were completed correctly. Points are lost for failure to complete the employability requirements (see Non-Task-Specific criteria). When all criteria are evaluated, tally the points for a total at the bottom of each column.

Tasksheet Scoring

Evaluation Items	Test		Retest	
	Pass	Fail	Pass	Fail
Task-Specific Evaluation	**(1 pt)**	**(0 pts)**	**(1 pt)**	**(0 pts)**
Student properly observed warning lights and gauges and checked the operation of all electrical accessories.				
Student properly extracted and recorded the engine monitoring information.				
Student properly used the diagnostic tools monitoring function to record miscellaneous engine/system functions.				
Student accurately listed any results that did not meet the manufacturer's specifications and rectified them if instructed by their supervisor/instructor.				
Non-Task-Specific Evaluation	**(0 pts)**	**(−1 pt)**	**(0 pts)**	**(−1 pt)**
Student successfully completed at least three of the non-task-specific steps.				
Student successfully completed all five of the non-task-specific steps.				
Total Score: <total # of points / 4 = %>				

Supervisor/Instructor:

Supervisor/instructor signature _____ Date _____

Comments:

Retest supervisor/instructor signature _____ Date _____

Comments:

CDX Tasksheet Number: 5.6b005

Student/Intern Information

Name _____ Date _____ Class _____

Machine, Customer, and Service Information

Machine used for this activity:

Make _____ Model _____

Hours _____ Serial Number _____

Materials Required
- Vehicle with possible engine concern
- Engine manufacturer's workshop materials
- Manufacturer-specific tools, depending on the concern/procedure(s)
- Vehicle/component lifting equipment, if applicable
- Digital multimeter (DMM)

Task-Specific Safety Considerations
- This task may require test driving the vehicle on the school grounds or on a hoist, both of which carry severe risks. Attempt this task only with full permission from your supervisor/instructor and follow all the guidelines exactly.
- Lifting equipment such as vehicle jacks and stands, vehicle hoists, and engine hoists are important tools that increase productivity and make the job easier. However, they can also cause severe injury or death if used improperly. Make sure you follow the manufacturer's operation procedures. Also make sure you have your supervisor's/instructor's permission to use any particular type of lifting equipment.
- Comply with personal and environmental safety practices associated with clothing; eye protection; hand tools; power equipment; proper ventilation; and the handling, storage, and disposal of chemicals/materials in accordance with federal, state, and local regulations.
- Always wear the correct protective eyewear and clothing and use the appropriate safety equipment, as well as wheel chocks, fender covers, seat protectors, and floor mat protectors.
- Make sure you understand and observe all legislative and personal safety procedures when carrying out practical assignments. If you are unsure of what these are, ask your supervisor/instructor.

▶ TASK Test engine sensors.

AED 5.6

Time off_____

Time on_____

Total time_____

Student Instructions: Read through the entire procedure prior to starting. Prepare your workspace and any tools or parts that may be needed to complete the task. When directed by your supervisor/instructor, begin the procedure to complete the task, and comment or check the box as each step is finished. Track your time on this procedure for later comparison to the standard completion time (i.e., "flat rate" or customer pay time).

Note: This tasksheet may require the student to check the condition of miscellaneous vehicle fluids, some of which may be flammable and could damage the environment or cause health problems if not handled properly. Observe all safety precautions and follow local regulations for the proper disposal of fluids.

Procedure	Step Completed
1. While referencing the manufacturer's workshop materials, use the DMM to test the boost pressure sensor for proper operation.	☐
a. Meets the manufacturer's specifications: Yes ☐ No ☐	☐
b. If no, list your recommendations for rectification:	☐
2. While referencing the manufacturer's workshop materials, use the DMM to test the engine position sensor for proper operation.	☐
a. Meets the manufacturer's specifications: Yes ☐ No ☐	☐
b. If no, list your recommendations for rectification:	☐
3. While referencing the manufacturer's workshop materials, use the DMM to test the engine speed sensor for proper operation.	☐
a. Meets the manufacturer's specifications: Yes ☐ No ☐	☐
b. If no, list your recommendations for rectification:	☐
4. While referencing the manufacturer's workshop materials, use the DMM to test the throttle position sensor for proper operation.	☐
a. Meets the manufacturer's specifications: Yes ☐ No ☐	☐
b. If no, list your recommendations for rectification:	☐

5. While referencing the manufacturer's workshop materials, use the DMM to test the manifold pressure sensor for proper operation.	☐
a. Meets the manufacturer's specifications: Yes ☐ No ☐	☐
b. If no, list your recommendations for rectification:	☐
6. While referencing the manufacturer's workshop materials, use the DMM to test the fuel pressure sensor for proper operation.	☐
a. Meets the manufacturer's specifications: Yes ☐ No ☐	☐
b. If no, list your recommendations for rectification:	☐
7. While referencing the manufacturer's workshop materials, use the DMM to test the high-pressure oil sensor for proper operation.	☐
a. Meets the manufacturer's specifications: Yes ☐ No ☐	☐
b. If no, list your recommendations for rectification:	☐
8. Discuss your findings with your supervisor/instructor.	☐

Non-Task-Specific Evaluation	Step Completed
1. Tools and equipment were used as directed and returned in good working order.	☐
2. Complied with all general and task-specific safety standards, including proper use of any personal protective equipment (PPE).	☐
3. Completed the task in an appropriate time frame (recommendation: 1.5 or 2 times the flat rate).	☐
4. Left the workspace clean and orderly.	☐
5. Cared for customer property and returned it undamaged.	☐

Student signature _____ Date _____

Comments:

Have your supervisor/instructor verify satisfactory completion of this procedure, any observations made, and any necessary action(s) recommended.

Evaluation Instructions: The scoring box below is intended to act as a guide for both student and supervisor/instructor. Each criterion listed will help students to understand what is expected of them and help supervisors/instructors to articulate the level of success at a particular task. The scoring is set up to allow a second attempt at each task (see the Test and Retest columns). Scoring is designed only to award students points for task criteria that were completed correctly. Points are lost for failure to complete the employability requirements (see Non-Task-Specific criteria). When all criteria are evaluated, tally the points for a total at the bottom of each column.

Tasksheet Scoring

Evaluation Items	Test		Retest	
	Pass	**Fail**	**Pass**	**Fail**
Task-Specific Evaluation	**(1 pt)**	**(0 pts)**	**(1 pt)**	**(0 pts)**
Student properly tested at least two of the sensors.				
Student properly tested at least four of the sensors.				
Student properly tested all seven of the sensors.				
Student accurately listed any necessary rectifications.				
Non-Task-Specific Evaluation	**(0 pts)**	**(−1 pt)**	**(0 pts)**	**(−1 pt)**
Student successfully completed at least three of the non-task-specific steps.				
Student successfully completed all five of the non-task-specific steps.				
Total Score: <total # of points / 4 = %>				

Supervisor/Instructor:

Supervisor/instructor signature _____ Date _____

Comments:

Retest supervisor/instructor signature _____ Date _____

Comments:

Chapter 49: Diagnostics; Understand Proper Diesel Engine Diagnostic Procedures

Learning Objective/Task	CDX Tasksheet Number	AED Reference Number
• Diagnose exhaust smoke.	5.7002	AED 5.7
• Test engine fails to start problem.	5.7003	AED 5.7
• Troubleshoot engine low power problems.	5.7005	AED 5.7
• Perform cylinder contribution test utilizing electronic service tool(s).	5.7006	AED 5.7
• Troubleshoot cooling system.	5.7007	AED 5.7
• Test cooling system.	5.7008	AED 5.7

Materials Required

- Vehicle with possible engine concern
- Vehicle manufacturer's workshop materials
- Manufacturer-specific tools, depending on the concern/procedure(s)
- Vehicle/component lifting equipment, if applicable

Safety Considerations

- This task may require test driving the vehicle on the school grounds or on a hoist, both of which carry severe risks. Attempt this task only with full permission from your supervisor/instructor and follow all the guidelines exactly.
- Lifting equipment such as vehicle jacks and stands, vehicle hoists, and engine hoists are important tools that increase productivity and make the job easier. However, they can also cause severe injury or death if used improperly. Make sure you follow the manufacturer's operation procedures. Also make sure you have your supervisor's/instructor's permission to use any particular type of lifting equipment.
- Comply with personal and environmental safety practices associated with clothing; eye protection; hand tools; power equipment; proper ventilation; and the handling, storage, and disposal of chemicals/materials in accordance with federal, state, and local regulations.
- Always wear the correct protective eyewear and clothing and use the appropriate safety equipment, as well as wheel chocks, fender covers, seat protectors, and floor mat protectors.
- Make sure you understand and observe all legislative and personal safety procedures when carrying out practical assignments. If you are unsure of what these are, ask your supervisor/instructor.

CDX Tasksheet Number: 5.7002

Student/Intern Information

Name _____ Date _____ Class _____

Machine, Customer, and Service Information

Machine used for this activity:

Make _____ Model _____

Hours _____ Serial Number _____

Task-Specific Safety Considerations
- This task may require test driving the vehicle on the school grounds or on a hoist, both of which carry severe risks. Attempt this task only with full permission from your supervisor/instructor and follow all the guidelines exactly.
- Lifting equipment such as vehicle jacks and stands, vehicle hoists, and engine hoists are important tools that increase productivity and make the job easier. However, they can also cause severe injury or death if used improperly. Make sure you follow the manufacturer's operation procedures. Also make sure you have your supervisor's/instructor's permission to use any particular type of lifting equipment.
- Comply with personal and environmental safety practices associated with clothing; eye protection; hand tools; power equipment; proper ventilation; and the handling, storage, and disposal of chemicals/materials in accordance with federal, state, and local regulations.
- Always wear the correct protective eyewear and clothing and use the appropriate safety equipment, as well as wheel chocks, fender covers, seat protectors, and floor mat protectors.
- Make sure you understand and observe all legislative and personal safety procedures when carrying out practical assignments. If you are unsure of what these are, ask your supervisor/instructor.

▶ **TASK** Diagnose exhaust smoke.   **AED 5.7**

Time off_____

Time on_____

Student Instructions: Read through the entire procedure prior to starting. Prepare your workspace and any tools or parts that may be needed to complete the task. When directed by your supervisor/instructor, begin the procedure to complete the task, and comment or check the box as each step is finished. Track your time on this procedure for later comparison to the standard completion time (i.e., "flat rate" or customer pay time).

Total time_____

Note: This tasksheet may require the student to check the condition of miscellaneous vehicle fluids, some of which may be flammable and could damage the environment or cause health problems if not handled properly. Observe all safety precautions and follow local regulations for the proper disposal of fluids.

Procedure	Step Completed
1. Start the engine and bring it to operating temperature.	☐
a. List any hard starting problems (extended cranking, etc.):	☐
2. Observe and record the exhaust color.	
a. Exhaust color upon initial start-up: _____	☐
b. Exhaust color after engine is at operating temperature at idle: _____	☐
c. Exhaust color after engine is at operating temperature at governed rpm (high idle): _____	☐
3. Record the quantity of smoke coming from the exhaust (e.g., short burst, then cleared; longer burst, then cleared; large amount after start-up, at idle, and at governed rpm):	☐
a. List the possible causes for excessive exhaust (e.g., white, blue, black in color):	☐
b. Determine what action is required for an engine's possible excessive exhaust problems:	☐
4. With the engine running at operating temperature, record the following:	☐
a. Record the idle rpm: _____ rpm	☐
b. Record the governed rpm (high idle): _____ rpm	☐
5. Record any mechanical, whistling, knocking, or grinding noises at idle and governed rpm:	☐

a. List possible causes for mechanical, whistling, knocking, or grinding noises. (**Note:** Shut down the engine immediately and notify your supervisor/instructor if you hear any of the above noises.)	☐
b. Determine what action is required for an engine's knocking, whistling, or grinding noise:	☐
6. Record excessive vibrations at idle, governed rpm with the clutch disengaged (pushed in) and engaged (released):	☐
a. List possible causes for excessive vibrations:	☐
b. Determine what action is required for excessive vibrations:	☐
7. Return the vehicle to its beginning condition and return any tools you used to their proper locations.	☐
8. Discuss your findings with your supervisor/instructor.	☐

Non-Task-Specific Evaluation	Step Completed
1. Tools and equipment were used as directed and returned in good working order.	☐
2. Complied with all general and task-specific safety standards, including proper use of any personal protective equipment (PPE).	☐
3. Completed the task in an appropriate time frame (recommendation: 1.5 or 2 times the flat rate).	☐
4. Left the workspace clean and orderly.	☐
5. Cared for customer property and returned it undamaged.	☐

Student signature _____ Date _____

Comments:

Have your supervisor/instructor verify satisfactory completion of this procedure, any observations made, and any necessary action(s) recommended.

Evaluation Instructions: The scoring box below is intended to act as a guide for both student and supervisor/instructor. Each criterion listed will help students to understand what is expected of them and help supervisors/instructors to articulate the level of success at a particular task. The scoring is set up to allow a second attempt at each task (see the Test and Retest columns). Scoring is designed only to award students points for task criteria that were completed correctly. Points are lost for failure to complete the employability requirements (see Non-Task-Specific criteria). When all criteria are evaluated, tally the points for a total at the bottom of each column.

Tasksheet Scoring

Evaluation Items	Test Pass (1 pt)	Test Fail (0 pts)	Retest Pass (1 pt)	Retest Fail (0 pts)
Task-Specific Evaluation	**(1 pt)**	**(0 pts)**	**(1 pt)**	**(0 pts)**
Student properly started the engine, brought it to operating temperature, and listed any hard starting problems.				
Student properly observed and recorded exhaust color and quantity at idle and governed rpm.				
Student properly observed and recorded unusual noises and excessive vibrations at idle and governed rpm.				
Student accurately determined what actions were required for each situation.				
Non-Task-Specific Evaluation	**(0 pts)**	**(−1 pt)**	**(0 pts)**	**(−1 pt)**
Student successfully completed at least three of the non-task-specific steps.				
Student successfully completed all five of the non-task-specific steps.				
Total Score: <total # of points / 4 = %>				

Supervisor/Instructor:

Supervisor/instructor signature _____ Date _____

Comments:

Retest supervisor/instructor signature _____ Date _____

Comments:

CDX Tasksheet Number: 5.7003

Student/Intern Information

Name _____ Date _____ Class _____

Machine, Customer, and Service Information

Machine used for this activity:

Make _____ Model _____

Hours _____ Serial Number _____

Materials Required
- Vehicle manufacturer's workshop materials

Task-Specific Safety Considerations
- This task may require test driving the vehicle on the school grounds or on a hoist, both of which carry severe risks. Attempt this task only with full permission from your supervisor/instructor and follow all the guidelines exactly.
- Lifting equipment such as vehicle jacks and stands, vehicle hoists, and engine hoists are important tools that increase productivity and make the job easier. However, they can also cause severe injury or death if used improperly. Make sure you follow the manufacturer's operation procedures. Also make sure you have your supervisor's/instructor's permission to use any particular type of lifting equipment.
- Comply with personal and environmental safety practices associated with clothing; eye protection; hand tools; power equipment; proper ventilation; and the handling, storage, and disposal of chemicals/materials in accordance with federal, state, and local regulations.
- Always wear the correct protective eyewear and clothing and use the appropriate safety equipment, as well as wheel chocks, fender covers, seat protectors, and floor mat protectors.
- Make sure you understand and observe all legislative and personal safety procedures when carrying out practical assignments. If you are unsure of what these are, ask your supervisor/instructor.

▶ TASK Test engine fails to start problem. **AED 5.7**

Time off _____

Time on _____

Student Instructions: Read through the entire procedure prior to starting. Prepare your workspace and any tools or parts that may be needed to complete the task. When directed by your supervisor/instructor, begin the procedure to complete the task, and comment or check the box as each step is finished. Track your time on this procedure for later comparison to the standard completion time (i.e., "flat rate" or customer pay time).

Total time _____

Note: This tasksheet may require the student to check the condition of miscellaneous vehicle fluids, some of which may be flammable and could damage the environment or cause health problems if not handled properly. Observe all safety precautions and follow local regulations for the proper disposal of fluids.

Procedure	Step Completed
1. Reference the manufacturer's workshop materials for the common causes of a no crank situation (the engine will not turn over using the starter motor).	☐
a. List all possible causes for a no crank situation:	☐
b. Determine what action is required for a no crank situation:	☐
2. Reference the manufacturer's workshop materials for the common causes of a cranks but fails to start situation (the engine turns over by the starter motor but fails to run).	☐
a. List all possible causes for a cranks but fails to start situation:	☐
b. Determine what action is required for a cranks but fails to start situation:	☐
3. Reference the manufacturer's workshop materials for the common causes of a hard starting situation (the engine will run but takes longer than usual to start).	☐
a. List all possible causes for a hard starting situation:	☐
b. Determine what action is required for a hard starting situation:	☐
4. Reference the manufacturer's workshop materials for the common causes of a starts but does not continue to run situation.	☐
a. List all possible causes for a starts but does not continue to run situation:	☐

	Step Completed
b. Determine what action is required for a starts but does not continue to run situation:	☐
5. Return the vehicle to its beginning condition and return any tools you used to their proper locations.	☐
6. Discuss your findings with your supervisor/instructor.	☐

Non-Task-Specific Evaluation	Step Completed
1. Tools and equipment were used as directed and returned in good working order.	☐
2. Complied with all general and task-specific safety standards, including proper use of any personal protective equipment (PPE).	☐
3. Completed the task in an appropriate time frame (recommendation: 1.5 or 2 times the flat rate).	☐
4. Left the workspace clean and orderly.	☐
5. Cared for customer property and returned it undamaged.	☐

Student signature _____ Date _____

Comments:

Have your supervisor/instructor verify satisfactory completion of this procedure, any observations made,

and any necessary action(s) recommended.

Evaluation Instructions: The scoring box below is intended to act as a guide for both student and supervisor/instructor. Each criterion listed will help students to understand what is expected of them and help supervisors/instructors to articulate the level of success at a particular task. The scoring is set up to allow a second attempt at each task (see the Test and Retest columns). Scoring is designed only to award students points for task criteria that were completed correctly. Points are lost for failure to complete the employability requirements (see Non-Task-Specific criteria). When all criteria are evaluated, tally the points for a total at the bottom of each column.

Tasksheet Scoring

Evaluation Items	Test		Retest	
	Pass	Fail	Pass	Fail
Task-Specific Evaluation	**(1 pt)**	**(0 pts)**	**(1 pt)**	**(0 pts)**
Student accurately listed the common causes and the actions required for a no crank situation.				
Student accurately listed the common causes and the actions required for a cranks but fails to start situation.				
Student accurately listed the common causes and the actions required for a hard starting situation.				
Student accurately listed the common causes and the actions required for a starts but does not continue to run situation.				
Non-Task-Specific Evaluation	**(0 pts)**	**(−1 pt)**	**(0 pts)**	**(−1 pt)**
Student successfully completed at least three of the non-task-specific steps.				
Student successfully completed all five of the non-task-specific steps.				
Total Score: <total # of points / 4 = %>				

Supervisor/Instructor:

Supervisor/instructor signature _____ Date _____

Comments:

Retest supervisor/instructor signature _____ Date _____

Comments:

CDX Tasksheet Number: 5.7005

Student/Intern Information

Name _____ Date _____ Class _____

Machine, Customer, and Service Information

Machine used for this activity:

Make _____ Model _____

Hours _____ Serial Number _____

Materials Required
- Vehicle manufacturer's workshop materials

Task-Specific Safety Considerations
- This task may require test driving the vehicle on the school grounds or on a hoist, both of which carry severe risks. Attempt this task only with full permission from your supervisor/instructor and follow all the guidelines exactly.
- Lifting equipment such as vehicle jacks and stands, vehicle hoists, and engine hoists are important tools that increase productivity and make the job easier. However, they can also cause severe injury or death if used improperly. Make sure you follow the manufacturer's operation procedures. Also make sure you have your supervisor/instructor's permission to use any particular type of lifting equipment.
- Comply with personal and environmental safety practices associated with clothing; eye protection; hand tools; power equipment; proper ventilation; and the handling, storage, and disposal of chemicals/materials in accordance with federal, state, and local regulations.
- Always wear the correct protective eyewear and clothing and use the appropriate safety equipment, as well as wheel chocks, fender covers, seat protectors, and floor mat protectors.
- Make sure you understand and observe all legislative and personal safety procedures when carrying out practical assignments. If you are unsure of what these are, ask your supervisor/instructor.

▶ **TASK** Troubleshoot engine low power problems. _____ **_AED_** **5.7**

Time off_____

Time on_____

Student Instructions: Read through the entire procedure prior to starting. Prepare your workspace and any tools or parts that may be needed to complete the task. When directed by your supervisor/instructor, begin the procedure to complete the task, and comment or check the box as each step is finished. Track your time on this procedure for later comparison to the standard completion time (i.e., "flat rate" or customer pay time).

Total time_____

Note: This tasksheet may require the student to check the condition of miscellaneous vehicle fluids, some of which may be flammable and could damage the environment or cause health problems if not handled properly. Observe all safety precautions and follow local regulations for the proper disposal of fluids.

Procedure	Step Completed
1. Reference the manufacturer's workshop materials for the common causes of a surging situation.	☐
a. List all possible causes of surging (uneven or rolling idle):	☐
b. Determine what action is required for any surging problems:	☐
2. Reference the manufacturer's workshop materials for the common causes of an engine's rough operation situation.	☐
a. List all possible causes for an engine's rough operation:	☐
b. Determine what action is required for a rough operation situation:	☐
3. Reference the manufacturer's workshop materials for the common causes of an engine's misfiring situation.	☐
a. List all possible causes for an engine's misfiring:	☐
b. Determine what action is required for a misfiring situation:	☐
4. Reference the manufacturer's workshop materials for the common causes of an engine's low-power situation.	☐
a. List all possible causes for an engine's low-power situation:	☐
b. Determine what action is required for a low-power situation:	☐

5. Reference the manufacturer's workshop materials for the common causes of an engine's slow deceleration and/or slow acceleration situation.	☐
a. List all possible causes for an engine's slow deceleration and/or slow acceleration situation:	☐
b. Determine what action is required for a slow deceleration and/or slow acceleration situation:	☐
6. Reference the manufacturer's workshop materials for the common causes of an engine's shutdown problems.	☐
a. List all possible causes for an engine's shutdown problems:	☐
b. Determine what action is required for any shutdown problems:	☐
7. Discuss your findings with your supervisor/instructor.	☐

Non-Task-Specific Evaluation	Step Completed
1. Tools and equipment were used as directed and returned in good working order.	☐
2. Complied with all general and task-specific safety standards, including proper use of any personal protective equipment (PPE).	☐
3. Completed the task in an appropriate time frame (recommendation: 1.5 or 2 times the flat rate).	☐
4. Left the workspace clean and orderly.	☐
5. Cared for customer property and returned it undamaged.	☐

Student signature _____ Date _____

Comments:

Have your supervisor/instructor verify satisfactory completion of this procedure, any observations made, and any necessary action(s) recommended.

Evaluation Instructions: The scoring box below is intended to act as a guide for both student and supervisor/instructor. Each criterion listed will help students to understand what is expected of them and help supervisors/instructors to articulate the level of success at a particular task. The scoring is set up to allow a second attempt at each task (see the Test and Retest columns). Scoring is designed only to award students points for task criteria that were completed correctly. Points are lost for failure to complete the employability requirements (see Non-Task-Specific criteria). When all criteria are evaluated, tally the points for a total at the bottom of each column.

Tasksheet Scoring

	Test		Retest	
Evaluation Items	**Pass**	**Fail**	**Pass**	**Fail**
Task-Specific Evaluation	**(1 pt)**	**(0 pts)**	**(1 pt)**	**(0 pts)**
Student accurately listed the common causes for at least three of the situations.				
Student accurately listed the common causes for all six of the situations.				
Student accurately listed the actions required for at least three of the situations.				
Student accurately listed the actions required for all six of the situations.				
Non-Task-Specific Evaluation	**(0 pts)**	**(−1 pt)**	**(0 pts)**	**(−1 pt)**
Student successfully completed at least three of the non-task-specific steps.				
Student successfully completed all five of the non-task-specific steps.				
Total Score: <total # of points / 4 = %>				

Supervisor/Instructor:

Supervisor/instructor signature _____ Date _____

Comments:

Retest supervisor/instructor signature _____ Date _____

Comments:

CDX Tasksheet Number: 5.7006

Student/Intern Information

Name _____ Date _____ Class _____

Machine, Customer, and Service Information

Machine used for this activity:

Make _____ Model _____

Hours _____ Serial Number _____

Materials Required
- Vehicle with possible engine concern
- Vehicle manufacturer's workshop materials
- Manufacturer-specific tools, depending on the concern/procedure(s)
- Vehicle/component lifting equipment, if applicable

Task-Specific Safety Considerations
- This task may require test driving the vehicle on the school grounds or on a hoist, both of which carry severe risks. Attempt this task only with full permission from your supervisor/instructor and follow all the guidelines exactly.
- Lifting equipment such as vehicle jacks and stands, vehicle hoists, and engine hoists are important tools that increase productivity and make the job easier. However, they can also cause severe injury or death if used improperly. Make sure you follow the manufacturer's operation procedures. Also make sure you have your supervisor's/instructor's permission to use any particular type of lifting equipment.
- Comply with personal and environmental safety practices associated with clothing; eye protection; hand tools; power equipment; proper ventilation; and the handling, storage, and disposal of chemicals/materials in accordance with federal, state, and local regulations.
- Always wear the correct protective eyewear and clothing and use the appropriate safety equipment, as well as wheel chocks, fender covers, seat protectors, and floor mat protectors.
- Make sure you understand and observe all legislative and personal safety procedures when carrying out practical assignments. If you are unsure of what these are, ask your supervisor/instructor.

▶ TASK Perform cylinder contribution test utilizing electronic service tool(s).

AED 5.7

Time off_____

Time on_____

Student Instructions: Read through the entire procedure prior to starting. Prepare your workspace and any tools or parts that may be needed to complete the task. When directed by your supervisor/instructor, begin the procedure to complete the task, and comment or check the box as each step is finished. Track your time on this procedure for later comparison to the standard completion time (i.e., "flat rate" or customer pay time).

Total time_____

Note: This tasksheet may require the student to check the condition of miscellaneous vehicle fluids, some of which may be flammable and could damage the environment or cause health problems if not handled properly. Observe all safety precautions and follow local regulations for the proper disposal of fluids.

Procedure	Step Completed
1. While referencing the manufacturer's workshop materials, record the procedure for performing a cylinder contribution test:	☐
2. While referencing the manufacturer's workshop materials, record any special instructions and/or conditions that must be met before performing a cylinder contribution test:	☐
3. While referencing the manufacturer's workshop materials, record any safety precautions to be observed while performing a cylinder contribution test:	☐
4. While referencing the manufacturer's workshop materials, connect the electronic service tool (EST) and record any fault codes that may prohibit performing a cylinder contribution test:	☐
a. If directed by your supervisor/instructor, repair the above fault codes.	☐
5. While referencing the manufacturer's workshop materials and using the EST, perform a cylinder contribution test.	☐
a. Meets the manufacturer's specifications: Yes ☐ No ☐	☐
b. If no, list your recommendations for rectification:	☐
6. While referencing the manufacturer's workshop materials, record the procedure for performing a cylinder cutout test:	☐

7. While referencing the manufacturer's workshop materials, record any special instructions and/or conditions that must be met before performing a cylinder cutout test:	☐
8. While referencing the manufacturer's workshop materials, record any safety precautions to be observed while performing a cylinder cutout test:	☐
9. While referencing the manufacturer's workshop materials, connect the EST and record any fault codes that may prohibit performing a cylinder cutout test:	☐
a. If directed by your supervisor/instructor, repair the above fault codes.	☐
10. While referencing the manufacturer's workshop materials and using the EST, perform a cylinder cutout test.	☐
a. Meets the manufacturer's specifications: Yes ☐ No ☐	☐
b. If no, list your recommendations for rectification:	☐
11. Discuss your findings with your supervisor/instructor.	☐

Non-Task-Specific Evaluation	Step Completed
1. Tools and equipment were used as directed and returned in good working order.	☐
2. Complied with all general and task-specific safety standards, including proper use of any personal protective equipment (PPE).	☐
3. Completed the task in an appropriate time frame (recommendation: 1.5 or 2 times the flat rate).	☐
4. Left the workspace clean and orderly.	☐
5. Cared for customer property and returned it undamaged.	☐

Student signature _____ Date _____

Comments:

Have your supervisor/instructor verify satisfactory completion of this procedure, any observations made, and any necessary action(s) recommended.

Evaluation Instructions: The scoring box below is intended to act as a guide for both student and supervisor/instructor. Each criterion listed will help students to understand what is expected of them and help supervisors/instructors to articulate the level of success at a particular task. The scoring is set up to allow a second attempt at each task (see the Test and Retest columns). Scoring is designed only to award students points for task criteria that were completed correctly. Points are lost for failure to complete the employability requirements (see Non-Task-Specific criteria). When all criteria are evaluated, tally the points for a total at the bottom of each column.

Tasksheet Scoring

Evaluation Items	Test		Retest	
	Pass	**Fail**	**Pass**	**Fail**
Task-Specific Evaluation	**(1 pt)**	**(0 pts)**	**(1 pt)**	**(0 pts)**
Student accurately recorded the procedures for performing a cylinder contribution test and a cylinder cutout test.				
Student accurately recorded any special instructions and safety precautions to be observed before and during each test.				
Student properly checked (and repaired, if directed) any fault codes that may have prohibited either test.				
Student properly performed both tests and noted any necessary rectifications.				
Non-Task-Specific Evaluation	**(0 pts)**	**(−1 pt)**	**(0 pts)**	**(−1 pt)**
Student successfully completed at least three of the non-task-specific steps.				
Student successfully completed all five of the non-task-specific steps.				
Total Score: <total # of points / 4 = %>				

Supervisor/Instructor:

Supervisor/instructor signature _____ Date _____

Comments:

Retest supervisor/instructor signature _____ Date _____

Comments:

CDX Tasksheet Number: 5.7007

Student/Intern Information

Name _____ Date _____ Class _____

Machine, Customer, and Service Information

Machine used for this activity:

Make _____ Model _____

Hours _____ Serial Number _____

Materials Required

- Vehicle with possible engine concern
- Vehicle manufacturer's workshop materials
- Manufacturer-specific tools, depending on the concern/procedure(s)
- Vehicle/component lifting equipment, if applicable

Task-Specific Safety Considerations

- This task may require test driving the vehicle on the school grounds or on a hoist, both of which carry severe risks. Attempt this task only with full permission from your supervisor/instructor and follow all the guidelines exactly.
- Lifting equipment such as vehicle jacks and stands, vehicle hoists, and engine hoists are important tools that increase productivity and make the job easier. However, they can also cause severe injury or death if used improperly. Make sure you follow the manufacturer's operation procedures. Also make sure you have your supervisor's/instructor's permission to use any particular type of lifting equipment.
- Comply with personal and environmental safety practices associated with clothing; eye protection; hand tools; power equipment; proper ventilation; and the handling, storage, and disposal of chemicals/materials in accordance with federal, state, and local regulations.
- Always wear the correct protective eyewear and clothing and use the appropriate safety equipment, as well as wheel chocks, fender covers, seat protectors, and floor mat protectors.
- Make sure you understand and observe all legislative and personal safety procedures when carrying out practical assignments. If you are unsure of what these are, ask your supervisor/instructor.

▶ TASK Troubleshoot cooling system.

Time off_____

Time on_____

Student Instructions: Read through the entire procedure prior to starting. Prepare your workspace and any tools or parts that may be needed to complete the task. When directed by your supervisor/instructor, begin the procedure to complete the task, and comment or check the box as each step is finished. Track your time on this procedure for later comparison to the standard completion time (i.e., "flat rate" or customer pay time).

Total time_____

Note: This tasksheet may require the student to check the condition of miscellaneous vehicle fluids, some of which may be flammable and could damage the environment or cause health problems if not handled properly. Observe all safety precautions and follow local regulations for the proper disposal of fluids.

Procedure	Step Completed
1. Reference the manufacturer's workshop materials and record the engine coolant operating temperature: _____ °F/°C	☐
2. While referencing the manufacturer's workshop materials, test the engine temperature with an infrared thermometer at or near the coolant temperature sensor while cold. Compare the reading to the operation of the original equipment manufacturer (OEM) temperature sensor and gauge.	☐
a. Engine coolant temperature (cold): _____ °F/°C	☐
b. Meets the manufacturer's specifications: Yes ☐ No ☐	☐
c. If no, list your recommendations for rectification:	☐
3. While referencing the manufacturer's workshop materials, bring the engine to operating temperature. Test the engine temperature with an infrared thermometer at or near the coolant temperature sensor. Compare the reading to the operation of the OEM temperature sensor and gauge.	☐
a. Engine coolant temperature (hot): _____ °F/°C	☐
b. Meets the manufacturer's specifications: Yes ☐ No ☐	☐
c. If no, list your recommendations for rectification:	☐
4. Reference the manufacturer's workshop materials and check the operation of the coolant level sensors.	☐
a. Meets the manufacturer's specifications: Yes ☐ No ☐	☐
b. If no, list your recommendations for rectification:	☐
5. Discuss your findings with your supervisor/instructor.	☐

Non-Task-Specific Evaluation	Step Completed
1. Tools and equipment were used as directed and returned in good working order.	☐
2. Complied with all general and task-specific safety standards, including proper use of any personal protective equipment (PPE).	☐
3. Completed the task in an appropriate time frame (recommendation: 1.5 or 2 times the flat rate).	☐
4. Left the workspace clean and orderly.	☐
5. Cared for customer property and returned it undamaged.	☐

Student signature _____ Date _____

Comments:

Have your supervisor/instructor verify satisfactory completion of this procedure, any observations made, and any necessary action(s) recommended.

Evaluation Instructions: The scoring box below is intended to act as a guide for both student and supervisor/instructor. Each criterion listed will help students to understand what is expected of them and help supervisors/instructors to articulate the level of success at a particular task. The scoring is set up to allow a second attempt at each task (see the Test and Retest columns). Scoring is designed only to award students points for task criteria that were completed correctly. Points are lost for failure to complete the employability requirements (see Non-Task-Specific criteria). When all criteria are evaluated, tally the points for a total at the bottom of each column.

Tasksheet Scoring

Evaluation Items	Test		Retest	
	Pass	**Fail**	**Pass**	**Fail**
Task-Specific Evaluation	**(1 pt)**	**(0 pts)**	**(1 pt)**	**(0 pts)**
Student accurately recorded the engine coolant operating temperature.				
Student properly checked the cooling system temperature (cold).				
Student properly checked the cooling system temperature (hot).				
Student properly checked the cooling system level sensor.				
Non-Task-Specific Evaluation	**(0 pts)**	**(−1 pt)**	**(0 pts)**	**(−1 pt)**
Student successfully completed at least three of the non-task-specific steps.				
Student successfully completed all five of the non-task-specific steps.				
Total Score: <total # of points / 4 = %>				

Supervisor/Instructor:

Supervisor/instructor signature _____ Date _____

Comments:

Retest supervisor/instructor signature _____ Date _____

Comments:

CDX Tasksheet Number: 5.7008

Student/Intern Information

Name _____ Date _____ Class _____

Machine, Customer, and Service Information

Machine used for this activity:

Make _____ Model _____

Hours _____ Serial Number _____

Materials Required
- Vehicle with possible engine concern
- Vehicle manufacturer's workshop materials
- Manufacturer-specific tools, depending on the concern/procedure(s)
- Vehicle/component lifting equipment, if applicable

Task-Specific Safety Considerations
- This task may require test driving the vehicle on the school grounds or on a hoist, both of which carry severe risks. Attempt this task only with full permission from your supervisor/instructor and follow all the guidelines exactly.
- Lifting equipment such as vehicle jacks and stands, vehicle hoists, and engine hoists are important tools that increase productivity and make the job easier. However, they can also cause severe injury or death if used improperly. Make sure you follow the manufacturer's operation procedures. Also make sure you have your supervisor's/instructor's permission to use any particular type of lifting equipment.
- Comply with personal and environmental safety practices associated with clothing; eye protection; hand tools; power equipment; proper ventilation; and the handling, storage, and disposal of chemicals/materials in accordance with federal, state, and local regulations.
- Always wear the correct protective eyewear and clothing and use the appropriate safety equipment, as well as wheel chocks, fender covers, seat protectors, and floor mat protectors.
- Make sure you understand and observe all legislative and personal safety procedures when carrying out practical assignments. If you are unsure of what these are, ask your supervisor/instructor.

▶ **TASK** Test cooling system. **AED 5.7**

Time off_____

Time on_____

Student Instructions: Read through the entire procedure prior to starting. Prepare your workspace and any tools or parts that may be needed to complete the task. When directed by your supervisor/instructor, begin the procedure to complete the task, and comment or check the box as each step is finished. Track your time on this procedure for later comparison to the standard completion time (i.e., "flat rate" or customer pay time).

Total time_____

Note: This tasksheet may require the student to check the condition of miscellaneous vehicle fluids, some of which may be flammable and could damage the environment or cause health problems if not handled properly. Observe all safety precautions and follow local regulations for the proper disposal of fluids.

Procedure	Step Completed
1. Reference the manufacturer's workshop materials and identify the proper engine coolant type, level, condition, and consumption.	☐
a. Coolant type: _____	☐
b. Coolant quantity: _____ quarts/gallons	☐
c. Cooling system pressure cap: _____ psi/kPa	☐
2. Check the coolant level.	☐
a. Meets the manufacturer's specifications: Yes ☐ No ☐	☐
b. If no, list your recommendations for rectification:	☐
3. Pressure test the cooling system pressure cap and record the results: _____ psi/kPa	☐
a. Meets the manufacturer's specifications: Yes ☐ No ☐	☐
b. If no, list your recommendations for rectification:	☐
4. Pressure test the cooling system.	☐
a. Meets the manufacturer's specifications: Yes ☐ No ☐	☐
b. If no, list your recommendations for rectification:	☐
5. Reference the manufacturer's workshop materials and list the possible causes for excessive coolant consumption:	☐
6. Discuss your findings with your supervisor/instructor.	☐

Non-Task-Specific Evaluation	Step Completed
1. Tools and equipment were used as directed and returned in good working order.	☐
2. Complied with all general and task-specific safety standards, including proper use of any personal protective equipment (PPE).	☐
3. Completed the task in an appropriate time frame (recommendation: 1.5 or 2 times the flat rate).	☐
4. Left the workspace clean and orderly.	☐
5. Cared for customer property and returned it undamaged.	☐

Student signature _____ Date _____

Comments:

Have your supervisor/instructor verify satisfactory completion of this procedure, any observations made, and any necessary action(s) recommended.

Evaluation Instructions: The scoring box below is intended to act as a guide for both student and supervisor/instructor. Each criterion listed will help students to understand what is expected of them and help supervisors/instructors to articulate the level of success at a particular task. The scoring is set up to allow a second attempt at each task (see the Test and Retest columns). Scoring is designed only to award students points for task criteria that were completed correctly. Points are lost for failure to complete the employability requirements (see Non-Task-Specific criteria). When all criteria are evaluated, tally the points for a total at the bottom of each column.

Tasksheet Scoring

Evaluation Items	Test		Retest	
	Pass	**Fail**	**Pass**	**Fail**
Task-Specific Evaluation	**(1 pt)**	**(0 pts)**	**(1 pt)**	**(0 pts)**
Student accurately identified the engine coolant type, level, condition, and consumption.				
Student properly checked the coolant level.				
Student properly performed a pressure test on the cooling system pressure cap.				
Student properly performed a pressure test on the cooling system.				
Non-Task-Specific Evaluation	**(0 pts)**	**(−1 pt)**	**(0 pts)**	**(−1 pt)**
Student successfully completed at least three of the non-task-specific steps.				
Student successfully completed all five of the non-task-specific steps.				
Total Score: <total # of points / 4 = %>				

Section 6: Air-Conditioning/Heating

Chapter 50: Fundamental Knowledge

Learning Objective/Task	CDX Tasksheet Number	AED Reference Number
• Measure the effects of pressures on liquids.	6.1003	AED 6.1

Materials Required

- Vehicle with possible air-conditioning (A/C) concerns
- Vehicle manufacturer's service information
- Manufacturer-specific tools, depending on the concern/procedure(s)

Safety Considerations

- This task may require test driving the vehicle on the school grounds or on a hoist, both of which carry severe risks. Attempt this task only with full permission from your supervisor/instructor and follow all the guidelines exactly.
- Comply with personal and environmental safety practices associated with clothing; eye protection; hand tools; power equipment; proper ventilation; and the handling, storage, and disposal of chemicals/materials in accordance with federal, state, and local regulations.
- Always wear the correct protective eyewear and clothing and use the appropriate safety equipment, as well as fender covers, seat protectors, and floor mat protectors.
- Make sure you understand and observe all legislative and personal safety procedures when carrying out practical assignments. If you are unsure of what these are, ask your supervisor/instructor.
- While working on the vehicle, wheel chocks must be placed on both sides of one set of tires or as directed by your supervisor/instructor.
- When running any vehicles in the shop, make sure you use the shop's exhaust ventilation system to discharge all exhaust gas safely outside.

CDX Tasksheet Number: 6.1003

Student/Intern Information

Name _____ Date _____ Class _____

Machine, Customer, and Service Information

Machine used for this activity:

Make _____ Model _____

Hours _____ Serial Number _____

Task-Specific Safety Considerations

- This task may require test driving the vehicle on the school grounds or on a hoist, both of which carry severe risks. Attempt this task only with full permission from your supervisor/instructor and follow all the guidelines exactly.
- Comply with personal and environmental safety practices associated with clothing; eye protection; hand tools; power equipment; proper ventilation; and the handling, storage, and disposal of chemicals/materials in accordance with federal, state, and local regulations.
- Always wear the correct protective eyewear and clothing and use the appropriate safety equipment, as well as fender covers, seat protectors, and floor mat protectors.
- Make sure you understand and observe all legislative and personal safety procedures when carrying out practical assignments. If you are unsure of what these are, ask your supervisor/instructor.
- While working on the vehicle, wheel chocks must be placed on both sides of one set of tires or as directed by your supervisor/instructor.
- When running any vehicles in the shop, make sure you use the shop's exhaust ventilation system to discharge all exhaust gas safely outside.

▶ **TASK** Measure the effects of pressures on liquids.

AED
6.1

Time off_____

Time on_____

Student Instructions: Read through the entire procedure prior to starting. Prepare your workspace and any tools or parts that may be needed to complete the task. When directed by your supervisor/instructor, begin the procedure to complete the task, and comment or check the box as each step is finished. Track your time on this procedure for later comparison to the standard completion time (i.e., "flat rate" or customer pay time).

Total time_____

Procedure	Step Completed
(**Note:** Steps 1–3 must be completed before moving on to Step 4.)	☐
1. Research and describe the effect of atmospheric pressure on the boiling point of water:	☐
2. Using the above effect, describe how and why water is removed from an A/C system that has been opened to the atmosphere:	☐
3. Using an online resource, find a R134A refrigerant pressure calculator and fill in the required information below.	☐
a. 1 psig _____ ° F	☐
b. 109.4° F _____ psig	☐
c. 54 psig _____ ° F	☐
d. 178.2° F _____ psig	☐
e. 62 psig _____ ° F	☐
f. 54.82° F _____ psig	☐
g. (22) psig _____ ° F	☐
h. -14.92° F _____ psig	☐
4. Using an infrared thermometer, take the temperature at the following locations and convert those readings to pressure.	☐

a. Compressor inlet
    _____ ° F
    _____ psig
	☐

b. Compressor outlet
    _____ ° F
    _____ psig
	☐

c. Evaporator inlet
    _____ ° F
    _____ psig
	☐

d. Evaporator outlet
    _____ ° F
    _____ psig
	☐

	Step Completed
e. Condenser inlet _____ ° F _____ psig	☐
f. Condenser midpoint _____ ° F _____ psig	☐
g. Condenser outlet _____ ° F _____ psig	☐
h. Drier/accumulator inlet _____ ° F _____ psig	☐
i. Drier/accumulator outlet _____ ° F _____ psig	☐
j. TXV(H-Block)/metered orifice inlet _____ ° F _____ psig	☐
k. TXV(H-Block)/metered orifice outlet _____ ° F _____ psig	☐
5. Discuss your findings with your supervisor/instructor.	☐

Non-Task-Specific Evaluation	Step Completed
1. Tools and equipment were used as directed and returned in good working order.	☐
2. Complied with all general and task-specific safety standards, including proper use of any personal protective equipment (PPE).	☐
3. Completed the task in an appropriate time frame (recommendation: 1.5 or 2 times the flat rate).	☐
4. Left the workspace clean and orderly.	☐
5. Cared for customer property and returned it undamaged.	☐

Student signature _____ Date _____

Comments:

Have your supervisor/instructor verify satisfactory completion of this procedure, any observations made,

and any necessary action(s) recommended.

Evaluation Instructions: The scoring box below is intended to act as a guide for both student and supervisor/instructor. Each criterion listed will help students to understand what is expected of them and help supervisors/instructors to articulate the level of success at a particular task. The scoring is set up to allow a second attempt at each task (see the Test and Retest columns). Scoring is designed only to award students points for task criteria that were completed correctly. Points are lost for failure to complete the employability requirements (see Non-Task-Specific criteria). When all criteria are evaluated, tally the points for a total at the bottom of each column.

Tasksheet Scoring

	Test		Retest	
Evaluation Items	**Pass**	**Fail**	**Pass**	**Fail**
Task-Specific Evaluation	**(1 pt)**	**(0 pts)**	**(1 pt)**	**(0 pts)**
Student accurately described the effect of atmospheric pressure on the boiling point of water.				
Student accurately described how and why water is removed from an A/C system that has been opened to the atmosphere.				
Student accurately converted the given temperature/pressure measurements.				
Student properly took the temperature at each location and converted the readings to pressure.				
Non-Task-Specific Evaluation	**(0 pts)**	**(−1 pt)**	**(0 pts)**	**(−1 pt)**
Student successfully completed at least three of the non-task-specific steps.				
Student successfully completed all five of the non-task-specific steps.				
Total Score: <total # of points / 4 = %>				

Chapter 51: Servicing A/C Systems

Learning Objective/Task	CDX Tasksheet Number	AED Reference Number
• Identify refrigerant type and capacity.	6.3001	AED 6.3
• Use refrigerant ID tool (gas analyzer) to identify refrigerant.	6.3002	AED 6.3
• Connect and disconnect gauge manifold sets.	6.3003	AED 6.3
• Evacuate and dehydrate an A/C system.	6.3005	AED 6.3
• Recover and charge an A/C system.	6.3007	AED 6.3
• Add oil, dye, and refrigerants to an A/C system.	6.3010	AED 6.3

Materials Required

- Vehicle with possible A/C concerns
- Vehicle manufacturer's service information
- Manufacturer-specific tools, depending on the concern/procedure(s)

Safety Considerations

- This task may require test driving the vehicle on the school grounds or on a hoist, both of which carry severe risks. Attempt this task only with full permission from your supervisor/instructor and follow all the guidelines exactly.
- Comply with personal and environmental safety practices associated with clothing; eye protection; hand tools; power equipment; proper ventilation; and the handling, storage, and disposal of chemicals/materials in accordance with federal, state, and local regulations.
- Always wear the correct protective eyewear and clothing and use the appropriate safety equipment, as well as fender covers, seat protectors, and floor mat protectors.
- Make sure you understand and observe all legislative and personal safety procedures when carrying out practical assignments. If you are unsure of what these are, ask your supervisor/instructor.
- While working on the vehicle, wheel chocks must be placed on both sides of one set of tires or as directed by your supervisor/instructor.
- When running any vehicles in the shop, make sure you use the shop's exhaust ventilation system to discharge all exhaust gas safely outside.

CDX Tasksheet Number: 6.3001

Student/Intern Information

Name _____ Date _____ Class _____

Machine, Customer, and Service Information

Machine used for this activity:

Make _____ Model _____

Hours _____ Serial Number _____

Materials Required

- Vehicle with possible air-conditioning (A/C) concerns
- Vehicle manufacturer's service information
- Manufacturer-specific tools, depending on the concern/procedure(s)

Task-Specific Safety Considerations

- This task may require test driving the vehicle on the school grounds or on a hoist, both of which carry severe risks. Attempt this task only with full permission from your supervisor/instructor and follow all the guidelines exactly.
- Comply with personal and environmental safety practices associated with clothing; eye protection; hand tools; power equipment; proper ventilation; and the handling, storage, and disposal of chemicals/materials in accordance with federal, state, and local regulations.
- Always wear the correct protective eyewear and clothing and use the appropriate safety equipment, as well as fender covers, seat protectors, and floor mat protectors.
- Make sure you understand and observe all legislative and personal safety procedures when carrying out practical assignments. If you are unsure of what these are, ask your supervisor/instructor.
- While working on the vehicle, wheel chocks must be placed on both sides of one set of tires or as directed by your supervisor/instructor.
- When running any vehicles in the shop, make sure you use the shop's exhaust ventilation system to discharge all exhaust gas safely outside.

▶ TASK Identify refrigerant type and capacity. **AED 6.3**

| Time off_____ |
| Time on_____ |
| Total time_____ |

Student Instructions: Read through the entire procedure prior to starting. Prepare your workspace and any tools or parts that may be needed to complete the task. When directed by your supervisor/instructor, begin the procedure to complete the task, and comment or check the box as each step is finished. Track your time on this procedure for later comparison to the standard completion time (i.e., "flat rate" or customer pay time).

Procedure	Step Completed
1. Record the equipment's make and model:	☐
2. Using service literature or an A/C data plate, record the following.	
a. Refrigerant type	☐
b. Refrigerant capacity	☐
c. Refrigerant oil type	☐
d. Refrigerant oil capacity	☐
3. Discuss your findings with your supervisor/instructor.	☐

Non-Task-Specific Evaluation	Step Completed
1. Tools and equipment were used as directed and returned in good working order.	☐
2. Complied with all general and task-specific safety standards, including proper use of any personal protective equipment (PPE).	☐
3. Completed the task in an appropriate time frame (recommendation: 1.5 or 2 times the flat rate).	☐
4. Left the workspace clean and orderly.	☐
5. Cared for customer property and returned it undamaged.	☐

Student signature _____ Date _____

Comments:

Have your supervisor/instructor verify satisfactory completion of this procedure, any observations made, and any necessary action(s) recommended.

Evaluation Instructions: The scoring box below is intended to act as a guide for both student and supervisor/instructor. Each criterion listed will help students to understand what is expected of them and help supervisors/instructors to articulate the level of success at a particular task. The scoring is set up to allow a second attempt at each task (see the Test and Retest columns). Scoring is designed only to award students points for task criteria that were completed correctly. Points are lost for failure to complete the employability requirements (see Non-Task-Specific criteria). When all criteria are evaluated, tally the points for a total at the bottom of each column.

Tasksheet Scoring

	Test		Retest	
Evaluation Items	**Pass**	**Fail**	**Pass**	**Fail**
Task-Specific Evaluation	**(1 pt)**	**(0 pts)**	**(1 pt)**	**(0 pts)**
Student accurately identified the refrigerant type.				
Student accurately identified the refrigerant capacity.				
Student accurately identified the refrigerant oil type.				
Student accurately identified the refrigerant oil capacity.				
Non-Task-Specific Evaluation	**(0 pts)**	**(−1 pt)**	**(0 pts)**	**(−1 pt)**
Student successfully completed at least three of the non-task-specific steps.				
Student successfully completed all five of the non-task-specific steps.				
Total Score: <total # of points / 4 = %>				

Supervisor/Instructor:

Supervisor/instructor signature _____ Date _____

Comments:

Retest supervisor/instructor signature _____ Date _____

Comments:

CDX Tasksheet Number: 6.3002

Student/Intern Information

Name _____ Date _____ Class _____

Machine, Customer, and Service Information

Machine used for this activity:

Make _____ Model _____

Hours _____ Serial Number _____

Materials Required
- Vehicle with possible air-conditioning (A/C) concerns
- Vehicle manufacturer's service information
- Manufacturer-specific tools, depending on the concern/procedure(s)

Task-Specific Safety Considerations
- This task may require test driving the vehicle on the school grounds or on a hoist, both of which carry severe risks. Attempt this task only with full permission from your supervisor/instructor and follow all the guidelines exactly.
- Comply with personal and environmental safety practices associated with clothing; eye protection; hand tools; power equipment; proper ventilation; and the handling, storage, and disposal of chemicals/materials in accordance with federal, state, and local regulations.
- Always wear the correct protective eyewear and clothing and use the appropriate safety equipment, as well as fender covers, seat protectors, and floor mat protectors.
- Make sure you understand and observe all legislative and personal safety procedures when carrying out practical assignments. If you are unsure of what these are, ask your supervisor/instructor.
- While working on the vehicle, wheel chocks must be placed on both sides of one set of tires or as directed by your supervisor/instructor.
- When running any vehicles in the shop, make sure you use the shop's exhaust ventilation system to discharge all exhaust gas safely outside.

▶ **TASK** Use refrigerant ID tool (gas analyzer) to identify refrigerant.

AED 6.3

Time off_____

Time on_____

Student Instructions: Read through the entire procedure prior to starting. Prepare your workspace and any tools or parts that may be needed to complete the task. When directed by your supervisor/instructor, begin the procedure to complete the task, and comment or check the box as each step is finished. Track your time on this procedure for later comparison to the standard completion time (i.e., "flat rate" or customer pay time).

Total time_____

Procedure	Step Completed
1. Research the types of refrigerant and lubricant types and list them below.	
a. Refrigerant types	☐
b. Lubricant types	☐
2. Determine the refrigerant and lubricant types in the machine assigned for this task. Refrigerant and lubricant types can be identified by the factory sticker or placard.	
a. Refrigerant identified on factory sticker or placard: Yes ☐ No ☐	☐
b. If the refrigerant could not be identified this way, use a refrigerant identifier. Locate the high- and low-side pressure ports. Connect the refrigerant identifier to the low-side port and open the service valve. Follow the prompts on the refrigerant identifier. Record refrigerant type below:	☐
3. Determine whether the refrigerant is contaminated.	
a. Locate the high- and low-side pressure ports. Connect the sealant identifier to the low-side port and open the service valve. Follow the prompts on the sealant identifier. Are there contaminants present? Yes ☐ No ☐	☐
4. Return the vehicle to its beginning condition and return any tools you used to their proper locations.	☐
5. Discuss your findings with your supervisor/instructor.	☐

Non-Task-Specific Evaluation	Step Completed
1. Tools and equipment were used as directed and returned in good working order.	☐
2. Complied with all general and task-specific safety standards, including proper use of any personal protective equipment (PPE).	☐
3. Completed the task in an appropriate time frame (recommendation: 1.5 or 2 times the flat rate).	☐
4. Left the workspace clean and orderly.	☐
5. Cared for customer property and returned it undamaged.	☐

Student signature _____ Date _____

Comments:

Have your supervisor/instructor verify satisfactory completion of this procedure, any observations made,

and any necessary action(s) recommended.

Evaluation Instructions: The scoring box below is intended to act as a guide for both student and supervisor/instructor. Each criterion listed will help students to understand what is expected of them and help supervisors/instructors to articulate the level of success at a particular task. The scoring is set up to allow a second attempt at each task (see the Test and Retest columns). Scoring is designed only to award students points for task criteria that were completed correctly. Points are lost for failure to complete the employability requirements (see Non-Task-Specific criteria). When all criteria are evaluated, tally the points for a total at the bottom of each column.

Tasksheet Scoring

Evaluation Items	Test		Retest	
	Pass	**Fail**	**Pass**	**Fail**
Task-Specific Evaluation	**(1 pt)**	**(0 pts)**	**(1 pt)**	**(0 pts)**
Student accurately listed the different types of refrigerant.				
Student accurately listed the different types of lubricant.				
Student properly determined the refrigerant type for their vehicle.				
Student properly tested for contaminants present in the refrigerant.				
Non-Task-Specific Evaluation	**(0 pts)**	**(−1 pt)**	**(0 pts)**	**(−1 pt)**
Student successfully completed at least three of the non-task-specific steps.				
Student successfully completed all five of the non-task-specific steps.				
Total Score: <total # of points / 4 = %>				

Supervisor/Instructor:

Supervisor/instructor signature _____ Date _____

Comments:

Retest supervisor/instructor signature _____ Date _____

Comments:

CDX Tasksheet Number: 6.3003

Student/Intern Information

Name _____ Date _____ Class _____

Machine, Customer, and Service Information

Machine used for this activity:

Make _____ Model _____

Hours _____ Serial Number _____

Task-Specific Safety Considerations

- This task may require test driving the vehicle on the school grounds or on a hoist, both of which carry severe risks. Attempt this task only with full permission from your supervisor/instructor and follow all the guidelines exactly.
- Comply with personal and environmental safety practices associated with clothing; eye protection; hand tools; power equipment; proper ventilation; and the handling, storage, and disposal of chemicals/materials in accordance with federal, state, and local regulations.
- Always wear the correct protective eyewear and clothing and use the appropriate safety equipment, as well as fender covers, seat protectors, and floor mat protectors.
- Make sure you understand and observe all legislative and personal safety procedures when carrying out practical assignments. If you are unsure of what these are, ask your supervisor/instructor.
- While working on the vehicle, wheel chocks must be placed on both sides of one set of tires or as directed by your supervisor/instructor.
- When running any vehicles in the shop, make sure you use the shop's exhaust ventilation system to discharge all exhaust gas safely outside.

▶ **TASK** Connect and disconnect gauge manifold sets. **AED 6.3**

Time off_____

Student Instructions: Read through the entire procedure prior to starting. Prepare your workspace and any tools or parts that may be needed to complete the task. When directed by your supervisor/instructor, begin the procedure to complete the task, and comment or check the box as each step is finished. Track your time on this procedure for later comparison to the standard completion time (i.e., "flat rate" or customer pay time).

Time on_____

Total time_____

Procedure	Step Completed
1. Pressure gauge sets are determined based on the refrigerant type used. High- and low-pressure side gauges are further identified by the size of the coupler, with high and low side being of different sizes.	
a. Determine the refrigerant type from the placard in the engine bay or by testing the system with a refrigerant identifier. Record the refrigerant type below:	☐
2. Before attaching hoses to the test ports, make sure the service knobs are in the closed position. Then attach the hoses to the proper test ports.	☐
3. Record the procedure for purging service tool hoses to prevent cross-contamination and the introduction of noncondensables:	☐
a. Have your supervisor/instructor approve your recording of the procedure above. Supervisor's/instructor's initials: _____	☐
b. Once Step 3 is approved, purge the service tool hoses.	☐
4. Start the machine, turn the A/C to max and record the high- and low-side pressures: High _____ Low _____	☐
a. Are the pressures within specifications? Yes ☐ No ☐	☐
5. Turn off the machine and allow the pressures to stabilize. Following proper safety and environmental procedures, remove A/C service hoses.	☐
6. Discuss your findings with your supervisor/instructor.	☐

Non-Task-Specific Evaluation	Step Completed
1. Tools and equipment were used as directed and returned in good working order.	☐
2. Complied with all general and task-specific safety standards, including proper use of any personal protective equipment (PPE).	☐
3. Completed the task in an appropriate time frame (recommendation: 1.5 or 2 times the flat rate).	☐
4. Left the workspace clean and orderly.	☐
5. Cared for customer property and returned it undamaged.	☐

Student signature _____ Date _____

Comments:

Have your supervisor/instructor verify satisfactory completion of this procedure, any observations made,

and any necessary action(s) recommended.

Evaluation Instructions: The scoring box below is intended to act as a guide for both student and supervisor/instructor. Each criterion listed will help students to understand what is expected of them and help supervisors/instructors to articulate the level of success at a particular task. The scoring is set up to allow a second attempt at each task (see the Test and Retest columns). Scoring is designed only to award students points for task criteria that were completed correctly. Points are lost for failure to complete the employability requirements (see Non-Task-Specific criteria). When all criteria are evaluated, tally the points for a total at the bottom of each column.

Tasksheet Scoring

Evaluation Items	Test		Retest	
	Pass	Fail	Pass	Fail
Task-Specific Evaluation	**(1 pt)**	**(0 pts)**	**(1 pt)**	**(0 pts)**
Student accurately determined the refrigerant type for their vehicle.				
Student accurately recorded the procedure for purging service tool hoses and properly performed the purge.				
Student accurately recorded the high- and low-side pressures.				
Student allowed the pressures to stabilize and properly removed the hoses.				
Non-Task-Specific Evaluation	**(0 pts)**	**(−1 pt)**	**(0 pts)**	**(−1 pt)**
Student successfully completed at least three of the non-task-specific steps.				
Student successfully completed all five of the non-task-specific steps.				
Total Score: <total # of points / 4 = %>				

Supervisor/Instructor:

Supervisor/instructor signature _____ Date _____

Comments:

Retest supervisor/instructor signature _____ Date _____

Comments:

CDX Tasksheet Number: 6.3005

Student/Intern Information

Name _____ Date _____ Class _____

Machine, Customer, and Service Information

Machine used for this activity:

Make _____ Model _____

Hours _____ Serial Number _____

Task-Specific Safety Considerations

- This task may require test driving the vehicle on the school grounds or on a hoist, both of which carry severe risks. Attempt this task only with full permission from your supervisor/instructor and follow all the guidelines exactly.
- Comply with personal and environmental safety practices associated with clothing; eye protection; hand tools; power equipment; proper ventilation; and the handling, storage, and disposal of chemicals/materials in accordance with federal, state, and local regulations.
- Always wear the correct protective eyewear and clothing and use the appropriate safety equipment, as well as fender covers, seat protectors, and floor mat protectors.
- Make sure you understand and observe all legislative and personal safety procedures when carrying out practical assignments. If you are unsure of what these are, ask your supervisor/instructor.
- While working on the vehicle, wheel chocks must be placed on both sides of one set of tires or as directed by your supervisor/instructor.
- When running any vehicles in the shop, make sure you use the shop's exhaust ventilation system to discharge all exhaust gas safely outside.

▶ **TASK** Evacuate and dehydrate an A/C system. **AED 6.3**

Time off_____

Time on_____

Student Instructions: Read through the entire procedure prior to starting. Prepare your workspace and any tools or parts that may be needed to complete the task. When directed by your supervisor/instructor, begin the procedure to complete the task, and comment or check the box as each step is finished. Track your time on this procedure for later comparison to the standard completion time (i.e., "flat rate" or customer pay time).

Total time_____

Procedure	Step Completed
1. Using the appropriate service information, state and federal requirements, and safety data sheets (SDS) for the types of refrigerant in your workshop, research and record how to handle, label, and store refrigerant:	☐
2. Evacuate, label, and store refrigerant.	
a. Obtain a US Department of Transportation (DOT)–approved refrigerant container. There are several sizes, from 15- to 500-lb (6.8- to 226.8-kg) tanks. The recommended size for most repair shops is a 60-lb (27.2-kg) container.	☐
b. Connect the A/C machine's hoses to the tank with the appropriate adapters in an A/C retrofit kit. Use the high- or low-side adapters from the retrofit kit to connect the quick chuck fittings to the $\frac{1}{4}$-in (6.4-mm) Society of Automotive Engineers (SAE) fittings on the tank.	☐
c. Open the tank valves. Open the quick chuck Schrader depressors on the quick chucks. At this point, you are ready to charge the tank just as you would charge a vehicle.	☐
d. Use the keypad on the A/C machine and select the "charge" mode. Determine the amount of refrigerant you want to evacuate from the piece of equipment, then enter that weight into the recovery machine.	☐
e. Begin the process of evacuating the system. Do not fill the tank to more than 60% of the total gross capacity of the tank. The total gross capacity is written on the tank, and the technician must mathematically determine what 60% of that capacity is.	☐
f. After the tank is filled with refrigerant, label the tank with the type and weight of the refrigerant. By labeling the tank with the type and weight, the next technician can determine the type and whether there is enough free space to charge any more refrigerant into the tank.	☐
g. Close the tank valves and disconnect the hoses from the tank.	☐
h. Store the refrigerant in a cool, dry place where the sunlight cannot directly hit it.	☐
3. Identify the type of equipment to be used to properly dehydrate the A/C system (vacuum pump and gauge set or A/C machine):	☐

	Step Completed
4. Once identified, record the procedure for properly dehydrating the A/C system, then perform the procedure:	☐
a. Was the task successful? Yes ☐ No ☐	☐
b. If no, list your recommendations for rectification:	☐
5. Return the machine to its beginning condition and return any tools you used to their proper locations.	☐
6. Discuss your findings with your supervisor/instructor.	☐

Non-Task-Specific Evaluation	Step Completed
1. Tools and equipment were used as directed and returned in good working order.	☐
2. Complied with all general and task-specific safety standards, including proper use of any personal protective equipment (PPE).	☐
3. Completed the task in an appropriate time frame (recommendation: 1.5 or 2 times the flat rate).	☐
4. Left the workspace clean and orderly.	☐
5. Cared for customer property and returned it undamaged.	☐

Student signature _____ Date _____

Comments:

[ ]

Have your supervisor/instructor verify satisfactory completion of this procedure, any observations made, and any necessary action(s) recommended.

Evaluation Instructions: The scoring box below is intended to act as a guide for both student and supervisor/instructor. Each criterion listed will help students to understand what is expected of them and help supervisors/instructors to articulate the level of success at a particular task. The scoring is set up to allow a second attempt at each task (see the Test and Retest columns). Scoring is designed only to award students points for task criteria that were completed correctly. Points are lost for failure to complete the employability requirements (see Non-Task-Specific criteria). When all criteria are evaluated, tally the points for a total at the bottom of each column.

Tasksheet Scoring

	Test		Retest	
Evaluation Items	**Pass**	**Fail**	**Pass**	**Fail**
Task-Specific Evaluation	**(1 pt)**	**(0 pts)**	**(1 pt)**	**(0 pts)**
Student accurately recorded how to handle, label, and store the refrigerant.				
Student properly evacuated, labeled, and stored the refrigerant.				
Student accurately identified the equipment to use to dehydrate the A/C system.				
Student accurately recorded the procedure for dehydrating the A/C system, then properly performed the procedure.				
Non-Task-Specific Evaluation	**(0 pts)**	**(−1 pt)**	**(0 pts)**	**(−1 pt)**
Student successfully completed at least three of the non-task-specific steps.				
Student successfully completed all five of the non-task-specific steps.				
Total Score: <total # of points / 4 = %>				

Supervisor/Instructor:

Supervisor/instructor signature _____ Date _____

Comments:

Retest supervisor/instructor signature _____ Date _____

Comments:

CDX Tasksheet Number: 6.3007

Student/Intern Information

Name _____ Date _____ Class _____

Machine, Customer, and Service Information

Machine used for this activity:

Make _____ Model _____

Hours _____ Serial Number _____

Materials Required
- Vehicle with possible air-conditioning (A/C) concerns
- Vehicle manufacturer's service information
- Manufacturer-specific tools, depending on the concern/procedure(s)

Task-Specific Safety Considerations
- This task may require test driving the vehicle on the school grounds or on a hoist, both of which carry severe risks. Attempt this task only with full permission from your supervisor/instructor and follow all the guidelines exactly.
- Comply with personal and environmental safety practices associated with clothing; eye protection; hand tools; power equipment; proper ventilation; and the handling, storage, and disposal of chemicals/materials in accordance with federal, state, and local regulations.
- Always wear the correct protective eyewear and clothing and use the appropriate safety equipment, as well as fender covers, seat protectors, and floor mat protectors.
- Make sure you understand and observe all legislative and personal safety procedures when carrying out practical assignments. If you are unsure of what these are, ask your supervisor/instructor.
- While working on the vehicle, wheel chocks must be placed on both sides of one set of tires or as directed by your supervisor/instructor.
- When running any vehicles in the shop, make sure you use the shop's exhaust ventilation system to discharge all exhaust gas safely outside.

▶ **TASK** Recover and charge an A/C system. _____ **AED 6.3**

Time off_____

Time on_____

Student Instructions: Read through the entire procedure prior to starting. Prepare your workspace and any tools or parts that may be needed to complete the task. When directed by your supervisor/instructor, begin the procedure to complete the task, and comment or check the box as each step is finished. Track your time on this procedure for later comparison to the standard completion time (i.e., "flat rate" or customer pay time).

Total time_____

Procedure	Step Completed
1. Research how to properly recover and charge the A/C system refrigerant.	☐
2. Identify the A/C system refrigerant and record it below:	☐
a. Locate the high- and low-side pressure service ports. Connect the refrigerant identifier to the low side of the A/C system and open the service valve. Follow the prompts on the refrigerant identifier, and record the refrigerant type and amount of air, if any: Refrigerant type _____ Amount of air _____	☐
3. Ensure that the refrigerant type listed on the under-the-hood sticker matches that on the refrigerant identifier. Turn off the service valve and disconnect the refrigerant identifier.	☐
4. Recover, evacuate, and charge the A/C system.	
a. Start the reclaim process by hooking up the A/C machine to the low- and high-side service ports.	☐
b. Open the valves and turn on the A/C machine. Select the reclaim mode and follow the prompts on the screen.	☐
c. When the refrigerant has been removed, record the amount of refrigerant removed and compare it to the amount listed on the sticker or in the service information:	☐
5. The A/C machine will drain any excess oil that might have been reclaimed. The refrigerant oil that is drained should be minimal or nonexistent. Record the amount of oil that is discharged and install the same amount if the total oil removed is less than 1 ounce (29.6 mL). If the oil drain discharges more than 1 ounce, the A/C system will need to be flushed using a flush machine, removing all of the oil from the system.	☐
6. Using either a recovery machine or a vacuum pump and gauges, dehydrate the system. Watch the vacuum gauge to ensure that it does not bleed up. If no leaks appear after 5 minutes, install the required oil. Open the oiling valve as recommended by the A/C machine's service information.	☐
7. Shut off the valve when the proper amount of oil has been added. Recharge the A/C system with the amount of refrigerant noted on the under-the-hood A/C sticker or in the service information.	☐
8. Return the vehicle to its beginning condition and return any tools you used to their proper locations.	☐
9. Discuss your findings with your supervisor/instructor.	☐

Non-Task-Specific Evaluation	Step Completed
1. Tools and equipment were used as directed and returned in good working order.	☐
2. Complied with all general and task-specific safety standards, including proper use of any personal protective equipment (PPE).	☐
3. Completed the task in an appropriate time frame (recommendation: 1.5 or 2 times the flat rate).	☐
4. Left the workspace clean and orderly.	☐
5. Cared for customer property and returned it undamaged.	☐

Student signature _____ Date _____

Comments:

Have your supervisor/instructor verify satisfactory completion of this procedure, any observations made,

and any necessary action(s) recommended.

Evaluation Instructions: The scoring box below is intended to act as a guide for both student and supervisor/instructor. Each criterion listed will help students to understand what is expected of them and help supervisors/instructors to articulate the level of success at a particular task. The scoring is set up to allow a second attempt at each task (see the Test and Retest columns). Scoring is designed only to award students points for task criteria that were completed correctly. Points are lost for failure to complete the employability requirements (see Non-Task-Specific criteria). When all criteria are evaluated, tally the points for a total at the bottom of each column.

Tasksheet Scoring

Evaluation Items	Test		Retest	
	Pass	**Fail**	**Pass**	**Fail**
Task-Specific Evaluation	**(1 pt)**	**(0 pts)**	**(1 pt)**	**(0 pts)**
Student accurately identified the A/C system's refrigerant.				
Student properly recovered, evacuated, and charged the A/C system.				
Student accurately recorded the amount of discharged oil and flushed the A/C system if necessary.				
Student properly dehydrated the A/C system, installed the oil, and recharged the system.				
Non-Task-Specific Evaluation	**(0 pts)**	**(−1 pt)**	**(0 pts)**	**(−1 pt)**
Student successfully completed at least three of the non-task-specific steps.				
Student successfully completed all five of the non-task-specific steps.				
Total Score: <total # of points / 4 = %>				

Supervisor/Instructor:

Supervisor/instructor signature _____ Date _____

Comments:

Retest supervisor/instructor signature _____ Date _____

Comments:

CDX Tasksheet Number: 6.3010

Student/Intern Information

Name _____ Date _____ Class _____

Machine, Customer, and Service Information

Machine used for this activity:

Make _____ Model _____

Hours _____ Serial Number _____

Materials Required

- Vehicle with possible air-conditioning (A/C) concerns
- Vehicle manufacturer's service information
- Manufacturer-specific tools, depending on the concern/procedure(s)

Task-Specific Safety Considerations

- This task may require test driving the vehicle on the school grounds or on a hoist, both of which carry severe risks. Attempt this task only with full permission from your supervisor/instructor and follow all the guidelines exactly.
- Comply with personal and environmental safety practices associated with clothing; eye protection; hand tools; power equipment; proper ventilation; and the handling, storage, and disposal of chemicals/materials in accordance with federal, state, and local regulations.
- Always wear the correct protective eyewear and clothing and use the appropriate safety equipment, as well as fender covers, seat protectors, and floor mat protectors.
- Make sure you understand and observe all legislative and personal safety procedures when carrying out practical assignments. If you are unsure of what these are, ask your supervisor/instructor.
- While working on the vehicle, wheel chocks must be placed on both sides of one set of tires or as directed by your supervisor/instructor.
- When running any vehicles in the shop, make sure you use the shop's exhaust ventilation system to discharge all exhaust gas safely outside.

▶ **TASK** Add oil, dye, and refrigerants to an A/C system.

AED
6.3

Time off_____

Time on_____

Student Instructions: Read through the entire procedure prior to starting. Prepare your workspace and any tools or parts that may be needed to complete the task. When directed by your supervisor/instructor, begin the procedure to complete the task, and comment or check the box as each step is finished. Track your time on this procedure for later comparison to the standard completion time (i.e., "flat rate" or customer pay time).

Total time_____

Procedure	Step Completed
(**Note:** Pressure gauge sets are determined based on the refrigerant type used. High- and low-pressure side gauges are further identified by the size of the coupler, with high and low sides being of different sizes.)	
1. Identify the type of service valve:	☐
2. Before attaching hoses to the test ports, make sure the service knobs are in the closed position. Then attach the hoses to the proper test ports.	☐
3. Record the procedure for purging service tool hoses to prevent cross-contamination and the introduction of noncondensables:	☐
a. Have your supervisor/instructor approve your recording of the procedure above. Supervisor's/instructor's initials: _____	☐
b. Once Step 3 is approved, purge the service tool hoses.	☐
4. Record the procedure for adding refrigerant to the system, then perform the task:	☐
a. Was the refrigerant successfully added? Yes ☐ No ☐	☐
b. If no, list your recommendations for rectification:	☐
5. Record the procedure for adding refrigerant oil to the system, then perform the task:	☐
a. Was the refrigerant oil successfully added? Yes ☐ No ☐	☐

b. If no, list your recommendations for rectification:	☐
6. Record the procedure for adding refrigerant dye to the system, then perform the task:	☐
a. Was the refrigerant dye successfully added? Yes ☐ No ☐	☐
b. If no, list your recommendations for rectification:	☐
7. Turn off the machine and allow the pressures to stabilize. Following proper safety and environmental procedures, remove the A/C service hoses.	☐
8. Discuss your findings with your supervisor/instructor.	☐

Non-Task-Specific Evaluation	Step Completed
1. Tools and equipment were used as directed and returned in good working order.	☐
2. Complied with all general and task-specific safety standards, including proper use of any personal protective equipment (PPE).	☐
3. Completed the task in an appropriate time frame (recommendation: 1.5 or 2 times the flat rate).	☐
4. Left the workspace clean and orderly.	☐
5. Cared for customer property and returned it undamaged.	☐

Student signature _____ Date _____

Comments:

Have your supervisor/instructor verify satisfactory completion of this procedure, any observations made, and any necessary action(s) recommended.

Evaluation Instructions: The scoring box below is intended to act as a guide for both student and supervisor/instructor. Each criterion listed will help students to understand what is expected of them and help supervisors/instructors to articulate the level of success at a particular task. The scoring is set up to allow a second attempt at each task (see the Test and Retest columns). Scoring is designed only to award students points for task criteria that were completed correctly. Points are lost for failure to complete the employability requirements (see Non-Task-Specific criteria). When all criteria are evaluated, tally the points for a total at the bottom of each column.

Tasksheet Scoring

	Test		Retest	
Evaluation Items	**Pass**	**Fail**	**Pass**	**Fail**
Task-Specific Evaluation	**(1 pt)**	**(0 pts)**	**(1 pt)**	**(0 pts)**
Student accurately recorded the procedure for purging service tool hoses, then properly performed the purge.				
Student accurately recorded the procedure for adding refrigerant to the system, then properly performed the task.				
Student accurately recorded the procedure for adding refrigerant oil to the system, then properly performed the task.				
Student accurately recorded the procedure for adding refrigerant dye to the system, then properly performed the task.				
Non-Task-Specific Evaluation	**(0 pts)**	**(−1 pt)**	**(0 pts)**	**(−1 pt)**
Student successfully completed at least three of the non-task-specific steps.				
Student successfully completed all five of the non-task-specific steps.				
Total Score: <total # of points / 4 = %>				

Supervisor/Instructor:

Supervisor/instructor signature _____ Date _____

Comments:

Retest supervisor/instructor signature _____ Date _____

Comments:

Chapter 52: Testing, Troubleshooting, Diagnosing, and Repairing A/C Systems

Learning Objective/Task	CDX Tasksheet Number	AED Reference Number
• Perform a visual inspection of an A/C system.	6.4002	AED 6.4
• Identify the type of A/C system (e.g., an H-block TXV [receiver/drier] or a metered orifice [accumulator]).	6.4003	AED 6.4
• Identify climate control systems and components.	6.4004	AED 6.4
• Troubleshoot A/C systems.	6.4005	AED 6.4
• Troubleshoot metering devices and limit switch malfunctions.	6.4006	AED 6.4
• Detect refrigerant leaks.	6.4007	AED 6.4
• Determine contaminants in a system due to system component failure.	6.4008	AED 6.4
• Replace or repair A/C system components.	6.4009	AED 6.4
• Test the cooling capabilities of an A/C system.	6.4010	AED 6.4

Materials Required

- Vehicle with possible air-conditioning (A/C) concerns
- Vehicle manufacturer's service information
- Manufacturer-specific tools, depending on the concern/procedure(s)

Safety Considerations

- This task may require test driving the vehicle on the school grounds or on a hoist, both of which carry severe risks. Attempt this task only with full permission from your supervisor/instructor and follow all the guidelines exactly.
- Comply with personal and environmental safety practices associated with clothing; eye protection; hand tools; power equipment; proper ventilation; and the handling, storage, and disposal of chemicals/materials in accordance with federal, state, and local regulations.
- Always wear the correct protective eyewear and clothing and use the appropriate safety equipment, as well as fender covers, seat protectors, and floor mat protectors.
- Make sure you understand and observe all legislative and personal safety procedures when carrying out practical assignments. If you are unsure of what these are, ask your supervisor/instructor.
- While working on the vehicle, wheel chocks must be placed on both sides of one set of tires or as directed by your supervisor/instructor.
- When running any vehicles in the shop, make sure you use the shop's exhaust ventilation system to discharge all exhaust gas safely outside.

CDX Tasksheet Number: 6.4002

Student/Intern Information

Name _____ Date _____ Class _____

Machine, Customer, and Service Information

Machine used for this activity:

Make _____ Model _____

Hours _____ Serial Number _____

Materials Required

- Vehicle with possible air-conditioning (A/C) concerns
- Vehicle manufacturer's service information
- Manufacturer-specific tools, depending on the concern/procedure(s)

Task-Specific Safety Considerations

- This task may require test driving the vehicle on the school grounds or on a hoist, both of which carry severe risks. Attempt this task only with full permission from your supervisor/instructor and follow all the guidelines exactly.
- Comply with personal and environmental safety practices associated with clothing; eye protection; hand tools; power equipment; proper ventilation; and the handling, storage, and disposal of chemicals/materials in accordance with federal, state, and local regulations.
- Always wear the correct protective eyewear and clothing and use the appropriate safety equipment, as well as fender covers, seat protectors, and floor mat protectors.
- Make sure you understand and observe all legislative and personal safety procedures when carrying out practical assignments. If you are unsure of what these are, ask your supervisor/instructor.
- While working on the vehicle, wheel chocks must be placed on both sides of one set of tires or as directed by your supervisor/instructor.
- When running any vehicles in the shop, make sure you use the shop's exhaust ventilation system to discharge all exhaust gas safely outside.

▶ **TASK** Perform a visual inspection of an A/C system.

Student Instructions: Read through the entire procedure prior to starting. Prepare your workspace and any tools or parts that may be needed to complete the task. When directed by your supervisor/instructor, begin the procedure to complete the task, and comment or check the box as each step is finished. Track your time on this procedure for later comparison to the standard completion time (i.e., "flat rate" or customer pay time).

Time off_____

Time on_____

Total time_____

Procedure	Step Completed
1. Check for loose or missing service caps.	☐
a. Note any problems you found below:	☐
b. If problems exist, list your recommendations for rectification:	☐
2. Inspect hoses and connections for signs of leaks (e.g., oil spots).	☐
a. Note any problems you found below:	☐
b. If problems exist, list your recommendations for rectification:	☐
3. Inspect the evaporator drain tube for blockages.	☐
a. Note any problems you found below:	☐
b. If problems exist, list your recommendations for rectification:	☐
4. Check the condition and proper tension of the A/C pump drive belt.	☐
a. Meets the manufacturer's specifications: Yes ☐ No ☐	☐
b. If no, list your recommendations for rectification:	☐

5. Check the exterior of the condenser for blockages or damage.	☐
a. Note any problems you found below:	☐
b. If problems exist, list your recommendations for rectification:	☐
6. Check the condition of the cabin air filter.	☐
a. Note any problems you found below:	☐
b. If problems exist, list your recommendations for rectification:	☐
7. Using a refrigerant identifier, determine the refrigerant type:	☐
8. Discuss your findings with your supervisor/instructor.	☐

Non-Task-Specific Evaluation	Step Completed
1. Tools and equipment were used as directed and returned in good working order.	☐
2. Complied with all general and task-specific safety standards, including proper use of any personal protective equipment (PPE).	☐
3. Completed the task in an appropriate time frame (recommendation: 1.5 or 2 times the flat rate).	☐
4. Left the workspace clean and orderly.	☐
5. Cared for customer property and returned it undamaged.	☐

Student signature _____ Date _____

Comments:

[ ]

Have your supervisor/instructor verify satisfactory completion of this procedure, any observations made, and any necessary action(s) recommended.

Evaluation Instructions: The scoring box below is intended to act as a guide for both student and supervisor/instructor. Each criterion listed will help students to understand what is expected of them and help supervisors/instructors to articulate the level of success at a particular task. The scoring is set up to allow a second attempt at each task (see the Test and Retest columns). Scoring is designed only to award students points for task criteria that were completed correctly. Points are lost for failure to complete the employability requirements (see Non-Task-Specific criteria). When all criteria are evaluated, tally the points for a total at the bottom of each column.

Tasksheet Scoring

Evaluation Items	Test		Retest	
	Pass	**Fail**	**Pass**	**Fail**
Task-Specific Evaluation	**(1 pt)**	**(0 pts)**	**(1 pt)**	**(0 pts)**
Student properly checked for loose/missing service caps and properly inspected hoses and connections for signs of leaks.				
Student properly inspected the evaporator drain tube and properly checked the condition and tension of the A/C pump drive belt.				
Student properly checked the exterior of the condenser and the condition of the cabin air filter.				
Student accurately identified the refrigerant type.				
Non-Task-Specific Evaluation	**(0 pts)**	**(−1 pt)**	**(0 pts)**	**(−1 pt)**
Student successfully completed at least three of the non-task-specific steps.				
Student successfully completed all five of the non-task-specific steps.				
Total Score: <total # of points / 4 = %>				

Supervisor/Instructor:

Supervisor/instructor signature _____ Date _____

Comments:

Retest supervisor/instructor signature _____ Date _____

Comments:

CDX Tasksheet Number: 6.4003

Student/Intern Information

Name _____ Date _____ Class _____

Machine, Customer, and Service Information

Machine used for this activity:

Make _____ Model _____

Hours _____ Serial Number _____

Materials Required

- Vehicle with possible air-conditioning (A/C) concerns
- Vehicle manufacturer's service information
- Manufacturer-specific tools, depending on the concern/procedure(s)

Task-Specific Safety Considerations

- This task may require test driving the vehicle on the school grounds or on a hoist, both of which carry severe risks. Attempt this task only with full permission from your supervisor/instructor and follow all the guidelines exactly.
- Comply with personal and environmental safety practices associated with clothing; eye protection; hand tools; power equipment; proper ventilation; and the handling, storage, and disposal of chemicals/materials in accordance with federal, state, and local regulations.
- Always wear the correct protective eyewear and clothing and use the appropriate safety equipment, as well as fender covers, seat protectors, and floor mat protectors.
- Make sure you understand and observe all legislative and personal safety procedures when carrying out practical assignments. If you are unsure of what these are, ask your supervisor/instructor.
- While working on the vehicle, wheel chocks must be placed on both sides of one set of tires or as directed by your supervisor/instructor.
- When running any vehicles in the shop, make sure you use the shop's exhaust ventilation system to discharge all exhaust gas safely outside.

▶ **TASK** Identify the type of A/C system (e.g., an H-block TXV [receiver/drier] or a metered orifice [accumulator]).

AED 6.4

Time off_____

Student Instructions: Read through the entire procedure prior to starting. Prepare your workspace and any tools or parts that may be needed to complete the task. When directed by your supervisor/instructor, begin the procedure to complete the task, and comment or check the box as each step is finished. Track your time on this procedure for later comparison to the standard completion time (i.e., "flat rate" or customer pay time).

Time on_____

Total time_____

Procedure	Step Completed
1. Using available service literature, determine the type of A/C system and refrigerant charge.	☐
a. H-block TXV (receiver/drier) ☐ Metered orifice (accumulator) ☐	☐
b. Refrigerant charge	☐
2. Once identified in the service literature, confirm on the applicable machine.	☐
a. H-block TXV (receiver/drier) ☐ Metered orifice (accumulator) ☐	☐
b. Refrigerant charge shown on label	☐
3. Discuss your findings with your supervisor/instructor.	☐

Non-Task-Specific Evaluation	Step Completed
1. Tools and equipment were used as directed and returned in good working order.	☐
2. Complied with all general and task-specific safety standards, including proper use of any personal protective equipment (PPE).	☐
3. Completed the task in an appropriate time frame (recommendation: 1.5 or 2 times the flat rate).	☐
4. Left the workspace clean and orderly.	☐
5. Cared for customer property and returned it undamaged.	☐

Student signature _____ Date _____

Comments:

Have your supervisor/instructor verify satisfactory completion of this procedure, any observations made, and any necessary action(s) recommended.

Evaluation Instructions: The scoring box below is intended to act as a guide for both student and supervisor/instructor. Each criterion listed will help students to understand what is expected of them and help supervisors/instructors to articulate the level of success at a particular task. The scoring is set up to allow a second attempt at each task (see the Test and Retest columns). Scoring is designed only to award students points for task criteria that were completed correctly. Points are lost for failure to complete the employability requirements (see Non-Task-Specific criteria). When all criteria are evaluated, tally the points for a total at the bottom of each column.

Tasksheet Scoring

Evaluation Items	Test		Retest	
	Pass	Fail	Pass	Fail
Task-Specific Evaluation	**(1 pt)**	**(0 pts)**	**(1 pt)**	**(0 pts)**
Student accurately determined the type of A/C system using the service information.				
Student accurately determined the refrigerant charge using the service information.				
Student accurately confirmed the type of A/C system.				
Student accurately confirmed the refrigerant charge.				
Non-Task-Specific Evaluation	**(0 pts)**	**(−1 pt)**	**(0 pts)**	**(−1 pt)**
Student successfully completed at least three of the non-task-specific steps.				
Student successfully completed all five of the non-task-specific steps.				
Total Score: <total # of points / 4 = %>				

Supervisor/Instructor:

Supervisor/instructor signature _____ Date _____

Comments:

Retest supervisor/instructor signature _____ Date _____

Comments:

CDX Tasksheet Number: 6.4004

Student/Intern Information

Name _____ Date _____ Class _____

Machine, Customer, and Service Information

Machine used for this activity:

Make _____ Model _____

Hours _____ Serial Number _____

Materials Required

- Vehicle with possible air-conditioning (A/C) concerns
- Vehicle manufacturer's service information
- Manufacturer-specific tools, depending on the concern/procedure(s)

Task-Specific Safety Considerations

- This task may require test driving the vehicle on the school grounds or on a hoist, both of which carry severe risks. Attempt this task only with full permission from your supervisor/instructor and follow all the guidelines exactly.
- Comply with personal and environmental safety practices associated with clothing; eye protection; hand tools; power equipment; proper ventilation; and the handling, storage, and disposal of chemicals/materials in accordance with federal, state, and local regulations.
- Always wear the correct protective eyewear and clothing and use the appropriate safety equipment, as well as fender covers, seat protectors, and floor mat protectors.
- Make sure you understand and observe all legislative and personal safety procedures when carrying out practical assignments. If you are unsure of what these are, ask your supervisor/instructor.
- While working on the vehicle, wheel chocks must be placed on both sides of one set of tires or as directed by your supervisor/instructor.
- When running any vehicles in the shop, make sure you use the shop's exhaust ventilation system to discharge all exhaust gas safely outside.

▶ TASK Identify climate control systems and components. _____ **AED 6.4**

Time off_____

Time on_____

Student Instructions: Read through the entire procedure prior to starting. Prepare your workspace and any tools or parts that may be needed to complete the task. When directed by your supervisor/instructor, begin the procedure to complete the task, and comment or check the box as each step is finished. Track your time on this procedure for later comparison to the standard completion time (i.e., "flat rate" or customer pay time).

Total time_____

Procedure	Step Completed
1. With your supervisor/instructor present, identify the following components and describe their functions.	☐
a. A/C compressor	☐
b. A/C drier or accumulator	☐
c. Restricted orifice or TXV	☐
d. Service fittings	☐
e. Low-side hoses	☐
f. High-side hoses	☐
g. Evaporator	☐
h. Condenser	☐
i. Heater core and hoses	☐

j. High-pressure cutout switch	☐
k. Low-pressure switch	☐
l. Cycling switch	☐
m. Water pump	☐
n. Heater core	☐
o. Coolant control valve(s)	☐
p. Coolant lines	☐
q. Engine thermostat	☐
r. Temperature control valve	☐
2. Discuss your findings with your supervisor/instructor.	☐

Non-Task-Specific Evaluation	Step Completed
1. Tools and equipment were used as directed and returned in good working order.	☐
2. Complied with all general and task-specific safety standards, including proper use of any personal protective equipment (PPE).	☐
3. Completed the task in an appropriate time frame (recommendation: 1.5 or 2 times the flat rate).	☐
4. Left the workspace clean and orderly.	☐
5. Cared for customer property and returned it undamaged.	☐

Student signature _____ Date _____

Comments:

Have your supervisor/instructor verify satisfactory completion of this procedure, any observations made, and any necessary action(s) recommended.

Evaluation Instructions: The scoring box below is intended to act as a guide for both student and supervisor/instructor. Each criterion listed will help students to understand what is expected of them and help supervisors/instructors to articulate the level of success at a particular task. The scoring is set up to allow a second attempt at each task (see the Test and Retest columns). Scoring is designed only to award students points for task criteria that were completed correctly. Points are lost for failure to complete the employability requirements (see Non-Task-Specific criteria). When all criteria are evaluated, tally the points for a total at the bottom of each column.

Tasksheet Scoring

Evaluation Items	Test		Retest	
	Pass	**Fail**	**Pass**	**Fail**
Task-Specific Evaluation	**(1 pt)**	**(0 pts)**	**(1 pt)**	**(0 pts)**
Student accurately identified and described the functions of at least four components.				
Student accurately identified and described the functions of at least eight components.				
Student accurately identified and described the functions of at least 13 components.				
Student accurately identified and described the functions of all 18 components.				
Non-Task-Specific Evaluation	**(0 pts)**	**(−1 pt)**	**(0 pts)**	**(−1 pt)**
Student successfully completed at least three of the non-task-specific steps.				
Student successfully completed all five of the non-task-specific steps.				
Total Score: <total # of points / 4 = %>				

Supervisor/Instructor:

Supervisor/instructor signature _____ Date _____

Comments:

Retest supervisor/instructor signature _____ Date _____

Comments:

CDX Tasksheet Number: 6.4005

Student/Intern Information

Name _____ Date _____ Class _____

Machine, Customer, and Service Information

Machine used for this activity:

Make _____ Model _____

Hours _____ Serial Number _____

Materials Required
- Vehicle with possible air-conditioning (A/C) concerns
- Vehicle manufacturer's service information
- Manufacturer-specific tools, depending on the concern/procedure(s)

Task-Specific Safety Considerations
- This task may require test driving the vehicle on the school grounds or on a hoist, both of which carry severe risks. Attempt this task only with full permission from your supervisor/instructor and follow all the guidelines exactly.
- Comply with personal and environmental safety practices associated with clothing; eye protection; hand tools; power equipment; proper ventilation; and the handling, storage, and disposal of chemicals/materials in accordance with federal, state, and local regulations.
- Always wear the correct protective eyewear and clothing and use the appropriate safety equipment, as well as fender covers, seat protectors, and floor mat protectors.
- Make sure you understand and observe all legislative and personal safety procedures when carrying out practical assignments. If you are unsure of what these are, ask your supervisor/instructor.
- While working on the vehicle, wheel chocks must be placed on both sides of one set of tires or as directed by your supervisor/instructor.
- When running any vehicles in the shop, make sure you use the shop's exhaust ventilation system to discharge all exhaust gas safely outside.

▶ **TASK** Troubleshoot A/C systems. _____ **AED 6.4**

Time off_____

Time on_____

Student Instructions: Read through the entire procedure prior to starting. Prepare your workspace and any tools or parts that may be needed to complete the task. When directed by your supervisor/instructor, begin the procedure to complete the task, and comment or check the box as each step is finished. Track your time on this procedure for later comparison to the standard completion time (i.e., "flat rate" or customer pay time).

Total time_____

Procedure	Step Completed
1. Using an infrared thermometer, record the temperature at the following locations and, using the appropriate P-T chart, convert the temperature to pressure.	☐
2. Evaporator inlet Temperature _____° F Converted pressure _____ psi	☐
a. Meets the manufacturer's specifications: Yes ☐ No ☐	☐
b. If no, list your recommendations for rectification:	☐
3. Evaporator outlet Temperature _____° F Converted pressure _____ psi	☐
a. Meets the manufacturer's specifications: Yes ☐ No ☐	☐
b. If no, list your recommendations for rectification:	☐
4. Condenser inlet Temperature _____° F Converted pressure _____ psi	☐
a. Meets the manufacturer's specifications: Yes ☐ No ☐	☐
b. If no, list your recommendations for rectification:	☐

5. Condenser outlet	☐
Temperature _____° F	
Converted pressure _____ psi	
a. Meets the manufacturer's specifications:	☐
Yes ☐ No ☐	
b. If no, list your recommendations for rectification:	☐
6. Receiver drier or accumulator inlet	☐
Temperature _____° F	
Converted pressure _____ psi	
a. Meets the manufacturer's specifications:	☐
Yes ☐ No ☐	
b. If no, list your recommendations for rectification:	☐
7. Receiver drier or accumulator outlet	☐
Temperature _____° F	
Converted pressure _____ psi	
a. Meets the manufacturer's specifications:	☐
Yes ☐ No ☐	
b. If no, list your recommendations for rectification:	☐
8. Restricted orifice or H-block TXV inlet	☐
Temperature _____° F	
Converted pressure _____ psi	
a. Meets the manufacturer's specifications:	☐
Yes ☐ No ☐	
b. If no, list your recommendations for rectification:	☐

9. Restricted orifice or H-block TXV outlet Temperature _____ ° F Converted pressure _____ psi	☐
a. Meets the manufacturer's specifications: Yes ☐ No ☐	☐
b. If no, list your recommendations for rectification:	☐
10. Compressor inlet Temperature _____ ° F Converted pressure _____ psi	☐
a. Meets the manufacturer's specifications: Yes ☐ No ☐	☐
b. If no, list your recommendations for rectification:	☐
11. Compressor outlet Temperature _____ ° F Converted pressure _____ psi	☐
a. Meets the manufacturer's specifications: Yes ☐ No ☐	☐
b. If no, list your recommendations for rectification:	☐
12. Discuss your findings with your supervisor/instructor.	☐

Non-Task-Specific Evaluation	Step Completed
1. Tools and equipment were used as directed and returned in good working order.	☐
2. Complied with all general and task-specific safety standards, including proper use of any personal protective equipment (PPE).	☐
3. Completed the task in an appropriate time frame (recommendation: 1.5 or 2 times the flat rate).	☐
4. Left the workspace clean and orderly.	☐
5. Cared for customer property and returned it undamaged.	☐

Student signature _____ Date _____

Comments:

Have your supervisor/instructor verify satisfactory completion of this procedure, any observations made, and any necessary action(s) recommended.

Evaluation Instructions: The scoring box below is intended to act as a guide for both student and supervisor/instructor. Each criterion listed will help students to understand what is expected of them and help supervisors/instructors to articulate the level of success at a particular task. The scoring is set up to allow a second attempt at each task (see the Test and Retest columns). Scoring is designed only to award students points for task criteria that were completed correctly. Points are lost for failure to complete the employability requirements (see Non-Task-Specific criteria). When all criteria are evaluated, tally the points for a total at the bottom of each column.

Tasksheet Scoring

Evaluation Items	Test		Retest	
	Pass	Fail	Pass	Fail
Task-Specific Evaluation	**(1 pt)**	**(0 pts)**	**(1 pt)**	**(0 pts)**
Student properly measured the temperature for at least three of the locations.				
Student properly measured the temperature for at least six of the locations.				
Student properly measured the temperature for all 10 locations.				
Student accurately converted all temperatures to pressure.				
Non-Task-Specific Evaluation	**(0 pts)**	**(−1 pt)**	**(0 pts)**	**(−1 pt)**
Student successfully completed at least three of the non-task-specific steps.				
Student successfully completed all five of the non-task-specific steps.				
Total Score: <total # of points / 4 = %>				

CDX Tasksheet Number: 6.4006

Student/Intern Information

Name _____ Date _____ Class _____

Machine, Customer, and Service Information

Machine used for this activity:

Make _____ Model _____

Hours _____ Serial Number _____

Task-Specific Safety Considerations

- This task may require test driving the vehicle on the school grounds or on a hoist, both of which carry severe risks. Attempt this task only with full permission from your supervisor/instructor and follow all the guidelines exactly.
- Comply with personal and environmental safety practices associated with clothing; eye protection; hand tools; power equipment; proper ventilation; and the handling, storage, and disposal of chemicals/materials in accordance with federal, state, and local regulations.
- Always wear the correct protective eyewear and clothing and use the appropriate safety equipment, as well as fender covers, seat protectors, and floor mat protectors.
- Make sure you understand and observe all legislative and personal safety procedures when carrying out practical assignments. If you are unsure of what these are, ask your supervisor/instructor.
- While working on the vehicle, wheel chocks must be placed on both sides of one set of tires or as directed by your supervisor/instructor.
- When running any vehicles in the shop, make sure you use the shop's exhaust ventilation system to discharge all exhaust gas safely outside.

▶ **TASK** Troubleshoot metering devices and limit switch malfunctions. **AED 6.4**

Time off_____

Time on_____

Student Instructions: Read through the entire procedure prior to starting. Prepare your workspace and any tools or parts that may be needed to complete the task. When directed by your supervisor/instructor, begin the procedure to complete the task, and comment or check the box as each step is finished. Track your time on this procedure for later comparison to the standard completion time (i.e., "flat rate" or customer pay time).

Total time_____

Procedure	Step Completed
1. Measure the temperature at the restricted orifice or H-block TXV inlet, then convert it to pressure: Temperature _____ ° F Converted pressure _____ psi	☐
a. Meets the manufacturer's specifications: Yes ☐ No ☐	☐
b. If no, list your recommendations for rectification:	☐
2. Measure the temperature at the restricted orifice or H-block TXV outlet, then convert it to pressure: Temperature _____ ° F Converted pressure _____ psi	☐
a. Meets the manufacturer's specifications: Yes ☐ No ☐	☐
b. If no, list your recommendations for rectification:	☐
3. Check the supply voltage and operation of the high-pressure cutout switch and record it below: _____ vdc	☐
a. Meets the manufacturer's specifications: Yes ☐ No ☐	☐
b. If no, list your recommendations for rectification:	☐
4. Check the supply voltage and operation of the low-pressure/cycling switch and record it below: _____ vdc	☐
a. Meets the manufacturer's specifications: Yes ☐ No ☐	☐
b. If no, list your recommendations for rectification:	☐

	Step Completed
5. Check the supply voltage and operation of the binary/trinary switch and record it below: _____ vdc	☐
a. Meets the manufacturer's specifications: Yes ☐ No ☐	☐
b. If no, list your recommendations for rectification:	☐
6. Discuss your findings with your supervisor/instructor.	☐

Non-Task-Specific Evaluation	Step Completed
1. Tools and equipment were used as directed and returned in good working order.	☐
2. Complied with all general and task-specific safety standards, including proper use of any personal protective equipment (PPE).	☐
3. Completed the task in an appropriate time frame (recommendation: 1.5 or 2 times the flat rate).	☐
4. Left the workspace clean and orderly.	☐
5. Cared for customer property and returned it undamaged.	☐

Student signature _____ Date _____

Comments:

Have your supervisor/instructor verify satisfactory completion of this procedure, any observations made, and any necessary action(s) recommended.

Evaluation Instructions: The scoring box below is intended to act as a guide for both student and supervisor/instructor. Each criterion listed will help students to understand what is expected of them and help supervisors/instructors to articulate the level of success at a particular task. The scoring is set up to allow a second attempt at each task (see the Test and Retest columns). Scoring is designed only to award students points for task criteria that were completed correctly. Points are lost for failure to complete the employability requirements (see Non-Task-Specific criteria). When all criteria are evaluated, tally the points for a total at the bottom of each column.

Tasksheet Scoring

	Test		Retest	
Evaluation Items	**Pass**	**Fail**	**Pass**	**Fail**
Task-Specific Evaluation	**(1 pt)**	**(0 pts)**	**(1 pt)**	**(0 pts)**
Student properly measured the temperature at both locations and converted the temperature to pressure.				
Student properly checked the supply voltage and operation of the high-pressure cutout switch.				
Student properly checked the supply voltage and operation of the low-pressure/cycling switch.				
Student properly checked the supply voltage and operation of the binary/trinary switch.				
Non-Task-Specific Evaluation	**(0 pts)**	**(−1 pt)**	**(0 pts)**	**(−1 pt)**
Student successfully completed at least three of the non-task-specific steps.				
Student successfully completed all five of the non-task-specific steps.				
Total Score: <total # of points / 4 = %>				

Supervisor/Instructor:

Supervisor/instructor signature _____ Date _____

Comments:

Retest supervisor/instructor signature _____ Date _____

Comments:

CDX Tasksheet Number: 6.4007

Student/Intern Information

Name _____ Date _____ Class _____

Machine, Customer, and Service Information

Machine used for this activity:

Make _____ Model _____

Hours _____ Serial Number _____

Materials Required

- Vehicle with possible air-conditioning (A/C) concerns
- Vehicle manufacturer's service information
- Manufacturer-specific tools, depending on the concern/procedure(s)

Task-Specific Safety Considerations

- This task may require test driving the vehicle on the school grounds or on a hoist, both of which carry severe risks. Attempt this task only with full permission from your supervisor/ instructor and follow all the guidelines exactly.
- Comply with personal and environmental safety practices associated with clothing; eye protection; hand tools; power equipment; proper ventilation; and the handling, storage, and disposal of chemicals/materials in accordance with federal, state, and local regulations.
- Always wear the correct protective eyewear and clothing and use the appropriate safety equipment, as well as fender covers, seat protectors, and floor mat protectors.
- Make sure you understand and observe all legislative and personal safety procedures when carrying out practical assignments. If you are unsure of what these are, ask your supervisor/ instructor.
- While working on the vehicle, wheel chocks must be placed on both sides of one set of tires or as directed by your supervisor/instructor.
- When running any vehicles in the shop, make sure you use the shop's exhaust ventilation system to discharge all exhaust gas safely outside.

▶ TASK Detect refrigerant leaks. **AED 6.4**

Time off_____

Time on_____

Student Instructions: Read through the entire procedure prior to starting. Prepare your workspace and any tools or parts that may be needed to complete the task. When directed by your supervisor/instructor, begin the procedure to complete the task, and comment or check the box as each step is finished. Track your time on this procedure for later comparison to the standard completion time (i.e., "flat rate" or customer pay time).

Total time_____

Procedure	Step Completed
1. Perform one or more of the following tests to check for leaks in a machine's A/C system.	☐
2. Review the manufacturer's instructions for the correct use of an electronic leak detector and check the A/C system for leaks.	☐
a. Note any problems you found below:	☐
b. If problems exist, list your recommendations for rectification:	☐
3. Review the manufacturer's instructions for the correct use of a dye test and check the A/C system for leaks.	☐
a. Note any problems you found below:	☐
b. If problems exist, list your recommendations for rectification:	☐
4. Discuss your findings with your supervisor/instructor.	☐

Non-Task-Specific Evaluation	Step Completed
1. Tools and equipment were used as directed and returned in good working order.	☐
2. Complied with all general and task-specific safety standards, including proper use of any personal protective equipment (PPE).	☐
3. Completed the task in an appropriate time frame (recommendation: 1.5 or 2 times the flat rate).	☐
4. Left the workspace clean and orderly.	☐
5. Cared for customer property and returned it undamaged.	☐

Student signature _____ Date _____

Comments:

Have your supervisor/instructor verify satisfactory completion of this procedure, any observations made,

and any necessary action(s) recommended.

Evaluation Instructions: The scoring box below is intended to act as a guide for both student and supervisor/instructor. Each criterion listed will help students to understand what is expected of them and help supervisors/instructors to articulate the level of success at a particular task. The scoring is set up to allow a second attempt at each task (see the Test and Retest columns). Scoring is designed only to award students points for task criteria that were completed correctly. Points are lost for failure to complete the employability requirements (see Non-Task-Specific criteria). When all criteria are evaluated, tally the points for a total at the bottom of each column.

Tasksheet Scoring

Evaluation Items	Test		Retest	
	Pass	Fail	Pass	Fail
Task-Specific Evaluation	**(1 pt)**	**(0 pts)**	**(1 pt)**	**(0 pts)**
Student chose one of the three tests to perform.				
Student reviewed the instructions for the test.				
Student properly performed the test.				
Student accurately identified any necessary rectifications.				
Non-Task-Specific Evaluation	**(0 pts)**	**(−1 pt)**	**(0 pts)**	**(−1 pt)**
Student successfully completed at least three of the non-task-specific steps.				
Student successfully completed all five of the non-task-specific steps.				
Total Score: <total # of points / 4 = %>				

Supervisor/Instructor:

Supervisor/instructor signature _____ Date _____

Comments:

Retest supervisor/instructor signature _____ Date _____

Comments:

CDX Tasksheet Number: 6.4008

Student/Intern Information

Name _____ Date _____ Class _____

Machine, Customer, and Service Information

Machine used for this activity:

Make _____ Model _____

Hours _____ Serial Number _____

Materials Required
- Vehicle with possible air-conditioning (A/C) concerns
- Vehicle manufacturer's service information
- Manufacturer-specific tools, depending on the concern/procedure(s)

Task-Specific Safety Considerations
- This task may require test driving the vehicle on the school grounds or on a hoist, both of which carry severe risks. Attempt this task only with full permission from your supervisor/instructor and follow all the guidelines exactly.
- Comply with personal and environmental safety practices associated with clothing; eye protection; hand tools; power equipment; proper ventilation; and the handling, storage, and disposal of chemicals/materials in accordance with federal, state, and local regulations.
- Always wear the correct protective eyewear and clothing and use the appropriate safety equipment, as well as fender covers, seat protectors, and floor mat protectors.
- Make sure you understand and observe all legislative and personal safety procedures when carrying out practical assignments. If you are unsure of what these are, ask your supervisor/instructor.
- While working on the vehicle, wheel chocks must be placed on both sides of one set of tires or as directed by your supervisor/instructor.
- When running any vehicles in the shop, make sure you use the shop's exhaust ventilation system to discharge all exhaust gas safely outside.

▶ TASK Determine contaminants in a system due to system component failure.

AED 6.4

Time off_____

Student Instructions: Read through the entire procedure prior to starting. Prepare your workspace and any tools or parts that may be needed to complete the task. When directed by your supervisor/instructor, begin the procedure to complete the task, and comment or check the box as each step is finished. Track your time on this procedure for later comparison to the standard completion time (i.e., "flat rate" or customer pay time).

Time on_____

Total time_____

Procedure	Step Completed
1. Using available service literature, record the procedure for checking the A/C system for degrading hoses, then perform the check:	☐
a. Note any problems you found below:	☐
b. If problems exist, list your recommendations for rectification:	☐
2. Using available service literature, record the procedure for checking the A/C system for a defective receiver dryer/accumulator, then perform the check:	☐
a. Note any problems you found below:	☐
b. If problems exist, list your recommendations for rectification:	☐
3. Using available service literature, record the procedure for checking the A/C system for faulty compressor seals, then perform the check:	☐
a. Note any problems you found below:	☐

	Step Completed
b. If problems exist, list your recommendations for rectification:	☐
4. Discuss your findings with your supervisor/instructor.	☐

Non-Task-Specific Evaluation	Step Completed
1. Tools and equipment were used as directed and returned in good working order.	☐
2. Complied with all general and task-specific safety standards, including proper use of any personal protective equipment (PPE).	☐
3. Completed the task in an appropriate time frame (recommendation: 1.5 or 2 times the flat rate).	☐
4. Left the workspace clean and orderly.	☐
5. Cared for customer property and returned it undamaged.	☐

Student signature _____ Date _____

Comments:

Have your supervisor/instructor verify satisfactory completion of this procedure, any observations made,

and any necessary action(s) recommended.

Evaluation Instructions: The scoring box below is intended to act as a guide for both student and supervisor/instructor. Each criterion listed will help students to understand what is expected of them and help supervisors/instructors to articulate the level of success at a particular task. The scoring is set up to allow a second attempt at each task (see the Test and Retest columns). Scoring is designed only to award students points for task criteria that were completed correctly. Points are lost for failure to complete the employability requirements (see Non-Task-Specific criteria). When all criteria are evaluated, tally the points for a total at the bottom of each column.

Tasksheet Scoring

	Test		Retest	
Evaluation Items	**Pass**	**Fail**	**Pass**	**Fail**
Task-Specific Evaluation	**(1 pt)**	**(0 pts)**	**(1 pt)**	**(0 pts)**
Student accurately recorded the procedure for each check.				
Student properly performed each check.				
Student accurately noted any problems.				
Student accurately identified any necessary rectifications.				
Non-Task-Specific Evaluation	**(0 pts)**	**(−1 pt)**	**(0 pts)**	**(−1 pt)**
Student successfully completed at least three of the non-task-specific steps.				
Student successfully completed all five of the non-task-specific steps.				
Total Score: <total # of points / 4 = %>				

Supervisor/Instructor:

Supervisor/instructor signature _____ Date _____

Comments:

Retest supervisor/instructor signature _____ Date _____

Comments:

CDX Tasksheet Number: 6.4009

Student/Intern Information

Name _____ Date _____ Class _____

Machine, Customer, and Service Information

Machine used for this activity:

Make _____ Model _____

Hours _____ Serial Number _____

Materials Required

- Vehicle with possible air-conditioning (A/C) concerns
- Vehicle manufacturer's service information
- Manufacturer-specific tools, depending on the concern/procedure(s)

Task-Specific Safety Considerations

- This task may require test driving the vehicle on the school grounds or on a hoist, both of which carry severe risks. Attempt this task only with full permission from your supervisor/instructor and follow all the guidelines exactly.
- Comply with personal and environmental safety practices associated with clothing; eye protection; hand tools; power equipment; proper ventilation; and the handling, storage, and disposal of chemicals/materials in accordance with federal, state, and local regulations.
- Always wear the correct protective eyewear and clothing and use the appropriate safety equipment, as well as fender covers, seat protectors, and floor mat protectors.
- Make sure you understand and observe all legislative and personal safety procedures when carrying out practical assignments. If you are unsure of what these are, ask your supervisor/instructor.
- While working on the vehicle, wheel chocks must be placed on both sides of one set of tires or as directed by your supervisor/instructor.
- When running any vehicles in the shop, make sure you use the shop's exhaust ventilation system to discharge all exhaust gas safely outside.

▶ TASK Replace or repair A/C system components.

AED 6.4

Time off_____

Student Instructions: Read through the entire procedure prior to starting. Prepare your workspace and any tools or parts that may be needed to complete the task. When directed by your supervisor/instructor, begin the procedure to complete the task, and comment or check the box as each step is finished. Track your time on this procedure for later comparison to the standard completion time (i.e., "flat rate" or customer pay time).

Time on_____

Total time_____

Procedure	Step Completed
1. Using available service literature, record the procedure for replacing the A/C compressor, then perform the replacement using the proper tools and procedures:	☐
a. Have your supervisor/instructor verify satisfactory completion of the task. Supervisor's/instructor's initials: _____	☐
2. Using available service literature, record the procedure for replacing the A/C compressor clutch, then perform the replacement using the proper tools and procedures:	☐
a. Have your supervisor/instructor verify satisfactory completion of the task. Supervisor's/instructor's initials: _____	☐
3. Using available service literature, record the procedure for replacing metering valves, then perform the replacement using the proper tools and procedures:	☐
a. Have your supervisor/instructor verify satisfactory completion of the task. Supervisor's/instructor's initials: _____	☐
4. Using available service literature, record the procedure for replacing A/C condenser, then perform the replacement using the proper tools and procedures:	☐
a. Have your supervisor/instructor verify satisfactory completion of the task. Supervisor's/instructor's initials: _____	☐
5. Using available service literature, record the procedure for replacing the receiver drier or accumulator, then perform the replacement using the proper tools and procedures:	☐

	Step Completed
a. Have your supervisor/instructor verify satisfactory completion of the task. Supervisor's/instructor's initials: _____	☐
6. Using available service literature, record the procedure for replacing the A/C pressure control switches, then perform the replacement using the proper tools and procedures:	☐
a. Have your supervisor/instructor verify satisfactory completion of the task. Supervisor's/instructor's initials: _____	☐
7. Using available service literature, record the procedure for replacing the A/C lines, then perform the replacement using the proper tools and procedures:	☐
a. Have your supervisor/instructor verify satisfactory completion of the task. Supervisor's/instructor's initials: _____	☐
8. Discuss your findings with your supervisor/instructor.	☐

Non-Task-Specific Evaluation	Step Completed
1. Tools and equipment were used as directed and returned in good working order.	☐
2. Complied with all general and task-specific safety standards, including proper use of any personal protective equipment (PPE).	☐
3. Completed the task in an appropriate time frame (recommendation: 1.5 or 2 times the flat rate).	☐
4. Left the workspace clean and orderly.	☐
5. Cared for customer property and returned it undamaged.	☐

Student signature _____ Date _____

Comments:

Have your supervisor/instructor verify satisfactory completion of this procedure, any observations made,

and any necessary action(s) recommended.

Evaluation Instructions: The scoring box below is intended to act as a guide for both student and supervisor/instructor. Each criterion listed will help students to understand what is expected of them and help supervisors/instructors to articulate the level of success at a particular task. The scoring is set up to allow a second attempt at each task (see the Test and Retest columns). Scoring is designed only to award students points for task criteria that were completed correctly. Points are lost for failure to complete the employability requirements (see Non-Task-Specific criteria). When all criteria are evaluated, tally the points for a total at the bottom of each column.

Tasksheet Scoring

Evaluation Items	Test		Retest	
	Pass	**Fail**	**Pass**	**Fail**
Task-Specific Evaluation	**(1 pt)**	**(0 pts)**	**(1 pt)**	**(0 pts)**
Student accurately recorded each procedure.				
Student used the proper tools for each replacement.				
Student properly performed at least three of the replacements.				
Student properly performed all seven of the replacements.				
Non-Task-Specific Evaluation	**(0 pts)**	**(−1 pt)**	**(0 pts)**	**(−1 pt)**
Student successfully completed at least three of the non-task-specific steps.				
Student successfully completed all five of the non-task-specific steps.				
Total Score: <total # of points / 4 = %>				

Supervisor/Instructor:

Supervisor/instructor signature _____ Date _____

Comments:

Retest supervisor/instructor signature _____ Date _____

Comments:

CDX Tasksheet Number: 6.4010

Student/Intern Information

Name _____ Date _____ Class _____

Machine, Customer, and Service Information

Machine used for this activity:

Make _____ Model _____

Hours _____ Serial Number _____

Task-Specific Safety Considerations

- This task may require test driving the vehicle on the school grounds or on a hoist, both of which carry severe risks. Attempt this task only with full permission from your supervisor/instructor and follow all the guidelines exactly.
- Comply with personal and environmental safety practices associated with clothing; eye protection; hand tools; power equipment; proper ventilation; and the handling, storage, and disposal of chemicals/materials in accordance with federal, state, and local regulations.
- Always wear the correct protective eyewear and clothing and use the appropriate safety equipment, as well as fender covers, seat protectors, and floor mat protectors.
- Make sure you understand and observe all legislative and personal safety procedures when carrying out practical assignments. If you are unsure of what these are, ask your supervisor/instructor.
- While working on the vehicle, wheel chocks must be placed on both sides of one set of tires or as directed by your supervisor/instructor.
- When running any vehicles in the shop, make sure you use the shop's exhaust ventilation system to discharge all exhaust gas safely outside.

▶ **TASK** Test the cooling capabilities of an A/C system. **AED 6.4**

Time off_____

Student Instructions: Read through the entire procedure prior to starting. Prepare your workspace and any tools or parts that may be needed to complete the task. When directed by your supervisor/instructor, begin the procedure to complete the task, and comment or check the box as each step is finished. Track your time on this procedure for later comparison to the standard completion time (i.e., "flat rate" or customer pay time).

Time on_____

Total time_____

Procedure	Step Completed
1. Turn on the machine.	☐
2. Place a fan so that air is directed across the machine's condenser to simulate the airflow that occurs when the machine is in operation. (**Note:** If the engine's cooling fan is a hydraulic drive, this step can be skipped.)	☐
3. Close all windows and turn the A/C to its maximum setting.	☐
4. Raise the engine rpm to 1200–2000.	☐
5. Record the vent temperature in the cabin using a thermometer: _____° F	☐
a. Meets the manufacturer's specifications: Yes ☐ No ☐	☐
b. If no, list your recommendations for rectification:	☐
6. Record the high- and low-side pressures: High side _____ psi Low side _____ psi	☐
a. Meets the manufacturer's specifications: Yes ☐ No ☐	☐
b. If no, list your recommendations for rectification:	☐
7. Return the machine to its beginning condition and return any tools you used to their proper locations.	☐
8. Discuss your findings with your supervisor/instructor.	☐

Non-Task-Specific Evaluation	Step Completed
1. Tools and equipment were used as directed and returned in good working order.	☐
2. Complied with all general and task-specific safety standards, including proper use of any personal protective equipment (PPE).	☐
3. Completed the task in an appropriate time frame (recommendation: 1.5 or 2 times the flat rate).	☐
4. Left the workspace clean and orderly.	☐
5. Cared for customer property and returned it undamaged.	☐

Student signature _____ Date _____

Comments:

Have your supervisor/instructor verify satisfactory completion of this procedure, any observations made,

and any necessary action(s) recommended.

Evaluation Instructions: The scoring box below is intended to act as a guide for both student and supervisor/instructor. Each criterion listed will help students to understand what is expected of them and help supervisors/instructors to articulate the level of success at a particular task. The scoring is set up to allow a second attempt at each task (see the Test and Retest columns). Scoring is designed only to award students points for task criteria that were completed correctly. Points are lost for failure to complete the employability requirements (see Non-Task-Specific criteria). When all criteria are evaluated, tally the points for a total at the bottom of each column.

Tasksheet Scoring

Evaluation Items	Test		Retest	
	Pass	**Fail**	**Pass**	**Fail**
Task-Specific Evaluation	**(1 pt)**	**(0 pts)**	**(1 pt)**	**(0 pts)**
Student properly simulated airflow with a fan, if necessary, and turned the A/C to the maximum setting.				
Student properly raised the engine rpm.				
Student accurately recorded the vent temperature in the cabin.				
Student accurately recorded the high- and low-side pressures.				
Non-Task-Specific Evaluation	**(0 pts)**	**(−1 pt)**	**(0 pts)**	**(−1 pt)**
Student successfully completed at least three of the non-task-specific steps.				
Student successfully completed all five of the non-task-specific steps.				
Total Score: <total # of points / 4 = %>				

Supervisor/Instructor:

Supervisor/instructor signature _____ Date _____

Comments:

Retest supervisor/instructor signature _____ Date _____

Comments:

Chapter 53: Heating System Operation

Learning Objective/Task	CDX Tasksheet Number	AED Reference Number
• Replace a water pump.	6.5002	AED 6.5

Materials Required

- Vehicle with possible air-conditioning (A/C) concerns
- Vehicle manufacturer's service information
- Manufacturer-specific tools, depending on the concern/procedure(s)

Safety Considerations

- This task may require test driving the vehicle on the school grounds or on a hoist, both of which carry severe risks. Attempt this task only with full permission from your supervisor/instructor and follow all the guidelines exactly.
- Comply with personal and environmental safety practices associated with clothing; eye protection; hand tools; power equipment; proper ventilation; and the handling, storage, and disposal of chemicals/materials in accordance with federal, state, and local regulations.
- Always wear the correct protective eyewear and clothing and use the appropriate safety equipment, as well as fender covers, seat protectors, and floor mat protectors.
- Make sure you understand and observe all legislative and personal safety procedures when carrying out practical assignments. If you are unsure of what these are, ask your supervisor/instructor.
- While working on the vehicle, wheel chocks must be placed on both sides of one set of tires or as directed by your supervisor/instructor.
- When running any vehicles in the shop, make sure you use the shop's exhaust ventilation system to discharge all exhaust gas safely outside.

CDX Tasksheet Number: 6.5002

Student/Intern Information

Name _____ Date _____ Class _____

Machine, Customer, and Service Information

Machine used for this activity:

Make _____ Model _____

Hours _____ Serial Number _____

Materials Required
- Vehicle with possible air-conditioning (A/C) concerns
- Vehicle manufacturer's service information
- Manufacturer-specific tools, depending on the concern/procedure(s)

Task-Specific Safety Considerations
- This task may require test driving the vehicle on the school grounds or on a hoist, both of which carry severe risks. Attempt this task only with full permission from your supervisor/instructor and follow all the guidelines exactly.
- Comply with personal and environmental safety practices associated with clothing; eye protection; hand tools; power equipment; proper ventilation; and the handling, storage, and disposal of chemicals/materials in accordance with federal, state, and local regulations.
- Always wear the correct protective eyewear and clothing and use the appropriate safety equipment, as well as fender covers, seat protectors, and floor mat protectors.
- Make sure you understand and observe all legislative and personal safety procedures when carrying out practical assignments. If you are unsure of what these are, ask your supervisor/instructor.
- While working on the vehicle, wheel chocks must be placed on both sides of one set of tires or as directed by your supervisor/instructor.
- When running any vehicles in the shop, make sure you use the shop's exhaust ventilation system to discharge all exhaust gas safely outside.

▶ **TASK** Replace a water pump. **AED 6.5**

Time off_____

Time on_____

Student Instructions: Read through the entire procedure prior to starting. Prepare your workspace and any tools or parts that may be needed to complete the task. When directed by your supervisor/instructor, begin the procedure to complete the task, and comment or check the box as each step is finished. Track your time on this procedure for later comparison to the standard completion time (i.e., "flat rate" or customer pay time).

Total time_____

Procedure	Step Completed
1. Using available service literature, record the procedure for inspecting the water pump for leaks or damage, then perform the inspection:	☐
a. Note any problems you found below:	☐
b. If problems exist, list your recommendations for rectification:	☐
2. Using available service literature, record the procedure for removing the water pump, then perform the removal using the proper tools and procedures:	☐
a. Have your supervisor/instructor verify satisfactory completion of the removal. Supervisor's/instructor's initials: _____	☐
3. Using available service literature, record the procedure for installing the water pump, then perform the installation using the proper tools and procedures:	☐
a. Have your supervisor/instructor verify satisfactory completion of the installation. Supervisor's/instructor's initials: _____	☐
4. Complete a work order covering the 3 Cs (complaint, cause, and correction).	☐
5. Discuss your findings with your supervisor/instructor.	☐

Non-Task-Specific Evaluation	Step Completed
1. Tools and equipment were used as directed and returned in good working order.	☐
2. Complied with all general and task-specific safety standards, including proper use of any personal protective equipment (PPE).	☐
3. Completed the task in an appropriate time frame (recommendation: 1.5 or 2 times the flat rate).	☐
4. Left the workspace clean and orderly.	☐
5. Cared for customer property and returned it undamaged.	☐

Student signature _____ Date _____

Comments:

Have your supervisor/instructor verify satisfactory completion of this procedure, any observations made, and any necessary action(s) recommended.

Evaluation Instructions: The scoring box below is intended to act as a guide for both student and supervisor/instructor. Each criterion listed will help students to understand what is expected of them and help supervisors/instructors to articulate the level of success at a particular task. The scoring is set up to allow a second attempt at each task (see the Test and Retest columns). Scoring is designed only to award students points for task criteria that were completed correctly. Points are lost for failure to complete the employability requirements (see Non-Task-Specific criteria). When all criteria are evaluated, tally the points for a total at the bottom of each column.

Tasksheet Scoring

| | Test | | Retest | |
Evaluation Items	Pass	Fail	Pass	Fail
Task-Specific Evaluation	**(1 pt)**	**(0 pts)**	**(1 pt)**	**(0 pts)**
Student accurately recorded the procedure for inspecting the water pump and properly performed the inspection.				
Student accurately recorded the procedure for removing the water pump and properly performed the removal.				
Student accurately recorded the procedure for installing the water pump, then properly performed the installation.				
Student properly completed a work order.				
Non-Task-Specific Evaluation	**(0 pts)**	**(−1 pt)**	**(0 pts)**	**(−1 pt)**
Student successfully completed at least three of the non-task-specific steps.				
Student successfully completed all five of the non-task-specific steps.				
Total Score: <total # of points / 4 = %>				

Supervisor/Instructor:

Supervisor/instructor signature _____ Date _____

Comments:

Retest supervisor/instructor signature _____ Date _____

Comments:

Chapter 54: Servicing Heating Systems

Learning Objective/Task	CDX Tasksheet Number	AED Reference Number
• Install heater core and coolant lines.	6.6001	AED 6.6
• Replace heater system control valves.	6.6002	AED 6.6
• Reinstall engine thermostat(s).	6.6003	AED 6.6

Materials Required

- Vehicle with possible air-conditioning (A/C) concerns
- Vehicle manufacturer's service information
- Manufacturer-specific tools, depending on the concern/procedure(s)

Safety Considerations

- This task may require test driving the vehicle on the school grounds or on a hoist, both of which carry severe risks. Attempt this task only with full permission from your supervisor/instructor and follow all the guidelines exactly.
- Comply with personal and environmental safety practices associated with clothing; eye protection; hand tools; power equipment; proper ventilation; and the handling, storage, and disposal of chemicals/materials in accordance with federal, state, and local regulations.
- Always wear the correct protective eyewear and clothing and use the appropriate safety equipment, as well as fender covers, seat protectors, and floor mat protectors.
- Make sure you understand and observe all legislative and personal safety procedures when carrying out practical assignments. If you are unsure of what these are, ask your supervisor/instructor.
- While working on the vehicle, wheel chocks must be placed on both sides of one set of tires or as directed by your supervisor/instructor.
- When running any vehicles in the shop, make sure you use the shop's exhaust ventilation system to discharge all exhaust gas safely outside.

CDX Tasksheet Number: 6.6001

Student/Intern Information

Name _____ Date _____ Class _____

Machine, Customer, and Service Information

Machine used for this activity:

Make _____ Model _____

Hours _____ Serial Number _____

Materials Required
- Vehicle with possible air-conditioning (A/C) concerns
- Vehicle manufacturer's service information
- Manufacturer-specific tools, depending on the concern/procedure(s)

Task-Specific Safety Considerations
- This task may require test driving the vehicle on the school grounds or on a hoist, both of which carry severe risks. Attempt this task only with full permission from your supervisor/instructor and follow all the guidelines exactly.
- Comply with personal and environmental safety practices associated with clothing; eye protection; hand tools; power equipment; proper ventilation; and the handling, storage, and disposal of chemicals/materials in accordance with federal, state, and local regulations.
- Always wear the correct protective eyewear and clothing and use the appropriate safety equipment, as well as fender covers, seat protectors, and floor mat protectors.
- Make sure you understand and observe all legislative and personal safety procedures when carrying out practical assignments. If you are unsure of what these are, ask your supervisor/instructor.
- While working on the vehicle, wheel chocks must be placed on both sides of one set of tires or as directed by your supervisor/instructor.
- When running any vehicles in the shop, make sure you use the shop's exhaust ventilation system to discharge all exhaust gas safely outside.

▶ **TASK** Install heater core and coolant lines. _____ **AED** 6.6

Time off_____

Student Instructions: Read through the entire procedure prior to starting. Prepare your workspace and any tools or parts that may be needed to complete the task. When directed by your supervisor/instructor, begin the procedure to complete the task, and comment or check the box as each step is finished. Track your time on this procedure for later comparison to the standard completion time (i.e., "flat rate" or customer pay time).

Time on_____

Total time_____

Procedure	Step Completed
1. Using available service literature, record the procedure for inspecting the heater core and coolant lines for leaks or damage, then perform the inspection:	☐
a. Note any problems you found below:	☐
b. If problems exist, list your recommendations for rectification:	☐
2. Using available service literature, record the procedure for removing the heater core and coolant lines, then perform the removal using the proper tools and procedures:	☐
a. Have your supervisor/instructor verify satisfactory completion of the removal. Supervisor's/instructor's initials: _____	☐
3. Using available service literature, record the procedure for installing the heater core and coolant lines, then perform the installation using the proper tools and procedures:	☐
a. Have your supervisor/instructor verify satisfactory completion of the installation. Supervisor's/instructor's initials: _____	☐
4. Complete a work order covering the 3 Cs (complaint, cause, and correction).	☐
5. Discuss your findings with your supervisor/instructor.	☐

Non-Task-Specific Evaluation	Step Completed
1. Tools and equipment were used as directed and returned in good working order.	☐
2. Complied with all general and task-specific safety standards, including proper use of any personal protective equipment (PPE).	☐
3. Completed the task in an appropriate time frame (recommendation: 1.5 or 2 times the flat rate).	☐
4. Left the workspace clean and orderly.	☐
5. Cared for customer property and returned it undamaged.	☐

Student signature _____ Date _____

Comments:

Have your supervisor/instructor verify satisfactory completion of this procedure, any observations made, and any necessary action(s) recommended.

Evaluation Instructions: The scoring box below is intended to act as a guide for both student and supervisor/instructor. Each criterion listed will help students to understand what is expected of them and help supervisors/instructors to articulate the level of success at a particular task. The scoring is set up to allow a second attempt at each task (see the Test and Retest columns). Scoring is designed only to award students points for task criteria that were completed correctly. Points are lost for failure to complete the employability requirements (see Non-Task-Specific criteria). When all criteria are evaluated, tally the points for a total at the bottom of each column.

Tasksheet Scoring

	Test		Retest	
Evaluation Items	**Pass**	**Fail**	**Pass**	**Fail**
Task-Specific Evaluation	**(1 pt)**	**(0 pts)**	**(1 pt)**	**(0 pts)**
Student accurately recorded the procedure for inspecting the heater core and coolant lines and properly performed the inspection.				
Student accurately recorded the procedure for removing the heater core and coolant lines and properly performed the removal.				
Student accurately recorded the procedure for installing the heater core and coolant lines, then properly performed the installation.				
Student properly completed a work order.				
Non-Task-Specific Evaluation	**(0 pts)**	**(−1 pt)**	**(0 pts)**	**(−1 pt)**
Student successfully completed at least three of the non-task-specific steps.				
Student successfully completed all five of the non-task-specific steps.				
Total Score: <total # of points / 4 = %>				

CDX Tasksheet Number: 6.6002

Student/Intern Information

Name _____ Date _____ Class _____

Machine, Customer, and Service Information

Machine used for this activity:

Make _____ Model _____

Hours _____ Serial Number _____

Materials Required

- Vehicle with possible air-conditioning (A/C) concerns
- Vehicle manufacturer's service information
- Manufacturer-specific tools, depending on the concern/procedure(s)

Task-Specific Safety Considerations

- This task may require test driving the vehicle on the school grounds or on a hoist, both of which carry severe risks. Attempt this task only with full permission from your supervisor/instructor and follow all the guidelines exactly.
- Comply with personal and environmental safety practices associated with clothing; eye protection; hand tools; power equipment; proper ventilation; and the handling, storage, and disposal of chemicals/materials in accordance with federal, state, and local regulations.
- Always wear the correct protective eyewear and clothing and use the appropriate safety equipment, as well as fender covers, seat protectors, and floor mat protectors.
- Make sure you understand and observe all legislative and personal safety procedures when carrying out practical assignments. If you are unsure of what these are, ask your supervisor/instructor.
- While working on the vehicle, wheel chocks must be placed on both sides of one set of tires or as directed by your supervisor/instructor.
- When running any vehicles in the shop, make sure you use the shop's exhaust ventilation system to discharge all exhaust gas safely outside.

▶ TASK Replace heater system control valves. _____ **AED 6.6**

Time off_____

Student Instructions: Read through the entire procedure prior to starting. Prepare your workspace and any tools or parts that may be needed to complete the task. When directed by your supervisor/instructor, begin the procedure to complete the task, and comment or check the box as each step is finished. Track your time on this procedure for later comparison to the standard completion time (i.e., "flat rate" or customer pay time).

Time on_____

Total time_____

Procedure	Step Completed
1. Using available service literature, record the procedure for testing the heater control valves, then perform the test:	☐
a. Meets the manufacturer's specifications: Yes ☐ No ☐	☐
b. If no, list your recommendations for rectification:	☐
2. Using available service literature, record the procedure for removing the heater control valves, then perform the removal using the proper tools and procedures:	☐
a. Have your supervisor/instructor verify satisfactory completion of the removal. Supervisor's/instructor's initials: _____	☐
3. Using available service literature, record the procedure for installing the heater control valves, then perform the installation using the proper tools and procedures:	☐
a. Have your supervisor/instructor verify satisfactory completion of the installation. Supervisor's/instructor's initials: _____	☐
4. Complete a work order covering the 3 Cs (complaint, cause, and correction).	☐
5. Discuss your findings with your supervisor/instructor.	☐

Non-Task-Specific Evaluation	Step Completed
1. Tools and equipment were used as directed and returned in good working order.	☐
2. Complied with all general and task-specific safety standards, including proper use of any personal protective equipment (PPE).	☐
3. Completed the task in an appropriate time frame (recommendation: 1.5 or 2 times the flat rate).	☐
4. Left the workspace clean and orderly.	☐
5. Cared for customer property and returned it undamaged.	☐

Student signature _____ Date _____

Comments:

Have your supervisor/instructor verify satisfactory completion of this procedure, any observations made, and any necessary action(s) recommended.

Evaluation Instructions: The scoring box below is intended to act as a guide for both student and supervisor/instructor. Each criterion listed will help students to understand what is expected of them and help supervisors/instructors to articulate the level of success at a particular task. The scoring is set up to allow a second attempt at each task (see the Test and Retest columns). Scoring is designed only to award students points for task criteria that were completed correctly. Points are lost for failure to complete the employability requirements (see Non-Task-Specific criteria). When all criteria are evaluated, tally the points for a total at the bottom of each column.

Tasksheet Scoring

	Test		Retest	
Evaluation Items	**Pass**	**Fail**	**Pass**	**Fail**
Task-Specific Evaluation	**(1 pt)**	**(0 pts)**	**(1 pt)**	**(0 pts)**
Student accurately recorded the procedure for testing the heater control valves and properly performed the test.				
Student accurately recorded the procedure for removing the heater control valves, then properly performed the removal.				
Student accurately recorded the procedure for installing the heater control valves, then properly performed the installation.				
Student properly completed a work order.				
Non-Task-Specific Evaluation	**(0 pts)**	**(−1 pt)**	**(0 pts)**	**(−1 pt)**
Student successfully completed at least three of the non-task-specific steps.				
Student successfully completed all five of the non-task-specific steps.				
Total Score: <total # of points / 4 = %>				

Supervisor/Instructor:

Supervisor/instructor signature _____ Date _____

Comments:

Retest supervisor/instructor signature _____ Date _____

Comments:

CDX Tasksheet Number: 6.6003

Student/Intern Information

Name _____ Date _____ Class _____

Machine, Customer, and Service Information

Machine used for this activity:

Make _____ Model _____

Hours _____ Serial Number _____

Materials Required

- Vehicle with possible air-conditioning (A/C) concerns
- Vehicle manufacturer's service information
- Manufacturer-specific tools, depending on the concern/procedure(s)

Task-Specific Safety Considerations

- This task may require test driving the vehicle on the school grounds or on a hoist, both of which carry severe risks. Attempt this task only with full permission from your supervisor/instructor and follow all the guidelines exactly.
- Comply with personal and environmental safety practices associated with clothing; eye protection; hand tools; power equipment; proper ventilation; and the handling, storage, and disposal of chemicals/materials in accordance with federal, state, and local regulations.
- Always wear the correct protective eyewear and clothing and use the appropriate safety equipment, as well as fender covers, seat protectors, and floor mat protectors.
- Make sure you understand and observe all legislative and personal safety procedures when carrying out practical assignments. If you are unsure of what these are, ask your supervisor/instructor.
- While working on the vehicle, wheel chocks must be placed on both sides of one set of tires or as directed by your supervisor/instructor.
- When running any vehicles in the shop, make sure you use the shop's exhaust ventilation system to discharge all exhaust gas safely outside.

▶ **TASK** Reinstall engine thermostat(s).

AED
6.6

Time off_____

Student Instructions: Read through the entire procedure prior to starting. Prepare your workspace and any tools or parts that may be needed to complete the task. When directed by your supervisor/instructor, begin the procedure to complete the task, and comment or check the box as each step is finished. Track your time on this procedure for later comparison to the standard completion time (i.e., "flat rate" or customer pay time).

Time on_____

Total time_____

Procedure	Step Completed
1. Using available service literature, record the procedure for testing the engine thermostat(s), then perform the test:	☐
a. Meets the manufacturer's specifications: Yes ☐ No ☐	☐
b. If no, list your recommendations for rectification:	☐
2. Using available service literature, record the procedure for removing the engine thermostat(s), then perform the removal using the proper tools and procedures:	☐
a. Have your supervisor/instructor verify satisfactory completion of the removal. Supervisor's/instructor's initials: _____	☐
3. Using available service literature, record the procedure for installing the engine thermostat(s), then perform the installation using the proper tools and procedures:	☐
a. Have your supervisor/instructor verify satisfactory completion of the installation. Supervisor's/instructor's initials: _____	☐
4. Complete a work order covering the 3 Cs (complaint, cause, and correction).	☐
5. Discuss your findings with your supervisor/instructor.	☐

Non-Task-Specific Evaluation	Step Completed
1. Tools and equipment were used as directed and returned in good working order.	☐
2. Complied with all general and task-specific safety standards, including proper use of any personal protective equipment (PPE).	☐
3. Completed the task in an appropriate time frame (recommendation: 1.5 or 2 times the flat rate).	☐
4. Left the workspace clean and orderly.	☐
5. Cared for customer property and returned it undamaged.	☐

Student signature _____ Date _____

Comments:

Have your supervisor/instructor verify satisfactory completion of this procedure, any observations made, and any necessary action(s) recommended.

Evaluation Instructions: The scoring box below is intended to act as a guide for both student and supervisor/instructor. Each criterion listed will help students to understand what is expected of them and help supervisors/instructors to articulate the level of success at a particular task. The scoring is set up to allow a second attempt at each task (see the Test and Retest columns). Scoring is designed only to award students points for task criteria that were completed correctly. Points are lost for failure to complete the employability requirements (see Non-Task-Specific criteria). When all criteria are evaluated, tally the points for a total at the bottom of each column.

Tasksheet Scoring

Evaluation Items	Test		Retest	
	Pass	**Fail**	**Pass**	**Fail**
Task-Specific Evaluation	**(1 pt)**	**(0 pts)**	**(1 pt)**	**(0 pts)**
Student accurately recorded the procedure for testing the engine thermostat(s) and properly performed the test.				
Student accurately recorded the procedure for removing engine thermostat(s) and properly performed the removal.				
Student accurately recorded the procedure for installing engine thermostat(s), then properly performed the installation.				
Student properly completed a work order.				
Non-Task-Specific Evaluation	**(0 pts)**	**(−1 pt)**	**(0 pts)**	**(−1 pt)**
Student successfully completed at least three of the non-task-specific steps.				
Student successfully completed all five of the non-task-specific steps.				
Total Score: <total # of points / 4 = %>				

Supervisor/Instructor:

Supervisor/instructor signature _____ Date _____

Comments:

Retest supervisor/instructor signature _____ Date _____

Comments:

Chapter 55: Pressurized Cabs

Learning Objective/Task	CDX Tasksheet Number	AED Reference Number
• Replace cab air filter(s).	6.7002	AED 6.7

Materials Required

- Vehicle with possible air-conditioning (A/C) concerns
- Vehicle manufacturer's service information
- Manufacturer-specific tools, depending on the concern/procedure(s)

Safety Considerations

- This task may require test driving the vehicle on the school grounds or on a hoist, both of which carry severe risks. Attempt this task only with full permission from your supervisor/instructor and follow all the guidelines exactly.
- Comply with personal and environmental safety practices associated with clothing; eye protection; hand tools; power equipment; proper ventilation; and the handling, storage, and disposal of chemicals/materials in accordance with federal, state, and local regulations.
- Always wear the correct protective eyewear and clothing and use the appropriate safety equipment, as well as fender covers, seat protectors, and floor mat protectors.
- Make sure you understand and observe all legislative and personal safety procedures when carrying out practical assignments. If you are unsure of what these are, ask your supervisor/instructor.
- While working on the vehicle, wheel chocks must be placed on both sides of one set of tires or as directed by your supervisor/instructor.
- When running any vehicles in the shop, make sure you use the shop's exhaust ventilation system to discharge all exhaust gas safely outside.

CDX Tasksheet Number: 6.7002

Student/Intern Information

Name _____ Date _____ Class _____

Machine, Customer, and Service Information

Machine used for this activity:

Make _____ Model _____

Hours _____ Serial Number _____

> ## Materials Required
> - Vehicle with possible air-conditioning (A/C) concerns
> - Vehicle manufacturer's service information
> - Manufacturer-specific tools, depending on the concern/procedure(s)

Task-Specific Safety Considerations
- This task may require test driving the vehicle on the school grounds or on a hoist, both of which carry severe risks. Attempt this task only with full permission from your supervisor/instructor and follow all the guidelines exactly.
- Comply with personal and environmental safety practices associated with clothing; eye protection; hand tools; power equipment; proper ventilation; and the handling, storage, and disposal of chemicals/materials in accordance with federal, state, and local regulations.
- Always wear the correct protective eyewear and clothing and use the appropriate safety equipment, as well as fender covers, seat protectors, and floor mat protectors.
- Make sure you understand and observe all legislative and personal safety procedures when carrying out practical assignments. If you are unsure of what these are, ask your supervisor/instructor.
- While working on the vehicle, wheel chocks must be placed on both sides of one set of tires or as directed by your supervisor/instructor.
- When running any vehicles in the shop, make sure you use the shop's exhaust ventilation system to discharge all exhaust gas safely outside.

▶ **TASK** Replace cab air filter(s). _____

Student Instructions: Read through the entire procedure prior to starting. Prepare your workspace and any tools or parts that may be needed to complete the task. When directed by your supervisor/instructor, begin the procedure to complete the task, and comment or check the box as each step is finished. Track your time on this procedure for later comparison to the standard completion time (i.e., "flat rate" or customer pay time).

Time off_____

Time on_____

Total time_____

Procedure	Step Completed
1. Using available service literature, record the procedure for removing the cabin air filter, then perform the removal using the proper tools and procedures:	☐
a. Have your supervisor/instructor verify satisfactory completion of the removal. Supervisor's/instructor's initials: _____	☐
2. Inspect the cabin air filter box for damaged/missing seals and fasteners.	☐
a. Note any problems you found below:	☐
b. If problems exist, list your recommendations for rectification:	☐
3. Remove any foreign material from the cabin filter air box.	☐
4. If able, inspect the heater core and/or evaporator core for excessive debris.	☐
a. Note any problems you found below:	☐
b. If problems exist, list your recommendations for rectification:	☐
5. Reinstall the cabin air filter.	☐

	Step Completed
6. Turn the fan motor on high and check for any air leaks around the cabin filter air box.	☐
a. Note any problems you found below:	☐
b. If problems exist, list your recommendations for rectification:	☐
7. Discuss your findings with your supervisor/instructor.	☐

Non-Task-Specific Evaluation	Step Completed
1. Tools and equipment were used as directed and returned in good working order.	☐
2. Complied with all general and task-specific safety standards, including proper use of any personal protective equipment (PPE).	☐
3. Completed the task in an appropriate time frame (recommendation: 1.5 or 2 times the flat rate).	☐
4. Left the workspace clean and orderly.	☐
5. Cared for customer property and returned it undamaged.	☐

Student signature _____ Date _____

Comments:

Have your supervisor/instructor verify satisfactory completion of this procedure, any observations made, and any necessary action(s) recommended.

Evaluation Instructions: The scoring box below is intended to act as a guide for both student and supervisor/instructor. Each criterion listed will help students to understand what is expected of them and help supervisors/instructors to articulate the level of success at a particular task. The scoring is set up to allow a second attempt at each task (see the Test and Retest columns). Scoring is designed only to award students points for task criteria that were completed correctly. Points are lost for failure to complete the employability requirements (see Non-Task-Specific criteria). When all criteria are evaluated, tally the points for a total at the bottom of each column.

Tasksheet Scoring

Evaluation Items	Test		Retest	
	Pass	Fail	Pass	Fail
Task-Specific Evaluation	**(1 pt)**	**(0 pts)**	**(1 pt)**	**(0 pts)**
Student accurately recorded the procedure for removing the cabin air filter, then properly performed the removal.				
Student properly inspected the cabin air filter box and removed any foreign material.				
Student properly inspected the heater core and/or evaporator core.				
Student properly reinstalled the cabin air filter and checked for any air leaks.				
Non-Task-Specific Evaluation	**(0 pts)**	**(−1 pt)**	**(0 pts)**	**(−1 pt)**
Student successfully completed at least three of the non-task-specific steps.				
Student successfully completed all five of the non-task-specific steps.				
Total Score: <total # of points / 4 = %>				

Supervisor/Instructor:

Supervisor/instructor signature _____ Date _____

Comments:

_____

Retest supervisor/instructor signature _____ Date _____

Comments:

_____

Appendix A

AED Standards for Construction Equipment Technology 2017

AED Standard Reference	AED Competency / Performance Statement	FMHE Chapter Reference	Tasksheet Number
AED 1	**SAFETY/ADMINISTRATIVE**		
AED 1a	**Safety**		
AED 1a.1	Identify and correctly name the basic hand tools.	5	1a1001
AED 1a.1	Emphasis on safety will be demonstrated with all tool usage.		1a1002a
AED 1a.1	Emphasis on safety will be demonstrated with all tool usage.		1a1002b
AED 1a.1	Emphasis on safety will be demonstrated with all tool usage.		1a1002c
AED 1a.1	Emphasis on safety will be demonstrated with all tool usage.		1a1002d
AED 1a.1	Emphasis on safety will be demonstrated with all tool usage.		1a1002e
AED 1a.1	Demonstrate the proper use, care and maintenance of each tool, and safe operating procedure for each.	5	1a1003
AED 1a.1	Demonstrates proper use, care and maintenance, and calibration of precision hand tools.	5	1a1004
AED 1a.1	Review assignments, evaluation of identification exercises. Written examinations that will determine the competency on many items unable to check by hands-on exercises. Emphasis on safety should be demonstrated with tool usage.		No tasksheet
AED 1a.1	Test students' use of tools/equipment to check comprehension. Demonstrate all torque and de-torque methods with hands-on exercises.		1a1006
AED 1a.1	The student should be able to demonstrate that they can accurately read all precision measuring tools and gauges.		1a1007
AED 1a.1	Convert standard to and from metric measurements, both pressure and distance.		No tasksheet
AED 1a.1	Determine engine speed and pulses per revolution.		1a1009
AED 1a.1	Perform tasks related to measuring, understanding, and recording pressure, flows, and temperature.		1a1010

AED 1a.1	Perform tasks related to measuring specific gravity of fuel, coolant, and electrolyte.		1a1011
AED 1a.2	Identify and correctly name the electrical tool.	11	1a2001
AED 1a.2	Demonstrate the proper use of the designed application and safe operating procedure for each.	11	1a2002
AED 1a.2	Demonstrate the proper inspection, care, and storage for electric hand tools.		Included in 1a2002
AED 1a.2	Understand and exhibit the safe and proper use of ground fault circuits.		1a2004
AED 1a.3	Identify and correctly name the basic air tool.	5	1a3001
AED 1a.3	Demonstrate the proper use of the designed application and safe operating procedure for each.	5	1a3002
AED 1a.3	Demonstrate the proper inspection, care, maintenance, and storage for air tools.	5	Included in 1a3002
AED 1a.4	Identify and correctly name the basic hydraulic tools.		1a4001
AED 1a.4	Demonstrate the proper inspection, care, maintenance, and storage as applicable.		Included in 1a4003
AED 1a.4	Demonstrate the proper use of the designed application and safe operating procedure as applicable.		1a4003
AED 1a.5	Identify and correctly name the various types of lifting equipment.	1, 2, 8	1a5001
AED 1a.5	Demonstrate the proper inspection, care, maintenance, and storage for each.	8	1a5002
AED 1a.5	Demonstrate the proper use of the designed application and safe operating procedure for each.	2	1a5003
AED 1a.5	Students show understanding of current regulations and standards for use, inspection, and certification of lifting equipment.	8	No tasksheet
AED 1a.5	Identify and correctly name the basic cleaning equipment used in our industry.		1a6001
AED 1a.6	Demonstrate the proper use of the designed application and safe operating procedures for each.		1a6002
AED 1a.6	Demonstrate the proper inspection, care, maintenance, and storage for cleaning equipment.		Included in 1a6002
AED 1a.6	Identify the various solvents and solutions used in the cleaning process.		1a6004

AED 1a.6	Identify the risks, hazards, and precautions for cleaning materials, both personal and environmental.	3	No tasksheet
AED 1a.6	Demonstrate an understanding of Safety Data Sheets (SDS) and requirements to meet OSHA standards.	3	1a6006
AED 1a.7	Identify and correctly name the various types of fluid pressure test equipment and the accessories required for proper testing.		1a7001
AED 1a.7	Describe the proper use of the designated application and safe operation of each type of equipment.		1a7002
AED 1a.7	Demonstrate a proper source for calibration of precision test equipment and accessories.		Included in 1a1004
AED 1a.7	Identify and correctly name the use of the personal protective equipment required for the various types of fluid pressure testing equipment.		1a7004a
AED 1a.7	Identify and correctly name the use of the personal protective equipment required for the various types of fluid pressure testing equipment.		1a7004b
AED 1a.7	Describe multiple dangers of working with fluids under pressure.	3	No tasksheet
AED 1a.8	Identify the various types of exhaust systems used in repair facility.		1a8001
AED 1a.8	Demonstrate the proper use of the designed application and safe operation of each type of system.		1a8002
AED 1a.8	Demonstrate the proper inspection, care, maintenance, and storage of the systems and the equipment required for operation.		Included in 1a8002
AED 1a.8	Explain why carbon monoxide and diesel smoke can be hazardous to your health and the precautions required for eliminating injury or death.	3	No tasksheet
AED 1a.8	Recognize symptoms of exposure to carbon monoxide, diesel smoke, and other hazardous materials.	3	No tasksheet
AED 1a.9	Identify the various types of construction equipment and forklifts, using the standard industry names accepted by equipment manufacturers.	1, 2	1a9001
AED 1a.9	Demonstrate and explain the proper, safe, and fundamental operation of the various types of machinery.	2	1a9002

AED 1a.9	Translate from a user's perspective the importance of and reasons for caution/warning lights, backup alarms, seat belts, safety instructions, decals, and other customer-related safety information.	17	No tasksheet
AED 1a.9	Recognize hybrid systems and/or machines as they relate to safety concerns.		1a9004
AED 1a.10	Identify and correctly name the various types of equipment required for mandated regulations.		1a10001
AED 1a.10	Demonstrate and explain the principles and procedures for each of the regulations.		1a10002
AED 1a.10	Demonstrate the operation, inspection, proper care, and maintenance of the various equipment required for conforming with federal and state OSHA and MSHA regulations.		Included in 1a10002
AED 1a.10	Identify the different types of fire extinguishers and know the applications and correct use of each type.	3	1a10004a
AED 1a.10	Identify the different types of fire extinguishers and know the applications and correct use of each type	3	1a10004b
AED 1a.10	Demonstrate how to find, explain, and use an SDS for a product.	3	1a10005
AED 1a.10	Recall and identify underground utility hazard marking that would commonly be encountered on a job site.		1a10006
AED 1a.10	Explain why working safely is important, and explain the procedures for reporting unsafe working conditions and practices.	3	No tasksheet
AED 1a.11	Identify safe work practices in each situation.	3	1a11001
AED 1a.11	Demonstrate safe work practices in the shop or in the field.	3	1a11002
AED 1a.11	Identify proper lifting and pulling techniques to avoid personal injury.	3	No tasksheet
AED 1a.11	Demonstrate proper lifting and pulling techniques.	3	1a11004
AED 1a.11	Demonstrate proper shop/facility cleanliness/appearance to dealer standards.	3	1a11005
AED 1a.11	Identify potential hazards and develop a plan to deal with them.		1a11006
AED 1a.12	Demonstrate safe mounting and dismounting practices on construction machinery.		1a12001

AED 1a.12	Explain proper types of chains and binders used in securing loads.		1a12002
AED 1a.12	Demonstrate proper lockout/tagout procedures.	3	1a12003
AED 1a.12	Demonstrate understanding of the HazCom standard and how to use safety data sheet (SDS) and chemical labels.	3	1a12004
AED 1a.12	Write about or discuss from personal or team experience (shop, workplaces, etc.), common safety hazards and what you would have done to eliminate them.	3	No tasksheet
AED 1a.12	Demonstrate proper work procedures in handling wheel assemblies safely. Refer to industry standard procedures.	36	1a12006
AED 1a.12	Identify when tethering is necessary and proper use of the fall protection equipment.		1a12007
AED 1b	**Administrative**		
AED 1b.1	Exhibit the ability to use parts and service reference/technical materials and safety materials in print or computer format.	3	No tasksheet
AED 1b.1	Exhibit the ability to follow written instructions.		No tasksheet
AED 1b.1	Exhibit the ability to complete forms, time cards, work orders, accident reports, sales leads, technical bulletins, parts requisitions, and other related written forms of communication.		No tasksheet
AED 1b.1	Exhibit the ability to perform basic math functions, including measurement in both US and metric, calculations, conversions, and currency.		No tasksheet
AED 1b.2	Develop and exhibit good listening skills.		No tasksheet
AED 1b.2	Exhibit the ability to use a computer, related hardware, current software, Internet, and technology currently in use.		1b2002
AED 1b.2	Demonstrate efficient, effective, correct, and timely communications to a customer and coworker utilizing telephone, fax, computer, word processing, and e-mail.		No tasksheet
AED 1b.2	Using a computer, demonstrate the ability to retrieve specifications, part numbers, bulletins, schematics, produce reports, and similar types of information using manufacturers' software and Internet-based resources.		1b2004

AED 1b.3	Exhibit the ability to work toward achieving established goals while in a diversified environment.		No tasksheet
AED 1b.3	Recognize organizational chart.		No tasksheet
AED 1b.3	Demonstrate understanding of how product support activities contribute to the overall profitability of the company.		No tasksheet
AED 1b.3	Identify expense control requirements.		No tasksheet
AED 1b.3	Maintain awareness of sexual harassment policy, safety rules, environmental regulations, disciplinary action policy, and equal opportunity policy.	3	No tasksheet
AED 1b.3	Explain the need for performance reviews and the impact of different performance levels.		No tasksheet
AED 1b.3	Maintain confidentiality as required.		No tasksheet
AED 1b.3	Explain the need for quality performance and the impact on customer satisfaction and profitability.		No tasksheet
AED 1b.3	Demonstrate a positive attitude toward the company and other contacts.		No tasksheet
AED 1b.3	Define impact of not meeting the customers' needs in a timely manner.		No tasksheet
AED 1b.3	Recognize customer retention policies and procedures.		No tasksheet
AED 1b.3	Exhibit the ability to communicate to coworkers and customers in a courteous, professional manner.		No tasksheet
AED 1b.3	Demonstrate time management and organizational skills.		No tasksheet
AED 1b.3	Develop an awareness of stressful situations and the ability to handle and resolve problems with difficult internal and external customers.		No tasksheet
AED 1b.3	Exhibit the ability to listen and follow verbal and written instructions.		No tasksheet
AED 1b.3	Respect authority and accept the responsibilities of the position.		No tasksheet
AED 1b.3	Demonstrate proper appearance to dealer standards.		No tasksheet
AED 1b.5	Identify and establish both short- and long-term goals and the requirements to achieve them (business and personal).		No tasksheet
AED 1b.5	Describe parts inventory control, procurement, and accountability.		No tasksheet

AED 1b.5	Demonstrate knowledge of factors that can determine shop labor rates.		No tasksheet
AED 1b.5	Demonstrate the ability to accurately complete work orders/repair orders and other related reports, including parts and consumables.		1b5004
AED 1b.5	Demonstrate the ability to write a thorough and comprehensive service report, including warranty repairs.		No tasksheet
AED 1b.5	Describe tool procurement procedures.		No tasksheet
AED 1b.5	Describe time tracking.		No tasksheet
AED 1b.5	Demonstrate the ability to use correct industry terminology.		No tasksheet
AED 2	**ELECTRONICS/ELECTRICAL SYSTEMS**		
AED 2.1	**Fundamental Knowledge**		
AED 2.1a	Define the basic structure of conductors, insulators, and semiconductors.	9	No tasksheet
AED 2.1a	Describe the reaction of like and unlike charges.	9	No tasksheet
AED 2.1b	Describe the differences of conventional and electron theory current flow.	9	No tasksheet
AED 2.1b1	Demonstrate the principles of operation and the correct usage of the various types of meters to measure volts, amps, and ohms.	9	No tasksheet
AED 2.1b1	Demonstrate the ability to convert between kilo, milli, and micro units.		No tasksheet
AED 2.1b2	Demonstrate knowledge of the laws governing permanent magnets, electro-magnets, and magnetic fields.	9	No tasksheet
AED 2.1b2	Demonstrate knowledge of the effects of magnetic forces on current-carrying conductors.	9	No tasksheet
AED 2.1b3	Describe the basic parts and operation of the basic types of storage batteries.	12	No tasksheet
AED 2.1b3	Describe knowledge and laws of electromagnetic induction as it applies to generating electrical current using a magnetic field.	15	No tasksheet
AED 2.1c	Define remote monitoring systems and the ability to remotely diagnose electrical/electronic issues. Define what they are and what are their capabilities.	21	No tasksheet

AED 2.2	Ohm's Law		
AED 2.2a	Demonstrate the mathematical relationship of the various terms in ohms law as they pertain to series, parallel, and series/parallel circuits.	10	No tasksheet
AED 2.2b	Measure voltage, amperage, and resistance values in series, parallel, and series/parallel DC circuits.	10	2.2b001
AED 2.3	**12/24 Volt Cranking Circuits**		
AED 2.3a	Describe the basic components that make up the various types of 12/24 volt cranking systems.	14	No tasksheet
AED 2.3b	Demonstrate the sequence of operation of the components contained within a cranking system. The emphasis is on how each component effects the system's overall operation.	14	No tasksheet
AED 2.3c	Demonstrate the ability to isolate problems using voltage drops and other diagnostic methods.	14	2.3c001
AED 2.3d	Demonstrate the ability to correctly test, evaluate, and replace the following components: conductors, relays/solenoids, and starters, using manufacturers' service publications and specifications.	14	2.3d001
AED 2.4	**12/24 Volt Charging Circuits**		
AED 2.4a	Describe the basic components that make up the various types of 12/24 volt charging systems.	10, 15	No tasksheet
AED 2.4b	Demonstrate the sequence of operation of the components contained within a charging system. The emphasis is on how each component effects the system's overall operation.	15	No tasksheet
AED 2.4c	Demonstrate/emphasize the ability to isolate problems using voltage drops and other diagnostic methods.	15	2.4c001
AED 2.4c	Demonstrate understanding of 5V reference voltage and its effect on all sensors in the same circuit.		No tasksheet
AED 2.4d	Demonstrate the ability to properly test, evaluate, and replace the following components: conductors, alternators, and regulators, using manufacturers' service publications and specifications.	15	2.4d001

AED 2.5	Lighting, Accessory, and Control Systems		
AED 2.5a	Describe the basic components that make up the various types of lighting, accessory, and control systems.		No tasksheet
AED 2.5b	Demonstrate the sequence of operation of the components contained within various lighting, accessory, and control systems. The emphasis is on how each component effects the system's overall operation.		No tasksheet
AED 2.5c1	Demonstrate the ability to isolate problems within various lighting, accessory, and control systems, emphasizing voltage drops and other diagnostic methods. NEW TASK–Troubleshoot lighting, accessory, and control systems.		No tasksheet
AED 2.5d	Demonstrate the ability to correctly disassemble, test, assemble, replace, or repair lighting, accessory, and control system components using manufactures' service publications and specifications. Examples of the components are as follows: 1. Wiring harness/connectors 2. Fuses/circuit breakers 3. Lights/bulbs 4. Hall effects systems: switches, sensors, and other 5. Gauges 6. Meters 7. Horns and buzzers 8. Relays 9. Diodes 10. Resisters 11. Potentiometers 12. Solenoids 13. Rheostats 14. Switches 15. Electric motors 16. Transformers/converters 17. Preheat devices, for example, glow plugs, intake heaters 18. Sensors 19. Monitors 20. Controllers 21. HID/LED 22. Transducers 23. Transistors (NEW TASK–Test and determine whether replacement is necessary for lighting, accessory, and control system components)		No tasksheet

AED 2.6	Electrical Schematics/Diagrams		
AED 2.6a	Demonstrate the ability to identify basic electrical/electronic symbols. Ensure newer symbols like all effect sensors are covered.		No tasksheet
AED 2.6b	Demonstrate the ability to trace various circuits using wire schematics/diagrams.		2.6b001
AED 2.6c	Diagnose machine electrical system faults using schematics/diagrams.		2.6c001
AED 2.7	**SAE Computer Can-Bus Standards**		
AED 2.7a	Demonstrate a working knowledge of the different systems used on computer-controlled machinery. Examples: LIN, CAN	19, 20	No tasksheet
AED 2.7a	Understand the logic of wake-up and timed shutdown circuits.	19	No tasksheet
AED 2.7b2	Understand the importance of twisted and shielded wire systems.	19, 20	No tasksheet
AED 2.7b	Demonstrate a working knowledge of the codes to identify errors within the different systems. Demonstrate the understanding of the logic and theory of how a processor generates a code. Inputs versus outputs.		No tasksheet
AED 2.8	**Diagnostics Systems Troubleshooting**		
AED 2.8	Describe the complaint prior to beginning diagnostic tests.	20	No tasksheet
AED 2.8	Demonstrate the ability to perform a diagnostic procedure with emphasis on arriving at the root cause of failure.	19	2.8002
AED 2.8	Demonstrate the ability to reason with regard to a specific malfunction in the system.	20	No tasksheet
AED 2.8	Demonstrate the use of proper tools, including flex probes and back probing.	11	No tasksheet
AED 2.8	Demonstrate mastering the use of all test equipment, including digital volt-ohmmeter (DVOM), laptop computers, and other system-specific troubleshooting devices.	11	No tasksheet
AED 2.8	Demonstrate the ability to do voltage drop testing to determine available versus potential voltage.	11	No tasksheet
AED 2.8	Demonstrate the ability to use schematic diagrams and follow troubleshooting flowcharts in selected technical manuals.		2.8007

AED 2.8	Utilize an interactive equipment diagnostic program.	20	2.8008
AED 2.8	Demonstrate technical write-up competency.		2.8009
AED 3	**HYDRAULICS/HYDROSTATICS**		
AED 3.1	**Theory and Operation**		
AED 3.1	Demonstrate knowledge that fluids have no shape of their own, are practically incompressible, apply equal pressure in all directions, and provide great increases in workforce.	22, 28	No tasksheet
AED 3.1	Describe the function of a reservoir, pump, filters, relief valve, control valve, and cylinder in relation to each other.	23, 24, 25, 26, 28	No tasksheet
AED 3.1	Describe how open and closed center systems are determined by one or all of the following: (a) the type of control valve, (b) the type of pump, (c) use of unloading valve, (d) path of oil return to reservoir from pump.	23, 32	No tasksheet
AED 3.1	Describe a basic, but complete, open center hydraulic system, explaining the operation of the system, the route of fluid during the use of a function, and the route of the fluid while the machine is running when no hydraulic function is being used.	32	No tasksheet
AED 3.1	Describe a basic, but complete, closed center load sensing hydraulic system, explaining the operation of the system, the route of fluid during the use of a function, and the route of the fluid while the machine is running when no hydraulic function is being used.	32	No tasksheet
AED 3.1	Identify applications and benefits of those applications on construction equipment.	32	No tasksheet
AED 3.1	Demonstrate knowledge of hydrostatic systems, including closed- and open-loop systems.	23	No tasksheet
AED 3.1	Understand the various types of cooling circuits.	30	No tasksheet
AED 3.1	Understand the purpose of a charge circuit and how charge pressure relates to hydrostatic system efficiency.		No tasksheet
AED 3.1	Explain the differences between hydraulic and hydrostatic systems.		No tasksheet
AED 3.1	Demonstrate the ability to identify applications and benefits of those applications on construction equipment.		No tasksheet

AED 3.1	Explain the different characteristics between various types of pumps and exhibit the ability to follow the oil flow through each pump, both with and without hydraulic function used.	23, 25, 31	No tasksheet
AED 3.1	Demonstrate the ability to identify a gear pump, name all parts, follow the oil flow through a gear pump, identify inlet and outlet ports, and identify the direction of rotation of the pump.	23, 25, 31	3.1b001
AED 3.1	Identify a vane pump, name all parts of a vane pump, follow the oil flow through a vane pump, identify inlet and outlet ports of a vane pump, and identify the direction of rotation of the pump. Explain how a vane pump can be changed to operate in the opposite direction, when applicable.	23, 25, 31	3.1b002
AED 3.1	Identify various piston pumps, name all parts of a piston pump, follow the oil flow through a piston pump, identify inlet and outlet ports of a piston pump (both variable and fixed), and identify the direction of rotation of the pump.	23, 25, 31	3.1b003
AED 3.1	Identify types of swash plate control (manual, servo piston, electronic, etc.).	31	No tasksheet
AED 3.1	Explain the different characteristics between the various motors; exhibit the ability to follow the oil flow through each motor while using a hydraulic function.		No tasksheet
AED 3.1	Identify a gear motor, name all parts of a gear motor, follow the oil flow through a gear motor, identify inlet and outlet ports of a gear motor, and identify the direction of rotation of the motor.	23, 25, 31	3.1b006
AED 3.1	Identify a vane motor, name all parts of a vane motor, follow the oil flow through a vane motor, identify inlet and outlet ports of a vane motor, and identify the direction of rotation of the motor.	23, 25, 31	3.1b007
AED 3.1	Identify radial and axial piston motors, name all parts of these piston motors, follow the oil flow through these piston motors, identify inlet and outlet ports of these piston motors (both variable and fixed), and identify the direction of rotation of the motors.	23, 25, 31	3.1c001
AED 3.1	Identify a gerotor motor, name all parts, and understand its operation.	25, 31	3.1c002

AED 3.1	Describe the differences between these three major types:
	  a. Pressure control valves
	  b. Directional control valves
	  c. Flow-control valves
		26	No tasksheet

AED 3.1	Exhibit knowledge of the uses and functions of the following valves:
	  a. Direct-acting relief valves
	  b. Pilot-operated relief valves
	  c. Cartridge relief valves
	  d. Pilot-operated valves
	  e. Sequence valves
	  f. Unloading valves
	  g. Multifunction valves
	  h. Counterbalance valves
	  i. Pressure-reducing valves
	  j. Pressure-limiting valves
	  k. Pressure differential valves
	  l. Crossover relief valves
		26	No tasksheet

AED 3.1	Exhibit knowledge of the uses and functions of the following valves:
	  a. Check valves
	  b. Rotary valves
	  c. Spool valves
	  d. Pilot-controlled poppet valves
	  e. Electrohydraulic valves
	  f. Electrohydraulic control systems
	  g. Pulse-width-modulated valves
		32	No tasksheet

AED 3.1	Exhibit knowledge of the uses and functions of the following valves:
	  a. Flow-control valves
	    1. Compensated
	    2. Noncompensated
	  b. Flow divider valves
	    1. Priority
	    2. Nonpriority
	    3. Proportional
		26, 31, 32	No tasksheet

AED 3.1	Explain the uses and movements of the two types of cylinders.	27	No tasksheet
AED 3.1	Identify a single-acting cylinder, name all of its parts, and follow the oil flow through the cylinder.	27	3.1e002
AED 3.1	Understand operation of a cushioned cylinder.	33	No tasksheet
AED 3.1	Identify a double-acting cylinder, name all of its parts, and follow the oil flow through the cylinder.	27	3.1e004

AED 3.1	Explain how accumulators store energy, absorb shocks, build pressure, and maintain a constant pressure within a system.	30	No tasksheet
AED 3.1	Explain where and why gas, pneumatic, spring-loaded, and weighted accumulators are used.	30	No tasksheet
AED 3.1	Explain and practice all accumulator safety.	30	3.1f003
AED 3.2	**Fluids, Transfer Components, and Filtering**		
AED 3.2	Exhibit the ability to select the proper hose for a given function, taking into consideration the flow needed, pressures to be used, routing, clamping, fittings required, and pulsating of lines.	29	No tasksheet
AED 3.2	Exhibit knowledge of the understanding of hydraulic fittings, the importance of selecting the proper fitting, and their relationship to noise and vibration.	29	No tasksheet
AED 3.2	Demonstrate the ability to identify various fittings and thread styles, examples: O-ring boss, NPT, NPTF, British Metric, O-ring flange, ORFS, etc. Proper procedure to torque fittings and flanges. NEW TASK—Correctly identify different styles of hydraulic fittings and provide torque installation specifications for them.	29	3.2003
AED 3.2	Demonstrate the ability to crimp hydraulic fittings onto hose.	29	3.2004
AED 3.2	Know the construction and function of filters used in hydraulic/hydrostatic systems.	28, 31	No tasksheet
AED 3.2	Describe the use of various filters in hydraulic and hydrostatic systems.	28, 31	No tasksheet
AED 3.2	Demonstrate an understanding of the concept of auxiliary bypass filtration and its benefits to a total system cleanliness.		No tasksheet
AED 3.3	**Maintenance Procedures**		
AED 3.3	Demonstrate familiarity with, and practice good hydraulic maintenance/safety practices.	22, 34	3.3a001
AED 3.3	Perform all hydraulic functions and repairs in a clean atmosphere.	34	No tasksheet
	Exhibit the ability to follow the proper flushing procedure using the correct technical manual/service information.		No tasksheet

AED 3.3	Exhibit the proper maintenance techniques to prevent internal and external leaks.	27	No tasksheet
AED3.3	Demonstrate the procedure for cleaning hoses after cutting and crimping.		3.3a005
AED 3.3	Demonstrate knowledge of overheating conditions. Prevent overheating by keeping the oil at the proper levels, cleaning dirt and mud from around lines and cylinder rods, keep relief valves adjusted properly, do not overload or overspeed systems, and do not hold control valves in a stalled position longer than necessary.	35	No tasksheet
AED 3.3	Identify and recognize the root causes of "blistering" or frayed hoses and procedures to avoid these problems.		No tasksheet
AED 3.3	Understand oils and show familiarity with various fluids and their effects on hydraulic systems.	4	No tasksheet
AED 3.3	Understand the effects of mixing oil types.		No tasksheet
AED 3.3	Understand ISO cleanliness code principles. Identify key elemental categories.	28, 35	No tasksheet
AED 3.3	Understand the proper way to obtain fluid samples from a system.		3.3c002
AED 3.3	Identify key elements found in oil analysis and the types of failures related to each.		No tasksheet
AED 3.3	Identify key indicators on a fluid analysis report that illustrate: 1. The proper fluid type is being used. 2. Fluid types have not been mixed. 3. Indicators of fluid degradation. 4. Trend analysis.		No tasksheet
AED 3.3	Demonstrate the ability to identify aeration and determine the root cause.		No tasksheet
AED 3.3	Describe how reactions of some sealant materials differ among types of hydraulic fluids.		No tasksheet
AED 3.3	Describe the applications of various types of sealants.		No tasksheet
AED 3.3	Demonstrate that safety practices are followed.		No tasksheet

AED 3.4	Component Repair and Replacement		
AED 3.4	Following the proper technical manual/service information, exhibit the ability to remove, disassemble, diagnose failure, evaluate, repair, or replace/reinstall, and test operate any given component, including, but not limited to: • Gear, vane, and piston pumps • Gear, vane, and piston motors • Pressure control valves • Directional control valves • Volume control valves • Single-acting, double-acting cylinders (If OEM recommends or allows: gas, pneumatic, spring, and weight-loaded accumulators.)	25, 26, 27, 30	3.4001
AED 3.4	Following the proper technical manual/service information, exhibit the ability to remove and replace any given component, including, but not limited to: • Gear, vane, and piston pumps • Gear, vane, and piston motors • Pressure control valves • Directional control valves • Volume control valves • Single-acting, double-acting cylinders • Gas, pneumatic, spring, and weight-loaded • Accumulators • Hoses, steel lines, and fittings • Oil coolers • Reservoirs	25, 26, 27, 30	No tasksheet
AED 3.4	Describe proper system flushing/cleanup procedures to achieve ISO cleanliness code.		No tasksheet
AED 3.4	Follow proper bleeding and priming procedures.		No tasksheet
AED 3.5	Hydraulic schematics		
AED 3.5	Exhibit knowledge of symbol identification through demonstration.	23, 33	No tasksheet
AED 3.5	Given a selected schematic, exhibit your knowledge of schematics by using JIC, ISO, and various symbols to identify locations of various components.	23, 33	No tasksheet
AED 3.6	Diagnostics Systems and Component Troubleshooting		
AED 3.6	Exhibit the ability to reason with regard to a specific malfunction.	35	No tasksheet
AED 3.6	Use proper oils and fluids as per manufacturer's specifications.		No tasksheet

AED 3.6	Exhibit proficiency in the use of all test equipment including flowmeters, pressure gauges, vacuum gauges, and temperature measuring devices, in both the metric and standard scales.	32, 35	3.6003
AED 3.6	Demonstrate the ability to use schematic diagrams and follow a troubleshooting flowchart using a selected technical manual.	35	3.6004
AED 3.6	Demonstrate the ability to follow an operational check procedure using a selected technical manual.	35	3.6005
AED 3.6	Troubleshooting of load-sensing hydraulics.	32	3.6006
AED 3.6	Demonstrate technical write-up competency • Demonstrate logic and critical thinking in identifying, evaluating, and diagnosing customer complaint • Identify the root cause of failure • Correction procedure • Machine inspection	35	3.6007
AED 4	**POWER TRAINS**		
AED 4.1	**Theory and Operation**		
AED 4.1	Demonstrate knowledge of basic powertrain components and how those components, as a whole, relate to one another. Demonstrate by following a power flowchart from flywheel to ground.		4.1a001
AED 4.1	Recognize hybrid and electric drive systems and/or machines as they relate to safety concerns.		4.1a002
AED 4.1	Demonstrate knowledge by identifying the various types of gears using a matching test.		4.1a003
AED 4.1	Explain the benefit of one type of gear versus other types of gears using factors such as cost, strength, quietness, bulkiness, and capability of ratios.		No tasksheet
AED 4.1	Identify types of bearings through matching tests.	4	4.1a005
AED 4.1	Demonstrate an understanding of various types of bearings and proper adjustment procedures.		4.1a006
AED 4.1	Identify components of a torque converter and describe the relationship of those components to one another.	47	4.1a007

AED 4.1	Describe the operation of a given torque converter and various stages of operation.	47	4.1a008
AED 4.1	Use OEM manuals/service information to test a torque converter unit and determine whether operation is within specifications.	47	4.1a009
AED 4.1	Exhibit your understanding of "sliding gear" transmissions by identifying components, explaining operation, and demonstrating power flow though all gear sets.	45	4.1b001
AED 4.1	Exhibit your understanding of "collar shift" transmissions by identifying components, explaining operation, and demonstrating power flow through all gear sets.	45	4.1b002
AED 4.1	Exhibit your understanding of "synchromesh" transmissions by identifying components, explaining operation, and demonstrating power flow through all gear sets.	45	4.1b003
AED 4.1	Identify shifting control components and explain their operation.	45	4.1b004
AED 4.1	Demonstrate the ability to perform adjustments to transmissions as instructed in the OEM service manual/information.	45	4.1b005
AED 4.1	Demonstrate your understanding of the operation of powershift transmissions by explaining which clutches and/or brakes are engaged and which planetary gear sets are being used during a specific gear selection.	45, 48	4.1c001
AED 4.1	Explain the differences, advantages, and disadvantages of planetary and countershaft transmissions.	45, 48	No tasksheet
AED 4.1	Use service manual/information to test and/or troubleshoot a powershift transmission (on-highway truck transmissions do not qualify), and verify if it is within OEM specifications.	48	4.1d001
AED 4.1	Demonstrate the ability to set and measure preload, end play, and backlash for a specific component using OEM manuals/service information.		4.1d002a
AED 4.1	Demonstrate the ability to set and measure preload, end play, and backlash for a specific component using OEM manuals/service information.		4.1d002b

AED 4.1	Identify all components in a single- and multiple disc and plate-type clutch, including flywheel, pilot and release bearings, disc and pressure plate parts, and powertrain input shaft. Also, explain differences and benefits of solid and button-type clutches.	43	4.1d003
AED 4.1	Explain operation of a selected clutch.	43	4.1d004
AED 4.1	Demonstrate knowledge and operation of single and multiple disc clutches by explaining the relationship of the clutch components to each other and their roles in the transfer of power.	43	4.1d005a
AED 4.1	Demonstrate knowledge and operation of single and multiple disc clutches by explaining the relationship of the clutch components to each other and their roles in the transfer of power.	43	4.1d005b
AED 4.1	Describe the relationship of the number of discs, types of discs (wet or dry), and type of clutch material to the transfer of torque and horsepower to the ground.	43	No tasksheet
AED 4.1	Demonstrate an understanding of overrunning clutches by identifying the different types of clutches, their operation, and various applications.		4.1d007
AED 4.1	Explain the operation of magnetic clutches and name various applications.	43	4.1d008
AED 4.1	Explain the operation of modulating clutches and name various applications.		4.1d009
AED 4.1	Exhibit knowledge of electronic control systems by identifying components used on a specific unit.	46, 48	No tasksheet
AED 4.1	Demonstrate an understanding of a specific unit's operation by explaining the functions of all components and their relationships to one another.	46, 48	No tasksheet
AED 4.1	Demonstrate the ability to follow flow and troubleshooting charts to correctly identify the operation of a specific unit's system and troubleshooting methods used by the OEM.		No tasksheet
AED 4.1	Demonstrate understanding of theory and principles of hydrostatic systems by explaining, in writing, how a basic hydrostatic system functions.	31	No tasksheet

AED 4.1	Exhibit knowledge of hydrostatic transmission operation by explaining the flow of fluids through the charge circuit, pump, motor, control, and loop circuits.	31	No tasksheet
AED 4.1	Explain the differences between fixed and variable pumps and motors and the effects of their various combinations.	31	No tasksheet
AED 4.1	Explain various adjustment procedures for straight travel.		4.1f004
AED 4.2	**Driveshaft Function and Construction**		
AED 4.2	Demonstrate knowledge of driveshafts by recognizing components, realizing the effects of driveline angle, and studying why driveline failures occur.	49	4.2a001a
AED 4.2	Demonstrate knowledge of driveshafts by recognizing components, realizing the effects of driveline angle, and studying why driveline failures occur.	49	4.2a001b
AED 4.2	Demonstrate knowledge of driveshafts by recognizing components, realizing the effects of driveline angle, and studying why driveline failures occur.	49	4.2a001c
AED 4.2	Exhibit understanding of basic differential operation by identifying the components and explaining how pinion, ring, and bevel gears operate in relationship to each other.	50	4.2b001a
AED 4.2	Exhibit understanding of basic differential operation by identifying the components and explaining how pinion, ring, and bevel gears operate in relationship to each other.		4.2b001b
AED 4.2	Identify each type of differential locking device and explain in detail how each one operates.	50	4.2b002a
AED 4.2	Identify each type of differential locking device and explain in detail how each one operates.	50	4.2b002b
AED 4.2	Given a specific component and proper manuals/information, perform all adjustments on a differential with a new ring and pinion, and also perform all adjustments with original ring and pinion but with new bearings.	50	4.2b003a

AED 4.2	Given a specific component and proper manuals/information, perform all adjustments on a differential with a new ring and pinion, and also perform all adjustments with original ring and pinion but with new bearings.	50	4.2b003b
AED 4.2	Given a specific component and proper manuals/information, perform all adjustments on a differential with a new ring and pinion, and also perform all adjustments with original ring and pinion but with new bearings.	50	4.2b003c
AED 4.2	Given a specific component and proper manuals/information, perform all adjustments on a differential with a new ring and pinion, and also perform all adjustments with original ring and pinion but with new bearings.	50	4.2b003d
AED 4.2	Given a specific component and proper manuals/information, perform all adjustments on a differential with a new ring and pinion, and also perform all adjustments with original ring and pinion but with new bearings.	50	4.2b003e
AED 4.2	Given a specific component and proper manuals/information, perform all adjustments on a differential with a new ring and pinion, and also perform all adjustments with original ring and pinion but with new bearings.	50	Included in 4.1d002a
AED 4.2	Given a specific component and proper manuals/information, perform all adjustments on a differential with a new ring and pinion, and also perform all adjustments with original ring and pinion but with new bearings.	50	4.2b003g
AED 4.2	Given a specific component and proper manuals/information, perform all adjustments on a differential with a new ring and pinion, and also perform all adjustments with original ring and pinion but with new bearings.	50	4.2b003h
AED 4.2	Given a specific component and proper manuals/information, perform all adjustments on a differential with a new ring and pinion, and also perform all adjustments with original ring and pinion but with new bearings.	50	4.2b003i

AED 4.2	Given a specific component and proper manuals/information, perform all adjustments on a differential with a new ring and pinion, and also perform all adjustments with original ring and pinion but with new bearings.	50	4.2b003j
AED 4.2	Identify the most common root causes of failure with differentials.	50	4.2b004
AED 4.2	Exhibit knowledge of final drives by identifying the different types and the components that make up final drives.	52	4.2c001
AED 4.2	Perform adjustments according to OEM standards.	52	4.2c002a
AED 4.2	Perform adjustments according to OEM standards.	52	4.2c002b
AED 4.3	**Fundamental Theory of Hydraulic and Pneumatic Braking Systems**		
AED 4.3	Describe fundamental theory, adjustments, and repair of hydraulic braking systems used primarily in mobile construction equipment.	54, 55	4.3001a
AED 4.3	Describe fundamental theory, adjustments, and repair of hydraulic braking systems used primarily in mobile construction equipment.	54, 55	4.3001b
AED 4.3	Describe fundamental theory, adjustments, and repair of hydraulic braking systems used primarily in mobile construction equipment.	54, 55	4.3001c
AED 4.3	Demonstrate knowledge of basic brake components of a dry external system.		4.3002a
AED 4.3	Demonstrate knowledge of basic brake components of a wet internal system.		4.3002b
AED 4.3	Explain and sketch hydraulic and pneumatic brake systems, internal and external.		No tasksheet
AED 4.4	**Understanding Maintenance Practices in Power Trains**		
AED 4.4	Demonstrate procedures to follow in keeping a work area, and the parts worked with, clean.		No tasksheet
AED 4.4	Describe proper flushing procedures, including when components are replaced.		4.4002
AED 4.4	Describe scheduled oil sampling and cite several reasons why it is necessary.		4.4003

AED 4.5	**Power Train Schematics and Flow Diagrams**		
AED 4.5	Be able to identify all electrical/hydraulic, pneumatic, and mechanical symbols used in powertrain units.		4.5001
AED 4.5	Demonstrate the ability to use schematics and flow diagrams to follow both control circuits and power flow of a given piece of equipment using the corresponding OEM manual/service information.		No tasksheet
AED 4.6	**Troubleshooting and Failure Analysis**		
AED 4.6	Describe steps in solving a problem related to a powertrain system, decisions required to perform work and analysis as to why problem occurred and how it could have been prevented.		No tasksheet
AED 4.6	Describe common reasons for parts failure and be able to discuss symptoms of wear, corrosion, etc. of actual parts.		4.6002
AED 4.6	Demonstrate the ability to follow reference information, and test, and determine whether unit is within specifications for a hydraulic/hydrostatic trainer or equipment with a hydrostatic drive using service manuals/information/software; demonstrate the ability to follow a diagnostic troubleshooting chart for a specific system.	54, 55	No tasksheet
AED 4.6	Use proper oils and fluids as per manufacturer specifications.		4.6004
AED 4.6	Demonstrate technical write-up competency • Demonstrate logic and critical thinking in identifying, evaluating and diagnosing customer complaint. • Identify the root cause of failure • Correction procedure • Machine inspection		4.6005
AED 5	**DIESEL ENGINES**		
AED 5.1	**Safety**		
AED 5.1	Explain safety issues specifically related to engine applications.		No tasksheet
AED 5.1	Review assignments, evaluation of identification exercises. Successfully complete written examinations that will determine the competency on many items unable to check by hands-on exercises. Emphasis on safety is to be demonstrated through tool usage.		No tasksheet

AED 5.2	Theory and Operation		
AED 5.2	Demonstrate competency in the application of engine theory and operation. Written tests designed for this purpose. Possible task list.		No tasksheet
AED 5.2	Understanding and comprehension of formulas to calculate engine performance criteria.		No tasksheet
AED 5.2	Understand the relationship between engine HP and torque.		No tasksheet
AED 5.2	Describe the differences between spark ignited and compression-ignition engines.		No tasksheet
AED 5.2	Determine engine/component motion and speed ratios.		No tasksheet
AED 5.2	Explain diesel four-stroke engine cycle.		No tasksheet
AED 5.2	Memorize the order of strokes. Identify the specific stroke of each cylinder during engine rotation.		No tasksheet
AED 5.2	Determine the number of degrees between power strokes on various engines.		No tasksheet
AED 5.2	Understand diesel combustion principles and the effects of preignition, detonation, and misfire.		No tasksheet
AED 5.2	Demonstrate glow plug operation and testing.		5.2010
AED 5.2	Determine engine rotation by valve overlap.		5.2011
AED 5.2	Identify the various combustion chambers and know the advantages/disadvantages of each type.		No tasksheet
AED 5.2	Perform basic valve and injection timing tasks.		5.2013
AED 5.2	Understand the theory of injection pump timing.		No tasksheet
AED 5.2	Understand the functions of various cooling system components.		5.2015a, 5.2015b, 5.2015c
AED 5.2	Understand the functions of various cooling system components.		5.2015b
AED 5.2	Understand the functions of various cooling system components.		5.2015c
AED 5.2	Understand measurement and properties of the engine fluids. Understand cross-contamination root causes and effects of each.		

AED 5.2	Understand the functions and components of diesel engine lubrication systems and the effects of machine operating angle versus oil pan and pump design.		5.2017a
AED 5.2	Understand the functions and components of diesel engine lubrication systems and the effects of machine operating angle versus oil pan and pump design.		5.2017b
AED 5.2	Understand the effects of lubrication system levels (over and under).		5.2018a
AED 5.2	Understand the effects of lubrication system levels (over and under).		5.2018b
AED 5.2	Understand the functions and components of diesel engine fuel and governing systems, including mechanical, electronic, and computer-controlled systems.		5.2019
AED 5.2	Understand common rail fuel systems.		5.2020
AED 5.2	Understand the functions and components of emission control systems and governmental regulations (i.e. EPA and CARB).		5.2021a
AED 5.2	Understand the functions and components of emission control systems and governmental regulations (i.e. EPA and CARB).		5.2021b
AED 5.2	Understand penalties for non-compliance to emission regulations to the dealer, equipment owner, and technician.		No tasksheet
AED 5.2	Understand how emissions systems impact engine life and repairs.		No tasksheet
AED 5.3	**Maintenance Practices**		
AED 5.3	Locate maintenance specifications including fluid change intervals, fluid specifications (SAE/API, etc.), fuel specifications, filter replacement intervals, proper filter replacement procedures, other maintenance guidelines, etc.		5.3001
AED 5.3	Understand commonly used methods for maintenance records keeping and their importance.		No tasksheet
AED 5.3	Demonstrate how to obtain proper oil, fuel, and coolant samples.	12, 13, 15, 33	5.3003a
AED 5.3	Demonstrate how to obtain proper oil, fuel, and coolant samples.		5.3003b
AED 5.3	Demonstrate how to obtain proper oil, fuel, and coolant samples.		5.3003c
AED 5.3	Demonstrate understanding in how to interpret fluid analysis results.		No tasksheet

AED 5.3	Demonstrate how to inspect used filters for early warning signs of potential problems.		5.3005
AED 5.3	Demonstrate preventative maintenance tasks performed to industry standards; completion of an inspection tasksheet.		5.3006
AED 5.4	**Component Repair**		
AED 5.4	Demonstrate via practical exercises, parts reusability procedures, and guidelines.		5.4001
AED 5.4	Demonstrate understanding of industry remanufactured component guidelines and how to determine when to use remanufactured components.		No tasksheet
AED 5.4	Remove and replace commonly serviced external components. Know the inspection, service, and cleaning techniques associated with replacement of these items.		5.4003
AED 5.5	**Engine Subsystems**		
AED 5.5	Locate and identify various external components.		5.5a001
AED 5.5	Demonstrate knowledge of vibration fundamentals. • Linear characteristics • Rotational characteristics		5.5a002
AED 5.5	Demonstrate understanding of the basic theory of exhaust after-treatment systems like: • Diesel Particulate Filter (DPF) • Diesel Oxidation Catalyst (DOC) • Selective Catalytic Reduction (SCR) • Diesel exhaust fluid (DEF) • Regeneration process		5.5a003
AED 5.5	Demonstrate comprehension of the removal, inspection, and installation techniques associated with basic internal components.		5.5b001
AED 5.5	Perform identification and inspection of all internal components.		5.5b002
AED 5.5	Describe tasks associated with the removal, inspection, and installation of internal engine components (i.e., cylinder packs).		5.5b003
AED 5.5	Describe bearing "roll-in" and tasks associated with in-frame overhauls.		5.5b004
AED 5.5	Describe valve and injector adjustments, as well as timing and idler gear installations.	11	5.5b005a

AED 5.5	Describe valve and injector adjustments, as well as timing and idler gear installations.		5.5b005b
AED 5.5	Demonstrate knowledge of hydraulic accessories driven or operated by the engine.		5.5b006
AED 5.5	Demonstrate understanding of cold weather starting aids and block heaters.		5.5b007
AED 5.6	**Fuel and Governing Systems, Mechanical and Electronic Systems**		
AED 5.6	Perform basic maintenance and diagnosis of the different fuel delivery systems available today. Demonstrate a basic understanding of the adjustment and repair of various governing systems used by the major manufacturers.		Included in 5.6a008
AED 5.6	Understand basic hydraulic principles and fluid transfer technology.		5.6a002
AED 5.6	Measure specific gravity of fuel and determine proper grade and/or contamination. Understand the use of fuel conditioners, fuel coolers, and heaters. Recognize waste oil/fuel blends.		5.6a003
AED 5.6	Measure fuel pressure/volume with correct diagnostic tools and compare to specifications. Determine and understand the problems with the basic supply systems.		5.6a004
AED 5.6	Explain how contamination, such as air, water, and dirt, can enter a fuel system and the effect it can have.		5.6a005
AED 5.6	Proper replacement of fuel transfer pumps, filters, lines, and hoses including proper bleeding/priming procedures.		5.6a006
AED 5.6	Identify misfiring cylinders with appropriate tooling. Emphasis on cleanliness and safety.		5.6a007
AED 5.6	Replacement and timing of various injection pumps including inline, distributor, and unit injector pumps.		5.6a008
AED 5.6	Perform tasks associates with troubleshooting, adjusting, and replacing governor components.		Included in 5.7005
AED 5.6	Identification exercises and demonstrations of system operation.		Included in 5.6a008
AED 5.6	Understanding operation of mechanical governors and hydraulic/servo systems.		No tasksheet

AED 5.6	Troubleshooting and programming principles of electronic governors should be emphasized. Use of scan tools and PCs should be demonstrated to illustrate the self-diagnosing capabilities of the system.		5.6b004
AED 5.6	Be able to demonstrate the ability to locate and test the following sensors: boost pressure, engine position, engine speed, throttle position, manifold pressure, fuel pressure, and high pressure oil sensor.		5.6b005
AED 5.7	**Diagnostics**		
AED 5.7	Tasks associated with troubleshooting emission controls and basic adjustments.		Included in 5.5a003
AED 5.7	Visual basic exhaust analysis, white, gray, or black, as applicable.	7, 8, 17, 18, 26, 28	5.7002
AED 5.7	Practical exercises in identification of common diesel engine problems using proper diagnostic tools and procedures.		5.7003
AED 5.7	Determine root causes of failure, establish reusability, and know the recommended repair options available.		No tasksheet
AED 5.7	Demonstrate proper use of special tools and equipment utilized in engine repair.		5.7005
AED 5.7	Tasks using technical service manuals, service information, bulletins, and special instructions. Proficient use of service manuals, desktop PCs, and laptops for retrieval of specifications and service procedures.		5.7006
AED 5.7	Troubleshooting common problems caused by a malfunctioning engine subsystem.		5.7007
AED 5.7	Testing of the engine cooling system, including overheating issues and testing procedures, especially the flow through the radiator, correct temperature drops.		5.7008
AED 5.7	Use proper oils and fluids as per manufacturer's specifications.		Included in 5.2018b
AED 5.7	Demonstrate technical write-up competency -Demonstrate logic and critical thinking in identifying, evaluating, and diagnosing customer complaint. -Identify the root cause of failure -Correction procedure -Machine inspection		No tasksheet

AED 6	AIR-CONDITIONING/HEATING		
AED 6.1	**Fundamental Knowledge**		
AED 6.1	Demonstrate knowledge of heat sources, types of heat transfer, and how humidity affects heat transfer. Emphasis will be placed on factors that affect heat transfer and how to measure heat energy.		No tasksheet

AED 6.1	Demonstrate knowledge of the following terms:
	   1. Sensible heat
	   2. Change of state
	   3. Saturation temperature
	   4. Latent heat (Hidden heat)
	   5. Latent heat of fusion
	   6. Latent heat of evaporation
	   7. Latent heat of condensation
	   8. Superheated
	   9. Subcooled
	  10. Vapor
	  11. Gas
			No tasksheet

AED 6.1	Measure and calculate the effects of pressures on liquids. Emphasis will be placed on understanding and using pressure and temperature (P/T) charts.		6.1003
AED 6.1	Describe refrigerant characteristics in relation to environmental damage. Emphasis will be placed on identification, labeling, and handling of refrigerants in accordance with EPA 609 regulations.		No tasksheet
AED 6.1	Demonstrate knowledge of the types of oils used in A/C systems.		No tasksheet
AED 6.1	Demonstrate knowledge on handling and storing of refrigerant oils.		No tasksheet
AED 6.1	Demonstrate knowledge on recovery, recycle, and reclaiming of refrigerants with respect to identifying the refrigerant currently in the system and the amounts of oil, water, and particulates that are removed.		No tasksheet
AED 6.2	**A/C Systems Operation**		

AED 6.2	Demonstrate knowledge of the following system components:
	   1. Compressor
	   2. Condenser
	   3. Metering device
	   4. Evaporator
	   5. Service values
	   6. Schrader valves
	   7. Receiver-drier
	   8. Accumulator
	   9. Lines
			No tasksheet

AED 6.2	Demonstrate knowledge of refrigerant flow and states through an A/C system.		No tasksheet
AED 6.2	Demonstrate knowledge of the state (superheated vapor, saturated mixture, and subcooled liquid) of the refrigerant at various points in an A/C system. Emphasis will be placed on the locations in the system that the refrigerant exists as a saturated mixture.		No tasksheet
AED 6.3	**Servicing A/C Systems**		
AED 6.3	Identify various types and refrigerant capacities of A/C systems. Emphasis will be placed on the ability to identify types and capacities by using manufactures' service publications along with equipment tags, labels, and specifications.		6.3001
AED 6.3	Demonstrate use of a refrigerant ID tool (gas analyzer).		6.3002
AED 6.3	Demonstrate the ability to properly connect and disconnect gauge manifold sets. Emphasis will be placed on using proper procedures to purge hoses to prevent cross-contamination and introduction of noncondensables.		6.3003
AED 6.3	Demonstrate the ability to connect gauge sets to systems having either Schrader or quick disconnect type service valves.		No tasksheet
AED 6.3	Demonstrate the ability to properly evacuate and dehydrate an A/C system.		6.3005
AED 6.3	Demonstrate knowledge of the damage caused to A/C systems by noncondensables and moisture. Emphasis will be placed on having knowledge of using micron gauges and establishing minimum evacuation pressure based on altitude as well as maximum evacuation time periods to completely dehydrate A/C systems.		No tasksheet
AED 6.3	Demonstrate the ability to properly recover and charge A/C systems with refrigerants.		6.3007
AED 6.3	Emphasis placed on properly connecting and operating gauge manifold sets, recovery, and charging equipment.		No tasksheet
AED 6.3	Demonstrate knowledge and ability to describe the conditions that need to exist to charge A/C systems with refrigerant existing as a liquid or vapor into the high or low side.		No tasksheet
AED 6.3	Demonstrate the ability to add oil, dye, and refrigerants to operating A/C systems.		6.3010

AED 6.4	Testing, Troubleshooting, Diagnosing, and Repairing A/C Systems		
AED 6.4	Describe the complaint prior to beginning diagnostic tests. Describe and utilize an industry-accepted diagnostic process.		No tasksheet
AED 6.4	Demonstrate the ability to perform a visual inspection of an A/C system. a. Loose or missing service caps b. Oily spots – connections – evaporator drain tube c. Belt tension d. Condenser condition e. Cab filter condition f. Determine refrigerant type.		6.4002
AED 6.4	Demonstrate the ability to visually identify the type of A/C system and determine the amount of refrigerant charge. a. TXV (H-Block) – Receiver/drier b. Metered orifice – accumulator		6.4003
AED 6.4	Demonstrate the ability to identify climate control systems and components.		6.4004
AED 6.4	Demonstrate the ability to troubleshoot and diagnose A/C systems by converting system pressures to saturated mixture temperatures and comparing this to temperature readings taken at key points in the system.		6.4005
AED 6.4	Demonstrate the ability to troubleshoot and diagnose metering devices and limit switch malfunctions.		6.4006
AED 6.4	Demonstrate the ability to detect refrigerant leaks.	37	6.4007
AED 6.4	Demonstrate the ability to determine contaminants in a system due to system component failure, for example, hoses, desiccants, or compressor seal material.		6.4008
AED 6.4	Replace or repair A/C system components i.e. compressor, compressor clutch, seals, metering valves, condenser, receiver-drier, accumulator, limit switches, and lines.		6.4009
AED 6.4	Demonstrate the ability to test the cooling capabilities of an A/C system including controls. Emphasis will be placed on demonstrating the knowledge to determine the operational conditions needed to validate a performance test.		6.4010

AED 6.4	Demonstrate technical write-up competency • Demonstrate logic and critical thinking in identifying, evaluating, and diagnosing customer complaint. • Identify the root cause of failure • Correction procedure • Machine inspection		No tasksheet
AED 6.5	**Heating System Operation**		
AED 6.5	Identify and describe the following system components: 1. Water pump 2. Heater core 3. Coolant control valve(s) 4. Coolant lines 5. Engine thermostat 6. Temperature control valve		No tasksheet
AED 6.5	Inspect, remove, and replace a water pump. Emphasis will be placed on covering the 3 Cs (complaint, cause, correction) on a repair order.		6.5002
AED 6.5	Describe coolant flow direction.		No tasksheet
AED 6.5	Demonstrate knowledge of the function of different thermostats and designs, and common troubleshooting methods.		No tasksheet
AED 6.6	**Servicing Heating Systems**		
AED 6.6	Remove and install heater core and coolant lines. Emphasis will be placed on covering the 3 Cs (complaint, cause, correction) on a repair order.		6.6001
AED 6.6	Describe how to correctly remove and install heater system control valves.		6.6002
AED 6.6	Demonstrate how to correctly remove, test, and install engine thermostats. Emphasis will be placed on covering the 3 Cs (complaint, cause, correction) on a repair order.		6.6003
AED 6.7	**Pressurized Cabs**		
AED 6.7	State the purpose and function of pressurized cab systems.		No tasksheet
AED 6.7	Demonstrate how to correctly remove, inspect, and replace cab air filters.		6.7002

Appendix B

ASE Standards for Master Truck Service Technology 2018

I	DIESEL ENGINES	
I.A	**General**	
I.A.1	Research vehicle service information, including fluid type, vehicle service history, service precautions, and technical service bulletins.	MHT1A001
I.A.2	Inspect level and condition of fuel, oil, diesel exhaust fluid (DEF), and coolant.	MHT1A002
I.A.3	Inspect engine assembly for fuel, oil, coolant, air, and other leaks; determine needed action.	MHT1A003
I.A.4	Diagnose engine operation (starting and running) including noise, vibration, smoke, etc.; determine needed action.	MHT1A004
I.A.5	Use appropriate electronic service tool(s) and procedures to diagnose problems; check, record, and clear diagnostic codes; check and record trip/operational data; reset maintenance monitor (if applicable); interpret digital multimeter (DMM) readings.	MHT1A005
I.A.6	Identify system components, configurations, and types of the following: cylinder head(s), valve train, engine block, engine lubrication, engine cooling, air induction, exhaust, fuel, and engine braking.	MHT1A006
I.A.7	Diagnose engine no-crank, cranks but fails to start, hard starting, and starts but does not continue to run problems; determine needed action.	MHT1A007
I.A.8	Diagnose engine surging, rough operation, misfiring, low power, slow deceleration, slow acceleration, and/or shutdown problems; determine needed action.	MHT1A008
I.B	**Cylinder Head and Valve Train**	
I.B.1	Inspect electronic wiring harness and brackets for wear, bending, cracks, and proper securement; determine needed action.	MHT1B001
I.B.2	Inspect cylinder head for cracks/damage; check mating surfaces for warpage; check condition of passages; inspect core/expansion and gallery plugs; determine needed action.	MHT1B002
I.B.3	Inspect injector sleeves and seals; determine needed action.	MHT1B003
I.B.4	Inspect valve train components; determine needed action.	MHT1B004
I.B.5	Inspect, measure, and replace/reinstall camshaft; measure/adjust end play and backlash.	MHT1B005
I.B.6	Adjust valve bridges (crossheads); adjust valve clearances and injector settings.	MHT1B006
I.B.7	Disassemble cylinder head; inspect valves, guides, seats, springs, retainers, rotators, locks, and seals; determine needed action.	MHT1B007

II.B.7	Inspect and/or replace clutch brake assembly; inspect input shaft and bearing retainer; determine needed action.	MHT2B007
II.B.8	Inspect, adjust, and/or replace self-adjusting/continuous-adjusting clutch mechanisms.	MHT2B008
II.B.9	Inspect and/or replace pilot bearing.	MHT2B009
II.B.10	Identify causes of clutch noise, binding, slippage, pulsation, vibration, grabbing, dragging, and chatter problems; determine needed action.	MHT2B010
II.B.11	Remove and install flywheel; inspect mounting area on crankshaft; inspect rear main oil seal; measure crankshaft end play; determine needed action.	MHT2B011
II.B.12	Inspect flywheel and starter ring gear; measure flywheel face; measure pilot bore runout; determine needed action.	MHT2B012
II.B.13	Inspect flywheel housing-to-transmission housing/engine mating surface(s); measure flywheel housing face and bore runout; determine needed action.	MHT2B013
II.C	**Transmission**	
II.C.1	Inspect transmission shifter and linkage; inspect and/or replace transmission mounts, insulators, and mounting bolts.	MHT2C001
II.C.2	Inspect transmission for leakage; determine needed action.	MHT2C002
II.C.3	Replace transmission cover plates, gaskets, seals, and cap bolts; inspect seal surfaces and vents; determine needed action.	MHT2C003
II.C.4	Check transmission fluid level and condition; determine needed action.	MHT2C004
II.C.5	Inspect transmission breather; inspect transmission oil filters, coolers, and related components; determine needed action.	MHT2C005
II.C.6	Inspect speedometer components; determine needed action.	MHT2C006
II.C.7	Inspect and test function of REVERSE light, NEUTRAL start, and warning device circuits; determine needed action.	MHT2C007
II.C.8	Inspect, adjust, and replace transmission covers, rails, forks, levers, bushings, sleeves, detents, interlocks, springs, and lock bolts/safety wires.	MHT2C008
II.C.9	Identify causes of transmission noise, shifting concerns, lockup, jumping out-of-gear, overheating, and vibration problems; determine needed repairs.	MHT2C009
II.C.10	Inspect, test, repair, and/or replace air shift controls, lines, hoses, valves, regulators, filters, and cylinder assemblies.	MHT2C010
II.C.11	Remove and reinstall transmission.	MHT2C011
II.C.12	Inspect input shaft, gear, spacers, bearings, retainers, and slingers; determine needed action.	MHT2C012
II.C.13	Inspect and adjust power take-off assemblies, controls, and shafts; determine needed action.	MHT2C013
II.C.14	Inspect and test transmission temperature gauge, wiring harnesses, and sensor/sending unit; determine needed action.	MHT2C014

II.C.15	Inspect and test operation of automatic transmission, components, and controls; diagnose automatic transmission system problems; determine needed action.	MHT2C015
II.C.16	Inspect and test operation of automated mechanical transmission, components, and controls; diagnose automated mechanical transmission system problems; determine needed action.	MHT2C016
II.D	**Driveshaft and Universal Joints**	
II.D.1	Inspect, service, and/or replace driveshafts, slip joints, yokes, drive flanges, support bearings, universal joints, boots, seals, and retaining/mounting hardware; check phasing of all shafts.	MHT2D001
II.D.2	Identify causes of driveshaft and universal joint noise and vibration problems; determine needed action.	MHT2D002
II.D.3	Inspect driveshaft center support bearings and mounts; determine needed action.	MHT2D003
II.D.4	Measure driveline angles; determine needed action.	MHT2D004
II.E	**Drive Axles**	
II.E.1	Check and repair fluid leaks; inspect drive axle housing assembly, cover plates, gaskets, seals, vent/breather, and magnetic plugs.	MHT2E001
II.E.2	Check drive axle fluid level and condition; check drive axle filter; determine needed action.	MHT2E002
II.E.3	Inspect, adjust, repair, and/or replace air-operated power divider (inter-axle differential) assembly including: diaphragms, seals, springs, yokes, pins, lines, hoses, fittings, and controls.	MHT2E003
II.E.4	Inspect drive axle shafts; determine needed action.	MHT2E004
II.E.5	Remove and replace wheel assembly; check rear wheel seal and axle flange for leaks; determine needed action.	MHT2E005
II.E.6	Inspect, repair, or replace drive axle lubrication system pump, troughs, collectors, slingers, tubes, and filters.	MHT2E006
II.E.7	Identify causes of drive axle(s) drive unit noise and overheating problems; determine needed action.	MHT2E007
II.E.8	Inspect and test-drive axle temperature gauge, wiring harnesses, and sending unit/sensor; determine needed action.	MHT2E008
II.E.9	Remove and replace differential carrier assembly.	MHT2E009
II.E.10	Identify causes of drive axle wheel bearing noise and check for damage; determine needed action.	MHT2E010
II.E.11	Inspect and/or replace components of differential case assembly including spider gears, cross shaft, side gears, thrust washers, case halves, and bearings.	MHT2E011
II.E.12	Inspect and replace components of locking differential case assembly.	MHT2E012
II.E.13	Inspect differential carrier housing and caps, side bearing bores, and pilot (spigot, pocket) bearing bore; determine needed action.	MHT2E013
II.E.14	Inspect and replace ring and drive pinion gears, spacers, sleeves, bearing cages, and bearings.	MHT2E014

II.E.15	Measure ring gear runout; determine needed action.	MHT2E015
II.E.16	Measure and adjust drive pinion bearing preload.	MHT2E016
II.E.17	Measure and adjust drive pinion depth.	MHT2E017
II.E.18	Measure and adjust side bearing preload and ring gear backlash.	MHT2E018
II.E.19	Check and interpret ring gear and pinion tooth contact pattern; determine needed action.	MHT2E019
II.E.20	Inspect, adjust, or replace ring gear thrust block/screw.	MHT2E020
III	**BRAKES**	
III.A	**General**	
III.A.1	Research vehicle service information, including fluid type, vehicle service history, service precautions, and technical service bulletins.	MHT3A001
III.A.2	Identify brake system components and configurations (including air and hydraulic systems, parking brake, power assist, and vehicle dynamic brake systems).	MHT3A002
III.A.3	Identify brake performance problems caused by the mechanical/foundation brake system (air and hydraulic).	MHT3A003
III.A.4	Use appropriate electronic service tool(s) and procedures to diagnose problems; check, record, and clear diagnostic codes; interpret digital multimeter (DMM) readings.	MHT3A004
III.B	**Air Brakes: Air Supply and Service Systems**	
III.B.1	Inspect, test, repair, and/or replace air supply system components such as compressor, governor, air drier, tanks, and lines; inspect service system components such as lines, fittings, mountings, and valves (hand brake/trailer control, brake relay, quick release, tractor protection, emergency/spring brake control/modulator, pressure relief/safety); determine needed action.	MHT3B001a
III.B.1	Inspect, test, repair, and/or replace air supply system components such as compressor, governor, air drier, tanks, and lines; inspect service system components such as lines, fittings, mountings, and valves (hand brake/trailer control, brake relay, quick release, tractor protection, emergency/spring brake control/modulator, pressure relief/safety); determine needed action.	MHT3B001b
III.B.1	Inspect, test, repair, and/or replace air supply system components such as compressor, governor, air drier, tanks, and lines; inspect service system components such as lines, fittings, mountings, and valves (hand brake/trailer control, brake relay, quick release, tractor protection, emergency/spring brake control/modulator, pressure relief/safety); determine needed action.	MHT3B001c

III.B.1	Inspect, test, repair, and/or replace air supply system components such as compressor, governor, air drier, tanks, and lines; inspect service system components such as lines, fittings, mountings, and valves (hand brake/trailer control, brake relay, quick release, tractor protection, emergency/spring brake control/modulator, pressure relief/safety); determine needed action.	MHT3B001d
III.B.1	Inspect, test, repair, and/or replace air supply system components such as compressor, governor, air drier, tanks, and lines; inspect service system components such as lines, fittings, mountings, and valves (hand brake/trailer control, brake relay, quick release, tractor protection, emergency/spring brake control/modulator, pressure relief/safety); determine needed action.	MHT3B001e
III.B.1	Inspect, test, repair, and/or replace air supply system components such as compressor, governor, air drier, tanks, and lines; inspect service system components such as lines, fittings, mountings, and valves (hand brake/trailer control, brake relay, quick release, tractor protection, emergency/spring brake control/modulator, pressure relief/safety); determine needed action.	MHT3B001f
III.B.1	Inspect, test, repair, and/or replace air supply system components such as compressor, governor, air drier, tanks, and lines; inspect service system components such as lines, fittings, mountings, and valves (hand brake/trailer control, brake relay, quick release, tractor protection, emergency/spring brake control/modulator, pressure relief/safety); determine needed action.	MHT3B001g
III.B.2	Test gauge operation and readings; test low pressure warning alarm operation; perform air supply system tests such as pressure buildup, governor settings, and leakage; drain air tanks and check for contamination; determine needed action.	MHT3B002a
III.B.2	Test gauge operation and readings; test low pressure warning alarm operation; perform air supply system tests such as pressure buildup, governor settings, and leakage; drain air tanks and check for contamination; determine needed action.	MHT3B002b
III.B.2	Test gauge operation and readings; test low pressure warning alarm operation; perform air supply system tests such as pressure buildup, governor settings, and leakage; drain air tanks and check for contamination; determine needed action.	MHT3B002c
III.B.2	Test gauge operation and readings; test low pressure warning alarm operation; perform air supply system tests such as pressure buildup, governor settings, and leakage; drain air tanks and check for contamination; determine needed action.	MHT3B002d
III.B.3	Demonstrate knowledge and understanding of air supply and service system components and operations.	MHT3B003
III.B.4	Inspect air compressor drive gear components (gears, belts, tensioners, and/or couplings); determine needed action.	MHT3B004

III.B.5	Inspect air compressor inlet; inspect oil supply and coolant lines, fittings, and mounting brackets; repair or replace as needed.	MHT3B005
III.B.6	Inspect and test air tank relief (safety) valves, one-way (single) check valves, two-way (double) check valves, manual and automatic drain valves; determine needed action.	MHT3B006
III.B.7	Inspect and clean air drier systems, filters, valves, heaters, wiring, and connectors; determine needed action.	MHT3B007
III.B.8	Inspect and test brake application (foot/treadle) valve, fittings, and mounts; check pedal operation; determine needed action.	MHT3B008
III.C	**Air Brakes: Mechanical/Foundation Brake System**	
III.C.1	Inspect, test, repair, and/or replace service brake chambers, diaphragms, clamps, springs, pushrods, clevises, and mounting brackets; determine needed action.	MHT3C001
III.C.2	Identify slack adjuster type; inspect slack adjusters; perform needed action.	MHT3C002
III.C.3	Check camshafts (S-cam), tubes, rollers, bushings, seals, spacers, retainers, brake spiders, shields, anchor pins, and springs; perform needed action.	MHT3C003
III.C.4	Inspect rotor and mounting surface; measure rotor thickness, thickness variation, and lateral runout; determine needed action.	MHT3C004
III.C.5	Inspect, clean, and adjust air disc brake caliper assemblies; inspect and measure disc brake pads; inspect mounting hardware; perform needed action.	MHT3C005
III.C.6	Remove brake drum; clean and inspect brake drum and mounting surface; measure brake drum diameter; measure brake lining thickness; inspect brake lining condition; determine needed action.	MHT3C006a
III.C.6	Remove brake drum; clean and inspect brake drum and mounting surface; measure brake drum diameter; measure brake lining thickness; inspect brake lining condition; determine needed action.	MHT3C006b
III.C.7	Diagnose concerns related to the mechanical/foundation brake system including poor stopping, brake noise, premature wear, pulling, grabbing, or dragging; determine needed action.	MHT3C007
III.D	**Air Brakes: Parking Brake System**	
III.D.1	Inspect, test, and/or replace parking (spring) brake chamber.	MHT3D001
III.D.2	Inspect, test, and/or replace parking (spring) brake check valves, lines, hoses, and fittings.	MHT3D002
III.D.3	Inspect, test, and/or replace parking (spring) brake application and release valve.	MHT3D003
III.D.4	Manually release (cage) and reset (uncage) parking (spring) brakes.	MHT3D004
III.D.5	Identify and test anti-compounding brake function; determine needed action.	MHT3D005

III.E	Hydraulic Brakes: Hydraulic System	
III.E.1	Check master cylinder fluid level and condition; determine proper fluid type for application.	MHT3E001
III.E.2	Inspect hydraulic brake system for leaks and damage; test, repair, and/or replace hydraulic brake system components.	MHT3E002
III.E.3	Check hydraulic brake system operation including pedal travel, pedal effort, and pedal feel; determine needed action.	MHT3E003
III.E.4	Diagnose poor stopping, premature wear, pulling, dragging, imbalance, or poor pedal feel caused by problems in the hydraulic system; determine needed action.	MHT3E004
III.E.5	Test master cylinder for internal/external leaks and damage; replace as needed.	MHT3E005
III.E.6	Test metering (hold-off), load sensing/proportioning, proportioning, and combination valves; determine needed action.	MHT3E006
III.E.7	Test brake pressure differential valve; test warning light circuit switch, bulbs/LEDs, wiring, and connectors; determine needed action.	MHT3E007
III.E.8	Bleed and/or flush hydraulic brake system.	MHT3E008
III.F	Hydraulic Brakes: Mechanical/Foundation Brake System	
III.F.1	Clean and inspect rotor and mounting surface; measure rotor thickness, thickness variation, and lateral runout; determine necessary action.	MHT3F001
III.F.2	Inspect and clean disc brake caliper assemblies; inspect and measure disc brake pads; inspect mounting hardware; perform needed action.	MHT3F002a
III.F.2	Inspect and clean disc brake caliper assemblies; inspect and measure disc brake pads; inspect mounting hardware; perform needed action.	MHT3F002b
III.F.3	Remove, clean, and inspect brake drums; measure brake drum diameter; measure brake lining thickness; inspect brake lining condition; inspect wheel cylinders; determine serviceability.	MHT3F003
III.F.4	Check disc brake caliper assembly mountings and slides; replace as needed.	MHT3F004
III.G	Hydraulic Brakes: Parking Brake System	
III.G.1	Check parking brake operation; inspect parking brake application and holding devices; adjust, repair, and/or replace as needed.	MHT3G001
III.H	Power Assist Systems	
III.H.1	Check brake assist/booster system (vacuum or hydraulic) hoses and control valves; check fluid level and condition (if applicable).	MHT3H001
III.H.2	Check operation of emergency (backup/reserve) brake assist system.	MHT3H002
III.H.3	Identify concerns related to the power assist system (vacuum or hydraulic), including stopping problems caused by the brake assist (booster) system; determine needed action.	MHT3H003
III.H.4	Inspect, test, repair, and/or replace hydraulic brake assist/booster systems, hoses, and control valves.	MHT3H004

III.I	Vehicle Dynamic Brake Systems (Air and Hydraulic): Antilock Brake System (ABS), Automatic Traction Control (ATC) System, and Electronic Stability Control (ESC) System	
III.I.1	Observe antilock brake system (ABS) warning light operation including trailer and dash mounted trailer ABS warning light; determine needed action.	MHT3I001
III.I.2	Observe automatic traction control (ATC) and electronic stability control (ETC) warning light operation; determine needed action.	MHT3I002
III.I.3	Identify stopping concerns related to the vehicle dynamic brake systems: ABS, ATC, and ESC; determine needed action.	MHT3I003
III.I.4	Diagnose problems in the vehicle dynamic brake control systems; determine needed action.	MHT3I004
III.I.5	Check and test operation of vehicle dynamic brake system (air and hydraulic) mechanical and electrical components; determine needed action.	MHT3I005
III.I.6	Test vehicle/wheel speed sensors and circuits; adjust, repair, and/or replace as needed.	MHT3I006
III.I.7	Bleed ABS hydraulic circuits.	MHT3I007
III.I.8	Verify power line carrier (PLC) operation.	MHT3I008
III.J	Wheel Bearings	
III.J.1	Clean, inspect, lubricate, and/or replace wheel bearings and races/cups; replace seals and wear rings; inspect spindle/tube; inspect and replace retaining hardware; adjust wheel bearings; check hub assembly fluid level and condition; verify end play with dial indicator method.	MHT3J001
III.J.2	Identify, inspect, and/or replace unitized/preset hub bearing assemblies.	MHT3J002
IV	SUSPENSION AND STEERING	
	For every task in Suspension and Steering, the following safety requirement must be strictly enforced: • Comply with personal and environmental safety practices associated with eye/foot/hand/hearing protection, clothing, hand tools, power equipment, lifting practices, and ventilation. Handle, store, and dispose of fuels/chemicals/materials in accordance with federal, state, and local regulations. • The first tasks in Suspension and Steering are to listen to and verify the operator's concern, review past maintenance and repair documents, and determine necessary action.	
IV.A	General	
IV.A.1	Research vehicle service information, including fluid type, vehicle service history, service precautions, and technical service bulletins.	MHT4A001
IV.A.2	Disable and enable supplemental restraint system (SRS); verify indicator lamp operation.	MHT4A002
IV.A.3	Identify suspension and steering system components and configurations.	MHT4A003

IV.A.4	Use appropriate electronic service tool(s) and procedures to diagnose problems; check, record, and clear diagnostic codes; interpret digital multimeter (DMM) readings.	MHT4A004
IV.B	**Steering Column**	
IV.B.1	Check steering wheel for free play, binding, and proper centering; inspect and service steering shaft U-joint(s), slip joint(s), bearings, bushings, and seals; phase steering shaft.	MHT4B001
IV.B.2	Diagnose causes of fixed and driver adjustable steering column and shaft noise, looseness, and binding problems.	MHT4B002
IV.B.3	Check cab mounting and adjust cab ride height.	MHT4B003
IV.B.4	Remove the steering wheel (includes steering wheels equipped with electrical/electronic controls and components); install and center the steering wheel.	MHT4B004
IV.B.5	Inspect, test, replace, and calibrate steering angle sensor.	MHT4B005
IV.C	**Steering Pump and Gear Units**	
IV.C.1	Check power steering pump and gear operation, mountings, lines, and hoses; check fluid level and condition; service filter; inspect system for leaks.	MHT4C001
IV.C.2	Flush and refill power steering system; purge air from system.	MHT4C002
IV.C.3	Diagnose causes of power steering system noise, binding, darting/oversteer, reduced wheel cut, steering wheel kick, pulling, nonrecovery, turning effort, looseness, hard steering, overheating, fluid leakage, and fluid aeration problems.	MHT4C003
IV.C.4	Inspect, service, and/or replace power steering reservoir, seals, and gaskets.	MHT4C004
IV.C.5	Inspect and/or replace power steering system cooler, lines, hoses, clamps, mountings, and fittings.	MHT4C005
IV.C.6	Inspect and/or replace power steering gear(s) (single and/or dual) and mountings.	MHT4C006
IV.D	**Steering Linkage**	
IV.D.1	Inspect, service, repair, and/or replace tie-rod ends, ball joints, kingpins, pitman arms, idler arms, and other steering linkage components.	MHT4D001
IV.E	**Suspension Systems**	
IV.E.1	Inspect, service, repair, and/or replace shock absorbers, bushings, brackets, and mounts.	MHT4E001
IV.E.2	Inspect, repair, and/or replace leaf springs, center bolts, clips, pins, bushings, shackles, U-bolts, insulators, brackets, and mounts.	MHT4E002
IV.E.3	Inspect, repair, and/or replace axle and axle aligning devices such as radius rods, track bars, stabilizer bars, and torque arms; inspect related bushings, mounts, shims, and attaching hardware; determine needed action.	MHT4E003
IV.E.4	Inspect, repair, and/or replace tandem suspension equalizer components; determine needed action.	MHT4E004

IV.E.5	Inspect, repair, and/or replace air-springs, mounting plates, springs, suspension arms, and bushings.	MHT4E005
IV.E.6	Inspect, test, repair, and/or replace air suspension pressure regulator and height control valves, lines, hoses, dump valves, and fittings; check and record ride height.	MHT4E006
IV.E.7	Inspect and service kingpins, steering knuckle bushings, locks, bearings, seals, and covers.	MHT4E007
IV.E.8	Measure, record, and adjust ride height; determine needed action.	MHT4E008
IV.E.9	Diagnose rough ride problems; determine needed action.	MHT4E009
IV.F	**Wheel Alignment Diagnosis and Repair**	
IV.F.1	Demonstrate understanding of alignment angles.	MHT4F001
IV.F.2	Diagnose causes of vehicle wandering, pulling, shimmy, hard steering, and off-center steering wheel problems.	MHT4F002
IV.F.3	Check, record, and adjust camber.	MHT4F003
IV.F.4	Check, record, and adjust caster.	MHT4F004
IV.F.5	Check, record, and adjust toe settings.	MHT4F005
IV.F.6	Check rear axle(s) alignment (thrust line/centerline) and tracking.	MHT4F006
IV.F.7	Identify turning/Ackerman angle (toe-out on turns) problems.	MHT4F007
IV.F.8	Check front axle alignment (centerline).	MHT4F008
IV.G	**Wheels and Tires**	
IV.G.1	Inspect tire condition; identify tire wear patterns; measure tread depth; verify tire matching (diameter and tread); inspect valve stem and cap; set tire pressure; determine needed action.	MHT4G001
IV.G.2	Diagnose wheel/tire vibration, shimmy, pounding, and hop (tramp) problems; determine needed action.	MHT4G002
IV.G.3	Check wheel mounting hardware; check wheel condition; remove and install wheel/tire assemblies (steering and drive axle); torque fasteners to manufacturer's specification using torque wrench.	MHT4G003
IV.G.4	Inspect tire and wheel for proper application (size, load range, position, and tread design); determine needed action.	MHT4G004
IV.H	**Frame and Coupling Devices**	
IV.H.1	Inspect, service, and/or adjust fifth wheel, pivot pins, bushings, locking mechanisms, mounting hardware, air lines, and fittings.	MHT4H001
IV.H.2	Inspect frame and frame members for cracks, breaks, corrosion, distortion, elongated holes, looseness, and damage; determine needed action.	MHT4H002
IV.H.3	Inspect, install, and/or replace frame hangers, brackets, and cross members; determine needed action.	MHT4H003
IV.H.4	Inspect, repair, or replace pintle hooks and draw bars (if applicable).	MHT4H004
IV.H.5	Inspect, service, and/or adjust sliding fifth wheel, tracks, stops, locking systems, air cylinders, springs, lines, hoses, and controls.	MHT4H005

V	ELECTRICAL/ELECTRONIC SYSTEMS	
V.A	**General**	
V.A.1	Research vehicle service information, including vehicle service history, service precautions, and technical service bulletins.	MHT5A001
V.A.2	Demonstrate knowledge of electrical/electronic series, parallel, and series/parallel circuits using principles of electricity (Ohm's Law).	MHT5A002
V.A.3	Demonstrate proper use of test equipment when measuring source voltage, voltage drop (including grounds), current flow, continuity, and resistance.	MHT5A003
V.A.4	Demonstrate knowledge of the causes and effects of shorts, grounds, opens, and resistance problems in electrical/electronic circuits; identify and locate faults in electrical/electronic circuits.	MHT5A004
V.A.5	Use wiring diagrams during the diagnosis (troubleshooting) of electrical/electronic circuit problems.	MHT5A005
V.A.6	Measure parasitic (key-off) battery drain; determine needed action.	MHT5A006
V.A.7	Demonstrate knowledge of the function, operation, and testing of fusible links, circuit breakers, relays, solenoids, diodes, and fuses; perform inspection and testing; determine needed action.	MHT5A007
V.A.8	Inspect, test, repair (including solder repair), and/or replace components, connectors, seals, terminal ends, harnesses, and wiring; verify proper routing and securement; determine needed action.	MHT5A008
V.A.9	Use appropriate electronic service tool(s) and procedures to diagnose problems; check, record, and clear diagnostic codes; interpret digital multimeter (DMM) readings.	MHT5A009
V.A.10	Diagnose faults in the data bus communications network; determine needed action.	MHT5A010
V.A.11	Identify electrical/electronic system components and configuration.	MHT5A011
V.A.12	Check frequency, pulse width, and waveforms of electrical/electronic signals using appropriate test equipment; interpret readings; determine needed repairs.	MHT5A012
V.A.13	Understand the process for software transfer, software updates, and/or reprogramming of electronic modules.	MHT5A013
V.B	**Battery System**	
V.B.1	Identify battery type and system configuration.	MHT5B001
V.B.2	Confirm proper battery capacity for application; perform battery state of charge test; perform battery capacity test, determine needed action.	MHT5B002
V.B.3	Inspect battery, battery cables, connectors, battery boxes, mounts, and hold-downs; determine needed action.	MHT5B003
V.B.4	Charge battery using appropriate method for battery type.	MHT5B004

V.B.5	Jump-start vehicle using a booster battery and jumper cables or using an appropriate auxiliary power supply.	MHT5B005
V.B.6	Check low-voltage disconnect systems; determine needed action.	MHT5B006
V.B.7	Inspect, clean, and service battery; replace as needed.	MHT5B007
V.B.8	Inspect and clean battery boxes, mounts, and hold-downs; repair or replace as needed.	MHT5B008
V.B.9	Test and clean battery cables and connectors; repair or replace as needed.	MHT5B009
V.B.10	Identify electrical/electronic modules, radios, and other accessories that require reinitialization or code entry after reconnecting vehicle battery.	MHT5B010
V.C	**Starting System**	
V.C.1	Demonstrate understanding of starter system operation.	MHT5C001
V.C.2	Perform starter circuit cranking voltage and voltage drop tests; determine needed action.	MHT5C002
V.C.3	Inspect and test starter control circuit switches (key switch, push button, and/or magnetic switch), relays, connectors, terminals, wires, and harnesses (including over-crank protection); determine needed action.	MHT5C003
V.C.4	Diagnose causes of no-crank or slow crank condition; differentiate between electrical and engine mechanical problems; determine needed action.	MHT5C004
V.C.5	Perform starter current draw tests; determine needed action.	MHT5C005
V.C.6	Remove and replace starter; inspect flywheel ring gear or flex plate.	MHT5C006
V.D	**Charging System**	
V.D.1	Identify and understand operation of the generator (alternator).	MHT5D001
V.D.2	Test instrument panel mounted voltmeters and/or indicator lamps; determine needed action.	MHT5D002
V.D.3	Inspect, adjust, and/or replace generator (alternator) drive belt; check pulleys and tensioners for wear; check fans and mounting brackets; verify proper belt alignment; determine needed action.	MHT5D003
V.D.4	Inspect cables, wires, and connectors in the charging circuit.	MHT5D004
V.D.5	Perform charging system voltage and amperage output tests; perform AC ripple test; determine needed action.	MHT5D005
V.D.6	Perform charging circuit voltage drop tests; determine needed action.	MHT5D006
V.D.7	Remove, inspect, and/or replace generator (alternator).	MHT5D007
V.E	**Lighting Systems**	
V.E.1	Diagnose causes of brighter-than-normal, intermittent, dim, or no-light operation; determine needed action.	MHT5E001
V.E.2	Test, replace, and aim headlights.	MHT5E002
V.E.3	Inspect cables, wires, and connectors in the lighting systems.	MHT5E003

V.E.4	Diagnose faults in tractor-to-trailer multi-wire connector(s), cables, and holders; determine needed action.	MHT5E004
V.E.5	Diagnose faults in switches, relays, bulbs/LEDs, wires, terminals, connectors, sockets, and control components/modules of exterior lighting systems; determine needed action.	MHT5E005
V.E.6	Diagnose faults in switches, relays, bulbs/LEDs, wires, terminals, connectors, sockets, and control components/modules of interior lighting systems; determine needed action.	MHT5E006
V.E.7	Diagnose faults in switches, relays, bulbs/LEDs, wires, terminals, connectors, sockets, and control components/modules of auxiliary lighting circuits; determine needed action.	MHT5E007
V.F	**Instrument Cluster and Driver Information Systems**	
V.F.1	Check gauge and warning indicator operation.	MHT5F001
V.F.2	Diagnose faults in the sensor/sending units, gauges, switches, relays, bulbs/LEDs, wires, terminals, connectors, sockets, printed circuits, and control components/modules of the instrument cluster, driver information systems, and warning systems; determine needed action.	MHT5F002
V.F.3	Inspect, test, replace, and calibrate (if applicable) electronic speedometer, odometer, and tachometer systems.	MHT5F003
V.G	**Cab and Chassis Electrical Systems**	
V.G.1	Diagnose operation of horn(s), wiper/washer, and occupant restraint systems.	MHT5G001
V.G.2	Understand operation of safety systems and related circuits (such as speed control, collision avoidance, lane departure, and camera systems).	MHT5G002
V.G.3	Understand operation of comfort and convenience systems and related circuits (such as power windows, power seats, power locks, remote keyless entry, steering wheel controls, and cruise control).	MHT5G003
V.G.4	Understand operation of entertainment systems and related circuits (such as radio, DVD, navigation, speakers, antennas, and voice-activated accessories).	MHT5G004
V.G.5	Understand the operation of power inverter, protection devices, connectors, terminals, wiring, and control components/modules of auxiliary power systems.	MHT5G005
V.G.6	Understand operation of telematics systems.	MHT5G006
V.G.7	Diagnose faults in engine block and engine oil heater(s); determine needed action.	MHT5G007
VI	**HEATING, VENTILATION, AND AIR-CONDITIONING (HVAC)**	
VI.A	**General**	
VI.A.1	Research vehicle service information, including refrigerant/oil type, vehicle service history, service precautions, and technical service bulletins.	MHT6A001
VI.A.2	Identify heating, ventilation, and air-conditioning (HVAC) components and configuration.	MHT6A002

VI.A.3	Use appropriate electronic service tool(s) and procedures to diagnose problems; check, record, and clear diagnostic codes; interpret digital multimeter (DMM) readings.	MHT6A003
VI.A.4	Diagnose heating and air-conditioning problems; determine needed action.	MHT6A004
VI.A.5	Identify refrigerant type; test for contamination; select and connect proper gauge set/test equipment; record temperature and pressure readings.	MHT6A005a
VI.A.5	Identify refrigerant type; test for contamination; select and connect proper gauge set/test equipment; record temperature and pressure readings.	MHT6A005b
VI.A.5	Identify refrigerant type; test for contamination; select and connect proper gauge set/test equipment; record temperature and pressure readings.	MHT6A005c
VI.A.6	Perform A/C system performance test; determine needed action.	MHT6A006
VI.A.7	Perform A/C system leak test; determine needed action.	MHT6A007
VI.A.8	Inspect condition of refrigerant oil removed from A/C system; determine needed action.	MHT6A008
VI.A.9	Determine oil and oil capacity for system application and/or component replacement.	MHT6A009
VI.B	**Refrigeration System Components**	
VI.B.1	Inspect, remove, and replace A/C compressor drive belts, pulleys, and tensioners; verify proper belt alignment.	MHT6B001
VI.B.2	Check A/C system operation including system pressures; visually inspect A/C components for signs of leaks; check A/C monitoring system (if applicable).	MHT6B002
VI.B.3	Inspect A/C condenser for airflow restrictions; determine needed action.	MHT6B003
VI.B.4	Inspect, test, service, and/or replace A/C compressor and clutch assembly; check compressor clutch air gap; determine needed action.	MHT6B004
VI.B.5	Inspect, service, and/or replace A/C system hoses, lines, fittings, O-rings, seals, and service valves.	MHT6B005
VI.B.6	Inspect, remove, and/or replace receiver/drier or accumulator/drier.	MHT6B006
VI.B.7	Inspect, remove, and/or replace expansion valve or orifice (expansion) tube.	MHT6B007a
VI.B.7	Inspect, remove, and/or replace expansion valve or orifice (expansion) tube.	MHT6B007b
VI.B.8	Inspect evaporator housing water drain; perform needed action.	MHT6B008
VI.B.9	Diagnose A/C system conditions that cause the protection devices (pressure, thermal, and/or control module) to interrupt system operation; determine needed action.	MHT6B009
VI.B.10	Determine procedure to remove and reinstall evaporator.	MHT6B010
VI.B.11	Determine procedure to inspect and/or replace condenser.	MHT6B011

VI.C	Heating, Ventilation, and Engine Cooling Systems	
VI.C.1	Inspect engine cooling system and heater system hoses and pipes; determine needed action.	MHT6C001
VI.C.2	Inspect HVAC system heater ducts, doors, hoses, cabin filters, and outlets; determine needed action.	MHT6C002
VI.C.3	Identify the source of A/C system odors; determine needed action.	MHT6C003
VI.C.4	Diagnose temperature control problems in the HVAC system; determine needed action.	MHT6C004
VI.C.5	Determine procedure to remove, inspect, reinstall, and/or replace engine coolant and heater system components.	MHT6C005
VI.D	Operating Systems and Related Controls	
VI.D.1	Verify HVAC system blower motor operation; confirm proper air distribution; confirm proper temperature control; determine needed action.	MHT6D001
VI.D.2	Inspect and test HVAC system blower motors, resistors, switches, relays, wiring, and protection devices; determine needed action.	MHT6D002
VI.D.3	Diagnose A/C compressor clutch control systems; determine needed action.	MHT6D003
VI.D.4	Diagnose malfunctions in the vacuum, mechanical, and electrical components and controls of the HVAC system; determine needed action.	MHT6D004
VI.E	Refrigerant Recovery, Recycling, and Handling	
VI.E.1	Understand correct use and maintenance of refrigerant handling equipment.	MHT6E001
VI.E.2	Understand how to identify A/C system refrigerant; test for sealants; recover, evacuate, and charge A/C system; add refrigerant oil as required.	MHT6E002
VI.E.3	Understand how to recycle, label, and store refrigerant.	MHT6E003
VII	CAB	
VII.A	General	
VII.A.1	Research vehicle service information, including vehicle service history, service precautions, and technical service bulletins.	MHT7A001
VII.A.2	Use appropriate electronic service tool(s) and procedures to diagnose problems; check, record, and clear diagnostic codes; check and record trip/operational data; reset maintenance monitor (if applicable); interpret digital multimeter (DMM) readings.	MHT7A002
VII.B	Instruments and Controls	
VII.B.1	Inspect mechanical key condition; check operation of ignition switch; check operation of indicator lights, warning lights and/or alarms; check instruments; record oil pressure and system voltage; check operation of electronic power take-off and engine idle speed controls (if applicable).	MHT7B001

VII.B.2	Check operation of all accessories.	MHT7B002
VII.B.3	Understand operation of auxiliary power unit/electric power unit.	MHT7B003
VII.C	**Safety Equipment**	
VII.C.1	Test operation of horns (electric and air); test warning device operation (reverse, air pressure, etc.); check condition of spare fuses, safety triangles, fire extinguisher, and all required decals; inspect seat belts and sleeper restraints; inspect condition of wiper blades, arms, and linkage; determine needed action.	MHT7C001
VII.D	**Hardware**	
VII.D.1	Test operation of wipers and washer; inspect windshield glass for cracks or discoloration; check sun visor; check seat condition, operation, and mounting; check door glass and window operation; verify operation of door and cab locks; inspect steps and grab handles; inspect mirrors, mountings, brackets, and glass; determine needed action.	MHT7D001
VII.D.2	Record all physical damage.	MHT7D002
VII.D.3	Lubricate all cab grease fittings; inspect and lubricate door and hood hinges, latches, strikers, lock cylinders, safety latches, linkages, and cables.	MHT7D003
VII.D.4	Inspect cab mountings, hinges, latches, linkages, and ride height; determine needed action.	MHT7D004
VII.D.5	Inspect quarter fender, mud flaps, and brackets; determine needed action.	MHT7D005
VIII	**HYDRAULICS**	
VIII.A	**General**	
VIII.A.1	Research vehicle service information, including vehicle service history, service precautions, fluid type, and technical service bulletins.	MHT8A001
VIII.A.2	Verify placement of equipment/component safety labels and placards; determine needed action.	MHT8A002
VIII.A.3	Identify hydraulic system components; locate filtration system components; service filters and breathers.	MHT8A003
VIII.A.4	Check fluid level and condition; purge and/or bleed system; take a hydraulic fluid sample for analysis; determine needed action.	MHT8A004
VIII.A.5	Inspect hoses and connections for leaks, proper routing, and proper protection; determine needed action.	MHT8A005
VIII.A.6	Use appropriate electronic service tool(s) and procedures to diagnose problems; check, record, and clear diagnostic codes; interpret digital multimeter (DMM) readings.	MHT8A006
VIII.A.7	Read and interpret system diagrams and schematics.	MHT8A007
VIII.A.8	Perform system temperature, pressure, flow, and cycle time tests; determine needed action.	MHT8A008
VIII.A.9	Perform system operational tests; determine needed action.	MHT8A009

VIII.B	**Pumps**	
VIII.B.1	Identify causes of pump failure, unusual pump noises, temperature, flow and leakage problems; determine needed action.	MHT8B001
VIII.B.2	Determine pump type, rotation, and drive system.	MHT8B002
VIII.B.3	Remove and install pump; prime and/or bleed system.	MHT8B003
VIII.B.4	Inspect pump inlet and outlet for restrictions and leaks; determine needed action.	MHT8B004
VIII.C	**Filtration/Reservoirs (Tanks)**	
VIII.C.1	Identify type of filtration system; verify filter application and flow direction.	MHT8C001
VIII.C.2	Service filters and breathers.	MHT8C002
VIII.C.3	Identify causes of system contamination; determine needed action.	MHT8C003
VIII.C.4	Inspect, repair, and/or replace reservoir, sight glass, vents, caps, mounts, valves, screens, supply, and return lines.	MHT8C004
VIII.D	**Hoses, Fittings, and Connections**	
VIII.D.1	Diagnose causes of component leakage, damage, and restriction; determine needed action.	MHT8D001
VIII.D.2	Inspect hoses and connections for leaks, proper routing, and proper protection; determine needed action.	MHT8D002
VIII.D.3	Assemble hoses, tubes, connectors, and fittings.	MHT8D003
VIII.E	**Control Valves**	
VIII.E.1	Pressure test system safety relief valve; determine needed action.	MHT8E001
VIII.E.2	Perform control valve operation pressure and flow tests; determine needed action.	MHT8E002
VIII.E.3	Inspect, test, and adjust valve controls (electrical/electronic, mechanical, and pneumatic).	MHT8E003
VIII.E.4	Identify causes of control valve leakage problems (internal and external); determine needed action.	MHT8E004
VIII.E.5	Inspect pilot control valve linkages, cables, and power take-off controls; adjust, repair, or replace as needed.	MHT8E005
VIII.F	**Actuators**	
	Comply with manufacturers' and industry accepted safety practices associated with equipment lockout/tagout, pressure line release, implement support (blocked or resting on ground), and articulated cylinder devices/machinery safety locks.	
VIII.F.1	1. Identify actuator type (single-acting, double-acting, multi-stage, telescopic, and motor).	MHT8F001
VIII.F.2	2. Identify the cause of seal failure; determine needed action.	MHT8F002
VIII.F.3	3. Identify the cause of incorrect actuator movement and/or leakage (internal and external); determine needed action.	MHT8F003

VIII.F.4	4. Inspect actuator mounting, frame components, and hardware for looseness, cracks, and damage; determine needed action.	MHT8F004
VIII.F.5	5. Remove, repair, and/or replace actuators.	MHT8F005
VIII.F.6	6. Inspect actuators for dents, cracks, damage, and leakage; determine needed action.	MHT8F006
IX	**Cutting and Welding**	
IX.A	**Basic Cutting and Welding**	
IX.A.1	Describe the type of protection that must be worn when welding and cutting.	MHT03
IX.A.2	Identify and demonstrate the basic types of weld joints, which are the butt, t-joint, and lap joint.	MHT04
IX.A.3	Identify and explain the main features of a weld and the correct welding positions.	MHT05
IX.A.4	Demonstrate and explain how to set up and operate a MIG Welder.	MHT06
IX.A.5	Identify some common problems encountered in MIG welding and be able to solve them correctly.	MHT07
IX.A.6	Demonstrate simple metal cutting by using the oxyacetylene combination torch.	MHT08
IX.A.7	Weld rosettes or plugs in all welding positions.	MHT09